Perspectives

in American Indian Culture Change

Perspectives

in American Indian Culture Change

EDITED BY EDWARD H. SPICER

Studies in the Acculturation of the

YAQUI · *Edward H. Spicer*

RIO GRANDE PUEBLOS · *Edward P. Dozier*

MANDAN · *Edward M. Bruner*

NAVAHO · *Evon Z. Vogt*

WASCO-WISHRAM · *David French*

KWAKIUTL · *Helen Codere*

 *The University of Chicago Press*

Chicago and London

Library of Congress Catalog Card Number: 60-14358

THE UNIVERSITY OF CHICAGO PRESS, CHICAGO 60637
The University of Chicago Press, Ltd., London W. C. 1

Acknowledgment

The authors wish to express their gratitude to the Social Science Research Council for making possible the Interuniversity Summer Research Seminar on which this book is based, to Joseph B. Casagrande for his personal interest and aid in furthering the project, to the University of New Mexico for generous provision of facilities, to Ronald Kurtz for his efficient and conscientious service as recorder, and to W. W. Hill and other members of the Department of Anthropology of the University of New Mexico for their wonderful hospitality. We are grateful to Rosamond B. Spicer, who has provided us with the maps for chapters ii, iii, v, and vi.

Contents

List of Illustrations

List of Tables

CHAPTER 1

Introduction

Amid all the variety of custom among present-day Indian communities in the United States and Canada, an impression of similarity grows as one becomes acquainted with successive reservations. The surviving native languages, persisting and revived crafts, house types, foods, and ceremonials differ in such fascinating ways that it is easy for a student of Indian life to become absorbed in the details of these modern modifications of aboriginal customs. On the other hand, as knowledge of life on the reservations deepens, the repetition of certain combinations of Indian and Anglo-American ways becomes unmistakable. Similar trends in the replacement of material culture, similarities in dialects of English, likenesses in kinship behaviors and types of extended families, comparable growths of nativism and adaptations of ceremonial life, and even what one feels to be nearly identical constellations of personality traits thrust themselves on one's attention. As one goes from reservation to reservation, the feeling grows that what one sees today is what one saw not long before on some other reservation.

To be sure there is variation in the ways the clothes are worn or the houses built or the dances performed. The whole inventory of culture traits, for example, on the Fox Reservation in Iowa is different from that among the Hopis in Arizona, but nevertheless one feels that somehow one is moving among the same people in the two places; attitudes and views of life seem essentially the same; and, perhaps most definitely, the way of dealing with non-Indians has the same quality. In other words, "culture contact" feels very much the same in these two widely separated places where the people have had such different historical experiences. This sense of coming repeatedly into the same situations intensifies as one goes from, let us say, the San Carlos Apache Reservation in Arizona to the Rosebud Sioux Reservation in South Dakota and so on throughout the country.

It is not that there are no markers to indicate which is which, but that underlying the obvious and specific differences are patterns of behavior that are nearly identical. It is further not that all reservations are felt to be the same; certainly Ute does not feel like Hopi and Hopi does not feel like Cherokee. It is rather that one begins to feel that there are only a few patterns which keep cropping up under the diversity of detail. One senses that the varied surfaces of life, while real enough in their uniqueness for each group, obscure the fact that there are fewer than a half dozen, perhaps no more than three or four, ways of life, or that is to say distinctive cultures, in all the reservations of the United States and Canada.

The growing number of careful studies of the acculturation of North American Indians reinforces these impressions and points to the existence of similar social and cultural processes at work under the surfaces of reservation life. Studies like those of the White Knife Shoshonis in Nevada (Linton 1940), the Makahs in Washington (Colson 1953), the Chickahominies in Virginia (Stern 1952), the Southern Utes in Colorado (Linton 1940), the Delawares in Oklahoma (Newcomb 1956), the Blackfoot in Alberta (Hanks 1950), and similar research have begun to provide the data from which the identification of recurrent processes may be made. It is such perspectives on Indian response to contact, showing the conditions under which redefinition of purpose has taken place or old values have prevailed, that may be expected to move us toward the systematic comparison on which understanding of cultural change depends.

The accounts of the six American Indian cultures in the present volume were undertaken as a contribution to the comparative study of acculturation (Bruner 1957). They were conceived as carrying further the analysis of change under contact conditions inaugurated in 1935 by the Social Science Research Council with the Memorandum for the Study of Acculturation (Redfield *et al.* 1936). That memorandum was produced as a piece of committee work. It was essentially a guide for the collection and classification of data, a preliminary basis for gathering comparable materials. In 1953 the Social Science Research Council sponsored another group of students interested in acculturation. Their work was conceived as an effort at the formulation of working concepts and a theoretical approach based on the large amount of acculturation data from all over the world gathered in the interval since the memorandum of 1936 (Broom *et al.* 1954). Two years later the Social Science Research Council arranged to bring together the contributors to the present volume in order to encourage the systematic comparison of detailed acculturation materials through close collaboration of persons actively engaged in research.

The form which the collaborative effort took was that of an Interuniversity Summer Research Seminar. As originally planned the work was focused with the following statement of problem:

We know that in every contact situation some aspects of the native culture change more than others, but we do not adequately understand why this is so, nor how to characterize that which has changed and that which has not in categories that have cross-cultural validity. . . . We think that this problem area is much in need of conceptual assessment and codification, and that the time is ripe for a systematic approach which would (*a*) attempt to develop a cross-cultural analytical scheme, (*b*) apply the scheme to a selected number of diverse North American Indian cases where the facts are well known, and (*c*) isolate general propositions that would serve as directives for further research in the Americas and in other areas.

Following some correspondence during the winter of 1955–56, the six participants in the seminar came together in Albuquerque at the University of New Mexico during the summer of 1956. Each had been engaged in field research over several years with the Indian group on which he reported during the seminar. None had prepared in advance an account of the material presented to the group. The form of the report was worked out only after the seminar had met for a week of intensive discussions concerning the scheme of analysis and the objectives of the comparative study.

The approach adopted sought to discover relations between the changes in Indian cultures and the conditions of contact under which those changes had taken place. This involved the seminar group in two major enterprises: first, the description of contact conditions in comparable terms and, second, the identification of types of change.

Discussion of the first often centered on the concept "contact community." The participants were by no means agreed on the content of the concept or even on whether it was a usable tool of comparative analysis. One view held that the essential conditions of contact could be stated with reference to the network of roles in those communities where Indians lived and which linked Indians and non-Indians in a social structure. Another view held that a contact community should be broadly conceived as embracing the total network of social relations in which Indians were involved. The total network in this conception included, for example, the roles of the Viceroy of New Spain or the United States Secretary of the Interior even though there was no direct interaction of Indians with them. It was agreed that there was no essential difference in theoretical approach whether analysis were limited to Indian communities or included the larger social structure of which Indian communities became a part in the course of political incorporation; what was involved was merely a difference in level of analysis within the same framework of approach.

Ultimately the seminar members assembled their data for comparison chiefly in terms of the types of role relationships in the communities in which Indians lived. A check list of features of contact communities was employed for organizing the six sets of data. It included the following categories: (1) definition of significant groups in contact or, that is, how each of the groups in a contact situation classified and characterized other groups in relation to themselves; (2) demographic features, especially population trends and settlement patterns; (3) community structure in the sense of functional relations among the significant groups, the strategy of each group in relation to the others, and intergroup attitudes; and (4) the intercultural role network described in terms of (*a*) reciprocals, such as trader-trader or missionary-neophyte, (*b*) the characteristics of the roles especially with reference to frequency of interaction, affective tone, incidence of authority, and ideal and real patterns, and (*c*) situational contexts such as trading posts, ceremonies, reservation agencies.

As descriptions were worked out in these terms, it became apparent that quite different types of contact communities succeeded one another for each of the six Indian groups over the span of their recorded history. Marked changes in types and numbers of contact roles, group strategies, intergroup attitudes, population trends, and settlement patterns became the basis for defining "periods" in the contact conditions. The data in each of the six cases were presented to the seminar in terms of these period demarcations. There is consideration in the final chapter of the nature of the periods and their employment in the interpretation of changes in Indian culture.

The task of delineating types of change in the Indian cultures offered more complex problems. The range in results of contact in the six cases was wide. At one extreme the Rio Grande Pueblos maintained during four hundred years a social and religious life which differed only in detail from that which the Spaniards first reported. At the opposite extreme were the Kwakiutl among whom nearly all aspects of native custom seemed to have undergone extensive replacement. In between were the Navahos whose life had been profoundly altered but who had synthesized their borrowings, such as sheepherding from the Spaniards and religious ideas from the Pueblos, into what could justifiably be called a distinctive Navaho way of life. In a different way, under conditions of greater intimacy with Spaniards, the Yaquis had also created a new synthesis which was not Spanish and which did not become wholly Mexican. The Mandans, shifting from compact village life to reservation farmsteads, underwent a profound transformation which amounted to the achievement of a new identity despite the near extinction of the culture which had characterized them. The Wascos and Wishrams, subjected to similar conditions but starting from a different cultural base, were in somewhat the same fashion as the Mandans in process of merging with neighboring Indians while nevertheless maintaining some sense of distinctive identity. In view of such variety it would have been possible to treat each tribal experience as a unique historical development, but that was not the aim of the seminar.

The aim was rather to discover whether there were any fundamental similarities in the responses of the different Indian groups to similar conditions of contact. The comparison of the six groups in terms of the successive types of contact community in which each lived enabled the seminar members to see some similarities and hence to suggest some types of change. Those identified were described in terms of social and cultural integration, or as forms of linkage and combination of the societies and the cultural traditions which came into contact. Most of 'the half-dozen types of social and cultural integration to which the seminar paid special attention were represented in each of the cases, but during one period or another there was usually dominance of a single kind. In the case studies which follow names are given to each of the types, and the conditions under which they occurred are described in detail.

In the final chapter, the editor has sought to compare the cases systematically and to go as far as the data permit in generalization. The definitions of types of acculturative change which appear there were in large part worked out while the seminar was still in session and to a lesser degree this is also true of the delineation of types of contact conditions. Proceeding from the base which the seminar developed the editor has attempted analysis of the relationship between type of contact and type of change and to advance some general propositions regarding this relationship. Each member of the seminar would undoubtedly have written a somewhat different chapter, but all have approved the present one as substantially summing up and relating to the existing theory of culture change the main themes on which the seminar touched.

CHAPTER **2**

These people seem to be highly
intelligent, curious, and knowledgeable
about what they desire.

Yaqui

By Edward H. Spicer

In the 1950's one of the major regions of enclaved native cultures in North America lay in the arid southwestern part of the continent. Within the area of four of the current political divisions—Chihuahua, Sonora, New Mexico, and Arizona—some twenty-five Indian groups had survived contact with Europeans. The fact that they had preserved, or developed, a tribal name and sense of distinct identity did not mean that they had maintained intact their aboriginal cultures. A few, like the Western Pueblos of Arizona and New Mexico, held to many customs which were not far different from those practiced at the time White men entered their country. Some, such as the Pimas of Arizona and Opatas of Sonora, had preserved little of their native way and were in the final stages of cultural assimilation. Most others, like the Navahos of Arizona and the Yaquis of Sonora, had altered their ways of life profoundly under the influence of Europeans. The cultures of all were thus in greater or less degree combinations of customs and beliefs derived from both the Indian and the European streams of tradition.

There appeared to be a limited number of types of response to contact. Each involved different modes of combining or integrating the cultural traditions concerned. The Yaquis, one of the larger tribes both at the beginning and at the end of the period under consideration, exhibited during a large part of their contact history a type which could be called fusion or synthesis, that is, a combination of cultural traditions resulting in a new, emergent cultural system.

7

The relationship of the conditions of contact to the type of cultural response of the Yaquis is the subject of this study. Over the four centuries of contact with Spaniards and Mexicans the Yaquis gained a reputation, unique among Indians of northern Mexico, for active "resistance to civilization." It is true that military activity was an important theme in Yaqui cultural history and that Yaquis undertook

TABLE 1

YAQUI CONTACT HISTORY

Period	Events	Contact Communities	General Type of Change
IV Relocation 1887—	1956 Main irrigation canal completed 1939 Tribal title to land by presidential decree 1927 Last "uprising" 1919 Resettlement begins 1910 Deportation program ends 1906 First Easter ceremony in Arizona 1897 Peace of Ortiz 1887 Mexican military occupation	Urban segments in Sonora and Arizona Relocated river towns	Assimilation Cultural revival
III Autonomous 1740–1887	1875 Cajeme appointed alcalde 1868 Massacre of Yaquis at Bacum 1833 Banderas executed 1824 First Banderas revolt 1771 Secularization of missions 1767 Expulsion of Jesuits 1740 First Yaqui-Mayo revolt	Autonomous river towns	Cultural resynthesis Cultural fusion
II Mission 1617–1767	1684 Alamos silver mines opened 1623 Founding of the Eight Towns 1617 Entrance of Jesuits	Mission communities	Acceptance of Spanish innovation
I Rancheria 1533–1617	1610 Yaquis defeat Hurdaide 1564 Ibarra prospecting expedition 1533 Guzmán slave raid	Rancherias	

military action as late as 1927. Moreover their military success was exceptional against both Spaniards and Mexicans. Nevertheless it will become clear that an interpretation of their behavior in terms such as "resistance to civilization" sheds little light on the nature of their successive adaptations to Western cultures.

We may distinguish four phases in Yaqui contact history. During their first sporadic encounters with Spaniards from 1533 until 1617, Yaquis maintained the aboriginal type of community which the

Spaniards called *rancherias*. No substantial changes in their way of life took place. Yet important conditions were established for the following period in the form of attitudes toward Spaniards and evaluations of features of Spanish culture with which they were as yet very imperfectly acquainted.

The next 150 years, from 1617 until 1767, constituted a phase in which Yaquis experienced intensive contact with a limited number of Spaniards. The setting of the contact was largely in a new form of community established by Jesuit missionaries. Centered around Jesuit-managed churches, the mission communities crystallized into tightly organized local groups which contrasted strongly with the looser rancherias. The mission communities persisted until the expulsion of the Jesuits from the New World in 1767.

In the early 1700's conditions on the Yaqui frontier began to change, so that even before the expulsion of the missionaries the circumstances of contact altered. The new situation took definite form in 1740 at the outbreak of a hard-fought revolt by Yaquis. For nearly another 150 years no effective political dominance over Yaquis was maintained either by the Spanish or the Mexican government. Yaqui communities existed through most of the period as practically autonomous entities. Military and political control was not established by Mexicans until 1887.

Decisive defeats of Yaquis in the 1880's inaugurated a whole new set of contact conditions. Military control of the Yaqui territory resulted in dispersal of Yaquis throughout Mexico and the southwestern United States. Almost wherever Yaquis went, despite necessary acceptance of political and economic integration into larger national wholes, they attempted to rebuild communities along the lines of the autonomous towns of the previous phase. The relocated communities maintained a variety of distinctive cultural ways, and the Yaquis who lived in them identified themselves as a distinctive people. By the middle of the twentieth century such communities were widely scattered over Sonora and Arizona.

The four phases of Yaqui contact history saw the development of four different systems of cultural behavior. So different were their total patterns that it would be unsatisfactory for purposes of cross-cultural comparison to speak of each simply as "Yaqui culture." It will be useful to employ such terms as Yaqui rancheria culture, Yaqui mission culture, Yaqui autonomous culture, and Yaqui relocated culture.

Yaqui Culture about 1600

As the Spaniards reported the situation in the late 1500's, little difference existed in the ways of life of the inhabitants of what is now northern Sinaloa and southern Sonora in northwestern Mexico (Pérez de Ribas 1645). The 115,000 people (Sauer 1935: 5; Beals 1943: 2) living along the bottom lands of the Sinaloa, Fuerte, Mayo, and Yaqui rivers all spoke dialects of a language—Cahita, as the Spaniards mistakenly named it—which varied little from tribe to tribe (Mason 1940: 68). Their economies were based solidly in agriculture, and they were all vigorously interested in organized warfare in connection with which they practiced forms of ceremonial cannibalism (Pérez de Ribas 1645: I, 132–33). Yet, similar as they were in language and culture, these Cahitan-speaking people by no means constituted a single unified population. On the contrary, they thought of themselves as at least sixteen distinct tribal groups (Beals 1943: 1). The warfare in which they exhibited so much interest was carried on chiefly among themselves. At the time of their first contacts with Spaniards, they were in a phase of instability with respect to tribal division and territorial identification.

The northernmost and the most populous of the Cahitan tribes were the Yaquis. They differed in no important ways in their inventory of culture traits from the other Cahitans (Beals 1943: 2). Their dialect was intelligible to the tribes on the Fuerte River 150 miles to the south and was almost identical with that of the Mayos, their immediate Cahitan neighbors. The Yaquis seem to have been no more warlike than the other Cahitans, but they distinguished themselves from the beginning as more successful in fighting off the Spaniards. The Spaniards who first reached them in 1533 consisted of a party of slave-raiders under Diego de Guzmán. The Yaquis forced Guzmán to retire to the south; the Spanish recorder of the battle wrote that his party had encountered no Indians in New Spain so valiant as the Yaquis (Bancroft 1884: I, 57; Troncoso 1905: 37). During the rest of the century contacts with Spaniards were very occasional and uniformly friendly. Meanwhile the Yaquis seem to have been sporadically at war with all their immediate neighbors, including the Guaymas on the west, the Lower Pimas on the north and east, and even the Cahitan-speaking Mayos on the southeast. It seems probable that their hostility to Pimas and Mayos was a result of dispute or uncertainty concerning the eastern boundaries of the territory which they claimed.

The interest in warfare had nothing directly to do with subsistence. Like all the Cahitans, the Yaquis were settled agriculturalists deriving

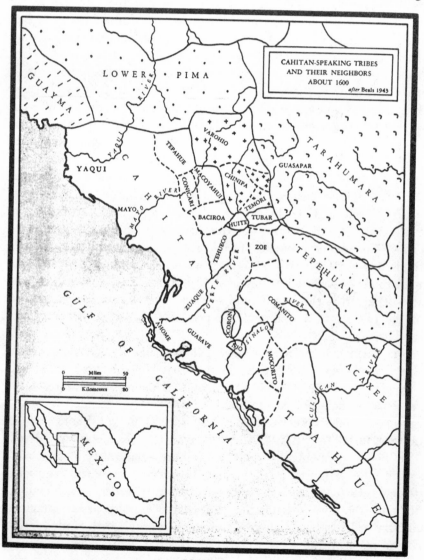

MAP 1

their living primarily from the planting of corn, beans, and squash (Beals 1943: 10 ff.). They lived in and along the well-defined flood-plain of the Yaqui River, occupying both sides of the lower course of the river from the Gulf of California to some sixty miles upstream. They made no irrigation works, but relied on the annual overflows of the river and on the rainfall to soak the ground for planting. The Yaqui River, like the other rivers along which the Cahitan people lived, had its source in the high Sierra Madre Mountains to the east and hence produced floods at least twice a year following the spring thaws and at the time of the heavy summer rains. It was possible for Yaquis to raise two crops a year on the highly fertile alluvial flood-plain. In addition, there was an abundance of wild foods and game. The beans of mesquite trees grew in profusion, a dozen different species of cactus yielded quantities of fruit, and many other kinds of wild fruits, seeds, and roots were available. Deer were numerous in the mountains bordering the river to the north, as were many forms of small game. Near the mouth of the river, the gulf produced various species of fish and shellfish. All such sources of wild foods were utilized, and the hunting of deer in organized parties was an especial interest of Yaquis, but the major reliance was on cultivated crops. No reliable estimate of the proportion of cultivated to wild foods was made by early observers, but it would seem doubtful that wild foods constituted as much as 40 per cent of Yaqui subsistence. We believe that the Yaqui economy was one of abundance, in view of the two crops a year and the profusion of supplementary wild foods.

The Spaniards reported 30,000 Yaquis living in eighty rancherias along the lower Yaqui River in the early 1600's (Pérez de Ribas 1645: II, 62; cf. Sauer 1935: 5). These settlements were located in or immediately adjacent to the bottom lands which extended for from two to ten miles on either side of the river. Thus the Yaqui population was concentrated in an area approximately sixty miles by fifteen. This meant a population density of more than thirty persons per square mile. It must be emphasized, however, that what Yaquis regarded as their territory extended over a vastly wider area, including not only the bottom lands but also a large expanse of mountainous country called the Bacatete Mountains to the north and a great coastal plain on the south. Thus the resources which they exploited covered an area of more than 3,500 square miles.

If, as Pérez de Ribas, the first missionary to enter Yaqui territory, said, the whole Yaqui population was comprised in the eighty rancherias, then settlements may have averaged between 300 and 400 persons. There is no clear indication that there was any great variation in the size of the rancherias. It seems rather that we may think of the Yaqui population as concentrated close to the river in settlements of about equal size. These were fairly evenly distributed from the gulf coast northeastward to where the floodplain pinched out and the river emerged from a gorge. Although all the early Spaniards reported encounters with Yaquis only at the river, it seems likely that there were many temporary and some more or less permanent camps, as bases for wild food gathering and hunting, scattered through the mountains. However, the Yaqui "rural" population must have been relatively very small.

A rancheria, as the Spaniards used the term, was to be distinguished from a pueblo (town or village) on the one hand and a camp on the other. In both permanence of location and compactness of dwelling units it stood somewhere between. Since the Yaqui settlements were at first described as rancherias, we may assume that the location of a group of dwellings was not necessarily fixed from year to year and that houses were not contiguous. There are no data regarding the number of buildings in a Yaqui rancheria. There were no permanent structures used as ceremonial centers. The form of the dwelling units varied, ranging from circular, dome-shaped, mat-covered houses of unknown size to rectangular, flat-roofed structures with woven cane or wattle and daub walls. Every cluster of dwelling units was also characterized by ramadas, or pole-supported roofs without walls, which served as shades for food preparation, lounging, and sleeping.

The location of any cluster of houses and shades constituting the households of a rancheria probably varied considerably over a period of years. Shifts in the course of the river, with consequent changes in the location of areas suitable for planting, were frequent, especially in the delta lands nearest the gulf coast. Adjustment to these vagaries of the river flow must have resulted in periodic changes in the location of the rancherias. What the organization of land use was we do not know. The considerable density of population, the active interest in farming, and the evident tribal unity (which will be discussed below) must have required a system of regulation which promoted co-operation among the rancherias. Yet no head rancherias or hierarchies of the Yaqui settlements were mentioned by the Spaniards. We may infer well-defined rancheria territories within which the local group was free to move in its adjustments to the changes in flow of the river. That there were well-recognized means of settling boundary disputes after floods had obliterated landmarks may also be inferred. It seems unlikely, however, in view of the very large area outside the floodplain that similar precision existed in defining the total tribal territory.

The rancherias were exogamous (Beals 1943: 52). The kinship terminology which survives to the present suggests an absence of lineages and points to a bilateral extended family as the basic social unit (Beals 1943: 47–52). Probably several such households made up each rancheria, and it is likely that they regarded themselves as related, in view of the rule of exogamy. Precisely what the character and strength of kinship ties were we do not know. The immediate acceptance of the Spanish program of "reduction" and the evidences of tribe-wide military organization point to the interpretation that segmentation on a kinship basis was not strongly developed.

The Spanish recording of events gives no information specifically for the Yaquis about the nature of organization wider than the rancheria. Nevertheless there are some data for other Cahitans and sufficient chronicling of Yaqui behavior in war and peacemaking to provide some basis for a general understanding. In 1533 and again in the first decade of the 1600's Yaquis were able to put in the field a fighting force which the Spaniards regarded as truly formidable. This force was reported to consist of as many as 5,000–7,000 warriors (Pérez de Ribas 1645: II, 68). Out of a population of 30,000 this must have included all the men of fighting age. In other words all the eighty rancherias during this whole period could be mobilized for defense of the Yaqui territory. That such complete mobilization was based on some system of military associations which put organized companies of young men into the field on short notice is indicated in the accounts of the Cahitans farther south. The companies of warriors fought under a unified leadership focused in a single field commander according to the earlier Spanish records, but this is not indicated at the time of the final conflict with Spaniards under Captain Hurdaide in 1609–10. The fighting was nevertheless highly effective and resulted in a Yaqui victory. The peace negotiations which followed the Yaqui military triumph, although initiated by Mayo leaders with a single named Yaqui leader, were carried through in a way that indicated wide participation on the part of Yaquis. In fact general assemblies took place in the Yaqui country in which older men had to outtalk younger men, and ultimately a party of 150 attended the making of the final offensive and defensive agreement with the Spanish captain (Pérez de Ribas 1645: II, 76–83).

The fact that this peace, once made, was never broken by Yaquis indicates a high degree of tribal unity with respect at least to external relations of the tribe. However, it cannot be concluded that any peacetime tribal-wide political organization existed. The general participation of the principal men of the rancherias in the making of the peace suggests an absence of political hierarchy. Moreover, during the subsequent reception of missionaries by the Yaquis, it became clear that, despite a unity of feeling among Yaquis regarding the desirability of admitting the missionaries, there was no one powerful individual who would or could guarantee safe reception of the Jesuits from one end of the Yaqui country to the other. The missionary advance was rather rancheria by rancheria (Pérez de Ribas 1645: II, 88–109).

We may infer that when there was no threat to the land area which Yaquis regarded as their collective territory, there was no tribal organization. It was only when threat appeared that Yaquis acted as a unity, and under such circumstances their organization was based on an assemblage of specialized military associations. In peacetime every rancheria was an autonomous unit in control of its own affairs. Rancheria government was in the hands of the adult males who met when occasion required in assemblies in which all had the right to speak. While the nature of leadership in the rancherias remains unrecorded, it is nevertheless fairly certain that there was no highly formalized command power vested in one or a few individuals. On the other hand, there is abundant indication that within the military organizations there were ranked offices and that the occupants of the higher ranks were distinguished by special insignia such as shell-embroidered capes and foxskins (Beals 1943: 41–42).

Life in the rancherias was characterized by simple subsistence activities with direct production and consumption, with no system of food storage and no trade in food (Beals 1943: 10–31). The only specialization in food production consisted in the emphasis on fishing in the rancherias which bordered the gulf. Men were the major food producers. They hunted small and larger game, usually in groups with specialized ritual. They carried out what fishing was done. They also did the greater part of the planting and cultivating of crops. The women were important in the gathering of wild food plants and fruits, and of shellfish. Together with the men they participated in the harvesting of the corn, beans, and squash. While men and women together engaged in house-building, the women only engaged in the making of mats, baskets, and pottery and wove the cotton and fiber textiles. There were no markets in which exchange of food or crafts took place, although a gift-exchange system for supplying the food necessary at large ceremonial gatherings was well developed. A more or less regular trade among Yaquis and with neighboring tribes was carried on in shell and stone ornaments and birds whose feathers could be used for ornament and ritual.

The religious life of the Yaquis was very inadequately reported, despite the fact that the first missionaries evidently took some interest in it and witnessed a good deal of ceremonial. The missionaries were impressed by what they reported as a comparative absence of "idols" among the Cahitans generally (Pérez de Ribas 1645: I, 138–39). Occasionally they saw stone or wooden figures, but these were stored away from the rancherias when not in use. Apparently the ritual connected with such objects escaped the notice of or was kept hidden from the Jesuits. The missionaries noted that it was a common practice to make ground paintings, that is, representations of animals or other figures in colored earth or other materials on the ground (Beals 1943: 65). These ceremonial paintings, which were laid out on the floors of special temporary ramadas, were destroyed, along with the buildings, when the ceremonies were over (Beals 1943: 60, 66). They, therefore, were not continuously obtruded on the attention of the missionaries. The Spaniards learned that individuals believed in spirits with which they had special personal relationships, a concept not strange to the Europeans. Much of Yaqui supernaturalism was concerned with such "guardian spirits" (Beals 1943: 59). Knowledge of them came to individuals under various circumstances, usually described as dreams. There were no recorded special techniques for inducing such visions. The fact that there were no permanent idols set up in the rancherias and that ceremonial activity centered about either ordinary dwellings or structures which were destroyed on completion of the ceremonies must have given the missionaries the feeling that they had rather less to combat than did their co-workers farther south in New Spain, where elaborate pantheons were represented in permanent and tangible form.

It was true nevertheless that Yaquis and other Cahitans believed in a wide variety of supernaturals (Beals 1943: 58–62). The sun as a male and the moon as a female deity were both the object of food offerings. A horned water serpent, a black dwarf associated with the rainbow, the horned toad associated with all land animals, an old woman who was patroness of all the humanlike beings of the sea, a supernatural deer, and a great variety of forms of guardian spirits were all important in Yaqui belief. The guardian spirits might appear to any individual as coyotes, dogs, mountain sheep, snakes, beautiful women, or winged beings. They gave power of different kinds, one of the most important of which was for curing disease.

Several kinds of ritual specialists existed, although all were usually called "witches" by the missionaries who became aware of them. There were diagnosticians who through dream or trance determined the cause of an illness or a misfortune and prescribed the cure; curing practitioners who employed singing, blowing, sucking, and other techniques; hunting specialists who knew the proper songs, dances, and invocations for the good will of the supernatural leader of the deer; men and women who knew the formulas for the ground paintings; and speakers who talked at great length in the open spaces between the houses in the rancherias. These last may have been moral exhorters or even tellers of news rather than ritual specialists proper, but they were reported by the Spaniards as connected with the supernatural beliefs of the Yaquis. Nothing clear emerges concerning the organization of these specialists, except the fact that some of them worked as individual practitioners rather than as part of any systematically organized ceremonial groups. It appears, however, that there were organized groups whose nature the missionaries did not discover or neglected to record.

It would be dangerous to draw positive conclusions from the Spanish accounts concerning the major ceremonial interests of Yaquis. It is indicated that agricultural activities and the germination of seeds were not, at least directly, the focus of ceremony. There is further no indication that rain-making or other weather-control rites had any important place. This is easy to accept when we consider the conditions under which Yaqui agriculture was pursued. There was an abundant and regular supply of water, and the soil was extremely fertile. If there were ritual concerned with natural phenomena related to crop production, we might expect it to have dealt with flood prevention, for unexpected floods were the major source of crop destruction and consequent shortage of cultivated foods. Ceremonies which were noted especially were of three kinds. One recurrent type for Cahitans generally consisted in war ceremonies. They took place both before and after battles and included dances, feasting, and intoxication on maguey or other forms of fermented drink. Hunting rites were also important. These varied but included usually animal impersonation or representation by dancers; drums and cane whistles were the musical instruments employed. A third type of ceremony reported by eye witnesses among the Spaniards involved some type of initiation or ceremonial sponsoring rites; the erection of two separate temporary houses, ground paintings, and ceremonial dances centering around the latter characterized such rites. Along with these indications of ceremonial interests should be included the numerous individually conducted curing rituals.

The culture of the Yaqui rancherias in the period before intensive contact with Europeans cannot be characterized with certainty. The Spanish records provide only information on a few selected aspects. Modern reconstructions of the culture in the light of Cahitan customs generally help to round out the picture. Points on which we can rely in our analysis of the three and a half centuries of culture change following 1600 are: (1) Yaqui population had attained a fairly high degree of density; (2) yet the level of organization for most purposes was that of the local group of not more than 400. (3) However, a strong sense of tribal solidarity existed and could be translated into tribal-wide organization under threat of invasion. (4) The tribal organization appeared to be based on a system of military associations with ranked offices. (5) The economic level of development was that of the small self-sufficient settlement engaged in subsistence agriculture with much wild food supplementation. Neither markets nor extensive individual or regional specialization had developed. (6) As indicated in ceremonial activity major orientations of the culture consisted in warfare, "initiation" rites, hunting, and curing; at least these were the chief ceremonially emphasized interests reported by the early Spanish observers. (7) Ritual techniques emphasized the individual vision as a source of supernatural power and among ceremonials a variety of group and individual dances often connected with animal representation either in the dance or in ground paintings. (8) Yaqui relations with outsiders at the time Spaniards encountered them uniformly involved warfare; that is, all immediately neighboring tribes were regarded as threats to Yaqui security and as sources of ritual power through organized warfare. (9) The Spaniards were promptly met by the Yaquis on the same basis as they were currently dealing with other tribes in their vicinity.

The Mission Communities—1617–1767

To the Jesuit missionaries who worked their way up the west coast of Mexico beginning in 1590 the Cahitans appeared as "rude and barbarous" people. The Jesuits were shocked by the ceremonial cannibalism, the nakedness, and the group intoxication. They thought the mat-covered round houses were crude and saw great opportunity for improving Indian farming by introducing plows and livestock. They assumed that no religion existed; they were pleased at the relative lack of "idols" and felt great sympathy for the "witch"-ridden Indians. They themselves believed deeply in demons and other evil spirits and welcomed the chance to introduce faith in good spirits. The interests of the missionaries were focused on eliminating warfare, improving agriculture, and providing a faith in heaven and a benevolent deity. These ends were realized with remarkable rapidity among the Yaquis. Within a half-dozen years after the first entry of missionaries in 1617 the foundations of a new type of community had been laid (Pérez de Ribas 1645:II, 121–28). For a century and a quarter thereafter the Jesuit leadership was accepted by Yaquis and the life of the rancherias was transformed. The transformation is the more interesting when we realize that the initial and basic changes were not effected as a result of forcible, military conquest and that the following century of continued growth of a new way of life took place without the presence of Spanish soldiers in the Yaqui communities.

The generally enthusiastic reception of the Jesuits in 1617 was the culmination of a series of events which had prepared Yaquis in a very special way for intensive contact with the missionaries. The first contact with Spaniards in 1533 was a hard-fought battle which forced Diego de Guzmán, a slave-raider, out of Yaqui territory. A second contact thirty-one years later was of a quite different character. Francisco de Ibarra, exploring for minerals from headquarters in Zacatecas, found Yaquis peaceful and helpful to his expedition (Mecham 1927: 179). His party spent some time on the Yaqui River, joined the Yaquis in a fight against Mayos, and when they departed were urged to come back. Ibarra had sixty soldiers, three hundred horses, and two friars in his party. They evidently stayed long enough among Yaquis for the latter to gain some knowledge of Spanish artifacts and religious and military behavior. They already knew something about the dangerousness of Spaniards as fighting men; Ibarra's party provided an acquaintance with peaceful aspects of Spanish culture. During the 1590's Spaniards advanced steadily up the west coast of Mexico, establishing missions under Jesuit management and presidios for their protection. About 1600 Captain Diego Martínez de Hurdaide was appointed Captain-General of Sinaloa and took command of the Spanish town and presidio of San Felipe y Santiago on the Fuerte River, 150 miles south of the Yaqui (Decorme 1941: II, 164). He was an especially vigorous man and set out to conquer rapidly all the Cahitan-speaking people of the Fuerte, Mayo, and Yaqui valleys. Most resisted briefly, but some, like the Mayos, entered into alliance with the Spaniards. Flourishing missions grew up rapidly along the Fuerte River, and Mayos sent delegations to inspect the new activities. They were very favorably impressed with what they saw among the Sinaloas, Tehuecos, Zuaques, and Ahomes (Acosta 1949: 37; Pérez de Ribas 1645: I, 310). The Yaquis, too, in view of the considerable communication between the various Cahitan tribes, must have been fairly well acquainted with the nature of the mission communities established by the Jesuits. They were nevertheless not led, like their enemies the Mayos, to form an alliance with Hurdaide.

Rather the Yaquis made it clear that they would not submit to Spanish power. In campaigns between 1608 and 1610 they met and defeated Captain Hurdaide three times. In the final encounter, for which Hurdaide raised the largest army yet seen under Spanish command on the west coast, the captain himself barely escaped capture. His fifty mounted Spaniards and 4,000 Indian troops were completely routed by the Yaquis. The Yaquis were reported to have put 7,000 fighting men in the field. So formidable did they seem to Hurdaide that he ceased campaigning against them (Pérez de Ribas 1645: II, 75–76; Alegre 1841:II, 33–36).

To Hurdaide's surprise, the victorious Yaquis then asked that Jesuit missionaries be sent to them and indicated that they were ready for further peace moves. In the extensive negotiations which followed the Yaquis agreed to maintain an alliance with the Spaniards and hence with their neighbors the Mayos. They also agreed to return captured horses and arms and emphasized their desire for missionaries. The Spanish chroniclers offered various interpretations for the behavior of the victorious Yaquis in seeking peace, such as that Yaquis feared the apparently magical powers of Hurdaide, who had escaped capture by a clever ruse. It seems likely that Yaquis saw an opportunity in their victory to secure what they had desired for several years, namely, Jesuit missionaries without military and political submission to the Spaniards. At any rate the missionaries were sent to them, seven years later, without military escort, and it was not until a full year after the Jesuits had worked among the Yaquis that Captain Hurdaide appeared for a brief visit to pay his respects (Decorme 1941: II, 328).

The first two Jesuits, Andrés Pérez de Ribas and Tomas Basilio, who undertook the missionization of the Yaquis were accompanied only by four baptized Zuaque Indians from the Fuerte River (Pérez de Ribas 1645: II, 88–90). Their reception was very favorable, although some Yaqui mothers were frightened by the baptism ceremony for children and had to be persuaded to accept it. The downriver rancherias were first reported as hostile, but the baptism of some headmen resulted in as friendly a reception in that part of the Yaqui country as had taken place elsewhere. Within two years almost the whole of the 30,000 population had been baptized. Within six years—by 1623—the eighty rancherias had been reduced to eight "pueblos," or towns. During the first months there were two attempts on the life of Basilio, and interference from persons called "witches" by the missionaries was not infrequent. Other than such occasional and individual opposition the Jesuits experienced no resistance. On the contrary the Yaqui leaders and the people generally offered the fullest co-operation. They not only submitted themselves for instruction and baptism, they also enthusiastically went to work, under the supervision of the missionaries, building simple adobe churches and houses for the Jesuits.

These initial contacts indicated a very high degree of prestige for the Jesuits. Knowledge of them and their work in introducing seeds and livestock farther south was possessed by Yaquis for at least twenty years before their arrival. Yaquis evidently had no single favorable or unfavorable stereotype for Spaniards. They distinguished between desirable Spaniards and Spaniards whom they wished to keep at a distance. While they rejected vigorously Spanish military control, they accepted just as positively the Jesuit program and were willing, in order to get one without the other, to include the Spaniards in their system of military alliances. The Jesuits who first came to the Yaquis spoke the Cahitan dialects of the Fuerte River tribes and at the same time had as assistants the Cahitan-speaking Zuaques. The missionaries thus not only began with the strong good will of Yaquis, but they were also able immediately to communicate effectively with them. All of these conditions no doubt contributed to good working relations from the first. The Jesuits were surprised and delighted with the Yaqui reaction to their program. They wrote that the Yaquis, whom they had expected to be savage and resistant, were equally with the "peaceful" Mayos most attentive to all preaching and instruction and that they showed exceptional ability not only in learning the new doctrines but also in teaching fellow Yaquis as soon as they had been instructed. During the whole of the 1600's and after, the Jesuits regarded the Yaqui missions as showplaces of their work in northwestern Mexico (Acosta 1949: 78–79).

The communities in which the Yaquis experienced their first intensive contacts with aspects of Spanish culture were basically creations of the Jesuit missionaries. It is difficult to imagine the rapid development of this type of community without the purposeful guidance of the Jesuits. It was uniform policy of the Jesuit Order, as of other missionary groups, in the early 1600's to "reduce" all Indians to settled life in "pueblos," as similar as possible to European towns. The Jesuits did not accept the Yaqui rancherias as sufficiently concentrated settlements. They proceeded immediately to stimulate the growth of more compact local groups by having Yaquis build eight mission churches at more or less regular intervals, some six or seven miles apart, throughout the length of the Yaqui country. They proposed then to have the whole thirty thousand Yaquis gather their dwellings close to one or the other of these new ceremonial centers. This, we are told, the Yaquis had pretty much done within six or seven years after the first baptisms. We need not believe that all Yaquis had complied with the Jesuit plan so quickly. Undoubtedly some families preferred to remain away from the new centers; devotion to old spots did not disappear in a few years. However, the spacing of the churches along the whole length of the settlement area enabled people to come to the churches easily without changing residence; each church could have served ten rancherias more or less without immediate change in house location. Whatever the rate of movement and whatever the number of families who preferred at first not to participate in the new ways, there is no doubt that well before 1700 a new settlement pattern had been created, a pattern which became so firmly established among Yaquis that they came to believe it sacred and established by supernatural mandate.

This new community type required a shift from one level of local group organization to another. Formerly probably the maximum size of a rancheria was not much above 400. Once the 30,000 Yaquis had moved into proximity around the eight churches, each new town consisted of between 3,000 and 4,000 inhabitants, or the population of as many as ten rancherias. What was involved was not simply a physical shift of house location, but the acceptance of a common governmental system, including management of farmlands. This meant realignment of family groups and loss of rancheria autonomy. That it was accomplished, as was evidently true, without the creation of cleavages and factionalism of importance in the new towns suggests strong leadership and lack of need for coercive measures. Yaqui population, in contrast with Mayo, did not decline during the first hundred years of contact, so that a population of 30,000 was involved in this shift.

Each of the new towns centered around an adobe church building surrounded by graveyard and plaza. Somewhere near were a simple residence for the missionary and such assistants as he required to live near him and corrals for the cattle and sheep and horses which were promptly introduced. No wall or other inclosure separated the mission establishment from the rest of the town. Houses of the residents were built in irregular arrangement in the general vicinity of the church; if the missionaries were interested in the grid plan of town layout, they were not successful in introducing it. The common territory of each town was marked off from its neighbors by groups of three large wooden crosses at the boundaries. There were eight

such towns, established and named within the first few years of
Jesuit activity (Acosta 1949: 63–64; Alegre 1841: II, 122). The eight
names, as well as the town territories, persisted for the next 300 years,
although, as we shall see, in later years only in Yaqui thought.

During the 1600's there were no more than ten missionaries in
residence at any time in the Yaqui towns. One or two lived at each
of the newly established mission churches. One of the first activities
organized by each missionary was the instruction of a Yaqui staff.
Men were selected to be trained as *temastianes,* that is, as catechists
and caretakers of the church (Bolton 1936: 10). Although they were
taught Spanish, the instruction of other Yaquis by them was carried
out in the Yaqui language. An Italian Jesuit, Father Jacobo Baisle,
prior to 1652 had translated the catechism, the standard prayers,
probably the Mass for the Dead, and other elements of Christian
doctrine into Yaqui (Acosta 1949: 73–74). These translations were
used regularly in the immense task of instructing the Yaqui population, and thus thousands of Yaquis who satisfied the missionaries as
being properly instructed did not have a command of the Spanish
language. We do not know how many temastianes were trained, but
a very considerable corps must have been necessary to enable the
missionaries to reach the large Yaqui population and maintain the
instruction of the new generations. There were, as a result, in every
town Yaquis who were literate in both Spanish and Yaqui.

The missionaries also carried on as part of their program the development of agriculture. This required the selection of individuals
to care for the stock and oversee the cultivation of the land which
was set aside for the support of the missionaries. Hoes, plows, and
new crops were introduced as well as livestock, and of course the
six-day workweek. The Jesuits had remarkable success in increasing
the agricultural production of the Yaquis. Their fertile and easily
irrigable lands were capable of high yield. The missionaries found
Yaquis willing to work under their direction. The result was that
by the 1680's a considerable surplus was being produced; a stone
warehouse was constructed at the town of Torim to take care of it
(Acosta 1949: 78; Spicer 1942: field notes). A port was established
at the mouth of the river, and the Yaqui country became a major
source of supply for the ever expanding Jesuit missions in Lower
California and to the northwest in Sonora.

Each missionary was also the actual head of government in his town of residence and other settlements which he regularly visited. The town officials were in theory appointed by the captain-general of the province, but in fact it was the missionary who appointed, or at least approved the choices for the major offices. Until the early 1700's there was little attempt on the part of the colonial administration to direct the affairs of the Yaqui towns.

All of these duties were in addition to the focal concern of the missionary, namely, the conduct of Christian services and the administration of sacraments. The Mass was said each Sunday and strict discipline was exercised in getting as many Yaquis to attend as possible. In this the missionary employed one or more *fiscales*, or church officials, who helped to bring people to church and gathered groups together for instruction. The fiscal was especially important in bringing children together for daily instruction in the saying of prayers and making of the sign of the cross. Failure to attend Mass was sometimes punished by whipping at a whipping post in the town. The missionary also taught music and dramatic representation of Christian belief, such as a form of Passion play, the Battle of the Moors and Christians, and a dance drama dealing with Malinche, the first Christian Indian in Mexico (Kurath 1949: 87–106).

In a population as large as the Yaqui, the Jesuits were heavily dependent on assistants. During much of the time there were no regularly resident missionaries at various towns. Under such circumstances direct and intimate relations were confined to a selected few, probably chiefly temastianes, fiscales, and the major officials in the town government. An active missionary in a town of 4,000 could not keep in constant touch with either the details of town government or the execution of the instruction and the dramatic representations which he initiated. In short, it must be presumed that to a very large extent, although the new organization of agricultural activities, ceremonial life, and government had been initiated by the Jesuits, it remained for Yaquis themselves to carry it out and interpret it to one another. Either as a result of Jesuit policy or because of the special circumstances, Jesuits relied heavily on persuasion rather than forcible prohibition for the elimination of religious practices which seemed wrong or distasteful to them (e.g., Beals 1943: 66–68). There is little record of destruction of any ceremonial materials or forcible break-up of ceremonies by the missionaries in the Yaqui country. There is rather indication of a tendency to discuss native ceremonies and to suggest Christian interpretations. The missionaries evidently succeeded in behaving in a manner which almost throughout the Jesuit period resulted in their being greatly liked and highly respected. Resentment of Yaquis toward Jesuits appeared only in the period just preceding the great revolt of 1740. Before and after that holocaust good will toward the Jesuits was general.

The Jesuits maintained a nearly unique position in the Yaqui country for something like a century. It was unique in its contrast with most other parts of the frontier of New Spain. There was no Spanish settlement within Yaqui territory during the Jesuit period. This meant that there were no *encomienda* grants and consequently an absence of the forced labor system which was so common elsewhere. There was not even Spanish settlement within sixty miles of the Yaqui towns until more than sixty years after the Jesuits had begun work. Mines at the edge of the Mayo country in the 1680's and later on the middle Yaqui River brought Spanish settlers within fifty miles of the Yaquis (Acosta 1949: 75), but the mines were not within Yaqui territory and consequently Yaquis remained relatively isolated. It was not until the 1730's, a century and a quarter after the founding of the Yaqui towns, that the characteristic conflict of the frontier of New Spain began to affect the mission communities in an important way. By that time, the growth of mining settlements on the south, east, and north of the Yaquis, and the development of haciendas on the Mayo River, less than fifty miles away, had reduced the long-existent isolation of the Yaquis.

Under the early conditions of isolation, the civil administrators had paid relatively little attention to what was going on in the Yaqui country. It had been possible for the Jesuits to work in accordance with their ideal of treating the Indian towns as transitional communities for as long as possible. It had been possible to avoid pressure from the civil authorities to divide up the Indian lands and require the payment of tribute. However, as soon as some Spaniards by the 1730's had established themselves as *hacendados*, or large agricultural proprietors, in the depopulated Mayo country, the conflict between missionaries and civil authorities broke out. To the latter the Yaquis, with their considerable surplus production of wheat and other crops, looked ready for the payment of tribute and no longer in need of the protective guidance of the missionaries. An anti-Jesuit captain-general touched off serious dispute in 1739 which led to the Yaqui revolt of 1740. During the war, although all other Spaniards were killed or chased out of the Yaqui country, the Jesuits were treated with a sort of proprietary tenderness (Decorme 1941: II, 337–38). One was kept prisoner for the purpose of maintaining the Catholic sacraments, the others were provided with food and given safe escort to the nearest Spanish settlements. The effects of the revolt on Yaqui-Spanish relationships were of profound importance and will be discussed at length below. But after peace was made, Yaqui relations with the Jesuits reshaped in accordance with the familiar mold of the preceding century.

Jesuits introduced a major innovation after the revolt of 1740, namely, an organized school system with its plant at Rajum in the western Yaqui country (Tamarón y Romeral 1765: 247–48). Two boys from each town were selected each year for advanced instruction at the Rajum school. Those who did well under the missionary teachers were then sent on to higher Jesuit schools, usually in Mexico City. This plan of higher education for selected male students had been in operation for about twenty-five years when in 1767 the Jesuits were expelled from New Spain, and the mission community era in Yaqui cultural history came to an end.

The Jesuit regime had stimulated a wider integration among Yaquis at the community level. The scale of Yaqui society as a whole was also very considerably widened between 1617 and 1767. Each Jesuit missionary was at the end of an administrative line linking him with the international hierarchy of the Order. This meant that there was a regular stream of Visitors and Inspectors coming to the Yaqui towns to collect information, give confirmations, and be entertained. The Yaqui mission communities were characterized by far more of this kind of link with the wider world than by visits of civil authorities with their military retinues. However, during the early part of the Jesuit regime Yaquis were enlisted with Spanish soldiers for a brief campaign against their old enemies the Lower Pimas. Yaquis also, even before the disastrous war of 1740, had begun to go out from the Yaqui country occasionally to work in mines. It seems probable that Yaquis were included among the numerous "Sonorans" listed as working in such mines as those at Parral in the 1600's (West 1949: 49, 55). About the time of the Jesuit departure, Yaquis were constant and valued workers in the mines at Soyopa on the middle Yaqui River. They had thus during this period begun to experience Spanish life in a variety of ways and places. A small proportion had become literate and had begun acquaintance with the liturgical literature of the Catholic Church, in Latin, in Spanish, and in Yaqui translations. Since Yaquis were considered Christians, they were not recruited for forced labor in the mines or elsewhere, but received wages for their work. In addition, the Yaqui horizon was expanded as a result of their accepting positions with the missionaries as the latter moved deeper into northwestern New Spain. Yaquis went as interpreters, stock foreman, catechists, and general handymen and women of all work to serve temporarily, or sometimes permanently, in the missions which were being established among the Opatas and Pimans.

We may summarize the significant conditions with respect to cultural changes which took place in the Jesuit mission communities. In contrast with the sharp declines in population characteristic of the Mayos and almost all other Indians of the region, the Yaqui population seems to have changed very little during the first century of Jesuit contact. There was decline thereafter, but the period of crystallization of the mission communities was one of population stability. Yaqui community life was rapidly reorganized on a wider basis with an increase in the average local group size to 3,000 or more. This wider level of community organization was not associated with any intensification of tribal organization along lines which had existed before the arrival of the Spaniards. There was, however, some linkage with the national life of Spain, chiefly through the ecclesiastical roles of the missionaries and their associates in the Jesuit Order. Through wage work for Spaniards in various capacities Yaquis also in some degree participated in the national economy of Spain and New Spain, but for the most part they were kept isolated in a small subsistence economy by the Jesuit-organized system of production in the tax-free Yaqui territory. For a period of some five generations, until the outbreak of the revolt of 1740, the Jesuit leadership was accepted by Yaquis in an atmosphere of cooperation and complete friendliness. There was no conquest of the Yaquis as an initial basis for resentment and hatred, and Jesuit behavior seems to have roused a minimum of antagonism. Under these conditions proceeded an intensive program of directed change. The limited segment of Spanish society in direct contact with Yaqui society consisted almost exclusively of missionaries with interest

focused on replacing the Yaqui religious system but with little awareness of the nature of that system. The program of directed change
was extremely limited in personnel; that is, the population to be
reached was extremely large in proportion to the number of innovators who sought to redirect Yaqui cultural development.

The Culture of the Mission Communities

Our knowledge of life in the eight towns during the 1600's
stems entirely from the reports of the Jesuits. And these are not
adequate for an understanding of the processes involved. The missionaries were too narrowly centered in their interests to be capable
of observing widely what went on about them. Like modern innovators of programs of directed change they were inclined to write
chiefly about their successes and to ignore the extensive areas where
their influence was felt in attenuated form or not at all. As a result
we have no accounts of Yaqui family life and little that reveals the
working of the town organization. Even ceremonial life remains
undescribed, since the missionaries took for granted what went on
in and about the churches and either closed their eyes to or were
uninformed about what took place elsewhere.

We are greatly limited, therefore, in what we can say about how
the introductions of the Jesuits were fitted to the culture of the
Yaquis or about modifications of Yaqui customs under the impact of
the Jesuit program. The culture of this period is in fact the least
known of any. What we can do is list the introductions which were
made, for it is clear from later descriptions of Yaqui culture which
elements could have been introduced only during this time.

The Jesuit period from 1617 to 1767 was one during which a very
large number of innovations were presented to the Yaquis. It might
give us the best possible perspective on Yaqui cultural history if we
think of this as the century and a half of Spanish innovation. In a
very short space of time Yaquis were made aware, through Jesuit
action, comment, and attitude, of a new evaluation of their established ways. Shelter, clothing, technology of cutting tools, cultivated
crops, farming methods, work habits, time counting, musical instruments, dance forms as Yaquis knew them were suddenly alternatives
rather than the only established and proper ways. The church and
agricultural headquarters of the missionary in each of the eight towns
became demonstration centers where adobe brick construction, the

six-day workweek, and all the other new ways of doing things stood as visible evidence of a different life. Wholly new techniques, for which there had been no equivalents among Yaquis, such as the use of domestic animals and writing, became with the same suddenness a part of daily life. At the same time new means of organization came into operation—peacetime authority of a single man over the population of what had been as many as ten rancherias, a roster of officials running to several score with sharply differentiated functions and new titles and insignia, sodalities for taking care of the church and its colorful images, sodalities for performing the new dances and playing the new music, stocks and whipping post for enforcing the new rules, and a somewhat mysterious authority in the background represented now and then in a Father Visitor. Related to all the rest through the person of the missionary, and obviously regarded by him as the most important of all, were the new religious symbols and ideas, such as the cross and the sign of the cross, the Virgin, Jesus, the saints, the five verbal formulas of the standard prayers, pageantry at Holy Week, a saint for the town's own and a great celebration for it, many ceremonies for honoring the dead, and scores of other ritual acts and concepts.

What came to the Yaquis from Spanish culture during this period was a selection by the missionaries. They were interested primarily in their mission program and were trained and commanded by their superiors to further it. While this had as its ultimate objective the saving of souls, there were necessary material means to that end. Foremost among these were food and equipment not only for each Yaqui mission but also for missions elsewhere and to-be-established. There was therefore heavy emphasis on the agricultural establishments and all that went with them, especially in the Yaqui country, where good land and tractable workers were abundant. Thus a strong focus on agricultural production characterized missionary behavior in the Yaqui towns. It was also true that the colonial authorities insisted on the organization of all reduced communities in accordance with a common plan. The missionaries were required to organize and maintain "pueblos" to insure that the Indians learned the ways of civilized government and that the provincial officials would have constituted authorities with whom to deal when they wished. Thus pressure for change lay strongly in the areas of agriculture and government, as well as in religion.

Vicfors

In general, it may be said that the Yaqui reaction to the host of new artifacts, behaviors, and ideas was one of ready acceptance. Nearly all of the cultural elements offered seem to have been accepted, for the well-described culture of the late nineteenth century included a very long inventory of elements which could have been introduced only by the Jesuits in the earliest period of contact. By acceptance we do not of course mean acceptance without modification. Most of the many Spanish-derived traits which became a part of Yaqui culture were altered, some slightly, some extensively. In general, the tendency was for Yaquis to accept readily the form of what was offered by the missionary and attach to it quite different meanings from those understood by the Jesuit. As an example, even the cross itself, which was certainly utilized from the earliest contact with the Jesuits, was not conceived simply as the missionaries understood it. Yaquis associated it with a female deity whom they called "Our Mother" and treated at least one form of the cross overtly as a female requiring dress and ornamentation at the spring festival of what became the Finding of the Holy Cross; such identification of cross and female deity continued into the 1950's (Spicer 1958: 434–36). This kind of reinterpretation of the new forms was pervasive, but it must be emphasized that nearly the whole inventory of religious beliefs and practices which the Jesuits introduced was accepted in some manner. No complete rejections can be pointed to, for even the belief in Hell, which was difficult for Yaquis to reconcile with their form of ancestral worship, was accepted even if in greatly modified form.

There is no indication that the first elements incorporated into Yaqui daily life were tools and techniques. It makes little sense to attempt to understand the processes of acceptance in terms of a supposed differential susceptibility to change of the "aspects" of culture. What seems to have been important at first was not so much the innovations as the innovators—Pérez de Ribas and Basilio in their roles as teachers of a novel way of life. Yaquis generally seem to have done what they asked, gaining increasing interest in and respect for what they instituted as their contacts with them developed. The first Yaqui gesture in greeting the Jesuits consisted in a mass welcome, the crowds holding small wooden crosses in their hands which they knew would please the Jesuits (Pérez de Ribas 1645: II, 89). What the missionaries presented to them first consisted in ideas, spoken in Cahita, about God and Heaven and individual rituals including recitation of short prayers, the making of the sign of the cross, and baptism. It was in an atmosphere of religious devotion and novel ritual that Yaquis proceeded to learn the techniques of adobe-making, writing, stock-raising, violin-playing, candle-making, dramatization of the Passion play, and all the other activities for which the mission churches became immediate centers.

It would be of immense interest if we knew something about how differing roles in Yaqui society influenced attitudes toward and participation in the new techniques and roles offered by the Jesuits. We do not however have any basis for inferring even differential behavior of men and women in the new situation. We do know that the Jesuits offered nearly as many opportunities for women to be active in the new church organization as for men and that there were important places for children as well as adults (Spicer 1954: 78–93). One can guess that the many roles in town government made possible an easy adjustment of prestige in the old rancherias to the new town organization and consequently no resistance from a former elite. There was reported some slight resistance by individual ritual practitioners who opposed and were opposed by the Jesuits. Our view of how the innovations came into Yaqui culture, the steps in their acceptance, must remain cloudy unless more information can be gleaned from historical documents. The picture which is permitted us at present is a simple one—Yaquis generally accepted whatever the missionaries urged on them and showed them how to do. This view is inescapable when we consider the assemblage of traits in later periods.

While some of these traits have been mentioned, and will be again, it may be useful to summarize them here. In doing so, we are forced for lack of data, to do it in the form of an inventory; we know very little about the interrelationships of these traits during the Jesuit era.

In the first place there was a great enrichment of the vocabulary of the Yaqui language (Spicer 1943: 410–26). There is very little indication that Yaquis pursued any course except that of borrowing directly the Spanish words for those new tools and ideas which they began to employ. If there was any tendency to make up words in Yaqui to designate the new traits, this did not result in lasting contribution to the Yaqui vocabulary. It seems likely that good communication between Jesuits and Yaquis they gathered about them as assistants played a part in this transfer of Spanish words; it is also suggested that the high prestige of the missionaries led to borrowing of the words they used. Words borrowed during this earlier period, when Yaquis were not widely accustomed to the hearing of Spanish, consisted of such forms as *Lios* (for *dios,* God), *kus* (for *cruz,* cross), *loria* (*Gloria,* heaven), *aasul* (*azul,* blue), *tiiko* (*trigo,* wheat), *kabayum* (*caballo,* horse), *nabasum* (*navaja,* knife), and a hundred or more others, besides a long list of Christian given names, such as *Pahsiko* (Francisco) and *Tiniran* (Trinidad), and titles of church and town officials such as *alawasin* (for *alguacil,* constable), *kobanao* (for *governador,* governor), and *pihkan* (*fiscal,* church official). Two hundred years after this borrowing began the Spanish-derived words had become solidly integrated into the Yaqui lexicon and were regarded by Yaquis as no more foreign than the rest of their vocabulary.

The constant focus of each missionary on religious instruction and the maintenance of church ritual brought about the rapid introduction of Christian verbal and behavioral forms. These forms, as we have seen, had to diffuse outward from the missionary through his immediate associates, the newly trained temastianes, to various levels of appointed ceremonial officials, and thence to the townspeople at large. We may assume that this process resulted in much wider acquaintance with the ritual forms than with the meanings which the Jesuits attached to those forms. It must not be assumed therefore that the list of forms which follows had meanings for Yaquis at this time that were closely similar to those held by the missionaries, or indeed that there was always a generally accepted meaning among Yaquis this early in the process of introduction.

Very probably the Jesuit religious ideas constituted alternatives for most Yaquis during most of the period. The new conception of the supernatural world with its centralization of power in the mysterious Trinity, its division of an afterworld into good and bad regions, its separation of men and animals and exclusive reservation of power to human spirits must have taken a good deal of reconciling with the earlier conception of the supernatural world held by Yaquis. In the 1940's the process of reconciliation was still in progress (Spicer 1940: 196–99). Nevertheless the various supernaturals, even if only as alternatives to the native forms, were early accepted and became familiar, at least in certain contexts, to most Yaquis. The Trinity as three Gods, the Blessed Mary, Saint John the Baptist, Saint Michael, Saint Ignatius, many other saints, guardian angels, and angels in general became part of Yaqui life. The missionaries sought vigorously to secure paintings and three dimensional representations for the churches and so made them tangible (Acosta 1949: 64). Especially Jesus, represented in many forms ranging from a red-robed figure entering Jerusalem on a donkey to Ecce Homo on the cross, became a focus of Yaqui interest and ceremonial activity (Spicer 1954: 117–19). The concept of obligation and duty to the supernaturals who were all human in form was juxtaposed with the Yaqui conception of the whole natural world as a source of power through mystical experience and magical formula. It would be interesting to know their relations in Yaqui thinking during this period, but we do not.

A calendar of ceremonial events characterized by a new short rhythm in the weekly Mass and associated services was introduced. Annual ceremonies such as Holy Week, All Souls, and the saint's days with their specific forms of procession, genuflection and kneeling, image-bearing and incensing became part of Yaqui life, and a new set of crisis rites was introduced which became, probably during Jesuit times, integrated with existing ones. One of the most important in Jesuit conception was baptism, which from the time of the first occasions (for which the Zuaques accompanying the missionaries served as godparents) was integrated with the existing ceremonial sponsorship rites and became of deep importance in Yaqui culture (Spicer 1940: 91–116).

New forms of ceremonial organization were a major interest of the Jesuits. Sodalities, or sisterhoods and brotherhoods of different types, were a part of European lay organization for assistance in church affairs. Organizations such as the Knights of Columbus, the Matachine dancers, the Judases or Pharisees, women's choir society, and others constituted important features of the church organization, in addition to the immediate assistants of the missionaries, the temastianes. The church organization was centralized under the direction of the Jesuit but gave much scope for Yaqui leadership with its various specialized associations of men and women.

The church was closely linked with the town government since in the conception of the missionary who was the head of both there was no real separation of civil and ecclesiastical affairs in the life of the community. The offices of governor and assistants, instituted in the first year after arrival of the missionaries, were properly filled by popular election each year, but nevertheless approval of elected officials by the Jesuits was customary (Acosta 1949: 83–86). In all decisions of any moment in town affairs the governors sat with the officials of the church organization and deliberated together. It would be dangerous to attempt any fuller description of the functioning of the towns in the 1600's.

The nature of the military organization during this period we do not know, but it is probable that it existed in some form continuously from the days of the rancherias.

The organizations mentioned superseded what organization there had been in the rancherias. In some fashion, under the authority of the missionary, the new wider integration of the local group from rancheria to town was achieved. Such organization was probably at the expense of some kinship group solidarity, but it became apparent in the revolt of 1740 that it in no way reduced the capacity for overall tribal action. The growth of these new forms of organization involved the acceptance of a large number of new status terms, many of them taken from Spanish military terminology (Spicer 1943: 417–18). If the missionaries, as seems likely, attempted to promulgate an authoritarian type of local organization, this was by no means successful. If such organization prevailed during the Jesuit period, it gave way immediately after to a governmental system with wide dispersion of powers and direct participation of all adult males.

An integral part of the new system of organization consisted of the agricultural establishment. Here tied in with the new discipline of weekly observance of Mass was the six-day workweek and foreman-managed crews of herders and farmers working for church benefit.

An important word accepted by Yaquis in this period was a term for work, namely, *tekil* and its verbal form *tekipanoa* (Spicer 1954: 177). These were adaptations of an Aztec word, introduced by the Jesuits. It is probable that through a system of rotation most of the adults in a Yaqui town in the course of a year had some experience of the new working schedule. It was under this system that the large surplus of food was produced in the Yaqui country during the period from about 1680 until 1739.

The transformation of Yaqui life brought about by the Jesuit introduction of so many innovations involved primarily an extensive enrichment of the content of Yaqui culture. Most of what has been mentioned, as well as the very large number of innovations not listed here, consisted of additions to the stock of Yaqui elements. In language, for example, the Uto-Aztecan linguistic structure and the traditional Yaqui vocabulary remained; there was merely an addition of a great store of new words from Spanish. The old basic crops of corn, beans, squash, and cotton were still planted along with wheat. Agricultural techniques were not in fact much changed; the dependence on overflow of the river continued, and no permanent ditch system was constructed. While Yaquis learned how to make adobe buildings and used them for churches, stables, and storage, few Yaquis changed their dwellings for such construction; sensitive to Jesuit disapproval of the round houses, they later were abandoned, but the old rectangular forms continued in use. Bodies were more generally covered, but the breechclouts and cloaks persisted. Ceremony was immensely augmented; there was persistent reworking of native ceremonials by the missionaries so that replacement gradually occurred, but this was primarily a replacement of form, while meanings persisted. Major replacements may have taken place in local government and in ceremonial organizations, but even here the data from later periods indicate only partial replacement. In general what happened was supplementation of earlier forms in all aspects of the culture, but most marked in religion and politico-ceremonial organization. The enrichment involved little replacement.

To what extent the acceptance of so many new ways resulted in any new view of life and the Yaqui place in it, in other words new orientations in Yaqui culture, cannot be known with much surety. There is no question that two basic changes in Yaqui life took place. These were something more than the acceptance of this or that new way of doing a particular activity or this or that idea about the supernatural world. Thus the whole orientation of Yaquis toward warfare as a necessary, stimulating, and important activity, if it persisted, did so in the absence of any actual fighting; for, from the 1620's on to 1739, more than a century, Yaquis are not reported to have taken up arms against anyone. In 1740 they did again go to war—and at first with their old success. But we do not know what form the old warrior societies had taken in the meantime. If they continued in existence, as seems probable in view of later evidence, did they focus their interest in some kind of military ritual? With so little to occupy them for so long in the way of real fighting, it would seem that something of the sort must have happened.

Another area of activity for which we have considerable evidence of change was that of farming, not only the additions of tools and crops which have been mentioned, but also the very considerable change in the level of production. All that has been said regarding the agricultural surplus which was produced from the 1680's for forty or fifty years can only be interpreted to mean that Yaqui economics had moved to a new basis. From subsistence farming and gathering in a fairly favorable environment with no need to produce any surplus from year to year, the Yaquis shifted to an exporting economy. We can imagine that the surplus was produced as a result of careful management on the part of the missionaries on those lands set aside for church use. We have no indication of whether these activities stimulated Yaquis generally to a new kind of economic interest or not. But Yaquis were participating in, were in fact the producers of, the surplus that began to come from the Jesuit fields. Did this bespeak a new orientation of Yaquis in economic life? If so, it was not a lasting change.

It seems very likely that another change in orientation took place. The concentration of more people into a single local group organization in the towns and the provision of new organizations for them to work in, together with the augmentation of ceremonials, could have resulted in a great intensification of ceremonial activities. This seems all the more likely with the decline in actual warfare and the general increase in prosperity. Undoubtedly much additional time was spent in farming. However, the stimulus of novel ceremonies and new dances and music, with the active encouragement of the Jesuits, could have brought about a new vigor in ceremonial affairs. Since ceremonies like Holy Week and all the other more important ones were matters of general community participation, requiring co-ordinated action of all the newly organized ceremonial associations, it also would appear likely that a high degree of solidarity characterized the new towns, and that town life and organization could itself have become a new orientation of the culture.

One feels that life in the mission communities was disciplined, but generally interesting and pleasant to the Yaquis who followed the leadership of the missionaries. One also gets the impression that this included nearly all Yaquis for the whole period up to the late 1730's. If there was a dissident minority there is no record of it. If there was a tendency for any sizable number of Yaquis to dissociate themselves from the increasingly complex activities of the town organizations, there is no record of it. Yet a rebellion did begin and sweep through the towns of both Mayos and Yaquis in 1739. Behavior during and immediately after this rebellion, however, points only toward the existence of a very high degree of solidarity among all Yaquis (Decorme 1941: II, 334–40). The fundamental causes of the revolt, which will be considered below, seem to have been external rather than internal.

The Autonomous Communities—1740–1887

While conditions established in the mission communities persisted until the expulsion of the Jesuits in 1767, the Mayo-Yaqui revolt of 1740 inaugurated such profoundly different conditions that we must regard the years from 1740 to 1767 as a period of overlapping tendencies. The system of relations between Spaniards and Yaquis which characterized the mission communities of the 1600's continued as a determinant of the culture of Yaqui towns as long as Jesuits were present in them. Nevertheless that system broke down temporarily during the revolt, and the aftermath of the war saw the beginning of the growth of a wholly new system of Yaqui-Spanish relations. While most Yaquis probably continued, until the Jesuit expulsion, to behave in terms of the mission system, most Spaniards on the frontier did not. The result was a new set of contact conditions which began to crystallize rapidly once the Jesuits were removed.

To call the period under consideration a period of autonomous communities is to stretch somewhat the meaning of the word "autonomous." The towns along the lower Yaqui River were at no time between 1740 and 1887 recognized by Spaniards or Mexicans as independent entities; they were regarded throughout as integral parts of the Spanish or Mexican nations. Nevertheless the Yaqui inhabitants of those towns did at three different times during the 150 years expel all non-Yaquis from their territory and gain military control of their own and surrounding lands. In the intervals between these three brief periods of full control by Yaquis, the military power of Spain and Mexico in the area was by no means well established. For all practical

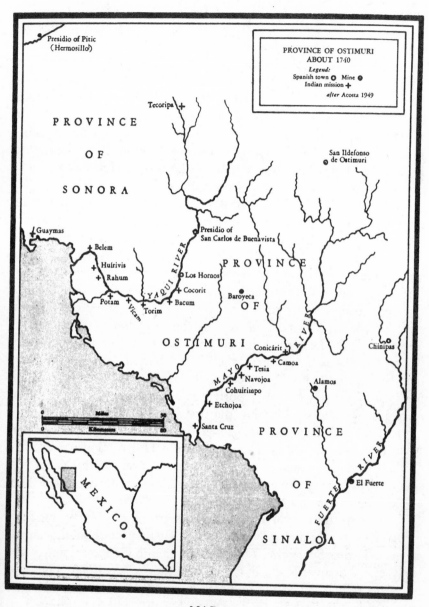

Presidio of Pitic
(Hermosillo)

PROVINCE OF OSTIMURI
ABOUT 1740
Legend:
Spanish town ◯ Mine ◎
Indian mission ✚
after Acosta 1949

Tecoripa ✚

PROVINCE

OF

SONORA

San Ildefonso
◯ de Ostimuri

Guaymas

Belem ✚

Huírivis ✚
Rahum ✚

Presidio of
San Carlos de Buenavista ◯✚

PROVINCE

Los Hornos ◯✚

Potam ✚
Vicam ✚   Torim ✚ Cocorit ✚
              Bacum ✚

Baroyeca ◎

OF

OSTIMURI

Conicárit ✚

Chinipas ◯

RIVER

Camoa ✚
Tesia ✚
Navojoa ✚
Cohuirimpo ✚

Alamos ◎

Etchojoa ✚

Santa Cruz ✚

PROVINCE

OF

El Fuerte ◯

SINALOA

MEXICO

Miles

Kilometers

MAP 2

purposes during most of the time, the Yaqui communities were in control of their own affairs. Moreover, the view of most Yaquis was that if their communities were not recognized by others as autonomous, that was simply a failure in perception.

The nature of the change in the relations between Yaquis and non-Yaquis during this period can best be made clear by describing the three wars which took place. The first was the revolt of 1740. The second occurred in the 1820's under the leadership of a Yaqui named Juan Banderas. The third was fought sixty years later during the 1880's. All three were hard-fought on both sides. Each contributed to uncompromising attitudes of mutual hostility.

The revolt of 1740 developed out of a controversy over the whipping of a Yaqui in one of the towns at the order of the missionary (Acosta 1949: 84; Decorme 1941: II, 333). It was fanned into a serious conflict by the actions of a strongly anti-Jesuit provincial governor. There is indication that the revolt gathered momentum as an effort to gain some reforms in the town governmental system, but it is far from clear whether the majority of Yaquis regarded the missionaries' or the civil authorities' role as the disturbing factor. All the Mayos and all the Yaquis joined and fought under the battle cry "Long live the King of Spain, the Blessed Virgin, and good government" (Acosta 1949: 86; Decorme 1941: II, 334–35). The Yaqui-Mayo fighting power was reported as 7,000 warriors. The Indians were highly successful during the first months and killed or drove out all Spaniards from the river towns and neighboring territory. Toward the end of 1740 at a spot called the Hill of Bones a decisive battle was fought which became an important event in the Yaqui version of their history. Five thousand Yaquis were reported killed there and resistance was no longer possible.

Yaqui unity during the revolt was very strong. While Yaquis dealt gently with the Jesuits, it became clear that they were solidly united against all other Spaniards. Their aim became to rid their country entirely of the Spaniards and in the process they killed 1,000. The train of events which led to the outbreak is imperfectly known. We can only conjecture that the encroaching Spanish frontier appeared to Yaquis as a threat to the relative independence which they had enjoyed in the mission communities. This threat became a definite and practical reality with their defeat. Their leaders were executed, controls were clamped on the towns, and a presidio was built at the eastern edge of the Yaqui country and manned with Spanish soldiers. The Yaqui country had finally become a typical outpost of New Spain.

That Yaqui hopes concerning political autonomy were by no means destroyed was indicated in the events of the 1820's. As Mexican independence of Spain was established, Yaquis together with neighboring Indian tribes including the Mayos, Opatas, and Pimas conceived the idea of an independent Indian nation in the northwest (Acosta 1949: 130–32; Bancroft 1884: II, 639–41; Hernandez 1902: 112–15). Leadership was supplied by a literate Yaqui, Juan Banderas, who was reported to have had a vision of the Virgin of Guadalupe and who led his troops under a flag bearing her likeness. Banderas organized several thousand fighting men from the four tribes, and, ineffectively opposed by the Mexicans, maintained control of southern Sonora for more than a year. Again non-Yaquis were driven out of the Yaqui territory. In 1833 Banderas was finally defeated and executed. The alliance with the Opatas and Pimas disintegrated. It became apparent, however, that the leadership of any one man was not essential to the existence of the Yaqui program for independence.

For the next fifty years, although the Sonoran government increased in strength and at different times asserted its dominance over the Yaqui towns, that dominance was never fully accepted. In the late 1870's a new leader appeared in the form of a Yaqui called Cajeme, who had had wide experience in the Mexican army and had been appointed *alcalde mayor*, the highest civil authority, of the Yaqui towns by the Sonoran government (Hernandez 1902: 125). Cajeme slowly built up a fighting force among Mayos and Yaquis; in 1885–86 he fought a brilliant campaign against federal and state troops. His defeat and execution in 1887 ended organized military operations by Yaquis, although various guerrilla activities continued from mountain strongholds for another twenty years.

Both Banderas and Cajeme evidently had the support of the great majority of those Yaquis who continued to live in the river towns. They fought in the name of the "Eight Towns" and to the very last, in their negotiations with Mexican commanders, insisted on the expulsion of all non-Yaquis from Yaqui country as the basic condition of peace (Hernandez 1902: 114–15, 142). This repeated the events of 1740, when the line was drawn just as sharply as it had been against the first slave-raiders and against Captain Hurdaide. There was no diminution in the intensity of feeling for autonomy in 1886 as compared with 1740. At both times Yaqui spokesmen made sharp distinctions between "*yoemem*" (we, the people) and "*yoris*" (non-Indians). At both times there was the strongest possible resistance to sharing their territory with any others. There was not so much a steady growth of such feeling, fanned by recurring conflict, but rather its continuance with no real change at a high level throughout the period.

In the intervals between the wars, conditions were such that no feeling of increasing political control by Spaniards or Mexicans could have been engendered among Yaquis. Following the revolt of 1740 the harsh measures and even the new presidio were short-lived. Soldiers were taken from the latter to fight the Seri Indians, and from then on throughout the Spanish regime the Spaniards were busy with attempts to control the Seris and the Apaches (Villa 1951: 116). With the departure of the Jesuits, Franciscan missionaries attempted to take over but were not successful either in winning the loyalty of Yaquis or in re-establishing the mission herds and farms which had been plundered by the civil authorities. The secularization of the mission communities which followed resulted in general in much less contact with Catholic Church representatives than under the Jesuits. Although the civil government announced the policy of requiring the Yaqui towns to pay tribute, it never enforced the policy. Similarly a feeble effort to survey the Yaqui territory preliminary to distributing the land as individual holdings was never carried through (Acosta 1949: 117–21). It must have been evident to Yaquis that Spanish power was disintegrating rather than increasing and that the desired independence might be possible.

With the failure of Banderas to gain independence, the new Sonora government announced a plan for incorporation of the Yaquis into the state on an entirely equal basis with Mexicans (Ezell 1955: 202). The incorporation required acceptance of the municipality form of administration which meant subordination of the Yaqui towns to Mexican controlled political units. It also meant the acceptance of taxation and agreement to divide the town lands into individual holdings. The Yaquis resisted these proposals with force, succeeding in staving off effective interference in their affairs until their defeat in 1886. At times there was military occupation of their territory and there was constant discussion in the Sonoran legislature of the threat which the "anomaly" (Troncoso 1905: 71) of the Yaqui towns offered to "civilization" in Sonora, but until 1887 the state of Sonora was too disorganized itself to effect continuous dominance.

It is apparent that there was a steadily decreasing participation of non-Yaquis in the life of the towns. From 1740 through 1767 some Jesuits were back at work with an intensified program of instruction. After their expulsion several secular priests served in the towns; one became very influential over a long period of years (Acosta 1949: 121–23) and, as an unusually highly educated man, constituted an important link with Spanish culture in its final phases in the region. He instituted new industrial enterprises, for example, a stocking factory in one town. But by the time of the war for independence, there were only two priests in touch with the Yaqui towns (Acosta 1949: 131). Some settlers moved into Yaqui country in the early 1800's and were one of the precipitating causes of Banderas' movement. But after the Banderas war, conditions remained too unsettled for Mexicans interested in the Yaqui land. There were probably no priests at all in residence in Yaqui towns from the late 1820's through the 1880's.

Thus, from the 1820's on, conditions were sharply different from what they had been under the Jesuits. The latter were an integral part of the town organization and controlled its operation at many points. They were also consistently vigorous innovators. With them and the later priests eliminated, all official posts in the towns were occupied by Yaquis and there were no non-Yaqui innovators seeking to change and replace religious or other customs. So long as Mexican civil administration remained unorganized at the local level, there were no outsiders of any kind in the Yaqui towns. One might in fact hold that Yaquis were no longer subject to a program of directed change.

The fact must be emphasized, however, that there was constant threat to the autonomy of the town governments and to their traditional communal control over the land. While there were no officials in regular contact with Yaquis pushing such changes, there were periodic attempts to carry them out by force. Yaquis were thus well aware that this was the program first of the Spanish civil government and later of the Sonoran government. Awareness of that fact, we may believe, was the basis of continuing Yaqui hostility.

At the same time that Yaquis were gaining control of their own affairs in a more complete manner than under the Jesuit regime, there was a considerable decline in population. Yaquis had somehow escaped the early smallpox and measles epidemics which decimated the Mayos and other Indian groups, so that their population remained nearly constant during the 1600's (Garcia Cubas 1876: 72). The first serious reduction in population came with the wiping out of the reported 5,000 at the Hill of Bones. This was a temporary reduction, but it nevertheless marked a new era of decline in Yaqui population. By 1765, toward the end of the Jesuit period, the population in the river towns was barely 23,000 (Tamarón y Romeral 1765: 244–47). In 1830, as the Banderas war drew to a close, Yaqui population was listed as 12,000 (Bancroft 1884: II, 647, n. 83; 652, n. 12; Nye 1861: 28). In the 1870's it had declined to 8,000 or 9,000 (Troncoso 1905: 65; cf. Garcia Cubas 1876: 74), and in 1887 after the defeats of Cajeme there was a population along the river of only 4,000 (Troncoso 1905: 148).

There is no doubt of a considerable population decline among Yaquis during this hundred-and-fifty-year period, but these figures should not be taken too literally. The most accurate are probably the first and the last, but the decline indicated in these was definitely a measure of decline in the population of the river towns only. At the time the count of 23,000 was made in 1765, there were "thousands" of Yaquis away from the towns working in mines at Soyopa on the middle Yaqui River and elsewhere (Tamarón y Romeral 1765: 246). This trend of working away from the towns had been intensified as a result of the revolt of 1740. Throughout the late 1700's there was some scattering of Yaqui population (Acosta 1949: 112). The population figure for 1830 is an estimate and hard to evaluate. European diseases had caught up with the Yaquis before this date; it is possible that there had been as drastic a decline as this indicates. The later figures are definitely not to be considered as including the whole Yaqui population. From the 1830's on there was some seasonal migration out of the Yaqui country and also a steady movement of Yaqui families to take up residence permanently, in Guaymas, Hermosillo, and elsewhere. The low figure for the 1870's is an indication, probably, of how many Yaquis had grown weary of the constantly unsettled conditions on the river and had migrated. The final figure for 1887 is of course the count of Yaquis who remained in the river towns and submitted to the Mexican military occupation. There were at the time this count was made hundreds of Yaquis who had taken refuge in the mountains north of the river, other thousands who had been shipped out by the Mexicans to work on haciendas and ranches in Sonora, and those Yaquis who had already taken up residence more or less permanently on a voluntary basis during earlier years in various parts of Sonora.

We may conclude on a basis of such data that there were fewer and fewer Yaquis who regarded life in the river towns as desirable under the circumstances. By the time Cajeme began to assume leadership in the 1870's, probably the average size of a town was little above 1,000 or about one-third the size of a town in the days of the Jesuits.

The emigration of Yaquis, which played an important part in the reduction of town size, was not a purely nineteenth-century phenomenon. Some Yaquis had served as mine-workers as early as the late 1600's. After the revolt of 1740, hundreds of Yaquis were reported to have gone to work for Spaniards either in the mining towns or the ranches and haciendas of Sonora and Sinaloa. The break-up of the Jesuit agricultural operations in the Yaqui country resulted in an increasing number of Yaquis seeking wages, and probably new experience, elsewhere. As tension and recurrent disorder grew in the Yaqui towns during the nineteenth century, more and more Yaquis took up residence in various parts of Sonora. It became common practice for most Yaqui families to work for a season or a year or two on some hacienda in the Mayo country or neighboring the Yaqui territory. Yaquis worked as pearl-divers and fishermen along the coast of the Gulf of California. They were generally highly regarded as workers by Mexican employers in whatever employment they entered. Their good reputation as workmen persisted through all the period of conflict and hostility. The leadership of Cajeme itself stimulated many Yaquis to leave the towns and take up residence in Mexican communities, for Cajeme's exercise of the office of chief judge, which was not a recognized Yaqui institution, antagonized many Yaquis. Often Yaquis who worked outside the Yaqui country had no intention of staying away permanently. Many came back for various reasons, but many also became assimilated into the general population of the state of Sonora. We can have no precise data on the numbers who returned or who were assimilated, but we can be sure that there was a steady growth in the heterogeneity of the population of the Yaqui towns throughout the nineteenth century. The increased heterogeneity was in terms of extent of command of the Spanish language, miscegenation, experience of a wide variety of work techniques, and knowledge of and intimate acquaintance with the heterogeneous population of the growing Sonoran frontier.

This heterogeneity was already apparent in the towns as early as the 1820's, at the time of the development of the Banderas movement for political independence (Hernandez 1902: 115). There was at that time a faction of Yaquis who were opposed to the program of Banderas. Its leader advocated co-operation rather than war with the Mexicans, although it is unlikely that he and his followers were any less devoted to the type of community government and institutions which had grown up under Jesuit tutelage than were Banderas and his followers. Submerged in the temporary great success of the Banderas movement, the opposing faction came back into prominence after Banderas' defeat and for a time co-operated with the Sonoran *caudillo*, General Gándara (Hernandez 1902: 115). It appears, however, that there was too little in the way of stable advantage offered by alliance with any of the Sonoran contenders for political power during the nineteenth century for the growth of such a faction to be encouraged. In the 1870's there was a rapid growth of sentiment in the towns against any peaceful co-operation with Mexicans (Hernandez 1902: 126–27). It became increasingly impossible for any advocate of such a course to remain in the towns. In other words, the movement of Yaquis out of the towns resulted in an increase in the homogeneity of the town population with respect to hostility toward Mexicans and to the sacredness of traditional institutions.

Nevertheless there is no reason to suppose that those Yaquis who supported Cajeme in his bid for Yaqui control of their towns were necessarily those who had the least experience of Mexican life. The contrary seems more likely. Cajeme himself was an example (Hernandez 1902: 121–25). Although he was born and spent part of his early childhood in one of the western Yaqui towns, most of his youth was spent in Hermosillo, where he gained a good command of Spanish and learned to read and write in that language. He went with his father to the goldfields of California in 1849 and later served in the Mexican army in various parts of Mexico. He rose to the rank of captain in the army and as a result of such background had been appointed to office as judge and intercessor between Mexicans and Yaquis by the governor of Sonora. Cajeme was probably not typical of the Yaqui men of the towns in the 1880's, but neither was he unrepresentative. We may think of Yaquis who supported Cajeme's military leadership as having considerable direct or indirect knowledge of life in Sonora. Many had lived in the Sonora towns, including the state capital of Hermosillo, as well as on the haciendas and ranches. Many had fought in the armies of Sonoran political leaders seeking power by force, such as Manuel Gandara. All had experienced at one time or another contacts with soldiers of invading forces of Sonoran governors. Some Yaquis had by the 1880's begun to make all or part of their living as traders, driving strings of burros to market in Guaymas at the western edge of the Yaqui country (Spicer: field notes). An unknown number had become thoroughly literate in Spanish and many were literate in Yaqui, which since Jesuit days had been a written language. Yaqui isolation had, in short, been greatly reduced over what it was in the Jesuit period.

The Yaquis who remained in the river towns did so through choice, or at least as a result of influence and decisions in Yaqui family and other groups in which they participated. There were no bars to movement out of the Yaqui towns set up from the Mexican side. There was in fact a steady and growing demand for Yaquis as laborers throughout Sonora. The Sonoran population was racially heterogeneous. Opportunities were restricted only on a class basis, and even this was not rigid or highly restrictive in a frontier state.

We may sum up the period of "autonomous communities" as one in which the conditions of contact were characterized by recurrent conflict between Yaquis and Spaniards and later Mexicans. The dominance of non-Yaquis over Yaquis was not wholly clear for any extended period. Yaquis did not accept their position as one of subordination and Mexicans did not accept the Yaqui attempts to define their position in terms of a high degree of autonomy. The Spanish and Mexican focus of interest with respect to changing Yaqui culture shifted, as compared with the previous period, from religion and agricultural development to town government and land control. Contacts between Yaquis and non-Yaquis continued and intensified. Yaquis became acquainted with non-Yaquis in a far wider variety of roles than in the previous period, and in some of these, such as that of fellow worker, an even greater degree of intimacy than had obtained between Jesuits and their immediate assistants. Interbreeding and some intermarriage took place between Yaquis and Mexicans and between Yaquis and other Sonoran Indians, especially Mayos.

The whole structure of contact was vastly more complex than in the previous period. Not only was there increased interaction in a wide variety of roles with Spaniards and Mexicans, there was also a marked shift in the relations between Yaquis and other Indians of the region. Most important in this connection was the appearance of solidarity with Mayos against Spaniards. This identification of interests with other Indians was expressed in intertribal military organization and at least a conception of political federation. This was in contrast with the prevailing intertribal hostility which preceded the coming of the Spaniards.

Of great importance in the new structure of contact was the change in the leadership of Yaqui communities. While the general form of governmental and ceremonial organization remained the same as under the Jesuits, no cross-cultural equivalent of the missionaries participated any longer in town affairs. Every office was occupied by Yaquis and hence no pressure for change to conformity with Spanish or Mexican culture operated directly within the towns. All such pressure was felt, when it was felt, indirectly rather than through any member of the town organization.

In general it may be said that there were two levels of contact. One consisted in the often intimate relationships that developed in the work groups which Yaquis joined outside of Yaqui country. Here much knowledge of Mexican culture was gained by Yaquis and much intimate borrowing took place. On the other hand there was a level at which conflict prevailed, namely, in the relations between the town governments and the state of Sonora.

The Culture of the Autonomous Communities

What the way of life in the Yaqui towns had become by 1887 is fairly well known, from accounts by Yaqui individuals who lived in the towns in the 1880's (Spicer: field notes). Its major features could be described as an intricate fusion of Spanish and Indian cultural elements in most aspects of life, a highly organized social and ceremonial life at the level of the local community, and close integration of the culture through sacred sanctions.

At what point in Yaqui cultural history this kind of tight integration of society and culture was achieved is not known from direct evidence. There are two possibilities. One is that it took place during the mission period and was an accomplished fact by the beginning of the autonomous community period. This certainly is within the realm of possibility, if we consider the long period of peaceful interaction between a limited number of Spanish innovators and highly receptive Yaqui communities under conditions of relative isolation. No doubt much of the form of cultural life which characterized the later nineteenth-century towns did crystallize in the Jesuit period. However, much of the content of Yaqui culture in the 1880's seems inexplicable on this basis. The view is taken here that Yaqui cultural life underwent important transformations from 1740 on, and that what we know as the culture of the 1880's, with its characteristic forms of integration and orientation, came into existence under the conditions of the autonomous communities. We shall view the culture as a product not only of the processes of innovation and fusion of the Jesuit period but also of the processes of resistance to directed change and of cultural reorientation in the autonomous period.

The interpretation which seems most plausible is that the great number of innovations of the first century of contact did not become fully integrated with the various elements of aboriginal culture until at least the early 1800's. The stimuli for this reorganization of the mission period culture consisted primarily of the new set of pressures for economic and political integration of the Yaquis. This program required a fundamental shift in the mission community adjustment and was resisted as a clear and obvious threat to the way of life which had developed over the previous century. Since neither the Spanish government nor the Sonoran government was successful in imposing conditions of directed change, Yaquis were able to focus on the preservation of the threatened institutions and reorganize their culture along new lines. As we shall see, an important part of the specific content of Yaqui culture of the 1880's, including features most securely integrated within the whole, were elements unlikely to have been introduced by the Jesuits.

The culture of the nineteenth-century river towns took form among a steadily declining population. There was at least one period, just after the expulsion of the Jesuits, when community size declined as a result of break-up of towns and re-formation of rancherias (Acosta 1949: 112, 127). This trend ceased some time later, so that during the 1800's most Yaquis in the river country lived at one or another of the eight town sites. There was by the 1820's a return to the settlement pattern of the late 1600's, but each town was much reduced in size.

There was also a change in economic life, marked by a decline in farming and crafts. The decline in farming set in immediately after the expulsion of the Jesuits and was much noted by the Franciscans and civil officials. The considerable agricultural surplus characteristic of the Jesuit period was never again produced in the Yaqui country. Many Yaquis continued subsistence farming all through the period and raised small herds of cattle, but after the 1770's more and more Yaquis found it necessary or desirable to work outside the Yaqui country. From the 1820's warfare was a major cause for such activities. Fighting, often within the boundaries of the Yaqui territory, became steadily more frequent and more devastating. Even if crops were planted, they often were not harvested. The dry weather of the late winter and spring was favorable for military campaigns so that the spring crop was never planted. Weaving, which had been encouraged by the Jesuits and was again stimulated in the 1780's by a secular priest in Torim, also declined. By the 1880's weaving was almost a lost art among Yaquis (Spicer: field notes; Beals 1945: 23). Yaquis continued to manufacture pottery for their own use, but they became increasingly dependent on the Mexican economy for clothing, blankets, and other textiles. It was true then that by the end of the autonomous period, Yaqui economic life was not self-sufficient, as it had been in Jesuit times; although Yaquis still controlled a sufficient amount of land to provide adequate food for the whole population, they were not using the land consistently. Their needs had developed in such a way that they also found it necessary to trade constantly for clothing, hoes, and other goods. During peaceful periods, no doubt, most Yaquis raised sufficient food for subsistence and some trade, but peaceful periods became increasingly shorter and the expectation of a crop became less certain.

Yaquis continued to raise corn and wheat as well as beans, watermelons, pumpkins, and squash. They fished and gathered oysters. In all these activities metal implements, including hoes and plows, had become important elements. Horses and cattle had become important resources both for transportation and food. Irrigation ditch systems were still far less important than the traditional natural flooding technique. To Mexicans their agriculture appeared crude and inefficient, but it was basically the same as that of the other Sonorans and embodied when possible all that had been learned from the Jesuits. Moreover, work habits which characterized the Yaquis in the Jesuit period continued into this period. While considered by Mexicans to be inefficient on their own land, Yaquis were highly valued as workmen wherever they were known. They had by the 1880's a very high reputation for industry in fishing, in mines, and on haciendas (Troncoso 1905: 342).

The distinctive features of Yaqui culture in this period may be best appreciated through a description of the local group, or town, organization and the functions of its various parts. Yaqui culture of the 1880's was a classic example of the folk culture; and the social unit in which that culture was expressed was the autonomous town (Spicer 1954: *passim*). The town consisted of persons who worked land in a defined territory surrounding a church. There were in the 1880's, as there had been in the 1600's, eight such units among the Yaquis. Most of the townspeople were scattered about within a distance of a half-mile or less of the church building; surrounding the church was an irregularly shaped bare area several hundred yards in diameter which was the scene of numerous ceremonies. The church was of adobe or burned brick, at least 125 feet long and 30 wide, by far the most imposing structure on the town site. The houses were not arranged along streets, for the grid plan of town layout still was being resisted by Yaquis. Houses were for the most part rectangular, wattle and daub, dirt-roofed, simple structures of one or two rooms. The dome-shaped house had disappeared. There was, however, a good deal of variation in house type, some with adobe brick and some with mat walls. Houses were grouped in household units of from one to three or four with associated structures, such as open-sided rectangular shelters for cooking and living during most of the year, and raised mesquite pole platforms for storage of corn, squash, and other crops. Most house groups were surrounded by cane fences, giving considerable privacy from neighboring households. Within each household unit a short distance from the main building and to the east, embedded in the ground was a wooden cross three to six feet high. This cross was an important feature of each household as the center of all family ceremonies.

Everyone who called himself a Yaqui was identified with one of the towns, usually the town in which he was born. But individuals did move from their native towns, commonly upon marrying, and came to identify themselves with the town of residence. The new identification carried with it obligation to participate in the socio-ceremonial organization of the town.

Each town had a supernatural foundation explained in myth and a biblical association (Spicer 1954: 125–28). Thus one town was associated with the Garden of Eden and another with Bethlehem. Each town was believed to have been founded by a "prophet" who had a Yaqui name and who had had a vision at some spot within the town territory, usually near the site of the church. The vision was of a saint or a biblical character, who gave some instruction on the founding of the town. If a saint had appeared in the vision, that saint was accepted as the patron of the town and honored in an elaborate ceremony on the saint's day. Thus the location of every town was sacred and a well-developed mythology supported the concept of sacredness. The church was located on a high spot within the territory to insure that it would not be washed away by the periodic heavy floods which sometimes inundated the whole Yaqui delta. This high spot whether or not it was the scene of the founding vision was regarded as being located on especially sacred ground and it was here immediately surrounding the church that the dead of the community were buried. It followed from this conception of the town territory as sacred and the mandate of a prophet's vision that the location of a town could not be changed. Churches were occasionally moved and with them the main settlement of people, but this was only a shifting of church site within the sacred territory. The territory itself could not be altered and its boundaries, marked at intervals by three crosses since the days of the Jesuits, were fixed for all time. Mexicans were forever excluded from possessing land within the territory of any town.

The government of the town was composed of five separate authorities, or *ya'uram*, each of which had distinct functions (Spicer 1954: 55 ff.). These authorities were the civil, the military, the church, the fiesta, and the customs. The officers of the five authorities decided in joint meeting all matters of general concern; no one authority was autonomous even within its own realm of jurisdiction, although in practice each did make decisions without consultation with others. Consensus was sufficiently developed so that each authority was clearly aware when consultation was and was not required.

The civil authority consisted of five governors each with an assistant, elected annually in a general town meeting, and taking office in January. The formal pattern was in general a Spanish one. The functions, too, were Spanish; the governors were responsible for maintaining law and order (using as ultimate sanction the stocks, the whipping post, and death), for resolving disputes between families, and for the equitable assignment of the lands of the town. In this last function the Yaqui governors managed all lands, in contrast with the Spanish colonial plan which included individually held lands. Also derived from the Spanish system was an official called the "town elder" (*pueblo mayor* in Spanish, *yo'owe* in Yaqui) who had a voice in all meetings of the governors and who was the spokesman for all the people of the town who held no official positions.

The military authority consisted of an organization of specially dedicated individuals formally promised to the service of the Virgin of Guadalupe, usually for life. The organization ideally had at least two captains (the highest administrative office), a flag-bearer (the highest ritual office), a drummer, several lieutenants, sergeants, numerous corporals, and an indefinite number of common soldiers. Also every able-bodied man in the town was subject to draft for sentry duty or other activities; every man was expected to serve, when war was declared, under the leadership of the promised members of what may be called the military society. Like the captains and lieutenants of the Spanish colonial town organization, the Yaqui military society carried out the orders of the First Governor in maintaining law and order. The military society also had full responsibility for the safety of the governors and their assistants; this required that a contingent of soldiers with at least one captain accompany the governors whenever they engaged in formal meeting or made any movement as a group. Thus soldiers always accompanied the governors to and from church on the regular Sunday ceremonial observances, and to and from fiestas or other occasions which the governors attended.

Of fundamental importance in the ceremonial life of the towns by the 1880's was the ritual of the military society. Whether it was a part of the culture of the mission communities is not certain, but it is very likely that it was in some form, for the dancing and ceremonial costumes of the military society in the 1880's and later were very similar to military leaders' costumes mentioned by the earliest Spanish chroniclers of the Yaquis in 1533. The military society was dedicated to the Virgin of Guadalupe, who was the supernatural seen by Juan Banderas in a vision and under whose aegis the wars of the 1820's were carried out. Much of the important ritual of the military society, as on each Sunday, involved the Virgin of Guadalupe, but much of the rest of it, as at all fiestas of general importance, was related to the sun and its movements. In addition the military society was proprietor of the Coyote dances and songs, which were also an important, if less sacred, part of major ceremonies. The military society with its Spanish military titles and its function of wielding the whip at the whipping post combined with the most ancient shell-decorated headdresses, foxskin capes, and aboriginal animal-imitating dances, was a good example of the kind of fusion that had taken place between the Spanish and the native traditions.

The church authority constituted a complex, highly specialized structure with many parts. We can only indicate very briefly its nature here. While its official positions, open to both men and women, were unlimited in number, it required for its adequate operation perhaps a minimum of sixty-five to seventy formally dedicated officers. Each town regarded its own church as an independent unit, unrelated to any higher ecclesiastical authority; Yaqui officials known as *maestros*, or *malestos*, took full responsibility for managing the church affairs. Such officers, trained through both oral and written tradition, had since the time of the expulsion of the Jesuits in 1767 maintained an independent church embodying what had been learned from the Jesuits. The maestro's position as counterpart of the Jesuit missionary was indicated not only in his management of purely ceremonial affairs, but also in the fact that he, as representative of the church, had the privilege of nominating persons for the offices of the five governors each year.

The top of the church heirarchy consisted of a council of the eldest from among the maestros, the *sacristans* or *temastim* (in charge of maintenance of church property and treasury), and *kiyohteim* (from Spanish *prioste*, or female caretakers of the church images). Two administrative officers operated below the policy level, a church governor (*teopo kobanao*) and *pihkan* (from Spanish *fiscal*), the former having responsibility for co-ordination of all ceremonies of the church and the latter being in charge of the doctrinal and ritual instruction of all children of the town. Within this framework three male groups and three female groups led the church ceremonies, including one group of important male dancers, the *matachinis*.

The fiesta authority was composed of twenty-four men and women annually chosen by their predecessors to manage the very elaborate ceremony for the patron saint of the town. The *fiesteros* (*pahkome* in Yaqui) were also in charge of burial arrangements for all residents of the town. In addition they performed exacting duties in connection with the weekly Sunday ceremonies, duties which were regarded as a penance.

The customs authority derived its name from its important functions in maintaining what Yaquis regarded as the most vital of their ceremonial customs, namely, the dramatic representation of the Passion of Christ during Lent and Holy Week and all the associated ceremonies and activities. This authority took over complete control in a town during the latter part of Lent, including law and order and the church, so that symbolically all the other authorities were under its power and direction. This especially significant authority was composed of two men's secret societies called the Horsemen and the Judases, the latter derived on the one hand from the devil-clowns of medieval Spain and on the other from the native helmet-masked impersonators of benevolent supernaturals.

The officials of these five authorities, and any rank and file members who cared to, constituted the town council which deliberated on all matters of general concern. There was a formal seating arrangement which included places for any persons, known as *kia pueblo*, who were not currently members of any of the formal organizations. Deliberations were opened and closed by the first civil governor, but in their course anyone was permitted to speak. Thus a completely democratic system of expression of opinion prevailed. Action was only through feeling of general consensus or unanimity, never by majority vote. The governors and their assistants, the town elder and other older men, and the officials of the military society met at least weekly, on every Sunday morning, and anyone was privileged to bring any matter before them. After the weekly meeting the civil authorities and the military society moved from their headquarters to the church to participate in the regular Sunday ceremony called the "Surrounding," which symbolized the Yaqui maintenance of control over their tribal lands.

Tribal organization during the autonomous period, as in pre-Spanish times, had only intermittent overt existence. During periods of fighting exceptionally able men like Juan Banderas and Cajeme took command of the military societies of all the towns and of the whole fighting force of young men. Banderas and Cajeme likewise commanded Mayo troops, for no Mayo seems ever to have attained this kind of intertribal leadership. It is a mistake, however, to assume that such supreme military commanders took control of the towns as civil-ceremonial units. The civil-ceremonial organization remained intact during the periods of warfare, and Yaquis regarded the "Eight Towns" rather than the fighting command as the legitimate peace-making bodies. This was illustrated over and over again, especially in the 1880's and later (Hernandez 1902: 126, 132, 142, 169). There was never any single representative or commander of all the towns. Peace could be made only with consent of the town councils. It seems to have been the case that until the time of Cajeme, able military leaders either had to accept positions in the traditional hierarchy of the town military societies with their attendant ritual duties during times of peace or accept status as ordinary citizens of the towns. Cajeme made an effort during peaceful years to create an over-all position of judge (Spicer: field notes). He functioned in this capacity but the office did not have general acceptance by Yaquis and remained a source of friction and dissatisfaction. Channels of communication and formal co-operation were well established between the different parts of the town organizations, so that all eight towns were capable of co-ordinate action, but during peacetime this was accomplished without any one town being recognized as dominant and without any one individual assuming leadership.

It seems probable that the town organization just described must have come into existence in somewhat similar form during the Jesuit regime. That is, an elected set of governors, working closely with a church organization introduced by the Jesuit, must have been the basic pattern. These were both innovations of the period. It seems probable also that the customs authority, at least the two male ceremonial organizations, had prominence in Jesuit times. The names of these organizations are Spanish; the organization is the Spanish military form; part of the costuming and much of the meaning as evil

Judases and good soldiers were Spanish-derived. However, the forms of recruiting, by trespass and vow, much of the costuming detail, most of the specific ritual forms, such as backward behavior, were clearly Indian in origin. We do not know whether their dominance in the town structure during Lent was the same in Jesuit times, nor do we know whether they were then called the "customs authority." It may be suggested that their key position in ceremonial organization and their meaning as protectors of the most important customs developed only after the mission type community existence was threatened. If that is true, then their role in the 1880's was one result of a reorientation of Yaqui culture under the threat of the Mexican program for change. It seems probable also, that the prominent and major role of the military society in each town government was a nineteenth-century development. Certainly the dedication of the military societies to the Virgin of Guadalupe seems to have been a result of the Banderas period influences. The existence of pre-Spanish warrior organizations and the persistence of costumes and ritual from the aboriginal period in the warrior societies suggest that military organizations never died out, but it is here suggested that their high importance as protectors of the town officials and prominent place in the town councils was not a feature of the Jesuit period, but rather a nineteenth-century development. The fiesta authority very probably was a fusion of the Jesuit period, but it seems likely that its incorporation into the town government was another result of the tightening of integration which is posited for the 1800's. The vision-sanctioned concept of the town as sacred, with its biblical and Catholic elements, was also probably a development of the later period. Not that a sacred man-land relationship was not a part of the pre-Spanish culture; it undoubtedly was; but the specific form of application of this concept to the Jesuit-founded eight towns must necessarily have postdated the mission community period. It represented a closer fusion and tighter integration of the Spanish innovations with the surviving aboriginal elements of culture.

Little can be said about changes in the kinship system. The specific composition of households is not known, except for the indication from informants that there was no consistency with regard to matrilocal or patrilocal residence. The wedding ceremony suggests an earlier patrilocal residence, which may have persisted into the autonomous period (Spicer 1940: 74–76). Bilateral kinship terminology was in general use through the 1880's. Household groups were large and consisted not only of kin but also of ritual kin. Large groups of kin and ritual kin co-operated in producing the great amount of food necessary for the annual fiestas. That ritual kinship, or the *compadrazgo*, was of considerable importance is indicated in many informant accounts from the river towns. The ritual kinship system was, like the military societies and men's organizations of the customs chieftainship, an outstanding example of the combination into a single pattern of many Spanish and aboriginal elements.

Just as the organization of the towns revealed a close-knit social integration in Yaqui life with reference to the activities of warfare, local government and land management, and ceremonialism, so the system of religious belief and ritual revealed a close-knit integration of the cultural values and interests of the Yaquis who participated in it. It was throughout each of its aspects a fusion of the Christian innovations and aboriginal beliefs and practices. It was sufficiently different from even the folk Catholicism of Sonorans generally to cause representatives of the Catholic Church to regard it as still essentially pagan. Yet in formal features it was obviously closer to being a variant of Christian than of aboriginal Indian religion.

From the time of the departure of the Jesuits, Yaquis had had only intermittent contact with the Catholic Church. As conflict with Mexicans increased through the nineteenth century, Yaquis increasingly regarded themselves as separate from the Catholic Church. They found that priests who came to them more consistently than not allied themselves with Mexicans and sought to persuade Yaquis to accept the program of the Sonoran government. So deep was the cleavage by the 1830's that the Sonoran and the federal governments entertained for a time the idea of bringing Jesuits back to live in the towns in an effort to restore the co-operative relationship of the colonial period; the plan was never realized. Yaquis called themselves Catholics, as well as Yaquis, but they managed their own religious affairs, even administering their own versions of the sacraments.

While the religion of the eight towns was a closely integrated whole, it may perhaps best be comprehended as four cults. The "cults" were specialized ceremonial activities which rested on the conception of the Yaqui tribal territory as a sacred entity in which Yaquis had lived from the first and the boundaries of which had been imperishably delimited in mythical times. The ancestors of all

Yaquis had survived a flood which inundated all but some peaks in the Bacatete Mountains. After the flood a group of angels and Yaqui prophets had traversed the boundaries of the Yaqui country, singing hymns and establishing landmarks. Sometime after this a mysterious talking tree foretold coming events, including baptism and such modern miracles as the telegraph (which was brought through Yaqui country in 1885). Yaquis were then divided into the baptized and the unbaptized, the latter having eternal life within the Yaqui country, where they became the invisible inhabitants of the un- tamed country surrounding the fields and the town sites and the source of special powers for vision, song, and dance. Prophets then founded the towns, establishing them for eternity to the number of eight. Later, perhaps not in mythical times, Jesus was born in one of the towns, Belem, and in the face of hostility and persecution by evil beings went about the Yaqui country curing and helping people. Baptized people gave him shelter for the night and gained his favor. Still later, after the mythical times, a contest with the King of Spain reaffirmed the boundaries of the Yaqui country when the Yaqui hero outdid the King by shooting an arrow farther. After that times were hard and there was much fighting and suffering, but Yaquis had learned the right way to live and would forever follow this way.

It does violence to the Yaqui understanding of their religion to discuss it in terms of four cults, and yet there is little alternative if we are to present it in small compass. That which was accorded the greatest importance was a cult of Jesus, most commonly called the Lord, or *El Señor*. Both the male ceremonial societies of the Horse- men and the Judases were dedicated to Jesus. They, as the customs authority, were regarded ritually as the highest authority in the town; their taking direction of all activities during Lent symbolized their position. All members of these organizations were promised to the service of Jesus, the Horsemen as devotees of Christ the child and the Judases of the crucified Christ. Each group had a sacred image of its patron. Members were promised to serve for life or for three- or six-year periods in return for help in curing some illness. These two societies were active during only a part of the year, from Ash Wednesday until May 3, and during this season took over the duties of the fiesta authority, including burials. They performed the heavy work, such as cutting wood and carrying water for all fiestas given in their period of ascendancy, as well as organized and carried out the complex set of ceremonies during Lent and Holy Week which involved the representation of the last days of Christ. All their work was regarded as a penance. At any given time in a town of a thousand the dedicated members of the customs chieftainship might run as high as two hundred; in addition the maestros and sacristans of the church, who sometimes numbered twenty-five to thirty, were also dedicated to Jesus and might be regarded as maintainers of this cult specifically, as well as of the church ritual in general.

The cult of Jesus could be understood only with reference to the mythology which had developed around Jesus, myths which placed his birth, life, and death in the Yaqui country, localized his curing journeys in the eight towns, and identified "Our Mother," the old female deity, with the Virgin. Here again there was extensive fusion of Christian and native elements. The localization of the Christian supernatural gave him meaning as part of the Yaqui conception of sacred territory which must be defended against the encroachments of non-Yaquis.

Also closely related to the Yaquis' conception of themselves as an integral part of the land was what might be called the cult of the Virgin. Derived from the native North Mexican female divinity associated with rainy season growth and from Mary, mother of Jesus, the Yaqui supernatural was called both "Our Mother" and "Blessed Mary." Represented by conventional Catholic images of wood or plaster, she was also represented by a rough wooden cross of mesquite which, dressed in skirt and necklaces, was the object of special devotion in the spring, when the winter ceremonial season dominated by the customs chieftainship gave way to the summer season dominated by the matachinis. Also, the crosses in the house yards were called "Our Mother" in Yaqui, so that the identification of cross and Virgin was general. There were many other associations, linking her with both Christian-derived and aboriginal ritual concepts. Her cult was marked, in contrast with the relatively somber cult of Jesus, by flowers and bright colors. Most important in the devotions to the Virgin was the matachin dance society. This was a part of the church organization, but a distinct unit within it. The members were promised to serve the Virgin through a sacred vow in return for help in curing. The dance of the matachinis was originally an introduction of the Jesuits, a dance drama depicting the conversion of the first Mexican Indian, Malinche, to Christianity; but this set of meanings connected with Malinche had disappeared by the later nineteenth century and such Christian associations as it had were with the Holy Family (Spicer 1940: 253–56). The fusion of Indian and Spanish had produced a new emergent ritual, the aboriginal Indian dance of devotion in the shell of European music, choreography, and costuming.

A third cult of great importance and one which was integrated with the other two through church and fiesta activities could be called the cult of the dead. The great Yaqui interest in the ancestral dead was colored by respect, warmth, and friendliness, even though the dead were not without their element of dangerousness. The cult involved family records of the dead ancestors, books which were required to be handled in ritual ways at fiestas. It enjoined gatherings once a month at the village graveyard surrounding the church and had a focus in the annual All Souls feasts in November, as prescribed in the Catholic calendar.

The fourth distinguishable cult might perhaps be regarded as an aspect of the cult of the Virgin. However, it bears earmarks of being quite distinct in Yaqui thought, despite the fact that its supernatural patroness was the Virgin of Guadalupe. For Yaquis Guadalupe was the patroness of the military societies and in each town they maintained devotions to her which were exclusively their privilege and obligation. The conventional Mexican representation of Guadalupe as a figure surrounded by golden rays was the one used by Yaquis either in picture or three dimensional form. The military society, besides carrying this figure in most important ceremonies in the required processions, performed rituals directed to the sun, at dawn, noon, and sunset during any fiesta at which they were in attendance. The rituals of the military society, as devotees of the Virgin of Guadalupe and the sun, were an amalgam of Spanish-derived and aboriginal elements—bows and arrows, guns, and rosaries were all employed in their part of the ritual within the church building; the ritual to the sun involved a special form of the sign of the cross, the sounding of the drum, and the waving of the ceremonial banner introduced by the Jesuits; a military society dance was called the Coyote dance and showed some of the most definitely aboriginal features of music and costume. Since the military society of each town was the standing army, its cult was of high importance in the

village life and in the maintenance of a disciplined nucleus for a
fighting force. It may be repeated here that its integration as a cult
of the Virgin of Guadalupe and incorporation into the town organization in these terms seems most likely to have been a result of the
forces making for tighter integration of Yaqui culture during the
nineteenth century.

While the cults which have been described would probably have
been offered by most Yaquis as the content of their religion, it was
true nevertheless that there was another area of supernaturalism
which was at least as important as any one of the four described.
This was the set of beliefs and ritual behaviors associated with the
pascola and deer dancers and a few other animal-representative
dances (Spicer 1940: 173–203). These dancers appeared at all the
most important town ceremonials, where they were as essential as
maestros and matachin dancers and others whose work was organized
by the church officials. Nevertheless they were not managed and
directed by any church officials, but had their separate organization.
Their mythical foundations were, moreover, different, or at least
contained essential elements which did not appear in the mythology
of Jesus and the Virgin. In these ways it was clear that there was a
difference between the pascola-deer role in Yaqui life and that of
the four cults described. Yet the animal dance complex was linked
in terms of form and meaning very closely to the whole system of
the four cults, in fact must be described as an integral part of that
system. It was not only that such a ritual act as making the sign of
the cross was prescribed for deer dancers and pascolas as well as for
maestros and matachinis. The linkage existed also at a much deeper
level of meaning. Thus the aboriginal Yaqui concept of the "flower
patio," or area of ceremonial activity blessed by being sung over or
danced upon, was of equal importance in the deer-pascola ceremonials and in those at the church where the matachin dancers also
blessed the ground by dancing. The concept of flowers (Painter
et al. 1955: 12) was also one of these master integrating principles
which ran through the whole of Yaqui ceremonialism. The flowers
of the "dawn world" of the mythological counterpart of the deer
appealed to by the deer dancer were sacred symbols and these were
the same ritually as the flowers used in the matachin dancers' headdresses and the Virgin's dress. Flowers were equally the grace of

God and the mythical setting of the ancient supernatural deer. The ceremonial context made either, or both at once, appropriate; they were the same. Through many other such concepts, the five cults were integrated into a single religious system.

The pascola-deer cult however had functions not duplicated by the other major parts of the Yaqui religious system. It was the liveliest area of popular art in Yaqui culture. The pascolas were entertainers—the hosts at most important ceremonials. In this capacity they functioned to amuse the crowds. Their dances and accompanying music could be practiced by members of the crowd at a stated time just after dawn. Most important was the oral literature which constituted the pascola dancers' most vivid and varied contribution. As tellers of tales, and particularly of humorous ones, the pascolas maintained a constant exchange with the crowds all night in the intervals between their dances. In these the passing stream of town activities was commented on, twisted into odd forms through the license accorded pascolas, and tossed back for added comment to the more articulate persons in the crowd. This proceeded at the same time under the same ramada in which the singers for the deer dancer gave continuous vitality in poetic form to the sacred and semisacred mythology of the deer. The pascola-deer arts were the important focus of Yaqui aesthetic interests, channeling them in the direction of music, dance, poetry, fiction, and humorous tale. While these flourished as a major Yaqui cultural interest, the plastic and pictorial arts were largely ignored.

Yaqui oral tradition, outside the pascola dance ramadas, turned during the 1800's to a major concern with history. The conflicts with Spaniards and Mexicans suffused with deep meaning such events as the Battle of the Hill of Bones which ended the revolt of 1740, the massacre of Yaquis in the church of Bacum in 1868, and the disastrous fighting at Capitamaya in the Mayo country in 1883 (Spicer 1954: 23–38). These and many other lesser events were knitted systematically into a narrative of Yaqui suffering. The actual historical events were combined with the growing myths of the period, such as the Singing of the Boundary by a band of angels and prophets and the founding of the towns through prophetic vision. The real events and the mythical ones became fused into a single whole, which did not until the following period begin to be disentangled, as Mexican books on Yaqui history were published and the Yaqui historical tradition began the slow shift, under guidance of literate men, from oral to written tradition.

Literacy increased greatly over what it had been in the Jesuit period; it became a steadily more important means of linkage not only between Yaquis and Mexicans, but also among Yaquis. The important nineteenth-century leaders in the conflicts with Mexicans, such as Banderas and Cajeme, were literate and communicated in writing with Mexican military leaders. The Jesuits had established a tradition of literacy in training their catechists and other assistants. This continued as the temastianes assumed the positions of the Jesuits in the church leadership. The prayers and hymns were written out in Spanish, Latin, or Yaqui and passed down in written form from maestro to maestro. Thus the religious as well as the military leaders were literate, both in Spanish and in the written form of Yaqui for which the Jesuits had laid foundations. Increasingly, as families moved to different parts of Sonora, the written form of Yaqui was used in maintaining communication.

The increased familiarity with Mexicans in everyday pursuits outside the towns had two major effects on language use. On the one hand, the phonology of Spanish became much better known to Yaquis; many individuals like Cajeme spent parts of their childhood among Mexicans and learned to speak Spanish in the manner of the Mexicans. We do not know the number of Yaqui bilinguals during this period, but that there were many is certain. Secondly, Yaquis borrowed an increasing number of Spanish words, incorporating them into the everyday speech of the towns. This borrowing, as a result of familiarity with Spanish phonetics, involved relatively little modification of the words borrowed as compared with those taken over during the Jesuit period. Consistently Yaquis borrowed the terms for new cultural items along with the items themselves, rather than constructing circumlocutions in the Yaqui language. Verb forms, as well as substantives, entered Yaqui from Spanish, and these began to be employed in combinations with Yaqui morphological elements, such as the usual prefixes and suffixes of the Yaqui language (Johnson 1943: 427–34).

One area of Yaqui culture, in addition to the vocabulary, was notably characterized by innovations from Mexican culture. This was the area of warfare, which was greatly enriched by direct bor-

*[handwritten: this warfare seems highly mixed with ideal of autonomy and self direction and control.
No warfare with Jesuits because it was not needed - Jesuits invited and welcomed.]*

rowing especially during the period of Cajeme's leadership (Hernandez 1902: 127). Cajeme's service in the Mexican army gave him intensive experience of military techniques. He organized cavalry units, which he combined with the traditional infantry, and trained them to fight with swords as well as guns. He also adopted the system of building forts at strategic points, especially to cover possible lines of retreat. He equipped these not only with breastworks and other defensive devices, but also with food and water to permit withstanding siege. This involved a complete reorganization of Yaqui warfare. *[handwritten: borrowed from Mexican army]*

It should be clear from the foregoing that there were two notable shifts in the orientations of Yaqui culture which constituted reversals of orientations developed during the Jesuit period. The production of an agricultural surplus ceased to be an important focus of Yaqui interest. That a negative valuation of surplus production was involved seems doubtful. It was rather a matter of the interest in military activities taking precedence over farming. It was in war that the other important reversal of the trend during Jesuit times was apparent. War became an important interest of all those Yaquis who maintained residence in the river towns, although it was also true that many Yaquis refused to accept this orientation and moved from the towns to escape such involvement. To call the vigorous activity in warfare a shift from the earlier period may be misleading. It was apparent that some sort of organization for carrying on warfare existed among Yaquis before the close of the mission period. The growth of warfare activities during the subsequent period may have involved merely a shift from ritualized to practical war interest, with the ritual valuation of warfare having been expressed continuously in the ceremonial associations into which the Jesuits converted the pre-Spanish warrior societies. It should also be noted that the ideology of nineteenth-century warfare was defensive and did not involve the growth of war interest either in the direction of warfare as an organized game or as a means to conquest of others.

The other orientations which were clearly important until 1887 consisted of (1) the ceremonies devoted to the Christian-derived cults with a focus in the customs chieftainship, (2) the pascola arts with their associated fiesta complex, and (3) the organization and ideology of the autonomous town. The first very probably was also a major orientation during the mission period and was fostered by

the Jesuits. If there was change, it might well have been in an en-
hancement in the importance of the customs chieftainship. We could
posit such an intensification of that focus on the basis of the threat
to the whole town organization of which the Christian-derived ceremonialism was such an integral part. Elsewhere in Mexico the relaxation of control by the Catholic Church resulted in development
of a cultural orientation called "The Customs" (Beals in Tax
1952: 230), the content of which consisted of selected ways from
the teachings of the missionaries in combination with older customs
to form a new sacred amalgam. The Christian elements in this orientation served to link Yaquis with rather than distinguish them from
Mexicans. Superficially, the devotions to all the supernaturals involved were very similar to those of Mexicans. It was in meaning
rather than forms that the distinctive features of Yaqui religious life
were abundant.

The pascola arts, on the other hand, were distinctive of Yaquis as
compared with Mexicans, although not as compared with other Indians of the region. One important meaning or value which they
served in the milieu of increasing hostility between Yaquis and
Mexicans must have been as symbols and expressions of Yaqui distinctiveness, and to some extent of Yaqui kinship with Mayos,
Pimas, and Opatas. The pascola arts being closely integrated with
fiesta giving, in fact being themselves the traditional context of the
fiesta, helped to sustain the structure of community co-operation
which was involved in every fiesta.

The orientation of greatest intensity during the period of autonomous communities was that of the town ideology. The pressure
for political and economic integration of the town into the Mexican
system led to a focus on the town as the major value of the late
nineteenth century. It was the political autonomy and collective land
use pattern which Yaquis were ready to fight for all during that
century. It was always under the collective title of the Eight Towns
that peace negotiations were carried on. This spiritual, or ideological,
entity had become extremely sacred by the 1880's. Each town within
this entity was also sacred, and one of the notable developments of
the early nineteenth century consisted in the mythology of the divinely ordained town sites. Since the close-knit ceremonial organization and pascola arts were practically inseparable in function, there
was a high degree of reinforcement among the several cultural ori-

entations. The foundations had been laid during the period of Spanish innovation for the growth of this orientation. Its specific form in the late 1800's would seem, however, to have been a development following the introduction of the cult of the Virgin of Guadalupe. That seems to have taken place during the 1820's after Juan Banderas' vision. The Yaquis who remained in the river towns and ultimately fought the battles with the Mexicans for control of the Yaqui country were those for whom the Christian cults, the pascola arts, the Eight Towns, and the degree of militarism necessary to maintain them took precedence over all else. The peace and the material advantages of wage labor outside the Yaqui country attracted many Yaquis during this period, but it was also true that, while they avoided the fighting themselves, they contributed supplies to the defense of the Eight Towns.

The turn which Yaqui–non-Yaqui relations took during the 1740 revolt had continued with ever increasing intensity to 1887. Yaqui culture had changed, both in details of content and in general structure and orientation, as the contact relations had altered. The third phase of contact with the Western world had resulted in the emergence of a new culture, in many respects Spanish so far as specific formal elements went, but unmistakably different from either Yaqui rancheria culture or seventeenth-century Spanish village culture.

The Relocated Communities, 1887–1956

The seventy years following the defeat of Cajeme was a period of wide dispersal of Yaquis. By the 1950's Yaquis were to be found in most of the states of Mexico and in a half-dozen states in the United States. In Sonora and Arizona six new permanent settlements had been established. In addition, in railroad section houses and cotton camps Yaquis lived and worked as temporary members of those heterogeneous laborers' communities, and in most of the towns and communities of the region there were hundreds of Yaquis in various stages of cultural assimilation. In cities as far from the Yaqui homeland as Tlaxcala in central Mexico and Los Angeles in California there were resident Yaqui families. At the same time the homeland had been resettled by Yaquis after a phase of emigration which lasted for thirty years from 1887 until 1918. Wherever Yaquis lived in the 1950's, they were in process of building new communities, for only a very few families had lived continuously in the home-

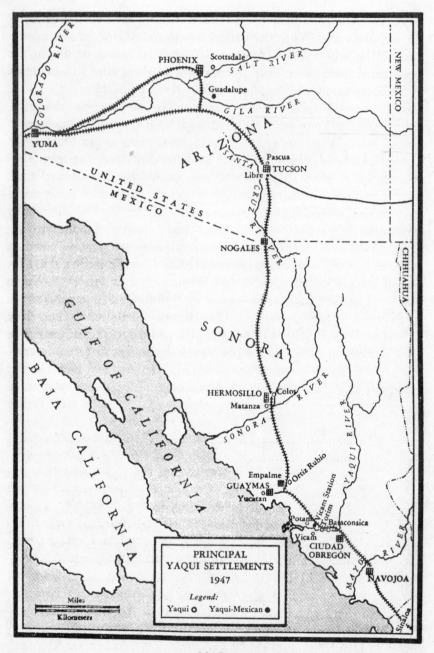

COLORADO RIVER

NEW MEXICO

PHOENIX Scottsdale SALT RIVER

Guadalupe

GILA RIVER

YUMA

A R I Z O N A

SANTA CRUZ RIVER

Pascua
Libre TUCSON

UNITED STATES
MEXICO

NOGALES

CHIHUAHUA

G U L F   O F   C A L I F O R N I A

B A J A   C A L I F O R N I A

S O N O R A

YAQUI RIVER

HERMOSILLO Colos
Matanza

SONORA RIVER

Empalme Ortiz Rubio
GUAYMAS
Yucatan

Vicam Station
Potam Torim Bataconsica
Vicam
CIUDAD
OBREGÓN

MAYO RIVER

NAVOJOA

Sinaloa

PRINCIPAL
YAQUI SETTLEMENTS
1947

Legend:
Yaqui ○   Yaqui-Mexican ●

Miles

Kilometers

MAP 3

land, and those who had, had not been able to maintain residence at the old town sites. Thus the period was characterized by the relocation of the whole Yaqui population. The conditions of life in the new communities bore little resemblance to those that had obtained in the autonomous communities of the previous period.

The dispersal was a direct consequence of the irreconcilable positions taken by Yaqui and Mexican leadership during the nineteenth century. Yaqui leadership, with great consistency, insisted on the sacred, inviolable relationship of Yaquis to their land. Sonoran leaders, not only when they wielded real power but even when they were conscious of their military impotence, refused to accept any compromise with complete political subordination. The defeats of the Yaquis in the 1880's produced no basic change in the leadership of the Eight Towns, except possibly to intensify the existing negative attitudes toward Mexican domination. Immediately after the execution of Cajeme, Mexican troops assumed control of the lower Yaqui Valley. The land was surveyed and distribution of farms was made to a colony of Mexican settlers (Hernandez 1902: 150). A program of water development was inaugurated providing for an extensive canal system on both sides of the Yaqui River. But despite real control of the Yaqui country by Mexicans for the first time, it was evident that Yaquis had not accepted defeat. Paying no attention to a large-scale nativistic religious movement which swept their earlier defeated allies, the Mayos (Troncoso 1905: 181–84), Yaquis inaugurated a systematic harassment of the Mexicans settled in and around the Yaqui country. A force of four hundred to five hundred guerrillas based for ten years at waterholes in the Bacatete Mountains kept the Yaqui country in a state of constant conflict. Relentless and destructive raids and massacres increased the Yaqui-Mexican hatred. Only a few hundred Yaquis remained along the river; the other thousands scattered over Sonora to work on haciendas and in the cities but often with the aim of providing supplies for the guerrillas.

Meanwhile the Mexican government, balked in its attempt at peaceful colonization, decided on a policy of large-scale deportation of Yaquis out of the state of Sonora. It had already shipped many Yaquis involuntarily to work on Sonora haciendas. Now it saw as the only hope for peace the deportation of Yaquis to Yucatan and Oaxaca as forced laborers. Some 5,000 were rounded up and shipped out (Turner 1910: 17–19, 45), a decisive defeat was dealt the guerrillas in the Bacatete Mountains, and an intensive military occupation was carried through. The new measures established Mexican political control of the land, but the Yaquis still residing in the river towns continued an underground organization for revolt. The majority of Yaquis wherever they had escaped deportation in Sonora or by migration to Arizona continued to give what aid they could to the few bands of guerrillas who survived. In short, there was still a Yaqui leadership who refused to accept the reality of Mexican domination.

By the time of the Mexican Revolution of 1910 no stabilization of Yaqui-Mexican relations had been attained. The deportation program was still in progress. Tiny groups of guerrillas in the mountains north of the river towns continued to fight sporadically. Several thousand Yaquis had escaped across the border into Arizona where they still dreamed, and even sometimes acted, in terms of restoration of Yaqui autonomy (Spicer 1940: 19–22). Although hundreds of Yaquis joined the forces of the Sonoran revolutionary General Alvaro Obregón and fought in his final victories, it was necessary for Obregón in 1916 to send troops into the Yaqui country to subdue a last Yaqui effort to establish military control of their territory (Weyl 1939: 53). It was not until the end of 1918 that Yaquis ceased to fight, when Obregón promised aid in agricultural development and commissioned the new governor of Sonora, Adolfo de la Huerta, to help rebuild the Yaqui towns.

From this point on, the federal government, usually supported by the state of Sonora, encouraged resettlement of the Yaqui territory. The plan called for colonization by Mexicans as well as Yaquis. Some Yaqui leaders, who had risen to high rank in Obregón's army, co-operated and helped guide the resettlement. Two new towns, Mexican in character, were built in the heart of the Yaqui country along the railroad which had been built in the area since the late 1880's. Slowly Yaquis returned from the United States and various parts of Mexico where they had been deported or served in the revolutionary army. An interruption occurred in 1926–27, when a final military outbreak of Yaquis took place in connection with a visit of General Obregón to the Yaqui country (Spicer 1954: 34–35). The result of the outbreak was a systematic military occupation of the whole territory which was maintained into the 1950's. It was under conditions of military occupation that the heaviest resettlement during the 1930's took place. By 1950 the Yaqui population of the lower river valley approached 10,000 (Fabila 1940: 113–14; Spicer 1947: 11–12). There were in addition 3,000–4,000 Mexicans concentrated for the most part in one of the new railroad towns.

Yaqui resettlement was confined to only a portion of the old tribal territory. During the period of intensive conflict and depopulation of the Yaqui country, Mexicans had taken over the extensive and fertile coastal plain south of the Yaqui River and converted it into highly productive irrigated farmland. As Yaquis returned to the homeland in the 1930's, they found only the north bank of the river available for resettlement. In 1939, President Cárdenas, by executive decree, established the north bank and the Bacatete Mountains, perhaps half of the original territory, as exclusively for Yaquis (Fabila 1940: 295–310). Within this area during the 1930's and 1940's five predominantly Yaqui and one predominantly Mexican settlements developed. The Mexican settlement—Vicam Station—had a population of about 4,000. The Yaqui settlements ranged from 100 to 3,500 (Spicer 1947: 11). Only three of the Yaqui settlements were in approximately the same locations as the mission communities whose names they bore—Torim, Vicam, and Potam. The other five towns either had been taken over by Mexicans, if on the south side of the river, or had ceased to exist because of failing water supply resulting from diversion of water to the flourishing Mexican farms in the coastal plain. As resettlement progressed Yaquis made desperate efforts to reconstitute the five lost towns on the north side of the river.

In all of the Yaqui communities there was an effort to re-establish the form of the nineteenth-century towns. It was obvious, however, that, in each, two different settlement patterns were competing. The old plan of fenced households irregularly clustered in the vicinity of a church was in part realized, but at the same time portions of the communities were laid out in a grid plan with houses flush with the streets and patios behind. The fact was that most of the Yaqui communities had two civic centers, one the church and the headquarters of the civil governors and the other the Mexican army headquarters, a federal rural school, small stores, bakeries, and perhaps a pool hall. Around the latter, houses were placed in the Mexican way, around the church in the older Yaqui way.

The mixed physical plan of the community was a reflection of the social and political structure. The Mexican army headquarters had its counterpart in the *guardia* of the Yaqui military society. The Yaqui church might be considered as having its counterpart in the federal school. The open air gathering place of the Yaqui governors and other officials was matched by a Mexican style adobe building in which the Mexican commissioner of police maintained his office. The Yaqui towns, even though the percentage of Mexicans living in them was small, were dual societies, and the settlement pattern was an expression of the condition.

The river towns were heterogeneous, considerably more so than towns of similar size generally in Sonora. In the first place, the ethnic composition was mixed. Each contained some Mexicans, and the larger ones several hundred. A sharp distinction existed between the Indian majority—the yoemem—and the Mexican minority—the yoris; the two Yaqui terms which had been employed during the period of autonomous communities were still in use by both groups. The Indians, too, were accustomed to make distinctions among themselves with reference to Mayo or Yaqui ancestry, although their cultural and racial traits were not distinctive. Among Yaquis there were great differences in fluency in Spanish, although nearly all, as a result of residence elsewhere had some command of Spanish and were classed as bilingual by the census takers. As a result of residence in the United States, 15 or 20 per cent of the Yaquis also knew English. The great variety of life experiences of Yaquis resulted in great differences in occupational skills, although a majority had been agricultural laborers. A majority were literate, although with little or no formal schooling. The population of any community contained individuals whose combined backgrounds included knowledge not only of Mexicans and Anglo-Americans but also other Indians such as Papagos, Seris, Apaches, Zunis, and Tarahumaras. Their rating of themselves in relation to these other ethnic groups was complex, but in general on a scale of "civilized" (a term which they employed often in such matters) they regarded themselves as more civilized than any of the Indian groups or the Mexicans and as at least the equal, except in technical skills, of the Anglo-Americans.

Within the towns closest relations with non-Yaquis were with Mexican storekeepers. They traded what corn and beans they could spare for cloth, coffee, sugar, and metal and enamelware containers. They obtained credit from them and transportation to neighboring cities in the storekeepers' trucks. The storekeepers generally learned no more than a few words of Yaqui, so that all but the most elementary communication was in the Spanish language. Most storekeepers were interested in acquiring land or cattle of their own and generally in the expansion of their economic holdings and power. All were interested in seeing the Yaqui country come under actual political domination of Mexicans rather than remain in the equivocal status in which it existed, yet none pursued a course of action directly connected with political change.

Other important areas of interaction between Yaquis and non-Yaquis were in military affairs and with the technically trained persons engaged in various government programs. Yaquis were paid as "auxiliary troops" on the army payroll, an arrangement regarded by Yaquis as due them because of past injustices and by Mexicans as bribery to maintain peace. The officers of the occupation army were often as interested as storekeepers in obtaining economic advantage and engaged in extralegal use of Yaqui lands. Under army supervision a medical program came into operation which brought modern medical practices and ideas into the towns. Until the early 1950's Yaquis showed little interest in the federal schools, but gradually enrolment increased. A federal program of irrigation development on the north side of the river got under way in the 1930's, bringing Yaquis into contact intensively with agricultural technicians (Fabila 1940: 33–59). It was not, however, until 1956 that the canal system was ready for use. Thus Yaquis, even in their towns, were thrown into contact with a wide variety of Mexicans, and these varied relationships increased in intensity as the federal programs gained momentum.

The pressures to change were quite different from what they had been in either of the two preceding periods. On the one hand, at the level of daily routine there was no direct pressure to change. No missionaries were present and the agents of Mexican culture did not exercise coercive power on specific individuals. Nevertheless the stores with their desirable goods, and medical officers with their medicines, the schoolteacher with his books and knowledge, the schoolhouse with its Saturday night dancing for fun, the Mexicans in general with their interest in material comfort were there constantly as a part of town life. On the other hand, there was tangible evidence of envelopment everywhere which amounted to a diffuse pressure for change. The Yaqui military societies still functioned, but every meeting was in plain sight of the Mexican army headquarters.

Yaquis went out to their fields daily, engaging in the traditional floodwater farming, but periodically, when federal funds were available, work proceeded on the canal system and slowly the main canal reached deeper into the north bank farmlands. The civil governors were elected annually and took office on the Day of the Kings in January, but notices were also posted regularly of the elections for officers in the municipalities which now included the whole of the Yaqui country. Military, economic, and political affairs had much the form of the nineteenth-century towns, but a different scheme of life reached always into the relocated communities. Knowledge of the steady growth of that new order was inescapable.

Outside the river towns in Sonora another 3,000 to 4,000 Yaquis lived more intimately with the Mexican order of things (Spicer 1947: 11–12). Small settlements had grown up at the edges of Empalme, Guaymas, and Hermosillo. They maintained their own independent churches and something of their annual round of ceremonial life, including the Easter ceremony. Economically, they were entirely dependent on employers in the cities where they worked as domestic help and laborers. They thought of themselves as Yaqui communities and called their settlements "*barrios*" of the larger community. From them there was constant, slow movement into the larger communities as processes of assimilation encouraged loss of identity.

In Sonora generally the attitudes of Mexicans toward Yaquis developed along two distinct lines. Rural dwellers who lived closest to Yaquis and those whose relatives had suffered in the protracted fighting maintained attitudes of superiority and hostility. Settlers and storekeepers who moved into the Yaqui country beginning in the 1920's shared such attitudes, despite close personal relations with individual Yaquis. Nourished by such feelings, an elaborate tradition of rumor and fiction concerning Yaqui savagery gained currency throughout Sonora (Spicer 1945: 283–85; Spicer 1954: 175–76). This tradition supported a stereotyped adverse judgment of Yaquis as fanatically religious, lazy and improvident, and hopelessly incompetent in managing their land and public affairs. The judgment of Yaquis as lazy and incompetent coexisted with the widespread belief in Sonora that Yaquis were able and industrious workers, when employed by others. On the other hand, at the level of national thought and literature a quite different image of Yaquis grew up. Novels widely read in the 1920's, such as those of the Sonoran Djed Borquez, dramatized the conflict of Yaquis and Yoris and created a view of Yaquis as courageous underdogs (Borquez 1929). This conception gained great support through exaggerated stories of Yaqui participation with Obregón's troops in the victorious final phase of the 1910 revolution. The favorable national stereotype led to the inclusion of the figure of the Yaqui deer dancer in the official seal of the state of Sonora. The recognition of Yaquis as an important element in the population of Sonora received not only symbolic expression, but led also to a program of educational and agricultural development during the administration of President Cárdenas in the 1930's.

Yaquis had begun to cross the border into the United States as early as 1887 (Spicer 1940: 20). As the deportation program intensified, more and more crossed; the migration reached a peak in the years just before the 1910 revolution. By the 1950's there were approximately 4,000 in Arizona who identified themselves as Yaquis. Like the Sonora Yaquis they had established themselves at the edges of cities in what they called "barrios." During early years in the United States they were fearful of being identified as Yaquis and sent back for deportation. It was 1906 before they realized that they had been granted political asylum and could freely reinstitute the Easter ceremony and other customs which would reveal them as Yaquis (Spicer 1948). The settlements which they established were considerably smaller than the nineteenth-century river towns, averaging in the neighborhood of 400 to 500 persons. Like the Sonora Yaquis who lived near the cities, they established themselves first as squatters and only slowly acquired title to house sites. They remained entirely dependent on Anglo-American employers for their living.

In the Arizona settlements Yaquis were thrown most closely with Mexican Americans, but also to some extent with Papago, Pima, and other Indians. They sought from the first to keep from identification with Papago and other Indians whom they regarded as inferior to themselves. As soon as the fear of being returned to Mexico for deportation had dissipated, they sought also to keep themselves distinct from Mexican Americans. The traditional feelings of hostility and superiority to Mexicans remained strong. This was true despite the fact that their closest association as workers and in the places where they found residence was with Mexicans. Many already spoke Spanish; rapidly all became Spanish speakers, although they retained

Yaqui as the language of the home. Intermarriage with Mexicans and close association with them through godparent relations and the compadrazgo steadily increased.

The Yaqui communities were never completely segregated areas composed only of Yaqui residents. Each shaded into adjoining residential areas of Mexican Americans. Nevertheless each Yaqui settlement, like those in Sonora, built a church, often of discarded railroad ties, and maintained it as a community center. Anglo-Americans, who generally viewed the refugee Yaquis with pity mingled with a good deal of respect for their warlike past, took an interest in establishing Yaquis in something like a reservation system. However, a land base for such a system was lacking, and attempts by Yaquis to set up either tribal or town organizations did not work out. The general friendliness of Americans did, however, result in encouraging the old ceremonial organization. In the 1930's the Tucson Chamber of Commerce appointed a special committee to work with Yaquis in organizing their annual Easter ceremony. This collaboration continued into the 1950's, as the Easter ceremony at one of the Tucson settlements became a national tourist attraction.

Within the Yaqui communities there were periodic efforts by missionaries of various Christian denominations to convert the Yaquis, and the Catholic Church in one Arizona city made a special effort to bring Yaquis to Catholic orthodoxy. Only a few Protestant converts were made. The overwhelming majority of Yaquis who maintained residence in the barrios continued to participate in and support their own independent churches. Other than the missionary efforts there was little direct pressure for cultural change. The most important consisted in schools. Schools were built especially for Yaquis in two of their communities. Attendance was irregular at first, but by the 1950's had become as consistent as that of Arizonans generally.

Constant communication was maintained between the Arizona and the Sonora Yaquis. Much of the communication was by mail, but there was also frequent visiting, since members of the same family lines in the course of dispersal had become established on different sides of the international line. Sonora Yaquis were constantly drawn to settle in Arizona because of the possibility of higher wages, but it was also true that there was a constant migration of Arizona Yaquis back to Sonora. The attraction of the homeland was still a powerful force in the 1950's. The Arizona settlements also became dependent on the re-established river towns for certain ceremonial performers, such as deer dancers.

The Culture of the Relocated Communities

The disruption of the way of life of the river towns was not complete for ten years after the defeat of Cajeme. In 1898 General Luis Torres instituted a paternalistic regime of rigid controls over all aspects of life among the 3,000 Yaquis who remained in the homeland (Hernandez 1902: 162–70). A priest and a group of Sisters of Josephine were placed at Bacum in the expectation that the peaceful and co-operative relationships of the Jesuit period might be restored. The almost immediate result was a new military outbreak by Yaquis, the renewal of demands (by a leadership signing itself as "the eight towns") for evacuation of the Yaqui territory by Mexicans, and, in sequence, the tightening of repressive measures by General Torres. This inaugurated the final exodus of Yaquis from the river country.

The river towns no longer existed as organizations of persons pursuing a way of life in a sacred homeland. Nevertheless during the next twenty-five years they continued to exist as models of community life in the minds of thousands of Yaquis. The possibility of restoring this ideal was denied the ragged families of the few hundred seminomadic guerrillas in the mountains of the Yaqui territory. Until after the 1910 revolution had begun, most Yaquis elsewhere in Sonora were subject to deportation and hence afraid to call attention to themselves as Yaquis. It was in the Arizona settlements, which grew rapidly after 1900, that the revival of customs first got under way.

The revival was a slow, but accelerating, process (Spicer 1948). Extended, and even nuclear, families had been broken apart during the dispersal. Scores of persons found themselves in Arizona as individuals with no relatives. Knowledge of a ritual kinship bond, through the godparent system, led many to seek one another out and settle together. Slowly clusters of Yaquis associated themselves at the edges of the Arizona towns or on ranches where they could find employment. Funerals were reported to be the first ceremonies revived. It was found that every cluster of families and individuals had members who had retained some knowledge of the ritual. The little groups became dependent on one another for the services of persons who knew different elements of the ceremonies. In 1906, aware of the friendliness of Anglo-Americans, one group went beyond the revival of the crisis rites and instituted an Easter ceremony. It was found that the necessary knowledge and skills were present among those families and individuals who had settled in the vicinity of Tucson. In each river town the Easter ceremony, as the annual focus of activities of the customs chieftainship, had been a major foundation of community solidarity. It became so now in Arizona for all those Yaquis who lived at the north edge of Tucson. Over the next few years the Easter ceremony was revived among Yaquis settled at the south edge of Tucson and those living near Phoenix. From this time on into the 1950's there were three permanent centers of Yaqui life in Arizona—the sites of these three annual ceremonials.

The regrouping of Yaquis in Arizona had a certain basis in common town affiliation in the homeland, but this applied only to the original small clusters. Individuals who came together as a result of actual and ritual kinship connections usually, but not always, had been residents of the same towns. But in each of the three centers which ultimately crystallized in Arizona there were people from all of the eight towns. The ties which reconstituted them as communities in Arizona crosscut the river town memberships. These new ties were residence in the same general area in Arizona and ceremonial interests which could be served only by pooling ritual skills learned in the various river towns.

After the revival of the Easter ceremonies there was a strong tendency to concentrate into more compact local groups. On the one hand, the intensification of interests resulting from the ceremonial activities encouraged the tendency. On the other hand, pressures came from non-Yaquis. The latter were of two sorts. An effort to establish better administrative control of Yaqui immigration into Arizona played a part. This led to the setting aside of tracts of land near Phoenix and Tucson for Yaqui settlement. Two such tracts did become the territorial basis of two of the permanent Yaqui communities. There was also a tendency on the part of Anglo-Americans to assume that Yaquis, as Indians, ought to be organized as a "tribe." Hence they were encouraged to choose a "chief," who could be, from the point of view of the Anglo-Americans, the liaison between Yaquis and immigration officials. Some Yaquis who had been born in the United States or who had lived only briefly in the river towns attempted to co-operate. For a time there was an individual who assumed the title of "chief of the Yaquis," but it was clear that he had no important influence with the great majority of Yaquis. The residents of the developing Yaqui communities equated the Anglo-American conception of chief with captain of a military society and immediately found themselves in conflict over method of selection, term of office, extent of jurisdiction, and the functions themselves. The essential incompatibility consisted in jurisdiction. While Yaquis from various river towns did unite into new local groups, the new grouping took on the characteristics of the old autonomous town. An organizational level beyond that of local group, under conditions of peace, still had no meaning. Hence even under the circumstances of encouragement by the dominant Anglo-Americans, no "tribal" organization took lasting form.

The Yaqui communities tried briefly, under the stimulus of the outside interest and of a few Yaqui individuals, to revive the war captain and the military societies. The attempt was unsuccessful. Similarly in one of the communities a town council with jurisdiction over family disputes was in operation for a few years. It, too, failed to find lasting functions. In both cases of unsuccessful revival, it was evident that most Yaquis regarded police and court functions as the proper prerogative of the political organization which had given them shelter. In contrast with their refusal to accept political integration in Sonora, they regarded it as proper under conditions in which their sacred land was not involved.

The failure of those aspects of the culture connected with the ideology of the autonomous town and the sacred land to be revived included not only the military and civil organization, but extended also to features of ceremonial life. Thus the weekly Sunday ceremony of The Surrounding, symbolic of possession of the tribal territory, did not become a part of the revived ceremonies. Moreover, the whole fiestero system focused on the annual ceremony honoring the patron saint of the town remained absent from the life of the Arizona settlements. This was true despite the use of patron saints for the churches.

It was clear, then, that a process of selection in the movement for revival was constantly in operation. That this was not a selection dictated by attitudes or controls of the dominant Anglo-Americans is also clear when we consider the latter's favorable interest in town council and war captain. The selection would seem to have been a result of the Yaqui conception of themselves in relation to the Anglo-Americans. The relationship was quite different from that to Mexicans. Yaqui conceptions of land rights and proprietorship required that they see themselves as guests of Anglo-Americans. Some effort to restore the customs connected with town autonomy were to be expected in view of the strength of the image of the Eight Towns, but meaning for such customs was lacking in the Arizona situation, and they did not persist.

Thus, while integration took place politically in a way that had never developed in Sonora and with it the disappearance of large sectors of the river town culture, the revival of elements of the town ceremonial system proceeded at an accelerating rate. In terms of the "cult" terminology employed above, it may be said that all cults except that of the Virgin of Guadalupe were revived in essential form. Even the latter appeared in very attenuated character in the Arizona settlements. The Easter ceremony was in itself the major expression of the cult of Jesus, and it was the first large scale ceremonial revival. Complementary to it, in terms of seasonal organization as well as ceremonial meaning, was the cult of the Virgin. This was developed in much the same way as in the river towns, with the matachin dancers as the chief devotees and an annual ceremony in May as a major expression. The cult of the dead was interwoven with both the others; while not all customs and rituals connected with it were revived in Arizona, nevertheless the Books of the Dead with their associated rituals and the annual All Souls devotions were revived and became important features of Arizona Yaqui ceremonial life. As a basic mechanism of the whole system, the custom of promising young children to service in the organizations was employed, as it had been in the river towns. Most of what was revived bore surface resemblance to the customs of folk Catholicism common among the neighbors of Yaquis in Arizona. Nevertheless there were fundamental differences; these were, if anything, emphasized by Yaquis.

Moreover, it was not only the strongly Christianized features of Yaqui ceremonial life which were revived. Yaquis took at least equal interest in reviving the whole complex of the pascola arts and the household fiesta system associated with it. In these, costuming, dance, and music, as well as specific features of ritual behavior of pascola and deer dancer, were sufficiently different from Mexican or Anglo-

American practice to encourage newspaper writers to use the words "savage" and "barbaric" in describing them. They were also sufficiently different from what most inhabitants of Arizona knew as "Indian" to prevent classification of Yaquis in the same category with Papagos, Apaches, or others. It was the current scene in Arizona which the pascolas commented on in their ritual roles, as well as on the golden age of the river towns. In this way they kept themselves related in a meaningful manner to the Arizona milieu, as the deer dancer did not. The deer ritual tended steadily toward obsolescence in Yaqui culture, despite achieving considerable spectacle value in Anglo-American life (Spicer 1948).

A Yaqui community, then, in Arizona became a truncated version of a river town, organized in terms of only two rather than all five major orientations of nineteenth-century Yaqui culture. The total town organization did not exist and even the church, which embraced three of the four major cults, tended in Arizona to be less a single over-all organization than a number of distinct sodalities. In addition an atomistic tendency developed whereby the important images employed in church activities were controlled by particular owning families rather than the church as a whole (Spicer 1954: 205).

Despite the fact that all the organizational features of river towns were not revived in Arizona the concept of the Eight Towns was of major importance in Yaqui life. While the mythology of the tribal territory and the founding of the towns was imperfectly known by Arizona-born Yaquis in the 1940's, the history was known in a general way and the phrases for the Eight Towns and associated concepts were regularly used as sacred words in the ritual (Spicer 1948); in this form they were a part of common knowledge. A sense of Yaqui identity as sharply distinct from Mexican neighbors, and as well from all other Indians of the region, was supported by the sacred words and the awareness of history.

By the 1940's there was, as compared with towns in the Sonora homeland, declining interest in complete reconstitution of the nineteenth-century culture. Effort was focused rather on the maintenance of those elements of the culture which had been revived by the 1930's. Arizona Yaquis were aware of difficulties in recruiting persons for the roles necessary even for what they had by that time revived.

Through the 1930's Yaqui had remained the language of most of the households. By the 1950's a minority used Yaqui as the dominant language of the home. Spanish rather tended to take its place, but most young adults had about the same command of all three languages of daily life, namely, Yaqui, Spanish, and English (Barber 1952). The Yaqui language showed marked vocabulary enrichment from English; borrowing took place in the same manner that it had earlier from Spanish. Yaqui was tending to be used by all Arizona-born Yaquis in fewer daily situations than either of the other two languages. It was still the major language of the organized ceremonial life, but was losing out to Spanish in frequency of use in homelife situations. The use of Yaqui was still a basic criterion for evaluating the degree of "Yaqui-ness" of any individual (Spicer 1948).

By the 1950's kinship terminology and usages had been largely replaced by Mexican forms, although elementary family terms persisted in many households. The basic kinship unit through the 1930's was an extended family of loose composition, with no consistent patterns of residence after marriage. It included ritual as well as actual kin and changed composition in response to employment opportunities. By the 1950's the extended family was still general, but there was a growing number of nuclear families as household units. The ritual kinship system retained strength and constituted an important, because immensely flexible, mechanism for insuring co-operation and financial help in connection with employment fluctuations and demands of ceremonial obligations. The ritual kinship system also functioned, however, as a mechanism for integration of Yaquis with neighboring Mexican-American families.

From the first, Arizona Yaquis depended for their living on non-Yaqui employers. No distinctive patterns of subsistence developed. Yaquis possessed no land, except house sites, and consequently became completely participant in the general economic system, gradually assuming a spread into the skilled as well as the unskilled levels of occupation. While maintaining a few distinctive customs of economic distribution through ceremonial obligation, they otherwise participated fully in the money economy. Adjustments of ceremonial schedule were made as required to the demands of job-holding, so that only ceremonial leadership produced occasional conflicts between their ceremonial and economic life. In material culture, masks, musical instruments, and some other ceremonial paraphernalia persisted as the only distinctive elements, and in these there were numerous specific adaptations to the different materials available.

A notable characteristic of Yaqui life in Arizona consisted in a wide variation in the participation of individuals in the distinctive Yaqui ways (Spicer 1948). At any given time in one of the ceremonially defined communities there might be from fifty to sixty households in residence around the church. At other times, as during cotton-picking season in the fall, not more than a dozen families might be in residence. Families moved in and out of the community in accordance with their job requirements. Many families divided their time about equally between living in their houses near the church and living on some ranch where they had permanent relations with an employer. Other families moved away from the church communities for months at a time, sometimes two or three years, to work on the railroad or live in the section houses. Residence on jobs often threw them with non-Yaqui families with whom they became as intimate as with Yaqui families. While seasonal residence away from the church community did not involve complete suspension of participation in the ceremonial round, the more protracted residences did. Such conditions resulted in the acceptance of a flexible standard in the meeting of ceremonial obligations. It was also common for young men to engage in several years of wandering through various states, suspending meanwhile whatever ceremonial obligations they had contracted. Many returned eventually to marry and settle in or near the church communities where they re-established their ceremonial connections. Such variation in participation in the community, family, and ritual kinship obligations characterized most Yaquis. It became an acceptable mode of adjustment to the exigencies of living in a larger society. It also promoted the learning of the ways of that larger society. A number of persons never returned to any participation in Yaqui life and became assimilated to the culture of the larger society. Others intensified their Yaqui participation after a youthful lapse.

In Sonora the reconstitution of Yaqui culture proceeded along considerably different lines. There was a lag of fifteen or twenty years behind the Arizona settlements. Resettlement, as the reverse trend to dispersal, did not begin actually until after 1918, when fighting finally ceased in Yaqui territory. During the next forty

years there was steady growth of Yaqui population in the river
country except for some decline after the 1927 "uprising," when
many Yaquis were impressed into military service in the Mexican
army.

The aim of the Yaqui resettlers in the homeland was definitely to
re-establish all the eight towns as near the traditional sites as possible,
certainly somewhere within the divinely revealed town territory,
and in all details like the nineteenth-century ideals. The relocation
of those towns whose water supply had been interfered with by the
new irrigation developments proceeded against great odds. By 1955
there were counterparts of all the old towns, but the former approximate equality in size and character was far from realized. The
new Cocorit was a place of about 200, in contrast with Potam with
a population of nearly 4,000. Moreover, the town structure of the
latter included the politico-ceremonial organization of Huirivis,
whose town site was so lacking in water that nearly all the
Huirivis resettlers were forced to maintain residence at Potam. There
was a very considerable mixture of town affiliation among the residents of the relocated communities.

Despite such variation from the earlier pattern each settlement
moved steadily in the direction of more and more complete duplication of the older town organization. Officials of the different town
organizations visited with one another and discussed proper procedures and rituals. Copies of ceremonial paraphernalia possessed by
one town organization were made and used by another. The process
of borrowing and mutual influence was still in progress in the 1950's.
By that time three of the larger settlements had revived what must
have been nearly the whole complement of nineteenth-century military and politico-ceremonial organizational forms. This included the
full set of offices and the whole set of rituals of the military societies,
the whole church organization serving the four cults, the governor
system of civil authority including land management, the annual
patron saint's fiesta with its elaborate organization, and the pascola
and deer complex of arts and ritual. The last seems to have been the
only one of the major areas of formal culture which lost important
elements in the process of revival; a number of ritual animal dances
were not revived and seemed as late as the 1950's unlikely to be.
One other institution of considerable importance, which had been
part of the church organization, was revived, but seemed unaccepta-

ble and was already falling into disuse by the late 1940's. This was the *pihkan* system of child indoctrination (Spicer 1954: 87–88). The office of *pihkan ya'ut* was re-created in at least two towns, but failed to function. Aside from these few, but significant, losses, the revival was nearly complete.

What differed from the nineteenth-century towns were the setting and the human materials of the revived organization. Nearly perfect though it might appear to a Yaqui using as a standard the golden age of the Eight Towns, there was no escaping the reality of the dual character of each town. Even though there might be complete participation (and this was rare in the 1940's) of Yaquis in the Easter and patron saint celebrations, there were always the Mexican residents of the town. Some of the women participated, but not the men. The military societies and the group of governors did not have jurisdiction over the army colonel and the police commissioner. Dual organization was the fact. The sacred town site, divinely set aside for exclusive Yaqui use, was not wholly under the control of the Yaqui hierarchy. Not only Mexicans could live in the town under another jurisdiction, but also Yaquis who became dissatisfied with the controls of the town system. Yet, it was not so easy for a Yaqui in one of the towns to withdraw as it was in Arizona, for the line between Yaquis and Yoris was much more sharply drawn in Sonora. There was an organization with harsh sanctions at its disposal to keep the line well-defined. Nevertheless there were Yaquis in every town who did dare to express their dissatisfactions and to be branded as Yori. There were many more who shrank from such formal identification and kept their negative feelings and thoughts to themselves while they continued to meet their obligations to relatives and godparents. The town organization was far less flexible than in Arizona, in that it forced participation of dissident individuals in this way.

In Arizona Yaquis accepted political integration into the larger society, maintaining an autonomy only in religious life. In the river towns in Sonora the dual organization was a product of continuing Yaqui refusal to accept political integration. Despite the dominant military power of the Mexicans, Yaqui revival of their institutions was allowed. Yaqui officials spoke of the "Yaqui Law" as superior to Mexican, using the term along with the "Eight Towns" as a sacred phrase; they employed the whipping post for punishment, a practice long since discarded in the Mexican penal system. The clash of political systems within the framework of the town was obvious, yet Yaquis were no longer forcibly directed to change their political organization. There was instead the constant and unmistakable presentation of an alternative system. Children grew up with the alternative tangibly present. It was not easy for all to accept the idea of the sacred exclusiveness of the Yaqui land with the fact of Mexican power on that land always before them.

The economic basis of the re-established river towns was essentially subsistence farming. The Mexican government's efforts to aid Yaqui agricultural development begun in the early 1920's received more and more financial support, but the canal system was not completed until 1956. Consequently Yaqui agriculture continued for thirty-five years on the uncertain floodwater basis. Very little in the way of mechanized farming took place. Yaqui economy existed on an unstable basis and with considerable range in income and production among families (Spicer 1954: 39–54). The range in productive capacity was a result not only of the great variation in water supply, but also of the tremendously varied backgrounds of the resettlers and their knowledge of farming. The techniques employed varied little from those of the nineteenth century. Nevertheless Yaqui interest in trade goods had greatly increased. Their demand for goods with which they were acquainted as a result of residence in various parts of Mexico and the United States generally exceeded their ability to purchase. The result was a persistent sense of poverty as characteristic of Yaquis and a negative evaluation of themselves in relation to Mexicans in this regard. At the same time a very strong sense of moral superiority to Mexicans prevailed generally and was regarded as being expressed in their fighting capacity and in the solemnity and large number of ceremonial devotions.

Much of Yaqui material culture was distinctive as compared with that of the Mexicans of the towns. The wood and cane technology of the early nineteenth century characterized house-building and furnishing and agricultural implements. This varied little, however, from that of rural people elsewhere in the state and was generally evaluated by Mexicans as lower class and not necessarily "Indian." Crafts, such as weaving and pottery-making, were not revived.

The social organization was in most respects like that in the Arizona "barrios." The older kinship system had been largely replaced. Households were of miscellaneous composition with reference to the kinship of the members. An economic unit consisting of several nuclear families was, however, well established. The networks of generalized kin relations and ritual kinship were to a much larger extent than in Arizona functional with respect to economic distribution. This was notable especially in the annual town-wide effort to carry out the fiesta for the patron saint; but it was also important in the considerably more frequent subsistence crises of the yearly routine. It was also true that in Sonora groups of relatives larger than nuclear families functioned together as units more regularly and frequently than in Arizona, especially in connection with monthly ceremonies honoring the dead ancestors—observances which were part of the cult of the dead and which were not revived in Arizona.

There was what amounted to a revival of the Yaqui language in the river towns. Nearly all the resettlers had learned Spanish, English, or both in the course of the dispersal. Resettlement in the homeland did not mean the complete discontinuance of daily relations with non-Yaqui speakers, but it did mean that many people, and particularly children, found themselves in situations in which all communication could be carried on in Yaqui. The result was a more intensive and general use of the Yaqui language. It meant also that some children grew up with a knowledge of Yaqui only, so that the number of monolinguals increased. The language continued receptive to the introduction of Spanish words, including verb forms.

An organized myth-history of Yaquis from pre-Spanish times was maintained in oral form by specialists in some of the towns. It was enriched by extracts from published histories of Sonora in Spanish. Portions of the account were written out in Yaqui. Older men held special classes of young men for instruction in their interpretation of history (Spicer 1954: 24). There was marked contrast between the Sonora and Arizona settlements in the interest in tribal history. In Arizona little was known of Yaqui history except in the most general way by the 1950's.

The pascola arts were far richer in the Sonora towns than in Arizona. Dance, music, humorous monologue, and the art of fiction flourished and were characterized by more vigorous popular participation than in Arizona.

The Sonora barrio settlements near the cities were much more like the Arizona settlements than the new river towns. Like the Arizona barrios, they went through a process of revival. As in them, the

result was a truncated town structure in which little beyond the old
church organizations were revived.

Cultural Processes

The main outlines of Yaqui response to contact seem clear
enough. During the Mission Period Yaquis were extremely receptive
to a large number of European introductions in various aspects of
culture. The many innovations were integrated with Yaqui culture
elements partly during the Mission Period and partly during the
subsequent period of "autonomy." The modification of Spanish elements and their recombination with Yaqui resulted, before the close
of the Autonomous Period, in a cultural system which could not be
justly called a modified rancheria culture nor a variant of Spanish-
Catholic culture. A new folk culture had developed. This tightly
organized system of cultural behavior became extremely resistant to
further fundamental change. Even during dispersal, under very different conditions from those which obtained in the Autonomous
Period, various customs were revived and persisted. Under circumstances which prohibited revival of the whole folk culture, Yaquis
selected certain patterns and adapted them with minor modifications
to new economic and political conditions. After return to the homeland, however, Yaquis exerted vigorous effort to revive the whole.

The conditions to which the fusion of European and aboriginal
traditions was a response have been described and may be recapitulated here. In the first place stimulation of this process depended
heavily on the growth of Yaqui interest in the innovations. To a
large extent Yaquis were able to select, as a result of their military
position, those contacts with Spanish society which they wanted.
Having selected the missionaries with their agricultural and ritual
novelties, Yaquis and Jesuits developed a community of interest
which promoted an effective isolation from segments of Spanish
society with conflicting interests. The geographical situation contributed also to this relative isolation, which lasted for a period of
four or five generations.

The nature of the relations between Yaquis and the limited number
and types of innovators played an important part in the promotion
of the fusion. The Jesuits were accepted with high prestige and
authority. Nevertheless it was impossible for them to remake Yaqui
communities into duplicates of European agricultural villages, even

though the physical form of settlement tended under Jesuit leadership in that direction. The mission communities were so large as to require great dependence of the missionaries on existing Yaqui leadership and organization. Without military control or effective political coercion, the Jesuits worked through what became a fairly elaborate Yaqui hierarchy. The result was abundant opportunity for Yaqui reinterpretation of every innovation offered. Even the indoctrination of children, in which the missionaries were deeply interested, had to be organized through Yaqui assistants.

At the same time the Jesuit conception of their role inhibited the growth of antagonisms. They worked less in terms of the prohibition of existing Yaqui custom and belief than of suggested reinterpretations. The incipient hostility of Yaqui ritual specialists melted away rapidly under such permissive conditions. Most persons of prestige and authority in the Yaqui rancherias assumed equivalent positions in the new communities. Yaqui acceptance of the plan of reorganization of communities at a new wider level of integration gave the missionaries key positions in the remaking of Yaqui society. Nevertheless they were merely at the upper end of administrative lines and instructional systems extending out through the Yaqui-manned hierarchies.

It would be a mistake to assume that by the end of the Jesuit period the Yaqui folk culture of the Autonomous Period had taken form. The formation of that tightly integrated system was a result of new conditions of adaptation. By the end of the period of intensive Jesuit influence the mission communities were probably in a rather fluid state, still in process of adjusting to the flood of Spanish innovations. It was the nearly simultaneous application of new and different pressures for change and the disappearance of the Jesuits which constituted the decisive conditions for the formation of the Yaqui autonomous culture. The new pressures from Spanish society were direct and obvious threats to the political autonomy and exclusive possession of tribal territory which Yaquis had enjoyed under the mission system. These threats crystallized at precisely the time that Spaniards ceased to be an integral part of Yaqui community life. The pressures continued with greater intensity from the Mexicans, but with even less structuralization in Yaqui communities. In continuing isolation from the Mexican political system, Yaquis reoriented their community life around those interests which were threatened. The result was an intensification of the fusion process which had begun to operate in the mission communities.

Christian and aboriginal mythology, the already fused native-Christian ritual and the surviving more purely aboriginal ritual, the new interest in military action and the Jesuit-reinterpreted ritual of the former military societies—all of these and many other features of mission culture went through a further process of fusion. This was carried out in communities which had become reduced in size as a result of the total population decline. As the intensification of the new synthesis proceeded, it led to a steady homogenization of the communities. Those individuals who were closer to assimilation to Mexican culture and those who simply did not like the growing emphasis on warfare found few barriers to movement into Mexican communities. The final fusion of the folk culture of the Autonomous Period took place in a situation of growing social isolation and increasing sacredness of the threatened cultural interests. A hundred years after the departure of the Jesuits the resynthesis was probably complete.

Fusion, in the sense in which it has been used here, ceased to be the dominant process in Yaqui cultural adjustment during its fourth historical phase. The tendency to accept and reinterpret elements from other cultures in the manner described was inhibited by the growth of the sacred orientations of the nineteenth century. The tendency was rather to preserve whatever complexes or patterns could be preserved under circumstances prohibitive to the maintenance of the whole. The conditions under which this tendency asserted itself were markedly different from any preceding. The pressures for change bore no resemblance to those in the Mission or Autonomous Periods. In Arizona no non-Yaquis constantly urging new ways lived in what Yaquis regarded as their communities; rather Yaquis went out from their communities to participate in what was obviously a dominant society. There was no official hostility but rather a friendliness toward Yaqui attempts to maintain what autonomy they could. In the Sonora homeland there was ultimately a similar official permissiveness, although at the same time hostility of Yaquis was engendered by some intermittent pressures through military officials and government administrators. The effective pressures for change lay, however, in both areas in the constant and tangible presence of a functioning society alongside the Yaqui, participation in which brought obvious advantages to individuals.

The effects of these conditions in Arizona and in Sonora were quite different. In Arizona most of the features of the folk culture were abandoned through full acceptance of economic and political integration. Arizona Yaquis tended steadily, after efforts at revival, to assume the position of a religious sect. Under the encouragement of the dominant society, several of the ceremonial orientations of the folk culture were maintained. Adapted at many points to the requirements of the new economic and political environment, they nevertheless took much the form of their prototypes in the homeland. Participation in them gave expression to the sense of distinct identity as Yaquis which remained important through the third generation in Arizona. Even though the Yaqui language was disappearing as a source of Yaqui identity, the religion of the old folk culture persisted. It had nevertheless by the 1950's been integrated into what was otherwise the way of life of the dominant society. Out of the context of the sacred homeland, most of the other aspects of the old folk culture ceased to have meaning.

In Sonora it was otherwise. There in the face of the continued invasion of the homeland a dual society and culture developed in the re-established communities. The pervasive impingement of the invading society affected all Yaquis. Some shifted participation from Yaqui to Mexican culture. The general tendency, however, was toward an increasing rigidity of the revived folk culture.

REFERENCES CITED

ACOSTA, ROBERTO
    1949 *Apuntes Historicos Sonorenses. La Conquista Temporal y Espiritual del Yaqui y del Mayo.* México.
ALEGRE, FRANCISCO JAVIER
    1841–42 *Historia de la Compañía de Jesús en Nueva España.* 3 vols. Edición de CARLOS MARIÁ DE BUSTAMANTE. México.
BANCROFT, HUBERT HOWE
    1889 *History of the North Mexican States and Texas.* Vols. I and II. San Francisco.
BARBER, CARROLL
    1952 "Trilingualism in Pascua: The Social Functions of Language in an Arizona Yaqui Village." (Unpublished M.A. thesis, University of Arizona.)

BEALS, RALPH L.
1943   *The Aboriginal Culture of the Cahita Indians,* "Ibero-Americana," 19. Berkeley, Calif.
1945   *The Contemporary Culture of the Cahita Indians.* Bureau of American Ethnology, *Bulletin 142.* Washington.

BOLTON, HERBERT EUGENE
1936   *Rim of Christendom.* New York.

BORQUEZ, DJED
1929   *Sonot.* 2d ed. México.

DECORME, GERARD
1941   *La Obra de los Jesuítas Mexicanos durante la Época Colonial 1572–1767.* Tomo II, Las Misiones. México.

EZELL, PAUL
1955   "Indians under the Law: Mexico, 1821–47," *América Indígena,* XV, No. 3, 199–214.

FABILA, ALFONSO
1940   *Las Tribus Yaquis de Sonora, Su Cultura y Anhelada Auto-determinación.* México.

GARCÍA CUBAS, ANTONIO
1876   *The Republic of Mexico in 1876.* Translated by GEORGE F. HENDERSON. México.

HERNÁNDEZ, FORTUNATO
1902   *Las Razas Indígenas de Sonora y la Guerra del Yaqui.* México.

JOHNSON, JEAN BASSETT
1943   "A Clear Case of Linguistic Acculturation," *American Anthropologist,* XLV, 427–34.

KURATH, TULA
1949   "Mexican Moriscas: A Problem in Dance Acculturation," *Journal of American Folklore,* April–June. Pp. 87–106.

MASON, J. ALDEN
1940   "The Native Languages of Middle America" in *The Maya and Their Neighbors,* by CLARENCE L. HAY *et al.* New York.

MECHAM, J. LLOYD
1927   *Francisco de Ibarra and Nueva Vizcaya.* Durham, N.C.

NYE, WILLIAM F.
1861   *Sonora: Its Extent, Population, Natural Production, Indian Tribes, Mines, Mineral Lands, etc.* Translated from the Spanish of FRANCISCO VELASCO. San Francisco.

PAINTER, MURIEL THAYER, REFUGIO SAVALA, and IGNACIO ALVAREZ
1955   *A Yaqui Easter Sermon.* University of Arizona *Social Science Bulletin No. 26.* Tucson, Ariz.

PÉREZ DE RIBAS, ANDRÉS
1645   *Historia de Los Triunfos de Nuestra Santa Fé entre las Naciones más bárbaras y fieras del Nuevo Orbe . . .* 3 vols. Editorial Layac, México, 1944.

SAUER, CARL
1935   *Aboriginal Population of Northwestern Mexico,* "Ibero-Americana," 10. Berkeley, Calif.

SPICER, EDWARD H.
1940   *Pascua, a Yaqui Village in Arizona.* Chicago.

1943 "Linguistic Aspects of Yaqui Acculturation," *American Anthropologist*, XLV, 410–26.
1945 "El Problema Yaqui," *América Indígena*, V, 273–86.
1947 "Yaqui Villages Past and Present," *The Kiva*, Vol. XIII, No. 1. Arizona Archaeological and Historical Society, Tucson, Ariz.
1948 "People of Pascua, a Study of Participation in Yaqui Culture." (Unpublished manuscript.)
1954 *Potam, a Yaqui Village in Sonora.* American Anthropological Association, *Memoir No. 77.*
1958 "Social Structure and Cultural Process in Yaqui Religious Acculturation," *American Anthropologist*, LX, 433–41.

TAMARÓN Y ROMERAL, PEDRO
1765 "Demostración del Vastísimo Obispado de la Nueva Vizcaya–1765." In *Biblioteca Histórica Mexicana de Obras Inéditas* 7. México, 1937.

TAX, SOL
1952 *Heritage of Conquest: The Ethnology of Middle America.* Glencoe, Ill.

TRONCOSO, FRANCISCO P.
1905 *Las Guerras con las Tribus Yaqui y Mayo del Estado de Sonora.* México.

TURNER, JOHN KENNETH
1910 *Barbarous Mexico.* Chicago.

VILLA, EDUARDO W.
1951 *Historia del Estado de Sonora.* 2d ed. Hermosillo, Sonora.

WEST, ROBERT C.
1949 *The Mining Community in Northern New Spain: The Parral Mining District,* "Ibero-Americana," 30. Berkeley and Los Angeles.

WEYL, NATHANIEL and SYLVIA
1939 *The Reconquest of Mexico.* London and New York.

CHAPTER 3

Rio Grande Pueblos

By Edward P. Dozier

The Rio Grande Pueblos represent today a cultural type or condition[1] for which the term "compartmentalization" will be used in this paper.[2] Other terms for this situation such as "isolating" and the like have been suggested. Elsewhere we have characterized the Rio Grande Pueblo acculturative situation as a "dual tradition"—referring in this case to the fact that the two most prominent self-contained systems are the Spanish-Catholic tradition on the one hand and the native or indigenous tradition on the other (Dozier 1955).

The Rio Grande Pueblos experienced a definite program of directed culture change, forcefully imposed upon them by Spanish authorities. Spanish colonial officials, both secular and missionary, had a deliberate policy of exterminating pagan practices and substituting Spanish-Catholic patterns. Seventeenth-century records are replete with instances of attempts to eradicate native ceremonies by force. Kivas were raided periodically and masks and ceremonial paraphernalia of all kinds were burned and destroyed. Those Indian leaders who persisted in conducting ceremonies were executed or punished in a variety of ways. The *encomienda* system in New Mexico aggra-

[1] A pervasive and lasting outcome of acculturation (see Report of Social Science Research Council Summer Seminar 1954: 984). The "types" of acculturative situations discussed here refer to over-all patterns or "macro" characteristics of the culture, not to individual traits which may exhibit examples of reinterpretation, syncretism, and the like.

[2] The term used by Spicer, 1954, for this acculturative type.

vated conditions by exacting tribute from the Indians, while the missionary program vied with the encomienda system in forcing the Indians to abandon their native practices and was equally coercive and brutal. To supplant native ceremonial patterns and beliefs, missionaries baptized Indians, forced attendance at Mass and made instruction in Catholic doctrine compulsory in missionary establishments. A Spanish decree in 1620 permitted the creation of native officers among the Pueblos (Bandelier 1890–92: 200). These officers were expected to co-operate with Spanish civil and church officials in compelling their members to comply with the civilizing and Christianizing efforts of the Spaniards. But the fact unknown to the Spaniards was that the Indians who filled these positions were chosen by native priests and were individuals who owed primary allegiance to native ceremonial life. Thus the Spanish-imposed government system was converted into a tool that facilitated the preservation of native beliefs and rites, rather than a measure to serve the goals of the Spaniards.

The Pueblo Indians compromised by outwardly appearing to have accepted the Spanish-imposed cultural system. They adopted the externals of the new faith and conformed to the demands of labor and tribute, but they continued to practice their own indigenous religion and other customs behind closed doors, heavily guarded against church and civil authorities. In time, with succeeding generations who were brought up completely under the new order, the externally practiced Catholic religion and other Spanish patterns also became an important part of Pueblo culture. But the two traditions were kept distinct, partly because they had learned them in this manner but also because of the fear of reprisals.

Spanish-Catholic policy relaxed after the Pueblo Revolt of 1680, and with a rapidly increasing Spanish population in the succeeding century attention began to be diverted from the Pueblos. Raids of Apaches, Navahos, and Comanches on Spanish and Pueblo settlements alike also distracted Spanish attention from concern over the religious welfare of the Pueblos.

The relaxing of Spanish pressure permitted the Pueblo Indians to revive and reorganize their ceremonial patterns. Some of the more secret dances began to be practiced in the open again. But the coming of white Americans resulted in a return to earlier conditions. American missionaries and U.S. Indian Service officials were openly critical of the "obscene" and "immoral" practices of the Indians, and they took steps to stop them. The forced recruitment of Indian children to be enrolled in boarding schools at considerable distances from reservations was designed to wean Indian youngsters from their traditional culture. In these schools the use of the Indian language and all other "Indian" ways were prohibited. Infractions were dealt with brutally through a variety of physical punishments. During the early 1900's investigators were sent to the pueblos to study reported immoral and anti-Christian practices of the Indians. These investigators

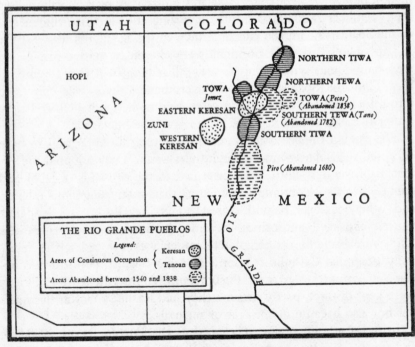

MAP 4

brought back reports of customs which violated Anglo-American standards of decency and morality. Under the religious Crimes Code, Indian Service officials were instructed to stop ceremonial practices which might be contrary to accepted Christian standards. These acts of church and U.S. Indian Service officials forced the Pueblos to reintrench their native ceremonial system and the pattern of compartmentalization was reinforced.

The different policy ushered in in the 1930's has not been in existence long enough to indicate changed reactions among the Pueblos. The unsuccessful attempts of recent ethnologists to break the Pueblo iron curtain appear to demonstrate that these Indians still believe that the release of ceremonial knowledge will be used against them. They, therefore, guard tenaciously their native ceremonial system from all outsiders, offering only the Spanish-Catholic and some less sacred aspects of the native system to public scrutiny.

Period I: Prehistoric[3]

CULTURAL EXCHANGE AMONG INDIANS: 1350–1540

The dates of this period cover the time from the establishment of the Keresans as neighbors of the Tanoans to the coming of the first Spanish expedition under Coronado in 1540.

Archeologists and ethnologists are generally agreed in deriving the culture of the Rio Grande Pueblos from two different prehistoric traditions, although there is yet no agreement on the particular archeological districts from which each stemmed. Reed (1949: 182) felt that the Keresan cultural antecedents were rooted in east central Arizona, while he derives the Tanoans from the Anasazi, Mesa Verde, and Chaco areas. Reed's conclusions have been criticized by Wendorf (1954), and Wendorf and Reed together later proposed an alternate reconstruction in which both Keresans and Tanoans are derived from the Anasazi but from different branches (Wendorf and Reed 1955).

Although it is not possible as yet to identify the prehistoric antecedents of the historical Tanoans and Keresans, there seems to be both archeological and ethnological evidence that at the time of our first cultural reading the Keresans had just established themselves in the Rio Grande Valley. On the other hand, the Tanoans, while also immigrants into the area, had preceded the Keresans by perhaps two hundred years (Reed 1950). The ethnological evidence comes primarily from an analysis of cultural differences between the two groups. The ethnological data suggest more pronounced differences between the two in the immediate prehistoric period but with continuous adjustments leveling off differences, as we approach the contemporary period.

The major difference between Keresan and Tanoan Pueblo inhab-

[3] The Pueblo "periods" discussed in this paper refer specifically to acculturative situations, each period differing significantly from another in terms of the kind of sociocultural reaction exhibited by the Rio Grande Pueblos to the contact situation. These periods have nothing to do with the time divisions set up by archeologists and cannot be correlated with them.

TABLE 2
Rio Grande Pueblo Contact History

Periods	Events	Contact Communities	General Type of Change
V Anglo-American dominance	1933 John Collier, Commissioner of Indian Affairs 1928 Radical changes in Federal Indian policy 1924 Pueblo Lands Act 1913 Sandoval Case—legal status of Pueblo Indians defined	Tourists Pueblo day schools Boarding schools Reservations without agents Anglo-American communities	Accelerated economic changes Continuing compartmentalization
IV Anglo-American intrusion	1881 Railway lines enter New Mexico 1881 Boarding school established at Albuquerque 1872 Primary schools in Pueblo villages begun 1869 Indian Bureau farmers for Pueblo villages 1852 Protestants begin missionary activity in Laguna Pueblo 1849 James S. Calhoun, first U.S. Indian agent 1846 U S. occupation of New Mexico 1822 Mexican Independence 1821 Anglo-American trade with New Mexico established 1812 Pino's *Exposición* 1804 First American citizen enters New Mexico	Conflict over land with Hispano and Anglo-American settlers Encroaching Anglo-American settlers Indian Bureau agents intrusive	Pueblo resistance patterns and compartmentalization reinforced
III Stabilized pluralism	1776 Fray Dominguez' visitation 1760 Bishop Tamaron's visitation 1737 Bishop Elzaecochea's visitation 1725 Bishop Crespo's visitation	Same as II	Compartmentalization established
II Spanish exploration and colonization	1693 De Vargas' reconquest of the Pueblos 1680 Pueblo Indian revolt 1630 Benavide's report 1593 Oñate, colonization 1582 Espejo expedition 1580 Rodriguez expedition 1540 Coronado expedition	Compact Pueblo villages with missions and chapels intrusive Spanish settlements	Forced directed culture change Pueblo resistance
I Prehistoric	*ca.* 1350 Keresan intrusion	Intrusion of Keresan settlers in Rio Grande area Relocated compact villages	Cultural exchange among Indians

itants was and is linguistic. Keresan is not considered related to Tanoan, and all authorities place these languages in completely different
stocks; the former is included in Hokan-Siouan and the latter in Aztec-Tanoan (Sapir 1929). Other important differences occur in political, social, and ceremonial organization. These differences will be
discussed in detail in the description of our base-line culture.

Settlement Pattern and Population.—From the narratives of Coronado and Espejo we derive a picture of numerous villages along the
Rio Grande and along the eastern foothills of the mountains all the
way from near El Paso in the south to Taos in the north. A century
later, in 1630, Benavides reported ninety villages with a population of
sixty thousand. This figure is probably too high; Scholes (1956, personal communication) estimates a more conservative number, about
thirty to forty thousand. Population figures for the individual pueblos varied from perhaps two thousand for Pecos to as low as fifty for
others, the average probably being around four hundred.

Present-day Keresan village plans are predominantly of the parallel
alignment type, like the Western pueblos, with no single central area.
The settlement pattern appears to be old and undoubtedly characterized Keresan pueblos in the immediate pre-Spanish period. For
Tanoans, generally, the single- or multiple-plaza type is characteristic
and is predominant in archeological sites (Reed 1956: 14–15). Kiva
patterns among Tanoans, as recently indicated by Florence Hawley
Ellis (Hawley 1950a), included one large and one small structure in
each village among the Tewa. Isleta and Sandía, also had two kivas,
one being larger than the other. Espejo (Bolton 1916: 177) reported
two *estufas* (kivas) as being characteristic of the southern Pueblos
(Piro and Tiwa). Keresans have two kivas of approximately equal
size and are the only Pueblos today with a consistent two-kiva pattern.

Rio Grande Pueblo houses were almost all of adobe, although away
from the valley sandstone slabs or pumice blocks were employed.
There is no evidence of the use of adobe bricks in the Rio Grande
region prior to Spanish contact.

Non-Pueblo Peoples.—During the period under consideration, there
were undoubtedly other peoples in the area. Whether the abandonment of the former archeological regions and concentration into the
historic positions of the pueblos can be attributed to the encroachment of predatory nomadic peoples is a controversial subject. We are

inclined to minimize enemy action as a significant reason for the reduction of the Pueblo area. It seems ill advised and foolhardy for a
people trying to escape predatory enemies to locate in open sites, less
easily defended than the communities they abandoned. Even the Hopi
were found by early explorers living at the foot of the mesas, for the
most part, rather than on top where they might better defend themselves against enemy attacks. Indeed the factors of drought and ar-
royo-cutting, for which there is abundant evidence (O'Bryan 1952;
Hack 1942), seem sufficient explanations for migration to the historical locations of the pueblos. Especially does this make sense when we
note that the movement was to areas of permanent or more dependable water supply.

There is no doubt that Apachean groups (see Vogt, *infra*) were
living near the Pueblos during the period under consideration. Cas-
tañeda in 1541 reported the following about relations between the
Pueblos and a nomadic tribe called the Teya, perhaps an Apache
tribe (Hodge 1907: Part 1, pp. 356–57):

These people (the Teya) knew the people in the settlements and were
friendly with them, and they went there to spend the winter under the
wings of the settlements. The inhabitants did not dare to let them come
inside, because they cannot trust them. Although they are received as
friends, and trade with them, they do not stay in the village over night,
but outside under the wings.

It is quite certain that Shoshonean-speaking nomadic Indians were
also impinging on the north during this period. Marvin Opler (Linton, ed., 1940: 123) places the ancestral Utes in the northern periphery of the Pueblo area in pre-horse days. The Espejo expedition in
1582 found the Pueblos wearing shoes and boots made from buffalo
hides and deerskin, further indications of trade relations between the
settled villages and nomadic hunters (Bolton 1916: 177). The sim-
plicity of Plains nomadic culture before the introduction of the horse
undoubtedly made them adhere to the Pueblos, whose economy was
more dependable and their culture generally richer. Opportunities
for more intensive borrowing by nomadic groups would, therefore,
seem to be indicated. The Tanoans who were closer to the open
Plains country appear within historic times to have more Plains Indian characteristics, manifested particularly in more aggressive and
individualistic personality traits of the Tanoans generally. Specific in-

stitutions such as the men's and women's warrior and scalp societies may have also been borrowed. Extensive visits of parties of Pueblo Indians, common in later periods, undoubtedly existed during this period, and we may conjecture the establishment of "friend-friend" visitation patterns between Pueblo families and nomadic ones. Some of these visits undoubtedly resulted in intermarriages, paving the way for more intensive cultural exchange.

BASE-LINE CULTURE, ABOUT 1500

Rio Grande Pueblo cultures of this period have been reconstructed from ethnographic accounts, ferreting out the patterns and institutions which appear to be tenacious and persisting. Assurance of the validity of this reconstruction is afforded by the compartmentalized nature of Pueblo cultures where indigenous patterns are fairly easily distinguished from Euro-American ones. It is, of course, important to emphasize that aboriginal elements of a culture are also subject to change and undoubtedly have changed. We are fully aware that no culture remains static. Hints of such changes and elaborations appear as we attempt to project backwards.

Environment, Economy, Technology.—The Rio Grande Pueblos are located along the Rio Grande and its tributaries and depend upon diverting the waters of these streams into their fields for farming activities. The climate is arid; the annual average rainfall is frequently less than ten inches. Moreover, the limited quantity of rain may not always fall when needed, or may fall in such torrents that crops are uprooted and destroyed. It has been necessary, therefore, in the past and at present to employ irrigation of some sort in order to insure a successful harvest. Unlike the Hopi and Zuni and the several prehistoric regions whence the ancestors of the Rio Grande Pueblos might have come, the Rio Grande region provides a permanent water supply. Hopi and Zuni depend more directly on rainfall for flood irrigation, or on springs. The tasks of clearing, terracing, braking, damming, and ditching thus require greater communal effort among the Rio Grande Pueblos. Among the Hopi and Zuni, and probably among the prehistoric Indians, irrigation for crops may have been done by small families or kin groups, perhaps lineage and clan members. In the Rio Grande area, the task of bringing the water to fields, located sometimes at considerable distance from the main streams, requires a large number of individuals, particularly since the technological achievements were simple. Women were required in most pueblos, until recently, to help in maintaining and constructing irrigation ditches.

Large-scale co-operation on irrigation projects has important implications for the nature of Rio Grande Pueblo socio-political and ceremonial organization. These implications have been recently elaborated by K. A. Wittfogel for oriental society and for ancient America (Wittfogel 1957). Wittfogel and Goldfrank (1943) have also presented a provocative article in which the importance of irrigation is discussed with respect to the nature of Pueblo societies. Cautioning that no proof is yet available in the Southwest that the introduction of large-scale waterworks had made revolutionary changes in Pueblo societies, the authors report: "If the Pueblos represent a waterwork society in miniature, then we should look for certain authoritative forms of civil and magic leadership, for institutionalized discipline, and a specific social and ceremonial organization" (*ibid.*: 20).

This suggestion has been examined in this paper and we feel that, in large part, the differences between Keresan and Tanoan sociopolitical and ceremonial organization may be explained by the Wittfogel-Goldfrank hypothesis. Before we analyze this basic proposition, however, other important data on Rio Grande Pueblo culture and society must be presented.

The aboriginal crops of the Rio Grande Pueblo Indians were maize, beans, gourds, cotton, and tobacco. Fields were cultivated close to the river and irrigated by ditches. The digging stick appears to be the only aid to planting and cultivation.

Men and women worked together in the construction and cleaning of irrigation ditches, the cleaning of villages and helping in the harvest—but at other times, division of labor was fairly rigidly prescribed. Men planted and tilled the fields and the gardens and cut and hauled firewood. Men also hunted, dressed the skins of animals they killed, made their own bows, arrows, shields and war clubs and wove baskets, blankets, and sashes. Women tended the children, did the cooking and other duties around the house and also made pottery. Whereas men constructed houses, both the living quarters and ceremonial chambers, women did the plastering.

There are no indications of craft specializations either by village, or by families or individuals within the village. Nor was the pueblo divided into a class structure. The sociopolitical organization did not allow for a privileged elite. Only the village chief may have been exempt from the ordinary duties required of all members of the pueblo. Given a more complex technology and a greater food surplus, it is likely that class and occupational stratifications might have risen, but there is no evidence of this development in the history of the Pueblos. Likewise there is no evidence of intra-village markets or even extensive trading between villages. Economic activities had hardly developed beyond reciprocal gift exchanges between pueblos and between Pueblos and nomadic tribes.

Turkeys and dogs were the only domesticated animals. Turkeys, as also captive eagles, were kept apparently primarily for feathers which were used ceremonially. The dog appears to have been a pet only, and not used for food or for other economic purposes.

The importance of hunting, although obviously secondary, is indicated by the presence in the villages of hunt societies. Communal rabbit hunts in which women and children joined the men were undoubtedly an important activity of all the Pueblos. Deer and antelope were available in nearby mountains, whereas periodic trips to the Plains for buffalo were also an important feature of Pueblo life. It is likely, however, that buffalo products were obtained primarily by trade or gift exchanges with friendly nomadic tribes.

Kin and Clan.—Our presentation of Rio Grande Pueblo kin and clan will first describe contemporary patterns and then briefly summarize the postulated forms at the time of our cultural base line. As over-all patterns, Keresan and Tanoan kinship systems are radically different and probably even more divergent in the period under discussion.

Tanoan kinship terms are descriptive and thoroughly bilateral. Parallel and cross cousins are treated similarly, either raised one generation or lowered one, depending on whether they are older or younger than Ego.[4] In Ego's generation and below, sex distinctions are not indicated. Reciprocals are employed with various sets of relatives in virtually all Tanoan pueblos, but are particularly characteristic of the Tewa.

The behavior of relatives is consonant with terminology. The basic social and economic unit of the Tanoan Pueblos is the bilocal extended family. The amount of extension varies; at Taos and Picurís

---

[4] Jemez is an exception to many of these generalizations as also to other features of social and ceremonial organization. See Parsons 1925; Ellis 1953.

the size of the family, although often extended, may sometimes include only members of the nuclear family. The unit in its most extended form, as among the Tewa, comprises a man and his wife, one or more married daughters and their husbands, and all unmarried sons and daughters of the married members of the household. Some daughters of the old couple and their children may align themselves with the households of their husbands, and occasionally one or more sons of the old couple may join his wife's extended household. Initially a couple may shift household allegiances, but once mutual work, food-sharing, and visiting patterns are established, the bilateral kin group takes on remarkable cohesiveness.[5]

Training and discipline follow the seniority pattern and the bilateral structure of the system is maintained with no hint of a lineage system. Thus disciplinary cases are handled by the oldest man in the household who may be a father, or a paternal or maternal grandfather. In the absence of a father or grandfather the oldest uncle, either on the mother's or father's side, may perform these functions. These male relatives also have the duty of training a male child or youth, while a mother or a paternal or maternal grandmother assumes responsibilities for training female children. Again, in the absence of such female relatives, the oldest aunt, on either the mother's or the father's side, may instruct, advise, and guide the vocational and avocational destinies of a girl. Serious cases of discipline as well as family troubles of an extreme sort are handled at the village level by duly appointed authorities or disciplinarians. Controversy over land, for example, is usually taken to village authorities. These factors reflect, as in other aspects of Tanoan society, the importance of the village over kin groups.

Land is in theory owned by the village and families have only use rights. These rights are passed on to both daughters and sons. The rights to the use of land and other property are usually transferred by the oldest surviving member of the household when he or she can no longer assume the responsibilities for caring for such property. Older members of the household are favored with the best plots of land or with choice pieces of property, but younger married members are not ignored. Younger members of a large extended

[5] This bilateral kin group fits Murdock's (1949: 56–57) description of the *kindred.* Although unnamed, the Tanoan bilocal extended kin group is a self-conscious, cohesive unit.

family who are allotted poor land or who cannot get land from older relatives may appeal to the War Captains or the governor for additional land.

There are no indications, terminologically or behaviorally, of a lineage system or of clans as kinship units among the Tanoans, with the single exception of Jemez. This pueblo because of its proximity to Keresan pueblos, and frequent intermarriage with Keresans has exogamous clans, although there are many indications in its kinship terminology of a former bilateral pattern (Parsons 1925). The "corn" groups among the Southern Tiwa, Isleta and Sandía, often called "clans" are clearly not kinship units but quasi-religious societies whose members are drawn through the mother's side and which function primarily in crisis rites for the individual (Ellis 1951a: 149). The Tewa "clan names" have even less right to be considered lineal kinship units. These names are merely sacred terms, inherited variously from the father or the mother. As with other property, a "clan" name seems to be the possession of the extended bilateral kin group and represents a case of undigested borrowing of the clan concept from Keresan neighbors.

Keresan kinship terms are arranged in a pattern that suggests affinity with the general Western Pueblo system (Hopi, Zuni, Acoma, Laguna; see Eggan 1950) and may be considered a form of the Crow type (White 1942: 159). The classificatory principle permeates the terminology. The use of separate terms in many instances by men and women for the same relative is also characteristic of the system. Inconsistencies appear in all areas, but, interestingly, toward patterns more consonant with Tanoan usages, and clearly indicate the breakdown of the lineage principle and the borrowing of the Tanoan model, perhaps as we suggest, under the pressure of ecological adjustment.

Although Keresan kinship behavior data are meager, the material shows correspondence with terminology and, as we may expect, the tendency to equalize maternal and paternal kin. The matrilineal, matrilocal extended family appears to be the important unit of Keresan social organization. Mother, mother's sisters and mother's brothers are most important in the socialization of the individual and in providing religious and economic training. The child is reared within the context of the matrilineal kin and, until he is married, spends the greater part of his life with them. Father and father's relatives have different relations to Ego. One of the father's sisters is especially important in this respect and sees to it that her niece or nephew is properly launched from one crisis period to another.

These behavioral patterns exhibit some inconsistencies in the various villages. In some households, notably at Cochiti, the father exercises disciplinary powers, while the mother's brother and father's brother are respected relatives but without specialized functions to Ego. In general, however, Keresan kinship behavior patterns follow basic Western Pueblo practices, that is, the greater importance of the matrilineal relatives, the singling out of mother's brother, and the specialized functions of father's relatives, particularly father's sister.

Indications of the former importance of the Keresan clan in terms of government, control of property, religion, and ceremonies are also clear. These functions have been assumed for the most part by the esoteric societies whose membership cuts across an entire village. Nevertheless there are still hints of clan roles and functions. In Zia, for example, the village chief must come from a specific clan. In Zia, also, clans conduct initiation ceremonies, and the leaders of certain religious societies come from specific clans (Hawley 1950*b*: 506–7). Thus, although many of the functions of the clan have lapsed, it is still an important institution in Keresan life at present. Actually, losses have been greatest in government, religion, and property control. The clan in all the Keresan villages still serves the important function of marriage control. Marriage into one's clan is strictly prohibited and violations appear to be nonexistent or minimal. Marriage with a member of father's clan is also denied, but such unions do occasionally occur without apparent serious social censure.

We may summarize briefly the nature of kin and clan in our baseline culture. Tanoan and Keresan clan and kin patterns were distinctly different, substantiating archeological and ethnological assumptions of different immediate origins of the two peoples. Tanoans classified kin bilaterally on a principle of generation, emphasized age, and generally ignored sex distinctions. Behavior of kin members reflected the basic terminological structure. Functions pertaining to government, landownership, religion, and ceremonies were vested in societies whose membership was drawn from the village without regard to kinship relations. The result was a tighter village integration

and more centralized direction. Conversely, Keresan kinship terminological patterns were of a lineage type with behavior consonant with
them. The clan was a matrilineal, matrilocal, exogamous unit, important in government, religion, and land control. Clans were essentially independent corporate entities loosely united into a village.

We would postulate that toward the end of the period of our
cultural base line, changes such as we have noted in our description
of contemporary patterns were beginning to take place. These
changes were undoubtedly accelerated after Spanish contact, but
the new environment into which the Keresans had moved had already set the changes in motion. The tendency to pattern social
organization along Tanoan lines was not a simple matter of borrowing. The new environment favored a sociopolitical system which
could compel larger numbers of people to cope with the demands of
farming based on irrigation. The changes were a response to new
environmental conditions which made imperative a different kind of
sociopolitical integration.

Sociopolitical and Ceremonial Organization.—In this area we again
note basic differences between our two major linguistic groups. It
is convenient here to describe recent or contemporary patterns and
to project back the features we believe characterized our base-line
cultures.

The important sociopolitical and ceremonial organization of
Tanoans generally, with Jemez excepted, is a dual division of the society, usually referred to as a moiety. Other characteristics include
three specialized types of associations or societies: (1) those with governmental and religious functions associated with the dual divisions;
(2) medicine societies embodying curing and exorcising practices;
(3) societies with special functions, such as war and hunting. In addition, Tanoan societies have a Katcina cult or some vestige of an organization concerned with supernatural beings vaguely connected
with ancestral spirits common among all Pueblo peoples.

The problem of kivas and dual divisions among the Rio Grande
Pueblos has been recently discussed by Hawley (1950*a*). The relationship of ceremonial structures to the socioceremonial organization
of the various Keresan and Tanoan Pueblo groups was also presented
(*ibid.*). For the Tewa, Hawley indicates that the pattern is clearly of
one large kiva and either a smaller one or the complete absence of a
second kiva. The Tewa, therefore, do not have a two-kiva system as

formerly reported (Parsons 1929: 99). Until recently among the Tewa, and still at Nambé and San Juan, masked performances were held in the large kiva. Tesuque performs its masked dances in the plaza, but rehearsals are held by both moieties in one kiva. Likewise, large group dances, such as the so-called "Corn" or "Tablita" dances, are rehearsed by both moieties in the large kiva and performed together in the plaza by San Juan, Nambé, and Tesuque. San Ildefonso and Santa Clara dropped the practice of inter-moiety co-operation and participation because of factional disputes which occurred about the turn of the century. These disputes took the form of a moiety split in both villages. In Santa Clara, one moiety, the Summer, went so far as to build its own kiva, thus giving the pueblo a two-kiva pattern. Tewa secret societies do not have special houses or kivas like Taos and Picurís. Meetings and retreats are held in dwelling rooms, usually in the homes of the society heads.

Parsons reported that Picurís and Taos each had six kivas, divided equally into a north- and south-side division, but according to Hawley each of these pueblos also has an additional round kiva, presumably a communal structure like the Tewa big kiva (Hawley 1950a: 287). The kivas in these two pueblos represent society chambers, the moiety division asserting itself in terms of spatial division, a double chieftainship, and rival relay races. Isleta has only one large round kiva; members of its six societies, apparently homologous to Northern Tiwa societies, meet in separate houses or rooms. Isleta has a dual division associated with "Summer" and "Winter" with double chieftainship and, above this, a town chief more important as a single chief than in any of the other Tanoan pueblos. Sandía, the other Southern Tiwa village, is also reported to have but a single round kiva like Isleta, but the absence of ethnological materials makes it impossible for us to report social organizational relationships.

Florence Hawley Ellis (Hawley 1950a: 287; Ellis 1951a: 150) suggests that the Northern Tiwa pattern of multiple kivas represents the older Tanoan system. The Southern Tiwa and the Tewa, she proposes, later gave up society kivas, using dwelling rooms for meetings and retreats, and borrowed the large kiva from Keresans in prehistoric times for communal affairs. This explanation she proposes to account for the several small kivas to a village in the ruins of the Mesa Verde area, whence she derives the Tanoans.

Hawley's reconstruction of Tanoan prehistoric kiva patterns seems plausible. We would, therefore, postulate a pattern of multiple society kivas, already changing to the use of simple dwelling rooms in our base-line culture. The possible use of the plaza as a place for communal religious performances should not be overlooked. This is especially pertinent in view of Reed's discovery of the plaza village pattern as the predominant type in the Tanoan Anasazi area. With the introduction of the Katcina complex among the Tewa, the adoption or borrowing of the big kiva is understandable. The need to keep children and women in ignorance of men's impersonation of Katcina supernaturals demands a large closed edifice among a people where the village rather than the clan is the political unit. Spanish contact would reinforce the need to safeguard ceremonials even with the Tiwa who did not impersonate Katcinas with masks. Undoubtedly kivas became larger in post-Spanish times in the Rio Grande area as ceremonials went "underground" and as the need for secrecy increased.

Among the Tewa and at Isleta everyone belongs in one moiety or the other. A Tewa individual inherits his moiety membership through the father, but affiliation may be changed later. Thus a woman upon marriage may change to her husband's moiety, or a man might as an adult undergo initiation into the opposite moiety to which his father belongs. The particular extended kin alignment seems to bring about moiety membership changes.[6]

Although the moiety is all-inclusive at Isleta, as among the Tewa, it differs considerably from the latter in other respects. Children take the moiety of parents but if the parents belong to different moieties their children are assigned alternately to one moiety and then the other. No information is available on the nature of the dual organization in Sandía, the other Southern Tiwa village. At Taos and Picurís dual division is in terms of kivas and with respect to north- and south-side divisions, with three kivas on each side. Male and female children are assigned by parents to Taos kivas, but only men are formally initiated. Assignment to kiva group or society membership at Taos is entirely optional with parents, while in Picurís an individual, male or female, joins the kiva group of his or her father.

Among the Tewa, both men and women undergo an initiation to

[6] There is a tendency to endogamy among Tanoans on the moiety or village level (see Murdock 1949: 62–63). There is, however, no conscious stated rule about whether a person should marry within his moiety or outside of it. Tanoan villages have a tendency toward endogamy, but inter-pueblo marriages, particularly within the same language group, occur and are not censured.

validate moiety membership. Initiation ceremonies occur about every four years and the ages of the initiates vary from six to ten, although an occasional adult changing moiety affiliations may also undergo the rite. The initiates are under various kinds of taboos and food restrictions.

At Taos initiates are about the same ages as they are among the Tewa, but in other respects Taos kiva groups appear to be more like Tewa esoteric societies. Isleta "corn" groups are also similar to Tewa societies. No information is available for Picurís and Sandía. Apparently kiva group initiations are absent at Jemez, where the moiety principle, as among Keresans, is extremely weak (see Parsons 1925: 74, 127–29).

Societies and their religious functions are essentially similar among all Tanoans. One type of society is closely related to the dual divisions. In composition all societies are similar. Like medicine societies and societies with special functions, dual division societies consist of a society head, assistants, and from one to a dozen members. Among the Tewa, women may become members, but they cannot become assistants or chief of the society; their main function appears to be as food carriers for the group when the society is in retreat. One woman member, however, has the role of pathmaker for the Katcina in the night kiva ceremonies among the Tewa. She leads the file of Katcina impersonators into the kiva by sprinkling a path of corn meal ahead of them. Women may also become members of societies among the Tiwa and their roles appear like those in Tewa societies.

Among the Tewa, the organization of any secret society is envisaged as a human being: the head is the chief, the arms are his right and left arm assistants and the body is made up of the members of the society. When a society leader dies, the right arm becomes the head, the left arm moves to right and a new member is chosen from the male members to fill the left arm vacancy. Should the right arm assistant die before the head, the left moves to right and a new member is chosen as above to fill the left arm position. It is not clear whether a society head has the sole right to select his left arm assistant or whether the selection entails a unanimous decision from all society members.

The Tewa composition and conception of a society as well as the method of selecting the society head would seem to apply for Isleta and even Jemez, but not for Taos. Taos societies do not have right and left arm assistants; a successor is therefore apparently selected directly from the members. Parsons discovered that the chiefs of the north-side and south-side kivas had been succeeded by their own sons; but in societies within the kivas the chief was selected by a committee of older men of the kiva acting with the chief of the moiety to which the kiva belonged. Parsons explains that the former system which is a hereditary pattern may arise from the fact that chiefs give one or more of their sons to their own kiva in the hope of training a successor within the family (Parsons 1936: 77–79).

Among all Tanoans the position of leaders or heads of societies is lifelong; indeed, membership in a society itself cannot be severed. The distinction between society people and non-society people is made in all Tanoan pueblos. Conceptually the distinction is between those who are "aware" and "know" and those who do not. Adults who do not belong to a society are considered like children, whereas society members are "men" and "women." Recruiting members into all Tanoan societies follows a similar pattern. A couple may dedicate a sick child, believing that by so doing the child will get well. If the child recovers, he is formally inducted after the age of puberty (in Taos earlier ages six to ten corresponding to the ages in Tewa moiety initiations) and after he has satisfactorily fulfilled a complex set of conditions. An adult who becomes ill may likewise dedicate himself to a moiety society and upon recovery be apprenticed to the society. Trapping is another manner by which members are recruited. When a society is in retreat or is in the performance of a ceremony, an area is marked off by corn meal around the altar containing the fetishes and other sacred objects. If an individual wanders into the area, he is "trapped" and must join the society. During the period of training or apprenticeship, the novitiate is confined to the pueblo for one to two years, and is required to observe ritual taboos and food restrictions. If a man, he is obliged to let his hair grow long and to have it braided (Tewa and Northern Tiwa) or tied in a club in back (Southern Tiwa and Jemez).

The conditions for membership described above apply to societies associated with the dual divisions as well as to societies with special functions. Parents of a child select the society which they want the child to join, usually one to which one of the parents belongs. Adults may also select a society of their choice, but most often adults are "called" to a specific society. Persistent thoughts or dreams about a society when one is ill is usually believed to be a summons to join that society.

Among all Tanoans two moiety or dual division chiefs are discernible. With the Northern Tiwa, Taos and Picurís, these are the chiefs of the two most important societies of the north-side and south-side divisions. The chief of the south-side division is the most important at Taos and considered the *cacique*.[7] At Isleta there is also a double chieftainship, but in addition a cacique above them. The two Tewa moiety society heads are equal in power and each rules the pueblo for half a year. In actuality the Tewa have the only true double chieftainship. The assistants of the cacique are the so-called War Captains —sometimes also referred to as War Chiefs. This is an unfortunate confusion since the term War Captain came from the Spanish *Capitán de la Guerra*, an office of the civil government system. The pueblos filled positions of "War Captain" primarily from the cacique's assistants, in order to keep the disciplinary characteristics of these newly created offices where they belonged in the native system. Properly, the term "War Chief" refers to the head of the war society, formerly an important position in the native societal system and, with modified functions, still important where the office occurs today. The term, for clarity's sake, should not be applied to the assistants of the cacique who have been since Spanish times called War Captains. The functions of the War Captains have been executive and disciplinary with respect to both the indigenous customs and secular affairs; for the latter duties, they are called "Outside Chiefs" by the Indians. The causes for disciplinary action taken against members of the pueblo include violations of harvesting and planting in season, refusal to work on cleaning irrigation ditches, sweeping the village plaza and other communal responsibilities.

Although societies associated with the dual divisions serve a curing function by virtue of the fact that members are dedicated to it to be cured, their more obvious and primary functions are governmental and religious. Among all Tanoans one or more of these societies, either singly or collectively have the following tasks to perform: (1) the maintenance of an annual solar calendar and the announcement of dates for fixed ceremonials during the year; (2) the organization

---

[7] A word of Arawakan origin applied by Spaniards to New World native religious and political leaders. In New Mexico, the term is customarily used to designate the highest-ranking chief and priest in an Indian pueblo.

and direction of large communal dances and ceremonies;[8] (3) the co-ordination of purificatory and cleansing rites for the village conducted by the medicine societies; (4) the co-ordination of communal hunts conducted by hunt societies; (5) the co-ordination of warfare ceremonies conducted by the war society, aided in some pueblos by a companion women's scalp society; (6) the organization and direction of planting and harvesting activities; (7) the cleaning and construction of irrigation ditches; (8) the repair and construction of communal kivas and cleaning of the plaza for communal ceremonies; (9) the nomination and installation of secular officials with responsibilities for compelling the population to participate in ceremonials and in communal projects of a more secular kind. The dual division societies nominate and select the officers of the civil government system imposed by Spanish colonial and church officials.

The functions enumerated above are the responsibilities of the kiva societies at Taos and Picurís and of similar societies at Isleta. Among the Tewa, the two moiety societies alternate seasonally in assuming these responsibilities. The Winter moiety society directs governmental and ceremonial affairs from the fall to the spring equinox, while the Summer moiety is in charge for the remaining half of the year. All members of the village, whether they are members of the moiety in power or not, are required to obey and conform to the governmental and ceremonial dictates of the moiety society leaders in office at any given time.

Medicine societies, where they exist among Tanoans, appear to be borrowed from the Keresans. Among the latter they are more numerous and more elaborately developed. Indeed, one of the names of the medicine societies among the Tewa and at Isleta clearly indicates its Keresan origin. At Isleta the medicine societies are the Laguna and Isleta Fathers, the former clearly borrowed from the Keresan pueblo of Laguna. Among the Tewa, the *Tema Kè*, or Cochiti Bear curing society was derived from this pueblo. There is also a medicine society among the Tewa called the Tewa Bear, whose name, like that of Isleta Fathers, implies a society with deeper roots in the indigenous culture, but its origin may also have been Keresan. Jemez has well-developed medicine societies patterned along Keresan models. In

[8] The Tablita dance, so popular today as the Saint's Day fiesta dance among Keresans, is a communal dance and may have been borrowed from Tanoans. The Tablita dance demands a centralized political control which we surmise did not characterize Keresans at an early date.

virtually all Tewa pueblos there is a Jemez Bear curing society, again indicating that the society was borrowed from Jemez, which is obviously most influenced by Keresan culture. At Taos, two Kiva societies perform curing rituals, but our information about the societal groups of this village is extremely meager (Parsons 1936: 59–60). Likewise, there is no information available about curing societies at Picurís. We may surmise, however, that the Keresan type curing societies are absent from these two pueblos for Tewa curing societies are popular with Taos and Picurís patients, who use their services frequently. In all Tanoan pueblos there are individual curers as well, that is, individuals who have no society affiliation.

Tewa, Jemez, and Isleta medicine societies use a variety of practices which are shamanistic: sucking of intruded objects, sleight of hand and other tricks of the magician, the use of fetishes and objects, the chasing of witches, and the like. They perform individual cures as well as cures in which the whole society participates. In the communal type of curing functions, all the curing societies of the village cooperate to rid the town of witches.

The composition of curing societies and the manner of selecting the leader or chief of the society is similar to the societies associated with the dual divisions.

Among all Tanoan pueblos at least three special societies exist or have recently become extinct; a hunt society, a war society, and one or two clown societies. In addition, Isleta and some of the Tewa have a women's war or "scalp" society whose activities are closely connected with the men's war society. Each of these societies holds separate retreats and conducts independent ceremonies periodically. Each one of them also conducts at least one major ceremony or directs an activity which in one way or another concerns and involves the whole community. Thus the hunt society may perform or direct small group animal dances and, before important kiva ceremonials, is responsible for a communal rabbit hunt into which the whole population is drawn. This activity is in co-operation with the dual division societies. The hunt society chief is also charged with installing a new cacique into office; this custom contrasts with Keresans, where medicine society leaders are charged with this function. The war society similarly directs small group war dances of various kinds but also assumes a major part in the communal relay and conditioning races and formerly in actual warfare. The women's scalp society has its own ceremonies, but also co-operates with the war societies. This society is custodian of scalps, which they feed and care for. The greater emphasis on hunting and war apparent among Tanoans generally may be due to their marginal position and proximity to the buffalo and Plains Indians (see Ellis 1951*b:* 187–88). The northern Tanoans are also in an area of more abundant game, the region of the southern Rockies and its eastern flanks, where grass is more plentiful.

The clown society has a number of special functions, but in the main is associated with the Katcina cult and large group dances. Clowns among the Tewa are most similar to Keresan clowns, both in appearance and function. Thus, for example, the very names, *Kosa* and *Kwirena* are related to those of Keresan clown societies. As among the Keresans, they are intimately connected with the Katcina societies and with large communal dances. The Kosa "bring" the Katcinas from a lake in the north. More attenuated are clown societies of the Northern Tiwa and Isleta, where they are associated with the equally attenuated maskless Katcina dances.

The Katcina cult in its most developed form, as at Jemez and among the Tewa, appears to be borrowed from the Keresans. The Tanoan villages nearest geographically and in terms of intimate relations with Keresans have borrowed most of the complex. Thus the Katcina cult (and the medicine and clown societies) are strongest at Jemez, then follow the Tewa, Isleta and finally Picurís and Taos. Jemez social and ceremonial patterns, for reasons elsewhere presented, fall more closely with Keresans.

The Tewa Katcina organization is a dual one but, now and in the past at San Juan and Nambé, the large kiva is used by both groups, while Tesuque uses the plaza. Formerly the other villages also employed the plaza, but the large kiva has been most frequently used, at least in the recent past. Until recently at Santa Clara, a place in the hills was also used for masked Katcina performances.

The number of participants is small—about five or six "line dancers" and as many side dancers. The cult is closely associated with the moiety societies but is under an independent supervisor, the Katcina Father, who co-operates closely with the moiety society head when engaged in cult activities. The Katcina Father is a lifelong position, but apparently he is appointed by the moiety society. The clowns, either *Koshare* or Kwirena or both, appear with the dancers at night; they "bring" the Katcina from underneath a lake in the north, apparently the mythological emergence lake (see Parsons 1936: 112).

All male individuals become members of the Katcina cult. The Tewa have one woman who acts as pathmaker for the Katcinas when the latter "visit" the pueblo during a ceremonial. This woman is not, however, a member of the cult, but a member of the moiety society. This Katcina organization is distinguished from other societies in that members are not recruited in the usual way by vow, dedication or trespass.[9] All males automatically become members, although a post-puberty initiation ceremony formalizes membership. The Katcinas are believed to be the bearers of rain, this is their primary role, but they are also believed to be bearers of good health and general well-being.

While the individual villages and the linguistic subgroups show considerable variation in details, there is a basic similarity in the over-all pattern of Tanoan political and ceremonial organization. Tanoan society revolves around four basic concerns: (1) weather control, (2) curing, (3) warfare and (4) the propitiation and control of wild game animals and fowl. While these four basic concerns also occupy Keresans, there is a difference in emphasis and, above all, in the approach toward the minimization of anxieties and difficulties that ensue from them. Keresans attempt to reduce anxieties by magical practices; Tanoans deal more directly with these concerns and, whereas magical rites are not absent, they are subordinated to secular activity.

The most important officers charged with political functions are the cacique and his assistants, the Outside Chiefs. The position of cacique among the Tiwa is a single office above the dual division chiefs; among the Tewa the dual chiefs have equal power and alternate seasonally in assuming the governmental and religious affairs of a village; they may thus both be properly called caciques. The Outside Chiefs have been appointive since Spanish times, but among the Tewa, at least, they are often the caciques' right and left arm assistants. These officers are the executives who see that the orders of the cacique are obeyed and that the responsibilities of the village are carried out.

Keresan socioceremonial organization attempts to serve the same functions as that of the Tanoans, and the institutions for carrying out

[9] This is also true among Keresans, except at Santa Ana, where the cult is similar to a medicine society and both men and women join by vow or trespass or by being dedicated to it by parents as the result of illness in early childhood and subsequent recovery (White 1942: 138–42).

these responsibilities are essentially similar. Differences between the two are in the emphases accorded specific functions and the characteristics of the institutions which are responsible for these duties. Thus, essentially similar functions such as weather-control, curing, war, and hunting receive different emphases. The specific institutions also differ in elaborateness of development.

Keresan social structural patterns and orientations appear to confirm the archeological record that Keresans arrived in the Rio Grande later than the Tanoans. These patterns also indicate that the former home of the Keresans was a more arid one, where farming depended more on the exigencies of rainfall. Keresans are far more preoccupied with magical rites to induce rainfall than are Tanoans and have specific institutions to bring moisture to planted fields. The Katcina cult, whose primary function is to bring rain, is more elaborately developed among Keresans than among Tanoans, where the cult is absent in a number of pueblos. Medicine societies also appear to be indigenous to the Keresans and are important in all villages. Among the Tanoans, Jemez excepted, they are weakly represented or absent. All Keresan villages have several such societies. These societies, while important in the curing of disease and the exorcism of witches, have primarily governmental and religious functions. Thus, for example, in virtually all Keresan villages the cacique must belong to one of these societies,[10] and in all of them he is installed in office by medicine societies. Governmental responsibilities like the maintenance of a solar calendar, the co-ordination of communal activities and the like which are clan duties at Hopi (and inferably of earlier Keresans) devolve to medicine societies. In Tanoan villages these functions are the responsibility of the moiety or dual division societies. Keresan societies whose earlier functions were probably curing and rain-making have, under the influence of the environment and of Tanoans, we believe, taken on governmental duties as well. The medicine societies, since their membership is drawn from the whole village without regard to clan affiliation, have thus given tight integration and centralized direction to Keresan villages.

Keresans, like Tanoans, have societies with special functions. Clown societies are especially strong among them and appear to have

---

[10] At Santa Ana the cacique is not obliged to be a member of a medicine society, yet the cacique at the time of White's study was said to "be acting as cacique because he is a member of a medicine society 'that can make new caciques'" (White 1942: 97).

diffused to Tanoans. It is difficult to determine the source of war and hunt societies; both of these associations are strong or have been strong in the recent past among both groups. Keresan pueblos have dual kiva groups which conduct dances and games, but these are not organizations which are authorized to co-ordinate governmental and ceremonial functions for the whole pueblo. The medicine societies control and direct communal aspects of government and religion. Thus despite surface resemblances, there are important organizational differences between Keresans and Tanoans.

Socialization.—Socialization practices are reconstructed from ethnographic descriptions of the recent past. For the accuracy of our socialization data we rely partly on the general conservative nature of Pueblo cultures and partly on the persistence of the agents and institutions of Pueblo socialization (see Thompson and Joseph 1944: 123, and Goldfrank 1945: 537). Although there appear to be some differences between Keresans and Tanoans in socialization practices and in the resultant personality structures, the overwhelming similarities far outweigh the differences. We may, therefore, discuss these factors for the Rio Grande Pueblos as a whole, noting differences only where they appear significant.

The period of infancy, the first two years, is a permissive one throughout the Pueblo area (Goldfrank 1945: 519). But while the child is not disciplined, the environment is pervaded with anxiety. Swaddling in the cradle board restricts movement and restrains the child. The cradle board is an obvious convenience to adults, but it is also rationalized as a training or educational device for the child. Other factors of anxiety in the atmosphere consist of constant angry admonitions meted out to older siblings in the presence of the infant. These scoldings are usually accompanied by threats of dire misfortune to befall a disobedient older sibling.

A sudden change in the permissive socialization pattern takes place when the child has begun to walk, at about the age of two. Parental admonition is directed to industry, to enduring discomfort without crying, working hard, not wasting food, and the like. Such admonitions are coupled with threats of ogres and giants who are said to visit the pueblo to carry away nagging, crying, and disobedient children.

As the child grows older he is made to see the village disciplinarians, a pair attired in buckskin clothes, wearing hideous masks and carrying whips. Although children under the age of puberty are made to hide indoors, parents permit them to steal a glimpse of the bogey men through an open door or window. Parents who feel that their child or children are especially prone to mischief and difficult to manage may ask the disciplinarians to visit their homes and discipline their children. Among the Tewa the disciplinarians make the child or children dance while they crack whips at their heels.

Between the ages of six and nine, girls and boys are initiated into a kiva group or moiety and undergo prescribed ritual training involving rigid physical and dietary restrictions. For boys, entrance into the Katcina cult requires the observance of additional ordeals, and in certain pueblos, a whipping ritual. Entrance into other esoteric societies after puberty involves further disciplinary measures and restrictions.

Besides the disciplines regularly practiced in the socialization of an individual from early childhood through puberty and the disciplinary demands of each society which is joined, other agents and practices constantly hem the individual in place and form him into the approved personality type. The clown societies exert a controlling influence on the individual by public and semipublic practices of ridicule, either verbal or by pantomine. The War Captains see to it that the individual observes all orders and demands of the religious hierarchy. Beyond this, and ever present, is the threat of damaging gossip, often promulgated by the War Captains themselves when an individual does not conform to approved Pueblo behavioral patterns. If deaths occur, epidemics develop, crops fail, hunts prove unrewarding, or the enemy wreaks destruction, the suspected "witch" is hunted out, whipped, expelled from the village, or even killed (cf. Bunzel 1932: 480).

Typically, Pueblo Indians exhibit reserve, restraint and frequently avoidance and rejection. These traits have been molded both by a permissive infancy period and later by rigid disciplines and controls. In view of the outwardly serene characteristics of the Pueblo individual and our knowledge of the rigid socialization techniques to which he has been subjected, we may expect frequent emotional outbursts and "mental breakdowns." There are, however, few records of "mental breakdowns" in past history, nor do we find that Pueblo Indians suffer serious personality disruptions in adjusting to modern American culture (Madigan 1956). We feel that an explanation for this phenomenon lies in two factors: (1) the large extended family where affections and loyalties are diffuse and resentment toward parents is watered down; and (2) supernaturals and priests exercise final authority and the child must ultimately defer to these, but so must adults.

Language.—The Rio Grande Pueblos fall into two language families unrelated to one another, Keresan and Tanoan (Hoijer 1946: 18, 22). Keresan has been classified with the broad Hokan-Siouan stock (Sapir 1929: 139), while Tanoan is linked with the equally widespread Aztec-Tanoan (Sapir 1929; B. L. Whorf and G. L. Trager 1937: 609–24). The Tanoan languages show greatest internal diversity, confirming the generally accepted belief that the Pueblos speaking these languages have occupied the region for a long period of time (see F. Hawley Ellis 1951a: 148–51; F. Eggan 1950: 311–13). Three mutually unintelligible subfamilies are distinguished at present among the Tanoans: Tiwa, comprising two villages north of Santa Fe, Taos and Picurís, and two others south, Sandía and Isleta, in the vicinity of Albuquerque; Tewa, including the villages of San Juan, Santa Clara, San Ildefonso, Pojoaque, Nambé, and Tesuque, plus Tewa Village, the latter a village on First Mesa, among the Hopi of Arizona; and Towa with only one representative Pueblo village today, Jemez. At the time of initial white contact in the mid-sixteenth century, the Tanoan linguistic family was more extensive. A southern dialect group of the Tewa known as Tano was spoken in the Galisteo Basin area, just south of Santa Fe. Tano is believed to have been mutually intelligible with Tewa (Espinosa 1940: 76, 80). Towa was also spoken at Pecos, a large village east of Santa Fe; the survivors of this village joined the pueblo of Jemez in 1838 (Hodge 1912: 261–62). The Tiwa villages extended from the vicinity of Bernalillo to Socorro along the Rio Grande and along the eastern flanks of the Sandia and Manzano Mountains. South of the Tiwa villages and extending to the vicinity of present Las Cruces were Piro villages, whose inhabitants spoke dialects related to Tiwa (Hodge 1912: 261–62).

Tiwa is fairly homogeneous, but speakers from the villages of the north frequently employ Spanish or English to communicate with their linguistic kin from the south; indeed even Picurís and Taos appear to understand one another with difficulty in the native idiom and often resort to Spanish or English. The Tiwa of Isleta and Sandía communicate freely in the native language, however.

Dialectical variations among the Rio Grande Tewa are minimal, suggesting recent separation or continued interaction. Rio Grande Tewa and Hopi-Tewa speakers have difficulty in conversing in the native language, however, and English is most commonly employed today. Towa and Tewa, although mutually unintelligible at present, appear quite close.

Keresan speakers are divided into an eastern group, including Zia, Santa Ana, San Felipe, Santo Domingo and Cochiti and a western group, comprising Acoma and Laguna. These two branches of Keresan are at present fairly distinct and speakers of one group have difficulty communicating in Keresan with the other. It is clear, however, that up to the time of the Pueblo revolt, there was no linguistic separation between the two, since Laguna is a colony of eastern Keresan villages drawn primarily from Santo Domingo, Cochiti and Zia (Bancroft 1889: 221). Geographical separation of approximately 250 years' duration would therefore appear to account for the differences between the two groups today. Although minor dialectical variations exist within each group of Keresan villages, frequent interaction between members of different villages is carried on in the native idiom.

In our base-line culture we may, therefore, postulate two distinct languages, Keresan and Tanoan, with a separation already under way in the latter part of the period in terms of historic Piro-Tiwa and Towa-Tewa, although perhaps with communication still possible within these two divisions. It is possible that these dialects diverged further after Spanish contact and the learning of Spanish, which quickly became a lingua franca throughout the Rio Grande Pueblo area. Historically and at present the Rio Grande Pueblos are known for their polylingualism; it is very probable, therefore, that Tanoans spoke Keresan and vice versa within the period under review, thus facilitating the social and cultural exchange evident today.

Values and Moral Concepts.—Although we have noted differences of an obvious nature between Tanoans and Keresans in the more explicit features of culture and society above, there appears to be no such clear-cut distinction in values and moral concepts between the two Pueblo groups. These concepts are deeply rooted in the basic concerns already discussed in relation to Pueblo ceremonialism. These concerns (illness, weather, animal life, and warfare) appear to be as important among Keresans as among Tanoans even though the emphasis placed on any one of them varies (Dozier 1956*a*).

The dominant integrating factor of Rio Grande Pueblo culture is the view of the universe as an orderly phenomenon. People or things are not merely "good" or "bad." "Evil" is a disturbance in the equilibrium that exists between man and the universe, while "good" is a positive frame of mind or action that maintains harmonious balance.

To keep man and the universe in harmonious balance, all must work together and with "good" thoughts. Unanimous effort of the body and mind is not only a key value, but it is also enforced. We have described the highly authoritarian nature of Rio Grande Pueblo societies. The cacique and the War Captains exert strict control over the activities of village members and see that all physically able members participate in a rigid calendric series of ceremonies. Among the members of a village there is serious concern over a neighbor's behavior and a perpetual watch is maintained over his or her activities. Any action, whether physical or verbal, which is construed by Pueblo authorities to be contrary to group concerns and the unanimous will of the village is promptly and severely punished.

Rio Grande Pueblo culture thus makes rigorous demands on the individual and fills him with deep anxiety and suspicion toward his fellow men. Not only is his personal behavior and social interaction strictly circumscribed, but his thoughts as well are rigidly harnessed. He is constantly plagued by an apprehension that he or his fellow man may break the harmonious balance of the universe and bring illness, famine, or some other form of dreaded disaster.

While the explicit features of the culture of Tanoans and Keresans differed in certain important respects, the mental patterns just described, we believe, characterized both groups at the time of our baseline culture.

Period II: Spanish Exploration and Colonization[11]
CONDITIONS OF CONTACT, 1540–1700

Explorations.—This period is ushered in by the expedition of Francisco Vasquez de Coronado in 1540. Coronado's party consisted of

[11] This section has been compiled from many sources, but chiefly from Hodge 1907; Winship 1896; Hammond 1926; Hammond and Rey 1927; Hammond and Rey 1929; and Bolton 1916, for the period concluding with the colonization of New Mexico. For the seventeenth century the chief sources consulted are Hodge, Hammond, and Rey 1945; Scholes 1930, 1935, and 1942; Hackett and Shelby 1942; J. M. Espinosa 1940.

five Franciscan missionaries and several hundred mailed and armed horsemen accompanied by Indian servants. The party established head-quarters at Tiguex, a large Tiwa pueblo near the present site of Bernalillo in the heart of the Pueblo country. For two years the expedition was supported by provisions supplied by the pueblo of Tiguex and probably by neighboring pueblos. Coronado and his party established a reputation for brutality and ruthlessness that later generations of Spaniards were to continue. For a minor rebellion, brought on by the incessant demands for provisions made by Cor-onado's party, the pueblo of Tiguex was "punished" by the execution of several hundred of its inhabitants (Winship 1896: 497). This news spread rapidly throughout the Pueblo country and laid the foundation for mistrust and antagonisms between the two peoples.

The next expedition forty years later was a small one. The party consisted of a Franciscan priest, Friar Augustin Rodriguez, two broth-ers of his order, and twelve volunteer soldiers under the command of Francisco Sanchez Chamuscado. This expedition appears to have found Coronado's Tiguex and explored the area rather thoroughly. The friars were left among the Pueblos—apparently in Tiwa pueblos— when the party returned to Mexico. These missionaries were appar-ently put to death soon after Chamuscado's return to Mexico.

Antonio de Espejo led the third expedition into New Mexico in 1582 with fourteen soldiers and one Franciscan priest. Specifically we know that Espejo visited Zia, Jemez, Acoma, Zuni and Hopi and then returned to the Rio Grande, passing again through Tiwa and Keresan territory and the Tanos of the Galisteo Basin. He returned to Mexico via the Pecos River.

Requests to colonize the Pueblo area began to be made to the crown soon after Espejo's return. While these proposals were being considered, two unauthorized expeditions entered the Pueblo country. The first, under Castano de Sosa, established headquarters at Pecos, but a military force was sent against Castano, and he and his party were returned to Mexico. Leyva de Bonilla and Antonio Gutierrez de Humana also tried to establish a colony at San Ildefonso pueblo, but both were killed while on an exploring trip in the Plains country.

Colonies Established.—The authorized and successful colonization of the Pueblo area began with the arrival of the settlers under the command of Juan de Oñate in 1598. Oñate brought several hundred Spaniards, Mexican Indians, and servants. There were eighty carts and wagons and more than a thousand head of cattle in the party.

Within a few months Oñate had received the submission of all the Pueblo Indians, including those of Acoma, Zuni, and Hopi.

The arrival of settlers in the Pueblo country added a significant population to the area. The first settlement was made at San Gabriel near San Juan Pueblo, but by 1610 the seat of the provincial government was moved to Santa Fe. From 1620 to the end of the century there were three main areas of colonization: (1) Santa Fe, (2) La Cañada, near present Santa Cruz in the Tewa Basin, and (3) the southern district from Santo Domingo south to approximately the position of modern Socorro. In addition to these settlements, the more populous Pueblo villages had resident priests and sometimes a small guard of soldiers. A report of ninety chapels in as many villages by Benavides in 1630 is probably correct, but only a few of these had resident missionaries. Most of the chapels were *visitas* to which a priest resident in another pueblo journeyed once a month to conduct Mass and other church services.

There were essentially two types of contact communities during the seventeenth century: (1) the Pueblo villages, in some of which were resident priests and perhaps a few soldiers and a missionary workshop, and (2) the three main areas of Spanish settlements, the most important of which was Santa Fe, where resided the provincial governor, and the garrison of soldier-citizens. These latter gradually accumulated an Indian or part Indian increment.

All of the Pueblo villages regardless of whether they had a resident missionary or not, however, became involved in the concerns and activities of the newcomers. Both civil authorities and missionaries abused the Indians either by exacting tribute or labor from them. Indeed, the competition for the services of the Indians resulted in a continuous conflict between civil and missionary authorities. This was a factor which contributed to the demoralization and disorganization of the New Mexico colony and in part, at least, paved the way for the Pueblo Revolt of 1680.

Missionaries.—From 1609 to 1674 there was a triennial mission caravan to Santa Fe, which brought supplies and replacements of personnel to New Mexico and returned goods and missionaries due for a transfer back to Mexico. Missionaries were constantly shifted from one place to another in the Pueblo area and transferred back to Mexico. Franciscan policy demanded that priests should not remain in one place too long, and there was considerable shifting of missionary personnel, especially after the mid-seventeenth century. This policy prevented close ties between the friars and their charges. With one or two exceptions none of the friars learned the indigenous languages, and they were not encouraged to do so. The number of priests serving the Pueblo area varied during the seventeenth century. Oñate in 1598 entered with eight Franciscan friars, two lay brothers, and three Mexican Indians dedicated to the order who had not taken the vows. In 1631 the total number of friars to be supported in New Mexico from the royal treasury was set at sixty-six. The peak in numbers of missionaries assigned to the area was probably in 1657. In that year the mission caravan was authorized to carry the full quota plus four extra friars to be assigned to the Manso and Suma missions (Scholes 1930). In 1680, at the time of the Pueblo Revolt, there were thirty-three; twenty-one of them were killed by the Indians.

No bishop had authority over the Franciscans in New Mexico during the period under consideration. The superior of the province, called a prelate, had some functions of a bishop but with limited powers. A prelate in New Mexico could administer confirmation, confer minor orders, consecrate church buildings and ornaments, issue indulgences, and give dispensation in certain matrimonial cases. The commissaries and custodians of the Franciscans in New Mexico were the prelates of the New Mexican Church. Until 1616 the Franciscan who supervised the activities of the missionaries was known as the "commissary"; in that year, however, New Mexico was elevated to a "custody"—the Custody of the Conversion of St. Paul and of the Holy Gospel Province—and the Franciscan supervisor became known thereafter as the *Custos* or *Custodio*. The commissary or custodian remained in the provincial capital at San Gabriel, but after the capital was moved to Santa Fe in 1610, the ecclesiastical capital of New Mexico became Santo Domingo and remained so throughout the seventeenth century. The commissary and later the custodian made the assignments of friars to the missions, received and distributed the provisions brought on the triennial mission caravan, and in general determined mission policy in New Mexico and was the intermediary between mission and civil interests in the province.

The work of the missionaries in the initial period of colonization consisted of enormous building programs. Mission establishments were imposing walled compounds within or just outside the Pueblo villages. They were constructed entirely by Indian labor under supervision of the friars. They were structures of adobe or, in the case of the eastern Tiwa and Piro pueblos, of sandstone slabs set in adobe mud. Timbers for beams and door and window frames were cut on steep mountain sides and brought a distance of twenty-five to thirty miles to mission sites.

Within the mission compound lived one or two missionaries and a number of Indian workers and servants. Although the missions were supposed to be training centers for Indians, they served more importantly as a place where priests might live in comfort. Indians were employed at weaving, leatherwork, blacksmithing, and as cooks and servants. The mission also had grazing lands outside the compound, where they kept sheep and cattle under the care of Indian herdsmen. Gardens and orchards were also a regular feature of the mission compound.

The religious duties of the missionaries consisted in saying Mass, conducting burial services, performing baptism and marriage, and conducting vesper services. A few Indians were taught prayers and made responsible for making the villagers attend church services. Instruction in reading and writing apparently was not a regular part of the program of the Franciscan friars. With rare exceptions, the missionaries did not learn the language of their charges and no attempt was made to translate prayers and Mass into the native languages.

Franciscan objectives in the Christianization program were the eradication of Pueblo customs and beliefs and the forced imposition of Catholic ideas and practices. Kivas were raided periodically and masks and prayer sticks burned. Pueblo religious leaders were whipped and hanged as witches if they persisted in carrying on native religious practices. Failure to attend Mass and other church services was dealt with promptly and severely.

The persistence of Indian customs and the power and influence of their leaders were vexing problems to the missionaries. In their desire to substitute Christian ideas and practices for pagan ones the missionaries resorted to drastic disciplinary measures. In the process they incurred the resentment of all the Indians who, instead of giving up their beliefs and customs, went "underground" but with no loss of fervor for the old ways.

Secular Authorities.—The supreme authority in the province of New Mexico was the governor and captain-general. He was appointed by the viceroy in Mexico City. France Scholes (1935: 75) reports in brief the responsibilities and duties of the governor:

It was the governor's function to promote the general advancement of the province, to secure the administration of justice, to defend the province from internal revolt and from attack by outside enemies, especially the marauding nomads, to foster and protect the missions, and to protect the settled Pueblo Indians from abuse and exploitation. The governor was at once the political leader of the province, the commander-in-chief of its military establishment, its legislator on all matters of local provincial policy, and its most important judicial officer. His powers were wide enough to permit an honest and energetic man to maintain discipline and secure justice, or to make it possible for a self-seeking official to become a local tyrant.

Although the governors were supposed to promote the general welfare of the province, they selfishly pursued their own interests. They failed to support the missionary program and followed a vacillating policy in enforcing mission discipline. The governors, moreover, engaged in diverse economic ventures for their own profit. In these ventures the labor and products of the Indian were used. Indians were made to spend long hours weaving cloth and blankets in workshops set up for the purpose in the pueblos and in Santa Fe. Other Indians were made to collect large quantities of piñon nuts, which brought a handsome price in Mexico. Still other Indians were employed to build wagons and carts for special caravans to Mexico to ship out the accumulated stocks of goods. In the caravan trains Pueblo Indians were pressed into service as servants and muleteers. The amount of goods transported in caravans to Mexico as early as 1638–39 indicates the tremendous production of Pueblo Indian labor.[12]

Generally the Indians were forced to perform these services without pay, and even when wages were paid, they were far below the standard scale of pay. The extremes to which Indian labor and production were exploited perhaps reached a peak during Mendizabal's term as governor, 1659–61. He was tried and found guilty on the general charge of the illegal use of Indian labor, but there is evidence that other governors were equally unscrupulous and abusive of Indian labor.[13]

For their profitable ventures, the governors and their cohorts, the "soldier-citizens," were under constant fire from the clergy. The

[12] See trade invoice of 1638 of goods shipped by Governor Rosas from Santa Fe to Mexico (Bloom 1935a: 242–48).

[13] For an excellent description of the profitable activities of New Mexico governors in the middle of the seventeenth century see Scholes 1935: 74 ff.

friars protested that the governor and the soldiers not only neglected to help the mission program but, in addition, aggravated conditions by the constant demand for Indian labor. The complaints of the missionaries were undoubtedly exaggerated, but as Scholes reports (1935: 86–87):

Even if we discount heavily the denunciations of the friars there remains ample proof of the fact that some of them [the Officials] were arbitrary in their conduct of the government, openly immoral, crass, and entirely unscrupulous. The most general complaint that can be laid up against them as a group was their eager and persistent desire to squeeze a profit out of their office. The salary was fairly good, as compared with other official salaries in New Spain, but it was not the salary that made men accept an appointment in a province fifteen hundred miles from Mexico City. It was the opportunity for gain. Their profits from trade, stock-raising, and exploitation of Indian labor were, in some cases, far in excess of their salary.

The enslavement of Pueblo Indians appears to have been rare, although during Governor Eulate's administration (1618–25) soldiers were given permission to keep Indian orphans as house servants. Whether the enslavement of Pueblo Indians was practiced at other times is not clear, perhaps the traffic in Apache captives countered the need for Pueblo slaves in later times. Legally the enslavement of Indians was forbidden by the crown, but this restriction was often abused, especially with respect to nomadic Indians.

In their economic exploits, the governors received full support from a group of *encomendero* soldier-citizens. These men, whose number was set at thirty-five, formed the core of the provincial military force. Their responsibilities were to protect settlers and missionaries and to quell uprising of the Indians. In times of trouble, they assumed command of several hundred settlers and Indian allies. At other times they and their families lived as quasi-lords from the proceeds of land and stock cultivated and tended by Indians. The soldier-citizens were, in fact, but instruments of the governors and served their interests more than the responsibilities with which they were charged. They received no pay, but the encomiendas which they received were far more profitable than salaries. The governor allocated the encomiendas to each soldier and determined the revenues to be derived from them. An encomienda in New Mexico entitled a soldier-citizen to the services of a number of Indians. Some of the Indians assigned to a soldier-citizen were used as household servants, but the main service performed by the Indians came from the farms and livestock which the Indians cultivated and tended. The encomendero was forbidden to live on the land used by Indians or on which his livestock grazed, but nevertheless he received most of the proceeds from the land. In addition to these services, it is very probable that many of the soldiers also joined with the governor in his ambitious and profitable economic ventures.

The civil government system in the province included a few other officials besides the governor and the soldier-citizen. These were the secretary of government and war, the lieutenant governor and the *alcaldes mayores*. All were appointed by the governor and held office at his pleasure.

The secretary was in charge of all documents and papers issued in the governor's name. In addition, he was the governor's adviser and intimate companion. The lieutenant governors performed services which the governor could not perform, represented the governor in his absence, and during the latter part of the century assumed contol over the southern district, Rio Abajo. The alcaldes mayores administered subdivisions of the province. During the sixteenth century there were six or eight such units in New Mexico. These people dealt directly with the settlers and the Indians. They were perhaps without exception instruments of the governor and carried out his explicit orders. They and the soldier-citizens kept the recruitment of Indians for labor and the flow of tribute going. None of the officials below the governor received direct pay, but they all profited from the collection of tribute and from the labor of the Indians.

In addition to the above, the villa of Santa Fe was governed by a *cabildo*. This body consisted of four councilmen and two magistrates. In general the cabildo represented the soldier-citizen group, which was the dominant class in the community. The civil administration and military group was thus a closely knit group with the governor at its head. The only check on the activities of the civil government were the missionaries, and we have already seen that this was not an effective one but a disorganizing factor which eventually paved the way to the successful Pueblo Revolt of 1680.

The nonaboriginal population, which was about twenty-five hundred throughout the seventeenth century, constituted a mixed group. We quote from Scholes (1935: 97–98):

It is impossible to estimate the proportions of Spaniards, creoles, and castes. In the beginning there was clearly a considerable number of Spanish born citizens and a sprinkling of foreigners such as Portuguese, Flemish and French, but in time this group became a small minority. In 1680–1681, it is evident that more than eighty per cent—perhaps ninety per cent—of the population were natives of the province itself. This fact itself illustrates clearly the lack of any considerable colonizing population. But in this majority of New Mexico born there were many who were of mixed blood. There is no way to determine the amount of mixture but there is reason to believe that it was considerable. The reader of the contemporary documents cannot fail to notice the incidental statements and evidence indicating that mixing of blood was frequent, and that many a man of pure European blood married an Indian, a mestiza, or even a negro caste. This was inevitable in a community which not only lived with the Indians and was outnumbered by them, but which received comparatively few new colonists. Moreover, many of the colonists were themselves mestizos.

. . . But despite the easy and free intermingling of classes and despite the fact also that no man could attain any great measure of wealth in New Mexico, there was clearly a well defined local aristocracy based on family, service to the Crown, and worldly possessions. . . . Sons followed fathers in the profession of arms and as holders of local political and military office. These men formed the core of that small caste of professional soldier citizens. . . .

Pueblo Indian-Spanish Relations.—The effect of Spanish control on the Pueblos and their reaction to church and civil authorities are characterized admirably by Scholes (1942: 15–16):

By 1650 the Indians were fully aware of the meaning and implications of Spanish supremacy and the mission system. Spanish supremacy had brought a heavy burden of labor and tribute and encroachment on the lands of the Pueblos. The mission system added to the burden of labor, but the most important phase of the program of Christianization was its effect on the old folk customs.

The friars sought not only to teach a new faith, but they zealously tried also to put an end to the practice of native religious ceremonial, to destroy the influence of the traditional leaders of the Indians, and to impose rigid monogamy on a people whose code of marital and sexual relationship was fairly flexible and elastic. In order to maintain mission discipline the friars often resorted to the imposition of physical punishment for such offenses as failure to attend religious services, sexual immorality, and participation in the native ceremonial dances.

But drastic disciplinary measures . . . could not force full allegiance to the new order. The efforts of the clergy to abolish the old ceremonial forms and to set up new standards of conduct merely caused greater resentment on the part of the Indians. . . . The Pueblos were not unwilling to accept externals of the new faith, but they found it difficult to understand the deeper spiritual values of Christianity. Pueblo religion served definite material and social ends, viz., the propitiation of those supernatural forces which they believed controlled their daily existence. They expected the same results from the Christian faith. But they soon realized that the new ways were no more successful in obtaining a good harvest than the old, and they realized too that the efforts to abolish their traditional ceremonials and destroy the influence of the old native leaders whose functions were both social and religious, raised serious problems concerning the entire fund of Pueblo civilization. Bewilderment soon turned into resentment, and resentment into a resurgence of loyalty to the traditional norms of folk-culture. The burden of labor and tribute might have been tolerated if off-set by recognized advantages, but if the new was no more efficient in guaranteeing a harvest or success in the hunt, what had been gained by accepting Spanish overlordship.

The fact that the Pueblos were permitted to remain in their villages was undoubtedly a major factor in the retention and continuity of Pueblo culture through the years. Had the Pueblo villages been broken up and the populations redistributed, reduced, and established in locations closer to the Spanish settlements, Pueblo culture might have been seriously modified. The situation might then have been much like central Mexico, where "Indian cultures" have survived as amalgams of Spanish and Indian elements. But in New Mexico, Indian populations remained in the old pueblos, and the attempts of missionaries to wipe out traditional practices and beliefs were largely ineffective. If the imposition of Christian and Spanish customs had been applied with sufficient force, a substitution of patterns might also have been effected, but a small group of dedicated and zealous friars could hardly accomplish this. We have seen also that the friars received only sporadic help in their Christianizing efforts from the civil authorities. Added to the difficulties of the mission program, and threatening the very lives of the settlers, were the increasing and devastating raids of the Apaches as the latter acquired horses.

A revolutionary change in the tactics of the missionaries might have also advanced the Christianizing and civilizing program. Reference is here made to the generally permissive, non-coercive methods employed by the Jesuit missionaries among the Yaquis. The missionary program of the Jesuits and the effect on Yaqui culture are discussed fully in Spicer's account in this volume. The Franciscan missionaries of the seventeenth century, however, defeated their own purpose by using force and drastic methods. Resentment toward friars and the Spaniards broke out in repeated minor rebellions, culminating finally in the successful revolt of 1680.

The revolt was planned by a Tewa of San Juan pueblo, Popé, who had been one of forty-seven Pueblo religious leaders brought to be punished by Spanish authorities in 1675. Smarting under the punishment, Popé planned a general revolt from his headquarters which he established in Taos pueblo. The news of the revolt leaked out before the day planned for its execution, and the revolt had to be put into effect prematurely. The northern Tanoan Indians were most active in the revolt, but many of the other pueblos co-operated by killing their resident missionaries and other Spaniards. The Apaches seem not to have participated actively, but the Spaniards were led to believe they were in the revolt pact and therefore succumbed more readily.

About one thousand settlers in the south took refuge in Isleta, a pueblo that remained friendly to the colonists. Believing that the Spaniards in Santa Fe and the northern area were all dead, this group retreated south to El Paso. The refugee group from Santa Fe, also numbering about one thousand, later joined the southern colonists in El Paso.

At the end of the revolt twenty-one out of thirty-three missionaries and about 380 colonists out of a total of about twenty-five hundred were dead (Hackett and Shelby 1942: 98). All missions were destroyed, together with furnishings and records.

Except for an abortive attempt to regain the area by Governor Otermín in the winter of 1681–82, and the equally unsuccessful forays by Governor Pedro Reneros de Posada in 1688 and Governor Cruzate in 1689, the Pueblos were free until the successful reconquest by De Vargas in 1693. During this period of twelve or thirteen years the Pueblo Indians abandoned many of their pueblos and retreated into more defensible areas in the mountains and mesas. Some of the Tano Indians moved north into the Tewa country while others entrenched themselves in Santa Fe, where De Vargas found them in 1693. The defensive measures of the Pueblos were undertaken for protection from the raids of Apaches as much as from the threat of Spanish invasion. While the Spaniards were away, the Apaches, realizing that

Spanish intervention was removed, descended on the marginal and more exposed villages with renewed fervor. Indeed, internal dissension among the Pueblos themselves also broke out. Native informants reported to the Spaniards that during the interim period Keresan and Pecos Indians became actively hostile toward the Tewa and Tano and that they warred with one another. Two brothers, natives of San Felipe pueblo, questioned by Governor Otermín's lieutenant, Juan Dominguez de Mendoza, in the attempted reconquest of New Mexico in 1681–82 described the conditions among the Pueblos after the revolt. The excerpt below contains part of the statement of the two brothers (Hackett and Shelby 1942: 251):

Asked what happened after the said rebellion, they said they saw that the said Indian, Popé, came down to the pueblo of San Felipe accompanied by many captains from the pueblos and by other Indians and ordered the churches burned and the holy images broken up and burned. They took possession of everything in the sacristy pertaining to divine worship, and said that they were weary of putting in order, sweeping, heating, and adorning the church; and that they proclaimed both in the said pueblo and in others that he who should utter the name of Jesus would be killed immediately; and that they (the Indians) were not to pray or to live with the wives whom they had taken in holy matrimony, all under the said penalty of death; and thereupon they could live contentedly, happy in their freedom, living according to their ancient custom. . . .

When De Vargas reached Santa Fe in 1693, the entrenched Tano in Santa Fe threatened resistance, but a bloodless surrender was eventually effected. A large number of these Indians were turned over to the soldiers and colonists as slaves, others were settled in Tewa villages. De Vargas persuaded the other Pueblos in hiding to return to their villages and in a few months settlers, missionaries, and the Indians had resumed a relationship similar to the pre-revolt period. But the situation was fraught with tension and new outbreaks seemed constantly imminent. Finally in 1694 the Tano and some of the Tewa retreated to the top of Black Mesa near San Ildefonso and from this stronghold harassed the Spanish settlements, even extending their raids to Santa Fe. These Indians withstood the attacks of De Vargas for nine months, but were finally compelled to sue for peace and agreed to return to their villages.

During the summer of 1696 some of the Tewa and the Indians of Taos, Picurís, Santo Domingo and Cochiti and the Tano rose in revolt. Twenty-seven Spaniards, six of them priests, were killed. De Vargas immediately took steps to stop the revolt. He succeeded in capturing some of the leaders, while large numbers fled to the Navaho and Hopi country.

After the abortive Pueblo revolt of 1696 the Pueblos settled down into outward peaceable relations with the Spaniards. In large measure, modified policies of the Franciscans and particularly those of the civil authorities were responsible for the changed conditions. Distrust and suspicion continued to characterize Pueblo and Spanish relations, but the coercive, forced policies gradually gave way to more humane treatment of the Pueblos in the succeeding generations. The specific details of these relations will be discussed in the next section; at the moment it is important to consider briefly the relation of the Pueblos to other peoples in the area.

Pueblo Relations with Other Peoples in the Seventeenth Century.— With the expedition of Oñate came a large number of Mexican Indians. These Indians appear to have been servants to Spanish soldiers and other prominent colonists, but the frontier conditions, coupled with the small numbers of Spanish and Creole colonists and especially the paucity of women among the latter made imperative the mixing of blood. At the time of the revolt few if any of the colonists could boast of a pure Spanish lineage. Nevertheless, even though mixing among Spaniards and Indians occurred, it is apparent that, from the time Santa Fe was established until the time of the revolt, there was a group of Mexican Indians who lived somewhat detached from the others in the village and also perhaps in the other areas of settlement. In Santa Fe these Indians lived in an area or "barrio" called Analco. That there was a more intimate tie between these Indians and the Pueblos than between the latter and the settlers is suggested in the quotation below, taken from Otermín's letter to Fray Francisco de Ayeta describing the siege of Santa Fe in the late summer of 1680. A party of Tanos, Pecos, and Keresan Indians surrounded the villa and had dispatched their leader, a Tano Indian who was from the villa, to confer with Governor Otermín:

... He [the Tano Indian] came back ... [from the enemy camp] saying that his people asked that all classes of Indians who were in our power be given up to them, both those in the service of the Spaniards and those of the Mexican nation of that suburb of Analco. He demanded also that his wife and children be given up to him, and likewise that all Apache men and women whom the Spaniards had captured in war be turned over to them, inasmuch as some Apaches who were among them were asking for them. If these things were not done they would declare war immediately, and they were not willing to leave the place where they were because they were awaiting the Taos, Pecuries, and Teguas nations, with whose aid they would destroy us. . . . (Hackett and Shelby 1942: I, 99.)

The Mexican Indians may have introduced the Montezuma legend, and they may have taught the Pueblos the pageant dances like Los Moros and the Matachina which had been taught them and their ancestors in Mexico by missionaries early in the sixteenth century. The Pueblos likewise may have learned from these Indians dances like the Sandaro or horse dance, performed in virtually all the Rio Grande pueblos, and the bull dance still enacted in Jemez pueblo by the descendants of Pecos pueblo. The Montezuma legend is known by many Spanish-Americans and the Matachina pageant is still performed in a number of Spanish-American villages. It is clear that some Mexican Indians, as well as others of mixed blood, joined the rebels in the Revolt of 1680 and remained in New Mexico after the colonists left. In January, 1682, when Governor Otermín decided to give up the reconquest of New Mexico and return to Mexico he reported that "Many mestizos, mulattoes, and people who speak Spanish have followed them [the rebellious Pueblos], who are skillful on horse back and who can manage firearms as well as any Spaniard" (Hackett and Shelby 1942: I, 355). It is probable, and the material suggests it, that the cultural elements taken over by the Pueblos during this period were those which the mixed bloods and Mexican Indians themselves had taken over from the frontier Spanish-Catholic culture.

Other peoples with whom the Pueblos came into contact during this century were Apaches and Navahos. Relations with these peoples were becoming increasingly hostile on the eve of the revolt. It is, therefore, unlikely that they figured prominently as allies in the revolt and certainly there was no friendliness later. Some Apache and Navaho slaves of the Spanish settlers may have, however, been freed during the revolt and adopted by Pueblo families. The number of such Indians would have been few, and it is unlikely that they would make much impression on Pueblo culture.

Finally the revolt, by intermingling Pueblo peoples of all linguistic and subcultural affiliations, undoubtedly cemented cultural ties among them, although there is evidence that political ambitions of the revolt leaders produced strained relationships among some groups of Pueblos. At the end of the seventeenth century the various Pueblos undoubtedly had a greater familiarity with one another's cultural patterns and greater cultural unity, if not political, than at any other time in their history.

Population and Settlement Patterns.—The population of the Pueblo Indians in 1600 was possibly between thirty and forty thousand. As the century wore on the population slowly decreased, and on the eve of the revolt had dropped by half, or to about sixteen thousand Hackett and Shelby 1942: xxi). The revolt reduced the population still further, as a result of deaths at the hands of Spaniards and losses by migration to the Hopi country and to the nomadic tribes. We may therefore estimate a Pueblo population in 1700 of about fourteen thousand.

Disease, particularly the periodic smallpox epidemics, and the raids of the Apaches, which had become increasingly destructive as these nomads acquired horses, were probably the two main factors responsible for population decrease. To these we must add, however, the forced labor program and the recruitment of servants for Spanish households which further reduced Pueblo population. The brutal punishments meted out by church and civil authorities to the Indians also drove hundreds to seek asylum among the Hopis, Apaches, and Navahos.

At the end of the revolt the Pueblo area had been drastically reduced. All of the Piro settlements were now uninhabited as were also Tiwa villages east of the mountains and along the Rio Grande south of Isleta pueblo. Some of the people from these pueblos joined the Spaniards, retreating south in 1680, and founded communities below El Paso, while others migrated to the Hopi country. The Tano were scattered among the Tewa pueblos north of Santa Fe and some of them had also joined the Hopi (see Dozier 1954). Early in the eighteenth century some of the dispersed Tano in New Mexico were resettled in the pueblo of Galisteo, but disease and nomadic Indian raids between 1782 and 1794 finally compelled the few surviving Tano to move to the pueblo of Santo Domingo. There were also some concentrations and shifting of Pueblo population in the period between 1680 and 1700. Some Keresan Indians from the Rio Grande pueblos moved west after the revolt, apparently in an attempt to get farther away from Spanish domination, and founded Laguna. The only southern

Tiwa pueblo that remained after the revolt was Isleta, although Tiwa refugees at Hopi were later returned and resettled at a newly created pueblo of Sandia, about twenty miles above Isleta in 1741.

The locations of the Rio Grande pueblos in 1700 were essentially in the sites they occupy today. Pecos, the large and important pueblo of the seventeenth century was, however, destined to be abandoned. Apache and Comanche raids reduced this pueblo during the eighteenth century to a few survivors who in 1838 moved to Jemez pueblo, a village which also spoke Towa (Hodge 1912: 221).

PUEBLO CULTURE, ABOUT 1700

The characteristics of Rio Grande Pueblo culture can best be described in terms of changes, additions, or losses from the base-line culture already presented. Basic changes in the agricultural economy were in techniques, particularly in methods of irrigation and in the addition of new crops and domesticated fowl and animals. The use of plows, oxen, and hoes became important alternatives to the old digging stick method of farming. Crops added were wheat, melons (cantaloupe and watermelon), apples, peaches, apricots, pears, tomatoes, and chile. The last two were aboriginal foods in Mexico but new to the Pueblos.

Mules, horses, and donkeys, along with the two-wheeled *carreta* or wagon, facilitated labor and revolutionized transportation and travel. Goats, sheep, and chickens added to the meat diet, while sheep, in addition, brought a new material for textile manufacture unknown in pre-Spanish times. Crafts were enriched by the addition of weaving in wool, blacksmithing (iron, tin, copper, bronze, and silver) and woodworking. These introductions included an assorted complex of tools like saddles, bridles, harnesses, metal knives, sickles, hoes, shovels, needles, axes, etc.

The changes in architecture and village layout patterns were not revolutionary. Although adobe bricks made by the use of a wooden form or mold were employed by the colonists, the Pueblos of the seventeenth century seem not to have adopted the technique extensively, if at all. Even the bread oven and corner fireplace, apparently, became fully established as a Pueblo architectural feature only in the succeeding period. It is instructive here to quote from N. C. Nelson who excavated a number of the major Tano pueblos of the Galisteo Basin early in the present century, exposing both prehistoric and seventeenth century, post-Spanish contact portions of these village sites (Nelson 1914: 112):

They [Tano] had the example and presumably the advice, as well as the occasional coercion of Spanish colonists and missionaries in reference to the execution of many common tasks for a century. Those who lived at Pueblo Galisteo enjoyed the privilege for about a hundred years more. Yet the architectural remains, so far examined, do not reveal any marked changes or improvements. The Tanos of historic times constructed the same style of building, retained the same room dimensions, the same sort of doors, fireplaces, etc., as their ancient forefathers.

For virtually every pueblo, of course, a Catholic chapel became a prominent feature of the community and with the more populous and important villages, the mission compound and workshops, as well. These additions should be considered impositions, however, rather than structures willingly accepted and incorporated into the pueblos. That they were not considered to be community structures is amply demonstrated by the wholesale destruction of the missions and mission equipment during and after the revolt.

It is more difficult to assess the amount of borrowing and acceptance in the less tangible areas of culture such as sociopolitical organizations, religion, and values. Land tenure, property control, and inheritance remained community responsibilities for Tanoans, while for Keresans the shift from clan to village in the assumption of these duties may have been accelerated. A centralized pueblo would be more effective than corporate clans or lineages to counteract the disruptive force of Spanish authorities or religion and land use.

Early in the seventeenth century the Pueblos experienced the imposition of the Spanish system of civil government. To facilitate the mission program and civil administration, native communities were required to appoint a set of officers to meet with outside agencies. Among the Pueblos, these officers were usually a governor, a lieutenant governor, *alguacil* or sheriff, *sacristan, mayordomos,* and *fiscales.* The governor was to represent the village in all important dealings with Spanish authorities. The lieutenant governor was to serve as assistant to the governor and represent him when absent, and, in the event of the governor's death, succeed him. The alguacil was to maintain law and order within the pueblo; the sacristan was church assistant and aid to the priest; the fiscales were responsible for mission discipline, while th: mayordomos were ditch superintendents.[14]

The importance of the civil organization cannot be denied among contemporary Pueblos, but this set of officers has not displaced the native sociopolitical organization in any of the present-day villages. The officers of the civil government are recognized in all of the pueblos today as an imposed set, but useful in meeting with outsiders and masking the identity and activities of the native officers. The latter are the *de facto* group of sociopolitical and ceremonial leaders in virtually all of the pueblos. We may conjecture that in 1700 the Spanish-imposed civil government system was even of less importance. This supposition is strengthened by the fact that the Hopi-Tewa community in Arizona whose members are descendants of the Tano refugees from Galisteo Basin have no vestige of the Spanish civil government system in their sociopolitical organization. The Tano being the nearest neighbors of the Spanish villa in Santa Fe throughout the seventeenth century, undoubtedly possessed a set of such civil officers. If no hint of such an organization exists among their descendants, who after the seventeenth century remained isolated from Spanish control in Arizona, it argues well for the unimportance of the Spanish civil government system among all the Pueblos in 1700.

The degree to which Spanish and Catholic values and beliefs were internalized and incorporated into Pueblo culture by the end of the seventeenth century also appears to be negligible. Pueblo Indians went to Mass, confessed, and received communion, attended vespers, were baptized and even married and buried by the friars for almost a century. These are all external acts, however: they do not reveal whether the Pueblos interpreted the acts and meanings of the Catholic religion in the same way as the friars. There is hardly any doubt that, in the beginning at least, the Indians wanted sincerely to know about the Catholic religion and wanted to perform correctly the prayers and rituals taught them by friars. But the ends desired by the Pueblos were different. As Dr. Scholes reports, Pueblo Indian religion serves definite material and social ends. In performing the rituals demanded by the Catholic religion, the Pueblo Indians hoped to reap practical results, but when the new religion was "no more efficient in guaranteeing a harvest or success in the hunt" than their own, they felt be-

[14] This is a generalized list of the officers and their duties—in the various pueblos the names and functions of the officers differ to some extent.

trayed and resentful. That the Pueblos had not internalized Spanish and Catholic values and beliefs is also shown by their actions during and after the revolt of 1680. There seemed to have been little guilt associated with the killing of priests and the destruction of chapels and mission furnishings, including images of the saints, crosses, and other blessed objects.[15]

Among the contemporary Pueblos, pageants and dances like the Matachina, the horse or Sandaro dance and the Pecos Bull ceremony are obviously of Spanish or Mexican derivation.[16] These ceremonies have a definite place in Pueblo ceremonialism as well, although their foreign derivation and separateness from native Pueblo ceremonies are recognized. Associated with these Spanish or Mexican derived ceremonies are masked clowns, called *Chapio* (also *K'apio, Tsabiyo*), who speak Spanish and Indian in falsetto. The masks have no resemblance to Katcina masks and are obviously of Mexican provenience. These masks, however, have a striking resemblance to masks worn by the *Chapaiyeka* in Mayo-Yaqui ceremonies. The behavior of both sets of clowns is also similar. The Matachina pageant itself, in variant form is danced by Tarahumara, Huicholes and Mayo-Yaqui (see Parsons 1939: 852, 1005–7). The Mexican origin of these ceremonies is further evidenced by their association with Montezuma. Among the Rio Grande Pueblos, Montezuma is a culture hero. This culture hero is called variously: Bocaiyanyi (Santa Ana), Poshaiyanki (Zuni) and Poseyemu (Tewa). He is champion of the Indian. Montezuma often assumes the physical form and personality of whites, speaks all languages, performs miracles, and foretells the future. Montezuma told the Pueblos of the coming of the Europeans, but admonished them to keep their own indigenous beliefs and customs. Parsons identifies the Pueblos' Montezuma with Jesus, but it is obvious that his behavior in the tales depict Indian characteristics as well.[17]

The ceremonies linked with the legend of Montezuma, although

15 For a vivid account of the activities of the Pueblos after the Spaniards were driven out of the province in 1680, see Hackett and Shelby, 1942: 247–53.

16 For description of the Matachina pageant among Rio Grande Pueblos see Parsons 1939: 852–56; for the Pecos Bull ceremony, Parsons 1925: 96–98; and for Sandaro dances Parsons 1939: 811–12, White 1942: 256–63. For an interesting and significant study of the Matachina and similar ceremonies see Kurath 1949.

17 For Montezuma legends see Parsons 1929: 276–77, 306–7; Dumarest 1919: 228–31. Parsons believes that "the Pueblos heard a good deal about Montezuma a 'god' that might be mentioned conveniently to white people" (1939: 1079).

recognized as foreign innovations among the Pueblos, are considered important and sacred. It is interesting that Catholic doctrine and ritual which was constantly drummed into the Indians by the friars did not become as intimately incorporated into Pueblo ceremonialism. It is very probable that the reason for the greater acceptance of the ceremonies associated with Montezuma is that they were introduced by Mexican Indians. Mexican Indians held no positions of authority and provided no threat to the Pueblos. If these Indians presented the ceremonies to the Pueblos, then it is easy to understand why the Pueblos accepted them. Perhaps the ceremonies already contained re-interpreted Spanish-Indian elements which would make them more palatable to the Pueblos.

The addition of the Spanish language to the Pueblo dialects must be considered an important acquisition. Undoubtedly not all Pueblo adults spoke Spanish, but the records reveal that during the revolt and after the reconquest communication between the Indians and Spaniards presented no difficulties. It is very probable that the Spanish language even at this early date, had become a lingua franca among the Pueblos. By adopting Spanish as the language for communicating with the outside world, the individual Pueblo linguistic communities retained their own indigenous languages as tools for retaining and perpetuating their cherished and closely guarded customs and beliefs. A study of the contemporary Pueblo languages reveals how effectively borrowing from the Spanish language has been resisted. This interesting, resistant nature of Pueblo languages we believe is a product of the seventeenth century; a result of the unpleasant experiences between Pueblos and the missionaries and colonists.

The use of the Spanish language undoubtedly also intensified the isolation and separation of the native dialects. We may, therefore, surmise that the three dialectical variations among the Tanoans grew apart more rapidly during this period and probably became unintelligible from one another.

At the end of the seventeenth century Rio Grande Pueblo Indians had added to their culture an impressive array of material items, domesticated animals and plants, and had learned numerous craft techniques. The Spanish language appears to have been firmly established as a second language and as an important communication tool not only with the colonists, but also with linguistically unrelated Pueblos. But Pueblo values, religious beliefs and ceremonialism, the areas under attack, remained essentially indigenous and resistant to change. These aspects of Pueblo culture became the "cultural focus" and in Hersko-vits' words: "that area of activity or belief where the greatest aware-ness of form exists, the most discussion of values is heard, the widest difference in structure is to be discerned" (1945: 164–65).

Period III: Stabilized Pluralism[18]

CONDITIONS OF CONTACT, 1700–1804

After the reconquest, Spanish attitudes and policies toward the Indians changed. In the seventeenth century the main concern had been to Christianize and to civilize the Indians, but in the succeeding century a series of political events directed attention away from the Indians and focused on colonization. Added to this was the fact that the encomienda system, which had been one of the main causes of the revolt, ceased to operate after the reconquest. The Spaniards or their heirs who lost encomiendas in 1680 never regained the traditional right to collect tribute from the Pueblo Indians. There was only one excep-tion, De Vargas, the reconqueror of New Mexico who was granted a large encomienda, but the encomienda was never put into operation, and finally, in 1726, De Vargas' heirs had it changed into a pension (Espinosa 1940: 38).

The friars resumed their Christianizing activities, but now the main concern was the welfare of the settlements. The forcing policies did not change immediately, and there were a few raids on Katcina masks and the punishment of native leaders during the first quarter of the seventeenth century. But the intensive raids of Apaches, and by 1705, those of the Comanches, as well, drew the attention of the Spaniards away from the Rio Grande Pueblos. The activities of the governors during the eighteenth century were concerned primarily with organ-izing and sending punitive expeditions against these Indians. In these expeditions they were joined by Pueblo Indians who were suffering as greatly from the raids. Although the friars deplored the religious deca-dence among the Pueblos, civil authorities largely ignored their ap-peals. Several of the governors, however, attempted to return the Rio Grande Pueblo refugees who fled to the Hopi country during the revolts of 1680 and 1696 to their original villages (Thomas 1932: 20;

[18] There were many sources consulted for this period, but the following were most extensively used: Thomas 1932; Bancroft 1884–89; Adams 1954; Adams and Chavez 1956.

Bloom 1931: 204–5). Most of these expeditions were unsuccessful, but in 1741 two friars, Fray Carlos Delgado and Fray Ignacio Pino succeeded in returning 441 Tiwa Indians and resettling them in their old pueblos, Paparito, Alameda, and Sandia (Thomas 1932: 160).

With the intervention of the civil authorities removed, the Rio Grande Pueblos returned to the practice of their ancient customs and ceremonies. Their participation in church activities was minimal and grudgingly performed. The remarks of Fray Atanasio Dominguez, Commissary Visitor of the missions of New Mexico in 1776, reveals the slight impression the work of the friars was making on the Indians. He reports (Adams and Chavez 1956: 254–58):

Even at the end of so many years since their reconquest, the specious title or name of neophytes is still applied to them. This is the reason their condition now is almost the same as it was in the beginning, for generally speaking they have preserved some very indecent, and perhaps superstitious, customs. . . .

Their repugnance and resistance to most Christian acts is evident, for they perform the duties pertaining to the Church under compulsion, and there are usually many omissions. They are not in the habit of praying or crossing themselves when they rise or go to bed, and consequently they have no devotion for certain saints as is customary among us. And if they sometimes invoke God and His saints or pray or pay for Masses, it is in a confused manner or to comply in their confusion with what the fathers teach and explain.

They use estufas [kivas], of which some pueblos have more, others less. . . . These estufas are the chapter, or council, rooms, and the Indians meet in them, sometimes to discuss matters of their government for the coming year, their planting, arrangements for work to be done, or to elect new community officials, or to rehearse their dances, or sometimes for other things.

Their customary dances usually resemble contredances or minuets as danced in Spain, or they are scalp dances. . . .[19]

There are other general customs observed by the Indians of these regions, but I have mentioned only the most noteworthy. I note, indeed, that although I stated above that the contredances, or minuets, do not appear

[19] The dances which Father Dominguez reports as resembling contredances and minuets are clearly the so-called Corn or Tablita dances of the Pueblos; see his description (*op. cit.*: 256–57). Scalp dancers also described by Father Dominguez (*op. cit.*: 257–58) were performed in the memory of the oldest informants among the Tewa, indeed the women's scalp society re-enacted activities similar to those described by Dominguez well into the present century and the society is still active in some of the Tewa pueblos (see Hill, MS; Parsons 1929: 212–14).

to be essentially wicked and are usual on solemn occasions during the year, here in the scalp ceremonial the dances are tainted by the idea of vengeance. The fathers have been very zealous in their opposition to this scalp dance, but they have only received rebuffs, and so the fathers are unable to abolish this custom and many others, because excuses are immediately made on the ground that (the Indians) are neophytes, minors, etc.

Pueblo Relations with the Hispanicized Population.—With the emphasis on colonization, the number and extent of the Spanish settlements increased by the middle of the century. These settlements numbered about thirty and extended from Alamillo in the south to Taos in the north along the Rio Grande.

The non-Pueblo colonial population during the eighteenth century was far from being uniformly Spanish. The settlements contained a core of Spanish or Mexican settlers and a larger number of mestizos (mixed Indian and Spanish, either with Mexican or local Indians) and *genízaros*. The latter are well characterized by Adams and Chavez (1956: 42, n. 71):

> In New Mexico [the term *genízaro*] was used to designate non-Pueblo Indians living in more or less Spanish fashion. Some of them were captives ransomed from the nomadic tribes, and their mixed New Mexico-born descendants inherited the designation. Church and civil records reveal such varied derivations as Apache, Comanche, Navajo, Ute, Kiowa, Wichita, and Pawnee. Many had Spanish blood, clandestinely and otherwise. They all bore Christian names from baptism and Spanish surnames from their former masters; belonging no longer to any particular Indian tribe they spoke Spanish. . . .

Genízaros were settled within or near the villages of the settlers, although at least three "pueblos de Genízaros" were established in the eighteenth century. These pueblos were at Abiquiu, Tomé, and Belen (Hodge 1912: 489).

In addition to the three groups described above, many Pueblo Indian servants and workers for the settlers and their descendants also became, in time, a part of the colonial population. There is evidence in the subsequent century that Pueblo individuals and families dissatisfied with Pueblo life also joined Spanish settlements or the genízaro villages. Undoubtedly this process started soon after the friars began active missionary work, and it was probably well established by the beginning of the eighteenth century.

During the period under discussion a separation between the

españoles, or people of predominantly Spanish blood, and the mixed and Indian groups was maintained. The españoles were the people with the best lands and the most livestock. It was this group which made an effort to keep up the Spanish way of life, as much as this was possible on the primitive frontier of New Mexico. The mestizos and the Indians in the settlements were in a menial position, both socially and economically. They looked up to the Spanish elite and took their cues of life, faith, and proper behavior from them.

The class-blood lines of the settlers were to become increasingly blurred in the succeeding century, and they finally became crystallized into the contemporary Spanish-American population. This population developed important cultural characteristics which will be described in our next period. The mixed group grew steadily in numbers, both by natural birth rate increases and by the continuous additions of genízaros and disaffected Pueblo Indians. By the end of the eighteenth century this population outnumbered the Rio Grande Pueblos almost two to one, viz.: Rio Grande Pueblos, 9,732; Spanish, 18,826 (Bancroft 1889: 279).

The relations between the Pueblos and the Hispanicized population during the eighteenth century appears to be outwardly friendly. The detailed description of Pueblo dances by Father Dominguez indicates that the performances were open to the attendance of the settlers (Adams and Chavez 1956: 256–58). Although the more sacred dances and ceremonies were undoubtedly concealed from the settlers,[20] dances like the ones observed by Father Dominguez surely provided opportunities for contact between the two populations.

Pueblo resentment toward Spanish civil authorities and the clergy remained. The alcaldes mayores, especially, were resented for the periodic demands they made upon the Indians for labor and other services. The animosity which the Pueblos bore the friars arose from the strict mission discipline and the periodic punishments they meted out through the fiscales. The following excerpts from a statement made by Father Ruiz at Jemez pueblo in 1776 (Adams and Chavez 1956: 308–15) is probably typical of missionary activities in most of the pueblos:

The bell is rung at sunrise. The married men enter, each one with his wife, and they kneel together in a row on each side of the nave of the

[20] The settlers were not permitted to enter estufas [kivas] early in the nineteenth century (Carroll and Haggard 1942: 29).

church. Each couple has its own place designated in accordance with the census list. When there are many, the married couples make two rows on each side, the two men in the middle and the women on the sides. This may seem a superficial matter, but it is not, for experience has taught me that when these women are together they spend all the time dedicated to prayer and Mass in gossip, showing one another their glass beads, ribbons, medals, etc., telling who gave them or how they obtained them, and other mischief. Therefore the religious who has charge of the administration must have a care in this regard. After all, it is a house of prayer, not of chitchat. . . .

The petty governor and his lieutenant have their places at the door so that the people may not leave during the hour of prayer and Mass.

When all are in their places, the fiscal mayor notifies the father, who comes down with his census lists and takes attendance to see whether everyone is there, whether they are in their proper places, and whether their hair is unbound. If anyone is missing, the petty governor goes to fetch him. If he is not in the pueblo, it is indicated by the thong and he is punished on the following Sunday or holy day of obligation. If the truant is a woman, her husband is sent to fetch her. . . .

After Mass is over, if the minister thinks that some have left, he summons them in accordance with the list and punishes anyone who does such a thing. He severely reprimands the petty governor who permits it. . . .

The lists of married men and widowers are so arranged that if anyone is guilty of absence, this is indicated by the thong. . . .

During the eighteenth century the Pueblos had adjusted tolerably well to the two sources of trouble from the colonial population: the alcaldes, or district supervisors, and the missionaries. After the abolishment of the encomienda system in New Mexico, only the alcaldes demanded and sometimes abused Indian labor. The evidence indicates, however, that these demands were diminishing toward the end of the century. Moreover, in the maintenance of their indigenous beliefs and customs, the Pueblos invariably received support from the alcaldes who denounced the forceful policies of the friars (Adams and Chavez 1956: 313–15, nn. 6, 7).

The primary source of irritation for the Pueblos was the clergy, but the Indians' attitude and bearing, amply documented in the records, indicate that they were aware that the influence and power of the Franciscans had been sapped. In 1725 the Bishop of Durango, Crespo, made a visit to New Mexico. It was the first official visit of a bishop to the province, and shortly thereafter New Mexico became a part of the diocese of Durango. This action indicated the end of the Franciscan monopoly over the religious affairs of New Mexico. Two other official visits by bishops followed: 1737, Elzaecochea; 1760, Tamaron, whose well-recorded tour has been preserved and is an excellent source of information on the missions and the people of New Mexico (Adams 1954).

The administrative change and the de-emphasis of the missionary program seriously affected the process of Christianization. The number of friars serving the area was reduced by more than one-third from the previous century. In 1776, Father Dominguez reported twenty friars in New Mexico, whereas at the time of the Pueblo revolt a century earlier there had been thirty-three. Some of the main pueblos like Pecos, Galisteo, and Tesuque had no missionaries in 1776. In addition the fathers were now responsible for a rapidly increasing non-Pueblo Christian population, almost double the size of the Pueblos.

The Pueblos developed a pattern of friendly co-existence with the colonial population which was to characterize relations between the two peoples for another century. Outwardly these relations were pleasant and amicable, but they never developed into more intimate understandings. The Pueblos reserved the inner core of their culture to themselves and effectively warded off influences which might have disorganized and disrupted the tightly integrated Pueblo way of life. There was obviously a socially developed protective mechanism to keep society and culture together which was undoubtedly a product of the previous period when the Pueblos experienced the ultimate in force and coercion. For latter periods we have detailed information on the "boundary maintaining mechanisms" that were employed to preserve Pueblo culture; it is clear, however, that they were developed during the century in review here.

Pueblo Relations with Other Indians.—Relations between the Pueblos and other peoples were sporadic and attenuated. Contacts with nomadic Indians occurred on occasional trading and buffalo hunting trips into the Plains country. During his term as governor in the late 1700's, Juan Bautista de Anza succeeded in making the Comanches allies of the New Mexicans (Thomas 1932: 83). This provided for friendly relations between the two populations. Virtually all the Rio Grande Pueblos today have "Comanche dances"; it is conceivable that such dances were borrowed during this period.

Fairs at Taos and Abiquiu also provided contacts with diverse Indian tribes. Father Dominguez' description of these fairs is interesting and significant for our purposes:

When the [Comanche] are on their good behavior, or at peace, they enter Taos to trade. At this fair they sell buffalo hides, "white elkskins," horses, mules, buffalo meat, pagan Indians (of both sexes, children and adults) whom they capture from other nations. (In Father Claramonte's [resident priest at Taos, during Father Dominguez' visit] time Christians from other places were also ransomed. He astutely cultivated the Comanche captain, his great friend, in order to get them out of captivity, for otherwise they carry them off again.) They also sell good guns, pistols, powder, balls, tobacco, hatchets, and some vessels of yellow tin (some large, others small) shaped like the crown of the friars' hats, but the difference is that the top of the hat is the bottom of the vessel. These have a handle made of an iron hoop to carry them. . . . They are great traders, for as soon as they buy anything, they usually sell exactly what they bought; and usually they keep losing, the occasion when they gain being very rare, because our people ordinarily play infamous tricks on them. In short, the trading day resembles a second-hand market in Mexico, the way people mill about. (Adams and Chavez 1956: 252.)

About the fair at Abiquiu, Father Dominguez reports:

Every year, between the end of October and the beginning of November, many heathen of the Ute nation come to the vicinity of this pueblo. They come very well laden with good deerskins, and they celebrate their fair with them. This is held for the sole purpose of buying horses. If one is much to the taste and satisfaction of an Indian (the trial is a good race), he gives fifteen to twenty good deerskins for the horse; and if not, there is no purchase. They also sell deer or buffalo meat for maize or corn flour. Sometimes there are little captive heathen Indians (male or female) as with the Comanches, whom they resemble in the manner of selling them. They usually sell deerskins for belduques only, and they are given two of the latter for a good one of the former. With the exception of fire arms and vessels, the Utes sell everything else as described with regard to the Comanches, but they are not so fond of trading as has been said of the latter. (Adams and Chavez 1956: 252–53.)

The diversity of the merchandise traded is remarkable. The fairs circulated as much European manufactured goods as Indian products. The former, of course, were obtained by the Comanches from the Pawnee who had direct contact with French traders.

Population.—The number and location of the Rio Grande villages were substantially the same as at the end of the preceding century. There was a drastic reduction in population, however, from an estimated 14,000 in 1700 to 9,732 in 1799 (Bancroft 1889: 279). The reduction is attributable to epidemic diseases, periodic attacks of nomadic Indians and to a slow, but steady movement of disaffected Pueblo Indians into the Hispanicized population.

PUEBLO CULTURE ABOUT 1800

Village and House Patterns.—Village and house patterns seem not to have changed significantly. A description of Tesuque pueblo by Father Dominguez in 1776 shows no appreciable difference in architecture and village plan from the previous period. This description was considered typical for all Rio Grande pueblos by Dominguez (Adams and Chavez 1956: 50):

> . . . the houses of which the pueblo is composed are adobe and like other Indian houses in these parts. All have upper and lower dwellings, but they are built like a dovecot, for the patio is communal like the plaza and street. The entrance to some houses is by little doors on the street; others have ladders, and some of these ascend to a door which resembles a little window torn in the wall of the upper apartment, while others rest on a portico-like jacal or on the roof of a small room that juts out from the lower dwelling and has a little flat roof which provides access to the upper dwelling. The fastenings are a wooden lock and key.

Possible additions from the previous period may be the entrance in some of the houses by "little doors" facing the street. Outside ovens, henhouses and livestock corrals, also reported by Father Dominguez (Adams and Chavez 1956), may also be eighteenth-century incorporations into the village plan. Nelson apparently did not find evidence of any of these structures in his excavation of seventeenth-century Tano pueblos.

Material and Technological Changes.—The agricultural complex with regard to techniques, tools, crops, and fowl indicates no pronounced additions or changes. Some French manufactured goods may have found their way into Pueblo homes, but it is more likely that such items were retained by the Hispanicized population.

Sociopolitical Changes.—The Pueblos had not endured strict mission discipline and punishments in the seventeenth century for naught. They had been impressed by the coercive techniques of the Spaniards

Spanish force
techinques

removal of transitional
people

and now began to employ them on their own people to enforce adherence to traditional Pueblo customs and practices. Indeed, the very officers, the fiscales and War Captains, who were charged with enforcing church discipline also compelled village members to adhere to Pueblo folkways. Offenders were punished by a variety of methods learned from their Spanish oppressors: whipping at the whipping-post, placing in stocks, standing upright in a circle, hanging by the arms from a roof beam, and other methods which are clearly of Spanish derivation. Witch trials and hangings, which were so common among their Hispanicized neighbors, were also adopted by the Pueblos. The Pueblos reasoned that only a "witch" would refuse to participate in a native dance or ceremony which was designed for the well-being of the entire community. The most extreme form of punishment was confiscation of land, house, and property. Those who suffered this final penalty were highly Hispanicized individuals and families who then moved into a community of settlers or into a genízaro village. Some of these malcontents undoubtedly remained and eventually became reconciled to Pueblo culture. Those who left removed a source of friction and change and thereby permitted the persistence of Pueblo culture in essentially its traditional form.

Pueblo Values.—The observations made by the friars amply demonstrate that the spiritual values of Catholicism were but imperfectly internalized, if at all. Pueblo values remained essentially aboriginal; indeed to this day, Pueblo Indians differ most profoundly from their neighbors in this area of their culture. During the period under review here, even the external acts, such as attendance at Mass, prayers, confession, participation in Church procession and the like, appear to have been observed only because of the threat of punishment.

Compartmentalization.—There is abundant evidence in the records of the eighteenth century that Pueblo indigenous practices were continuing with full force. It is interesting, however, that none of the reports in the latter part of the century mention masked dances or the exorcistic rites of the medicine societies. Of significance, too, is the fact that the descriptions of the dances reveal no Catholic elements or patterns which impressed the observers. That the Catholic church and Catholic ritual were distinct and separate from native ceremonialism is also clear from the reports of the missionaries. We may conclude that the Pueblos were already successfully concealing the esoteric rites of their ceremonial life and that the Pueblo leaders were insisting on the purity of indigenous practices, even in those ceremonies performed for general observation. It is evident, therefore, that compartmentalization had been fully established by the latter part of the eighteenth century. Compartmentalization was an obvious accommodating device which permitted the Indians to carry on their indigenous cultural practices behind a façade of activities acceptable or at least tolerable to Spanish authorities. We will discuss this phenomenon more fully in the concluding section.

Period IV: Anglo-American Intrusion[21]
CONDITIONS OF CONTACT, 1804–1900

This period covers the time between the arrival of the first Americans[22] and the definitive establishment of United States governmental supervision over the Pueblos. Although New Mexico became a part of the Republic of Mexico in 1821 and the United States took over the region in 1846, the amicable, but arms-length relations between the Hispanicized population and the Pueblos remained essentially unchanged. The few Anglo-Americans who entered New Mexico prior to the American occupation of New Mexico identified themselves with the Spanish "upper class" and often married into this group. Until 1850 the pressure on Pueblo lands had been minimal, and there was no conflict between the old residential populations or with the newcomers. Indeed, as we shall see, Hispanos and Pueblos were beginning to co-operate in a number of activities a decade or so before the American occupation. After the mid-century, however, the steadily increasing Hispanicized population and the influx of Anglo-Americans into the territory began to present difficulties. The pressure on Pueblo lands was the chief problem. In addition, the U.S. government's protective measures on the Indians and the special treatment the Pueblos were receiving began to set the Pueblos against both Anglo-Americans and the Hispanicized people.

Hispanos.—The dominant group in terms of population during this century was the "Hispano." This population, representing the people

[21] The main sources used for this period are the following: Bancroft 1889; Bloom 1935–38; Brayer 1938; Davis 1938; Carroll and Haggard 1942; Thwaites 1905: Vols. XIX and XX; Twitchell 1912.

[22] A Creole trader, Baptiste Lalande, was the first American citizen to enter New Mexico, in 1804 (Bancroft 1889: 291).

whom we have previously designated as Spanish, colonists, settlers, or the Hispanicized population, emerges with a distinctive culture by the beginning of the century. The term "Hispano" helps to differentiate this group from more recent migrants from Mexico who are also Spanish-speaking but whose way of life differs in many important respects from the Hispanos of New Mexico.

Barreiro (Carroll and Haggard 1942: 31) estimated the population of New Mexico as fifty thousand shortly after Mexican independence. This estimate did not take in the nomadic Indians, but it did include the Pueblo Indians, whose population during the nineteenth century never exceeded ten thousand. If we subtract the Pueblos, we still have forty thousand Hispanos. By 1880 this population had doubled (Bancroft 1889: 723), while the Pueblo population remained about the same (Hodge 1912: 325). The population increase was not by immigration from Mexico, but a local increase from three main sources: (1) natural birth rate, (2) the absorption of the genízaro populations, and (3) the addition of disaffected Pueblo Indians.

By the first quarter of the nineteenth century, through intermarriage among themselves, the Hispanos represented a fairly uniform physical type in which Indian ancestry was marked. There was an "upper class" group who claimed "pure" Spanish ancestry, but in actuality, the "upper class" represented the "ricos" or wealthy strata of the society rather than a group with any legitimate claim for a relatively pure Spanish genealogy. The "ricos" had large herds of sheep and some cattle which grazed over vast areas of north-central and northeastern New Mexico. The sheep were driven annually to markets in Chihuahua and Sonora, bringing in substantial profits to their owners (Thwaites 1905: XIX, 322–23). The bulk of the Hispano population was made up of poorer people, however, who supported themselves on small tracts of irrigated lands along the Rio Grande and its tributaries. These people, along with some Pueblo Indians, supplemented subsistence farming with earnings derived from working for the wealthy class.

The characteristics of Hispano culture are admirably drawn by Hawley and Senter (1946). Although they report conditions among contemporary Hispanos, the deeply rooted nature of the Hispano characteristics they describe suggest that the account would have applied equally well a hundred years ago. The following brief excerpt from Hawley and Senter (1946: 137) outlines the essential nature of Hispano culture:

The patrilineal pattern of village social organization is . . . modeled after the strongly patrilineal system of the church, in which authority comes down from God the Father to the Pope, then to the priests, and then to the fathers of families. As guardian and sponsor to each village, a patron saint received the special veneration of the people; his image is kept in the church and his day is celebrated by a fiesta. In a relatively parallel position in the secular organization is the *patron*, usually the head of a large family and of more wealth, prestige, political power, and experience than the other villagers. In return for their loyalty and support, his duty is to supply them with jobs, aid in emergencies, and proffer advice. He provides their contact with the outside world. . . .

Pueblo-Hispano Relations.—During the nineteenth century the Hispanos were little interested in changing or modifying the life of the Pueblo Indians, and the clergy, too, had withdrawn from intensive missionary work. Indeed the few missionaries in New Mexico had their hands full trying to serve the two populations and did not do justice to either. The inadequacy of the missionary program, and of the spiritual welfare of the Catholic people generally, during the first half of the nineteenth century is well described by Pino and Barreiro. Pino, a representative to the Spanish Cortes, reports in his *Exposición* of 1812 (Carroll and Haggard 1942: 50–51) that the 26 Indian pueblos and 102 Hispano settlements in New Mexico were served by only twenty-two friars. Pino told of the long distances between the pueblos where the missionaries resided and the Hispano settlements, a serious impairment to meeting the religious needs of the people. He reported that because of the tremendous distance to Durango, the bishopric, no bishop had visited the province for about fifty years. Pino made a plea for the establishment of a special bishopric for New Mexico and the construction of a college and primary schools. Two decades later Barreiro was even more emphatic about the deplorable religious situation in New Mexico, and for the Pueblo Indians, specifically he reported:

The religious care of these pueblos rests in the hands of the missionaries of the province of the Holy Gospel of Mexico; unfortunately, however, there exists the most doleful neglect because only five of the pueblos (out of twenty listed) have missionary fathers. If the government does not take active steps to remedy this evil, the vacant missions will never be filled, and the salvation of the souls of these unfortunate Indians shall continue, as it has for a long time, to be woefully neglected. (Carroll and Haggard 1942: 29.)

The conditions described by Pino and Barreiro continued until the American period, when John B. Lamy, bishop of the newly established diocese, reached Santa Fe in 1851. Lamy instituted a series of extensive reforms and launched a progressive program of education. The zealous, but coercive missionary program of the seventeenth-century Franciscan friars was not repeated, however. Lamy's reforms affected and benefited the non-Indian population primarily; for the Pueblos specifically, the missionary program continued essentially unchanged although the missionaries were better informed in Catholic doctrine than formerly.

The Pueblos also received little attention from the Spanish civil authorities during the first half of the nineteenth century. The latter were busy with commerce, troubled with the threat of a Texan or an American invasion and in futile attempts to control the constant ravages of the Apaches and Navahos. These factors, aside from the last, did not affect the Pueblos, and they were happy to be ignored by Spanish and Mexican officialdom. The surge of ceremonial activity which had started in the last century, continued through the Mexican period. With civil and missionary criticism and intervention virtually removed, the Pueblos began to relax their own surveillance measures. Ceremonies which had been restricted to the kivas were once again given in the plazas and open to observation by Hispanos.[23]

Although the Pueblos received little attention from Spanish and Mexican civil administrators and missionaries during this period, their associations with the Hispanos were developing more intimately. The participation of some Pueblo Indians with a segment of the Hispano population in an effort to take over the government of New Mexico in 1837 is illustrative of this close relationship. Albino Perez became the governor of New Mexico in 1835; he was the first governor under the Mexican rule who was not a native-born New Mexican. This fact, plus a rumor that circulated among the poorer Hispanos and Indians that heavy taxes were to be levied upon poultry, dogs, irrigation

[23] See Barreiro's statement on Pueblo Indian ceremonies, Carroll and Haggard 1942: 30.

ditches, and clothing, among other things, brought about a rebellion. An army of Hispanos and Pueblo Indians stormed Santa Fe and killed a number of citizens, including Governor Perez. They then elected one of their own participants, a Taos Pueblo Indian by the name of Jose Gonzales, as the governor of New Mexico. Gonzales' rule was brief; a force of "loyal citizens" under former governor Manuel Armijo recaptured Santa Fe, and Gonzales and several of his associates were captured and shot (Bancroft 1889: 317–19).

The co-operation of Pueblo Indians and Hispanos also manifested itself in the revolt of 1847 against American occupation. According to most historians, these rebels were "lower-class" Mexicans and Indians (Bancroft 1889: 432–37; Hallenbeck 1950: 271–74). This characterization, however, in no way detracts from the group's sincerity and loyalty to Mexican rule and demonstrates the suspicion and distrust of Americans held by a substantial portion of the Hispano and Indian population of New Mexico during this period.

Other examples of an amicable and co-operative relationship between the two peoples during the first half of the nineteenth century, are found in the reports of Pino and Barreiro. Pino speaks of the Pueblos as "hardly different from us" (Carroll and Haggard 1942: 9), while Barreiro reports favorably on the life, temperament, and intelligence of the Pueblos (*ibid.*: 29–30).

After American occupation Hispano-Pueblo relations began to change. The change was not abrupt, as competition for land and the specialized treatment of the Pueblos was not apparent in some areas, at least, until the end of the century. Land disputes which arose during the Mexican period and intensified after Anglo-American occupation were the chief sources of friction between the two peoples. The Spanish crown considered the Pueblo Indians wards and special protective measures were provided to prevent the alienation of their lands. During the seventeenth century Pueblo lands remained in the possession of the Indians, although such lands through the encomienda system and the missionary program provided for the support and economic gain of Spanish civil and church authorities. In the latter part of the eighteenth century the non-aboriginal population began to encroach on Pueblo lands, but since the population remained small the Pueblos did not experience severe deprivations. Difficulties began to

arise in the Mexican period, however, and loomed into enormous proportions after the first half of the nineteenth century.

The treaty of Guadalupe Hidalgo bound the United States to respect the land rights of all former citizens of Mexico, including Pueblo
Indians. A royal cedula published on June 4, 1687, authorizing the
grant of land one league, or 5,000 varas, in each direction became the
fundamental basis for Pueblo land grants in New Mexico. The grant
was four leagues square or 17,712 acres measured from the church.
However, no definite land grants were apparently made to the individual pueblos. Although eleven New Mexico pueblos were found to
possess documents indicating the granting of title to their lands, these
documents were found to be fraudulent in the late nineteenth century,
and the legal basis for pueblo grants reverted back to the royal cedula
of 1687.

When New Mexico became a territory in 1850 and the United
States assumed jurisdiction over Indian affairs, the land grants of virtually all the Pueblos had been invaded. In the beginning, the non-
Indians encroaching on Pueblo lands were Hispanos, but in time
Anglo-Americans also formed a substantial part of the people living
on Pueblo lands. The settlement of Pueblo Indian land disputes was
complicated further by the legal status of the Pueblo Indian. The Indian was a ward of the crown under Spanish rule and became a citizen
under Mexican regime. The United States considered Indians wards of
the government, but the Pueblos being a sedentary people and already
citizens, presented a special problem. The legal status of the Pueblo
Indian remained undefined until 1913, although before the turn of the
century he had begun to receive the specialized services provided for
other Indians in the United States. Non-Indians on Pueblo lands took
the position that since the Pueblos were citizens under Mexican rule,
with all the rights and privileges of citizens, they could therefore sell
or otherwise dispose of their land as they saw fit. The decisions of the
territorial courts upheld this argument; furthermore the courts also
declared that the non-intercourse acts of 1834 pertained only to wards
of the government, and since the Pueblos were citizens these acts did
not apply to the Pueblo Indians. The acts of 1834 were designed to
protect Indians and Indian land and prohibited settlers from entering
or making settlements on Indian reservations. The attorneys for the
government and the Indians tried repeatedly to change the decisions

of the territorial courts. The problem became further complicated when the United States Supreme Court in the Joseph case, in 1876, ruled that the Pueblo Indians had complete title to their lands and could therefore dispose of them to whomsoever they pleased.[24]

The decision of the United States Supreme Court in the Sandoval case in 1913 finally reversed the position taken by the territorial courts and placed the Pueblos in the same status as other Indians:

The people of the Pueblos, although sedentary rather than nomadic in their inclinations and disposed to peace and industry, are nevertheless Indians in race, customs, and domestic government, always living in separate and isolated communities, adhering to primitive modes of life, largely influenced by superstition and fetishism, and chiefly governed according to the crude customs inherited from their ancestors. They are essentially a simple, uninformed, and inferior people.[25]

This decision made it clear that the Pueblos could not alienate their land and that they were entitled to reclaim lands legally sold. The control of Pueblo lands was now in the hands of Congress and only an act of Congress could change the situation. The non-Indian settlers, mostly Hispanos, were dismayed. The former friendly relations between the two peoples were now severely strained. As a champion of the non-Indian settlers, Senator Holm O. Bursum of New Mexico introduced into the Senate of the Sixty-seventh Congress a bill to quiet title to lands within the Pueblo land grants. The Bursum bill, however, contained provisions which would allow clear title to landholdings for the non-Indians. The Bursum bill was defeated, but only after a long and concerted fight on the part of the friends of the Indians. In the forefront of the fight were the New Mexico Association on Indian Affairs and the general federation of Women's Clubs. The leaders of the fight were Mrs. Stella M. Atwood, Mr. Francis C. Wilson, legal counsel, and Mr. John Collier, who later became Commissioner of Indian Affairs.

The Pueblo Lands Act of 1924 provided the means by which a final solution was made of non-Indian claims to land on Pueblo grants. A commission known as the Pueblo Lands Board was established to review the status of all claims within the Pueblo grants. This board carefully reviewed the value of both land and improvements and com-

---

24 *United States* vs. *Joseph,* 94 U.S. 619.

25 *United States* vs. *Sandoval,* 231 U.S. 28.

pensated either claimants or Indians for lands lost. The special attorney for the Indians and the superintendent of the United Pueblos Agency were charged with the task of clearing the Indian lands of all persons who had no right upon them. This enormous task was completed in the mid-1930's, and a land controversy that had started over two hundred years before was finally settled.

We have gone beyond the period under consideration in order to present the land claims disputes to their culmination in the present century. These disputes were undoubtedly the primary factors that began to set the two populations apart. The breach widened toward the end of the century, particularly as the United States government made special services available to the Indians. The establishment of free schools and hospitals for the Indians and the assignment of "farmers" to teach the Pueblos improved methods of farming stirred bitter feelings of resentment in the Hispanos. The rural Hispanos, particularly, lived in a manner that hardly differed from that of the Pueblos in its economic and rural aspects. It was, therefore, difficult for the Hispanos to understand the separate treatment which the Pueblos received—a situation which could only be interpreted as discriminatory. The change in ethnic group status ratings was also disturbing to the Hispanos. The Pueblos had previously occupied the lowest stratum in the social scale, while the rural or poor Hispanos were just below the upper class of "ricos." Anglo-Americans and some of the ricos now formed the top stratum, but the masses of Hispanos were relegated to the same level as the Indians by the newcomers who were not always able to differentiate between the two peoples.

Pueblo–Anglo-American Relations.[26]—Only two years after the American occupation of New Mexico, James S. Calhoun was appointed Indian agent of the territory of New Mexico. He was also given the additional duties of territorial governor in 1851, but the offices were again separated in 1857. Calhoun wanted to establish reservations for the Indians immediately, but various matters, particularly the attempts to quell the nomadic Indian uprisings and the Civil War interfered. Pueblo land grants were not assigned or confirmed until the 1860's. While the reservation policy was rationalized as a measure to prevent white exploitation of the Indian, the main reason

[26] This section has been compiled primarily from Bancroft 1889, Bloom 1935–38, and Davis 1938.

for the policy was to protect the person and property of the white settler and to open up lands for settlement.

In New Mexico the reservation policy was complicated by the fact that much of the land was already occupied by a fairly large Hispano population and Pueblo Indians. Further, the Pueblos, though Indians, were sedentary farmers and already had lands assigned to them which the United States was obligated to respect under the provisions of the treaty of Guadalupe Hidalgo. These complications brought about the land controversy already discussed and resulted eventually in defining the status of the Pueblos in terms of other United States Indians.

Nevertheless, before the status of the Pueblo Indians was specifically determined, special services provided for other Indians were extended to the Pueblos. By 1869 Indian agents, called "farmers," were established for each of the pueblos. The duties of the "farmer" consisted in teaching the Indians better farming methods and in acting as a link between the Pueblos and the Indian agent in Santa Fe. Government funds were also made available for the construction of irrigation ditches, dams, and wells. In 1881 a boarding school in Albuquerque was established primarily for Pueblos, while primary schools began to function in many of the Indian pueblos from 1872 forward. Half of the salaries of the teachers in the Pueblo villages was met by the government and half by various Protestant denominations.

The condition of the Pueblos for the period between 1870 and 1885 is aptly summarized by Bancroft (1889: 741–42):

The Pueblos (including Zuni) may be regarded as having increased from about 8,500 to somewhat over 9,000 (from 1870 to 1885). They are still the same peaceable and inoffensive, industrious, simple, credulous and superstitious people that they have always been. In their character and primitive manner of life there has been no essential change. They were neglected during this later period by the priests, and the work of the Protestant missionaries has but slightly affected them; though at Laguna a body of so-called Protestants became strong enough to engage in certain controversies. Except in paying an agent's salary, appropriating $10,000 in 1871–2 for implements, and paying a part of teachers' wages, the government did nothing for them, and they have given the military and civil authorities no trouble. . . . In education, from about 1873, earnest efforts were made by the Presbyterians aided by the government; and schools were established at several pueblos and with considerable success, especially at Laguna, Zuni, and Jemes. Some 20 children were also sent to Carlisle, Pennsylvania, to be taught; and in 1881 an Indian boarding-school was founded at Albuquerque, where in later years over 100 pupils from all the tribes were gathered. . . .

During the nineteenth century contacts between Pueblos and Anglo-Americans were restricted mainly to Protestant missionaries and government agents. Such. relations appear not to have been frequent or intensive, but were essentially friendly. The Protestant missionaries used little or no coercion, at least in the beginning, to convert the Pueblos. They approached the Indians cautiously, afraid that an abrupt, bold technique might result in rejection. In almost every case, missionaries were permitted to remain in the pueblos because of their additional roles as teachers. Much of the opposition to Protestant missionaries in the pueblos came from Catholic priests who resented competition in a field over which they claimed priority. Protestant missionaries claimed that the priests were opposed to education, but the competition for Pueblo converts was undoubtedly the answer to the conflict between the two sets of missionaries. The Pueblos did not involve themselves in controversy; they remained nominally Catholic and steadfast Pueblos.

In addition to missionaries and government employees there was a small, but increasing, number of tourists who came to the Pueblo country. By 1881 two railway lines had entered New Mexico. The Atchison, Topeka and Santa Fe line ran conveniently within sight of the pueblos south of Santa Fe, while the narrow gauge Denver and Rio Grande road went near most of the Tewa pueblos in the north. John C. Bourke noted in his journal (Bloom 1937: 69) the following humorous remark he overheard at an inn in Pojoaque in 1881:

Mrs. Boquet, while I was eating supper, described with much vivacity the behavior of the American tourists who in shoals and swarms are now invading the Rio Grande valley: why, said she, do you believe me—they will buy everything from these Indians and an old Indian woman said to me yesterday—"what curious people these Americans are, one has just bought the stone which covered my chimney (i.e. to regulate the draught). What could he want with it?"

Bourke, himself, was collecting museum pieces and was on a special assignment, investigating the manner and customs of the Pueblos. It is interesting that he found the Pueblos no more willing to impart information about their religious beliefs and customs than at present.

Pueblo Relations with Other Indians.—The fairs at Taos and Abiquiu with Comanches and Utes, respectively, passed into history some-time during the Mexican period. The American monopoly of Plains Indian trade and the development of commerce on the Santa Fe trail stopped the flow of French goods via the Comanche. The prohibition of slavery during the Mexican period put an end to the other impor-tant commodity traded at the fairs, and a source of close contact be-tween the Hispanos, Pueblos, Utes, and Comanches disappeared.

Apaches and Navahos remained enemies to Pueblos[27] virtually throughout the period, but a lively trade went on with Comanches until about 1880. Some Pueblo Indians made annual trips into the Plains country to camp, visit, and hunt buffalo with Comanches and other Plains tribes. Individual Pueblo men also occasionally became *Comancheros*. This term was applied to Hispanos who carried on trade with Plains Indians, particularly Comanches. The contacts were apparently close and eagerly anticipated by both peoples. Old resi-dents of the pueblos as recently as a decade or two ago had nostalgic memories of sojourns into the Plains country. These relations became cemented into "friend-friend" associations and reciprocal visits con-tinued until the 1870's. The destruction of the buffalo and the placing of the Plains Indians on reservations abruptly broke up these amicable relations.

Toward the end of the century Pueblo Indian students in the board-ing schools were beginning contacts with Navahos, Apaches, Coman-ches and other Indians on a new plane and in a new environment. These relations did not affect Pueblo life in the nineteenth century to any appreciable degree, but they became important in our final period.

Population.—Pueblo population fell to an all-time low in the 1850's to about 7,000 but had gained again by the end of the nineteenth cen-tury to 9,026 (Hodge 1912: 325). Both figures include Zuni but not the Hopi. This is true of other census figures given in this paper, ex-cept where otherwise specified. Zuni population ranged between 1,500 and 2,000 from the Pueblo Revolt of 1680 to 1900. The low popula-tion figure at mid-century was probably due mainly to movement of disaffected Pueblo Indians into Hispano settlements which appear to have increased in the period just before American occupation.

---

27 Zuni and Jemez pueblos were perhaps exceptions; these pueblos apparently es-tablished friend-friend relations before the end of the nineteenth century with these tribes, Zuni with Navaho and Jemez with both Navaho and Apache. See also E. Z. Vogt's discussion of "guest-friend" relationships, below.

PUEBLO CULTURE ABOUT 1900

Village and House Patterns.—The number and location of Pueblo villages remained essentially the same as in the previous period. Some villages, notably Cuyumungue and Jacona were absorbed by Hispanos, while Pojoaque, although drastically reduced in numbers, survived with a few families into the twentieth century. Of interest is that the genízaro villages of Tomé, Abiquiu, and Belen became a part of the general Hispano population during this period. At the end of the nineteenth century the Pueblos were slowly increasing in numbers, but distinctly separated, geographically and socioculturally, from a rapidly growing Hispano population.

The following quotation from Bourke's journal reveals Pueblo architectural forms for the late nineteenth century (Bloom 1935: 313):

... We observed on our way that the chimneys of the houses were made of eathenware pots, placed one upon another and coated with mud, that upon the roofs in nearly all cases were bake-ovens, and that to enter any house it was necessary first to ascend a ladder to the roof of the first story and then descend to the living rooms ... the walls were not, as with us, flush with the front walls of the edifice. They receded in such a manner as to leave a platform in front; this was the roof of the first story and was formed of round pine logs, covered with small branches and afterwards plastered smoothly with mud.

Architectural changes were not pronounced, but the following innovations were apparent: an increasing number of windows of both selenite[28] and glass; doors beginning to compete with ladders for entrance from the outside; and the appearance of large, one-story rooms (Bloom 1935–38: 218).

Material and Technological Changes.—The Pueblos remained intensive farmers throughout the period. There was no change in crops or agricultural techniques, but superior United States manufactured tools such as plows, shovels, hoes, rakes, and pitchforks were beginning to make their appearance. These items were furnished by the government and eagerly taken over by the Pueblos. Government construction of irrigation dams and ditches was also an important innovation and added to agricultural efficiency and increased production.

[28] Transparent micaceous material, mined aboriginally in various parts of New Mexico.

Bourke's journal for the summer and fall of 1881 (Bloom 1935–38) mentions abundant crops and general prosperity for all the Pueblos.

Weaving, except cotton sashes, was discontinued either in the preceding period or early in the nineteenth century. These techniques were pursued intensively under the forceful policies of civil and church authorities and when the hold of these officials was relaxed, the Pueblos stopped weaving.

Socioceremonial Organization and Values.—Bourke's entries in his

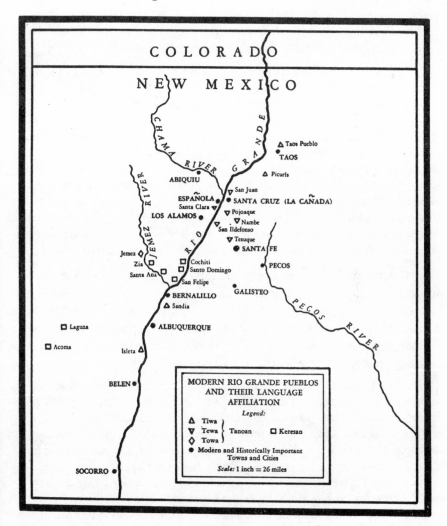

MAP 5

journal reveal tightly integrated, self-sustaining Pueblo communities living a full ceremonial life. In all the pueblos, kivas showed signs of active use—in contrast, for example, to the mission churches, several of which were in ruins. Bourke observed the remains of a "council fire" in some of the kivas, clear evidence that they had been used recently for secret rites. Bourke also witnessed a lively Corn or Tablita dance at Santo Domingo, where the Indians performed in full regalia and with religious fervor.

Catholic and Hispanicized values appear to be no stronger or more deeply internalized during this period than in the preceding one. Bourke's observations on the subject are worth quoting:

> An outward compliance with the requirements of law is never a difficult matter to effect. The eradication of ideas rooted in the traditions of centuries and entwined with all that a nation holds lovable and sacred is beyond the decree of a Council or the order of a military Commander. Unable to practice their ancient rites in public, the Pueblos cling to them in secret, and cling to them all the more tenaciously because the double halo of danger and mystery now surrounded them. The Pueblos became hypocrites; they never became Catholics. Instances without number could possibly be adduced to those among them who sloughed off the exuviae of Paganism; or of others again who modified early teachings by ingrafting upon them the doctrines of the missionaries; but the great bulk of the population remained and today remain, Pagan and Anti-Christian. (Bloom 1936: 262.)

That a strict watch was maintained over all members of a pueblo not to reveal ceremonial secrets was evident by the reception Bourke received everywhere. He was closely watched and very little of Pueblo beliefs and customs was revealed, except marginal and false information to satisfy Bourke's avid curiosity. His experiences led him to make the following remark:

> The Rio Grande Pueblos have become so shy and so timorous that duplicity and dissimulation are integral features of their character and in all conversations with strangers, especially such as bear upon their religion or their prehistoric customs and their gentile divisions, they maintain either an absolute reserve, or, if that be broken down, take a malicious pleasure in imparting information for no other object than to mislead and confuse. I had prepared myself for such an experience and determined that nothing should cause me to lose patience in the performance of my task; feeling that if at one pueblo I might be completely baffled, at another better fortune might await me. . . . (Bloom 1936: 257.)

Despite Bourke's hope that he would continue to make progress he left the Pueblo area with no more than a list of clan names for each village. Bourke's description of the externals of Pueblo life are excellent, but his meager ethnographic data are no contribution to Pueblo ethnology.

Final Period V: Anglo-American Dominance[29]
CONDITIONS OF CONTACT, 1900–1955

More profound changes in Pueblo culture occurred during this period than in the previous three hundred years. By 1881 railroads linked the Pueblo area with the rest of the United States. Railroads brought a steady stream of Anglo-American residents, who settled along the Rio Grande. The newcomers complicated the land problem already discussed, but they also upset the traditional economy. Anglo-Americans introduced two vital economic measures: a credit system and later a cash economy. Whereas, Pueblo economy was primarily subsistence farming in the pre-American period, the establishment of trading posts in the latter part of the nineteenth century involved Pueblo Indians in a credit system (S. D. Aberle 1948: 7).

The shift from a credit to a cash economy came later as the result of automobile travel which brought hundreds of tourists into the Pueblo area, who bought pottery and other handicrafts directly from the Indians, paying in cash. In the early thirties the U.S. Indian Service launched a construction program which brought the Indians into fuller participation with a cash economy (*ibid.*: 22). World War II opened up jobs all over the United States and brought dependency checks to the families of those in the armed services. The involvement of the Rio Grande Pueblos in wage work has continued since the war. For the most part, Pueblo Indians work locally and return to their pueblos in the evening and on weekends, but an increasing number are beginning to be absent seasonally on jobs at considerable distances from their homes.

With one or two exceptions, Pueblo communities continue in a farming economy, but small landholdings and the attraction of wage work are threatening the traditional economic system. These economic changes, plus frequent absenteeism and an increasing non-

[29] The following sources were used mainly in compiling this section: S. D. Aberle 1948; Bunker 1956; Collier 1947, 1949; Crane 1928; La Farge 1942; Lange 1953; Parsons 1939.

Indian population, have affected Pueblo culture profoundly. The specific relations which have developed between the Pueblos and their neighbors and the changes in Pueblo culture, will occupy us in following pages.

Inter-Pueblo and Other Indian Relations.—Intimate relations between members of different pueblos continue. Contacts are especially friendly on the annual saint's day feast, but intermittent contacts go on the year around. Vogt (1955: 820–39) and Lange (1952: 19–26) have presented detailed accounts of the Pueblo fiesta system.

Frequent interaction between Pueblos and other Indians occurs in boarding schools and in the jobs made available by the federal government in construction work. These situations bring individuals of different pueblos together, but they also provide relations between Pueblos and other Indians from distant tribes.

Other occasions in which Pueblo Indians meet Indians from other tribes occur in inter-Indian fairs and celebrations like the Gallup Intertribal Ceremonial and the Flagstaff Pow-wow. Pueblo-Navaho contacts, which are perhaps the most frequent, occur also on Pueblo feast days and in the urban centers of Albuquerque, Santa Fe, Gallup, and Phoenix. As the result of these contacts numerous intermarriages have taken place with Pueblos and other Indians; the non-Pueblo spouse sometimes comes to the pueblo to live, but the more typical pattern is for the couple to move into an off-reservation town and for the husband to take up unskilled or semi-skilled wage work. These movements are adding a significant Indian population to off-reservation towns.

The participation of Pueblo individuals in this network of inter-Indian relations is important in Pueblo acculturation. There are today greater opportunities for the exchange of ideas and information which affect not only the groups living away from the pueblos, but which also filter back to the home communities. Despite the efforts of Pueblo authorities to insulate their communities against the introduction of alien practices and ideas, these influences are modifying the traditional Pueblo way of life.

Pueblo-Hispano Relations.—Hispanos continue to be the closest neighbors of the Pueblos. Virtually all of the Pueblo villages are surrounded by Hispano communities whose populations far outnumber them. The breach between Hispanos and Pueblos noted in the previous section has widened since the turn of the century, as succeeding generations of Pueblo Indians have come more and more under direct contact with the dominant American culture.[30] The Pueblos have been quick to pick up negative Anglo-American attitudes toward Hispanos and Mexicans and regard themselves as in a superior status position. In some pueblos, Catholicism has been identified with Hispanos and in recent years a considerable number of Pueblos have left the church to embrace various Protestant sects (Dozier n.d.). Where Hispanicization set in early, intimate Hispano-Pueblo relations appear to be enduring. This is true at San Juan (Dozier n.d.) and at Cochiti (Goldfrank 1927: 9; Lange 1953: 681) where a number of Hispano-Pueblo marriages have taken place. But because of the conditions which keep Hispanos and Pueblos apart, it is unlikely that the two peoples will find a common meeting ground. If the process of cultural leveling continues, it is probable that each will assimilate separately into the dominant American culture. *has this happened?*

Pueblo–Anglo-American Relations.—One year after statehood in 1913, the population of New Mexico was reported as 300,000 (Crane 1928: 290). This figure included both Hispanos and Anglo-Americans in approximately equal proportions. New Mexico's population has doubled since 1913 and Anglo-Americans are now believed to exceed Hispanos.

Permanent Anglo-American residents, whether farmers, business people or in the professions, have little association with Pueblo Indians and only rarely attend Pueblo ceremonies. In their villages, Pueblo Indians come in contact most often with tourists, artists, and Indian Service personnel. Outside of the Pueblo communities, Pueblo Indians, as individuals, may deal directly with Anglo-Americans in the towns, usually in employer-employee relationships, but otherwise contacts are restricted to the groups just mentioned.

The visits of tourists are transient and of short duration, but there are numerous instances of a casual first visit developing into an enduring friendship between an individual Pueblo family and a family from a distant part of the country. Such friendships stimulate repeated visits. These friends are frequently drawn into siding with their Indian friends in petty disputes within the pueblo, a practice which has often

---

[30] For an excellent account of Hispano relations with other ethnic groups in New Mexico see E. K. Francis 1956: 86–87.

aggravated the trouble rather than helped matters. In a few instances, however, friends have helped the Pueblos tremendously in problems which affected them all. Thus the friends of the Indians, together with artists and writers,[31] joined the Pueblos in defeating the Bursum bill in the early twenties, which would have divested the Pueblos of most of their land.

The Bureau of Indian Affairs has probably affected the Pueblos more profoundly than any other source of change during the period under review. Before the mid-twenties Indian administration was committed to transforming Indian communities into variants of the dominant American culture as quickly as possible. After 1928 the situation was reversed, Indian administrators were to respect Indian ways of life, but assist the Indian in achieving equal footing in economy, education, and health.[32] Two men, Leo Crane and John Collier, exemplified these contrasting viewpoints. Both were intimately acquainted with the Pueblos. Crane was agent of the Pueblos from 1919 to 1929, while Collier served as Commissioner of Indian Affairs from 1933 to 1945. Crane accepted without question the superiority of Anglo-American culture and believed that the future of the Indian lay in cultural assimilation to Anglo-American standards. In a book he wrote about his experiences among the Pueblos, he briefly outlines his objectives as Indian agent:

. . . I had studied with considerable interest the history of the Pueblo Indians, and could look forward to the job of advancing their well-being. It seemed to me that they had a future, whereas it would be generations before the Hopi and the Navajo, as tribes, would advance clearly within the zone of civilization according to our standards. And however one views the Indian, with whatever of sentiment or admiration or affection, he cannot be diverted from laboring toward this proposed destination. (Crane 1928: 6.)

Collier propounded a philosophy of cultural pluralism and worked toward the reinstatement and perpetuation of Indian societies as differentiated cultures in the stream of American life. He believed with almost fanatical zeal that societies like the Pueblos could influence

[31] For an excellent discussion of the role of the artist in championing Indian cultures, see Spicer 1957: 222–26.

[32] Federal Indian policies appear again to have changed since 1950; these more recent changes are not considered in this paper.

Western cultures to recapture the serenity and meaningfulness of life which he felt the Pueblos possessed:

. . . how could [an industrial world] have a society anew, and freedom and power in and through it? . . . The question and answer of the Pueblos ring like bells in the heart of every human child, and ring like bells muffled by many veils and almost drowned in many noises, yet audible, in the foresworn deeps of the adults of our epoch which is rushing to its terminus. They tell that happy man, unwounded earth, and long, endless future can be had by our race still. (Collier 1949: 60.)

The Collier regime, however, brought able men into the Indian Service with more tempered notions about Indian societies and sound administrative procedures. Oliver La Farge's appraisal of the Collier administration by contrasting it with previous administrations is germane here:

For about a hundred years the Bureau of Indian Affairs, charged with the protection and advancement of the original inhabitants of the United States, functioned hit or miss, with good intentions, sometimes, by trial and error always, with a total disregard of everything that the steady march of scientific knowledge had to offer. In this country and abroad, medicine, anthropology, education, sociology, psychology, changed the whole thinking of civilized mankind, but the Indian Bureau ignored them all. The United States became a leader in many lines of knowledge and practice which bore directly upon the Indian problem—in public health, social service, education, and anthropology, to name a few. Bureaus dealing with all of these existed in our government. But it was a startling thing in the early 1920's to see how utterly the Indian Bureau remained insulated against all this, to see how it continued to exist and work not even in the nineteenth but in the eighteenth century . . . today, under Commissioner Collier's administration, a completely changed Indian Bureau is not only calling upon science for all that it can give but is also, through its testing of science in practical application to human life, contributing to our knowledge.

. . . We the United States, have undertaken a serious experiment. Belatedly, we have set out to help some four hundred thousand people—reared in a totally different culture under utterly different circumstances, the remnant that has survived our aggression—to adapt themselves to our culture with benefit to themselves and to us. (La Farge 1942: vii–ix.)

Among the Pueblos, the principle of self-government was applied with earnestness during the Collier regime. This basic philosophy of the new administration contrasted sharply with administrative policies of former Bureau officials. Agent Crane exemplified the older approach to Indian affairs. He alternately coerced and threatened the Pueblos toward a prescribed goal which he considered to be his "job of advancing their well-being.". On many occasions, like the proverbial "White Father," he fought the battles of the Pueblos for them (see Crane 1928: 149–80). Crane was openly disdainful of conservative pueblos like Santo Domingo, but exhibited genuine fondness and admiration for "progressive" Isleta.

A striking contrast to Crane's views and administrative activities is offered by Robert Bunker, an advocate of self-government and a Bureau official among the Pueblos during Collier's administration. Bunker also wrote a book. His views, although largely personal, illustrate rather dramatically policy differences between the Collier regime and former administrations. A quotation from Bunker's book will highlight the principles of self-government as he interpreted them:

Federal bureaucrats have done much "for" the Indians. Indians today are healthier and better educated than their fathers. Commissioner John Collier, in the 1930's gave them time and the confidence they desperately needed to learn to resist undue pressures. But the bureaucrats—and men of great good will among them—never got together on the next obvious step. They never found out where the Indians want to begin tackling their own problems. Indian action today is most often in spite of Indian Service, simply because Indian Service prejudges what "the Indians can do." I had to learn to look at Indians as individuals who might shape their own lives or who might, disastrously, not. (Bunker 1956: 11.)

The Pueblos have not digested the principles of self-government, and most Pueblo communities are not conscious that important or radical changes came about in the management of their affairs as a result of Collier's administration. A few communities in trouble, pueblos which had departed from the old cacique rule, benefited from the help of Bureau officials. Among these pueblos are Santa Clara and Isleta, where community government now operates along secular lines and whose political officials are "elected" by the people.

More comprehensible to the Pueblos are the Bureau's changed policies regarding the suppression of Indian customs and ceremonial activities which had characterized the administrations before 1928. The new regime permitted traditional authorities to relax controls that safeguard Pueblo ceremonial life. But the Pueblos *have not abandoned* these controls. The conservative communities are ever prepared to tighten social control mechanisms in the event of any threat to their indigenous way of life. The individual histories of Pueblo communities demonstrate this process vividly. When there are repeated violations of Pueblo patterns of behavior which endanger the ceremonial activities of the community, the War Captains and their assistants, the Pueblo gestapo, are alerted and an iron curtain descends over the pueblo. Within the village all but the rigid conformists are suspect and any deviant behavior is dealt with promptly and severely by a variety of social control measures.[33]

Population and Community Patterns.—The increase in Rio Grande Pueblo population in the last fifty years, although not so spectacular as the Navaho, is still impressive. Hodge's census figures (1912: 325) in 1901–5 for Rio Grande Pueblos exclusive of Laguna, Acoma and Zuni totaled 6,389. In 1950 these pueblos had a population of 11,470 (Tax 1956), an increase of almost 50 per cent in fifty years. This is almost completely by natural increase, since Pueblo communities strongly prohibited marriage with outsiders until recently. Even today, a marriage with a non-Pueblo Indian is looked upon with disfavor in the conservative pueblos. Thus, although spouses from other Indian tribes are ordinarily permitted to become members of the pueblo, the disapproval of marrying outsiders has restricted marriage choices to village members or to other Pueblo Indians. During the war and since, a number of marriages with Anglo-Americans have taken place in the less conservative pueblos like Santa Clara and Isleta, but the traditional pueblos have remained essentially endogamous. As Hispanos and Pueblos grew apart because of the factors already discussed, the movement of disaffected Pueblo Indians into the Hispano population decreased and has now virtually stopped. Today individual Pueblo Indians and families dissatisfied with life in the pueblo move to urban areas in the Southwest. The conservative pueblos still expel individuals and families who refuse to conform to traditional customs and practices. Only in the pueblos where cacique rule has been replaced by an elective or representational governmental system may individ-

[33] See Adair and Vogt (1949) for an excellent example of this process in the response of Zuni Pueblo to returning World War II veterans.

uals and families who refuse to participate in communal ceremonies remain in the pueblo. Santa Clara, Isleta, and perhaps Nambé are the only pueblos where the traditional leaders no longer exercise religious supervision over their members. In other pueblos like Taos (Fenton 1957; Siegel 1949), Cochiti (Lange 1953: 679, 691), and San Ildefonso, a progressive faction is challenging the right of the traditional leaders to exert political authority over the whole pueblo and to enforce ceremonial participation on all members of the pueblo. Marriage with a non-Pueblo Indian or white usually results in the confiscation of the Pueblo member's land and property and thus forces the couple out of the community. Formerly, nonconformists were individuals and families who came under the influence of Hispano neighbors and the Catholic Church; today, American culture and Protestant sects produce nonconformists. But the number of disaffected Indians alienated from individual pueblos is small, as evidenced by a steadily increasing Pueblo population. Pueblo culture is strong and enduring and Pueblo radicals often choose to conform to the demands of traditional leaders rather than to leave a pueblo (Crane 1928: 238–56). Among Pueblo Indians the rewards of community living are highly prized and in times of trouble all alternatives to keep the village together are explored (Bunker 1956: 37–52; French 1948; Dozier n.d.).

CONTEMPORARY PUEBLO CULTURE

Village and House Patterns.—Pueblo villages are still predominantly of adobe, but the compact village structures are beginning to give way to isolated, single-family dwellings. Multistoried houses are still characteristic of Taos, but in other pueblos only one or two such structures stand as lone remnants rapidly going to ruin. The less conservative villages are beginning new settlement areas where single-family structures have been patterned after American suburban homes, with a garage, yard, lawn, trees, and shrubbery. In these pueblos, but even in evidence in the more conservative villages, are an increasing number of houses whose interior and exterior walls are finished with hard plaster ranging in colors from tans to reds. New houses have three to four spacious rooms and ceilings are of milled lumber beams instead of the traditional round *vigas*. Floors are frequently covered with linoleum, laid either on a packed earth floor or over pine planks. At least a half-dozen pueblos now enjoy electricity. In a larger number of pueblos, water has been piped from wells and tanks to faucets within easy reach of the houses and in an increasing number of homes complete plumbing facilities have been installed.

Material and Technological Changes.—Houses, furniture, and other equipment inside the pueblos have undergone a complete revolution since the turn of the century. The items to be found within a pueblo home do not differ substantially from those encountered in a poorer Anglo-American home in New Mexico. In the pueblos which have electricity and plumbing, the furnishings and appliances of some families would equal those in middle-class American homes. Television antennas resemble a forest of bare trees above Santa Clara pueblo, and television programs have replaced the former gathering of the bilateral kin group to listen to old Tewa stories and legends. The arrangement of material possessions differs in many interesting respects from Anglo-American homes in all the pueblos. Pueblo walls are conspicuously cluttered with large pictures of saints, photographs, and snapshops of friends and relatives. Brightly colored Mexican shawls and blankets are popular coverings for sofas and chairs. It is interesting, however, that the Pueblos' own handicrafts, pottery, beadwork, and the like, are rarely displayed; instead, purchased items such as glass jars, vases, and bowls are used as containers and as decorative objects. A trunk or chest, containing ceremonial and dance paraphernalia, is a typical and prominent possession and provides a sitting place along with manufactured chairs and couches.

Greater adherence to traditional forms of dress distinguish the conservative pueblos from the "progressive" ones.[34] The brightly colored shawl is still much in evidence among girls and women, however, and a number of the old women and old men still wear the characteristic hair styles. Indian dress is distinctive essentially in the array of bright colors in shirts, skirts, and shawls where reds and blues predominate.

Automobiles are rapidly replacing horses and wagons as the mode of travel. Pickup trucks are the most popular of automobile body styles. Horses are in little evidence, although they still perform the bulk of farm work; only the most intensive farmers in such predominantly farming pueblos as Isleta and Sandia use tractors and other mechanical equipment.

Material possessions indicate economic changes among the Pueblos.

[34] See Roediger 1941 for traditional Pueblo dress styles.

While the majority of these Indians are still farmers, wage work and crafts, particularly pottery, have become important additional sources of income. Cash purchases and sales have now completely replaced the former practice of bartering and the credit system. Some villages like San Ildefonso and Santa Clara now derive the majority of their income from crafts and wage work. Employment in unskilled and semi-skilled labor has replaced farming as a way of life in these pueblos. Even in the predominately farming pueblos, however, wages from seasonal employment in nearby towns and cities are an important supplement to income.

Other Areas of Culture.—The Pueblos have retained to a remarkable degree the basic outline of the ceremonial and sociopolitical organization presented in our base-line culture. Nevertheless membership in the ceremonial societies has declined and there has been a definite weakening in the influence of traditional leaders. At the present time, sufficient members remain in the important medicine and moiety societies charged with governmental and ceremonial functions to keep the majority of the pueblos operating in the old way. But, as key societies become extinct or membership in them drops to low levels, a change to new patterns of civil and ceremonial organization becomes imperative. Pueblos like Santa Clara and Isleta point the direction in which all pueblos are likely to go. Considerable interaction with non-Indians and particularly intermarriage with outsiders would appear to be prerequisites for the reception of new concepts and practices which would result in fundamental changes. Doubts about the efficacy of the old system in a modern setting and the rise of "conservative" and "progressive" factions provide conditions for a shift from the old to the new.

English is now an important second language, but the native idioms continue to be dominant. Pueblo Indians are purists with regard to their language, a factor related to the phenomenon of compartmentalization. The native language is considered an area of culture that must not be polluted by foreign loans. The past generations of Pueblo speakers were also conversant in Spanish, and, just as they guarded the core of Pueblo ceremonialism against Spanish-Catholic contamination, so also they deleted terms of Spanish origin in the native language. Only a small portion of Pueblo words are of Spanish origin and the majority of these are nominal forms. Keresan and Tanoan morphology and syntax seem not to have been affected by Spanish, nor is there evidence that the phonology of these languages has been modified to any considerable degree (Dozier 1956b; Spencer 1947; Trager 1944). Pueblo speakers are keenly aware of borrowed terms and tend to delete or restrict their usage in the presence of outsiders (Harrington 1907–8: 97; Trager 1944: 144). The coinage of new words and the extension of old meanings to cover new cultural acquisitions are preferred to outright borrowing.

Retention of the native languages and the persistence of the large extended family as the primary unit of socialization, we believe, has tended to foster the continuity of a highly uniform personality structure throughout the Pueblos.[35] Similarly the persistence of a set of essentially indigenous values and moral concepts may be attributed to the continuity of the native languages and the basic unit of socialization. In recent years, particularly in the less conservative communities, the influence of the supernaturals, their impersonators, and the ceremonial priests have diminished, but the languages and the host of relatives involved in socialization have not changed significantly.

Rio Grande Pueblo Compartmentalization.—Compartmentalization, since it is employed in this paper to designate the Rio Grande Pueblo acculturative type, needs more explicit description. The term as used here refers to the presence in Pueblo culture of two mutually distinct and separate socioceremonial systems, each of which contains patterns not found in the other. These two systems are the indigenous and Spanish-Catholic traditions.

The indigenous or native system is an amalgam of Indian elements so thoroughly reworked that it is virtually impossible to trace the derivation of the parts. Several categories arranged in a sacred-profane continuum are identifiable, however. The sacred core of the system consists of the Katcina cult and the secret societies and the rites associated with them. This area of Pueblo ceremonialism is shrouded in secrecy and information regarding it is rigidly guarded. Another cate-

[35] The persistence and stability of indigenous psychological patterns in the acculturative context have also been noted in other American tribes; see especially Hallowell 1951: 112; Mekeel 1936; Spindler 1955. Spindler, however, found that the modal psychological structure of Menominee elite exhibited a psychological transformation toward American norms. His data, he believes, suggest that significant psychological changes occur when the barriers to achievement on the white man's terms are broken down, and the new adaptation thereby becomes rewarding rather than punitive. We would suggest that psychological patterns persist if the language and the basic units of socialization remain undisturbed.

Seems logical

gory of the native system is a set of communal ceremonies under the supervision of medicine societies (Keresan) and moiety societies (Tanoan) which are open to the public. The most popularly known of these ceremonies among whites are the so-called Tablita or Corn dances (Lange 1957). Within the native system, too, are small group dances open to the public, but under the supervision of secret societies like those of hunt, war, and clown. A final category of dances linked with the native system is essentially secular and performed primarily for entertainment. There is no limit to improvisation and to the introduction of novel forms in this last set, whereas such innovations are strongly discouraged and controlled in the other ceremonies. The Indian theme is retained in this final category of ceremonies for the songs and dance patterns exhibit essentially Pueblo or pan-Indian elements.

The Pueblos have not been completely successful in keeping non-Indian elements from invading the areas of native ceremonialism. In recent years, particularly, numerous changes in dress and costuming have taken place. It is remarkable, nevertheless, how much of the indigenous pattern has been retained, and even the casual white visitor is struck by the essentially "Indian" character of the public dances.[36] Of importance for the understanding of Pueblo compartmentalization, however, is not so much the degree to which the Pueblos have succeeded in keeping out foreign invasions, but in the *desire* and the *effort* expended to keep the native system "pure."

Life crisis rites, in the main, fall within the native system. It is significant that information about these practices is carefully guarded, an indication that these patterns belong to the sacred core of Pueblo culture. Certain practices in the life cycle are, of course, Spanish and Catholic; these deal with baptism, confirmation, and the *velorio*, or wake, at the death of an individual. There is no secrecy about these latter customs, and they are freely discussed with whites; indeed, they serve to screen the more esoteric practices. Knowlege of the Spanish language and, in recent years, English, has also proved an effective method for retaining the purity of the native rites which are conducted strictly in the indigenous language.

Coexisting with the native system is a set of introduced patterns of

[36] Compare, for example, Bourke's (1884) account of the Tablita dance in the early 1880's with that of Lange (1957).

Spanish derivation. This system is fitted in with Catholic ritual, such as the Mass, the velorio, and the saint's day celebration, which includes a procession and the erection of a bower in the pueblo plaza to contain the saint images or *santos*. Other important dates observed with processions, prayers, and vespers are: All Soul's Day on November 2 and the Christmas and Lenten seasons. The officers who are responsible for these ceremonies are from the Spanish-imposed civil government organization, primarily the fiscales, sacristans, governor, and War Captains. The ceremonies involve the "horse" or Sandaro dances and the Matachina pageant which are usually performed on important saints' days, frequently alternating with the Tablita-type dances. These dances are believed to "belong" and to have been brought by Montezuma, the mythological god from the south. Ceremonies associated with Montezuma are considered more sacred than activities connected with the Catholic Church, but they remain essentially distinct from the native ceremonial system.

[margin note: actually three levels then]

While there is a separation of Spanish and Indian traditions in the socioceremonial system of the Pueblos, there is no indication of a similar dichotomy in the beliefs, values, and moral concepts of the Indians. Pueblo Indians "explain" and "interpret" the purposes of the native and Spanish-Catholic systems in the same manner. When performed properly, but separately, they are believed to accomplish the same ends: health and well-being for all humanity (Dozier 1956a).

The compartmental model appears not to be satisfactorily adjusted to the incorporation of patterns of Anglo-American derivation. To a large extent, American contact has been experienced primarily in its economic, material, and technological aspects. Under Spanish domination the economy was not changed and material and technological aspects were added rather than compartmentalized. Similarly, under Anglo-American control, material items and techniques have been freely incorporated. Anglo-American contact has, however, brought about drastic economic changes and these are obviously threats to the unity of Pueblo communities, although thus far the conservative pueblos have not been disrupted. Protestantism seriously invaded only Jemez and Zia, and they solved the problem by expelling the Protestant converts. Santa Clara and Isleta may more appropriately indicate the trend in the future. These villages have separated religious and secular functions and remain united primarily on a secular and political level. Protestant members of these pueblos are permitted to live in the village. While a fairly substantial and increasing number appear to have become serious adherents, others switch back and forth, between the Protestant sects and the traditional compartmentalized Pueblo religion. The conservative Pueblos still dominate, however, and in these communities the compartmentalized character of the pueblo continues.

Concluding Discussion

[handwritten annotation: I felt this too in that they did receive some things w/cl.]

There is abundant evidence that the Pueblos were receptive to the borrowing of foreign cultural traits and complexes in the period just prior to Spanish contact. An early exchange of cultural items between the two major linguistic groups in the area is particularly clear. Thus Tanoans gave the moiety concept, perhaps animal and hunt societies to Keresans, while they received in return medicine societies, the Katcina cult, perhaps the clown societies and some notions of the clan. We have given considerable space to the important shift which we believe took place among Keresans, i.e., the movement from a clan to a village-based unit. The factors operative here, we believe, were ecological pressures reinforced by Spanish oppression, which produced a more centralized form of government, but the specific mechanism for giving the village central direction was the incorporation of governmental and religious functions into one or two medicine societies. The choice of medicine societies to integrate the village rather than other possible alternatives suggests the borrowing of a Tanoan pattern. That is, Keresans appear to have equated their own medicine societies with Tanoan governmental-ceremonial moiety societies and then invested them with governmental and ceremonial functions.

There are also many traits which Pueblos and Plains Indians share, such as scalp and war dances, dress and hair styles. These traits are, of course, most abundant in the marginal areas where Plains and Pueblo Indians came most frequently in contact with one another but occur in diffused form in all the villages.

Inter-pueblo cultural exchanges and Plains-Pueblo borrowing appear to be extremely old. The borrowed traits have become so well integrated and reworked among the Pueblos that their original proveniences are difficult to establish with certainty. Cultural exchange between these groups has not stopped. Inter-pueblo borrowing and co-operation is vigorous at present and, within the larger context of pan-Indian cultural exchange, Plains-Pueblo borrowing is a very live process.

There is little doubt that the Pueblos were likewise receptive to Spanish cultural introductions in the initial contact period. But when it became a matter of the complete eradication of their traditional customs and replacement by Spanish-Catholic patterns, the Pueblos resisted, rebelled, and eventually adjusted through the phenomenon we have designated as "compartmentalization." The Pueblos accommodated to Spanish pressures by separating the ceremonial practices which offended the Spaniards and concealing them behind a façade of the imposed Spanish-Catholic patterns.

Spanish efforts to civilize and Christianize the Pueblos have not undermined the locus of Pueblo socialization: the extended family and, more generally, the community itself. The traditional network of kin and community relations have remained essentially undisturbed. Present conditions threaten this area of Pueblo societies, but they have not, except in one or two villages, actually effected reorganization. The socializing units which fashioned Pueblo individuals from the time of initial White contact to the present have thus changed but little. It is not surprising, therefore, that the beliefs, moral concepts, values, and personality structure are highly uniform among the Pueblos and that they contrast sharply with those of their White neighbors.

The persistence of certain cultural complexes in Pueblo culture is easy enough to detect, but we do not hold the belief that these complexes have any innate qualities for stability in themselves. Indeed, our position with respect to persistences generally is that they are explainable in each given case as the result of the nature of the contact situation and the structure of the society. Briefly, among Pueblos, the following broad complexes appear to have extremely deep historical roots: the indigenous ceremonial system; the lexical and morphological forms of the languages; the extended family and the network of interpersonal relations in the community; and finally a system of beliefs, values, and moral concepts together with what may be called the personality structure. Since Spanish contact, Pueblo socioceremonial compartmentalization, particularly the Spanish-Indian dichotomy, appears to have great permanence.

The continuity of the indigenous ceremonial system and its separation and coexistence with the Spanish-Catholic system we attribute to
the forced policies of Spanish civil and church authorities. The retention of indigenous lexical forms and morphological characteristics of
the language may be similarly explained. This contention is reinforced
by the fact that the native system is clearly a syncretism (Herskovits
1938: 38–39) of Pueblo elements and those of Plains Indians and other
tribes.

On the other hand, Pueblo indigenous beliefs, values, and moral
concepts undoubtedly remained because the aboriginal family type
and the old community patterns were not disturbed. The persistence
of a homogeneous Pueblo personality structure may also be attributed
to the continuity of these units. Among the Pueblos the extended
family and the community are the units of socialization. Since they
were not disturbed, they molded the same type of personality structure through the years and continued to produce individuals loyal to
old Pueblo beliefs, values, and moral concepts.

Persistence of gross cultural elements and complexes are thus explained in terms of the situations in which they are found and not in
terms of themselves. A form of religious ritual, a kind of linguistic
morphological structure, a set of beliefs, and the like, may change
quickly or persist over a long period of time, depending on the total
environmental situation which either obstructs or permits continuity.

REFERENCES CITED

ABERLE, S. D.
    1948 *The Pueblo Indians of New Mexico, Their Land, Economy and Civil
          Organization.* American Anthropological Association, *Memoir No. 33.*
ADAIR, JOHN, and EVON Z. VOGT
    1949 "Navaho and Zuni Veterans: A Study of Contrasting Modes of Cul-
          ture Change," *American Anthropologist,* LI, 547–61.
ADAMS, ELEANOR B. (ed.)
    1954 *Bishop Tamaron's Visitation of New Mexico, 1760.* Historical Society
          of New Mexico, "Publications in History," Vol. XV.
ADAMS, ELEANOR B., and FRAY ANGELICO CHAVEZ (eds.)
    1956 *The Missions of New Mexico, 1776.* Albuquerque.
BANCROFT, HUBERT H.
    1889 *The Works of H. H. Bancroft.* Vol. XVII: *History of Arizona and
          New Mexico 1530–1888.* San Francisco.
BANDELIER, A. F.
    1890–92 *Final Report of Investigations among the Indians of the South-
          western United States.* Archaeological Institute of America, *Papers*
          ("American Series"), Vol. III, Part 1, and Vol. IV, Part 2. Cam-
          bridge, Mass.

BENNETT, JOHN
1946 "The Interpretations of Pueblo Culture: A Question of Values," *Southwestern Journal of Anthropology*, II, 361–74.
BLOOM, L. B.
1931 "A Campaign against the Moqui Pueblos," *New Mexico Historical Review*, VI, 158–226.
1935a "A Trade-Invoice of 1638," *New Mexico Historical Review*, X, 242–48.
1935–38 "Bourke on the Southwest," *New Mexico Historical Review*, X, 271–322; XI, 217–82; XII, 41–77; XIII, 192–238.
BOLTON, H. E.
1916 "The Espejo Expedition, 1582–1583," in H. E. Bolton, *Spanish Exploration in the Southwest, 1542–1706*. New York.
BRAYER, H. O.
1938 *Pueblo Indian Land Grants of the "Rio Abajo," New Mexico*. The University of New Mexico, *Bulletin 334*.
BUNKER, ROBERT
1956 *Other Men's Skies*. Bloomington.
BUNZEL, RUTH
1932 *Introduction to Zuni Ceremonialism. Forty-seventh Annual Report*, Bureau of American Ethnology, Washington.
CARROLL, H. BAILEY, and J. VILLASAUA HAGGARD
1942 *Three New Mexico Chronicles: The Exposición of Don Pedro Bautista Pino, 1912; the Ojeada of Lic. Antonio Barréiro, 1832; and the Additions by Jose Augustin de Escudero, 1849*. The Quivera Society, Albuquerque.
COLLIER, JOHN
1947 *The Indians of the Americas*. New York.
1949 *Patterns and Ceremonials of the Indians of the Southwest*. New York.
CRANE, LEO
1928 *Desert Drums: The Pueblo Indians of New Mexico, 1540–1928*. Boston.
DAVIS, W. W. H.
1938 *El Gringo, or New Mexico and Her People*. Santa Fe.
DOZIER, EDWARD P.
n.d. Unpublished field notes on Rio Grande Pueblos.
1954 *The Hopi-Tewa of Arizona*. Berkeley and Los Angeles.
1955 "Forced and Permissive Acculturation," *American Indian*, VII, 38–44.
1956a "The Values and Moral Concepts of Rio Grande Pueblo Indians," in *Encyclopedia of Morals*, VERGILIUS FERM (ed.), pp. 491–504. New York.
1956b "Two Examples of Linguistic Acculturation: The Yaqui of Sonora and Arizona and the Tewa of New Mexico," *Language*, XXXII, 146–57.
DUMAREST, FATHER NOEL
1919 "Notes on Cochiti, New Mexico." E. C. PARSONS (ed.). *Memoirs of the American Anthropological Association*, Vol. VI, No. 3.
EGGAN, DOROTHY
1953 In *Personality in Nature, Society and Culture*. New ed. CLYDE KLUCKHOHN, HARRY H. MURRAY, and DAVID M. SCHNEIDER (eds.). New York.
EGGAN, FRED
1950 *Social Organization of the Western Pueblos*. Chicago.

ELLIS, FLORENCE HAWLEY
  1951a "Pueblo Social Organization and Southwestern Archaeology," *American Antiquity*, XVII, 148–51.
  1951b "Patterns of Aggression and the War Cult in Southwestern Pueblos," *Southwestern Journal of Anthropology*, VII, 177–201.
  1953   "Authoritative Control and the Society System in Jemez Pueblo," *Southwestern Journal of Anthropology*, IX, 385–94.
ESPINOSA, J. M.
  1940   *First Expedition of Vargas into New Mexico, 1692.* Translated, with Introduction and notes by J. MANUEL ESPINOSA. "Coronado Historical Series," Vol. X. Albuquerque.
FENTON, WILLIAM N.
  1957   *Factionalism at Taos pueblo, New Mexico.* Bureau of American Ethnology *Bulletin 164*, 297–346. Washington.
FRANCIS, E. K.
  1956   "Multiple Intergroup Relations in the Upper Rio Grande Region," *American Sociological Review*, XXI, 84–87.
FRENCH, DAVID H.
  1948   *Factionalism in Isleta Pueblo.* American Ethnological Society, *Monograph 14.* New York.
GOLDFRANK, E. S.
  1927   *The Social and Ceremonial Organization of the Cochiti.* American Anthropological Association, *Memoir No. 33.*
  1945   "Socialization, Personality and the Structure of Pueblo Society," *American Anthropologist*, XLVII, 516–39.
HACK, J. T.
  1942   "The Changing Physical Environment of the Hopi Indians of Arizona," Peabody Museum of American Archaeology and Ethnology, *Papers*, Vol. XXXV, No. 1. Cambridge.
HACKETT, C. W., and C. C. SHELBY
  1942   *Revolt of the Pueblo Indians of New Mexico and Otermin's Attempted Reconquest, 1680–1682.* "Coronado Historical Series," Vols. VIII and IX. Albuquerque.
HALLENBECK, CLEVE
  1950   *Land of Conquistadores.* Caldwell, Idaho.
HALLOWELL, A. I.
  1951   "Ojibwa Personality and Acculturation," in SOL TAX (ed.), *Proceedings and Selected Papers of the Twenty-ninth International Congress of Americanists.* Chicago.
HAMMOND, G. P.
  1926   "Don Juan de Oñate, and the Founding of New Mexico," *New Mexico Historical Review*, I, 42–77; II, 156–92.
HAMMOND, G. P., and AGAPITO REY
  1927   *The Gallegos Relation of the Rodriguez Expedition to New Mexico.* Historical Society of New Mexico, "Publications in History," Vol. IV. Santa Fe.
  1929   *Expedition into New Mexico by Antonio de Espejo, 1582–1583, as Revealed in the Journal of Diego Perez de Luxan, a Member of the Party.* The Quivera Society, Los Angeles.

HARRINGTON, JOHN P.
1907–8   *The Ethnography of the Tewa Indians. Twenty-ninth Annual Report*, Bureau of American Ethnology, Washington.
HAWLEY, FLORENCE
1950a   "Big Kivas, Little Kivas and Moiety Houses in Historical Reconstruction," *Southwestern Journal of Anthropology*, VI, 286–302.
1950b   "Keresan Patterns of Kinship and Social Organization," *American Anthropologist*, LII, 499–512.
HAWLEY, FLORENCE, and DONOVAN SENTER
1946   "Group-designed Behavior in Two Acculturating Groups," *Southwestern Journal of Anthropology*, II, 133–51.
HERSKOVITS, M. J.
1938   *Acculturation: The Study of Culture Contact.* New York.
1945   "The Processes of Culture Change," in RALPH LINTON (ed.), *The Science of Man in the World Crisis.* New York.
HILL, W. W.
N.D.   Unpublished manuscript on Santa Clara pueblo.
HODGE, F. W. (ed.)
1907
and
1912   *Handbook of American Indians North of Mexico.* Bureau of American Ethnology, *Bulletin 30*, Parts 1 and 2. Washington.
HODGE, F. W., G. P. HAMMOND, and AGAPITO REY
1945   *Revised Memorial of Alonzo de Benavides, 1634.* "Coronado Historical Series," Vol. IV. Albuquerque.
HOIJER, HARRY
1946   "Introduction," in HARRY HOIJER and others, *Linguistic Structures of Native America.* Viking Fund "Publications in Anthropology," No. 6, New York.
KURATH, GERTRUDE
1949   "Mexican Moriscas: A Problem in Dance Acculturation," *Journal of American Folklore*, LXII, 87–106.
LA FARGE, OLIVER (ed.)
1942   *The Changing Indian.* Norman, Okla.
LANGE, CHARLES
1952   "The Feast Day at Zia Pueblo, New Mexico," *Texas Journal of Science*, IV, 19–26.
1953   "The Role of Economics in Cochiti Pueblo Culture Change," *American Anthropologist*, LV, 674–94.
1957   "Tablita or Corn Dances of the Rio Grande Pueblo Indians," *Texas Journal of Science*, IX, 59–74.
LINTON, RALPH (ed.)
1940   *Acculturation in Seven American Indian Tribes.* New York.
MADIGAN, LAVERNE
1956   *The American Indian Relocation Program.* Association on American Indian Affairs, New York.
MEKEEL, H. S.
1936   *The Economy of a Modern Teton Dakota Community.* Yale University "Publications in Anthropology," No. 6, New Haven, Conn.

MURDOCK, G. P.
1949   *Social Structure.* New York.
NELSON, N. C.
1914   *Pueblo Ruins of the Galisteo Basin, New Mexico.* American Museum of Natural History, *Anthropological Papers,* Vol. XV, Part 1. New York.
O'BRYAN, DERIC
1952   "The Abandonment of the Northern Pueblos in the Thirteenth Century," in SOL TAX (ed.), *The Indian Tribes of Aboriginal America: Selected Papers of the Twenty-ninth International Congress of Americanists.* Chicago.
OPLER, MARVIN K.
1940   "The Southern Ute of Colorado," in RALPH LINTON (ed.), *Acculturation in Seven American Indian Tribes.* New York.
PARSONS, E. C.
1925   *The Pueblo of Jemez.* Phillips Academy, Andover.
1929   *The Social Organization of the Tewa of New Mexico.* American Anthropological Association, *Memoir No. 36.*
1936   *Taos Pueblo.* "General Series in Anthropology," No. 2.
1939   *Pueblo Indian Religion.* 2 vols. Chicago.
REED, ERIK K.
1949   "Sources of Upper Rio Grande Pueblo Culture and Population," *El Palacio,* LVI, 163–84.
1950   "Eastern-Central Arizona Archaeology in Relation to the Western Pueblos," *Southwestern Journal of Anthropology,* VI, 120–38.
1956   "Types of Village-Plan Layouts in the Southwest," in GORDON R. WILLEY (ed.), *Prehistoric Settlement Patterns in the New World,* Viking Fund "Publications in Anthropology," No. 23. New York.
ROEDIGER, VIRGINIA M.
1941   *Ceremonial Costumes of the Pueblo Indians.* Berkeley and Los Angeles.
SAPIR, EDWARD
1929   "Central and North American Languages," *Encyclopedia Brittanica,* V, 138–41.
SCHOLES, FRANCE V.
1930   "The Supply Service of the New Mexico Missions in the Seventeenth Century," *New Mexico Historical Review,* V, 93–115, 186–98.
1935   "Civil Government and Society in New Mexico in the Seventeenth Century," *New Mexico Historical Review,* X, 71–111.
1942   *Troublous Times in New Mexico, 1659–1670.* Historical Society of New Mexico, "Publications in History," Vol. II. Albuquerque.
1956   Personal communication.
SEIGEL, BERNARD J.
1949   "Some Observations on the Pueblo Pattern at Taos," *American Anthropologist,* LI, 562–77.
SOCIAL SCIENCE RESEARCH COUNCIL (Summer Seminar on Acculturation, 1953).
1954   "Acculturation: An Exploratory Formulation," *American Anthropologist,* LVI, 973–1002.
SPENCER, ROBERT
1947   "Spanish Loanwords in Keresan," *Southwestern Journal of Anthropology,* III, 130–46.

SPICER, EDWARD H.
1954 "Spanish-Indian Acculturation in the Southwest," *American Anthropologist*, LVI, 663–78.
1957 "Worlds Apart, Cultural Differences in the Modern Southwest," *Arizona Quarterly*, XIII, 197–230.
SPIER, LESLIE
1928 *Havasupai Ethnology*. American Museum of Natural History, *Anthropological Papers*, Vol. XXIV, Part 2. New York.
SPINDLER, GEORGE D.
1955 *Sociocultural and Psychological Processes in Menominee Acculturation*. "Culture and Society Series," Vol. V. Berkeley.
TAX, SOL
1956 "The Distribution of Indians in the United States" (1950). Data compiled by SAMUEL STANLEY and ROBERT THOMAS for a paper presented by SOL TAX at annual meeting of the American Anthropological Association, December 1956.
THOMAS, A. B.
1932 *Forgotten Frontiers: A Study of the Spanish Indian Policy of Don Juan Bautista de Anza, Governor of New Mexico, 1777–1787*. Norman, Okla.
THOMPSON, LAURA, and ALICE JOSEPH
1944 *The Hopi Way*. United States Indian Service, Lawrence, Kan.
THWAITES, REUBEN GOLD (ed.)
1905 *Josiah Gregg's Commerce of the Prairies, 1831–1839. Early Western Travels 1748–1846*, Vols. XIX and XX, Part II. Cleveland, Ohio.
TRAGER, GEORGE
1944 "Spanish and English Loanwords in Taos," *International Journal of American Linguistics*, X, 144–58.
TWITCHELL, R. E.
1912 *Leading Facts of New Mexican History*, Vol. I. Cedar Rapids, Iowa.
UNITED STATES
United States vs. *Joseph*, 94 U.S. 619.
United States vs. *Sandoval*, 231 U.S. 28.
1950 Census for New Mexico
VOGT, E. Z.
1955 "A Study of the Southwestern Fiesta System as Exemplified by the Laguna Fiesta," *American Anthropologist*, LVII, 820–39.
WENDORF, FRED
1954 "A Reconstruction of Northern Rio Grande Prehistory," *American Anthropologist*, LVI, 200–227.
1956 "Some Distributions of Settlement Patterns in the Pueblo Southwest," in GORDON R. WILLEY (ed.), *Prehistoric Settlement Patterns in the New World*. Viking Fund "Publications in Anthropology," No. 23. New York.
WENDORF, FRED, and ERIK K. REED
1955 "An Alternative Reconstruction of Northern Rio Grande Prehistory," *El Palacio*, LXII, 131–73.
WHITE, LESLIE A.
1928 "A Comparative Study of Keresan Medicine Societies," *Proceedings of the Twenty-third International Congress of Americanists*, pp. 604–19.

WHITE, LESLIE A.
  1932a *The Acoma Indians. Forty-seventh Annual Report,* Bureau of Amer-
         ican Ethnology, Washington.
  1932b *The Pueblo of San Felipe.* American Anthropological Association,
         Memoir No. 38.
  1935   *The Pueblo of Santo Domingo.* American Anthropological Associa-
         tion, *Memoir No. 43.*   .
  1942   *The Pueblo of Santa Ana, New Mexico.* American Anthropological
         Association, *Memoir No. 60.*
WHORF, B. L., and G. L. TRAGER
  1937   "The Relationship of Uto-Aztecan and Tanoan," *American Anthro-
         pologist,* XXXIX, 609–24.
WILLEY, GORDON (ed.)
  1956   *Prehistoric Settlement Patterns in the New World.* Viking Fund
         "Publications in Anthropology," No. 23. New York.
WINSHIP, G. P.
  1896   "The Coronado Expedition, 1540–1542." *Fourteenth Annual Report,*
         Bureau of American Ethnology, Washington.
WITTFOGEL, KARL A.
  1957   *Oriental Despotism: A Comparative Study of Total Power.* New
         Haven, Conn.
WITTFOGEL, K. A., and E. S. GOLDFRANK
  1943   "Some Aspects of Pueblo Mythology and Society," *Journal of Ameri-
         can Folklore,* LVI, 1730.

CHAPTER 4

Mandan

By *Edward M. Bruner*

The most striking fact about the Mandan is that they are "extinct" (Will and Spinden 1906: 85; Lowie 1917; and Strong 1940: 391). In the year 1750 there were approximately nine thousand Mandan; when the smallpox epidemic of 1837 had passed, there were only twenty-three male survivors residing in the fertile bottom land near the confluence of the Knife and Missouri rivers in what is now the State of North Dakota. Today there is not one full-blood Mandan left, a result of the severe reduction in population combined with extensive intermarriage with Whites and other Indians. Nor has a distinctive and separate Mandan society existed within the past seventy years. The descendants of the Mandan are now scattered in mixed Hidatsa and Arikara communities on the Fort Berthold Indian Reservation. There can no longer be a resurgence of Mandan culture and identity; extinction is the most devastating and final result of culture contact situations.

Students of acculturation are interested in full documentation of known cases of extinction, not only because such cases are a most dramatic consequence of the contact of cultures, but also because they provide an opportunity to study the processes and mechanisms of change in their most extreme form. For extinction of human

I wish to thank Alfred W. Bowers and Wesley R. Hurt, Jr., who read the entire manuscript and made suggestions for its improvement, and John Landgraf, who made unpublished materials available.

groups rarely occurs as racial death alone—its most simple biological manifestation—but is a process with social, cultural, and psychological dimensions. The Mandan did not become extinct wholly as a result of the smallpox attacks, severe as they may have been. In fact, as we shall see, the Mandan attempted to preserve their own culture, and they consciously tried to replenish their depleted population. Men from other Plains Indian tribes were adopted into Mandan society and were offered Mandan women in marriage provided that the off-spring of such marriages be raised as Mandan. These efforts were not entirely unsuccessful. It was not until 1889, a half-century after the 1837 epidemic, that the first important Mandan ceremony, the Okipa, ceased to be performed. When I last did ethnological field work among the mixed descendants of the Mandan at Fort Berthold in 1953, I found some adults who still spoke the Mandan language.

Possibly these data raise questions about exactly what is meant by the term extinction and about the precise mechanisms of change and persistence involved in the Mandan case. We shall return to these questions in the concluding section of this chapter.

Historical Overview

Mandan culture history may be divided into five major periods as follows:

Most developed; largest population →

I. 1250–1500   Small Village
II. 1500–1750   Pre-Horse Coalescent
III. 1750–1862   Fur Trade
IV. 1862–1883   Military-Agency
V. 1883–1953   Reservation

Period I begins when the ancestors of the Mandan arrived in the Missouri River Valley from the southeast between 1200 and 1300 A.D. The archeological record, upon which our data for this period are based, indicates that the early Mandan borrowed heavily from the Plains-Woodland peoples, who formerly inhabited the area, as well as from Eastern Mississippi cultures. The Mandan soon developed the basic subsistence techniques for the exploration of the river valley environment and established small, widely separated villages over a large area along the waterways of the Dakotas.

During the 1500–1750 Pre-Horse Coalescent Period II the Mandan enjoyed the greatest power, most highly developed culture, and largest population of their entire history. Early in the period their culture was enriched by the penetration of elements from Upper Republican, a Proto–Pawnee-Arikara culture to the south, both through cultural diffusion and actual migration of peoples. Shortly thereafter, the displacement of eastern tribes led to a consolidation of the Mandan villages which culminated in the establishment of nine large towns in the vicinity of the Heart River in North Dakota (see Map 6).

Throughout the 1750–1862 Period III the Mandan suffered a de-

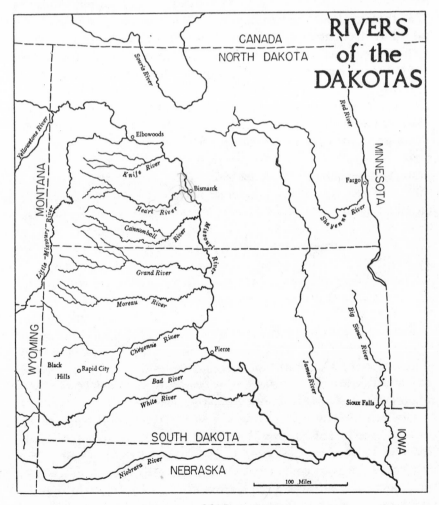

MAP 6

cline in power and population: the climax of cultural development had shifted from the eastern sedentary horticulturalists to the nomadic warriors of the High Plains. Their decline was set in motion by two new factors occurring at the very end of the previous period: the arrival of the Whites who brought the fur trade and smallpox, and the introduction of the horse which led to full equestrian nomadism. The data for Period III are based in large part upon historical documents. La Vérendrye, a Frenchman from Canada who visited the Mandan villages in 1738, was the first of many explorer-traders who left written accounts of their experiences. It may be noted that in 1738 the Mandan had no horses; in 1742 a son of La Vérendrye on a return visit obtained two horses from the Mandan; by 1750 there were horses in sufficient quantities on the Upper Missouri to produce a significant change in the total contact community (Burpee 1927: 337, 387).

At the beginning of the Military-Agency Period IV the remaining Mandan found themselves weakened by disease, facing starvation, and at the mercy of their enemy the Sioux. In 1862 they joined with the Hidatsa and Arikara in one village, Like-a-Fish-Hook, for mutual protection against hostile nomads. By 1868 the locus of power had shifted to the Whites with the erection of the Fort Stevenson Military Post eighteen miles below the Indian village, and the establishment of the first Indian Agency at Fort Berthold. Period IV ends in 1883 with the disappearance of the buffalo from the Northern Plains, the withdrawal of the military, and the coming of the railroad.

The abandonment of the combined Mandan, Hidatsa, and Arikara village under the provisions of the government Allotment Act marked the breakup of the traditional village life of the Indian people and the establishment of Reservation Period V. Each family was encouraged or forced to settle on its own plot of land. Starting in the latter part of the nineteenth century and continuing until the present, White homesteaders arrived on the Upper Missouri and with them came schools, churches, roads, stores, and cities.

The year 1953 was selected as a terminal date for this chapter not only because it was the last time I did field work among the Fort Berthold Indians, but also because 1953 marked the beginning of a new kind of contact community. In that year the government was in the process of constructing the Garrison Dam, a project requiring the establishment of a huge reservoir on both sides of the Missouri River

in the Berthold area. For the Indian people it meant flooding the agricultural bottom lands, the most fertile part or, as they put it, the very
"heart" of their reservation. They were forced to abandon the river
valley environment for which they had developed techniques of adjustment over the past seven hundred years and to relocate in the less
desirable upland region, an area unsuitable for farming. With the

TABLE 3

MANDAN CONTACT HISTORY

Period	Events	Contact Communities
V Reservation 1883–1953	1953 Garrison Dam constructed 1886 Breakup of village life; individual homesteads	American towns Reservation
IV Military- Agency 1862–1883	1883 Buffalo disappear; military leave; railroad com- pleted 1868 Fort Stevenson military post erected; first In- dian agency	Indian agency Military post
III Fur Trade 1750–1862	1862 Mandan, Hidatsa, and Arikara joined at Like- a-Fish-Hook village 1851 Fort Laramie Treaty; reservation lands granted 1837 Smallpox epidemic 1833 Maximilian and Catlin 1804 Lewis and Clark 1776 English fur traders 1764 First smallpox epidemic *ca.* 1750 Shift in cultural climax on Northern Plains	Fur traders in consoli- dated villages
II Pre-Horse Coa- lescent 1500–1750	1742 Horse introduced 1738 First recorded contact: La Vérendrye	Consolidated villages
I Small Village 1250–1500	*ca.* 1500 Proto–Pawnee-Arikara influence; village consolidation *ca.* 1250 Proto-Mandan settle Missouri River Valley	Small villages

Garrison Dam came improved roads, widespread use of electricity,
and more direct contact with local Whites. The discovery of oil in
the Williston Basin and on reservation lands has brought a new and
great wealth to many Indian families. It has been reported that the
Native American Church, the peyote cult, which had a temporary
success at Fort Berthold in 1912, has been revived within the last few
years. These developments will undoubtedly lead to vast changes in
Berthold society and culture, but it is too early to assess their precise
nature.

The Small Village Contact Community, 1250–1500

HISTORICAL BACKGROUND

Mandan prehistory is known only in dim outline: the two firm lines of evidence are linguistic and archeological. Mandan is a Siouan language tentatively classified by Voegelin (1941: 249) in a Mississippi Valley subgroup along with Chiwere and Dhegia Sioux and possibly Dakota. Wolff (1950: 61–62) places Winnebago in the same category as Chiwere and suggests that Mandan and Dakota coincide on many points of comparative phonology, although Mandan is definitely the more archaic. Mandan appears to have been among the first groups to separate from Proto-Siouan.

The Mandan origin legends and the archeological evidence indicate that separate groups entered the Missouri River Valley from the southeast starting about 1250 A.D. Their closest cultural affinities appear to be with the Cambria aspect of southern Minnesota and the Mill Creek complex of northeastern Iowa (Hurt 1953: 11; Strong 1935: 295). One group of Mandan arrived in South Dakota and moved upriver, the other entered North Dakota directly. Regional differences within the early village sites suggest a division between a northern branch centered in North Dakota and northern South Dakota, and a southern branch located in southeast South Dakota (Hurt 1953: 11; Bowers 1950: 16).

The archeological remains of early sedentary peoples situated in the river valleys of the Dakotas have been classified as Archaic and Middle Mandan by Will and Hecker (1944) and as the Middle Missouri Tradition by Lehmer (1954b). However, it is not known if all these early cultures in the Dakotas before 1500 A.D. were ancestors of the Mandan, as some may well have become Hidatsa or possibly other Siouan-speaking peoples (Jennings 1955: 51). It is difficult for the archeologist to connect an early site with one or another known historic tribe, due to the many similarities in socioeconomic institutions among all sedentary peoples of the Eastern Plains.

The more basic problem in understanding Mandan prehistory concerns the concept of "tribe" itself, and the modes of thought suggested by it. It seems reasonable that the picture of the Mandan as a unified tribe was a very late development. During the 1250–1500 period, the Proto-Mandan occupied a large area in both North and South Dakota and were organized in terms of small village communities with a relatively low level of sociopolitical integration. Clusters of hamlets exhibited marked cultural and linguistic variation. Bowers (1950: 25) and Maximilian (in Thwaites 1906) recognized distinct dialect differences within Mandan which must have either developed or been maintained during the Small Village Period. There were possibly many mergings and splittings of different Mandan groups, as well as both up- and down-river movements. To think of the thirteenth-century sedentary agriculturalists in terms of such nineteenth-century historic tribes as the Mandan, Hidatsa, Arikara, and Pawnee is probably a distortion. Diverse early peoples may well have amalgamated into the historic Mandan.

THE SMALL VILLAGE CULTURE

Despite the complexities of interpretation of Mandan prehistory, the basic socioeconomic institutions of the early cultures are fairly clear. The Small Village complex has been described by Will and Hecker (1944), Bowers (1948), Strong (1940), and Wedel (1956), among others. More specific and richer information is provided by the site reports on the Over Focus (Hurt 1951) and the first stages of the Fort Pierre Branch (Lehmer 1952, 1954a). There is evidence that the Indian people who occupied these sites were among or similar to those who eventually became Mandan (Spaulding 1956: 98–100; Wesley R. Hurt, Jr., personal communication, April 1, 1957).

Horticulture and hunting were of equal importance in the economy of the Small Village cultures, based upon exploitation of the dual environment of the Missouri River Valley. To the west of the Missouri are a series of east-flowing rivers and streams. The bottom lands along the river are well adapted to horticulture; the grasslands between the rivers support abundant large game. Heavily wooded areas in the valleys provide shelter for man and animal in the severe winters, as well as wood for fuel, housing, and artifacts.

The advantage of the dual economy for a people who develop the necessary technology and forms of social organization to exploit it fully is that it provides a degree of flexibility and adjustment to shifting conditions. When the game is scarce, greater emphasis can be placed upon the corn, bean, and squash horticulture. That the Small Village peoples had an economic surplus is indicated by the presence of underground cache pits to store grain. The bison scapula hoe was a simple but very effective agricultural implement. In times of drought, which occur periodically in the Eastern Plains, the emphasis shifted to hunting in the grasslands. Roughly 90 per cent of the total sample of animal bones found in Middle Missouri sites was bison (Lehmer 1954*b*: 145). Other animals whose remains have been found in the small villages include antelope, deer, elk, rabbit, raccoon, waterfowl, grouse, fox, beaver, coyote, prairie dog, gopher, skunk, ground squirrel, and badger (Hurt 1951, 1953).

The rivers and streams themselves not only provide water for drinking and washing, but also fresh water mussel, catfish, bullheads, sturgeon, and varieties of perch (Hurt 1951, 1953). Although shells, fish hooks, and fish bones are found in many sites, their limited quantity suggests that fishing was only of minor importance. Gathering of wild berries and roots was another supplement to the economy, as indicated by the presence of root diggers and wild vegetable products.

Skin-dressing and woodworking tools, household implements, ornaments, and other artifacts were made of stone, bone, horn, flint, shell, and wood. Pottery is found in abundance; arrowshaft smoothers indicate the use of the bow and arrow as the major hunting weapon; and large points suggest the knife and spear. The remains of bison skulls painted with red ochre, and of hawk, crow, and raven bones are certainly suggestive, but give us few clues to Mandan ceremonialism. Each village may well have had its own ceremonial lodge, since in the earlier sites one house much larger than the average dwelling has been found (Hurt 1953).

The majority of the villages were located on the higher terraces adjacent to the floodplains. The characteristic dwelling was the rectangular earth lodge, semisubterranean to a depth of three to four feet with primary roof supports of single or double rows (Lehmer 1954*b*: 143). The northern Mandan villages were unfortified and the houses widely spaced in the earlier stages but protected by ditches toward the end of Period I. Each northern village covered ten to twenty acres of ground and contained twenty to forty houses (Will and Hecker 1944: 63). The Swanson site, an early Over Focus village, in the southern Mandan area near the White River in South Dakota, was fortified by entrenchments and contained fifteen houses in a village area of approximately two and a half acres (Hurt 1951). In many villages the houses were arranged in fairly regular rows.

Thus far the description of the Small Village culture has been based rather firmly in archeological fact. It is possible to move to another level of interpretation, not of sheer guess, but of informed inference.

Two lines of evidence suggest that the rectangular earth lodges were occupied by extended families: their large size and the presence of multiple fireplaces. The living quarters of an average lodge in the Swanson site were thirty-four feet by twenty-two feet. If the ante-chamber is included, the exterior dimensions were forty-six feet by twenty-two feet. All houses but one in the Swanson site had two large central fireplaces (Hurt 1951). In other Mandan areas the lodges contained three fireplaces, and Bowers (1950: 16) reports that rectangular houses frequently reached the size of seventy-five feet by thirty-five feet.

If we grant that the earth lodges were occupied by extended families, it is possible to estimate how many people lived in a village. Hurt (1951: 4) suggests that the lodge group consisted of approximately ten individuals, which seems reasonable. On this basis, the range of the village populations was 150 to 400, with the average probably closer to 200 persons.

A composite picture of the Small Village emerges—tiny hamlets of approximately 200 people spread over a large area in the Dakotas, each containing twenty extended families residing in rectangular earth lodges, exploiting the river valley environment with a dual economy of horticulture and hunting, supplemented by fishing and gathering. The cultural and linguistic differences suggest that each hamlet, or cluster of hamlets, was relatively isolated and politically autonomous.

It would be tempting to go further; but to do so would be to make assumptions which it is the aim of this study to validate. One final inference may be permitted. The elaborate ceremonial structure, clan organization, and age-graded society system, which were such colorful and important features of historic Mandan culture, would not seem necessary as integrating mechanisms during the 1250–1500 period because of the small size of the community and low level of political integration.

The Pre-Horse Coalescent Contact Community, 1500–1750

HISTORICAL BACKGROUND

Mass population movements, shifts in the location and density of the sedentary villages, and changes in social, political, and ceremonial organization characterized all cultures of the Northern Plains during Period II. These events began by approximately 1500, and were apparently indigenous developments, uninfluenced by White contact. They were, however, greatly intensified during the seventeenth and early eighteenth centuries by the introduction of the horse, European trade goods, the displacement of eastern tribes, and direct White contact on the Plains. By 1710, the western tribes had the horse, the eastern tribes had the gun, the Mandan had neither; by 1750, the Mandan had both horse and gun (Secoy 1953: 105). In 1738, La Vérendrye visited the Mandan;[1] his was the first recorded contact and beginning of the historic period.

Throughout these exciting times the Mandan remained a large and powerful people, with a culture considerably more elaborate than that of their neighbors. The climax of cultural development on the Plains was located on the eastern margins, among the sedentary horticulturalists. No nomad group was considered a serious threat by the Mandan before 1750.

COMMUNITY ORGANIZATION

At the end of Period II the Mandan were concentrated into a number of large towns within twenty miles of one another in the Heart River area. Will and Spinden (1906: 90–92) are among those who have attempted to determine the exact number of Mandan villages. There appear to have been at least six, possibly thirteen, probably nine. Taking the latter figure, two villages were located on the east side of the Heart River, seven on the west side. Each village occupied approximately eight acres of land (Will and Hecker 1944: 7).

In 1738, La Vérendrye actually counted 130 earth lodges in one Heart River village. His son visited a second village and reported that it was larger, and hence would contain more than 130 lodges. Bowers (1948) presents lodge counts of five of the Heart River villages based upon archeological findings: in decreasing order there were 163, 130, 75, 72, and 64, for an average of 100 lodges per village.

David Thompson, who visited the Missouri in December 1797, estimated ten individuals per Hidatsa household and eight per Mandan household. He notes, however, that the Mandan had few children

[1] O. G. Libby (1908) argues that La Vérendrye actually visited the Hidatsa, not the Mandan, but his conclusions have not been accepted by later students (Bowers 1950).

(Tyrrell 1916: 228), undoubtedly as a result of the previous smallpox epidemics. The Hidatsa were the more nomadic and hence were less affected by epidemics. Using ten per household for 1750, before the smallpox, each Heart River village contained about a thousand people, with a total Mandan population of nine thousand. This is within the range of Bowers' (1950: 26) estimate, "possibly as much as seven or eight thousand," and Will and Spinden's (1906: 98), "at least fifteen thousand Mandans."

The larger Mandan community organization cannot be considered independently of the Hidatsa, with whom they had an especially close relationship. Linguistically, Mandan and Hidatsa are in separate branches of the Siouan stock and their languages mutually unintelligible; however, the two tribes had roughly similar cultural inventories, were neighbors, generally co-operated for defense, and each respected the other's territory. By 1750, three villages or bands of Hidatsa were located further upstream from the Mandan, in the vicinity of the Knife River. The three Hidatsa groups were relatively independent, one being much more nomadic than the other two and close to the River Crow. The nomadic Crow to the west were a recent offshoot of the Hidatsa and were usually allies of the Mandan. Hidatsa and Crow are mutually intelligible languages, differing only in relatively minor aspects of their phonemic systems (Bowers n.d.).

In the mid-eighteenth century the Mandan were in contact with many other Indian peoples around them: the Arikara, Pawnee, and Central Siouans to the south; the Dakota and Cheyenne to the east; the Cree and Ojibwa to the northeast; the Assiniboin to the north; the Crow, Blackfoot, and other nomads to the west. They had relationships with French traders from Canada and were at least aware of the Spaniards in the Southwest. The nature of these relationships emerges most clearly from an examination of La Vérendrye's visit in 1738. His account (in Burpee 1927) deserves extended treatment, because of the importance of the first White contact in all acculturation situations and because his is the only available eyewitness report on the Mandan until the 1790's.

EXTERNAL SOCIAL RELATIONSHIPS

La Vérendrye's dream was to discover an overland trading route to the Western Sea. As he could not obtain financing as an explorer, he associated himself with a group of Montreal merchants in the fur trade. In the 1730's he established trading posts on the Assiniboine River and on Lake of the Woods. La Vérendrye had heard from the Assiniboin and the Cree that the Mandan had an advanced civilization, and that they were White like the French. Remarkable and inaccurate tales about the Mandan were widespread. La Vérendrye asked the Assiniboin to make initial contacts with the Mandan on behalf of the French. The Assiniboin did so and reported to La Véren-drye in 1734:

They [the Mandan] were so pleased that the great chief said to me: "You are going to see the French. I request you to tell the chief from me that it would give me great pleasure to see him or any of his people, in order that we may establish a friendship [trading relation] with him. If he comes himself, or if he sends me one of his men, I beg him to let me know beforehand in order that I may send to meet him as he deserves." (Burpee 1927: 161.)

On December 3, 1738, La Vérendrye and his party of fifty-two, accompanied by over five hundred Assiniboin men and several women, arrived at the Mandan villages. Their entrance to the village was the occasion for a bit of display. At the head of the party was La Vérendrye's son, waving a French flag, followed by La Vérendrye himself carried on the shoulders of those Mandan who had been sent to receive him. The French were offered the ceremonial pipe, they shot off a three-volley salute, and marched in formation to the chief's lodge.

The next day at council meeting one of the chiefs begged La Vérendrye, whom he addressed as father, to adopt the principal Mandan men as his children. This he did, by placing his hands on the head of each chief. The Mandan replied with "shouts of joy and thankfulness" (331). La Vérendrye was embarrassed to find that the gifts he had brought for the Mandan had been stolen, but the chiefs reassured him that they had more than enough food stored in the village to provide for the needs of his party.

However, the Mandan did not particularly like the idea of feeding over five hundred Assiniboin. It was their practice to provide food to all who came to their village to trade. As the Assiniboin were consuming great quantities of grain and had already completed their trading, the Mandan were anxious for them to leave. This was accomplished by spreading the false rumor that the Sioux were approaching the Mandan villages. The Assiniboin were at war with the Sioux but apparently did not choose to fight them: they left the village in great haste.

The departure of the Assiniboin completely broke the chain of communication between the Mandan and their visitors. La Vérendrye's son spoke Cree, an interpreter in the party spoke Assiniboin, which several Mandan understood. To communicate, La Vérendrye spoke French to his son, his son translated it into Cree, the interpreter translated into Assiniboin, which was finally translated into Mandan. But the Cree interpreter left in order to be with an Assiniboin woman with whom he was enamoured—a great disappointment to La Vérendrye and to all later ethnologists, who would have appreciated a richer account of 1738 Mandan culture.

Because of the difficulty of communicating by sign and gesture, La Vérendrye left the village on December 13. Before his departure he assembled the Mandan chiefs and "made them a present of powder, ball and a number of small articles, to which they attach much value owing to the need they have of them" (350). To the principal chief he gave a flag and lead tablet in remembrance of his having taken possession of their land in the name of the King of France.

La Vérendrye's visit has very little intrinsic importance for Mandan culture history; its significance lies in what he tells us about Mandan relationships to other Indians and to Whites. To understand the bases of these relationships, we first turn to the pre–horse trading network on the Northern Plains.

Mandan trade faced two directions: from the eastern tribes they received guns and European goods, from the western tribes dressed skins and the products of nomadic life. These goods flowed through the Mandan villages because they had one commodity desired by all, a surplus of corn and other agricultural produce. In their role as middlemen, they sold the dressed skins received from the nomads to the eastern tribes; the guns and European objects received from the eastern tribes were sold to the western nomads. This trade network probably existed before 1700; possibly the pre-horse nomads and the sedentary Mandan had been exchanging skins and corn for centuries. The Mandan villages were the central market place in the Northern Plains (Will and Hyde 1917; Jablow 1951).

The Mandan received "guns, powder, ball, kettles, axes, knives and awls" from the Assiniboin for which they traded "grains, tobacco . . .

coloured buffalo robes, deer and buck skins, carefully dressed and
ornamented with fur and feathers, painted feathers and furs, worked
garters, head-bands, girdles" (Burpee 1927: 323, 332). "They said
also that every year, in the beginning of June, there arrive at the great
fort on the bank of the river of the Mandan, several savage tribes
which use horses and carry on trade with them; that they bring
dressed skins trimmed and ornamented with plumage and porcupine
quills, painted in various colours, also white buffalo-skins, and that the
Mandan give them in exchange grain and beans, of which they have
an ample supply" (*ibid.*: 366).

Trade structured the relationship between the Mandan and other
peoples. For their supply of European trade objects, the Mandan
were dependent upon those eastern tribes who were in direct contact
with the French, such as the Assiniboin, Cree, and Sioux. During La
Vérendrye's visit the Mandan wanted the Assiniboin band to leave
their village, yet they resorted to the trick of spreading a false rumor
about the Sioux rather than risk any overt offense or open break. It
was to their best interests to maintain their source of supply of manufactured goods.

The presence of French traders in the Mandan villages upset the
balance of trade among Indian peoples. The Mandan were gracious
and friendly to La Vérendrye and his party, not because they were
awed by the French, but because they were so eager to arrange for
direct trade with Whites. The Assiniboin, in turn, were anxious to
maintain their monopoly of European goods, as it placed them in an
advantageous position with reference to the Mandan. Each tribe attempted to prevent White traders from reaching Indian groups further west. Some time prior to 1760, a party of French Canadian traders was stopped by the Mandan, who prohibited further ascent into
their territory (from Newman 1950: 257).

In effect, the French and the Assiniboin were competing for Mandan trade and corn; the Assiniboin and the Mandan were in competition for French manufactured goods. Given this situation, it is not
surprising that the Assiniboin, Cree, and Sioux were at war with the
Mandan at the very same time that they were peacefully trading.
Whatever other factors may have precipitated extensive warfare on
the Plains, it is clear that the penetration of White traders increased
the hostility among Indian people.

The Mandan employed a series of social and ceremonial mechanisms to facilitate peaceful trade with those tribes with whom they were also at war. After the proper ritual, i.e., the presentation of a few ears of corn and some tobacco, and smoking the ceremonial peace pipe, the Indian groups who came to trade were given sanctuary in the Mandan villages. A Sioux who had killed a Mandan brave one day could freely trade with close relatives of the deceased Mandan warrior the very next day, provided that those relatives were compensated for their loss. During the trading period, visiting Indians were assured of a plentiful supply of Mandan food offered to them as a gift, but they were expected to reciprocate by presenting gifts of their own in exchange.

A father-son adoption ceremony was the key mechanism of social structure which enabled members of warring tribes to trade in peace. The Mandan were adopted by fictitious fathers, and in turn had adopted sons in the tribes with whom they dealt. Jablow (1951: 46) has distinguished two types of trade patterns: individual trade conducted by the women from house to house; and ceremonial tribal trade conducted by the men, in which large quantities of goods were exchanged between one tribe and another. Rituals of adoption were part of the latter. Plains Indian trade was accomplished by barter between fictitious relatives. From a larger perspective, a vast network of ritual kinship relationships extended throughout the entire Plains.

Many of the characteristics of experienced traders were developed by the Mandan. La Vérendrye reports they were "much more crafty than the Assiniboin in their commerce . . . and always dupe them"; many later visitors commented upon the Mandan shrewdness in bargaining (Burpee 1927: 324). The Mandan were also great linguists. We know that in 1738 they spoke Assiniboin; it is probable that some also spoke Hidatsa and Crow, possibly Sioux and Arikara. By the early nineteenth century they certainly understood all of these languages (Will and Spinden 1906: 188; Hayden 1863: 428).

The most general significance of the trading complex among the Mandan was that there emerged a series of behavior patterns to handle the "stranger," and White visitors for the next century were fitted into these patterns. The norms of social interaction to handle outsiders that were developed in the course of Indian trade were applied to all European contacting agents. That La Vérendrye was asked to adopt the principal Mandan men as his children was not a unique experience; the chiefs of the Assiniboin had probably done so before him.

THE PRE-HORSE COALESCENT CULTURE

Archeological reports and La Vérendrye's brief observations are the only sources which refer specifically to the 1750 Heart River Mandan culture. This account will be restricted to those sources. Our aim is to highlight the cultural changes from Period I to Period II, not to present a holistic description of Mandan culture. The more complete nineteenth-century material will be used for the next period, 1750–1862, to describe Mandan culture in its entirety.

Mandan economy was essentially similar to that described for the 1250–1500 period, with the possible exception of a greater reliance upon horticulture. La Vérendrye was very impressed with the abundance of grain and the scarcity of meat. Underground cache pits within and between the houses, and even outside the village, were stocked with surplus corn, beans, squash, pumpkins, and sunflower seeds.

Clothing consisted of a buffalo skin carelessly worn without any breechcloth for the men, and a buffalo robe, small loincloth, and sometimes a buckskin jacket for the women. Both men and women were tattooed. Material objects included catlinite pipes, wicker work, pottery, elaborately ornamented robes and headdresses, a wide variety of stone and bone tools (Will and Spinden 1906), and European trade objects.

In an oft-quoted passage, La Vérendrye (Burpee 1927: 339–40) describes the village fortifications:

All the streets, squares and cabins are uniform in appearance; often our Frenchmen would lose their way in going about. They keep the streets and open spaces very clean; the ramparts are smooth and wide; the palisade is supported on cross pieces mortised into the posts fifteen feet apart with a lining. For this purpose they use green hides fastened only at the top in places where they are needed. As to the bastions, there are four of them at each curtain well flanked. The fort is built on an elevation in mid-prairie with a ditch over fifteen feet deep and from fifteen to eighteen feet wide. Entrance to the fort can only be obtained by steps or pieces [of wood] which they remove when threatened by the enemy. If all their forts are similar you may say that they are impregnable to savages.

In addition to these elaborate fortifications, changes had taken place in village layout and house type. There was a large open space or ceremonial plaza in the center of each village. The houses, which had formerly been rectangular, were now circular, approximately 40 feet in diameter, and supported by four central posts set in a square around the fireplace. However, we know that although the residence lodges were circular, the Mandan ceremonial lodge remained rectangular.

PROCESSES OF CHANGE

The most striking change in Mandan culture during Period II was the new settlement pattern which involved a reduction in the number of villages, a decrease in the extent of the Mandan area of occupation, and an increase in population density. Formerly located in many small hamlets spread over a large area in North and South Dakota, the Mandan were now in nine large towns within twenty miles of one another along the banks of the Missouri. The population density increased from approximately 20 persons per acre of occupied village land to about 125 per acre.

Migrations of Pawnee-Arikara peoples from the south, the displacement of eastern tribes, acquisition of the horse and eventual emergence of equestrian nomadism contributed to the Mandan concentration in compact, heavily fortified villages for purposes of defense. Kroeber (1939: 87) has characterized the latter part of this period as follows: "Roughly about these village tribes there revolved the greatest turmoil of new contacts, clashes, readaptations, and importings. To these changes the villagers contributed, and they were not uninfluenced by them."

Fusion and mutual interchange of cultural elements undoubtedly occurred between the Mandan and other earth lodge peoples, particularly the Hidatsa who were their closest neighbors, and the Pawnee-Arikara. The shift from a rectangular to a circular earth lodge is directly attributable to Pawnee-Arikara influence. Lehmer (1954*b*) has marshaled the data to show that before 1500 two distinct cultural traditions existed on the margins of the Northern Plains, one in the Middle Missouri Mandan subarea of the Dakotas, and the other in the Central Plains Pawnee-Arikara subarea of Kansas and Nebraska; after 1500 there was a coalescent blending or fusion of the two (see also Hurt 1953; Wedel 1956). There is firm archeological evidence that some Central Plains groups settled in the Mandan area of South Dakota (Spaulding 1956), although much of the cultural interchange was probably the result of diffusion and contact rather than actual migration of peoples (Wedel 1956: 89).

One hypothesis of this study is that the basic fabric of historic Mandan culture had fully developed *after* the coalescence had taken place among the earth lodge tribes, and *before* the emergence of equestrian nomadism on the Plains. Mandan culture in 1750 was the result of five hundred years of adaptive response to the Missouri River Valley ecology, fusion with other earth lodge cultures of the Eastern Plains, contact with pre-horse nomads and internal adjustments to the new settlement pattern.

The concentration of villages and higher population density called for more elaborate means of societal integration and social control (Eggan 1952: 42; Wedel 1956: 90), accomplished by the age-grade society system, clan organization, and such elaborate ceremonials as the Mandan Okipa, which has many features in common with the traditional Plains Sun Dance. These institutions, which will be described in the next period, probably developed among the village tribes before the horse nomads occupied the Northern Plains (compare Lowie 1916; Spier 1921).

The new settlement pattern was also compatible with the importance of agriculture and with the historic Mandan practice of matrilineal descent. With the greater concentration of population the game near the villages would soon become exhausted. That the Mandan position in the trading network depended upon an economic surplus of maize was a positive factor favoring horticulture. Trading was a crucial part of the total Mandan economy, for it was one of the means by which they obtained the products of nomadic life. Among the nineteenth-century Mandan, agriculture was woman's work, hence its emphasis would strengthen the economic importance of women. As the determination of whether descent is through the male or the female line often depends upon which sex produces the economically valuable goods, during the 1500–1750 period the Mandan probably had matrilineal descent.

The horse nomads arrived too late to produce any fundamental alteration in Mandan culture; rather the influence was in the other direction. Even though the "vital ingredients" of typical Plains nomadism were widespread in the Eastern Woodlands before White

contact (Lowie 1954: 203), it is highly probable that the horse nomads adopted many aspects of material culture, hunting techniques,
social organization, and ceremonial practices from the well-established village tribes.

Weapons, skin dressing tools, and all those other traits which pertained
to the hunting phase of the village life appear again as the material culture of the horse tribes. In view of this, it also seems likely that many of
the more complex elements of the horse tribes' social organization were
also transpositions from the older village pattern. (Lehmer 1954*b*: 154.)

European contact and the introduction of the horse revolutionized
Plains life and thus changed the total situation in which the Mandan
people found themselves; but the actual changes in 1750 Mandan culture directly attributable to White contact and the horse were negligible. Manufactured goods, such as the gun and metal objects, were
simply alternatives, not replacements for the bow and arrow, pottery, and tools of stone, bone, and wood. The horse did increase mobility, extend the hunting range, and facilitate communication, but it
did not change the basic pattern of Mandan life.

The Cheyenne, Sioux, and other eastern peoples became nomads;
the Mandan stayed in their villages and cultivated their gardens. The
Mandan did not become nomads because there was no advantage in
doing so. They had developed a satisfactory adjustment to the river
valley environment, were numerous and fortified enough in their villages to withstand any attack, and received the products of nomadic
life through trade. Before 1750 they were neither lured by the buffalo nor pushed onto the High Plains. After 1750 the choice was not
theirs to make.

The Fur Trade Contact Community, 1750–1862
HISTORICAL BACKGROUND

A Western historian writing on the Mandan would distinguish between French, Spanish, British, and American contact, and between
such contacting agents as government employee, military man, missionary, explorer-naturalist, and trader. In the Mandan conception of
their own history until the last decades of Period III there would be
but one category, White man. This section begins with the historian's
view but approximates the Mandan conception in the analysis that
follows (see Map 7 for orientation).

French trade coming overland from Canada was virtually stopped
from 1756 to the end of the French and Indian War. In 1762, the
Mandan territory was part of the land transferred to Spain by France;
however, it was the British fur companies that revived the trade about
1766. The Hudson's Bay Company and the newly organized Northwest Company operating from their Canadian posts were fifteen days'
journey from the Mandan villages. A trader would leave the company post with a few hired men and a stock of goods, establish himself in an earth lodge in the Indian community or in the chief's house,
and would return after he had bartered his goods for furs and skins.
Keen competition developed between the Hudson's Bay and North-

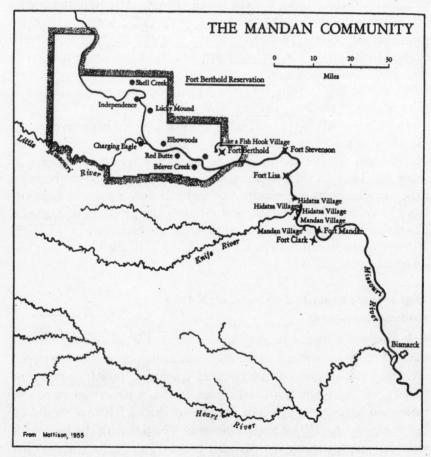

MAP 7

west Companies for the lucrative Mandan trade (Masson 1889; Hyde 1951–52).

Although the Upper Missouri was Spanish domain, traders from the Spanish center of St. Louis were hampered in their attempts to reach the Mandan villages by the Sioux and Arikara, who either demanded tribute or prevented passage. When the first representative of the Spanish traders, Jacques D'Église, reached the Mandan in August, 1790, he found one French Canadian employed by the British who had been living and trading in the Indian villages for fourteen years (Nasatir 1952: 82). John Evans made the first official Spanish contact with the Mandan in September, 1796. He distributed flags, medals, and presents to the chiefs, who promised to follow the counsels of "their Great Father the Spaniard" (Nasatir 1952: 496). The Spanish flag was hoisted over an English trading post which had been erected in 1794, and the British were ordered to return to Canada.

The story of John Evans is of interest in itself (Nasatir 1931). He had come to the United States in 1792 from Wales in order to find the Welsh Indians and attached himself to a Spanish expedition as a means of reaching the Mandan. Tales of supposed Welsh origin of the Mandan were widespread in the eighteenth century; were popularized by Catlin (1841) in the mid-nineteenth century; and were even repeated to me by Indian informants in 1953.

John Evans left the Mandan in the spring of 1797; the area was ceded by Spain back to France in 1800; and as part of the Louisiana Purchase was sold by Napoleon to the United States on April 30, 1803. Lewis and Clark, sent as official representatives of the United States for purposes of exploration and to assess the possibilities of trade, built Fort Mandan near the Indian villages and wintered there in 1804–5. Following the pattern established by the French, Spanish, and British before them, the American explorers distributed flags, medals, presents, and officers' uniforms to the Indian chiefs, who now promised to follow the counsel of their Great Father the President. Charles Mackenzie, a British trader, was told by the Indians that in the Lewis and Clark party there were "only two sensible men . . . , the worker of iron and the mender of guns" (Masson 1889: 330).

The British traders coming overland from Canada and the American traders traveling up the Missouri from St. Louis were prevented from establishing a permanent post among the Mandan by the surrounding tribes, the Assiniboin, Cree, Sioux, and Arikara. The trading post built by Manuel Lisa in 1809 for the Missouri Fur Company, in which Lewis and Clark had business interests, and the one erected by James Kipp in 1822 for the Columbia Fur Company had to be abandoned after brief and unsuccessful careers.

It was the American Fur Company which succeeded. They absorbed all opposition and maintained a virtual monopoly on the Upper Missouri trade from 1827 to the 1860's. John Jacob Astor sold out his interests in 1834 and eventually the concern came into the control of the Pierre Choteau Company of St. Louis, but it was still known as the American Fur Company, or simply as "the company" (Chittenden 1935). Their goods were shipped from St. Louis by keelboat and after 1832 by steamboat to their posts along the Missouri. The Mandan trade at Fort Clark, constructed in 1831, and at Fort Berthold, built in 1845.

The history of White relationships with the Mandan during the 1750–1862 period is essentially a history of the fur trade. Explorers and naturalists who visited the Mandan did so as "paying guests" of the fur companies. Bradbury and Brackenridge in 1811 accompanied Manuel Lisa; Catlin and Maximilian in 1832–34 obtained transportation, room and board, supplies, and interpreters through the head of the trading post at Fort Clark (Abel 1932).

United States government relationships with the Mandan were manipulated by the American Fur Company. The treaty of 1825 concluded by General Atkinson and Indian Agent O'Fallon with the Missouri tribes contained the provision that Indians were to deal only with licensed American traders (Reid and Gannon 1929). This provision was designed to curtail the activities of the Hudson's Bay Company which had merged with the Northwest Company in 1821. John Sanford, Indian agent from 1826 to 1834 with jurisdiction over the Mandan, worked zealously on behalf of the American Fur Company. He traveled on their boats, associated with their employees, and distributed presents to the Mandan in the company of the fur trader. The Indian agent from 1842 to 1846, Andrew Drips, was actually an employee of the company (Abel 1932).

It is not surprising that the Indian people equated scientist, military man, and government employee with trader (Coues 1897: 325; Catlin 1841: 98; Boller 1868: 55). From the Mandan point of view, to be White was to be a trader; there was no other kind of non-Indian in their social universe until the last decades of the Fur Trade Period. Only then did forces emerge more powerful than the American Fur Company.

The social roles of Indian agent and missionary or "Black Robe" developed in the 1850's. The Fort Laramie Treaty of 1851 established a 12,500,000 acre reservation for the Mandan, Hidatsa, and Arikara between the Yellowstone and the Missouri, their traditional hunting territory. The aim of the Laramie Treaty was to establish boundaries in preparation for the American expansion that was to follow (Billington 1949: 653). In compensation annuities were dispensed by the Indian agent for a period of ten years on behalf of the federal government. Through these annuity payments contact between Agent and Indian increased.

The first missionary to reach the Mandan was Father Hoecker who came on the annual steamboat to Fort Clark in 1840 and baptized seven half-breed children of the resident traders (Pfaller 1950). Father Pierre Jean DeSmet was the most respected and best-known Jesuit in the area (Chittenden and Richardson 1905). From the 1840's through the 1860's he made a number of very short visits to the Mandan. By the end of the Fur Trade Period most Mandans had been baptized, but these were mass conversions and the Jesuits were unable to solidify their initial gains.

Despite these forces for change, the one permanent White establishment in the Mandan villages was the trading post; Indian agency, military fort, mission, and White settlement developed after 1862. Others may have visited the Mandan but the fur trader learned their language and lived among them.

COMMUNITY ORGANIZATION

In 1750, there were nine thousand Mandan located in nine villages near the Heart River. In 1862, as a result of smallpox, whooping cough, cholera and measles, as well as hostile attacks by the Sioux, Arikara, Assiniboin, Cheyenne, Plains Cree, Plains Ojibwa, Blackfoot, and other tribes, the remnants of the Mandan, approximately 250, had joined with the Hidatsa and Arikara in Like-a-Fish-Hook village between the Knife and the Little Missouri.

Before the devastating diseases, the Mandan were numerous enough to resist hostile raids. There is some question about the precise date of the first smallpox attack; it may have been as early as 1764. But there is no doubt that, after a series of epidemics culminating in 1782, the Mandan population declined so severely that they became vulnerable to the nomads. The Teton Sioux, pressed from the east and in possession of horse and gun, were quick to take advantage of the weakened condition of the village tribes. In the 1780's they drove the Mandan from the Heart River area, crossed the Missouri, and adopted the High Plains life. The Teton bands were not merely playing the game of Plains Indian warfare; they attacked *en masse* and destroyed the Mandan villages (Will and Hecker 1944; Hyde 1951–52).

The Mandan resettled below the Hidatsa, who refused to give them permission to build their villages above the Knife River (Coues 1897: 334). According to Lewis and Clark, the two Heart River Mandan villages originally located on the east bank of the Missouri consolidated into one village; the original seven Mandan villages on the west bank were reduced to five, then two, then one. A group of Arikara, systematically harassed by the Sioux, fled to the Mandan and Hidatsa for protection, later joined the Sioux to fight against their protectors, and eventually moved downstream to South Dakota.

The Knife River contact community, consisting of the White traders, two Mandan and three Hidatsa villages, and visiting Indian bands from other areas, remained relatively stable until 1837. Although the community is described by many observers, the brief account presented here is based primarily upon Maximilian (in Thwaites 1906) and Chardon (Abel 1932).

The American Fur Company trading post, Fort Clark, was a one-story log building forty-four by forty-nine paces. James Kipp, the director of the fort in 1833, was married to a Mandan woman and spoke the Mandan language. Kipp received a salary of $600 a year (Abel 1932: xxiv). The number of company men located at the post varied by need and season; at times there was a total complement of fifteen to twenty. Two were interpreters, for Mandan and Sioux, one a smith, and the remainder French Canadian hired men, i.e., *engagés* or *voyageurs*. The two interpreters and most of the others were married to Indian women. One of the interpreters, Charboneau, had been employed by Lewis and Clark in 1804.

Three hundred paces from Fort Clark stood the first Mandan village, containing 65 earth lodges and 150 warriors. The second village with 38 lodges and 83 warriors was located three miles upstream. The combined Mandan population of the two villages was 900–1,000, according to Maximilian, who was an excellent observer but who nevertheless may have underestimated the Mandan population. In 1797 Thompson (Tyrrell 1916: 235) reports a population of 1,520; other reliable sources for the 1833–37 period place the number of Mandan at 1,600 (Lowie 1954: 10).

The Hidatsa villages were located within three miles of the Mandan in 1804, and within fifteen miles in 1833–34. During these thirty years, the Hidatsa had moved their villages farther up the Missouri. Each Hidatsa village may be considered as a relatively independent band, which differed slightly in culture and dialect from the others. Lewis and Clark considered one band, the Ahnahaways or Amahami— or in Bowers' orthography, the Awaxawi—as a separate tribe, but they spoke a dialect of Hidatsa and had simply diverged more widely.

MAP 8

Surrounding Indian tribes would come to the Knife River community to obtain corn from the Mandan and Hidatsa, and European trade objects from Fort Clark. The relative location of Plains Indian tribes is shown in Map 8, based upon Kroeber (1939), their populations in Table 4, adapted from Lowie (1954: 10–11). As a result of the extensive trade with other Indian groups, the quantity of goods at

TABLE 4

POPULATION OF PLAINS INDIANS
(Lowie 1954: 10–11)

Blackfoot..........	15,000	(1780)	Assiniboin.........	10,000	(1780)
	9,000	(1801)		8,000	(1829)
	7,600	(1855)		2,800	(1920)
	4,600	(1932)			
			Iowa..............	1,100	(1760)
Cheyenne..........	3,500	(1780)		800	(1804)
	2,695	(1930)		112	(1937)
Arapaho...........	3,000	(1780)	Oto..............	900	(1780)
	1,241	(1930)		500	(1805)
Gros Ventre.......	3,000	(1780)	Oto-Missouri......	931	(1843)
	809	(1937)		332	(1910)
				627	(1930)
Plains Cree........	4,000	(1835)			
	1,000	(1858)	Omaha...........	2,800	(1780)
				300	(1802)
Sarsi.............	700	(1670)		1,103	(1930)
	160	(1924)			
			Ponca............	800	(1780)
Pawnee...........	10,000	(1780)		939	(1930)
	4,686	(1856)			
	959	(1937)	Osage............	6,200	(1780)
				3,649	(1937)
Arikara...........	3,800	(1780)			
	2,600	(1804)	Kansa............	3,300	(1780)
	616	(1937)		1,850	(1822)
				515	(1937)
Kiowa............	2,000	(1780)	Wind River Sho-		
	1,050	(1930)	shone..........	1,500	(1820)
				1,250	(1878)
Hidatsa...........	2,500	(1780)			
	2,100	(1804)	Ute..............	4,500	(1845)
	528	(1930)			
			Jicarilla Apache....	800	(1845)
Crow.............	4,000	(1780)		714	(1937)
	2,173	(1937)			
			Kutenai..........	1,200	(1780)
Eastern and Central				1,087	(1905)
Dakota..........	15,000	(1780)			
Western Dakota....	10,000	(1780)	Nez Percé........	4,000	(1780)
	⎰25,000	(1780)		1,415	(1937)
All Dakota........	⎱27,175	(1904)			
	25,934	(1930)			

Fort Clark was far beyond that which would be necessary for the Mandan and Hidatsa alone. In 1833, the total stock was valued at $15,000; in 1835, a good year, there were 3,270 buffalo robes and 1,140 beaver skins, these two items themselves worth $13,000.

In 1837, the annual steamboat of the American Fur Company carried smallpox to all the Upper Missouri tribes. The disease had broken out at Pierre, South Dakota; nevertheless, the journey continued. When the boat docked at Fort Clark, the officers of the company attempted to keep the Indians away, but a Mandan stole the blanket of a watchman who was dying of the disease. Chardon, then director of Fort Clark, presents a vivid picture of the course of the epidemic (Abel 1932). At its peak eight to ten Indians died every day. It was impossible for those who remained to bury the dead; many were just thrown over a cliff. The Indians became desperate; some sought vengeance against the Whites, others committed suicide. Conditions were made worse by the Sioux and Assiniboin, whose war parties attacked the Mandan in November and December of 1837, at the height of the epidemic. Chittenden (1935: 847) states that by the spring of 1837 only thirty Mandan were left, but more liberal estimates place the number of survivors at twenty-three adult men, forty adult women, and sixty to seventy young people (Hayden 1863: 433). The unequal sex ratio was apparently not due to a differential susceptibility to smallpox. Before the epidemic, in 1832–33, Catlin reports that among the Mandan there were two or three women to each man.

One of the Mandan villages was burned by the Sioux in January, 1839. The survivors moved five miles above Fort Clark and managed to maintain themselves by making an arrangement with one band of Sioux whose leader was part Mandan and with whom they had many kinship relationships. The arrangement involved both protection and extortion. The second Mandan village was taken over by the Arikara, who had come to the Knife River area in 1837 seeking a new location. The occupation of their village and cornfields was resented by the remaining Mandan, but they were not in a position to resist. However, when the Hidatsa migrated upstream and constructed Like-a-Fish-Hook village in 1845, the Mandan gradually settled among them. The American Fur Company maintained Fort Clark for the Arikara and built Fort Berthold for the Hidatsa.

Between 1837 and 1860 some Mandan were in their own village, others were with the Arikara at Fort Clark, and still others with the

Hidatsa at Fort Berthold. Population figures for this period are generally unreliable, but the Indian agent's report for 1855 contains reasonable estimates: 252 Mandan in 21 lodges, 760 Hidatsa in 40 lodges, and 840 Arikara in 60 lodges. By 1860, all the Mandan were located at Like-a-Fish-Hook village; by 1862 the Arikara were forced to join them because of attacks by the Sioux.

EXTERNAL SOCIAL RELATIONSHIPS

The relationship between Indian and White man was structured by the nature of the situation in which the traders found themselves. The early traders were mostly illiterate, lower class, French Canadian *voyageurs* who were few in number and isolated from their own primary groups (Holder 1955). These men had to obtain their satisfactions within the Indian society; there was no White community to which they could turn. They learned the Indian language, intermarried with Indian women, participated in the Indian kinship system, and in effect, became acculturated to Indian ways. The comment made by David Thompson in 1797 (Tyrrell 1916: 230) about one French Canadian, that "he was in every respect as a Native," is repeated by others throughout the Fur Trade Period.

Chittenden (1935: xi) is probably correct when he writes that as a result of the extensive intermarriage, "It was only in these early years that the White man and the Indian truly understood each other." Some traders and trappers traveled widely from one Indian group to another, but many became attached to a particular tribe. Those who had intermarried and raised their children among the Mandan were fully identified and deeply committed to the Indian culture. They fought hostile nomads along with the Mandan, rejoiced in the victory celebrations and mourned at the death of Mandan warriors. Such men as Pierre Garreau, Jefferson Smith, Charles Malnouri, Frederick Gérard, and Peter Beauchamp spent most of their lives among the Indians; their descendants can be found today on the Fort Berthold Reservation.

When the giant concerns such as the Hudson's Bay Company and the American Fur Company became active among the Mandan, they employed French Canadian traders (Mekeel 1943). The American Fur Company had an administrative center in St. Louis, over twenty trading posts and approximately five hundred agents. They maintained their monopoly of the Upper Missouri trade by ruthless elimination of the opposition through underselling and cutthroat competition, force, or if these failed, merger. Despite the magnitude of their operation, it was the *voyageur* who had the routine daily interaction with the Indian people.

The nature of the relationship between Mandan and French trader was supported by the policies of the large trading companies. Their sole aim was profit, which they could best obtain by working through the established social order. The American Fur Company apparently made no effort whatsoever to civilize the Indian or to improve his condition. They were interested in material culture and economic change, but so were the Mandan. The Indians accumulated buffalo robes and beaver skins for the company because it brought them valued European goods.

White traders were subject to Indian law, mostly of necessity, but also as a matter of company policy (Maximilian in Thwaites 1906). White hunters obeyed the same regulations as the Indians on the organized buffalo hunts. Maximilian had to ask permission before leaving a Mandan ceremony, as did the Indian people. When a theft occurred at Fort Clark in 1834, the director of the post went to the Mandan Black Mouth society whose leaders saw that the missing objects were returned. During the fur trade period the balance of power remained with the Mandan; the American Fur Company may or may not have been able to upset it, but they never made the attempt.

The fur companies encouraged Indian-White intermarriage.

It becomes a matter of policy and almost of absolute necessity, for the white men who are Traders in these regions to connect themselves . . . to one or more of the most influential families in the tribe, which in a measure identifies their interest with that of the nation, and enables them, with the influence of their new family connections, to carry on successfully their business transactions . . . the young women of the best families only can aspire to such an elevation; and the most of them are exceedingly ambitious for such a connection . . . they flounce and flut about, the envied and tinselled belles of every tribe . . . almost every Trader and every clerk who commences in the business of this country, speedily enters into such an arrangement. . . . (Catlin 1841: 135–36.)

The traders played a crucial role as middlemen between the Mandan and the larger White society. They were the primary agents for the transmission of Western objects and ideas and provided the interpreters for almost all visitors during the Fur Trade Period (Mekeel 1943). A bilingual such as James Kipp was of great importance for our understanding of Mandan ethnology, as Kipp served as a key interpreter and informant for Catlin, Maximilian, Schoolcraft, Hayden, and Morgan (Will and Spinden 1906: 189).

The Mandan villages offered a number of advantages to the many White traders and explorers who came there. The Mandan were centrally located on the main transportation route between St. Louis and the Rockies, lived in settled villages, had tremendous quantities of surplus corn, were gracious hosts, and welcomed White visitors (Bowers 1950). The literature constantly refers to the "peaceful and friendly Mandan." They may have attacked an isolated trader on the prairies, but none were harmed within their villages. The heavily fortified Mandan villages also provided White visitors excellent protection against the Sioux and other hostile nomads.

The Mandan had one other attraction for the early traders, the availability of women. It is amply documented in the literature that many traders regarded all Mandan women as prostitutes.

Indeed both the girls and married women are so loose in their conduct, that they seem to be a sort of common stock; and are so easy and accessible that there are few among them whose favours cannot be bought with a little vermillion or blue ribbon. This kind of commerce is carried on to a great length by our young Canadian traders. (Truteau in Nasatir 1952: 258.)

The curse of the Mandanes is an almost total want of chastity: this, the men with me knew, and I found it was almost their sole motive for their journey hereto: the goods they brought, they sold at 50 to 60 p^r cent about what they cost; and reserving enough to pay their debts, and buy some corn: [they] spent the rest on Women. (Thompson in Tyrrell 1916: 234.)

The reader might expect us to

give some account of the fair sex of the Missouri, and entertain them with narratives of feats of love as well as of arms. Though we could furnish a sufficient number of entertaining stories and pleasant anecdotes . . . it might be observed generally that chastity is not very highly esteemed by these people, and that the severe and loathsome effects of certain French principles are not uncommon among them. The fact is, that the women are generally considered an article of traffic and indulgences are sold at a very moderate price. As a proof of this I will just mention that for an old tobacco-box, one of our men was granted the honor of passing a night with the daughter of the head chief of the Mandan nation. (Gass in Coues 1893: 74.)

Irrespective of its validity, the traders' conception that the favors of Mandan women could be purchased on a purely commercial basis is an important datum for our understanding of Indian-White relationships. However, other information suggests their conception to be in error. Alexander Henry (Coues 1897: 342) mentions that men offered their wives to strangers without solicitation and expected payment, but then states that "a mere trifle will satisfy them—even one single coat button." It does not seem reasonable that a shrewd trading people such as the Mandan would be satisfied with a coat button, an old tobacco-box, a little vermillion, or a blue ribbon. It was not the amount but simply the fact of payment that was important. The Mandan did sell women to the traders, but these were female prisoners captured from other tribes, never their own women (Masson 1889: 360). Finally, Mandan women offered themselves to distinguished Mandan men but always in a sacred or ceremonial context (Bowers 1950).

The sexual behavior of Mandan women toward White men was rooted in basic premises of the Indian culture; the interpretation of the White traders was a gross cultural misunderstanding. The Indian premises will be developed in the next section, but briefly, younger Mandan men seeking "power" offered their wives to those who had already accumulated much power, that is, to their ceremonial fathers, and to the older distinguished men of the tribe. Power was a quantity that could be transmitted through sexual intercourse, from the older man to the woman and ultimately to her husband. As Lewis and Clark (Coues 1893: 1217) state, "the Indians believed that these traders were the most powerful persons in the nation."

Mandan relationships to surrounding Indian tribes had developed by 1750 and remained essentially unchanged until the late 1820's. The Mandan received arms, ammunition, and European goods from the Canadian traders, from the Cree, and from the Assiniboin, all of whom were in competition with one another for the Upper Missouri trade. The Cree and Assiniboin pillaged and even murdered the Canadian traders en route to the village tribes (Coues 1897: 309), and in between their own trading sessions, were at war with the Mandan. Lewis and Clark report that the Mandan were dependent upon the

Assiniboin and Cree for their European goods, and hence were afraid to oppose them. A similar dependency relationship existed between the Sioux and the Arikara.

In return for manufactured goods, the Mandan traded corn as well as the products of nomadic life—horses, robes, furs, meat, and leather goods—which they received from the Crow, Cheyenne, Arapaho, Kiowa, and other western tribes. The Mandan attempted to prevent the British traders from going beyond their villages and establishing direct connections with the nomads. A tribe such as the Crow received all their guns and European supplies from the Mandan and Hidatsa, who had obtained them from the Cree, Assiniboin, and White traders.

Charles Mackenzie (Masson 1889: 346), after witnessing a transaction in which the village tribes gave the Crow 100 bushels of corn, 200 guns with 100 rounds of ammunition for each, kettles, axes, cloth, and other goods, in return for 250 horses, large parcels of buffalo robes, and leather goods, remarks, "It is incredible the great quantity of merchandise which the Missouri Indians have accumulated." This large tribal trade always involved father-son adoption and was accompanied by a ceremonial dance in which all tribes participated. Tabeau (Abel 1939: 165) was not exaggerating when he stated that "A post among the Mandanes would be a gathering-place for more than twenty nations."

When the American Fur Company established Fort Clark in 1831 and other trading posts throughout the Northern Plains, robes and furs were brought directly to these posts in exchange for European goods. Mandan corn and agricultural produce were still commodities desired by both trader and nomad, and the Mandan maintained a relatively favorable trading position.

After the smallpox epidemic of 1837, the Mandan population was so reduced that they became completely dependent upon their allies the Hidatsa and Arikara and upon their Great Father, the President. At first the Sioux were content to plunder the Mandan cornfields but by the late 1850's their attacks became increasingly severe. The Mandan still had not been vaccinated, for in 1856, seventeen Mandan died of smallpox.

The Indian agents for 1856 and 1858 report that the Mandan were afraid to leave their village because of the Sioux and "begged piteously" for government protection, and that "they appealed most earnestly to me to beg their Great Father to banish these diseases [smallpox and cholera] from their country forever."

If the reports of fur traders, explorers, Indian agents and other documentary sources for the 1750–1862 period are combined with the reconstructions of twentieth-century ethnologists, a holistic picture of Mandan culture emerges. Our aim is to present in brief capsule the major aspects of Mandan life; much of the detail and richness will necessarily be omitted. For a more complete picture of the aboriginal culture the reader is referred to Lewis and Clark (in Coues 1893), Catlin (1841, 1867), Will and Spinden (1906), Maximilian (in Thwaites 1906), De Land (1908), Curtis (1909), Lowie (1913, 1917), and Goplen (1946). This summary has borrowed heavily and paraphrased freely from Bowers (1950), the major work on Mandan culture.

As in earlier times the economy was based upon horticulture, hunting, fishing, gathering, and trade. The preferred food staple was buffalo meat, either roasted, broiled, boiled, smoked, or dried. Maximilian (in Thwaites 1906) reports that the Mandan were scarcely less dependent upon the buffalo than were the nomads and that agriculture was a small supplement to the food supply. Two major methods of hunting the buffalo were employed. In one the Mandan would encircle a herd, ride on horseback as close as possible to a selected animal, kill it with bow and arrow, and then go after another. The second method could more properly be called gathering rather than hunting the buffalo. Every spring when the ice broke on the Missouri River the buffalo which had drowned or were isolated on ice blocks floated downstream past the Mandan villages. The men would balance themselves on the ice or swim out to collect these buffalo; their rotten meat was considered a great delicacy.

A marked dichotomy existed in the division of labor between the sexes. The women performed the horticultural and household tasks; they worked the small garden plots, carried water, gathered fuel, tanned hides, cured meat, dried wild fruits, prepared food, made most of the household utensils and clothing, and repaired the lodge. The men hunted, fought hostile nomads, engaged in ceremonial activity, manufactured weapons, planted tobacco, and assisted in the harvest. The ownership of property reflected the division of labor. The females of the lodge group owned in common the household and garden equipment, the produce of the garden, the game killed by the men, and the dogs, mares, and colts. The men owned their weapons, personal effects and clothing, stallions, and geldings. The agricultural land, the house, and sacred ceremonial bundles belonged to the clan, not to individuals. However, of the children of a given family, the daughters inherited the land and house from their mothers, the sons inherited the sacred bundles from their mothers' brothers. In effect, the women's inheritance was economic, the men's ceremonial.

The annual cycle was adjusted to the severe North Dakota winters. At the end of October or in early November of each year, before the ice froze over the Missouri, the Mandan moved to winter villages located in the wooded bottom lands. This move preserved the wood supply in the summer villages, and provided protection against the elements. Particularly during the cold periods, the buffalo also sought shelter in the timber. Much of Mandan winter ceremonialism involved rites designed to "call" the buffalo, to lure them close to the village where they could be hunted with ease. Mandan parties went out in numerous small hunts of a few days or occasionally a few weeks' duration, but never on extended tribal hunts for an entire winter. The Mandan were not nomadic: however, they were semi-sedentary, as the village would be moved when the fields were exhausted, the game depleted, or the wood scarce.

A buffalo robe was the main article of dress for the men, a long leather garment with open sleeves for the women. Both sexes wore leggings and moccasins. All observers among the Mandan have commented upon the vanity of the men and the care they took in dressing. The men wore their hair long, sometimes down to the knees, carried feather fans, wore elaborate headdresses, and extensively ornamented buffalo robes depicting the heroic deeds which the wearer had performed, the number of sexual conquests he had made, and the quantity of valuable presents he had given to others. Porcupine quillwork, beads, bear claw necklaces, brass rings and tattooing all contributed to the desired masculine effect. To dress properly involved considerable expense; the tail feathers of an eagle were equal in value to one horse (Catlin 1841: 114).

Muskets, bows, arrows with iron heads, clubs and axes of various kinds, lances, shields, and knives were the Mandan weapons. Transportation over the water was by bullboat, made of bent willow frames about six feet in diameter covered with a buffalo hide, and over land by horse and dog. The horse did not replace the dog travois for transport, as the dog lasted longer, traveled farther, ate less, was easier to care for and less expensive than a horse.

Among the Mandan all technological skills, specialized knowledge, and ceremonial information was not freely given—it had to be paid for. When a mother taught her daughter to grind corn the daughter had to pay, even if only a few kernels of corn or a small bead. All technical knowledge concerning the manufacture of material objects, for example, arrowheads, pottery, houses, fish traps, was owned by specialists. Any person wishing to make these objects himself had to receive instruction from the specialist, to whom an appropriate payment was made.

The Mandan village was a major economic, political, and ceremonial entity. The village members hunted together and farmed in a common garden area. Each village was the exact duplicate of the others in terms of ceremonial organization. In the center of the village was an open plaza 60 to 150 feet in diameter. Located inside the plaza was a small wooden cylinder, open above, within which was the sacred cedar, representing the body of the culture hero, Lone Man. The inclosing wood cylinder symbolized the wall which Lone Man had used to protect the people from the flood. To the north of the plaza was the Okipa or ceremonial lodge. Outside of the ceremonial lodge there were various figures made of wood and skin, one of which, at the top of a high pole, represented the evil spirit. The residential lodges surrounding the plaza were occupied by the prominent men, those who owned bundle rights in the Okipa ceremony. The stratification system could be read from the lodge arrangement. The entire village was fortified by palisades, beyond which were the burial scaffolds.

The lodge group consisted of a matrilocal extended family, the smallest economic unit in Mandan society. Matrilocal residence was general although not universal. The lodge itself was held by the females of the lineage, although it belonged to the clan. The high status of certain families was expressed by the location of their lodge relative to the central plaza and by offerings placed on poles erected before their lodges.

The house itself, built of logs and earth, was circular, approximately forty feet in diameter with a covered entrance. The sleeping quarters were located along the wall to the left, the medicine shrine directly opposite, and a stall for horses to the right. In the center was the fireplace under the smoke hole, around which were the four central support posts.

The lodge group could change village affiliation at will, although generally members of related households or a lineage would move together. Reasons for moving included dissatisfaction with local leadership or disputes over the recognition of a chief, lack of adequate cornfields, or the desire to enhance social standing by taking residence in a new village.

Matrilineal descent and a widely extended Crow type of kinship system were the bases of Mandan social life and a key mechanism of tribal integration. The social world of the Mandan was a kinship world in which every individual was related to every other by consanguineous and affinal ties, clan and moiety affiliation, or ceremonial adoption. A constant theme in the mythology was that quarrels between relatives would bring chaos to the village. Sororal polygyny, the levirate, and sororate were practiced.

Catlin (1841: 133–35) has an insightful discussion of the value of polygyny among the upper class—the chiefs, war leaders, and medicine men of the tribe. He writes, "it becomes a matter of necessity for a chief (who must be liberal, keep open doors, and entertain, for the support of his popularity) to have in his wigwam a sufficient number of such handmaids or menials [wives] to perform the numerous duties and drudgeries of so large and expensive an establishment." The labor of women produced the economically valuable goods—corn and dressed buffalo robes for the fur traders—with which the chief could entertain, purchase additional sacred bundles, and assist in the performance of tribal ceremonies. A prominent man might have six or eight wives living together under one roof, although very few of the poor or ordinary men could afford more than a single wife. Polygyny also had a biological function in Mandan society, as Plains warfare led to an unequal sex ratio, sometimes as high as two or three women to each man. The economic importance of women was also a factor militating against possible change or loss of the matrilineal system.

The Mandan had thirteen matrilineal, exogamous, non-totemic clans divided into two moieties. The clan owned property, that is, the land, houses, gardens, and names. If a family died out the property reverted to the clan; if the entire clan died out the property was claimed by the moiety. The men of the clan took the personal property of the male members; the women took the earth lodge, cornfields, dogs, and personal property of the females. The clan controlled the performance of rituals and the transmission of medicine bundles. Marriage was regulated by the clan through the rule of exogamy.

Not all Mandan clans were of equal status. The Waxikena clan had the highest rank, since its members owned the major bundles in the Okipa ceremony. In the mythology the culture hero, Lone Man, was affiliated with the Waxikena clan.

Many social and economic functions were performed by the Mandan clans. Each was a corporate group, had recognized leaders, gave feasts, assisted those members who were old, poor, or orphaned, and disciplined the young. Those affiliated with a clan extended hospitality to all others, avenged the death of any member, and contributed goods toward the purchase or performance of a ceremony.

The Mandan sharply differentiated between the relationship to those in his own clan, and to those in his father's clan. Toward one's own clan members the basic theme was social and economic co-operation and interpersonal harmony. Toward one's father's clan, whose members were classificatory fathers and father's sisters, the basic relationship was ritual respect. A man acquired goods from his own lineage and clan and presented them as gifts to members of his father's clan. The clan fathers gave advice on ceremonial matters, prayed for their clan sons, conducted the son's funeral rites and disposed of the body, inserted thongs in their shoulder muscles during times of fasting, self-torture, and the Okipa, and gave a new name to a clan son when he returned from his first successful war expedition.

The Mandan had two types of medicine bundles, personal and tribal. Personal bundles were acquired by a vision experience, were individually owned, rarely inherited, and lacked a sacred myth or buffalo skull. To induce a vision a man fasted for four, seven, or nine days, during which time a guardian spirit appeared, adopted the faster as his son, and gave instructions concerning the composition of the bundle. These instructions had to be interpreted by a clan father.

The tribal bundles contained a buffalo skull and various objects symbolizing the characters and incidents of a myth. The performance of a ceremony dramatized the events related in the myth. Tribal bundles were most sacred: there were prescribed rules for displaying their contents, for the proper behavior in their presence, and for the feasts to be given in their honor. The owner would rarely tell others about the bundle and its associated myth and then only after an appropriate payment.

Tribal bundles were transmitted by inheritance or purchase; in either case a public feast had to be given to legitimize the transfer. Bundles were inherited within the clan, either by a sister's son, or by a son-in-law, if he were in the same clan as his father-in-law. When a bundle was sold the owner kept the original but made a duplicate bundle for the buyer, who then shared in the ownership of the myth and ceremony. Rights in the medicine bundle could be sold four times by the original owner, which served to widen the base of ceremonial knowledge and participation. Tribal bundles were purchased collectively by a lineage; a mother's brother was usually appointed as custodian. When a ceremony was given for one bundle, the custodians of related bundles and their respective lineages were expected to attend.

The complex of tribal bundles, taken together, provided the basis for Mandan ceremonial life. With the one exception of certain rights in the Okipa, each village was ceremonially independent, that is, each had an exact duplicate of the bundles owned by every other village. If a village split because of overpopulation or dissension, those who separated did not duplicate the ceremonial structure of the parent village immediately but returned for important rituals. With the passage of time, individuals in the appropriate clans were selected to purchase bundles, and eventually the complete ceremonial inventory existed in the new village. However, all recognized the original or primary bundle, the objects of which were thought to be the actual ones used by the mythological characters.

Mandan ceremonialism was designed to insure societal welfare, good crops, and success in buffalo hunting. Sacred beings created the Mandan people and would protect them only if the proper ceremonies were given; the ritual had to be performed to keep on good terms with the supernaturals. A lunar ceremonial calendar existed, but individuals could give ceremonies for doctoring, warfare, or to bring the buffalo at any time simply by announcing their intention and reserving a time for the performance. The Okipa, a four-day annual summer ceremony rich in symbolism, was the most important Mandan ritual (Catlin 1867). Its severe rites of self-torture served as an initiation ceremony for all the young men of the society; it dramatized the origin myth and brought general tribal well-being and buffalo fertility.

The Mandan were also organized in a system of secular societies or fraternities, organized named groups with external symbols of membership. The societies were graded into a series roughly corresponding to relative age. A group of young men would collectively purchase the first society including the songs, symbols, and ritual paraphernalia from those in the next higher age group, occupy it for a period of years, and eventually sell it to those younger than themselves. Most able-bodied persons belonged to one of the approximately ten men's societies or to one of the four women's societies (Lowie 1913).

The basic criterion of membership was not age but collective purchase, involving a large quantity of goods and lengthy bargaining. The transfer ritual was an elaborate affair sometimes lasting for forty nights and always ending with a public ceremony to symbolize the new status of the buyers. A fictitious kinship relationship facilitated the transfer. The buyers regarded the sellers as ceremonial fathers, the buyers' wives called the sellers "grandfather." In addition to the collective purchase, gifts were given individually to one ceremonial father who was in the same clan as the real father of the buyer. This ceremonial father gave special medicine, instruction, and power to his son. One feature of the transfer was the surrender of the buyer's wife to the ceremonial father. If a buyer was still single, he borrowed a friend's wife, usually the wife of a clan brother. The ceremonial father could avoid sexual intercourse with the woman offered to him by presenting her with a gift. Maximilian reports that this rarely happened.

One of the most important functions of the society system was that it established an individual's position in the social structure and defined the appropriate behavior for each age grade. The younger Mandan men were thought to be reckless and irresponsible. In the speeches made by the sellers to the young men the emphasis was upon bravery in warfare, courage and skill in hunting, and upon the performance of heroic personal exploits. The younger group achieved prestige in terms of the number of enemy scalps taken, horses stolen, and sexual conquests made. The societies of the middle-aged men preserved order, policed the hunts, settled difficulties, and were in charge of village administration and management. They acted with the authority

of an executive branch. The old people's societies made policy decisions, gave advice, acted as ceremonial leaders, and kept the traditions
(Lowie 1913).

In addition to defining the proper behavior throughout the life cycle, the society system performed an important educational function
in that instruction in tribal lore and societal values was a part of each
society transfer. The women's societies were similar in this respect, as
the younger groups were concerned with the military exploits of the
men, and the older group with agricultural activities. By giving unity
to the peer group, the system further integrated a society segmented
by clan and lineage ties.

The village leaders were those lineage and clan heads who owned
important tribal bundles. From them one peace leader was selected
who had performed many rites for village welfare, was thoughtful of
others, popular with the tribes coming to trade, could settle quarrels
amicably, was generous and well informed on tribal history and lore.
One war leader was also selected on the basis of his war record and
bundle ownership.

A chief's authority was dependent on his oratory ability, the length
of time his opinions were accepted, and the degree to which he reflected group opinion. No one individual leader was an absolute authority on all matters; particular leaders were chosen for different activities, for example, the performance of a ceremony, a buffalo hunt,
or an eagle-trapping expedition.

Each Mandan community was an independent entity. There was
no political organization above the village level. The villages often
acted collectively for defense and co-operated in matters of mutual
interest, but always informally and with reference to particular issues
as they arose. From the point of view of the individual, his primary
identifications were with lineage, clan, and village, not with the Mandan nation. Indian people in the twentieth century are still aware of
the original villages from which their ancestors came and the degree
to which their village differed in dialect and custom from all others.
On the tribal level, societal integration was based upon kinship extensions, clan affiliation, the society system, and ceremonial bundle ownership; cultural integration was based upon a common language and
culture.

Mandan society was stratified into classes based upon the inheritance of tribal bundles. Those who owned important bundles were

usually wealthy, as they received goods and property for performing the sacred rites and could marry two or more wives, who in turn produced corn, dressed skins and brought other economically valuable assets. The lineages in possession of tribal bundles tended to preserve their wealth by arranging selective marriages with other important families.

Those in the upper classes could achieve further recognition if they had certain desirable personality characteristics, such as consideration for others, and the ability to settle quarrels. But these characteristics were not essential; a family could be prominent but disliked (e.g., see Catlin 1841: 104). It was expected that the owners of important bundles would distribute goods freely and learn tribal lore. This could readily be accomplished by any man having sufficient property to be generous to others and to pay for sacred knowledge.

Those who were not eligible to inherit a tribal bundle could achieve recognition through personal achievements and military glory; the path was open, but it was difficult and uncertain. A young man who had no "medicine" could fast, engage in self-torture, perform acts for village welfare, and, if he were a member of a large kin group that could provide the necessary goods, he could give feasts to bundle owners. If he performed these acts, he would receive some sacred object or medicine associated with a ceremony which enabled him to become a war leader. Without the proper medicine and sacred knowledge a man could not lead a war expedition, as others would not follow.

The success or misfortune of an entire war party was directly attributed to the luck and power of the leader. If an expedition lost no men and obtained many scalps and horses, the reputation of the leader was established, especially if he gave away his horses and valuable articles in a large public display. He might then be a poor man, but people said of him that he had great power. However, if one person was killed on his war party, the leader lost prestige, which he could regain by fasting, cutting off a finger, gashing his legs, and making lavish gifts to the lineage of the deceased warrior. Unless a man already owned tribal bundles and came from a prosperous family, one unsuccessful war expedition was usually sufficient to end his career as a leader.

Basic to Mandan thought was the notion of "power" and the methods for its acquisition. Power was a dimensional substance, controlled by the supernaturals. It was acquired by fasting, self-torture, receiving visions, being kind to the old people, avoiding direct expressions of aggression in interpersonal relationships, purchasing sacred bundles, participating in tribal rituals, giving feasts to the bundles, being generous and giving gifts in public, obtaining ceremonial knowledge, and inviting older men to have sexual intercourse with one's wife. Power was spent by the performance of any dangerous act, such as crossing a river when the ice was thin, hunting buffalo, training wild horses, or leading a war party. The performance of these hazardous acts tended to validate the quantity of power possessed by an individual by demonstrating to others that he could complete these tasks successfully despite the power lost. Personal misfortune or unsuccessful experiences were evidence of the lack of adequate power.

The quantity of power possessed by an individual varied throughout his life career. Children had no power; they were not born with any. As a young man began to fast, engage in self-torture, and participate in the ceremonies, he gradually acquired power. His quantity of power was built up to its peak as he approached middle age, at about the time he became involved in village administration; thereafter there was a slow decline until, in old age, his power was gone. An old man who had completed the cycle was regarded with great respect; his material needs were provided by gifts from the young men just starting their power quest.

Those Mandan who followed the proper path throughout their life careers achieved personal satisfactions and cultural rewards at each step, lived up to the societal values, and, by the tasks they accomplished in the quest for power, kept the society going. When misfortune and death fell upon the Mandan, it was evidence of an infraction of tribal rule, of an error in the ritual, of insufficient fasting and self-torture, of the lack of generosity, of disrespect shown to the old people. The Mandan solution to misfortune was to intensify the power quest and increase the frequency of the ceremonials.

PROCESSES OF CHANGE

In 1862 Mandan society was intact and the culture continued to function with the exception of the economy which was severely disrupted. The traditional economy virtually collapsed as a result of attacks by the Sioux and other hostile nomads; it simply became too dangerous for the women to leave the villages to work their gardens or for the men to go out on hunting trips. The decline in both horticulture and hunting not only affected subsistence, but also Mandan relationships to other Plains tribes as they no longer had surplus corn and dressed skins to trade.

The pressure on the economy had been building up throughout the Fur Trade Period. In 1797 David Thompson (Tyrrell 1916: 229) was told "the enemies have never been able to hurt us when we are in our Villages; and it is only when we are absent on large hunting parties that we have suffered; and which we shall not do again." Catlin (1841: 143) reports that the Mandan were "unwilling to risk their lives by going far from home in the face of their more powerful enemies." By the middle of the nineteenth century the Sioux were stealing Mandan horses and plundering their crops at will, killing women working in the fields, and ambushing hunting parties. In some years the Mandan did not produce enough food for their own consumption. To meet these crises the government provided assistance in the form of annuities, not for humanitarian motives alone, but to compensate the Mandan for accepting reservation boundaries.

A century of continuous contact with White traders resulted in a decline in native technology, and in a few replacements, some additions, and many alternatives to the material culture inventory. The arts of making pottery and painting buffalo robes declined; the Indian men preferred the traders' tobacco to their home-grown variety; shields of buffalo bull hide were not used as they proved ineffective against a musket shot; coffee, tea, sugar, and the potato were introduced. Such small items as metal fishhooks, needles, axes, and files were eagerly accepted by the Mandan in preference to their stone and bone counterparts. Wool blankets, iron hoes, glass beads, and the log cabin became alternatives to buffalo robes, the shoulder-blade hoe, dyed porcupine quills, and the earth lodge. The gun was used for warfare and a possible encounter with a grizzly bear, but the bow and arrow was retained for hunting.

White contact also led to a series of changes in native secular knowledge. Western medicine was generally accepted and such specialists as the blacksmith were in great demand. The seeds of change in world view were introduced. When Maximilian told the Mandan that the earth was round and revolved about the sun, many rejected his notions as silly, but others were willing to consider the possibility that such seemingly incomprehensible ideas might be correct (in Thwaites 1906).

Two processes of change affected Mandan social and ceremonial organization; however, neither influenced the basic structure. The first was extensive intertribal borrowing of particular societies, dances, and ceremonies. In 1833, the Mandan performed a ceremony which they had obtained from the Hidatsa who had previously bought it from the Arikara. The purchase of a given society from the Sioux, Crow, Hidatsa, Arikara, or other Plains tribe was an important cultural addition for the Mandan, but it did not change the organization of the society system nor the cultural assumptions upon which it was based. Such purchases, sales, and borrowings were a very old and frequent occurrence on the Plains.

The second process of change in social and ceremonial organization might best be called consolidation, a consequence of the sharp reduction in the Mandan population from 9,000 to 250, and in the number of villages from nine to part of one. The process is illustrated most clearly in the clan system and in medicine bundle ownership. In 1750 there were thirteen Mandan clans, in 1782 there were nine, in 1837 there were seven, and in 1862 only four remained. In those cases in which all female members died the clan soon became extinct; in other cases there were so few survivors that they joined a larger clan of the same moiety. As the number of clans was reduced some means of adjustment had to be established if the ceremonial system was to function; for it was the clan that owned tribal medicine bundles. The Mandan were practical. Other clans and other individuals took over the ceremonial responsibility; and there were instances of father-son transmission of bundles, a radical but necessary departure from Mandan custom. Inevitably the process of clan consolidation led to a relaxation of marriage taboos, e.g., moiety exogamy was not continued after 1837.

The notion of equating the Mandan and Hidatsa clans developed, although this was not completely worked out until the next period. Each Mandan clan had a Hidatsa counterpart with whom it was affiliated, part of the attempt to develop a common social system to ease relationships between members of the two tribes.

As each village had previously been a ceremonial entity in itself with its own inventory of medicine bundles, after consolidation there were instances of multiple bundles and duplicate officers for important tribal ceremonies. In these instances the primary or original bundle was recognized and used, the secondary bundles that had been sold were put away and not transferred. This procedure reduced the total number of active Mandan bundles, but kept the ceremonial system going. It was a logical counterpart of the mechanism inherent in the system for the sale and duplication of bundles during periods of population expansion.

These then were the major changes in Mandan culture at the end of the Fur Trade Period.

It is somewhat remarkable that notwithstanding all the misfortunes that have befallen this tribe for so many years, it even to this time preserves its independence and individuality as a nation. . . . They will not . . . practice any customs but those of their ancestors. Their religious rites and ceremonies are preserved entire, and the system of self-inflicting tortures is practiced at the present day. (Clark 1885: 428, 434.)

Considering the severe population loss, Sioux attacks, enforced migrations up the Missouri, and other pressures to which they were subjected, one would almost have expected more extensive change: not necessarily change toward a Western model, as no functioning White society existed in the Mandan environment, but rather cultural extinction by absorption into one of the larger Plains societies.

The basic problem in the preservation of Mandan culture was the preservation of the Mandan community, that is, population replacement. We have previously stated that twenty-three men, forty women, and sixty to seventy children survived the 1837 smallpox epidemic. A total of only twenty-three adult males, some beyond the reproductive age, is a dangerously low number for any society.

The Mandan met this problem of their survival by the application of some shrewd social psychology and common sense. "They did not allow their women to marry into other bands or tribes unless the man would renounce his tribal relations, join them, and agree that the children should talk the Mandan language, and be reared in their customs and beliefs" (Clark 1885: 241).

The application of this rule, and the productivity of Mandan women, assured the preservation of Mandan culture. The mothers, the main agents of socialization, raised their children to become and to speak Mandan. In a matrilineal society it did not matter if the husband had no clan affiliation; the wife and consequently the children did. Land and houses were transmitted through the clan directly from mother to daughter; tribal bundles were inherited by males but within the clan. Marriage to alien men was also adaptive in a society in which there was a surplus of women, an unequal sex ratio due to Plains warfare.

Not all cultures can take in and assimilate men from other tribes; the Mandan could do so because of the nature of their social system. Mandan society was "open" in the sense that the mechanisms existed through ceremonial adoption for absorbing aliens into the kinship system. In a society in which social relationships are based upon kinship, to be adopted into the kinship system is the equivalent of being granted citizenship. Trading relationships with neighboring Plains tribes were eased by father-son adoption; the French Canadian traders and some recent anthropologists have been given Indian names, taken into clans, and therefore assigned to a position in the social structure. Female prisoners of war were either sold to White traders or adopted. It is as if all those who approached Mandan society from the outside were either absorbed into the system or expelled; one could not remain a neutral on the societal border.

By these means the Mandan population increased from approximately 150 in 1837 to approximately 250 in 1862. However in the process of population replacement, the biological identity, the gene pool, was changing radically. Actually from the middle of the eighteenth century there had been a constant flow of genes into the Mandan population from French, British, Canadian, Spanish, and American traders. The practice of ceremonial surrender of wives, trader-Indian intermarriage, the absorption of Indian men from alien tribes, and a rather permissive attitude toward sex in general—all operating for a long period of time on a small population—had undoubtedly created great change in the Mandan gene pool. Newman (1950) discusses this problem from the point of view of physical anthropology; for our purposes here it is sufficient to indicate that the gene flow may have been alien, but at this period in history the majority of offspring were culturally Mandan.

Possibly the most drastic change undergone by the Mandan was not cultural or biological, but psychological. In 1750, they were one of the most powerful and prosperous nations on the Northern Plains. By 1862, they fully realized that White man's diseases had almost annihilated them, that the buffalo were becoming scarce, and that Sioux attacks had precipitated an economic collapse (Annual Reports, Commissioner of Indian Affairs, 1856–58, 1862). The Mandan responded by an intensification of ceremonial activity as a means of relieving their anxiety. No major ceremonies were lost after the 1837 smallpox epidemic (Bowers 1950), yet the population was so reduced that the ceremonial load on each individual inevitably increased. Their aggressive feelings were released against the Whites, whom they held responsible for the smallpox attacks (Chittenden and Richardson 1905: 832; Abel 1932; Boller 1868: 55–56); against their enemies, whose slain bodies they mutilated (Matthews 1877: 58; Chittenden and Richardson 1905: 248); and against themselves, as indicated by an increase in self-torture. Father DeSmet did not see one adult male whose body was not scarred or who possessed his full number of fingers (Chittenden and Richardson 1905: 667).

The Military-Agency Contact Community, 1862–83
HISTORICAL BACKGROUND

Throughout the last decade of the Fur Trade Period the Mandan repeatedly asked for United States troops to protect them against the Sioux; they asked for financial assistance from the federal government; they asked for schools, and a missionary (Chittenden and Richardson 1905: 650–51, 828). The troops arrived in 1864, the first permanent Indian agency was established in 1868, a day school was started in 1870, and the first resident missionary arrived in 1876. Their requests were granted, but the consequences were not quite what the Mandan had originally envisioned.

Troops were sent to Fort Berthold in part because the Indians had requested protection, but primarily because of factors related to military control of the area during the Civil War. Many fur company employees were Confederate sympathizers and the government feared they might seize the Upper Missouri (Mattison 1951: 55); talk of an Indian war was common on the frontiers, especially after the outbreak of the Minnesota Sioux in 1862–63 (Billington 1949: 655–57). When the military arrived, the conflict which existed on the national and state level between the army and the Indian Bureau over who had control of the Indians (Lamar 1956: 36) was reflected on the local level. The civilian agent was forbidden to talk to Indians except in the presence of the military authorities, who also attempted to regulate trade, which in turn antagonized the fur company (Annual

Reports, Commissioner of Indian Affairs, 1865; Larpenteur in Coues 1898: 387). As a result of these disputes, the troops were located outside Fort Berthold in their own buildings.

A permanent military post, Fort Stevenson, was built in 1867–68 approximately eighteen miles below Fort Berthold on land ceded by the Mandan, Hidatsa, and Arikara. The general objectives of the post were to establish law and order, facilitate steamboat travel up the Missouri, and maintain mail and telegraph communication with the West. After the Civil War, emigrants passed through the Great Plains en route to the gold fields discovered in Montana; the military sought to channel part of this travel by way of the Missouri River (Mattison 1951: 56). In 1867, over forty steamers ascended the Missouri; previously only one or two of the American Fur Company boats had made the trip each year. Fort Stevenson was one link in a chain of military posts designed to protect the frontier and open the West for American expansion (Mattison 1951: 57).

During the last part of the Fur Trade Period the Indian agent visited the Upper Missouri tribes once a year to distribute annuities; in the summer and fall of 1866 the agent spent three months at Fort Berthold; he came again for three separate visits in the spring and summer of 1867; and in 1868 a resident agent arrived to direct the construction of a permanent agency (Annual Reports, Commissioner of Indian Affairs, 1867, 1868). The administrative unit included the Mandan, Hidatsa, and Arikara, known as the Three Affiliated Tribes, or the Fort Berthold Indians. The agent and his staff occupied part of the Fort Berthold trading post, for which the government paid rent to the trading company. The American Fur Company had retired and disposed of its interests; eventually a new company, Durfee and Peck, took over.

At the request of the headmen of the Three Tribes, who expressed a desire for education for their people, an agency day school was opened in December, 1870. The school was closed in 1872 as attendance was poor and it was felt that the Indians had little real interest in education; it was opened again in 1873, destroyed by fire in 1874, and reopened in 1875. The average school attendance varied from a low of twelve in 1877 to a high of thirty-two in 1883 (Annual Reports, Commissioner of Indian Affairs).

In the "Peace Policy" of President Grant, each Indian agency was to be assigned to one religious denomination so that all would eventually be brought under the influence of Christian missionaries. First given to the Episcopalians, who failed to supply a missionary, Fort Berthold was later passed to the Congregationalists. On May 9, 1876, Rev. Charles L. Hall and his wife arrived among the Three Tribes. At first, one building served as a residence, church, and school; by 1880 a chapel and schoolroom had been constructed. Church was held every Sunday, but not many came to the service, usually fifteen to twenty persons, sometimes only ten (Wilson 1914).

COMMUNITY ORGANIZATION

The Mandan lived in one section of Like-a-Fish-Hook village; the other two sections were occupied by the Hidatsa and Arikara Indians. Mandan population estimates for the Military-Agency Period vary from 228 to 479 (Annual Reports, Commissioner of Indian Affairs; Matthews 1877: 16–17; Bowers 1950: 1). Based upon the evidence available, approximately 300 seems most reasonable. There was certainly no decline in the Mandan population between 1862 and 1883 and probably a slight increase. The Hidatsa and Arikara population was approximately 1,200, for a combined total of about 1,500 Fort Berthold Indians.

The Indian village was built around Fort Berthold, within which the Durfee and Peck trading post and the Indian agency were located. In 1874 a fire destroyed all the agency buildings; the following year a new agency was constructed about a mile and a half below Fort Berthold, containing the offices and homes of the agent, a doctor, teacher, head farmer, head clerk, carpenter, blacksmith, and sawmill engineer. A boardinghouse operated by the agency provided for regular employees and transients. The main government building, still maintained in the Indian village, was an issue room for the distribution of annuities.

The military troops were located in Fort Berthold in 1864–65, in log buildings outside the fort in 1865–67, and about eighteen miles below Berthold in Fort Stevenson in 1867–83. The military post contained officers and company quarters, storerooms, shops, corrals, a guardhouse and prison, a hospital, and an officers' building. It was a two-company infantry post built for a maximum of 238 men, but the average number was only 110 with a range from 42 to 210 (Mattison 1951: 75). Indian scouts, mostly Arikara, were employed by the military and lived at the post. They served as mail carriers, herders, guards, escorts, and couriers (Mattison 1951).

The other White men living in and around Fort Berthold during the Military-Agency Period might be divided into three categories: first, those French Canadian traders who had intermarried with Indian women and who resided in a sort of half-breed community in a separate section of Like-a-Fish-Hook village (Kane 1951: 48); second, respectable Whites such as the missionary, official visitors, and civilian employees of the military and agency; third, lower-class Whites such as escaped criminals, army deserters, frontier drifters, some professional hunters, and woodhawks—those men who illegally cut wood on agency land for sale to the steamboat operators, from whom they obtained liquor for sale to the Indians (Mattison 1951; Kelly 1926). In reporting the White population at Fort Berthold, the agents made a distinction between those who were lawfully on the reservation—there were forty-four in 1877—and those who were unlawfully on the reservation—an annual average of twenty-two between 1879 and 1883 (Annual Reports, Commissioner of Indian Affairs).

The threefold categorization of Whites may have validity for the early years of the Military-Agency Period, but it is rather inappropriate for the situation in 1883. The lines of differentiation become blurred. Civilian employees at Fort Berthold took Indian wives; a number of army deserters also intermarried, settled down among the Indian people, and led very "respectable" lives; not all the French Canadians remained independent traders: some became woodhawks, while others sought permanent positions with the Indian Bureau.

Although various Indian tribes were constantly in the vicinity of Fort Berthold either trading or fighting, the Sioux were the most prominent group throughout the 1862–83 period. They came to exchange horses for Mandan corn—sometimes on terms which they themselves dictated—to harass the military, or to raid Like-a-Fish-Hook village. The Three Tribes were greatly outnumbered and not so well armed as the Sioux; nevertheless, they often took the offensive, sending out war parties to sneak up on a camp, steal horses, and run. De Trobriand (Kane 1951), the commander of Fort Stevenson from 1867 to 1869, remarked on one occasion when a Sioux scalp was brought to the Indian village, "there will be rejoicing in Berthold for a week." Indian warfare diminished after Custer's defeat in the Battle of the Little Bighorn in 1876 and virtually stopped by the early 1880's.

EXTERNAL SOCIAL RELATIONSHIPS

In his annual report for the year 1880, the Indian agent at Fort Berthold stated: "While the Indian loves his former habits of life, so in harmony with his uneducated tastes and desires, yet he seems to realize that the times are approaching when he must become a citizen and accept the lessons which teach him the better way of civilized life."

This quotation contains an assumption that the Indian is uncivilized, a basic postulate that the civilized, that is, the White way is better, a statement of policy that it is the responsibility of the agent to educate the Indian, to give him lessons in that civilized way of life, and by implication a statement of fact that the Indian has not yet learned that lesson—he has remained an Indian.

Agency personnel throughout the 1862–83 period generally agreed that the Indian was incompetent and that Indian culture contained no desirable qualities. Alternatives other than making the Indian people over in terms of an American image do not seem to have been considered.

My opinion is, that it is no longer well to consult their wishes, or the wishes of any tribe, to any great extent. They don't know what is best for them, and are incapable of making an intelligent and self-protecting treaty. Let the Government decide what is best for each tribe, and what it intends to do by it, and then let it be done, kindly, but decidedly and thoroughly. (Annual Reports, Commissioner of Indian Affairs, 1874.)

Indians are essentially conservative, and cling tenaciously to old customs and hate all changes: therefore the government should force them to scatter out on farms, break up their tribal organization, dances, ceremonies, and tom-foolery; take from them their hundreds of useless ponies, which afford them the means of indulging in their wandering, nomadic habits, and give them cattle in exchange, and compel them to labor or accept the alternative of starvation. (Annual Reports, Commissioner of Indian Affairs, 1879.)

That Indian women were very industrious and Indian men lazy was common knowledge among government agents; their basic problem became how to get the men to engage in productive enterprises.

Indian men were still occupied with their traditional tasks—warfare, hunting, and ceremonial activity—but these were not really "work" as defined by the agents. Farming was good work; therefore Indian men were taught agriculture in school and were given practical instruction on an agency farm supervised by a head farmer, also male. It may be noted that in 1953, farming was still regarded as "woman's work" by many Indian men, and that the varieties of corn developed over centuries by Mandan and Arikara women formed the basis of corn agriculture in modern North Dakota.

There arose in the minds of Indian Bureau personnel a crucial distinction between good and bad Indians. A good Indian was one who behaved as the government employees expected, who was becoming civilized, who was not lazy, who was a farmer. The agency had powerful sanctions to reward the good Indians and punish the bad ones, by differential distribution of government annuities. In 1875 flour, beef, and pork were issued to everyone, but coffee, tea, and sugar were only given as a reward. In the same year forty-three wagons and thirty-one carts were distributed to the most "industrious and deserving" of the Indians. In 1882, a man had to cultivate five acres by himself in order to get one wagon (Annual Reports, Commissioner of Indian Affairs, 1875, 1882). Especially good Indians were employed by the agency in various capacities.

Not only did the agency staff come to conceive of Indian people in terms of "good" and "bad," but other stereotypes arose. Women were "squaws," men "braves," horses "ponies," a conference a "pow-wow," the Indians "wild," the area "uncivilized." The literature of the period lacks the direct intimacy of warm personal relationships so prominent in the literature of fur trade times. Sarah Elizabeth Canfield, the wife of a lieutenant at Fort Stevenson, and one of the first White women among the Berthold Indians, wrote in her diary in 1867, "The robes were only held by the hands and had a way of Slipping down and displaying their Splendid brown Shoulders. They were magnificent Specimens of manhood" (Mattison 1953: 204). This was a new note in ethnographic descriptions of the Mandan.

The government employees withdrew physically as well as emotionally from the Indian people.

During the summer season the foul atmosphere, dust, smoke, fleas, flies, bed-bugs, and almost constant din of drum and dance, at times make sleep or comfort almost impossible, and though the six white ladies now here (wives of employees and the teacher) have endured it all thus far with remarkable patience and self-sacrifice, it is a shame to our Government and a disgrace to Christian culture to allow things to remain so another year. (Annual Reports, Commissioner of Indian Affairs, 1874.)

After the government buildings burned down on October 12, 1874, the new agency was constructed a mile and a half from Fort Berthold so that the staff would not have to live so close to Indians. Even after the relocation the agent left the following year:

The salary paid an Indian agent [$1,500] is entirely too small a consideration for the responsibility, service, and annoyance to which an agent is subjected—especially in such a climate as this and among such troublesome people. (Annual Reports, Commissioner of Indian Affairs, 1875.)

During the 1860's and early 1870's the position of agent at Fort Berthold was financially profitable, as the agency was thoroughly corrupt (Chittenden and Richardson 1905: 885; Kane 1951: 301; Taylor 1901; Mattison 1951; Lamar 1956). There was outright stealing of government annuities and collusion between agent and trader. High-quality merchandise supplied by the government was given by the agent to the trading company in return for condemned food and inferior goods. The trader sold the government goods at the company store and split the profits with the agent. All traders at Fort Berthold had to receive a license issued by the agent permitting them to do business with Indians; the agents refused to issue licenses to the independent French Canadian traders, ordered them to leave the reservation, and thus created a monopoly for Durfee and Peck. In 1870 and again in 1871, the Indian agents were removed from office by the President of the United States.

Fort Stevenson was generally an unsatisfactory enterprise from the point of view of all concerned. The Berthold Indians were not provided with the protection they had been promised, for as De Trobriand stated, U.S. troops were ineffective against Sioux horsemen (Kane 1951: 48). When there was a raid on Fort Berthold, a courier would be sent eighteen miles away to Fort Stevenson, but, by the time the troops arrived, the Sioux would be gone.

The military personnel were kept in a constant state of tension as the Sioux raided, stole horses, and killed stray soldiers but never attacked the fort. There was no open fight. The emigrants that were expected to travel up the Missouri on their way to the Montana gold fields never came; they took another route. The soldiers were not accustomed to the cold North Dakota winters, their lodgings were miserable, their health poor, the pay small, the work dull and routine, and the recreational facilities meager. As a result there was a high frequency of desertion, court martials, drinking, and fighting. By 1873, the Northern Pacific railroad had been completed to Bismarck, thereby replacing the steamboat and making the fort unnecessary as a communication link; by the 1880's the power of the Sioux was broken so that the troops were no longer needed for protection. In 1883, Fort Stevenson was declared obsolete and abandoned. (See Mattison 1951.)

The military did create one rewarding role, that of Indian scout. The army stated that their work was satisfactory; that the scouts liked the work was indicated by the fact that many kept re-enlisting; the Berthold people created a special cemetery near Like-a-Fish-Hook village for some 115 Indians who had served with the U.S. army. Although most scouts employed at Fort Stevenson were Arikara, all Berthold Indians shared in their glory. It was the only role relationship in the 1862–83 period, recognized and approved by all Whites, that also carried prestige and reward in the Indian culture.

Although the locus of power had shifted to the agency and military, and although new kinds of Indian-White interaction emerged in the 1862–83 period, some elements of the relationship between Indian and White man characteristic of the Fur Trade era persisted. French Canadian traders married Mandan women, lived in the Indian village, and learned the native language. Some of the Frenchmen, such as the Garreau family, could trace their ancestry back three generations; they had lived among Indian people since the time of Lewis and Clark (Reid 1943). These men were employed as interpreters and in other capacities by the fur company, the army, and the agency; they continued in the role of middlemen between the Indian and White cultures (Larpenteur in Coues 1898: 125).

From the perspective of the Mandan people, the Military-Agency Period was one of the most difficult in their entire history. They were harassed and hemmed in by the Sioux; the military did not provide them with protection; and the agent robbed them of their annuities (Chittenden and Richardson 1905: 885). They had never waged war on the Whites, had kept their agreements, and had always been friendly and peaceful. The Sioux, who had been hostile to the Whites, were strong, well-fed, received annuities, and were taken to Washington, D.C. The Whites had lied, cheated, and allowed them to starve (Mattison 1951, 1955). In 1851, they were given a reservation of 12,500,000 acres, on which they were told they could "live unmolested for all time" (Billington 1949: 653); by 1883, their reservation had been chopped to slightly under three million acres.

THE MILITARY-AGENCY CULTURE

Since the thirteenth century the Missouri River Valley environment had provided the Mandan with abundant game, wood for fuel and building purposes, and fertile fields for their crops. By 1883, the demands made upon the environment were far beyond those which the traditional techniques for its exploitation allowed. The game was depleted as the area around Fort Berthold had been hunted intensively for almost forty years. The completion of the Northern Pacific railroad in 1880 facilitated the shipment of buffalo hides to the East; by 1883, the remains of the northern buffalo herd had been almost entirely slaughtered by professional hunters. Timber had been cut in a ten- to fifteen-mile radius around the village, the fields were exhausted, and sanitary facilities completely inadequate. In the past the Mandan would have simply selected a new village site long before the situation became critical; during the 1862–83 period the Sioux and the agents prevented them from moving.

The Mandan hunted, planted gardens, stored crops in underground cache pits, engaged in intertribal trade with the Sioux and other nomads, and sold hides to the fur company (Matthews 1877); but these activities did not produce sufficient food for their own needs. Between 1865 and 1868 there was real famine and starvation at Berthold (Chittenden and Richardson 1905: 857; Kane 1951). Their economic problems were further multiplied when the agent in 1879 forbade hunting trips; he was against "wandering proclivities" (Annual Reports, Commissioner of Indian Affairs).

On an average of the nine years between 1875 and 1883, 56 per cent of the Berthold economy was supported by government annuities, 9 per cent by hunting and gathering, and 35 per cent by agriculture and other enterprises (Annual Reports, Commissioner of Indian Affairs, 1875–83). The range of government support varied from a high of 83 per cent in 1877 to a low of 20 per cent in 1875. The assistance provided by the federal government for the Indian people undoubtedly saved many from starvation during this difficult period, but it thoroughly undermined the Mandan economy. The government directly distributed some foodstuffs that were shipped in from the outside, such as coffee and tea. Others, wheat, corn, potatoes, and squash, were grown on the agency farm by Indian men working under the supervision of a head farmer. Approximately 500 to 600 head of cattle were purchased each year and butchered for distribution. The agency plowed a large field, divided the land into small plots of one to five acres each, and assigned the plots to separate families according to their size and ability (Matthews 1877: 11–12). Indians furnished coal, wood, and hay to the agency as needed, at prices, so the agent in 1876 tells us, much below that usually paid the White man.

During the Military-Agency Period, there was a transition from an economy based upon barter to one based upon money. Horatio H. Larned, in charge of Durfee and Peck from 1868 to 1870, reports that trade was entirely by barter with a buffalo robe as the unit of value. One robe was equivalent to two beaver skins, four deer skins, three wolf skins, one bear skin, two elk skins, six pint cups of sugar, and three pint cups of coffee (in Collins 1925: 31). A fairly good pony was equal to five buffalo robes, but a trained buffalo horse was worth 50 to 100 robes. By 1883, many Indian men had worked for wages, and cash was used in making purchases.

At the end of the Military-Agency Period, the customary occupations of the men either ceased to exist, for example, Indian warfare, or were severely curtailed, for example, hunting after the extinction of the buffalo. The Mandan women did not have this difficulty; they continued to plant gardens, raise children, and engage in household tasks. Some men found new occupations in working for the agency or military while others adopted what had been woman's work, farming. However, most Mandan men did not find wage work or agriculture congenial; the traditional masculine role conception persisted, but there was a scarcity of proper activities that could be performed to fulfil it.

The Mandan lived in Like-a-Fish-Hook village with the Hidatsa and Arikara for approximately eight months of the year; during the winter each tribal group usually moved a few miles away from Fort Berthold to its own separate quarters in the wooded bottom land. However, it is reported by Goodbird in his life story (Wilson 1914:

12–14) that although they usually built small earth lodges in the woods, "this winter we were to camp in our skin tents, like the Sioux." Matthews (1877: 6–7) states that because of the scarcity of game the people no longer occupied their winter villages but went on extensive winter hunts, traveled great distances, and lived in tipis. Both of these firsthand reports refer specifically to the Hidatsa during the 1870's, but possibly the Mandan also attempted extensive winter hunts. If this is so, it would not only represent a change in the annual cycle, but also a belated move in the direction of equestrian nomadism, prompted by the collapse of the traditional earth lodge economy.

It is difficult to establish a precise date when it can be said that an object made of native materials has been replaced by its Western counterpart. The Mandan were in possession of guns at the very end of the 1500–1750 Period II; they used the gun but preferred the bow and arrow for hunting throughout the 1750–1862 Period III. On a buffalo hunt which took place in the last years of the 1862–83 Period IV, everyone used the gun except one old man who had a bow and arrow (Wilson 1914). During the 1883–1953 Period V the bow and arrow was still used for sport and as a toy for children. In the 1870's the art of manufacturing bullboats, mats, baskets, wood bowls, spoons and ladles from horn, hair brushes, whistles, wooden instruments, dyed porcupine quillwork, flint and horn arrowheads, and the shoulder blade hoe were known and practiced by some (Matthews 1877: 18; Annual Reports, Commissioner of Indian Affairs, 1873), but their European alternatives were becoming more widely accepted in the Indian culture. Native pottery and most artifacts of stone and bone had been almost but not entirely replaced (Smith 1954: 31). Not only did the traders sell European goods, but the agency issued many items such as wagons, carts, harnesses, hoes, shovels, spades, rakes, scythes, axes, and grindstones. Western clothing was distributed by the government to those men who were employed by the agency but this clothing was worn only during working hours; when the men returned home in the evening, they changed to Indian dress.

Like-a-Fish-Hook village consisted of three separate social communities, as each of the three tribes maintained its own section of the village independently of the others. In the Mandan section the village layout was the same as in previous periods, with ceremonial lodge, open plaza, and sacred cedar (Matthews 1877: 9–10). The village itself was fortified by a stockade until 1865, when it was cut down for firewood. Scaffold burials still existed outside the village but the agent's report for 1880 states that earth burials were becoming more frequent. In 1862 most Mandan lived in earth lodges, in 1874 about one-half lived in log cabins, and by 1883 the log house had almost, but not completely, replaced the earth lodge. Those earth lodges that were constructed were done so in the traditional way with few nails or fastenings, except that in some the central fireplace had been replaced by iron stoves and chimney pipes. The Indian people built the log cabins themselves but the agency provided the furniture and made the doors, windows, and floors.

There were relatively few changes in social and ceremonial organization (Matthews 1877: 50–56; Bowers 1948, 1950). Kinship, residence, descent, and marriage rules remained; the proper rituals were performed; and the medicine bundles retained. As the agent for 1877 stated, "they have kept their religious ceremonies, medicine dances, feasts, and fasts." The Okipa ceremony was performed throughout the Military-Agency Period, although the very severe self-torture had been eliminated due to the pressure of local Whites to whom bodily mutilation was repugnant (Matthews 1877: 9–10; Kane 1951: 81).

The process of equating Mandan and Hidatsa clans and kinship concepts continued and was further extended to the society system and to ceremonial organization. Hidatsa women were admitted into the Mandan White Cow Society, and there was merging of those men's societies concerned with police work and village administration (Matthews 1877: 47). Some Hidatsa acquired Mandan medicine bundles and vice versa. In these cases there was a tendency to transmit the rites by the same method as they had been obtained, that is, a Hidatsa would transmit a Mandan bundle to the equated Mandan-Hidatsa clan, following Mandan practice. In the reverse case a Mandan would transmit a Hidatsa bundle from father to son, following traditional Hidatsa practice (Bowers 1948, 1950).

The Mandan clans were still functioning exogamous corporate groups; however, the ownership functions of the clan had been undermined by the agency. When the government plowed and assigned garden land, helped to build houses, and paid cash for services rendered, it interfered with traditional functions of the clan, weakened the unilineal emphasis in Mandan society, and increased the importance of the nuclear family.

It was a conscious Indian Bureau policy, on the national and local levels, to weaken the power of tribal unity and to deal with Indians as individuals (Billington 1949: 668).

The issuing of the annuity goods to the heads of families instead of the chiefs has been very satisfactory to all except said chiefs, who never miss an opportunity to request that their goods be given to them in the old way. While the poor people . . . say the agent's way is the best. It has done much to break up tribal relations, and there is a growing tendency on the part of the more intelligent to independence of thought and freedom of control from the chiefs. (Annual Reports, Commissioner of Indian Affairs, 1876.)

In every society there are some crucial aspects of culture so firmly integrated and interconnected that a change in one part ramifies to all others. The agency practice of issuing annuities directly to the heads of families—to the father of a nuclear family—hit one of these sensitive areas that set off a chain reaction. It started by undercutting the authority of the chiefs. In the past all visitors who came to the Mandan went directly to the chiefs with presents; that men with such authority and power as the Indian agents ignored the chiefs was a blow to their prestige. Traditionally the chiefs' position was validated by their generosity, by the gifts which they gave to the people of the village. Now, however, it was the Indian agent, as representative of the United States government, who distributed goods directly to the people. The attitudes and affect associated with a Mandan chief were thus transferred to the government, giving added depth to the entire paternalistic relationship.

The method of distribution of annuities increased the importance of the nuclear family, particularly in a matrilineal society. It created a large fund of property not under control of the unilineal descent groups. As the chiefs were hereditary bundle owners, and as the bundles were the property of the clan and the basis of the ceremonial system, to undercut the chiefs' authority was to undercut the entire clan system and ceremonial organization. Some of those in the lower strata of Mandan society became skeptical of the power inherent in the medicine bundles, for the chiefs, who were bundle owners, were no longer wealthy nor were they respected by the Whites. In a society in which other paths to leadership and recognition had recently become available, this skeptical attitude affected the bases of the traditional system of social stratification.

Toward the end of the Military-Agency Period, the government consciously used other techniques to disrupt the native political organization. In 1878, one person from each of the Three Tribes was selected as "captain of the working band." His task was to see that other members of his tribe cultivated their fields properly and to advise the agent in rewarding the industrious. Also in 1878, an Indian police force was organized, recruited from among those who were most "reliable and trustworthy." According to the agent's report for 1879, the force of about twenty men was needed because of the whiskey traders, tramps, and horse thieves on the reservation. The agency police force rapidly replaced its aboriginal counterpart, one of the Mandan men's societies. In 1883, an Indian Office order set up courts to relieve the native chiefs of their judicial functions; by 1885, federal courts had jurisdiction over Indians (Billington 1949: 668).

PROCESSES OF CHANGE

The outstanding features of the Military-Agency contact community were the shift in the locus of power to the White administrators, conscious efforts by the agency to destroy selected aspects of Indian culture, and a severe disruption of the ecological balance. The coming of the railroad led to rapid extinction of the buffalo; enforced confinement in Like-a-Fish-Hook village led to scarcity of wood and exhaustion of the fields; and the military put an end to intertribal warfare and trade.

Taken together, these features constituted a pressure for change more intense than any the Mandan had experienced before. The areas of Mandan culture most severely affected were the technological, economic, and political. Native arts declined and many material objects were replaced. When the Mandan subsistence base deteriorated, the gap was filled by the government through annuity distributions, which gave rise to the psychological attitudes of dependency usually associated with a paternalistic relationship. Wage work and a cash economy were introduced. Civil administration, police and judicial functions, and intergroup relations were in the hands of the American government. Those aspects of the clan system concerned with property ownership, and those aspects of the society and ceremonial systems concerned with political organization were disrupted by the agency program.

Other changes in Mandan culture can be traced directly to one or another particular feature of the contact community. For example, the self-torture rites and the fact that Mandan women did so much of the heavy work were especially disturbing to the local Whites. The warfare aspects of the society system and the buffalo calling rites of the ceremonial system no longer seemed necessary without warfare or buffalo. The enforced proximity of the Mandan and Hidatsa, and the necessity for establishing smooth patterns of interaction led to a further merging of their social and ceremonial systems.

Although the way of life of the Mandan had been substantially altered during the Military-Agency Period, it would be erroneous to assume that their culture had lost its distinctive qualities, or that the society had ceased to function. The people were together in a village, in extended families; men hunted antelope, elk, and deer; women farmed; descent was matrilineal, the clan a corporate exogamous group; polygynous marriages took place; the Crow kinship system structured social interaction; all men had personal medicine bundles; the important tribal bundles were respected, and the major ceremonies performed. The Mandan had not yet become a community of American farmers.

Mandan responses to the pressure created by the agency program of directed change and to the disruption of the ecological balance have been reviewed in terms of how the culture changed, from the perspective of cultural integration; but the situation may be examined from another perspective, that of societal integration. The Mandan responded not only by changing their culture but also by escaping from it. Individuals and family groups abandoned Mandan society and joined or identified with either the Plains nomadic or the larger American community. Let us first examine the evidence for the fact that some Mandan became nomads.

In the 1870's and 1880's almost 25 per cent of the total Mandan population left Fort Berthold and joined a nomadic group of Hidatsa. A controversy had developed among the Hidatsa over whether chiefs should be selected on the basis of inherited tribal bundles or warfare accomplishments (Annual Reports, Commissioner of Indian Affairs; Curtis 1909; Bowers 1948). Those who felt that a military record and vision experiences were more important accused the traditional ceremonial leaders of an unfair division of government rations. They left Like-a-Fish-Hook village and moved about a hundred miles away near Fort Buford. This disgruntled element came to be known as the Crow Flies High band. They refused to accept government annuities

and gave up agriculture, preferring to live by hunting, selling skins
to the fur trading companies, supplying fuel to the Missouri River
steamboats, and serving as U.S. army scouts. In 1885 there were approximately 185 members of the Crow Flies High band; 115 were
Hidatsa and 70 Mandan. Those 70 individuals represented a very
high proportion, almost 25 per cent, of the Mandan population. The
Crow Flies High band remained separated from their relatives at Fort
Berthold for about twenty years, until 1894, when a military detachment was sent to escort them back to the agency.

Some Mandan became Sioux. For many years Sitting Bull had tried
to enlist the support of the Berthold Indians in his war against the
Whites. The agent's report for the year 1864 quotes a letter from
Father DeSmet stating that although several attempts had been made
to induce the Arikara, Hidatsa, "and Mandan, to join the Sioux coali-
tion . . . only five or six of their youngsters have joined the enemy."
This number increased during the Military-Agency Period. In 1877,
when Sitting Bull's band was camped two days' ride from Fort
Stevenson, the army commander wrote that the Berthold Indians
were disposed to withhold information about the enemy and exhibited
a friendly spirit toward them, as so many had intermarried with the
Sioux (Mattison 1951, 1955).

That some Mandan left their own society to join nomadic bands
of Hidatsa and Sioux is not surprising when considered in the light
of three factors. First, the Mandan were subjected to intense pressures
in their village with Sioux attacks, the agency program of enforced
culture change, and the collapse of their economy. Second, the process of transfer from one society to another was facilitated as the
Mandan established kinship relationships with the nomads, visited
with them during intertribal trading sessions, and were well acquainted with the nomadic way of life. Since traditional Mandan
culture already contained the essential elements of the High Plains
life, the process of becoming nomad did not require the learning of
entirely new culture patterns. Third, the situation during Military-
Agency times intensified a basic conflict in the Mandan system of
social stratification. Disagreement arose between the younger men of
the commoner class who came from smaller, less wealthy kin groups,
who had no chance of obtaining a medicine bundle, and the older
well-established hereditary nobility who achieved prestige through
bundle ownership (Holder 1950; Bruner 1956b). The young men not

in possession of a tribal bundle, wanting attention, influence, and position, had to follow the path of excellence in warfare, as measured by horses stolen and scalps taken, and by seeking personal vision experiences (Kane 1951: 265). They had little opportunity for real leadership in Mandan society, found themselves in a generally frustrating situation, saw their traditional chiefs being ignored by the United States government, and became envious of the Sioux and other nomads, for in those societies what counted was a man's ability as a warrior, not his hereditary position. As acculturation pressures increased in the Mandan village, the image of the nomadic warrior life must indeed have been appealing and the desire to emulate that way of life most tempting.

It is a paradox that although the channel to membership in a nomadic society was open and available for the Mandan, the future of equestrian nomadism on the Plains was not particularly bright in the 1880's. The other possibility of escape from the sedentary village life—the choice of identifying with the invader and becoming like a White man—held great promise, but social barriers and limited opportunity prevented the free transfer of individuals from the Indian to the American community. Irrespective of his desires, the average Mandan had neither the means nor the opportunity of gaining entrance to the White world; the one segment of Indian society that had both the means and the opportunity was the offspring of Indian-White marriages.

The nature of mixed marriages changed in the Military-Agency contact community compared with the previous Fur Trade Period. In earlier times the French Canadian fathers had no other aspirations for themselves or for their children than to live in Mandan society as Indians; indeed, there was no alternative. During the Military-Agency Period the White men who took Indian wives were no longer all French *voyageurs;* there were also men from the agency and the trading company and those who left their homes in the East for the frontier after the Civil War and drifted to Fort Berthold (Reid 1943: 12). Some of these White men were not content to raise their children as Indians. They wanted and could afford to send their children to be educated in St. Louis or elsewhere, in the hope that they might have a better life as accepted members of White society (Kane 1951: 84). Thus individuals born at Fort Berthold left the reservation to seek their fortunes in the larger American society.

The Military-Agency Period has been examined from two different points of view, in terms of what happened to the culture, and what happened to members of the societies in contact. The processes of societal integration are not unrelated to the processes of cultural integration. That some Mandan became nomads provided a means of siphoning off those who were dissatisfied with sedentary life, either because of individual personality factors or because they occupied disadvantageous positions in the village social system. In either case the traditional culture was preserved for those who remained. However, a new and relatively progressive element also developed within Indian society. Some children of Indian-White intermarriages were not successful in finding a place for themselves in the surrounding American society; they returned to the reservation. Thus there emerged at Fort Berthold by the 1880's two distinct segments of Indian society: the most conservative of the Mandan population whose interests were best served by retaining the old culture, and the offspring of mixed marriages who formed the basis of a most highly acculturated and White-oriented group. To see how this situation developed we turn to the last period and the Reservation Contact Community.

The Reservation Contact Community
HISTORICAL BACKGROUND

The contemporary reservation situation arose in the 1880's with the scattering of the Fort Berthold Indians on individual allotments and the gradual transformation of North Dakota from a frontier community into a modern state. The allotment program was a logical extension of two basic principles of national Indian Bureau policy: (1) to isolate the Indian people on reservations as wards of the government where they could be educated to become civilized and to adopt the American rural life pattern, and (2) to weaken tribal political organization so that the government could deal with Indians as individuals (Billington 1949: 659–69). It was reasonable to extend these principles to land ownership, to place each Indian family on its own farm.

During the latter part of the Military-Agency Period, the agents at Fort Berthold realized that the old Indian culture was not broken and that the social-ceremonial organization continued to function. Some agents advocated that traditional Indian ways should be destroyed as quickly as possible, government annuities and other forms of pampering should be stopped, and the Indians should be given a start and then left alone to survive or starve. Other agents took just as extreme a position but in the opposite direction; as the Indian land was poor and the people uncivilized, it was the government's responsibility to continue annuity distribution and economic support. Actual Indian Bureau policy contained both of these views. Attempts were made to destroy Indian culture, the people were placed on allotments and given a start in farming and livestock enterprises, but direct government support continued.

The Berthold people were not anxious to give up their traditional village life but they realized it was no longer feasible for them to stay at Like-a-Fish-Hook (Wilson 1914). There was a scarcity of wood, game, and good farm land, and the economically valuable fur-bearing animals had been killed off. The danger of attack from hostile nomads had ceased, except for some Canadian Chippewa who raided the Berthold Indians and stole their horses (Annual Reports, Commissioner of Indian Affairs, 1884).

The exodus from Like-a-Fish-Hook began in 1882, when twenty nuclear families moved twenty-two miles west of Fort Berthold to build homes and farm 133 acres, and ended in 1886 with the agent's report that the Indian village was deserted. The Mandan were the last of the Berthold Indians to leave Like-a-Fish-Hook. A treaty between the government and the Three Affiliated Tribes, concluded in 1886 but ratified in 1891, allotted 160 acres to each family head and 80 acres to others. The allotments were not given outright to the Indians but were held in trust by the government for twenty-five years.

At the same time that the allotment program was in progress, the land in western North Dakota was opened for White settlement. Homesteaders, mostly of Canadian, Swedish, German, and Norwegian descent, were attracted to the Great Plains by what Billington (1949: 704) calls "the most effective advertising campaign ever to influence world migrations." The states, railroads, and other groups with commercial interests presented the Plains area as if it were a virtual paradise. They attracted many immigrants; in 1890 almost 45 per cent of the population of North Dakota was foreign born (Tanner 1906: 184–85). The two main vehicles of transportation were the Northern Pacific railroad, completed in 1883, and the Great Northern, completed in 1887. The majority of the new settlers were farmers; others were cattlemen quick to take advantage of the abundant grassland left vacant by the destruction of the buffalo.

COMMUNITY ORGANIZATION

When the people left Like-a-Fish-Hook, they established seven smaller villages on the Fort Berthold Reservation (see Map 7). One of the seven, Elbowoods, was selected in 1893 as the agency head-quarters and became the heart of the reservation community. In 1953 Elbowoods contained the Indian Bureau administrative offices and workshops; the homes of the agency staff; the offices of the Tribal Council; a Congregational and a Catholic church and the residences of the missionaries; two general stores operated by White merchants where groceries, clothing, gasoline, and other assorted goods could be purchased; a government grade school and a high school with dor-mitories; a hospital; post office; jail; and guest house. To one side of Elbowoods, physically separated from the main buildings, was an In-dian community consisting of those residents who either worked for the agency or preferred to live in the central part of the reservation.

The structure of the other six villages differed from that of El-bowoods. One of them, called Lone Hill by the Indian people, will be described as an illustration. Lone Hill was founded in 1885 by Wolf Chief, who led a group of Mandan and Hidatsa to the western segment of the reservation between the Missouri and the Little Mis-souri rivers. A government day school was built in 1894, a Congrega-tional church in 1912 and a Catholic church in 1919. In recent times the school building in Lone Hill consisted of two classrooms, a small apartment for the cook, and a kitchen and dining room in the base-ment where free lunches were served. Two government teachers, a man and wife, lived in a separate building adjacent to the school. Theirs was the only residence in Lone Hill with electricity, running water, and a telephone. Next to the Congregational church was a large rectangular hall where Indian give-away dances were held. The school, churches, and dance hall formed a community center. About fifteen Indian households were located within a mile radius of this center; the twenty-six remaining households were widely scattered along the river valley. The total population of Lone Hill was less than three hundred.

The demographic situation changed considerably in the Reserva-tion Period due to the allotment program, approaching in some re-spects what it had been in the 1250–1500 Small Village era. Formerly crowded into one large village the people were now dispersed into seven communities. The population of the Three Tribes was approximately 1500 at the end of the Military-Agency times, went down to below 1100 according to the agent's report for 1900, and thereafter rose sharply to about 2500 in the 1950's. The explanation of the drop is suggested by the medical report for 1894 (Annual Reports, Commissioner of Indian Affairs) that the death rate of the local White population was 11 per 1000 while the death rate of the Berthold Indians was 35 per 1000, mostly from tuberculosis. The Mandan population, which had been approximately 300 in 1883, was reduced to below 250 and then rose in the recent period. In the 1950's the average population of each village was approximately 350 people. The proportion of men to women, which had been unequal throughout the nineteenth century as a result of Indian warfare, stabilized early in the twentieth century. In 1896 there were 118 Mandan males and 144 females, but by 1905 there were 123 males and 126 females (Annual Reports, Commissioner of Indian Affairs).

One of the most significant social and demographic changes following the breakup of the traditional village life was the merging of separate tribal identities. Some new communities were founded by a particular tribal group and have been associated with that tribe in recent times, for example, Nishu with Arikara, Charging Eagle with Mandan, and Shell Creek with the Hidatsa of the Crow Flies High band. Nevertheless, there are members of each of the three tribes in every village on the Fort Berthold Reservation. The Arikara have remained somewhat apart from the others, but the intermarriage between the Mandan and Hidatsa has been so frequent that the two tribes have virtually merged. The Mandan people have not lived together in one community, nor has there been an identifiable Mandan society, for over seventy years.

For this reason it is difficult to evaluate the meaning of recent Mandan population figures or even to state precisely how many Mandan there were in 1953. Due to the high incidence of intermarriage with the Hidatsa, the Whites, and members of other Indian tribes, there is not one fullblood Mandan left. One Indian man listed on the agency records as 3/8 Crow and 5/8 Hidatsa married a woman listed as 1/4 Sioux, 1/2 Mandan, and 1/4 White; the children of that marriage would be 3/16 Crow, 5/16 Hidatsa, 1/8 Sioux, 1/4 Mandan, and 1/8 White, yet they would be counted in the tribal census as Mandan, since tribal affiliation is still inherited matrilineally.

The Mandan-Hidatsa social universe extends far beyond the bound-

aries of the Fort Berthold Reservation. Their most meaningful associations are with other Indians in North and South Dakota and Montana, primarily Sioux and Crow, and with White people from the
surrounding towns. A series of small farming communities encircle
the reservation. One of these, Van Hook, located ten miles from
the nearest Indian settlement, was established in 1914 and had a
population of 372 in 1930 and 380 in 1950. Beyond these White
towns are the big cities—Williston, Minot, and Bismarck—and beyond
them the larger American and world society. A few Indians have
made trips to Washington, D.C., Chicago, and Los Angeles; some of
those who served in the armed forces have been to Europe, the Near
East, and Asia. In the 1950's almost all the adults at Fort Berthold
spoke and understood English; they listened to world news on the
radio; were exposed to world history and geography in school; and
although they preferred cowboy and Indian movies, they saw the
same American shows in North Dakota theaters that were exhibited
in New York or London.

EXTERNAL SOCIAL RELATIONSHIPS

The basic aim of the agency throughout most of the Reservation
Period was to civilize the Fort Berthold Indians. Two major assumptions were involved: that the American way of life is superior to the
Indian way, and that assimilation into American society is inevitable.
The task of the Indian Bureau became one of determining the best
ways of facilitating the process of assimilation. There were two primary approaches, the direct application of force, more prominent in
earlier times, and the giving of help and assistance, which was emphasized in the recent period. Force and pressure on the one hand, and
help and paternalism on the other, characterize agency-Indian relationships between 1883 and 1953. Whether or not the Indian people
wanted to become civilized—integrated into American society—was
rarely considered.

During the early Reservation Period the Indian agent had great
power to apply pressure for cultural change: if the people did not
obey his orders they were either put in jail or subject to severe economic pressure, such as the withholding of subsistence support. A
network of agency-appointed police served as a spy system and means
of enforcing government regulations (Annual Reports, Commissioner
of Indian Affairs, 1890–99). The agent prohibited the performance

of all tribal ceremonies except on two occasions each year, July 4 and December 25. All forms of self-torture were absolutely forbidden. Fourteen Indians were appointed by the agent as assistant farmers in 1899 in order to insure that everyone at Berthold was engaged in productive economic enterprises in accordance with government directives. Goodbird (Wilson 1914: 61), who received one of these appointments, was given the assignment of measuring off ten acres for each man to plow and seed. If the task were not accomplished, Goodbird reported it to the agent who sent a policeman to investigate. The agent also exercised power in the personal life of the Indian people; in 1890 he directed a woman who had left her husband to return to him. An Indian court of justice was in existence but its decisions had to be approved by the agent.

The Indian Bureau made education compulsory: those children who chose not to attend school were forced to do so by the police; those parents who discouraged their children from attending found that their government assistance had stopped. When Fort Stevenson was abandoned by the military in 1883, the buildings were turned over to the agency for a boarding school, which had an enrolment of over 150 students before it was burned down in 1894. One of the students regarded the Fort Stevenson school as a combination prison reformatory and concentration camp; he has assured me, fifty-seven years later, that the fire was not accidental. A new boarding school was erected in Elbowoods; other children were sent off the reservation to Carlisle, Santee, and elsewhere; the Congregational and the Catholic missions operated their own schools; and eventually a day school for the primary grades was established in each Indian community.

Agency paternalism has been a constant theme in Indian-White relationships for almost a century. The Fort Berthold agency promoted farming and livestock enterprises, supervised the allotment, inheritance, and leasing of land, issued rations and relief, managed the individual Indian's financial facilities, took over the administration of internal political affairs, dispensed justice, and assumed jurisdiction of law and order problems.

In 1891, the reservation was reduced from 2,900,000 acres to 1,300,000 acres for which the Three Tribes were paid $80,000 per year for ten years. This money was to be used to further the agency objective of civilizing the Indians. Some of the funds went for education, social

See who negociated the deals then took the money!

welfare, and material goods; the remainder was spent to initiate a live-stock program for the Berthold people. The idea of making the Indians into sheepherders and cattlemen represented an important change in agency objectives. The agent purchased 400 cows, 16 bulls, 2,500 sheep, and 126 rams for distribution in 1891; at the completion of the program ten years later the agent reported that there were no livestock left, and the government must resort to rationing. Sixty years later, after repeated attempts, there were very few successful Indian farmers or cattlemen on the reservation, although local Whites have been successful in both enterprises.

According to the agency, the lack of success of economic develop-ment programs may be attributed, in part, to the fact that Mandan-Hidatsa men are lazy and irresponsible. "The Indians have had every-thing to learn. In the first place, they were lazy and naturally averse to labor, having lived by hunting and fishing, as inclination prompted or hunger pressed" (Annual Reports, Commissioner of Indian Affairs, 1896). Agency personnel in other years have not shared this notion of the Indian savage and have shown a better sense of historical per-spective, but most have found the men "averse to labor." Each new agent, and the turnover is relatively frequent, seems to begin with the assumption that he has to start anew to help the people on the path to civilization, which does not make for continuity in the agency pro-gram. When the agent leaves, he invariably reports that although the men have little sense of responsibility, some progress has been made for the welfare of the Indians.

It is not difficult to understand the attitudes of the government ad-ministrators. They distribute cattle to the Indian people, provide ev-ery possible means of assistance, and ask only to be repaid in kind out of the calf crop. However, the Indians do not seem to take care of the cattle, give them away to their relatives at Indian dances, butcher the cows for food, and then have the audacity to come and ask for more.

There are three main reasons for the failure of the program, an un-derstanding of which gives some insight into the paternalistic rela-tionship. First, the government employees themselves insist upon per-forming many of the operations necessary in the cattle business rather than allowing the Indian people to make mistakes and thereby learn in the process. The government farm agent contacts the state cattle-men's associations, investigates the latest scientific methods of vaccination, feed, and rotation of bulls, and oversees the purchase and distribution of stock. These activities of the agency prevent the Indians from having direct meaningful associations with outside Whites on matters of mutual concern, and create the feeling that it is an agency cattle program, not an Indian one. A second reason for failure is that the entire program is not administered through the indigenous Indian social organization, but is based upon atomistic relationships between individual Indians and an impersonal agency. There is a native social organization and leadership which organizes Indian dances, local rodeos, life crises rites, and other affairs, and which employs effective mechanisms of social control against those who are lazy or irresponsible. These mechanisms do not operate with reference to the agency-sponsored and -managed livestock program. The third reason stems from an Indian attitude, developed over many generations, that it is the responsibility of the government to provide economic assistance for the Berthold people. The agency distributes cattle, expecting repayment; the Indians take the cattle as a gift from their Great White Father. As is similar in many colonial areas of the world, the Berthold Indians resent the dependency but demand the protection. (See Rietz 1953.)

It is ironic that on the one hand the agency expended so much effort to civilize the Indians and make them into rural Americans, yet on the other hand defeated their own objectives by refusing to allow the Indian people to handle their own affairs and thereby have significant contact with local Whites. As a result of the paternalistic policy, the agency served as a buffer between the Three Tribes and members of the larger White society around them.

After the allotment program most of the government employees were concentrated in Elbowoods; the day school teachers were the only ones residing permanently in the Indian villages. This was a continuation of the tendency to withdraw which had begun in 1875, when the agency buildings were moved a mile and a half away from Like-a-Fish-Hook. The missionaries also lived in Elbowoods; they regularly visited each village once every five or six weeks to conduct Sunday services.

Nor were there any White homesteaders living near the Indian people. When civilization came to North Dakota in the last decades of the nineteenth century, it skirted around but did not penetrate the Fort Berthold Reservation. No railroad or major motor highway passed through Indian land. The White towns arose on the fringes of the reservation and remained enclaved White communities.

By and large, if the Indian people have contact with the larger White society, they do so through such impersonal mass media as newspapers, radios, and movies, or they themselves must leave the reservation boundaries. Except for the missionaries, the agency staff, and an occasional traveling salesman or local farmer, very few Whites come to the Indian villages. Those who do generally come only for business purposes and rarely stay overnight. The White world exists beyond the reservation; aspects of that world are available to the Berthold Indians, but they must go outside to seek it.

Indians tend to relate to White people for some specific and unitary purpose; they rarely develop warm friendships nor do they participate as full-fledged members in White social groups. Indian men are employed as cowboys or hired hands, and Indian women as domestics or secretaries by local Whites; they purchase necessary provisions from White shops and stores; and require the professional services of White doctors, dentists, and lawyers. Some of the most intimate Indian-White relationships occur in a recreational context, at rodeos, county fairs, or dances, but these contacts are not lasting, usually include only the young people, and tend to be disapproved by the elders of both cultures.

There are those local Whites who are strongly prejudiced against all Indians and others who seem to have the attitude that they would like to follow the Christian doctrine and help the poor Indians, if only those Indians were not so dirty and lower class. But many local White individuals, as well as civic and religious groups, sincerely want to help the Indian people. Usually they have a program of social or economic betterment designed to assist the Indian to become like a White man, presented with an implicit evaluation of Indian culture as unworthy, which the Indians either do not understand or refuse to accept.

The warmest and most rewarding external relationships are between the Fort Berthold people and Indians from other tribes. They are closest to the Arikara, the Crow, and their old enemy the Sioux. Only those over seventy years of age have lived in a society which engaged in intertribal warfare; stories and tales of those heroic times have become folklore. Intertribal visiting of friends and relatives on other reservations in North and South Dakota and Montana, contact with various Indian groups at off-reservation boarding schools, a sense of common problem and destiny, and a mutual spontaneous reaction to the popular conception of the "American Indian," have led to the development of a pan-Indian feeling which promises to become increasingly more important in the future.

The outstanding features of the Reservation Contact Community are the enforced culture change; the paternalism of the agency; the physical, social, and psychological isolation of the Berthold people from the surrounding Whites; the warm relationships among different Indian groups; and the emerging sense of pan-Indian identity.

THE RESERVATION CULTURE AND PROCESSES OF CHANGE

There is a functioning Indian culture on the Fort Berthold Reservation which is rich and satisfying to those who participate in it, but it is no longer distinctively Mandan. By the 1950's the Mandan were extinct; they had ceased to exist as a separate tribe and their descendants had merged with the Hidatsa. If the contemporary Mandan-Hidatsa culture is to be understood in a meaningful way, it must be described in terms of the four major processes by which it developed: the *extinction* of the Mandan, their *merger* with the Hidatsa, and the dual processes of *replacement* and *isolation* of the combined Mandan-Hidatsa culture with reference to local American culture.

Extinction is here considered as a process with biological, social, linguistic, cultural, and psychological dimensions. Focusing upon the members of any given group, we may speak of biological extinction when there are no living members, of social extinction when they lack a distinctive society, of linguistic extinction when they stop speaking their own language, of cultural extinction when the configuration of beliefs and customs ceases to function, and of psychological extinction when they no longer retain their original ethnic identity. Extinction is defined with reference to particular groups, for in the generic sense culture never dies as long as the most humble artifact is preserved in a museum, or as long as one isolated cultural element is still practiced. But specific cultures do die or become extinct.

The Mandan are an extinct tribe. There is no longer any group consisting of individuals racially identifiable as Mandan, living in a distinctively Mandan society, speaking the Mandan language, practicing Mandan culture, and claiming Mandan identity. This does not mean that everything uniquely Mandan has completely vanished. Certainly Mandan genes are present in the reservation breeding population; the mixed descendants of the Mandan are found scattered among the Hidatsa and Arikara at Fort Berthold; the Mandan language is known to a few bilingual adults, although it is not being taught to any children as a first language; some aspects of the old Mandan culture have been preserved; and there are individuals who recognize that they are of Mandan ancestry.

A general comparative problem requiring further research concerns the functional interrelationships between the five aspects of extinction; specifically, to what extent does a change in one necessarily lead to change in the others? For example, if a group became biologically extinct as a result of disease or warfare, there would be no individuals left to speak the language or carry on the traditions. In this extreme case there would necessarily be rapid total extinction. But if a given social group adopted a new language, to what extent could they maintain their own culture? Or if they were assimilated into a larger society, for how long could they retain their own identity? These and similar problems of the relationships between biological, social, linguistic, cultural, and psychological factors in acculturation are especially relevant in such areas of the world as Southeast Asia, where bold social experiments are being performed to nationalize many diverse ethnic groups.

In the Mandan case the crucial question is: why did they become extinct? The Mandan data provide an answer to this question if the merger with the Hidatsa is considered in conjunction with extinction. It is clear that biological extinction was not the significant factor. Despite the severity of the smallpox epidemics and the concomitant reduction in population from 9,000 to 150, the Mandan preserved their own society, language, culture, and identity long after the 1837 attack—until 1883—by a conscious program of population replacement. Because of the nature of their social system, their women could intermarry with men from the Hidatsa and other tribes and raise their offspring as Mandan. In the process they altered the gene frequencies in their population but that is evolution, not extinction.

The Mandan became extinct only when they could no longer maintain their own society. At the end of the Military-Agency Period in 1883 the Mandan were together in part of the village. All major elements of their culture remained intact, their society continued to function, and they preserved their own identity and language. By

1886, at the conclusion of the agency allotment program, the Mandan were no longer living together in one community but were intermingled with the Hidatsa in smaller communities. The agency program precipitated changes in settlement pattern and local group organization which dispersed the Mandan, destroyed their society, and led to their extinction and merger with the Hidatsa. The newly established Mandan-Hidatsa communities became the major units of social and ceremonial organization. It was increasingly difficult to re-affirm the solidarity of distinctively Mandan societies, clans, and religious groups. Within any one village the Mandan were closer to their Hidatsa neighbors than to their Mandan relatives in other communities. Residential proximity led to a marked increase in the frequency of intermarriage, which in itself had vast consequences: the children of the mixed marriages were exposed in the socialization process to two cultural traditions.

Although the merger occurred in the Reservation Period, there is no doubt that the process was facilitated by previous conditions of contact. When the Mandan and Hidatsa first met on the Upper Missouri, their cultures were similar in some respects, since both were Siouan-speaking peoples, part of the Eastern Plains earth lodge tradition. Thus from the very beginning there was a concordance of major cultural orientations. Thereafter intergroup relations were such as to favor further borrowing and diffusion: the two tribes were in continuous and friendly association for centuries, they joined together in opposition to the Sioux and could communicate, since many Mandan learned the Hidatsa language. In the historic period the Hidatsa had a dual economy based upon horticulture and hunting, a Crow kinship system, matrilineal descent, an age-grade society system, and many other institutions in common with the Mandan. Because of population reduction and the necessity of co-operating for defense, the two tribes came into even closer contact and lived together in separate parts of one village. By 1883 they had already moved in the direction of developing a common social system by equating their kinship, clan, society, and ceremonial organizations. Thus the basic patterns of social interaction and co-operation had emerged before the Reservation Period.

Once the processes of societal integration had proceeded far enough to develop a common society, there was no further barrier to the development of a common identity, language, and culture. A reaction against the agency—the *esprit de corps* that develops from fighting the same enemy—contributed to a new sense of Mandan-Hidatsa identity. The dominant local Whites did not recognize different Mandan or Hidatsa political entities, and the Fort Berthold people began to conceive of themselves as they were perceived by others—as Berthold Indians or simply as Indians. The Hidatsa language became the medium of communication, possibly because they had the larger population, or because the Mandan already knew the Hidatsa language. In 1933–34 only about forty people at Fort Berthold spoke Mandan, and every one of them also spoke Hidatsa (Kennard 1936). There were only three people living in the early 1930's who had come from homes in which both the parents were Mandan speakers. Under these conditions a distinctively Mandan culture ceased to exist, for there were no longer distinctively Mandan carriers of that culture.

As the merger of two originally separate groups is rather a rare occurrence in culture history, it is important to identify the significant causes in the Mandan-Hidatsa case as precisely as possible. It is here suggested that although a concordance of cultural orientations, continuous and friendly association for centuries in opposition to a common enemy, population reduction, and mutual patterns of social interaction may have *facilitated* the merger, it was the emergence of a common society associated with residence in the same community that *precipitated* the merger, and subsequently frequent intermarriage which *solidified* it. These data suggest that two separate cultures become one only after the development of a common society.

As the Mandan and Hidatsa cultures combined, the product, the merged Mandan-Hidatsa or Indian culture, confronted the larger American culture which existed around it. The conditions of contact between the Mandan-Hidatsa culture and the White culture were such that merger did not occur between them; the primary processes were replacement and isolation.

The merged Mandan-Hidatsa culture became less and less Indian as selected aspects of it were gradually replaced by comparable aspects of American culture. The best guide to the household goods, cooking utensils, and farm implements now found on Fort Berthold is a Sears, Roebuck mail order catalogue. Many Indian families have automobiles, kerosene-run washing machines, and battery-operated radios. A pair of cowboy boots, blue jeans, a long-sleeved Western shirt, and a Stetson hat are the standard masculine attire; almost all women wear plain cotton housedresses. However, the aboriginal material culture inventory has not been completely replaced. Those objects that have religious associations, such as medicine bundles, sacred amulets, special medicines and herbs for curing, have been retained.

The economy has changed as a result of the necessity for a cash income which is obtained by seasonal wage work off the reservation, leasing Indian land to White farmers and ranchers, government relief money, and the agency-sponsored commercial farming and livestock enterprises. The old village organization and practice of living in separate communities during the winter months has given way to the rural settlement pattern of fixed isolated households. The allotment of land to individuals broke up the matrilocal extended families, changed the residence pattern to neolocal, and upset the traditional system of land tenure as the matrilineal descent groups no longer owned property. Frame and log houses are now occupied by monogamous nuclear families. The aboriginal public ceremonials are no longer performed, the society system has ceased to function, and almost everyone at Fort Berthold is a member of either the Congregational or the Catholic church.

The merged Mandan-Hidatsa culture changed in many important respects as Indian elements were given up and Western elements accepted. This process of replacement was not carried to completion; if it had been, the communities at Fort Berthold would be indistinguishable from surrounding American communities. All observers unanimously agree that Berthold Indians differ in fundamental respects from local North Dakota farmers (Bruner 1953).

The Indian value system has been relatively unaffected by White influence. A good man was, and is, one who respects the old people, is brave and demonstrates fortitude, conforms to the obligations of the kinship system, is devoted to village co-operation and unity, is generous and gives away property in public, gets along well with others, and avoids overt expressions of aggression in interpersonal relationships (Bruner 1956a). The Indian's emotional security is dependent upon his relationships with his kinship, peer, and residential groups and not upon the demands of an absolute ethic; he listens to what others expect of him, not to his conscience.

The one public ceremony in which these values are expressed, reaffirmed, and maintained is the Indian give-away dance. It is a secular affair, held at life crisis rites, on Independence, Memorial, and Christ-

Freud would say conscience is what others expect of him.

mas days, and whenever someone leaves the village or returns after an extended stay. During the dance, gifts—war bonnets, horses, cattle, blankets, and money—are donated to the needy, to distinguished visitors, to the members of one's father's clan, and to various "societies," for example, the Antelope Society, the Congregational Society, the Catholic Society, and the American Legion Society. Those who give gifts have the opportunity of bragging about their war exploits, not with the Sioux, but in the First and Second World Wars and more recently in Korea. The give-away dance contains many replacements from American culture, but it is a rewarding and rich experience for the Mandan-Hidatsa participants, and in its meanings and combination of elements is distinctively Indian.

Mandan-Hidatsa society is still a kinship society. The aboriginal Crow type kinship system, both in terminology and behavior, persists relatively intact (Bruner 1955). The lineage is a socially relevant co-operating group, and although many of the clan functions have been replaced, it still extends hospitality, provides assistance, and disciplines members. The kinship system structures the interpersonal relationships between Indian people and provides the basis for a functioning Indian social organization. Within the context of that system in the village society hereditary political leaders function, social control is exercised, children are effectively socialized, and the Indian value system is maintained.

The old societal expectations of the proper behavior of men and women have persisted. Indian women conceive of themselves as housekeepers, mothers, and gardeners, and Indian men find most satisfaction in the roles of soldier, cowboy, athlete, and hunter. These masculine activities are economically unproductive but are personally rewarding roles in Mandan-Hidatsa society. The old power quest and society system are gone, but the expected behavior at each stage of the life cycle has remained. Young people under the age of thirty, married or not, are regarded by others and conceive of themselves as reckless and irresponsible. Only the older people speak up at meetings and assume positions of leadership and authority.

In many aspects of culture there have been both Western replacement and retention of old Indian patterns. All the aboriginal public ceremonies have long since been replaced; the Okipa was last performed in 1889 (Curtis 1909). The vast majority of Mandan-Hidatsa are now Christians. A few go to the Congregational and the

Catholic churches on Sunday, and many more attend special services at life crisis rites, Easter, and Christmas. The sermons are given in the English language and the behavior in church is similar in most respects to that in any North Dakota town. However, many of the private and less obvious aspects of aboriginal ceremonialism have been retained. Both personal and tribal medicine bundles are kept and respected. Feasts are given to the bundles and their power is used to cure the sick and insure the welfare of society.

The early agency objective of undermining the authority of the chiefs and replacing the aboriginal political organization was only partially successful. The Berthold Indians accepted the Reorganization Act of 1934 and now have a Tribal Council composed of elected representatives from each village. The Indian Bureau operates through the Tribal Council, but independent of it is an indigenous Indian political organization. Mandan tribal organization was always weak; the politically stronger social units were the unilineal descent groups; the political leaders were the clan heads who owned important medicine bundles. There was no authoritative and aggressive Indian leader who acted as representative of his people on all matters. The outstanding leader was thoughtful of others, generous, concerned with group welfare, and sensitive enough to act in terms of group opinion. These indigenous political leaders, hereditary bundle owners, still function informally at Fort Berthold.

A brief description of a modern Indian funeral illustrates the present-day importance of the clans and serves as an example of how Western replacement and Indian retentions operate together in a particular situation. Those individuals who are in the same clan as one's father are in charge of disposing of the body of the deceased. The funeral ceremony may be divided into three parts. Friends and clan relatives come to the home of the deceased, where the body is kept, bring lavish gifts, lament loudly for days, and participate in a common meal. This is followed by a Christian service in the church and an earth burial. When a selected member of the father's clan has asked the spirit of the deceased not to return to haunt the living, everyone goes to the Indian dance hall for a give-away feast. The gifts, brought by fellow clan members, are distributed to those in the same clan as the father of the deceased. The beginning and end of the funeral are Indian and are conducted in Hidatsa; the middle, from White culture, is conducted in English by the missionary.

The question emerges, how do we explain which aspects of Mandan-Hidatsa culture have been replaced and which have been retained? To answer this question we must first re-examine the aims and policies of the agency as they determined the conditions of contact in the Reservation Period. The basic aim of the agency was to civilize the Indians and to make them into American farmers; the policies designed to fulfil these aims were directed culture change and paternalism. The Mandan-Hidatsa were subject to considerable pressure backed by force; in the early part of the Reservation Period the agency jailed or withheld subsistence support from those who disobeyed government orders. But the pressure on the Indian people was never applied heavily enough to destroy them; whenever the situation became too difficult, the agency became paternalistic and provided assistance in the form of direct annuity distributions. Its policy was not consistent.

It is a Machiavellian principle that if an invader decides upon the use of force, it must be applied severely and continuously; vacillation in the application of force is almost always self-defeating. Certainly the program of enforced change was successful to some degree in that it led to many replacements in Indian culture. But the program also led the Mandan-Hidatsa to resist change and helped to maintain their sense of Indian identity. The vacillation in the insistence upon directed change combined with alternating periods of assistance enabled the Mandan-Hidatsa to consolidate and to preserve aspects of their traditional culture.

The allotment program may have precipitated the Mandan-Hidatsa merger, but it also created a kind of contact community that was rather favorable for the retention of selected Indian ways. After the movement from the overcrowded Like-a-Fish-Hook village, the Indian people found themselves physically, socially, and psychologically isolated from surrounding Whites. This was an unanticipated consequence of the allotment program. In the seclusion of their small villages the Mandan-Hidatsa could nurture and practice Indian ways in isolation. There were no authoritative White people near enough to interfere with how they raised their children, cared for a medicine bundle, or acted toward a clan relative. They were still located in the Missouri River Valley, a secure and known environment for which they had developed techniques of exploitation for centuries.

It is a harsh reality of the Reservation Contact Community that

Indian people eventually have to leave the isolation of their villages and relate to White people in the larger society around them. But this reality does not have to be faced in the early years of life. Not only are the villages isolated, but the Indian children and the agents of socialization are also isolated. The full implications of this finding are not apparent until the adult culture is viewed in terms of when, and from whom, it is transmitted to younger members of the society at different stages in the life career. For example, almost every Mandan-Hidatsa adult is bilingual with a knowledge of both Hidatsa and English. In the majority of cases Hidatsa is learned as the first language in the home; English is usually learned later in life, in government or mission schools. Hidatsa is learned from one's parents, close relatives, and neighbors, and is spoken in everyday interaction among Indian people in the village; English is learned from impersonal school teachers and is used at the agency headquarters, in the local towns, and in those situations in which White people are present. Cultural usage parallels, and is structured by, language usage.

The Mandan-Hidatsa learn two cultures and two languages. They keep them separate and use one or the other depending upon the context, but the two ways of life are learned at different stages in the life cycle and have different points of origin (Bruner 1956*b*). Indian ways are transmitted in the early formative years from close relatives within the security of the kinship group; White ways are learned in adolescence and adulthood. There is, in effect, a discontinuity in the Indian life career: the social world of the child at home and in the village among his kinship, peer, and residential groups is distinctively Indian. Only in the later years, primarily off the reservation, does he have direct contact with White people and direct exposure to acculturative influences.

When the Mandan-Hidatsa are with Whites they act in one way, and when they are with Indians in another (Bruner 1956*b*). This situational role specificity has become a perfectly natural routine procedure. It is not a source of confusion or disorganization, because the two ways of behavior are kept separate and do not merge or fuse. Indian people learn about White culture as a necessary accessory, as a technique of adjustment to the situation in which they find themselves. By alternating their behavior depending upon the context, the Indian people do not reveal much of their inner selves to local Whites: the practice serves as a cultural smoke screen.

As the social universe of the unacculturated village child is rich in positive affect and emotionally secure, those aspects of culture which he learns in his early life become so firmly internalized that they do not change in the adult years. In the later years the Indian finds himself adjusting to the White world but he does not change himself and his culture to emulate White ways. Those Indian ways, albeit merged Mandan-Hidatsa, that are learned early tend to persist (Bruner, 1956a).

There is no one-to-one correspondence between the cultural alternatives presented and pressures for change stemming from the contacting agents on the one hand and the actual changes in the Indian culture on the other. The Indian people do not automatically accept every change offered to or forced upon them; they are indifferent to a few, eagerly accept some, and strongly resist others. In the Mandan-Hidatsa case the agency applied pressure to all aspects of culture in the effort to make the Indians into American farmers. They were more successful in some areas of culture than in others. Kinship and values particularly, which were traditionally learned in the early years, have been most resistant to change. That which was learned early was continually reinforced throughout the life career, as experiences in the outside world were occasionally punishing and were rarely as richly rewarding as Indian behavior in the village.

Summary

If one takes the long view of seven hundred years of Mandan culture history, possibly the one most significant date would be 1868. In that year, with the establishment of a permanent Indian agency, the entire balance of military, political, and economic power was firmly in the hands of the Whites. For the first 130 years of contact, from 1738 to 1868, those Europeans who appeared in the Mandan villages adjusted to Mandan patterns and thereby revealed to the Indians only very limited aspects of the total inventory of Western culture. But in 1868 there arose in the Mandan environment a small but functioning White society, which enabled the Indian people to become aware of an entirely new cultural alternative. The members of the alien White community, whose attitude was that the Indian culture was inferior to their own, held great power, and had the explicit aim of educating the Indians to adopt the American way of life. A realistic cultural alternative was introduced which legitimized the efforts of some individuals to break away from the native system, to strive for leadership, and to seek rewards on a new basis—one provided by the American government. This tended to split the native population and was the beginning of modern factionalism.

Today there are vast differences in the degree of individual assimilation toward White ways among the population at Fort Berthold (Bruner 1955, 1956b). The majority speak the Indian language, defend their Indian identity, and despite the many replacements from American culture, conceive of themselves as following a distinctively Indian way of life. The minority who have become more assimilated have not done so by gradually accepting more and more replacements from American culture; they have made a cultural leap, as it were, from Indian to White ways. This is demonstrated by the fact that in every one of the more assimilated families there has been a White intermarriage within three generations, and the offspring of these unions have been raised from childhood to adopt the White way. Those who are more assimilated and who disregard Indian values and the traditional obligations of the kinship system are ostracized by the less assimilated majority.

It is a striking characteristic of the contemporary reservation community that an individual cannot be "progressive" and at the same time remain an accepted member of village society. The more assimilated tend to leave the Indian community for the White world beyond the reservation boundaries. Thus, an effective mechanism exists within Indian society itself which prevents full cultural assimilation to the American way of life. The goal of the superordinate Whites, of educating Indians to become like American farmers, has been blocked by the policies and attitudes of those Whites and by the kind of contact community which they created.

Mandan culture history, their extinction and merger with the Hidatsa, has very little intrinsic importance in world history. But possibly there is some significance in noting the parallels between White policy toward the Indian people and American policy toward other nations of the world. The same elements seem to reappear whenever Americans deal with non-Western peoples—the attitude that our own way of life is superior, alternating periods of paternalism and foreign aid on the one hand, and demonstrations of force and power on the other. It is apparently difficult for Americans to mix freely with other peoples and to accept them on an equal basis—

whether those Americans be stationed on an isolated Indian reservation in North Dakota or in capital cities of Asia and the Middle East.
Perhaps it is not too late to avoid repeating our past mistakes.

REFERENCES CITED

ABEL, ANNIE HELOISE (ed.)
  1921 "Trudeau's (Truteau's) Description," *Mississippi Valley Historical
        Review*, Vol. VIII.
  1932 *Chardon's Journal at Fort Clark, 1834–1839*. South Dakota State De-
        partment of History. Pierre.
  1939 *Tabeau's Narrative of Loisel's Expedition to the Upper Missouri*.
        Norman, Oklahoma.
AUDUBON, JOHN JAMES
  1897 *Audubon and His Journals*. ELLIOTT COUES (ed.). New York.
BILLINGTON, RAY ALLEN
  1949 *Westward Expansion: A History of the American Frontier*. New
        York.
BOLLER, HENRY A.
  1868 *Among the Indians: Eight Years in the Far West, 1858–1866*. Philadel-
        phia.
BOWERS, ALFRED W.
  N.D. "Hidatsa Social and Ceremonial Organization." Unpublished MS.
        Moscow, Idaho.
  1948 "A History of the Mandan and Hidatsa." Unpublished Ph.D. thesis.
        University of Chicago.
  1950 *Mandan Social and Ceremonial Organization*. Chicago.
BRACKENRIDGE, H. M.
  1811 *Journal of a Voyage up the River Missouri (in the year 1811)*. Re-
        printed in THWAITES, 1906, Vol. VI. Cleveland.
BRADBURY, JOHN
  1809–11 *Travels in the Interior of America in the Years 1809, 1810, 1811*.
        Reprinted in THWAITES, 1906, Vol. VI. Cleveland.
BRUNER, EDWARD M.
  1953 "Assimilation among Fort Berthold Indians," *American Indian*, VI,
        21–29.
  1955 "Two Processes of Change in Mandan-Hidatsa Kinship Terminology,"
        American Anthropologist, LVII, 840–50.
  1956a "Cultural Transmission and Cultural Change," *Southwestern Journal
        of Anthropology*, XII, 191–99.
  1956b "Primary Group Experience and the Processes of Acculturation,"
        American Anthropologist, LVIII, 605–23.
BURPEE, LAWRENCE J. (ed.)
  1910 *Journal of Larocque (from the Assiniboine to the Yellowstone 1805)*,
        Publication of the Canadian Archives, No. 3, pp. 1–82. Ottawa.
  1927 *Journals and Letters of Pierre Gaultier de Varennes de La Vérendrye
        and His Sons*. Champlain Society, Vol. XVI. Toronto.
BUSHNELL, D. I.
  1922 "Villages of the Algonquian, Siouan and Caddoan Tribes," Bureau of
        American Ethnology, *Bulletin* 77, pp. 122–40. Washington.

1927 "Burials of the Algonquian, Siouan, and Caddoan Tribes," Bureau of American Ethnology, *Bulletin 83*, pp. 65–73. Washington.

CATLIN, GEORGE
1841 *Illustrations of the Manners, Customs, and Condition of the North American Indians.* Vol. I. New York.
1867 *O-Kee-Pa.* Philadelphia.

CHITTENDEN, HIRAM MARTIN
1935 *The American Fur Trade of the Far West.* 2 vols. New York.

CHITTENDEN, HIRAM MARTIN, and ALFRED TALBOT RICHARDSON
1905 *Life, Letters and Travels of Father Pierre-Jean DeSmet, S.J., 1801–1873.* 4 vols. Cleveland.

CLARK, W. P.
1885 *The Indian Sign Language.* Philadelphia.

COLLINS, ETHEL A.
1925 "Pioneer Experiences of Horatio H. Larned," *North Dakota Historical Collections*, VII, 1–58. Grand Forks.

COMMISSIONER OF INDIAN AFFAIRS
Annual Reports of the Commissioner of Indian Affairs.

COUES, ELLIOTT (ed.)
1893 *History of the Expedition under the Command of Captains Lewis and Clark.* 4 vols. New York.
1897 *New Light on the Early History of the Greater Northwest: The Manuscript Journals of Alexander Henry and of David Thompson, 1799–1814.* 3 vols. New York.
1898 *Forty Years a Fur Trader on the Upper Missouri, 1833–72; The Journal of Charles Larpenteur.* 2 vols. New York.

CULBERTSON, T. A.
1952 *Journal of an Expedition to the Mauvaises Terres and the Upper Missouri in 1850.* JOHN FRANCIS MCDERMOTT (ed.). Bureau of American Ethnology, *Bulletin 147.* Washington.

CURTIS, EDWARD S.
1909 *The North American Indian.* Vol. V. Cambridge.

DELAND, CHARLES E.
1908 "The Aborigines of South Dakota, II." (Editorial Notes by DOANE ROBINSON.) *South Dakota Historical Collections*, IV, 273–730. Aberdeen.

DELAND, CHARLES E., and DOANE ROBINSON
1918 "Fort Tecumseh & Fort Pierre Journal and Letter Books," *South Dakota Historical Collections*, IX, 69–239. Aberdeen.

DENSMORE, F.
1923 "Mandan and Hidatsa Music," Bureau of American Ethnology, *Bulletin 80.* Washington.

DONALDSON, T.
1885 *The George Catlin Indian Gallery. Reports of the United States National Museum.* Washington.

DORSEY, JAMES OWEN
1890 "A Study of Siouan Cults," Bureau of American Ethnology, *Eleventh Annual Report*, pp. 501–13. Washington.
1894 "Siouan Sociology," Bureau of American Ethnology, *Fifteenth Annual Report*, pp. 242–43. Washington.

DORSEY, JAMES OWEN, and C. THOMAS
1907 "Mandan," Bureau of American Ethnology, *Bulletin 30*, pp. 769–99. Washington.

DOUGLAS, W. B.
1911 "Manuel Lisa," *Missouri Historical Society Collections*, III, 233–68, 367–406.

EGGAN, FRED
1952 "The Ethnological Cultures and Their Archeological Backgrounds," in JAMES B. GRIFFIN (ed.), *Archeology of Eastern United States*, pp. 35–45.

GASKIN, L.
1939 "A Rare Pamphlet on the Mandan Religious Ceremony," *Man*, XXXIX, 141–42.

GILLETTE, J. M.
1945 "North Dakota Weather and the Rural Economy," *North Dakota History*, XII, 5–98.

GOPLEN, ARNOLD O.
1946 "The Mandan Indians," *North Dakota History*, XIII, 153–75.

GRIFFIN, JAMES B. (ed.)
1952 *Archeology of Eastern United States*. Chicago.

HAINES, FRANCIS
1938 "The Northward Spread of Horses among the Plains Indians," *American Anthropologist*, XL, 429–37.

HARTLE, DON
1952 "Notes on the Chronology of the Hidatsa, Mandan and Arikara in the Northern Great Plains," Field Report, Smithsonian Institution. Lincoln.

HAXO, HENRY E. (trans.)
1941 "The Journal of La Vérendrye, 1738–39," *North Dakota Historical Quarterly*, VIII, 229–71.

HAYDEN, F. V.
1863 *On the Ethnography and Philology of the Indian Tribes of the Missouri Valley. Transactions of the American Philosophical Society*, Vol. XII. Philadelphia.

HEWES, GORDON W.
1948 "Early Tribal Migrations in the Northern Great Plains," *Plains Archaeological Conference–News Letter* (now *Plains Anthropologist*), I, 49–61. Lincoln.

HILLER, W. R.
1951 "Indian Village at Fort Berthold," *Minnesota Archaeologist*, XVII, 3–9.

HOLDER, PRESTON
1950 "The Role of Caddoan Horticulturalists in Culture History on the Great Plains." Unpublished Ph.D. thesis. Columbia University.
1955 "Some Patterns of French Colonial Penetration in Relation to Protohistoric Archeology on the Great Plains," *Plains Anthropologist*, No. 5, pp. 3–9.

HURT, WESLEY R., JR.
1951 "Report of the Investigation of the Swanson Site, 39BR16, Brule County, South Dakota, 1950," *Archaeological Studies, Circular 3*, State Archaeological Commission. Pierre.

1953 "Report of the Investigation of the Thomas Riggs Site, 39HU1, Hughes County, South Dakota, 1952," *Archaeological Studies, Circular 5*, State Archaeological Commission. Pierre.

HYDE, GEORGE E.
1951–52 "The Mystery of the Arikaras," *North Dakota History*, XVIII, 187–218; XIX, 25–58.

JABLOW, JOSEPH
1951 *The Cheyenne in Plains Indian Trade Relations 1795–1840*. American Ethnological Society, *Monograph 19*. New York.

JENNINGS, JESSE D.
1955 *The Archeology of the Plains: An Assessment*. University of Utah, for National Park Service. Salt Lake City.

KANE, LUCILE M. (ed.)
1951 *Military Life in Dakota: The Journal of Philippe de Trobriand*. St. Paul.

KELLY, LUTHER S.
1926 *"Yellowstone Kelly": The Memoirs of Luther S. Kelly*. MILO M. QUAIFE (ed.). New Haven.

KENNARD, EDWARD
1936 "Mandan Grammar," *International Journal of American Linguistics*, IX, 1–43.

KROEBER, A. L.
1939 *Cultural and Natural Areas of Native North America*. University of California "Publications in American Archeology and Ethnology," Vol. XXXVIII. Berkeley.

KURZ, RUDOLPH FRIEDERICH
1937 *Journal of Rudolph Friederich Kurz*. J. N. B. HEWITT (ed.). Bureau of American Ethnology, *Bulletin 115*. Washington.

LAMAR, HOWARD ROBERTS
1956 *Dakota Territory 1861–1889*. New Haven.

LANDGRAFF, JOHN
N.D. "Field Notes on the Fort Berthold Indians."

LA ROCQUE, FRANÇOIS-ANTOINE
1889 "The Missouri Journal, 1804–1805," in L. R. MASSON (ed.), *Les Bourgeois de la Compagnie du Nord-Ouest*, I, 299–313. Québec.

LEHMER, DONALD J.
1952 "The Fort Pierre Branch, Central South Dakota," *American Antiquity*, XVII, 329–36.
1954a *Archeological Investigations in the Oahe Dam Area, South Dakota, 1950–51*. Bureau of American Ethnology, *Bulletin 158*. Washington.
1954b "The Sedentary Horizon of the Northern Plains," *Southwestern Journal of Anthropology*, X, 139–59.

LE RAYE, CHARLES
1908 "The Journal of Charles Le Raye," *South Dakota Historical Collections*, IV, 150–80. Sioux Falls.

LIBBY, O. G. (ed.)
1906 "The Mandans and Grosventres (The Five Knife River Villages)," *North Dakota Historical Society Collections*, I, 431–36.
1908 "La Vérendrye's Visit to the Mandans in 1738–39. Typical Villages of the Mandan, Arikara and Hidatsa in the Missouri Valley, North Dakota," *North Dakota Historical Society Collections*, Vol. II.

LOWIE, ROBERT H.
1913   "Societies of the Hidatsa and Mandan Indians," American Museum of
       Natural History, *Anthropological Papers*, XI, 219–358. New York.
1916   "Plains Indian Age-Societies: Historical and Comparative Summary,"
       American Museum of Natural History, *Anthropological Papers*, XI,
       877–984. New York.
1917   "Social Life of the Mandan," American Museum of Natural History,
       Anthropological Papers, XXI, 7–16. New York.
1954   *Indians of the Plains*. New York.
LUTTIG, JOHN C.
1920   *Journal of a Fur-trading Expedition on the Upper Missouri, 1812–
       1813*. STELLA M. DRUMM (ed.). St. Louis.
McDERMOTT, JOHN FRANCIS (ed.)
1951   *Up the Missouri with Audubon: The Journal of Edward Harris*.
       Norman, Oklahoma.
McFARLING, LLOYD (ed.)
1955   *Exploring the Northern Plains, 1804–1878*. Caldwell, Idaho.
McGEE, W. J.
1894   "The Siouan Indians," Bureau of American Ethnology, *Fifteenth An-
       nual Report*, pp. 157–204. Washington.
MACKENZIE, CHARLES
1889   "The Mississouri Indians: A Narrative of Four Trading Expeditions to
       the Mississouri 1804, 1805, 1806," in L. R. MASSON (ed.), *Les Bour-
       geois de la Compagnie du Nord-Ouest*, I, 315–93.
MASSON, L. R. (ed.)
1889   *Les Bourgeois de la Compagnie du Nord-Ouest*, Vol. I, Québec.
MATTES, MERRILL J.
1947   "Historic Sites in Missouri Valley Reservoir Areas," *Nebraska His-
       tory*, XXVIII, 161–75.
MATTHEWS, WASHINGTON
1877   *Ethnography and Philology of the Hidatsa Indians*. U.S. Geological
       and Geographical Survey, "Miscellaneous Publications," Vol. VII.
       Washington.
MATTISON, RAY H.
1951   "Old Fort Stevenson—a Typical Missouri River Military Post," *North
       Dakota History*, XVIII, 53–91.
1953   "An Army Wife on the Upper Missouri," *North Dakota History*,
       XX, 191–220.
1955   "Report on Historic Sites in the Garrison Reservoir Area, Missouri
       River," *North Dakota History*, XXII, 5–73.
MAXIMILIAN, PRINCE OF WIED
1832–34   *Travels in the Interior of North America, 1832–1834*. Reprinted in
          THWAITES, 1906, Vols. XXII–XXIV.
MAYNADIER, LIEUTENANT HENRY E.
1867   *Report of General W. F. Raynolds. Exploration of the Yellowstone*.
       40th Cong., 1 sess., Senate Ex. Doc. 77, War Department. Washington.
MEKEEL, SCUDDER
1943   "A Short History of the Teton Dakota," *North Dakota Historical
       Quarterly*, X, 137–205.

MERRILL, R.
  1951 "Fort Berthold Relocation Problems." Unpublished M.A. thesis. University of Chicago.
MULLOY, WILLIAM
  1952 "The Northern Plains," in JAMES B. GRIFFIN (ed.), *Archeology of Eastern United States,* pp. 124–38.
NASATIR, A. P.
  1931 "John Evans, Explorer and Surveyor," *Missouri Historical Review,* XXV, 219–39, 432–60, 585–608.
  1952 *Before Lewis and Clark.* St. Louis.
NEWCOMB, W. W., JR.
  1950 "A Re-examination of the Causes of Plains Warfare," *American Anthropologist,* LII, 317–30.
NEWMAN, M. T.
  1950 "The Blond Mandan: A Critical Review of an Old Problem," *Southwestern Journal of Anthropology,* VI, 255–72.
PALLISER, JOHN
  1856 *The Solitary Hunter; or Sporting Adventures in the Prairies.* New York.
PFALLER, REV. LOUIS
  1950 "Catholic Missionaries and the Fort Berthold Indians to 1889." Unpublished M.A. thesis. Loyola University.
QUAIFE, MILO M. (ed.)
  1916 "Extracts from Capt. McKay's Journal—and Others," *Proceedings of the State Historical Society of Wisconsin,* pp. 186–210. Madison.
REID, RUSSELL
  1930 "The Earth Lodge," *North Dakota Historical Quarterly,* IV, 174–85.
REID, RUSSELL (ed.)
  1942–43 "Diary of Ferdinand A. Van Ostrand," *North Dakota Historical Quarterly,* IX, 219–42; X, 3–46, 83–124.
REID, RUSSELL, and CLELL G. GANNON
  1929 "Journal of the Atkinson-O'Fallon Expedition," *North Dakota Historical Quarterly,* IV, 5–56.
RIEFEL, B.
  1952 "A Relocation Program for Three Hundred Indian Families on the Fort Berthold Reservation, North Dakota." Unpublished Ph.D. thesis. Harvard University.
RIETZ, ROBERT W.
  1953 "Leadership, Initiative, and Economic Progress on an American Indian Reservation," *Economic Development and Cultural Change,* II, 60–70.
SCHOOLCRAFT, H. R.
  1854 *History, Condition, and Prospects of the Indian Tribes of the United States,* Vol. III. Philadelphia.
SECOY, FRANK RAYMOND
  1953 *Changing Military Patterns on the Great Plains.* American Ethnological Society, *Monograph 21.* New York.
SMITH, HUBERT G.
  1954 "Archeological Work at 32ML2 (Like-a-Fishhook Village and Fort Berthold), Garrison Reservoir Area, North Dakota, 1950–1954," *Plains Anthropologist,* No. 2, pp. 27–32.

SPAULDING, ALBERT C.
1956   *The Arzberger Site, Hughes County, South Dakota.* "Occasional Contributions from the Museum of Anthropology of the University of Michigan." Ann Arbor.

SPIER, LESLIE
1921   "The Sun Dance of the Plains Indians: Its Development and Diffusion," American Museum of Natural History, *Anthropological Papers,* Vol. XVI, Part VII. New York.

STRONG, WM. DUNCAN
1933   "The Plains Culture Area in the Light of Archeology," *American Anthropologist,* XXXV, 271–87.
1935   "An Introduction to Nebraska Archaeology," Smithsonian *Miscellaneous Collections,* Vol. XCIII. Washington.
1940   "From History to Prehistory in the Northern Great Plains," in *Essays in Historical Anthropology in North America, Published in Honor of John R. Swanton.* Smithsonian *Miscellaneous Collections,* C, 353–94. Washington.

TANNER, JESSE A.
1906   "Foreign Immigration into North Dakota," *North Dakota Historical Collections,* I, 180–200.

TAYLOR, JOSEPH HENRY
1897   *Sketches of Frontier and Indian Life on the Upper Missouri and Great Plains.* Bismarck.
1901   *Kaleidoscopic Lives.* Washburn, North Dakota.
1930   "Fort Berthold Agency in 1869," *North Dakota Historical Quarterly,* IV, 220–26.

THWAITES, REUBEN GOLD (ed.)
1906   *Early Western Travels, 1784–1846.* 32 vols. Cleveland.

TYRRELL, J. B. (ed.)
1916   *David Thompson's Narrative of His Explorations in Western America, 1784–1812.* Champlain Society, Vol. XII. Toronto.

VOEGELIN, CARL F.
1941   "Internal Relationships of Siouan Language," *American Anthropologist,* XLIII, 246–49.

WEDEL, WALDO R.
1949   "Some Provisional Correlations in Missouri Basin Archaeology," *American Antiquity,* XIV, 328–39.
1956   "Changing Settlement Patterns in the Great Plains," in *Prehistoric Settlement Patterns in the New World.* GORDON R. WILLEY (ed.). Viking Fund "Publications in Anthropology," No. 23, pp. 81–92. New York.

WILL, GEORGE F.
1910   "The Bourgeois Village Site," *American Anthropologist,* XII, 473–76.
1924   "Archeology of the Missouri Valley," American Museum of Natural History, *Anthropological Papers,* XXII, 285–344. New York.
1946   "Tree Ring Studies in North Dakota," *Bulletin 338,* Agricultural Experiment Station, North Dakota Agricultural College. Fargo.

WILL, GEORGE F. and THAD C. HECKER
1944   "The Upper Missouri River Valley Aboriginal Culture in North Dakota," *North Dakota Historical Quarterly,* XI, 5–126.

WILL, GEORGE F. and GEORGE E. HYDE
1917   *Corn among the Indians of the Upper Missouri*. St. Louis.
WILL, GEORGE F. and H. J. SPINDEN
1906   "The Mandans: A Study of Their Culture, Archeology, and Language," Peabody Museum of American Archeology and Ethnology, *Papers*, III, 81–219. Cambridge.
WILSON, GILBERT L.
1914   *Goodbird the Indian*. New York.
1924   "The Horse and the Dog in Hidatsa Culture," American Museum of Natural History, *Anthropological Papers*, XV, 125–311. New York.
1928   "Hidatsa Eagle Trapping," American Museum of Natural History, *Anthropological Papers*, XXX, 99–245.
1934   "The Hidatsa Earthlodge," American Museum of Natural History, *Anthropological Papers*, XXXIII, 341–420. New York.
WISSLER, CLARK
1914   "The Influence of the Horse in the Development of Plains Culture," *American Anthropologist*, XVI, 1–25.
WOLFF, HANS
1950   "Comparative Siouan," *International Journal of American Linguistics*, XVI, 61–66.
WORKS PROGRESS ADMINISTRATION, FEDERAL WRITERS' PROJECT
1950   *North Dakota: A Guide to the Northern Prairie State*. New York.

CHAPTER 5

Navaho

By Evon Z. Vogt

The Navaho are one of the Southern Athabascan tribes of the Southwest. They occupy a reservation of over 15 million acres in northeastern Arizona and northwestern New Mexico, and their population is now approaching 85,000, the largest Indian tribe in the United States.[1]

Navaho country, located on the Colorado Plateau, is noted for its great natural beauty but not for its economic productivity. Elevations range from about 3,500 feet to more than 10,000 feet above sea level, and hence altitude, rather than latitude, is the principal determinant of variations in the climate and in the character of the vegetative covering. In about half the area (at lower elevations) a warm, arid "desert" climate prevails, with an average of only eight inches of rainfall a year. In the middle elevation "steppe" regions (covering about two-fifths of the area) the average annual rainfall

I am grateful for the Fellowship at the Center for Advanced Study in the Behavioral Sciences, Stanford, California, during 1956–57, for making the writing of this chapter possible. I am also most grateful to David F. Aberle, Harry Basehart, Edward M. Bruner, Alan L. Bryan, Helen Codere, Edward P. Dozier, Malcolm Farmer, David French, W. W. Hill, Harry Hoijer, Dell H. Hymes, Clyde Kluckhohn, Ronald Kurtz, David G. Mandelbaum, Duane Metzger, Morris Opler, Frank D. Reeve, John M. Roberts, A. Kimball Romney, David M. Schneider, Mary Shepardson, Edward H. Spicer, and Robert W. Young, who carefully read an earlier draft and made many valuable suggestions for its improvement. Denis F. Johnston kindly provided data on Navaho population.

[1] It is believed that Navaho population is increasing at the rate of approximately 2.25 per cent per annum.

is more than twelve inches, and the vegetative cover is the typical pinyon-juniper-sagebrush combination of this Southwestern zone. The remainder of the area is mountainous, with a cold, subhumid climate that has rainfall averaging twenty-two inches a year and stands of pine, oak, aspen, and fir.

The desert and steppe regions are characterized by high temperatures in the summer and sub-zero weather during the winter, high winds and frequent sandstorms in the spring, and generally high evaporation rates. In the mountains the brief growing season of ninety days is often interrupted by killing frosts.

Precipitation comes in two seasons, in the form of snows during January through March, and in the form of rains, often cloudbursts, during July through September. The late spring and early summer dry season is especially critical, because although the winter snows may provide enough moisture for pasture grasses to start growing and planted seeds to sprout in the spring, the Navaho country faces a critical drought problem if the summer rains are delayed.

In this precarious environment the Navahos have developed an economic system based upon a combination of dry-land agriculture (especially maize) and flocks of sheep, supplemented by rug-weaving and silversmithing, and, increasingly, in recent years, by off-reservation wage work.

The cultural history of the Navaho can be divided into four major periods (see Table 5). The first period covers the time between the arrival of the Nadene stock in North America and the arrival of the Apacheans in the Southwest. Inasmuch as the reconstruction of this remote period is based wholly upon inferences from linguistic distributions, glottochronology, and scant archeological data, I shall discuss it under the general rubric of "Time Depths in the Growth of Navaho Culture."

The second period covers the time between the arrival of the Apacheans in the Southwest (400 to 900 B.P.[2]) and the first full and clear historical account of the Navaho Apaches in the chronicles of the Spaniards in 1630. Since during this period the Navahos were still beyond the range of historical reporting, I shall characterize it as the "Prehistoric Southwestern Period." In this period the Apacheans began to separate into different groups (which were the precursors of the contemporary Apachean tribes) as they came into varying

[2] B.P. is an abbreviation for "Before Present" in this chapter.

types of contact with the Southwestern Pueblos and adapted their cultures to different environmental niches in the Southwest. One group of Apacheans came under heavy influence from the Pueblos, began to adapt themselves to life on the Colorado Plateau, and by the end of the period were clearly identified as "Navajo Apaches." They stood out in the Spanish chronicles especially for their adoption of agriculture from their Pueblo neighbors.

TABLE 5

NAVAHO CONTACT HISTORY

Period	Events and Archeological Dates	Contact Communities	Cultural Readings
IV Anglo-American 1846–1955	1880 Railroad arrives 1864–68 Navahos in captivity 1846 Anglo-American conquest of Southwest	Anglo-American contact community	Navaho culture (*ca.* 1955)
III Spanish-Mexican 1630–1846	1746–50 Spanish mission attempt 1692 De Vargas reconquest 1680 Pueblo Rebellion 1630 Benavides Report	Spanish-Mexican contact community	Navaho culture (*ca.* 1846)
II Prehistoric Southwest 1000–1630	1622 Hogan date on Black Mesa 1598 Spanish colonization of Southwest begins 1540 Coronado expedition 1491–1540 Hogan dates in Governador Canyon, New Mexico	Prehistoric Southwest contact community	Navaho Apache culture (*ca.* 1630)
I Migration 3000 B.P.–A.D. 1300	1000–1300 B.P. 1300–1600 B.P. 2000 B.P. 3000 B.P.	Apachean migration toward Southwest Athabascan migration to Pacific Coast Breakup of Nadene Nadene arrival in North America	Apachean culture (*ca.* A.D. 1300)

[margin note:] Sheep, horses, weaving, pastoral culture

The third period covers the time between 1630 and the American conquest of the Southwest in 1846. Since the crucial new cultural and political factor in the Southwest during this period was the Spanish, and after the Mexican War of Independence, the Mexican occupation, I shall, following Kluckhohn and Leighton (1946: 4–8), characterize it as the "Spanish-Mexican Period." In this period the Navahos acquired sheep, horses, and weaving techniques partly from intensified contacts with the Pueblos and partly directly from the

Spanish and became one of the outstanding pastoral cultures in the New World. By the end of the period they constituted one of the dominant political and military forces in the Southwest and posed a threat to the settled Pueblo and Spanish villages that was broken only by the arrival of United States troops.

The fourth period opens in 1846, when political control of the Southwest passed into the hands of the United States during the Mexican War. During this "Anglo-American Period" the American army successfully captured over two-thirds of the Navahos and held them in captivity for four years (1864–68) at Bosque Redondo along the banks of the Pecos River in eastern New Mexico. The Bosque Redondo experience successfully eliminated the raiding complex from Navaho culture and brought them under the political control of the United States government. After their captivity, a reservation comprising about one-fourth its present size was established for the Navaho. The reservation grew to its present 15 million acres through a series of Executive Order Extensions and congressional acts beginning in 1878.

Throughout this treatment of Navaho cultural history I shall focus upon new data and upon fresh perspectives and syntheses that are now possible in the Navaho case, rather than attempt to describe Navaho history and culture in any period in detail. Summaries of Navaho history and culture are readily available in Underhill (1956), Kluckhohn and Leighton (1946), and McCombe, Vogt, and Kluckhohn (1951). Ethnographic details can be found in abundance in the large technical Navaho literature; see the bibliography compiled by Kluckhohn and Spencer (1940).

The two concluding sections of the chapter will present an interpretation of the processes of Navaho culture change by taking up first the "Decisive Factors in Navaho Cultural Continuity and Change" and then "The Incorporative Model as the Basic Integrative Process in Navaho Culture Change."

Time Depths in the Growth of Navaho Culture

Evidence is accumulating to support the hypothesis that the Nadene (who were ancestral to the Athabascans) were the last major linguistic group to cross the Bering Strait from Asia to North America. If so, it follows that the time depths involved are relatively shallow for Athabascans in the New World.

linguistic analysis

The postulated time depths based upon the best available evidence are summarized on Map 9. The following consistent sequence is beginning to emerge:

    3000 B.P.—Nadene arrival in North America.
    2000 B.P.—Separation of Tlingit from Athabascan, indicating the breakup of the Nadene.
    1600–1300 B.P.—Athabascan migration to Pacific Coast.
    1300–1000 B.P.—Athabascan migration toward the Southwest.
    500–400 B.P.—Definite presence of Apacheans in the Southwest and beginnings of differentiation in the direction of contemporary tribes.

The evidence for this postulated time sequence will be discussed under three headings: linguistic data, archeological data, and historical data.

LINGUISTIC DATA

Sapir's early hypothesis (1915) of the existence of a Nadene linguistic family is now accepted as reasonably proved by most linguists (cf. Newman 1954: 633; Hymes 1956: 632) who include four members in the family: Athabascan, Eyak, Tlingit, and Haida (Hymes 1956: 634).

Shafer (1952; 1957) and Swadesh (1952) are now also attempting to confirm Sapir's suggestion that Nadene is linked to Sino-Tibetan in Asia. This linkage is not yet accepted by many linguists, but the hypothesis is interesting and may eventually be established. At any rate, the northern center of Nadene distribution in North America leaves little doubt of their being immigrants from Eastern Asia.

The 3000 B.P. estimate for the migration across the Bering Strait is suggested by David Hirsch (1954: 831), who advances the intriguing theory that it was the Nadene, entering the New World later than the Eskimo-Aleut, who drove a wedge between the Eskimo-Aleut community in south Alaska at this time, pushing part of the group out into the Aleutians and part farther east and north. The Eskimo, then, presumably closed in along the Coast behind the Nadene, giving us the mistaken distributional impression that the Eskimo-Aleut, rather than the Nadene, were the most recent migrants to North America. Although this is purely a speculative hypothesis at present, it fits the archeological and glottochronological facts available on the time depth of the Eskimo-Aleut divergence (Swadesh 1954: 362; Collins 1954: 367), and Drucker's (1955) idea that the Eskimo and Northwest Coast cultures were both derived from the same subarctic fishing and sea hunting base of the coasts of the Bering Sea and Southwest Alaska. It is also consistent with the later sequence of events in the Nadene case.

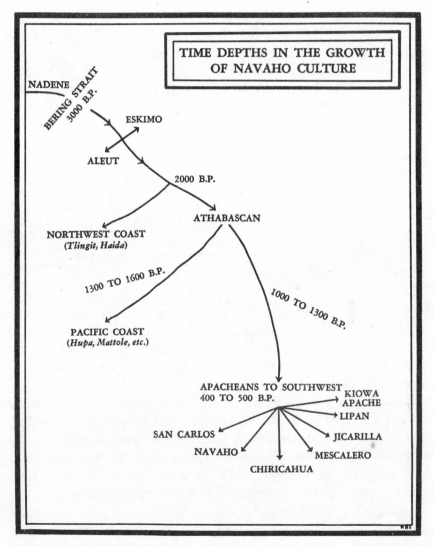

MAP 9

The 2000 B.P. date as a minimum estimate for the divergence of Nadene is suggested by Swadesh on the basis of glottochronological reckoning on the probable time of separation between Athabascan and Tlingit (Swadesh 1951: 14) and between Tlingit and Hupa (Swadesh 1954: 362). Kroeber (1955: 93) is inclined to attach a longer time depth to this divergence. He writes: "In spite of its wide geographic spread it is obvious that Athabascan has well-marked consistency; and yet I should expect at least 20 centuries of separation, quite probably up to fully 30, for some of the more divergent of its branches, rather than for Tlingit from Athabascan." More recently, Hoijer (1956a) has published a systematic glottochronological study of the Athabascan languages, using the 81 per cent retention rate.

TABLE 6

THE APACHEAN LANGUAGES*

	Navaho	Chiricahua	San Carlos	Jicarilla
Chiricahua......	205			
San Carlos......	387/424	311/348		
Jicarilla.........	387/311	274/205	460/424	
Lipan...........	460/348	311/168	579/460	311/205

* Where there are two figures, the first shows the recalculation of all of Hoijer's (1956a) 100-item list, while the second shows the recalculation for only those 78 items which are on Swadesh's original list (omitting the 22 supplementary items which Hoijer had to use). Both recalculations are with the 86 per cent retention rate.

Hymes's (1957) recalculation of Hoijer's data, using the 86 per cent retention rate, gives 16 centuries (with one case, Mattole-Kutchin, of 18 centuries) as the earliest time of divergence—a time depth which is more in line with the Swadesh figure of 20 centuries for the breakup of Nadene.

Hymes (1957) also calculates that the Athabascan movement to the Pacific Coast occurred between 13 and 16 centuries ago; the Apachean movement toward the Southwest between 10 and 13 centuries ago. The earliest divergence among the Apachean languages, according to Hymes (1957: 292), occurred only 400 to 500 years ago. His exact figures are given in Table 6. Hymes adds that:

The recalculations show San Carlos as most apart within the rather homogeneous Apachean group, as does the original study. The failure of the divergence to reflect the phonological isogloss (*t > t in Nav, Chir,

SC, *t > k in Jic, Lip) separating the western from the eastern languages may suggest that this isogloss, like the centum-satem split in Indo-European, is not an overriding diagnostic feature. Contact for the last two or three hundred years, as Hoijer points out, is also involved, and lexical borrowing may have obscured an actual split signalled by the t:k correspondence. (Hymes 1957: 295.)

At any rate, the time depths based upon linguistic evidence are beginning to emerge with consistency and with some clarity, if one grants that glottochronology can be used in a tentative way to provide the guidelines for analysis.

ARCHEOLOGICAL DATA[3]

The archeological evidence on time depths and relationships has been of two types: (*a*) specific archeological manifestations that are regarded as Athabascan, either along the probable routes of migration from the North, or in the Southwest; and (*b*) inferences from the defensive reactions of the Anasazi in the twelfth to fourteenth centuries which have suggested the arrival of warlike, nomadic, "enemy people" who began to harass them.

As matters now stand, there is not a shred of solid archeological evidence indicating which of a number of routes the Athabascans may have followed in their migration from Canada to the Southwest nor the time (or times) that the movement occurred. Although both the Promontory cultural assemblage, found in caves in the Salt Lake Valley in Utah (Steward 1937; 1940), and Dismal River culture, found in western Nebraska (Hill and Metcalf 1941; Champe 1949; Wedel 1949), are almost certainly Athabascan manifestations, it now appears they were both quite recent (approximately A.D. 1600–1700). In fact, the two cultures are probably related and represent an early protohistoric buffalo-hunting Athabascan group (Champe 1949; Gunnerson 1956; Jennings 1957) rather than evidence for early Athabascan movement toward the Southwest.

The appearance of pointed-bottom pottery (of the type which Navahos later made) in early sites, such as the Largo-Gallina Phase, dated at A.D. 1100–1250 (Keur 1941; Hall 1944*a* and *b*), can no longer

---

[3] The archeological picture of Navaho origins and cultural development will be much better understood when the data gathered by the late Richard Van Valkenburgh and his staff in connection with the Navaho Land Claims case are released for scientific use.

be used as specific evidence suggesting early Navaho occupations in the Southwest. It is now clear that essentially the same type of utility ware was also made by Southern Paiutes, Utes, and Western Apaches, and that it was similar to Northern Paiute pottery of the Owens Valley, and to the pottery of the Nevada Shoshoni (Baldwin 1950). As Baldwin concludes, "All this indicates that the ties of Southern Paiute utility ware are with the general Woodland type of the northern United States rather than with the Pueblo and Hohokam pottery" (Baldwin 1950: 54).

The discovery of ruins of circular or sub-rectangular stone structures with some associated pointed-bottom pottery in western and central Colorado (Huscher and Huscher 1942; 1943) have been regarded as Athabascan manifestations, perhaps dating back to a period before A.D. 1000. But whether these were Athabascan, Shoshonean, or some other group is still most unclear, especially in view of the nondiagnostic nature of the pointed-bottom pottery.

The first clear Apachean remains are the early Navaho hogans in the Governador Canyon in north central New Mexico, where Hall (1944*a* and *b*) reports tree-ring dates of 1491 to 1541, plus or minus 20 years.

The inferences made from the presumably defensive reactions of the Pueblos are based on the facts that the period A.D. 1150 to 1250 was characterized by compact surface pueblos in the open with a developing trend to move into cliff sites and other defensive locations (Reed 1954: 593; Farmer 1957); that late in the thirteenth century the Anasazi withdrew from the northern frontier of the Pueblo area; and that in the fourteenth century there occurred a similar constriction of the southern periphery (Gunnerson 1956: 346). It is still unclear whether these developments were related to the arrival of the Athabascans, pressure from Great Basin Shoshoneans, inter-Pueblo strife, or other factors.

In sum, if the Apacheans split from the Northern Athabascan block between 1000 and 1300 B.P. and began their movements toward the Southwest at this time, we still have no solid archeological evidence on this early migration. What we do have are Navaho hogans in north central New Mexico at A.D. 1500, a period that does fit approximately into 400–500 B.P. as the date suggested for the beginnings of Apachean differentiation in the Southwest. And we have the probably protohistoric Dismal River and Promontory manifestations suggesting that at least some of these Apacheans were hunting buffalo on the Plains and spilling over into the Basin about A.D. 1600–1700.

HISTORICAL DATA

The early historical data on the arrival of the Southern Athabascans in the Southwest has recently been summarized by Gunnerson (1956). It now seems quite possible that the Indian buffalo hunters, the Querechos and Teyas, encountered by Coronado's expedition on the plains east of the Pecos River were Southern Athabascans.[4] The evidence suggesting that Athabascans were west of the Rio Grande before 1600 is scantier. It is not until the Espejo account of 1583 that we have a Spanish record of groups which may be linked with Southern Athabascans—the Querechos near Acoma. The same group is described by Oñate in 1599 (Gunnerson 1956: 357).

Gunnerson (1956: 363) advances the theory that the Athabascans moved down the High Plains corridor, reaching the Texas–New Mexico plains about 1525; that the Eastern group remained on the Plains, while the Western group split off and settled west of the Rio Grande in northern New Mexico sometime after 1541; that the Eastern Lipanans expanded until they dominated the High Plains east of the Pueblos, while the Western Apacheans took possession of the area around and among the Western Pueblos.

This theory is certainly plausible in terms of the glottochronological and linguistic evidence and the archeological and historical evidence from Dismal River sites that Apacheans were strongly represented on the Plains in early protohistoric times. It does not fit the theory that the defensive reactions of the Anasazi in the twelfth and thirteenth centuries were due to Apachean pressure, but this "enemy people" theory is so far purely inferential. Hoijer's recent kinship reconstruction concludes that "In the Southwest, Nav, SC, Chir, and Mes were the result of the first migration, while Jic, Lip, and KA came somewhat later and perhaps by a different route. This conclusion must of course be regarded as highly tentative; the evidence on which it is based is admittedly both slender and incomplete" (Hoijer 1956b: 324). On the other hand, the Southern Athabascan kinship analyses of Opler (1936), Murdock (1949), Bellah (1952), White (1957), and Kaut (1957) all make differentiation from a single block

[4] See Tyler (1951) for an alternative theory that these groups were Shoshonean.

of proto-Apacheans seem plausible, and Kaut's study is especially impressive in maintaining that differences in kinship can be traced to differences in environmental adaptations that the groups have developed in the Southwest since the early seventeenth century.

While I would not rule out the possibility that one or more waves of Apacheans came either through the Great Basin or drifted southward just west of the crest of the Rockies—especially in view of Hoijer's kinship data and the phonological isogloss separating the western from the eastern languages—I think the burden of proof falls at present more upon those who propose a Great Basin or Rocky Mountain rather than High Plains route. The date of entry into the Southwest cannot yet be definitely set, but the outside limits would appear to be approximately A.D. 1000–1500.

APACHEAN CULTURE AT TIME OF ARRIVAL IN THE SOUTHWEST

Comparative study of Northern and Southern Athabascans leads to the following inferential reconstruction of Apachean culture at the time of their arrival in the Southwest.

The Apacheans were seminomadic hunters and gatherers, with men using the sinew-back bow to take deer, antelope, bison, and smaller game, such as rabbits, porcupines, and turkey, while the women did the wild plant gathering. They lived in scattered small encampments, probably composed of loosely organized bilocal (White 1957: 440) or matrilocal extended families, which moved with the game and up and down elevations following wild plant harvests. (Whether matrilocal residence patterns, which all Apacheans have now, were brought with them or were a later development in the Southwest, as Driver [1956] suggests, is a question that cannot yet be definitively answered.)

Descent was probably bilateral (White 1957: 441), although Murdock (1955: 86) provides an alternative suggestion that the ancestors of the Nadene peoples may have entered the New World with remnants of an old matrilineal organization. White (1957) concludes that the proto-Athabascan kinship system was probably Normal Hawaiian with Hawaiian cousin terminology and generation terminology for aunt-uncle—a conclusion which has been more recently challenged by Hymes and Driver (1958), who reaffirm Hoijer's (1956b) reconstruction of bifurcate collateral terms in the first ascending generation.

Material culture was simple and easily transportable. House types were probably of conical frames made of poles leaned together and covered with whatever materials were available. They built sweat houses similar in structure to their dwellings, but smaller in size. In addition to the bow, they had the fire drill, made undecorated pointed-bottom pottery and baskets, and wore skin clothing and moccasins. The dog was used as a beast of burden by the groups on the Plains.

Political organization beyond the limits of the extended family was minimal, with an older man in an encampment serving as headman to direct the movements of camps and to organize war and hunting parties.

Ceremonial organization was probably focused around a shaman who derived power from visions, or other supernatural manifestations, and performed curing ceremonies. Girls' puberty was emphasized ceremonially as an important rite of passage. Strong beliefs included fear of the dead and ghosts and that disease is caused by contact with lightning and with certain animals, such as the bear.

Prehistoric Southwestern Period   # 3

The Prehistoric Southwestern Period covers the time-span between the arrival of the Apacheans in the Southwest and the first clear description of Navahos in the 1630 report of Benavides. The period was characterized by Apachean contacts with Pueblos and the beginnings of Apachean differentiation due to variations in ecological setting and to variations in the Puebloan contact. The "Apaches de Navajo" emerge with a special culture by the end of the period, *contact* largely by virtue of more intensive contacts with the Pueblos and of *adaptation* adjustments to the Colorado Plateau environment. By 1630 these "Navaho Apaches" were practicing agriculture; they may have adopted some ceremonial ideas and procedures from the Pueblos along with the agricultural patterns.

PREHISTORIC CONTACT COMMUNITY

The outstanding feature of the prehistoric contact community was the interaction between the settled agricultural Pueblos living in compact villages during Pueblo III and Pueblo IV times and the Apacheans living in widely scattered and shifting encampments. This interaction must have taken place over a wide geographical front—from the Hopi country in Arizona to the Rio Grande Pueblos, and, conceivably, if one accepts an early entry date for the Apacheans, from the Zuni country (or beyond on the south) to southern Utah and Colorado on the north. Even if one favors a later entry date for the Apacheans, it is now clear that in the case of the Navaho Apaches alone, the range of contacts probably extended from the Rio Grande to the Hopi country by the end of the period. The tree-ring dates of 1491 to 1541 on hogan sites in the Governador (Hall 1944) and the 1626 reports of Zarate Salmeron (1856) and of Benavides in 1630 (Ayer 1916; Forrestal 1954; Reeve 1956) establish the presence of Navahos in contact with the Rio Grande pueblos; a recently dis-

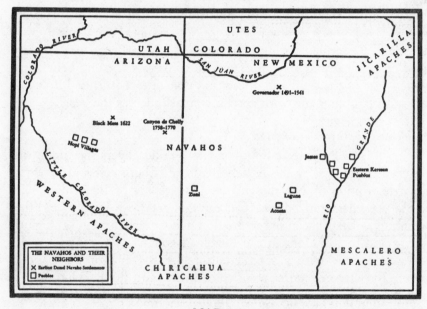

MAP 10

covered hogan site northeast of Pinyon on Black Mesa yields a tree-ring date of 1622 (Littel *et al.* 1957: Exhibit A–1) and definitely places the Navahos close to the Hopi villages at this time.

This early geographical range of the Navahos adds new significance to Kroeber's (1939: 35) concept of the Navahos as "Inter-Pueblo," since it is now evident that they have been in contact with Pueblo villages on the west, south, and east for over three hundred years (see Map 10). Even more significant, in view of Eggan's (1950:313) and Dozier's (see chapter iii of this book) thesis that the eastern Keresan Pueblos and Jemez previously had strong matrilineal clans and, only after moving to the east, changed from a clan-based to a village-based culture, is the fact that all the Pueblos which bordered Navaho country probably had strong matrilineal institutions. This means we no longer have the problem of wondering whether the Navahos came into contact with matrilineal Pueblo systems at an early date. It used to be assumed that not until the Navahos reached the western pueblos of Zuni and Hopi were they under strong influence from matrilineal systems. We now know from archeological evidence that they were probably in contact with the Hopi by the early half of the seventeenth century; we know from the ethnological evidence that the eastern Navaho were also in position to be influenced strongly by the matrilineal systems of Jemez and eastern Keresan.

Although difficult to interpret historically, the evidence from Navaho mythology (Spencer 1947, 1957) also suggests sustained early contacts with the Pueblos, who are specifically given credit in the origin myth for the introduction of agriculture to the Navahos.

Population sizes and trends during the period are difficult to estimate. It would appear that Pueblo population was undergoing a long-range contraction, and, with the introduction of agriculture, the best guess would be that Navaho population was slowly expanding—but there is as yet no systematic data on this problem.

The nature of Navaho-Pueblo relationships is also difficult to characterize during this prehistoric period. We can assume that the relationships involved raiding and trading. In raiding it is probable that the Navaho Apaches were on the offense, attempting to take Pueblo corn and other food supplies, while the Pueblos were on the defense, mustering only an occasional retaliatory raid. In trading one can imagine an active exchange of Navaho venison and buckskin for Pueblo corn, accompanied by much visiting and exchange of ideas. There is no evidence to suggest whether intermarriage occurred or whether slaves or captives were taken at this period.

Projecting back from later historical evidence, we can also infer that to the Navahos the Pueblos must have seemed to be sophisticated town-dwellers with impressive cultural features like agriculture, compact and multistoried stone architecture, and a colorful and complex ceremonial organization. The Pueblos probably regarded these Navaho Apaches as wild, uncivilized, and impoverished nomads. But, interestingly enough, it is extremely doubtful, judged from all we know now, that the Pueblos ever undertook any programs of directed culture change to "civilize" these new neighbors! The proselytizing programs were creatures of European culture, the Spanish and the Anglo-Americans who came later to the Southwest.

Even less can be said of the probable intercultural role network in this period, beyond the inference that the "warrior-warrior" and "trader-trader" intercultural role contacts were probably the most important, with most of the contacts occurring in or near the pueblos rather than out in the Navaho encampments.

NAVAHO APACHE CULTURE IN 1630

In 1630 we have our first historical glimpse of Navaho culture in the report of Fray Alonso de Benavides, who clearly differentiates the "Navajo Apaches" from the "Xila Apaches" and the "Vaquero Apaches of the Buffalo Herd" (Ayer 1916; Hodge, Hammond, Rey 1945; Forrestal 1954). The Xila Apaches are described as "living by the hunt," but the "Navajos are very skillful farmers, for the word *navajo* means 'large cultivated fields'" (Forrestal 1954: 45).

We also learn that the Navahos fight with bows and arrows to defend their territory, that "they have their own peculiar type of underground dwelling places, as well as a certain kind of hut for storing their grain" (Forrestal 1954: 46) and that "they have as many wives as they can support" (p. 50).

Benavides describes sending out twelve "Christian Indians" from Santa Clara to contact the Navahos. They took with them an arrow with a colored feather and a tobacco-filled reed to use in peace negotiations; they succeeded in bringing back an "Apache captain with four other of his captains" (pp. 47–49), which suggests a group of local headmen of the type that become familiar later in Navaho history. The Apache captain describes his own people as "going about these fields and mountains like deer and jack-rabbits" (pp. 49–50), a comparison that is also made by later Navaho leaders. Navaho curiosity about other cultures is clearly evident in the fact that the Apache captain was eager to see "God in the Mass"; however, Benavides refused to let him attend Mass because he had not been baptized (pp. 50–51).

The Navaho Apache captain also spoke of holding a great fair that would last three days and said the Navahos would bring their women and children, together with large quantities of dressed deerskins and "minerales de piedra lumbre" (best translated as "minerals of colored rock," according to Reeve 1956), and "thus a strong friendship would be established between them" (Forrestal 1954: 51). This suggests that trading patterns with the Pueblos had been established. It is not clear how the Navahos communicated with the people from Santa Clara pueblo, but they apparently did carry on quite sophisticated conversations, and my guess would be that the Pueblos had learned to speak some Navaho.

In sum, these Navaho Apaches (at least in the area near Santa Clara pueblo) had by 1630 acquired agriculture and developed some kind of structure for storing corn; they had developed a pattern for entering into peace negotiations and trading with the Pueblos; they had some kind of intercultural linguistic communication more sophisticated than sign language; they had a strong sense of possessing and defending a particular territory; they were clearly polygynous. Whether or not the Navahos had acquired Pueblo ritual and had begun the adoption (or development) of matrilineal institutions along with the agriculture is, unfortunately, not hinted at in Benavides' account.

Spanish-Mexican Period *1630 - 1846*

This period covers the time-span between 1630 and 1846, when the United States took possession of the Southwest during the Mexican War. The Spanish entered the Southwest with the Coronado Expedition of 1540, but colonization did not occur until 1598 under the leadership of the first Spanish governor, Don Juan de Oñate.

The period was characterized by important changes in Navaho culture that resulted from raiding and trading contacts with the Spanish, and, more importantly, from intensive contacts with Pueblo refugees from the Rio Grande Pueblos following the Pueblo Rebellion of 1680 and the reconquest in 1692. By 1846 the Navahos had integrated the Spanish horse and sheep into their culture and had become the most impressive pastoral culture in aboriginal America and one of the dominant military powers in the Southwest.

SPANISH-MEXICAN CONTACT COMMUNITY

The most significant groups in contact with the Navaho during the period were Pueblo and Spanish. Other cultural groups of variable importance included other Apaches, Utes, and Comanches. The Navaho settlement pattern appears to have been one of scattered encampments, or hogan clusters, throughout the period. The Rabal documents on the period 1706 to 1743 (Hill 1940*a*) describe the Navahos as living in "rancherías" on top of mesas. Kluckhohn and Leighton (1946: 5) interpret these statements to mean that the Navahos, having acquired agriculture, had settled down into "small, compact communities." While it is probable that agriculture, Pueblo influence (especially in the east where Pueblo refugees from the Spanish lived with Navahos), and pressure from Utes, Comanches, and the Spanish led to somewhat more residential stability and larger settlements, it is doubtful that the Navahos have ever lived in compact communities. Keur's (1941) archeological data from Big Bead Mesa, where maximum clustering occurred (in the period 1745–1812), shows only 32, 23, and 18 hogans in the largest three settlements. These clusters are scattered over rocky promontories for distances of one-eighth to one-fourth of a mile and are composed primarily of the stone-wall type of hogan, suggesting heavy Pueblo influence. Six other settlements on the same mesa contain only one to seven hogans, primarily of the forked-pole type. In the Governador, Keur (1944) also found many hogan clusters; in this case, many were in close association with "pueblitos," suggesting mixed Navaho and Pueblo occupation during the period 1670 to 1770. She does not, however, indicate how compact the clusters were.

If we can assume that Keur's Big Bead Mesa data represent the maximum clustering during this early period, the most we can say is that there was a tendency to greater clustering in limited areas for a limited period of time. Farmer (1942) does not indicate any compact settlements in the Upper Blanco and Largo Canyons, where tree-ring dates indicate an occupation during 1735 to 1777. Hurt's (1942) data on two groups of hogans that were occupied 1758–70, on the rim of Canyon de Chelly, clearly indicate a scattered settlement pattern in this area. It is my guess that further research will show that the predominant pattern during this early Spanish period, and throughout Navaho history, comes closer to the scattered hogan clusters (occupied by extended families) that are still found in Navaho country.

The Pueblos continued to live in compact villages, extending from the Hopi country to the Rio Grande, except for certain disturbances in the pattern during and after the Pueblo Rebellion. The Spanish settled in villages in the Upper Rio Grande Valley, with outlying ranches and with mission outposts in the various pueblos, and for brief periods in 1629 (Reeve 1957: 41) and in 1746–50 (Kelly 1941) at the edge of Navaho country. The other Apacheans lived in scattered encampments, south and east of Navaho country; the Utes in bands to the north, and the Comanches in bands on the Plains to the east.

Population sizes and trends are still difficult to estimate for this period. Navaho population for 1740 has been estimated at 4,000 (Hill 1940: 396); by 1846 the Navahos had increased to an estimated 13,500 (Graves 1866: 135). Pueblo population was almost certainly decreasing from an estimated 30,000 in 1630 to less than 10,000 in 1850. Spanish population markedly increased from an estimated 1,000 in 1630 to 2,500 in 1700 to 18,826 in 1799.

The structure and dynamics of the contact community became much more complex during this period with the arrival of the Spanish in the Southwest. I shall therefore attempt to characterize it under a number of subheadings.

NAVAHO-SPANISH RELATIONSHIPS

During these two centuries the Spanish had an almost continuous struggle to develop their colony in the province of New Mexico and to convert the Indians to Catholicism. Spanish-Navaho relations were characterized by periodic Navaho raids on settled Spanish villages and Spanish retaliatory expeditions into Navaho country, except for a peaceful fifty years from about 1720 to the mid-1770's.

From the Navaho point of view the most important feature of the Spanish colonists was their possession of horses, sheep, and goats which the Navahos began to acquire sometime between 1630 and 1706, when the presence of these domestic animals in Navaho rancherías is mentioned in the Rabal documents (Hill 1940a). It is not yet certain whether these animals were taken over by the Navahos at approximately the same or different times. The Rabal documents mention many sheep and goats, but few horses (Hill 1940a: 397). The archeological data from the Governador, 1670–1770 (Keur 1944), and from Canyon de Chelly, 1758–70 (Hurt 1942), yield horse bones, but no sheep or goat bones; while the data from the Upper Blanco and Largo, 1735–77 (Farmer 1942), and from Big Bead Mesa, 1745–1812 (Keur 1941), yield horse, sheep, and goat bones. Careful comparisons of these and other site reports may eventually answer the question whether horses or sheep came first, or were adopted at the same time by the Navaho.

At any rate, it is clear that Navaho raids against the Spanish were

primarily motivated by their desire for livestock; the Navahos sometimes took Spanish slaves, but this was secondary. More common was
the Navaho practice of trading slaves, captured elsewhere, to the
Spanish for horses.

The raiding of Spanish villages and ranches reached enormous proportions by the end of the period. For example, it is reported that in
1775 the herds of New Mexico were so depleted that the province
had to send to Spain for 1,500 additional horses (Hackett 1937: 486–
87). Between 1846 and 1850, it is estimated that the Navahos and
Apaches took over 450,000 Spanish sheep (Van Valkenburgh 1938:
11).

The Spanish had much to lose and little to gain in this early contact with the Navaho, except occasional slaves they captured on retaliatory expeditions. By 1799 Navaho blankets were being woven for
the Spanish market (Amsden 1934: 133), and the Navahos thus had
more to offer the Spanish late in the period.

Spanish strategy in dealing with the Navahos revolved around military and political efforts to reduce the number and intensity of Navaho raids, and missionary efforts to convert and "civilize" the Navahos. The punitive retaliatory campaigns into Navaho country began
in the early 1600's (Reeve 1957) and continued (with the exception
of the peaceful period from 1720 to the mid-1770's) until the U.S.
troops took over this function in 1846. Navaho activities during the
Pueblo Rebellion of 1680 are not well known, but there are implications that they took advantage of the situation by raiding the settled
villages for food and livestock (Reeve 1957: 51). It is also known that
the decade preceding the Pueblo Rebellion was a period of great difficulties with drought and pestilence and that during this time the
Apache onslaught on the livestock in the Rio Grande Valley reached
new heights. "It is quite possible that the well-known livestock (especially sheep) holdings of the Navaho Apaches in the eighteenth
century had their origins in these years immediately preceding the
Pueblo uprising" (Reeve 1957: 49). In fact, the whole period from
the 1670's through the Pueblo Rebellion in 1680 to the reconquest in
1692 appears to have been an era of flux and unsettled conditions in
which the Navahos could take sheep and horses from Spanish and
Pueblo settlements with maximum ease. The further importance of
the period in leading to more intensive contacts between Navahos and
Pueblos, especially after the reconquest in 1692, is discussed below.

The political efforts of the Spanish in the eighteenth century are interesting, especially since they did apparently result in a period of relatively peaceful relations. Under the leadership of Governor Anza, the Spanish attempted to make various treaties with Navaho "captains" or "generals" to restrain raiding parties. In particular, Antonio el Pinto, who was appointed a "general" in the Spanish army and received regular gifts, was successful in keeping at least some Navaho bands at peace with the Spanish. After his death the peace was broken and regular raids began again (Van Valkenburgh 1938: 6). The Spanish also made efforts to break an alliance between the Navahos and the Gila Apaches, who were apparently teaming up on some raids in the 1780's (Thomas 1932: 266).

In these political and diplomatic efforts the Spanish had the same difficulty the Americans experienced later. The Navahos never developed political unity on a tribal basis, so that treaties and agreements made with a Navaho "captain" or "general" were, in fact, being made with some *natani* (local headman) whose political power did not extend beyond the borders of his own band. It was usually impossible for him to restrain the raiding activities of another band which might be involved in the next raid.

The missionary efforts of 1629 and 1746–50 were the only two programs of directed culture change the Spanish undertook during the period. We know little about the 1629 effort except that shortly after the arrival of Fray Alonso Benavides in 1625 as Custodian of the Missions, serious efforts were made to strengthen relations with the Navahos with a view to converting them and maintaining peace between them and the Pueblos (Reeve 1957: 40). When Fray Pedro de Ortega, missionary of Santa Fe, learned that one of the Navaho captains named Quinia had been wounded by an arrow, he went to the Navaho country with a trained apothecary and surgeon to tend the wounded man. In 1627 Quinia came to Fray Pedro and asked to be baptized. "To console him, I went to his rancherías, as he had retired further inland, and planted there the first crosses," reported Fray Pedro. The following year he did baptize Quinia and a fellow chieftain named Manases. In the spring of 1629, the serious work of planting a mission was started. Captain Quinia came to the Rio Grande Valley to escort Fray Bartolomé Romero and Fray Francisco Muños; they were also accompanied by Governor Francisco de Sylva with a detachment of soldiers. "In one day they built a church of logs, which they hewed, and they plastered these walls on the outside." Then the Spanish departed, leaving Fray Bartolomé as resident missionary. But the Navahos soon tried to kill the friar and then moved away. It was then that Fray Alonso de Benavides attempted to repair the situation by sending the delegation from Santa Clara to bring in the Navaho captains (Reeve 1957: 41). The location of this first mission is uncertain, but it was presumably within four days' travel west or northwest of Santa Clara.

The second missionary effort has been summarized by Kelly (1941: 56–66). This effort began in March, 1744, when the priests from Isleta and Jemez penetrated Navaho country, in between trips to Hopi country and reported the conversion of five thousand Indians! They traveled west from Jemez four days and preached to the Navahos in their scattered rancherias. They stayed six days, "converting all the Indians." One of the padres admitted that their success "was made easier by the distribution of gifts in the form of cloth, beads, ribbons, tobacco, and other novel articles."

In the fall of 1745 one of the padres went again to Navaho country and came back with an exciting story about a great Indian kingdom, "El Gran Teguayo." This report, with the story about the conversion of five thousand Indians, led the viceroy to order the founding of four missions in Navaho country in 1746, protected by a garrison of thirty soldiers. The execution of the order was difficult because Governor Codallos found it impossible to furnish the soldiers. But Fray Juan Miguel Menchero, the Ecclesiastical Visitador, went into Navaho country anyway and induced five hundred Indians to return with him and settle at Cebolleta, just east of Mount Taylor. He baptized all the children, but refused baptism to the adults since they were trained in the rudiments of their own faith.

In 1749 the governor, in response to Father Menchero's request, received viceregal approval to found the missions, not in the inaccessible Navaho province, but in the more convenient region near Laguna, where the five hundred Navahos had already settled. Accordingly, the neighboring missions of Cebolleta and Encinal were established with a resident padre at each mission. This same year four other missionaries were working in the Navaho province.

But a series of difficulties followed. There were great delays in delivering the supplies Governor Cachupin promised to provide for the missions. Usually there were no supplies at all, and the padres were unable to fulfil their promises of gifts to the Navahos. On October 26, 1749, while passing through on a tour of inspection, Governor Cachupin picked up a bow and arrow and shot at a Navaho, striking him in the groin and drawing blood. The Governor left affairs simmering at Cebolleta.

In 1750 the Navahos increased the apprehension of the Acomas by petitioning the Governor for permission to move their residence to Cubero, where the water was more abundant. When the Acomas protested strongly, the Governor ordered a Spanish officer accompanied by Father Trigo to look into the trouble. On April 16, 1750, news was received that the Navahos had revolted at the two missions and driven out their padres. So the same day Father Trigo and his party hurried to Cebolleta and pleaded with the Navahos, promising them friendship and the reward of God and the Spaniards if they would return to the faith. The Navahos, said Father Trigo, would be molested in no way; they could build their pueblo in any spot they chose, and those Christians who wanted instruction could come to the padre, who would live nearby but apart from the Indians. The reply of the Navaho leader, as reported by Father Trigo, is a classic:

They, the Indians of Cebolleta, replied that they did not want pueblos now, nor did they desire to become Christians, nor had they ever asked for the fathers; and that what they had all said in the beginning to the Reverend Commissary, Fray Miguel Menchero in 1746 was that they were grown up, and could not become Christians or stay in one place because they had been raised like deer, that they would give some of their children who were born to have water thrown upon them and that these as believers might perhaps build pueblos and have fathers, but that now they did not desire either fathers or pueblos; that they would be, as always, friends and comrades of the Spaniards, and that if the father wished to remain there they would do him no harm, but that they could not be Christians. (Kelly 1941: 64–65.)

Father Trigo then offered more concessions, saying he would send them another priest. The Indians replied that they had no complaint about Father Vermejo, other than that he was so poor and could give them nothing. They repeated that they had not promised Father Menchero they would become Christians, and that they had only allowed water to be thrown upon their children because the parents who brought the children were rewarded with gifts of hoes and picks. At the mission at Encinal, Father Trigo's experience was much the same. The Navaho leader said that Father Menchero had not given them all the gifts he promised for bringing their children to be baptized. They said that Menchero had promised horses, mules, cows, sheep, and clothing and had not provided these things (Kelly 1941: 66). Although there is good evidence that this Navaho group remained in the Mount Taylor area and were at least partly the ancestors of Sandoval's band, that later co-operated with the Americans, this 1750 experience was apparently the end of the Spanish missionary effort among the Navaho.

The outlines of Navaho strategy in this period are clear. They took Spanish livestock by raiding and trading; they accepted gifts from Spanish missionaries and dealt with them only as long as there were practical gifts forthcoming; they made promises of peace and alliances when it was to their practical advantage to do so. In particular, it became typical practice for the Navahos to make promises about peace during the summer while they had to stay in one place to cultivate their crops. But as soon as the crops were harvested, raids began again in the fall (Underhill 1956: 73).

Intercultural attitudes are difficult to infer with precision, except that among the Spanish it is evident that the Navahos were strongly feared and were regarded as nomadic, heathen Indians. Among the Navahos, the Spanish appear to have been regarded very practically as a source of sheep, horses, and gifts.

Four major intercultural roles were involved in this Spanish-Navaho contact. The "missionary-neophyte" role connection has already been covered in the description of the missionary attempts. This role interaction was tenuous, to say the least. More important was the "raider-raided" interaction which persisted through most of the period, as did the "trader-trader" connection. The fourth point of contact was a "master-slave" relationship, in particular the relationship between the Spanish masters and an estimated 2,000 to 4,500 Navaho slaves they held in their households and on their ranches by 1846 (Underhill 1956: 80). These Navaho slaves were apparently well treated in the Spanish households, especially since most of them were women and children. Many of the women bore half-Spanish children who grew up serving as peons and learning Spanish culture. It is unclear how many of these slaves eventually returned to Navaho country; if many did, they were undoubtedly an important force for acculturation, as Underhill suggests (1956: 80). But there is no evidence to suggest that they did return to Navaho country in large numbers; more probably they were absorbed by the Spanish population in the Rio Grande Valley.

NAVAHO-PUEBLO RELATIONS

The raiding and trading contacts between the Navahos and Pueblos continued through most of the Spanish-Mexican Period, but the more important developments were the closer contacts following the Pueblo Rebellion of 1680 and reconquest in 1692, in the eastern Navaho zone, and the closer Navaho-Hopi contacts during drought and famine in the western Navaho zone during the 1700's.

The Spanish chronicles mention that many Pueblos fled from the Rio Grande villages to escape Spanish reprisals at the end of the seventeenth century (Twitchell 1911: 399, 412). According to the archeological data from the eastern Navaho zone, in particular in the Governador (Keur 1944; Hall 1944; Reed 1944), these Pueblo refugees settled with the Navahos from about 1700 to 1750 and built the "pueblitos" that are found in association with Navaho hogans in this area. In this situation one can infer that not only did Navahos and Pueblos work and fight together, but probably also intermarried (Underhill 1956: 41–57).

We are not yet certain of the magnitude and duration of this development, but our evidence suggests that it was a crucial period for Navaho culture change. The diffusion of Pueblo cultural elements to the Navahos which began in the Prehistoric Period must have been accelerated and extended to many more aspects of Navaho life. It was probably the time when the Navahos not only learned more about Pueblo technology (agriculture, animal husbandry, weaving, pottery), but also absorbed more Pueblo religious and social concepts and procedures: ceremonial masks, altars, prayer sticks, use of corn meal, sand paintings, the origin myth, and perhaps even selected aspects of the Pueblo matrilineal clan system. A number of contemporary Navaho clans had their origins in groups of Pueblo refugees who stayed with Navahos—for example, the Jemez clan, the Zia clan, the "Black Sheep People" reportedly derived from San Felipe (Van Valkenburgh 1938: 4–5; Haile 1941: 138–39).

A similar process occurred in the western Navaho zone during the 1700's when Hopis found refuge from drought and famine with the Navahos in Canyon de Chelly (Kluckhohn and Leighton 1946: 6).

The strategy and intercultural attitudes in these closer Navaho-Pueblo contacts in the late seventeenth and eighteenth centuries can only be approximately inferred from our scattered historical and archeological data. The Pueblos presumably had much to offer the Navahos as a source of livestock and food and in the way of practical economic knowledge, as well as social and religious knowledge. It is difficult to understand what the Navahos had to offer the Pueblos except refuge from Spanish oppression, and it is significant that, when sufficient Spanish force was applied, some groups of Pueblo Indians actually went to live with their erstwhile enemies. Again, as in the previous period, it is extremely doubtful that the Pueblos launched any programs of conscious and directed culture change to "civilize" the Navahos they lived with. Rather, the learning of new ideas and procedures probably occurred in an indirect, permissive manner as the two groups lived and worked together. The intermarriage that occurred added a new intercultural role to the Navaho-Pueblo relationship at this time and was especially important in cultural transmission.

NAVAHO RELATIONS WITH OTHER CULTURAL GROUPS

To date, we know even less about the relationships of the Navahos during the Spanish-Mexican Period to other Apacheans, Utes, and Comanches, except that contacts of variable importance occurred. The Navahos were in close touch with the Chiricahua Apaches, the Western Apaches, and the Mescaleros—all three of which apparently contributed to the development of Navaho clans by these names (Haile 1941: 139). Especially close contact between Navahos and Western Apaches is suggested by the fact that most of the Western Apache clans claim descent from one of three archaic clans which either are attributed to or are Navaho clans (Kaut 1956: 142; 1957: 40). It is, in fact, possible that at least part of the Western Apaches are descendants of a late split from westward moving Navaho groups (Kaut 1957: 57).

Although Navahos developed important trading patterns with the Utes (Hill 1948), the latter appear to have been strong enemies of the Navahos—and this was encouraged both by the Spanish and later by the Americans when Kit Carson recruited Utes to help him defeat the Navahos in the 1860's.

The Navahos met the Comanches at the Taos fair; they also encountered them when they went out on the Plains to hunt buffalo. More intensive contacts occurred in the next period during the time that Navaho were held in captivity at Fort Sumner.

To sum up, the event of major importance during this Spanish-Mexican Period for Navaho cultural development was the establishment and growth of the Spanish colony in the northern Rio Grande Valley. Direct, firsthand contacts between the Spanish and Navahos were not so important as the fact that the Spanish brought sheep and horses to the Southwest (which the Navahos acquired) and that they forced groups of Pueblos into closer contact with Navahos, thereby accelerating the process of cultural transmission from Pueblo to Navaho that had begun in the previous period. The results of this cultural transmission are clearly evident in the changes in Navaho culture that we see by the end of the period in 1846.

NAVAHO CULTURE IN 1846

By 1846 Navaho culture had absorbed most of the elements we have come to know in detail from later ethnographic study. Horses, sheep and goats, and Pueblo weaving and pottery techniques had all been added to the cultural inventory, while agriculture (with the addition of crops of wheat, melons, and peaches during the Spanish Period) and some hunting and gathering continued as important economic pursuits. The settlement pattern consisted of scattered small hogan clusters occupied by matrilocal extended families. The hogans were of three types, the forked-pole, rock-ring, and five- or six-sided log types, with the forked-pole variety the most common. Sweat houses, constructed like miniature forked-pole hogans, without the vestibule, were built near the hogan cluster. Sheep corrals and summer shades of poles and brush were also usually present. Special ceremonial hogans and dance grounds ringed with brush were constructed. All of these structures were typically oriented with the door or gate toward the rising sun.

Dress had shifted from entirely skin clothing to clothing of woven wool. The women wore black woolen dresses made like a double blanket, fastened at the shoulders and hanging down front and back. Early in the period the men wore skin breech clouts with shirt and leggings; late in the period the men shifted more to the Spanish style of dress, especially the wealthier Navahos who wore trousers that came halfway down to the calf and were split at the knee. These trousers were sometimes made of Spanish cloth, sometimes of tanned buckskin, and were decorated with silver buttons.

In their division of labor, the men owned and herded the horses, hunted, did most of the farming, and went on raids; the women owned and herded most of the sheep, with the assistance of the children (Letherman 1856: 294; Stephen 1893: 354; Franciscan Fathers 1910: 258; Roessel 1951: 50), butchered sheep, sheared them and did the weaving, and helped with the farming.

In social organization the Navahos had matrilineal clans with place names (e.g., Rock Pass, Close to Water), or personal or group identity names (e.g., Many Goats, Many Hogans, Red Forehead), or names indicating foreign origin (e.g., Jemez, Chiricahua, Apache, Ute, Mexican). The clan was exogamous, unified by a clan origin story, which might involve legendary, semi-legendary, or perhaps historical events, and served as a unit for the exchange of hospitality and favors (Aberle 1954: 11–15). The extent to which the clan was localized and formed a corporate group for the ownership of land and ritual property and for the control of crime is still an open question. Today, although the clans have wide geographical spread over Navaho country in individual membership, they still tend to be concentrated in certain regions (Kluckhohn and Leighton 1947: 64). At any rate, the important functional unit became what Aberle (1954: 16) has defined as "the local clan element," that is, those members of a given clan who live in a local Navaho community.

Aberle (1954: 11–12) suggests that if clans were borrowed from the Pueblos, it was stimulus diffusion; because the "totemism" and nature imagery of Pueblo clans are largely lacking. On the other hand, Kaut (1957) makes an impressive case for the development of Western Apache clans, and by implication also for Navaho clans, in response to more settled agricultural life. He writes:

The basic similarity of all the Apache systems of terminology is such that it is difficult to postulate a very early split of the ethnic divisions. It may well be that most of them were living in relatively close association in New Mexico and Colorado during the seventeenth century and that the segmentary process has occurred mostly since then. . . .

Taking Mescalero as a starting point, development of social organization among the Southern Athabascans may be seen as having proceeded in several directions. All the groups might have been organized in a fashion similar to the Mescalero just prior to 1600. At this time agriculture was of minor importance, and hunting and gathering organization was based upon bilateral local groups associated in loose bands. As the proto-Apache moved into the regions surrounding the heartland and adapted to different environments, changes occurred in social organization. The band became important to the Kiowa Apache, Mescalero, Chiricahua, and Lipan in their communal hunting activities. Jicarilla, Navaho, and Western Apache, on the other hand, began to depend somewhat less upon hunting and gathering as they *experimented* with agriculture. The resulting more settled conditions and intermarriage for several generations would strengthen the interrelationships between local groups, *temporarily emphasizing* territorial band organization among the Navaho and Western Apache.

. . . The nature of the country in which the Jicarilla settled did not allow the same degree of localization that was possible in Western Apache and Navaho country where plentiful game and wild crops reduced the necessary subsistence area. Thus, among the Jicarilla, local group and territorial bands remained as the important political groupings since the bands still operated, in relative independence of one another, with a large subsistence area. However, in the Navaho and Western Apache areas bands eventually ceased to exist because the relatively sedentary life brought about intermarriage and considerable interaction of all sorts between the members of formerly autonomous bands. The territorial bands gradually lost their importance as lineages became more or less permanently oriented toward particular agricultural sites and grew into clans. (Kaut 1957: 35–36.)

If this happened in the Navaho case, then presumably the later geographic spread of Navaho clans resulted from the adoption of sheep and/or military encounters with the Spanish and Americans which had the effect of dispersing the clan members.

While it is true that the Navaho clan system, which is matrilineal, exogamous, dispersed, unorganized, largely non-totemic, and named after a place or group, is what one would expect from their ecological adjustments with agriculture and later sheep, it would be premature to rule out Pueblo influence upon the development of this clan system. In the first place, we now know that Navahos had close associations with matrilineal Pueblos who bordered them on three sides; further, the Hopi-Tewa case (Dozier 1954) demonstrates that a clan system can be diffused to another group when the ecological conditions are similar and the association is close. On the other hand, we have the case of the Tanoan Pueblos who have a settled agricultural way of life but have never developed clans. In short, while the adoption of agriculture supplied the conditions for clans, and the acquisition of sheep may have strengthened the matrilineal emphasis, the Pueblo clan system probably provided some ideas and principles, especially during the period of very close intercultural association following the Pueblo Rebellion.

The extent to which Navaho clans were linked to other clans in 1846, as they are today, is unknown.

Political organization had developed to the point that there was apparently both a local band headman, or peace *natani*, chosen for life and inducted into office by a ceremony, and one or more war leaders whose choice was entirely dependent upon ritual attainment (Hill 1940*b*). To some extent during limited periods of time headmen from several bands may have been controlled by a pre-eminent natani, but it is extremely doubtful that the Navahos ever had any centralized authority until the recent emergence of the Navaho Tribal Council as a tribal political organization.

The raiding complex, which probably began, according to now available historical evidence (Reeve 1957), long before the Navahos acquired horses and became interested in sheep, was undoubtedly developed to a high point during the period. Horses enormously increased the mobility of the Navahos and made possible the mobilization of larger groups of men for raiding parties; the dependence upon sheep increased the motivation for mounting raids upon the Pueblos and Spanish. By 1846 the raiding and war potential of the Navahos was a major threat to peaceful life in the Rio Grande Valley.

There is interesting suggestive evidence that a system of social stratification had emerged by the end of this period (Roessel 1951). The *ricos* owned many sheep and horses; the *pobres* without sheep attached themselves to the encampments of the ricos and worked for them; the slaves were non-Navaho captives. Since the ricos could easily lose their sheep in retaliatory raids, the pobres could build up herds by raiding, and the descendants of slaves were free, the system was not rigid. But it may have been important in the dynamics of the raiding complex—the ricos wanted peace to maintain the herds they had; the young pobres wanted raids to build up their herds of horses and sheep.

In ceremonial organization, with the accelerated Pueblo borrowing during the period, the role of the "inspired" shaman was reduced in importance to include finally only the "hand-tremblers" who diag-nosed illnesses and recommended the type of ceremony to be used for the cure, and the role of the carefully taught singer became more im-portant. A complex set of two to nine night song ceremonials using sand paintings, masks, prayer sticks, and altars (derived from Pueblo ceremonialism) were being performed over patients. These ceremoni-als did not follow a calendric order, as among the Pueblos, but were performed when an individual became ill; certain ceremonials, how-ever, could only be held during the winter months. The mythological framework and the pantheon of Holy People also reflected heavy Pueblo influence, as for example, the affinity of the yeibichai to the Pueblo katchinas. Fear of the dead and strong ghost beliefs appear to be ancient Apachean features, but the witchcraft beliefs also have enough in common with the Pueblo pattern to suggest Pueblo affini-ties (Kluckhohn 1944: 42).

The Anglo-American Period

The Anglo-American Period covers the time from 1846, when the United States took possession of the Southwest, to the pres-ent. The major historical events include the conquest of the Navahos by United States troops and their captivity at Fort Sumner (1864–68); the establishment of the basic Navajo Reservation in 1868; the arrival of the transcontinental railroad in 1880, the subsequent growth of Anglo-American population on and off the reservation, and the con-sequent struggle with Americans for land; the forced reduction of livestock herds by the Collier administration in the 1930's; the spread of the peyote cult among the Navahos; the participation of the Nav-aho in World War II; and the recent efforts of the U.S. Indian Serv-ice to improve the situation of the Navahos. Needless to say, the pe-riod has been characterized by another series of important changes in Navaho culture and by increasingly complex relationships with An-glo-Americans as the Southwest has become involved in the modern world.

AMERICAN CONTACT COMMUNITY

The most significant groups in contact with the Navaho during the period have been Anglo-American, Pueblo, and Spanish-American. Other groups of variable importance include Apaches and other Southwestern Indians.

Except for the four-year period at Fort Sumner, when some 8,000 Navahos were settled in a forty-square-mile area along the banks of the Pecos River, the predominant Navaho settlement pattern has continued to be one of scattered hogan clusters. In agency towns, like Window Rock, Arizona, or Shiprock, New Mexico; near some of the missions, like Ganado; and in certain neighborhoods in White towns and cities of the Southwest, Navahos are found living under more compact conditions. But these are quite special developments in which the control of the settlement pattern is in the hands of Anglo-Americans. Where Navaho preferences prevail, over the rest of the reservation, the settlements continue to be scattered.

Pueblos and Spanish-Americans have continued to live in compact villages, but with some tendency to spread into outlying farming villages, as, for example, at Acoma, Laguna, and Zuni, and outlying ranch settlements, such as the Spanish-American ranches established along the southern border of Navaho country from Cubero, New Mexico, to St. Johns, Arizona, after Navaho power was broken by the Fort Sumner roundup. More recently, Pueblos and Spanish-Americans have also drifted into Anglo-American towns and cities, and in some towns, such as Flagstaff, Arizona, there are "across-the-tracks" neighborhoods composed of Indians, Spanish-Americans, and Negroes.

Anglo-Americans are settled in towns established south of the reservation (Grants, Gallup, Holbrook, Winslow, and Flagstaff) along the Santa Fe Railroad, which came through in 1880; in the towns of Aztec and Farmington in the San Juan Valley north of the reservation; and in Indian agency towns, trading posts, and mission stations on the reservation. Mormon communities established as missionary outposts from the Mormon settlements in Utah and northern Arizona brought additional Anglo-Americans into contact with Navahos in the 1870's and 1880's. Large Anglo-American ranches on all sides of the reservation began to be established about the same time.

The other Apachean tribes are now concentrated on reservations at considerable distance from Navaho country, except for the Jicarilla, whose reservation was established west of their aboriginal range and hence brought them closer to the Navahos. The Western Apaches are in the White Mountain country of Arizona; the Chiricahuas and Mescaleros are located in south central New Mexico. There is also some contact with Paiutes and Utes, living north of Navaho country, and the Upland Yumans living to the west. Comanche contacts were important during the Fort Sumner period.

Navaho population has grown enormously from an estimated 13,-500 in 1846 to nearly 85,000. By 1950, there were more than 100,000 Anglo-Americans (not counting the more distant urban centers like Albuquerque and Santa Fe) in the towns at the borders of Navaho country. The Spanish-American population significantly involved in the contact community is more difficult to calculate. Immediately after the Fort Sumner captivity there was an increase in Spanish-American population near Navaho country; more recently many small Spanish-American villages have declined in population as Anglo-Americans took over land and Spanish-Americans moved to more distant cities.

NAVAHO–ANGLO-AMERICAN RELATIONSHIPS

The relationships of Navahos with Anglo-Americans have moved through three important phases since 1846: (*a*) the phase of 1846 to 1863, before the Fort Sumner captivity, which was characterized by Navaho raids and American attempts to control the raids; (*b*) the Fort Sumner phase, 1864 to 1868, when a large proportion of the Navahos were held in captivity; and (*c*) the phase after the Fort Sumner captivity which has been characterized by an expanding Navaho population on the reservation and by complex relationships with white Americans including Indian agents, Indian traders, and missionaries, all having an impact upon Navaho life.

When General Kearny marched into Santa Fe in August, 1846, he met no resistance from the Mexican authorities: they had retreated down the Rio Grande Valley. His first difficulties were significantly enough with the Navahos, who in September, 1846, stole several head of cattle from General Kearny's beef herd at Algodones and raided settlements at various places near Albuquerque, killing seven or eight settlers, and stealing thousands of cattle, sheep, and horses. Exasperated by the conduct of the Navahos, Kearny ordered Colonel Doniphan to undertake what was to be the first in a series of expeditions against the Navaho during the next fifteen years (Keleher 1952: 23–33). Doniphan set out from Santa Fe in October with three hundred men and marched to Bear Spring, the present site of Fort Wingate, New Mexico, where over five hundred Navahos, and a number of chiefs, had been rounded up, and forced, at the point of the bayonet, to attend a meeting on November 21 with Doniphan.

Through an interpreter, Doniphan explained the purpose of the meeting. One of the young Navaho chiefs, Sarcilla Largo, responded for the Navahos saying that "He was gratified to learn the views of the Americans. He admired their spirit and enterprise, but detested the Mexicans" (Hughes 1847: 95). Speeches were delivered alternately during the whole day, and at sunset the parties adjourned to their respective camps. The following day there were more speeches; Doniphan explained that the United States had now taken military possession of New Mexico, that raids against the Mexicans must stop, and that he wished to enter into a treaty with the Navahos. He added that they should

. . . enter into no treaty stipulations unless they meant to observe them strictly and in good faith; that the United States made no second treaty with the same people; that she first offered the olive branch, and, if that were rejected, then powder, bullet, and the steel. (Hughes 1847: 95.)

The same Sarcilla Largo then responded:

Americans, you have a strange cause of war against the Navajos. We have waged war against the New Mexicans for several years. We have plundered their villages and killed many of their people, and made many prisoners. We have a just cause for all this. You have lately commenced a war against the same people. You are powerful. You have great guns and many brave soldiers. You have therefore conquered them, the very thing we have been attempting to do for so many years. You now turn upon us for attempting to do what you have done yourselves. We can not see why you have cause of quarrel with us for fighting the New Mexicans on the west, while you do the same thing on the east. Look how matters stand. This is our war. We have more right to complain of you for interfering in our war than you have to quarrel with us for continuing a war we had begun long before you got here. If you will act justly, you will allow us to settle our own differences. (Hughes 1847: 95–96.)

Then Colonel Doniphan explained that the New Mexicans had surrendered and that the war was over; all of New Mexico belonged to the United States, and if the Navahos stole property from the New Mexicans, it would be stealing from the Americans. Finally, the Navahos agreed to sign a mutual treaty which was drawn up for the signatures of twelve Navaho chiefs but significantly enough was actually signed (with an X) by fourteen chiefs (Hughes 1847: 96–97). Apparently two additional natanis took part in the actual signing—a clear indication that the Americans were not dealing with a structured hierarchy of authority among the Navaho, but only with a group of headmen from part of Navaho country. Colonel Doniphan and Sarcilla Largo exchanged gifts, and the troops departed. Within a few days, the Navahos had resumed their raids.

This first American encounter with the Navahos revealed the pattern that was to prevail for the next fifteen years. In 1847 and 1848 a number of small expeditions was sent against the Navahos; all were unsuccessful. In 1849, Colonel Washington, the military governor of New Mexico, accompanied by James S. Calhoun, the first Indian agent who later became the Civil Governor of the Territory, led a large expedition of 305 soldiers and 55 Pueblo Indians to the mouth of Canyon de Chelly. There were a few military skirmishes—as, for example, when Narbona, one of the natanis, was accidentally shot and killed during an argument between a soldier and a Navaho who had allegedly stolen his horse. But Colonel Washington's main service was simply to talk to whatever Navahos he could find. A meeting with a larger group was held at Canyon de Chelly. The Navahos claimed they had stolen no stock nor committed any crimes in the settlements and suggested that perhaps the Apaches were responsible for the depredations. Since Navaho settlement and political organization was so dispersed, the Canyon de Chelly Navahos may well have been truthful in their assertions of innocence. At any rate, after several days of talking, the Navahos entered into a treaty of peace and friendship, and army officers and Navaho chiefs exchanged gifts and the troops marched back to Santa Fe. But the raids continued (Keleher 1952: 46–50).

Smaller expeditions followed, and finally, in 1852, Fort Defiance was established, and troops were stationed in the heart of Navaho country. After a relatively peaceful period from 1852 to 1858, the killing of a slave owned by the post commander led to difficulties which climaxed on April 30, 1860, when a force of Navaho warriors, estimated between a thousand and three thousand men, attacked the fort. After an assault that lasted two hours, the warriors were repulsed by the U.S. garrison. Shortly thereafter, additional troops were moved into New Mexico from Utah to deal with the Indian problem, and by September, 1860, there were fifteen companies of regulars waging an active campaign in Navaho country (Bender 1934).

The following year the Civil War struggle reached into New Mexico, and the troops were withdrawn from Navaho country to deal with the Confederates. During 1862 the Navahos took advantage of the army's preoccupation with the Civil War to increase their raids again upon Rio Grande settlements.

In the meantime, General Carleton had marched across the desert from California to New Mexico with his California troops, only to find that the Confederates had already fled from New Mexico. For a time General Carleton kept his troops busy repairing streets and roads and rehabilitating army posts. But the soldiers soon grew tired, grumbling that they had enlisted to fight a war, not to work as laborers. The men demanded action, or a discharge. This led Carleton to look about for a task that would capture the imagination and harness the abilities of his fifteen hundred soldiers. It was at this point that he conceived the idea of fighting the Indians, and he and Governor Connelly in Santa Fe agreed to start a war against the Apaches and Navahos (Keleher 1952: 278–79).

The program that ensued was guided by probably the severest Indian policy ever carried out in the Southwest. Colonel Kit Carson, of Taos, was appointed as field commander, with orders to go after Mescalero Apaches and then Navahos. Both tribes were to be resettled at Bosque Redondo along the Pecos River where Fort Sumner was established in the center of the reserve as headquarters for the troops. The Indians were to be taught to build villages, learn to farm, and become "civilized" citizens.

The orders which went out to the soldiers in the field were: "All Indian men of the Mescalero tribe are to be killed whenever and wherever you can find them. The women and children will not be harmed, but you will take them prisoners, and feed them at Fort Stanton until you receive other instructions about them" (Keleher 1952: 286). By midsummer of 1863, most of the Mescaleros were imprisoned at Bosque Redondo, and Carson turned his attention to the Navahos. The Navahos were given until July 20, 1863, to surrender peacefully, when the orders were to shoot the men who resisted, bring in the women and children, destroy the crops and take the sheep. Carson astutely enlisted the aid of the Utes and also used many Mexicans, who were offered $20 for every horse and $1 for every Navaho sheep they delivered to the quartermaster.

Since the Navahos had only a few hundred Spencer rifles and Colt revolvers, owned by individuals in scattered parts of Navaho country, and only a small supply of lead and gunpowder acquired from Mexican traders, they were no military match for the U.S. troops (Keleher 1952: 306). Furthermore, they had no food surplus once the soldiers began systematically to destroy crops and take sheep; and this proved to be crucial strategy. It is significant that in 1863 the Navahos stole 24,389 sheep and the U.S. troops took 24,266 Navaho sheep; but in 1864, when the Navahos surrendered in large numbers, the Navahos only stole 4,250 sheep, while the troops took 12,284 sheep from the Navahos (United States Congress 1867: 247–67).

On March 6, 1864, 2,400 Navahos began the "Long Walk" to Fort Sumner. By the end of April, 3,500 more made the march. Eventually approximately 8,500 were held there. Other Navaho bands remained at large, in the Grand Canyon, on Black Mesa, north of the San Juan River, and elsewhere. But the Navahos had, in effect, been conquered.

Bosque Redondo was conceived as a place where the Navahos would begin a new way of life. Carleton described his program as follows:

To collect them together, little by little, on a reservation, away from the haunts and the hills and the hiding places of their country; there to be kind to them; there teach their children how to read and write; teach them the arts of peace, teach them the truths of Christianity. Soon they will acquire new habits, new ideas, new modes of life; and the old Indians will die off; and carry with them all latent belongings for murdering and robbing. The young ones will take their place without these belongings, and thus, little by little, they will become a happy and contented people; and Navajo wars will be remembered only as something that belongs entirely to the past. (Secretary of the Interior 1863: 230.)

The plan sounded good on paper, but from the beginning unforeseen obstacles arose which doomed the Bosque Redondo Reservation to failure as a permanent home for the Navahos. The community was composed of about 8,500 Navahos (Reeve 1938: 255) and 400 Mescaleros confined to a forty-mile-square, treeless plain and under the command of 400 U.S. troops. Technically the Navahos were prisoners of war; it was necessary for them to have passes to leave the reservation and tin ration tickets to procure food. Attempts to leave without permission were diligently prosecuted at first, but controls were relaxed in later years, and many Navahos left Bosque Redondo before the 1868 treaty was signed.

The Mescaleros had already dug an irrigation ditch and had the best piece of land along the river to farm. But they were displaced to make room for the Navahos, and friction between the two tribes was increased.

Although many Navahos continued to practice their more primitive types of agriculture, by 1866 some 2,000 acres were under cultivation using 47 plows. They planted corn, pumpkins, squash, and melons, but they never succeeded in raising more than about one-fifth of the food necessary to sustain themselves because the crops were destroyed by drought, floods, and invasion of worms (Secretary of the Interior 1866: 136–47). By 1866 the numbers of livestock had also decreased to a mere handful: 940 sheep, 1,025 goats, 550 horses, and 20 mules (Secretary of the Interior 1867: 203). The result was that the government had to continue to issue rations at great expense throughout the period.

Plans for a school and farming instruction failed to materialize. There were only occasional visits by Catholic priests, who were given precedence because Sandoval's band had supposedly been connected with Catholicism (Reeve 1938: 266–67). There were 1,276 lodges (hogans) reported for 1864, probably of cottonwood. There were attempts at making adobe houses like those of the Mexicans, and at times old army tents were used for dwellings. But the Navahos seemed to prefer their hogan structures (United States War Department 1880–1902, XLVIII: 523–25, 1259–60). The only fuel available was mesquite roots, which in time the Navahos had to travel six to twelve miles to procure.

There were plans to establish twelve village groups, half a mile apart, and to place each in the charge of one of the twelve principal Navaho chiefs (Reeve 1938: 266–67). The chiefs were appointed by the army selecting twelve natanis for these positions, but there is no evidence that the village organization ever developed. Indeed, the army reports indicate that the Navahos were scattered in extended family camps, unorganized in bands or other ways (United States War Department 1880–1902, XLVIII: 1259–60).

The Mescaleros became increasingly unhappy and by November 10, 1865, had all escaped from Bosque Redondo. The Navahos also had difficulty with the Comanches who raided their horse herds.

All of these problems were compounded by a governmental controversy which developed between the army and the civilian Indian agent, Michael Steck. Steck thought General Carleton's Indian policy was inhumane and unfruitful and that the Navahos should have been established on a reservation along the Little Colorado River. Annually, there was an insufficiency of funds to maintain good rations and a quarrel between the army and the Indian Bureau over which was to provide food and clothing. Finally, when American settlers in the area began to complain about the Navahos' occupying good land along the Pecos River, the whole issue came to a climax in the summer of 1868 (Keleher 1952).

General William Sherman was commissioned to draw up a treaty with the Navahos which was drafted and signed at Fort Sumner on June 1, 1868. The treaty provided that the Navahos would be allowed to leave Bosque Redondo at once and live on a reservation in northwestern New Mexico an northeastern Arizona. By July 20 they were back in their home country.

Although the ambitious program to teach the Navahos to become settled agricultural people living in villages like their Pueblo neighbors, to become literate, and to become Christians all failed completely, it is clear that the Fort Sumner experience did effectively bring the Navahos under the authority of the U.S. government and eliminate the raiding complex—the only major change in Navaho culture resulting from their five-year captivity (Green 1955).

The Navaho reservation community which has developed since Fort Sumner began with the provisions of the Treaty of 1868 which set aside a total of about 3,500,000 acres—much less than the Navahos had occupied for generations. This reservation has been extended from time to time until it now includes about 15,000,000 acres (Kluckhohn and Leighton 1946: 11). But at no point has the growth of the reservation kept pace with the growth of Navaho population which has increased from, at most, 15,000 in 1868 to nearly 85,000 today. Furthermore, there have been frequent reversals of policy and disappointing losses. For example, with the arrival of the railroad, all odd-numbered sections to a depth of 40 miles on each side of the right of way were granted to the Santa Fe railroad. This occurred in areas of heavy Navaho occupation, and they lost some of their best winter range land and finest watering places in the process. The lands added later as a compensatory measure were notably less desirable. In 1908, 3,500,000 acres were added to the reservation, but American ranchers brought political pressure to bear upon Congress, and the same amount of land was restored to the public domain in 1911. The Boundary Extension Act of 1934 cleared up the problem in Arizona by exchanging other parts of the public domain for land near the reservation, but action in New Mexico has been blocked by powerful economic and political interests (Kluckhohn and Leighton 1946: 11–12).

Whereas the principal intercultural role relationship during the early part of the Anglo-American Period was between American soldiers and Navaho warriors (or prisoners at Fort Sumner), the more recent contacts on the reservation have centered around Indian agents and the Indian Service, Indian traders, and missionaries.

Navaho relationships with Indian agents have moved through a number of phases in the ninety years since 1868. Up to 1901 the agents lived at and worked out of Fort Defiance. After 1901 the reservation began to be divided into independent agencies, of which there were eventually six. In 1934 the six independent agencies were unified and centralized into the Navajo Service with Headquarters at Window Rock, Arizona.

In the years following the Fort Sumner captivity the efforts of the agents were devoted to issuing rations, distributing sheep and seeds to help the Navahos re-establish their economic system, providing a school and trying to induce Navaho children to attend regularly, and providing some kind of medical care. The major goal of the government was to help the Navahos recover economically and then to educate them as rapidly as possible to American culture.

The Navahos willingly accepted the rations, seeds, sheep, and tools that were issued; they were quite unwilling to send their children to school. When, for example, the Indian Bureau passed a compulsory school regulation in 1887, the Navahos resisted strongly, even to the point of violence at Round Rock (Left-handed Mexican Clansman 1952). Between 1900 and 1930 boarding schools and mission schools were added; and during the Collier administration of the 1930's the day schools were established. But it is significant that it was not until the years following World War II that Navaho public opinion shifted to become predominantly in favor of schools, and Navahos began to demand schooling for their children. In 1955, for the first time in Navaho history, the Indian Service could report that almost all Navaho children of school age were enrolled in school (Young 1955).

A second crucial phase in Indian Service relationships began with the Collier administration in 1933 when policies forcing the Navahos in the direction of rapid acculturation and assimilation were reversed and emphasis was placed upon maintaining Navaho culture patterns. These policies removed some of the pressures on the Navahos; but at the same time the livestock reduction program which forced the Navahos to cut down their holdings of sheep, goats, and horses in the interests of long-range conservation added new pressures that led ultimately to a deterioration in Navaho–Indian Service relationships. The repercussions of the livestock reduction program were strongly felt in Navaho country, especially the increased use of peyote which appears to be, in large part, related to the difficulties generated by this livestock reduction (Aberle and Stewart 1957).

The third crucial phase in Indian Service relationships has in the past twenty years been characterized by three major developments: (*a*) a long-range program for rehabilitation, passed by Congress in 1950, which authorized an appropriation of $88,570,000 over a ten-year period for the purpose of "promoting the rehabilitation of the Navajo and Hopi Tribes of Indians and a better utilization of the resources of the Navajo and Hopi Indian Reservations"; (*b*) the growth of the Navaho Tribal Council as a politically effective tribal organization for the first time in Navaho history; and (*c*) the growth of mining and other business enterprises on the reservation and an enormous increase in off-reservation wage work.

The rehabilitation program is a full-scale effort to deal with the central Navaho problem—a rapidly expanding population on a limited resource base. Although full funds have not yet been appropriated for its implementation, much progress has been made on the program which includes plans for improvement of the range, the extension of irrigation projects and the development of water supplies, the development of coal and timber resources, the increased production of Navaho arts and crafts, construction of roads, the establishment of enterprises and industries, and the off-reservation resettlement of Navaho families.

Perhaps the most remarkable development in recent years has been the emergence of the Navaho Tribal Council as a politically effective and responsible organization. The development of an over-all organization has gone through a number of stages. Immediately after the Fort Sumner captivity, army officers and the first civilian agents appointed former war chiefs to positions of power in an effort to keep order and obtain co-operation for their programs. With the death of Manuelito in 1893, there was a complete breakdown in the organization, and the Indian agents attempted to run matters themselves. Later on Navaho leaders were chosen as advisers to the agents. With the discovery of oil on Navaho lands in 1923, it became urgent to create some body which could speak, at least in form, for the tribe as a whole; this led to the organization of a Navaho Council. Over the years, and especially since 1949, the Tribal Council, with strong Indian Service encouragement, has become an elected, representative body that has assumed major responsibility for Navaho affairs (Spicer n.d.). The Council is composed of a chairman, vice-chairman, and seventy-four delegates apportioned to the land management districts. An Advisory Committee of nine of the delegates normally meets for a week each month and attends to much of the business; the full Council normally meets on a quarterly basis (Young 1955).

The tribal budget, $3,368,333 for 1956, provides an idea of the magnitude of the business that is now conducted by the Tribal Council. The chairman receives a salary of $11,000 and, if re-elected, $15,000.

Since 1923, when oil was first discovered on Navaho lands near Shiprock, the Indian Service has also played an important role in assisting the Navahos with problems of leases on mineral rights, royalties on production of minerals, and the like. These functions have been gradually assumed by the Tribal Council, which now makes almost all of the major decisions on leases and royalties.

Oil and gas leases provided $1,544,062.08 of the tribal income during the fiscal year 1955, and the total payments since 1923 have been almost $18,500,000. Since 1942, vanadium-uranium leases and royalties have been important sources of tribal income, having provided a total of almost $2,400,000. These enterprises are also an important source of employment of Navahos on the reservation (Young 1955).

A program to establish a variety of small industries on the reservation, which was proposed in 1948 and attempted in 1951–54 with a number of small pilot operations, has not been generally successful (Young 1955). Emphasis has now shifted to a policy of encouraging outside industrial firms to build plants of various types near the reservation so that Navahos could be employed.

Finally, the Indian Service has been active in assisting Navahos to obtain off-reservation wage work, which has increased markedly in the past twenty years. According to Young (1955: 62–63), an estimated 19,602 Navahos were employed in off-reservation wage work during 1955: in railroad work, 6,571; in agricultural work, 8,839; and in non-agricultural wage labor, 4,192. This wage work has clearly become a major source of Navaho income in the 1950's.

The first trading post was opened for business on the reservation in 1871; by 1890 there were nine traders on the reservation and thirty more surrounding it at different points (Underhill 1956: 182); by 1943 there were 146 trading posts on and adjacent to the reservation (Kluckhohn and Leighton 1946: 38).

From the outset, Navaho relationships with the traders were of a different character from what they were with the Indian agents. As Underhill (1956: 184) expresses it:

He had the touchstone of friendly personal contact which opened the hearts of the Navajos. While the government was striving to civilize the Navajos by issuing orders that they should cut their hair and cease their heathen dances, and while the missionary was trying to convince them of their errors, the trader simply laid before them the possibilities of the new life.

The traders were soon doing a booming business in coffee, sugar, canned peaches, pocket knives, and cotton cloth in exchange for wool and Navaho blankets, and later on, silver jewelry. Indian trading became an enormously profitable business, if operated astutely, because the trader made a double profit. He made a handsome profit selling the goods that poured in from the outside world; and he also resold Navaho products at a good profit.

Some traders have been unscrupulous and unnecessarily forceful in dealing with their Navaho customers, but, on the whole, they have filled a useful and important role among the Navahos during the past ninety years. While they made handsome profits, they also ran risks in extending large amounts of credit to Navahos. They have also provided an important link between Navaho and American ways of life —a point which is clearly exemplified by the experience of the famous Wetherill family (Gillmor and Wetherill 1952).

Perhaps the greatest difficulty, in the long run, in this cultural role interaction is found in the propensity of many traders to continue to treat the Navahos as undependable credit risks unless their economic affairs are largely managed for them by the traders. This strategy clearly has the effect of maintaining a pattern of irresponsibility (by American standards) among the Navahos.

Anglo-American missionary activity in Navaho country began

during President Grant's administration. Grant was concerned about the Indian situation, and he took a suggestion from the Quakers: he asked the churches of the United States to nominate men fit to serve as agents (Underhill 1956: 169; Reeve 1941: 275). Each sect, after much discussion, decided on an area; the Navahos fell to the Presbyterians, who began their missionary work in Navaho country in the 1870's, with headquarters at Ganado, and who controlled both the appointment of Indian agents and the early schools on the reservation until the 1890's.

The Franciscans established a Catholic mission at St. Michaels near Fort Defiance in 1898 (Wilken 1955). The Mormons, working out of their settlements in southern Utah, had been active since before Fort Sumner days. By 1955 there were fifteen other denominations established in Navaho country: Episcopal, Seventh Day Adventist, American Baptist, Southern Baptist, Church of the Nazarene, Plymouth Brethren, Christian Reformed, Good News Mission, Navajo Gospel Mission, Navajo Bible School, Home Missions Council of North America, Methodist, Free Methodist, Brethren in Christ, and Wycliffe School of Bible Translators. The two strongest centers of mission activity are in the northeast along the San Juan River and along the southern fringe of the reservation, south of Fort Defiance and eastward.

The strategy of the missionaries has been to convert the Navahos to some brand of Christianity and to help them become "civilized," but there have been great variations in policy. The Catholics and Mormons represent one extreme in being permissive about native religion and patient about the length of time it will take to accomplish conversion. The other pole has been represented by sects like the Nazarenes, who have insisted that the Navahos immediately give up their "heathen" ceremonies and become Christians (Rapoport 1954). The others fall somewhere in between.

NAVAHO–SPANISH-AMERICAN RELATIONSHIPS

Although Navaho contacts with Anglo-Americans have overshadowed other intercultural relationships in the past century, there have been important continuing contacts with Spanish-Americans. Three special relationships require mention. Mexican (later called "Spanish-American" in the Southwest) traders were active in Navaho country and were apparently especially important in the years before the first Anglo-American trading posts were established in the 1870's. Mexican silversmiths were the source during this period of Navaho silversmithing, a skill which the Navahos began to acquire between 1853 and 1858 (Woodward 1938; Adair 1944). Later in the period, especially after Anglo-American law was seriously enforced in the United States and Navahos were prohibited from purchasing liquor, Mexicans were a principal source of liquor for the Navahos. This relationship continued until 1954, when the federal and state liquor laws prohibiting sale of liquor to Indians were finally repealed.

NAVAHO-PUEBLO RELATIONSHIPS

Pueblo contacts have also continued to be important during the American period, and, in particular, an institutionalized "guest-friend" relationship that has been developed since open hostilities ceased after the Fort Sumner episode. This relationship has recently been described by Kluckhohn and Leighton (1946: 76), Hill (1948: 389), and Vogt (1951: 18; 1955: 832–33). It depends upon patterns of mutual hospitality and reciprocity, and can be illustrated in the Navaho-Zuni case. Each Navaho family which visits Zuni (during large ceremonial occasions and at other times) has one or more Zuni families whom they regard as "friends." When the Navahos enter the pueblo, they invariably go to the house of their "friends" where they are expected to leave gifts of rugs, jewelry, or mutton. The Zuni family will house and feed the Navaho family during the visit and then return gifts of bread, corn, melons, or hay when the Navahos leave. The customary modes of interaction are highly patterned and communication ordinarily takes place in Navaho rather than in Zuni. At some other time during the year, the Zuni family may return the visit by going to the hogans of its Navaho friends where the Navahos provide hospitality, and gifts are again exchanged. These relationships are often enduring ones—sometimes persisting through two or more generations.

This interaction has provided the framework for continuing exchange of ideas and techniques, following probably some of the same types of cultural transmission that occurred during earlier periods of Navaho history.

CONTEMPORARY NAVAHO CULTURE

Navaho culture has undergone a series of important changes during the Anglo-American Period. Changes in material culture and economic system have been especially impressive. Silversmithing in the early part of the period and wage labor in recent decades added new elements to the economic system. Through the reservation trading posts and through economic exchanges in Anglo-American towns, Navahos have been drawn into our money and market economy. Wagons, and, more recently, automobiles, especially pickup trucks, have provided new modes of transportation (Vogt 1960). Factory-made metal tools and utensils have now almost entirely replaced older stone, wooden, basketry, and pottery forms (Tschopik 1938). Sewing machines and radios are common in Navaho homes. The forked-pole hogans, now rare except in the Dennehotso-Kayenta-Tuba city area, have been replaced by the hexagonal log hogan or round rock hogan. There has been a strong trend toward White-style cabins or frame or rock houses. Sweat houses, however, remain, and ceremonials cannot yet, in Navaho belief, be given in White-style houses but still require a hogan for effective performance. Men's clothing styles now tend to keep pace with Southwestern cowboy styles, with some distinctive Navaho substyles. Women's dress shifted to the velveteen blouse and calico skirt during and right after residence at Fort Sumner and has been more conservative.

In the kinship system there has been some obvious loss of the more remote kinship and clan ties and obligations (Kluckhohn n.d.). There has been an apparent increase in nuclear families living as units and a consequent decrease in the strength of the matrilocal extended family, but it is difficult to calculate how old this development actually is. In the 1930's an Indian Service survey described the following ratio of types of families: 53 per cent nuclear, 32 per cent matrilocal, 10 per cent bilocal, and 5 per cent patrilocal (Aberle 1954: 22). However, in these figures a nuclear family living by itself and a matrilocal extended family (composed of two or more nuclear families) are each counted as *one* family. If one were to ask about the percentage of the *total* number of nuclear families living by themselves, the figures would be quite different.

For the Ramah area, where we have the best available data, Kluckhohn (n.d.) reports that as of June, 1950, residence was as follows: uxorilocal, 47 cases; virilocal, 33 cases; ambilocal, 6 cases; neolocal, 8 cases; unclassifiable, 3 cases.[5] The composition of the 125 living

[5] "Uxorilocal" and "virilocal" mean residence in an area occupied by the family of the wife or husband, respectively. They do not necessarily mean residence within a stone's throw of wife's or husband's parents or parent.

units (135 if one counted the polygynous marriages separately) was:
(1) 39 simple nuclear families; (2) 25 nuclear families where one or
more of the children did not belong to both spouses; (3) 5 nuclear
families where one or more children did not belong to either spouse;
(4) 6 nuclear families plus one unmarried adult; (5) 11 units of
polygynous marriage; (6) 17 units where a single parent lives with
sub-adults; (7) 19 "relict" units;[6] and (8) 3 isolated individuals. Of
these units 53 are clearly embraced in 18 extended families; if one
used somewhat more flexible but still relevant criteria or considered a
period of a year or two earlier, one could speak of an additional 14
extended families embracing 30 other units. In other words, over
two-thirds of the Ramah Navaho living units are still embraced in
extended families, with uxorilocal residence more frequent than
virilocal by a margin of approximately 40 to 60 per cent.

These figures suggest that while there is now, and probably long
has been, a great deal of behavioral variation in the Navaho system
(Roberts 1951), the preferred pattern, especially in the more conservative areas, is the matrilocal extended family, with mother-in-law
avoidance and other associated customs. We also know that polygyny
is still practiced as a minor pattern, and that both polygyny and
matrilocal residence are more common in areas where sheep are more
important than farming as the basic economic pursuit (Kluckhohn
and Leighton 1946: 55). Clan membership continues to be of crucial
importance in reciprocal hospitality patterns and in regulating marriage. Clan incest taboos are strongly in force; for example, marriages
within a clan occur in only 1 per cent of the cases (Aberle 1954: 25).

In political organization the crucial changes have been the elimination of the raiding complex (by the Fort Sumner experience) and
the effective extension of Anglo-American political control over the
Navahos, followed recently by the emergence of the Tribal Council
as the first effective tribal organization in Navaho history.

The Navaho ceremonial system, with some losses under the impact
of White missionary influence, is still viable. Of the six groups of
ceremonials listed by Wyman and Kluckhohn (1938)—Blessing Way,
Holy Way, Life Way, Evil Way, War Ceremonials, and Game
Way—ceremonies in all but the last two (War and Game) are still

[6] A "relict" is a unit that lacks a single complete biological family but comprises
the "remains" of two or more marriages broken by death or divorce *or* the "relicts"
of one such marriage plus an unmarried adult.

being performed. Since there is no more war, and little hunting, the obsolescence of these ceremonies is understandable. There is also an observed tendency for shorter versions of ceremonies to be performed as the older chanters die and younger apprentices fail to learn as much of the ritual.

Navaho religious beliefs are still widely held in conservative areas, especially the basic elements of the origin myth, the pantheon of Holy People, the ghost and witchcraft beliefs. It is not known how many Navahos have become Christians in any deep-seated sense. Gifts of food and clothing and entertainment provided by Christian religious services are welcomed by Navahos, as is a good missionary who will assume the onerous responsibility of burying the dead, a task which Navahos have always abhorred. In some areas there are syncretistic tendencies to equate the Virgin Mary with Changing Woman and Jesus with one of the Hero Twins in the belief system (Rapoport 1954).

A more general tendency is the development of sophisticated combinations of beliefs about the cause and cure of disease—with the Hand-Tremblers, in some cases, recommending the White doctor, and Navahos recognizing that some ailments are better cured by their own chanters, others better treated in a hospital (Adair, Deuschle, and McDermott 1957).

Although Navaho is still the primary language for the majority of families, bilingualism is markedly increasing in recent years with the new educational program that has placed almost all Navaho children in school.

Decisive Factors in Navaho Cultural Continuity and Change

I shall now attempt to abstract some general features in the patterns of continuity and change in Navaho culture by indicating what I regard to be the decisive factors involved. I am using "decisive factors" in the Weberian sense that if these features had not been present the events we observe would presumably not have occurred (Weber 1949). These decisive factors were isolated by comparing periods within the Navaho sequence of change and comparing the Navaho with the other cases described in this volume.

FACTORS FOR CHANGE

Three interrelated factors leading to basic changes in Navaho culture appear to be decisive: (1) the economic differential between

value - he says health - I also would add a
practical material orientation or value.

the incoming Apacheans and the Pueblo, Spanish, and American
economic systems with which they came successively into contact in
the Southwest; (2) the presentation of new cultural materials to
the Navahos under indirect and permissive contact conditions; and (3)
certain key Navaho value patterns that have influenced the form the
changes took.

The enormous economic differential between the hunting and
gathering Apacheans and the Pueblo, Spanish, and American cultures
was undoubtedly a crucial factor in their cultural development. To
put it simply, the Apacheans arrived in the Southwest with little to
lose and almost everything to gain by borrowing economic and
technological patterns they successively came into contact with in
the Southwest. Economic advantage was clearly one of the driving
forces that led Navaho culture to become an outstanding case of an
"absorbing" or "borrowing" culture (Kluckhohn 1942*a*; Adair and
Vogt 1949).

Much of the presentation of new cultural materials to the Navahos
in the course of their history in the Southwest occurred under indirect and permissive contact conditions (Spicer 1954). During the
early period of contact with the Pueblos we can be relatively certain
that the Pueblos never developed a forced program of change to
"civilize" their wild Navaho neighbors. So far as I know the Spanish
never attempted to force the Navahos to take over horses and sheep—
in fact, if anything, the strategy was the reverse. The Spanish never
succeeded in bringing Navahos under their control, except on retaliatory punitive expeditions which affected only a few Navahos at a
time. The only real attempts at conscious and directed change were
the missionary endeavors of 1629 and 1746–50, and these efforts to
carry out programs of "reducción" and conversion were short-lived.
In the Anglo-American Period, more change again seems to have
resulted when the contact conditions were permissive rather than
forced. The application of force at Fort Sumner did eliminate the
raiding complex from Navaho culture, but all other crucial patterns
appear to have remained the same. The general point is that basic
change was, on the whole, more impressive and more lasting when
new cultural models were presented to the Navahos without any
attempt to force them to accept the new patterns.

Finally, certain key Navaho value patterns appear to have influenced the form and direction that the changes took as the new
cultural materials were incorporated in Navaho culture.

For purposes of illustration I shall discuss a value pattern of major significance in Navaho culture—the focus upon health and illness which has been described as the "type anxiety" in Navaho life (Kluckhohn 1942*b*) and the overwhelming emphasis upon curing ceremonies in Navaho religion. By comparison, concepts such as rain-making or fertility play a relatively minor role in the ceremonial system. As has been frequently pointed out, this focus upon illness and upon curing has been of crucial importance in giving form and direction to what the Navahos did with the ceremonial patterns they borrowed from the Pueblos. They are reworked into the ancient ceremonial system centered upon curing. A good case can also be made that the more recent additions to Navaho religion, the peyote cult and Christianity, have meaning for the Navahos insofar as they provide additional ways of preventing and curing illness and maintaining individual health about which the Navahos are so concerned.

It is highly significant, I think, that what promises to become one of the most successful improvement programs with the Navahos in recent decades has all three of these decisive factors present. This program is the Cornell University Medical College pilot project in field health at Many Farms, Arizona. The key features of this program are: (1) the Navaho leaders concerned clearly recognize the technological superiority of certain White medical practices; (2) the Navaho Tribal Council *invited* the Cornell group to set up the program, and there i evidence for greater acceptance of White medical practices on the part of the Many Farms community when permissive rather than coercive methods have been employed; and (3) the program is centered upon a central Navaho value pattern, the concern with bodily health (Adair, Deuschle, and McDermott 1957).

FACTORS FOR CONTINUITY

Three factors underlying basic continuities in Navaho culture appear to be decisive. Two of these factors are complementary to those discussed in the previous section, that is, (1) when little or no economic difference between old Navaho patterns and the new model being presented to them is perceived by the Navahos, they tend to continue with old patterns; (2) when force is applied to make the Navahos change, the result appears to lead more often to resistance and intensification of native patterns than to change.

The third factor is a resistant institutional core at the heart of

Navaho culture composed of a system of social relationships, ecological adjustments, and values that has formed a co'erent and distinctive Navaho pattern at least since about 1700. The crucial features of this institutional core include: the scattered settlement pattern; the matri- */.* local extended family and matrilineal exogamous clans; a material *2.* culture complex composed of a nuclear family hogan (sometimes *3.* now a house), a sweat house, and a sheep corral with openings to the *4.* east; political leadership based upon a local headman; a ceremonial *5.* system focused upon individual curing; ghost and witchcraft patterns *6.* as means of managing hostilities and aggression; values stressing *7.* "harmony," with bodily illness being an important manifestation of *8.* "disharmony," and "motion" (Kluckhohn 1949; Astrov 1950; Rei- *9.* chard 1950; Albert 1956); Navaho as the primary language; and a *10.* combination of farming and sheep husbandry, supplemented by weav- *11.* ing and, more recently, silversmithing as the basic economic pursuits.

The recent trend to wage labor in White American enterprises does not, in my judgment, yet belong in this institutional core. Wage labor is not yet regarded highly as a proper way to make a living, and it is significant that, by and large, the Navahos on the reservation are still maintaining farm acreages and sheep herds up to the limits set by the geographic and economic conditions and by the Indian Service system of grazing permits. Although only some 8,000 of the approximately 15,000 families have stock permits and the number of stock on such permits is rarely sufficient to provide a livelihood for the family without supplemental income, most Navaho families would still prefer a farming and grazing way of life on the reservation to a wage labor position off the reservation if economic conditions permitted.

It is also clear that *cultural content*, or the cultural inventory, has undergone impressive changes since about 1700, but insofar as I can determine, the structural framework of this institutional core has persisted with remarkable continuity.

It is instructive to review attempts to alter this institutional core, in particular, the Spanish mission attempt of 1746–50 and the American Fort Sumner program of 1864–68. Both programs attempted to persuade or force the Navahos to build pueblos, to settle down as irrigation farmers like their Pueblo neighbors, and to become "civilized" in terms of the dominant culture. In both cases the alternative models did not appeal to the Navahos from an economic point of view; they were forced programs; and they failed to alter the structural framework of Navaho culture as I have outlined it.

A more recent attempt to make the Navahos into settled irrigation farmers at Fruitland, New Mexico, has been conspicuously less successful than the settlements of Anglo-Americans on exactly the same kind of land immediately across the San Juan River (Sasaki 1950).

The self-conception mentioned by Navaho leaders at various points in their history to the effect that "they do not want pueblos but are like deer raised in the woods" apparently comes close to reality.

THE INCORPORATIVE MODEL AS THE BASIC INTEGRATIVE PROCESS

The Navaho case also appears to manifest a characteristic integrative process that has become stabilized through time. As a characteristic type or model I should like to advance the hypothesis that this process may be defined as "incorporative,"[7] as contrasted with the "fusional" model manifested in the Yaqui case, or the "compartmentalization" model in the Eastern Pueblo case (earlier chapters).

The essence of this process is that elements from other cultures are incorporated into Navaho culture in such a way that the structural framework of the institutional core (as I have described it above) is maintained, and the borrowed elements are fitted into place and elaborated in terms of the pre-existing patterns (Kluckhohn 1942a). The result has been a steady growth in cultural content throughout the Southwestern experience of the Navahos without important losses—except for fishing patterns, which the Athabascan ancestors of the Apacheans undoubtedly had in the North, and the elimination of the raiding complex by the Fort Sumner experience. Shifts of emphases in the culture occur as the growth proceeds; for example, hunting and gathering now occupy a minor place in the culture, but are still present. But the general process is one of expansion and growth around the central structural framework.

To provide some illustrations drawn from the historical materials, I begin with a quote from Woodward (1938: 10–11):

It has always seemed to me that the Navajo man is a living exponent of acculturation. He wears on his person in his various garments visible evidence of the accumulation of material culture from alien sources. First of all, a Navajo wears underneath his outer garments his native breech clout.

---

[7] This term was suggested to me by David Mandelbaum.

This he does not remove, unless he takes a bath, and even then some of the men do not take it off. Over the breech clout is a pair of calico drawers fashioned rather fully and being slightly more than knee length. These are slit up the outer seam from the bottom for about six or seven inches. These were his pantaloons in the days when Mexican costume was in vogue. . . . Over the aboriginal and Spanish-Mexican garb the Navajo has placed his latest acquisitions, the American jeans, shirt, shoes, and hat. Thus we have in him a living exponent of three layers of culture; he has absorbed them all and discarded none.   *wonderful example.*

This description is, of course, somewhat out of date for contemporary styles of dress, but it exemplifies clearly the process I am attempting to characterize.

In sociopolitical organization from the extended matrilocal family with local headman arrangements at the structural core, Navaho culture has added matrilineal clans, linked clans, and recently the Tribal Council. In religion, layers of Pueblo ceremonialism, Anglo-American Christianity, and Ute peyotism have been (and are still being) incorporated and reworked in terms of the central emphasis upon bodily health and curing ceremonies performed over one or more individual patients rather than upon communal ceremonies linked to lineages, clans, communities, or congregations. In modes of travel, the horse, the horse and wagon, and now the automobile have all been incorporated. In economics and technology, the incorporations over time have been agriculture, sheep husbandry, weaving, silversmithing, and wage labor. And, in the language, as Hoijer (1957) points out, such foreign elements as have been borrowed have been shaped into Navaho-like elements.

While the processes of growth and change in the Navaho case have become vastly more complex in the Anglo-American Period, and losses and replacements are recently more evident in the data, the incorporative model as a general type seems to represent a persisting and recurring phenomenon in Navaho cultural development for at least the past four hundred years. The basic conditions underlying this type of change appear to have been the economic and technological differences between the Navahos and the cultures with which they came in contact in the Southwest and, except for certain periods such as the Fort Sumner experience, the relative freedom the Navahos have had over the centuries to make selective adaptations to new cultural elements that were presented to them and which they successfully incorporated into their growing and expanding culture.

REFERENCES CITED

ABERLE, DAVID F.
   1954   "Navaho Kinship: A Trial Run." Unpublished MS. Prepared for SSRC Summer Seminar on Kinship, Harvard University.
ABERLE, DAVID F., and OMER C. STEWART
   1957   "Navaho and Ute Peyotism: A Chronological and Distributional Study," *University of Colorado Studies,* "Series in Anthropology," No. 6.
ADAIR, JOHN
   1944   *The Navajo and Pueblo Silversmiths.* Norman, Okla.
ADAIR, JOHN, and EVON Z. VOGT
   1949   "Navaho and Zuni Veterans: A Study of Contrasting Modes of Culture Change," *American Anthropologist,* LI, 547–62.
ADAIR, JOHN, KURT DEUSCHLE, and WALSH McDERMOTT
   1957   "Patterns of Health and Disease among the Navahos," *Annals of the American Academy of Political and Social Science,* Vol. CCCXI, May 1957.
ALBERT, ETHEL M.
   1956   "The Classification of Values: A Method and Illustration," *American Anthropologist,* LVIII, 221–48.
AMSDEN, CHARLES A.
   1934   *Navaho Weaving.* Santa Ana, Calif.
ASTROV, MARGOT
   1950   "The Concept of Motion as the Psychological Leitmotif of Navaho Life and Literature," *Journal of American Folklore,* LXIII, 45–56.
AYER, MRS. EDWARD E.
   1916   *The Memorial of Fray Alonso de Benavides 1630.* Chicago.
BALDWIN, GORDON C.
   1950   "The Pottery of the Southern Paiute," *American Antiquity,* XVI, 50–56.
BELLAH, ROBERT N.
   1952   *Apache Kinship Systems.* Cambridge, Mass.
BENDER, A. B.
   1934   "Frontier Defense in the Territory of New Mexico, 1846–1853," *New Mexico Historical Review,* IX, 249–73.
CHAMPE, JOHN L.
   1949   "White Cat Village," *American Antiquity,* XIV, 285–91.
COLLINS, HENRY B.
   1954   "Comments on Swadesh's 'Time Depths of American Linguistic Groupings,'" *American Anthropologist,* LVI, 364–71.
DOZIER, EDWARD P.
   1954   *The Hopi-Tewa of Arizona.* University of California "Publications in American Archaeology and Ethnology," XLIV, 259–376.
DRIVER, HAROLD E.
   1956   "An Integration of Functional, Evolutionary, and Historical Theory by Means of Correlations," Indiana University "Publications in Anthropology and Linguistics"; *Memoir 12 of the International Journal of American Linguistics.*

DRUCKER, PHILIP
1955 "Sources of Northwest Coast Culture," *New Interpretations of Aboriginal American Culture History*, Seventy-fifth Anniversary Volume of the Anthropological Society of Washington.

EGGAN, FRED
1950 *Social Organization of the Western Pueblos*. Chicago.

FARMER, MALCOLM F.
1942 "Navaho Archaeology of Upper Blanco and Largo Canyons, Northern New Mexico," *American Antiquity*, VIII, 65–79.
1957 "A Suggested Typology for Defensive Systems of the Southwest," *Southwestern Journal of Anthropology*, XIII, 249–66.

FORRESTAL, PETER P.
1954 *Benavides' Memorial of 1630*. Washington: Academy of American Franciscan History.

FRANCISCAN FATHERS
1910 *An Ethnologic Dictionary of the Navaho Language*. St. Michaels, Ariz.

GILLMOR, FRANCES, and LOUISA WADE WETHERILL
1952 *Traders to the Navahos*. Albuquerque.

GRAVES, J. K.
1866 "Abstract of Papers accompanying Report of J. K. Graves, Special Agent Relative to Indian Affairs in New Mexico," Documents No. 40 and 41, *Annual Report of the Commissioner of Indian Affairs*, 1866. Washington: U.S. Department of the Interior, Office of Indian Affairs.

GREEN, ROGER C.
1955 "The Navajo and Bosque Redondo, 1863–1868," Unpublished MS., Dept. of Anthropology, University of New Mexico.

GUNNERSON, DOLORES A.
1956 "The Southern Athabascans: Their Arrival in the Southwest," *El Palacio*, LXIII, 346–65.

HACKETT, CHARLES W. (ed.)
1937 *Historical Documents relating to New Mexico, Nueva Viscaya, and Approaches thereto, to 1773*, Vol. III. Washington: Carnegie Institution of Washington.

HAILE, BERARD
1941 *Learning Navaho*. Vol. I. St. Michaels, Arizona.

HALL, EDWARD T., JR.
1944a *Early Stockaded Settlements in the Governador New Mexico*, Columbia "Studies in Archaeology and Ethnology," Vol. II, Part I.
1944b "Recent Clues to Athabascan Prehistory in the Southwest," *American Anthropologist*, XLVI, 98–105.

HILL, A. T., and GEORGE METCALF
1941 "A Site of the Dismal River Aspect in Chase County, Nebraska," *Nebraska History*, XXII, 159–213.

HILL, W. W.
1940a "Some Navaho Culture Changes during Two Centuries," Smithsonian *Miscellaneous Collections*, C, 395–415.
1940b "Some Aspects of Navajo Political Structure," *Plateau*, XIII, 23–28.

HILL, W. W.
1948 "Navaho Trading and Trading Ritual: A Study of Cultural Dynamics," *Southwestern Journal of Anthropology*, IV, 371–96.
HIRSCH, DAVID I.
1954 "Glottochronology and Eskimo and Eskimo-Aleut Prehistory," *American Anthropologist*, LVI, 825–39.
HODGE, FREDERICK W., GEORGE P. HAMMOND, and AGAPITO REY (eds.)
1945 *Fray Alonso de Benavides' Revised Memorial of 1634*. Albuquerque.
HOIJER, HARRY
1951 "Cultural Implications of Some Navaho Linguistic Categories," *Language*, XXVII, 111–20.
1956a "The Chronology of the Athapaskan Languages," *International Journal of American Linguistics*, XXII, 219–32.
1956b "Athapaskan Kinship Systems," *American Anthropologist*, LVIII, 309–34.
1957 Personal communication, August 21, 1957.
HUGHES, JOHN T.
1847 *Doniphan's Expedition*. Cincinnati.
HURT, WESLEY R., JR.
1942 "Eighteenth-Century Navaho Hogans from Canyon de Chelley National Monument," *American Antiquity*, VIII, 89–104.
HUSCHER, BETTY H. and HAROLD A.
1943a "Athapaskan Migration via the Intermontane Region," *American Antiquity*, VIII, 80–89.
1943b "The Hogan Builders of Colorado," *Southwestern Lore*, IX, 1–92.
HYMES, DELL H.
1956 "Na-Déné and Positional Analysis of Categories," *American Anthropologist*, LVIII, 624–38.
1957 "A Note on Athapaskan Glottochronology," *International Journal of American Linguistics*, XXIII, 291–97.
HYMES, D. H., and HAROLD E. DRIVER
1958 "Concerning the Proto-Athapaskan Kinship System," *American Anthropologist*, LX, 152–55.
JENNINGS, JESSE D.
1957 *Danger Cave. Memoirs of the Society for American Archaeology*, Vol. XXIII, No. 2, Part 2.
KAUT, CHARLES R.
1956 "Western Apache Clan and Phratry Organization," *American Anthropologist*, LVIII, 140–46.
1957 *The Western Apache Clan System: Its Origins and Development*. University of New Mexico "Publications in Anthropology," No. 9.
KELEHER, WILLIAM A.
1952 *Turmoil in New Mexico, 1846–68*. Santa Fe.
KELLY, HENRY W.
1941 "Franciscan Missions of New Mexico, 1740–1760," *New Mexican Historical Review*, XVI, 41–70.
KEUR, DOROTHY LOUISE
1941 "Big Bead Mesa, an Archaeological Study of Navaho Acculturation, 1745–1812," *Memoirs of the Society for American Archaeology*, No. 1.
1944 "A Chapter in Navaho-Pueblo Relations," *American Antiquity*, X, 75–86.

KLUCKHOHN, CLYDE
1942*a* "The Navahos in the Machine Age," *Technology Review*, XLIV, 2–6.
1942*b* "Myths and Rituals: A General Theory," *Harvard Theological Review*, XXXV, 45–79.
1944 *Navaho Witchcraft*. Peabody Museum of American Archaeology and Ethnology, *Papers*, Vol. XXII, No. 2.
1949 "The Philosophy of the Navaho Indians," in *Ideological Differences and World Order*, ed. by F. S. C. NORTHROP, pp. 356–84. New Haven.
n.d. "The Ramah Navaho," in EVON Z. VOGT and JOHN M. ROBERTS (eds.), *The Peoples of Rimrock* (forthcoming).
KLUCKHOHN, CLYDE, and DOROTHEA LEIGHTON
1946 *The Navaho*. Cambridge, Mass.
KLUCKHOHN, CLYDE, and KATHERINE SPENCER
1940 *A Bibliography of the Navaho Indians*. New York.
KROEBER, A. L.
1939 *Cultural and Natural Areas of Native North America*. Berkeley.
1955 "Linguistic Time Depth Results so Far and Their Meaning," *International Journal of American Linguistics*, XXI, 91–105.
LEFT-HANDED MEXICAN CLANSMAN
1952 *The Trouble at Round Rock*. "Navajo Historical Series," 2. United States Indian Service.
LETHERMAN, J.
1856 "A Sketch of the Navajo Tribe of Indians, Territory of New Mexico," *Tenth Annual Report of the Smithsonian Institution*.
LITTEL, NORMAN M., *et al.*
1957 *Answer of the Navajo Tribe to the Petition by the Hopi Tribe to the Secretary of the Interior*. Washington.
McCOMBE, LEONARD, EVON Z. VOGT, and CLYDE KLUCKHOHN
1951 *Navaho Means People*. Cambridge, Mass.
MURDOCK, GEORGE P.
1949 *Social Structure*. New York.
1955 "North American Social Organization," *Davidson Journal of Anthropology*, I, 85–98.
NEWMAN, STANLEY
1954 "American Indian Linguistics in the Southwest," *American Anthropologist*, LVI, 626–35.
OPLER, MORRIS E.
1936 "The Kinship Systems of the Southern Athapaskan Speaking Tribes," *American Anthropologist*, XXXVIII, 620–33.
RAPOPORT, ROBERT N.
1954 *Changing Navaho Religious Values*. Peabody Museum of American Archaeology and Ethnology, *Papers*, Vol. XLI, No. 2.
REED, ERIK K.
1944 "Navajo Monolingualism," *American Anthropologist*, XLVI, 147–49.
1944 "Transition to History in the Pueblo Southwest," *American Anthropologist*, LVI, 592–97.
REEVE, FRANK D.
1938 "The Federal Indian Policy in New Mexico," *New Mexican Historical Review*, XIII, 14–62, 146–91, 261–313.

REEVE, FRANK D.
1941 "The Government and the Navaho, 1878–83,'" *New Mexican Historical Review,* XVI, 275–312.
1956 "Early Navaho Geography," *New Mexican Historical Review,* XXXI, 290–310.
1957 "Seventeenth Century Navaho-Spanish Relations," *New Mexican Historical Review,* XXXII, 36–52.

REICHARD, GLADYS
1950 *Navaho Religion.* "Bollingen Series," Vol. XVIII. New York.

RILEY, CARROLL L.
1954 "A Survey of Navajo Archaeology," *University of Colorado Studies,* "Series in Anthropology," No. 4, pp. 45–60.

ROBERTS, JOHN M.
1951 *Three Navaho Households: A Comparative Study in Small Group Culture.* Peabody Museum of American Archaeology and Ethnology, *Papers,* Vol. XL, No. 3.

ROESSEL, ROBERT A., JR.
1951 "Sheep in Navajo Culture." M.A. thesis, Washington University.

SAPIR, EDWARD
1915 "The Nadene Languages: A Preliminary Report," *American Anthropologist,* XVII, 534–38.
1936 "Internal Linguistic Evidence Suggestive of the Northern Origin of the Navaho," *American Anthropologist,* XXXVIII, 224–36.

SASAKI, TOM TAKETO
1950 "Technological Change in a Navaho Indian Farming Community: A Study of Social and Psychological Processes." Ph.D. thesis in Anthropology, Cornell University.

SECRETARY OF THE INTERIOR
1863 *Annual Report of the Commissioner of Indian Affairs.*
1866 *Annual Report of the Commissioner of Indian Affairs.*
1867 *Annual Report of the Commissioner of Indian Affairs.*

SHAFER, ROBERT
1952 "Athabaskan and Sino-Tibetan," *International Journal of American Linguistics,* XVIII, 12–19.
1957 "Note on Athabaskan and Sino-Tibetan," *International Journal of American Linguistics,* XXIII, 116–17.

SPENCER, KATHERINE
1947 *Reflection of Social Life in the Navaho Origin Myth.* University of New Mexico "Publications in Anthropology," No. 3.
1957 *Mythology and Values: An Analysis of Navaho Chantway Myths.* American Folklore Society, *Memoirs,* Vol. XLVIII.

SPICER, EDWARD H.
n.d. "A Cultural History of the Indians of the Southwest." Unpublished MS.
1954 "Spanish-Indian Acculturation in the Southwest," *American Anthropologist,* LVI, 663–78.

STEPHEN, A. M.
1893 "The Navajo," *American Anthropologist,* VI, 345–62.

STEWARD, JULIAN H.
1937 *Ancient Caves of Great Salt Lake Region.* Smithsonian Institution, Bureau of American Ethnology, *Bulletin 116.*

1940 "Native Cultures of the Intermontane (Great Basin) Area," Smithsonian *Miscellaneous Collections*, C, 445–502.

STRONG, WILLIAM DUNCAN
1935 "An Introduction to Nebraska Archaeology," Smithsonian *Miscellaneous Collections*, XCIII, No. 10.

SWADESH, MORRIS
1951 "Diffusional Cumulation and Archaic Residue as Historical Explanations," *Southwestern Journal of Anthropology*, VII, 1–22.
1952 "Review of R. Shafer, 'Athapaskan and Sino-Tibetan,'" *International Journal of American Linguistics*, XVIII, 178–81.
1954 "Time Depths of American Linguistic Groupings," *American Anthropologist*, LVI, 361–64.

THOMAS, A. B. (ed.)
1932 *Forgotten Frontiers: A Study of the Spanish Indian Policy of Don Juan Bautista de Anza, Governor of New Mexico.* Norman, Okla.

TSCHOPIK, HARRY, JR.
1938 "Taboo as a Possible Factor Involved in the Obsolescence of Navaho Pottery and Basketry," *American Anthropologist*, XL, 257–62.

TWITCHELL, RALPH E.
1911–17 *The Leading Facts of New Mexican History.* 5 vols. Cedar Rapids, Iowa.

TYLER, S. LYMAN
1951 "The Yuta Indians before 1680," *Western Humanities Review*, V, 153–64.

UNDERHILL, RUTH
1956 *The Navahos.* Norman, Okla.

UNITED STATES CONGRESS
1867 *Condition of the Indian Tribes.* Report of the U.S. Congress Joint Special Committee to Inquire into the Condition of the Indian Tribes.

UNITED STATES WAR DEPARTMENT
1880–1902 *The War of the Rebellion.* A Compilation of the Official Records of the Union and the Confederate Armies. 70 vols. Washington.

VAN VALKENBURGH, RICHARD
1938 *A Short History of the Navajo People.* Navajo Service, Window Rock, Ariz.

VOGT, EVON Z.
1951 *Navaho Veterans.* Peabody Museum of American Archaeology and Ethnology, *Papers*, Vol. XLI, No. 1.
1955 "A Study of the Southwestern Fiesta System as Exemplified by the Laguna Fiesta," *American Anthropologist*, LVII, 820–39.
1957 "The Acculturation of American Indians," *Annals of the American Academy of Political and Social Science*, CCCXI, 137–47.
1960 "The Automobile in Contemporary Navaho Culture," *Selected Papers of the Fifth International Congress of Anthropological and Ethnological Sciences*, ANTHONY F. C. WALLACE (ed.). Philadelphia.

WEBER, MAX
1949 *The Methodology of the Social Sciences.* Glencoe, Ill.

WEDEL, WALDO R.
1949 "Some Provisional Correlations in Missouri Basin Archaeology," *American Antiquity*, XIV, 328–39.

WHITE, CHARLES B.
1957 "A Comparison of Theories on Southern Athapaskan Kinship Systems," *American Anthropologist*, LIX, 434–48.
WILKEN, ROBERT L.
1955 *Anselm Weber, O.F.M. Missionary to the Navaho, 1898–1921*. Milwaukee.
WOODWARD, ARTHUR
1938 *A Brief History of Navajo Silversmithing*. Museum of Northern Arizona, *Bulletin 14*.
WYMAN, LELAND C., and CLYDE KLUCKHOHN
1938 *Navaho Classification of Their Song Ceremonials*. American Anthropological Association, *Memoir No. 50*.
YOUNG, ROBERT W. (ed.)
1955 *The Navajo Yearbook of Planning in Action*. Navajo Agency, Window Rock, Ariz.
ZARATE SALMERON, FRAY GERONIMO DE
1856 "Relaciónes de todas las Cosas que en el Nuevo México se han visto y sabido, asi por Mar como por Tierra, desde el Año de 1538 hasta el de 1626." *Documentos para la Historia de México* (3d sér.), III, 30–38. México.

CHAPTER 6

Wasco-Wishram

By *David French*

The names Wasco and Wishram refer to Indians who lived on either side of the Columbia River near the site of the present city of The Dalles, Oregon. Since the river was a highway rather than a barrier, it is not surprising that cultural differences between the two groups were slight, nor that they were culturally similar to other Chinookan-speakers down the river to the west. Today, Wascos are those whose ancestors lived on the south side of the river or were assigned to the Warm Springs Reservation more than 50 miles south of their traditional home, while Wishrams are associated with the north side of the river and with the Yakima Reservation in Washington.

Oregon and Washington can be divided into markedly contrasting geographic areas. As a result of rains from the Pacific, there are heavy forests in the western third of each state. Within the forested region, running north and south, is the Cascade Range. Much of the eastern portion of the two states is a semi-arid plateau, drained by the Columbia River and its tributaries. The higher parts of this eastern region have open stands of timber, mainly yellow (or ponderosa) pine. A belt of junipers is sometimes found at intermediate altitudes. Except

I am indebted to my fellow members of the Social Science Research Council Seminar on Differential Culture Change, to my students at Reed College, and to Robert Benson, Evelyn French, Kathrine French, Frank Fussner, Melville Jacobs, Dorothy Johansen, Howard Jolly, Richard Jones, Herbert Landar, John Pock, and Carl Reynolds. I am also grateful for past research support from the American Philosophical Society, the Social Science Research Council, and the Wenner-Gren Foundation.

near streams, the vegetation at lower altitudes is predominantly grasses
and such shrubby plants as sagebrush and rabbit brush. In the southeast, the plateau breaks into the even more arid Great Basin.

The Columbia is the only river cutting through the Cascade Mountains; the gorge thus formed was an Indian travel route. Rapids and
falls, wherever they occurred, were important fishing places and portage points for canoe travel. The Wasco and Wishram lived in the
vicinity of such a series of rapids and were concentrated especially at

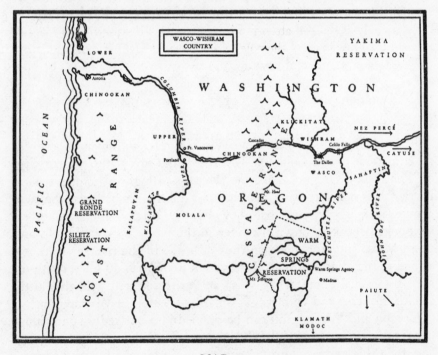

MAP 11

Fivemile Rapids (or the Long Narrows), at the eastern entrance to
the gorge. In contrast to the Lower Chinookans near the mouth of
the river and various intermediate Upper Chinookan groups,[1] the
Wasco and Wishram villages were thus in an unforested area. They
were, however, within easy traveling distance of the Cascade Mountains, and the people were not wholly dependent on the semi-arid
plateau for hunting and gathering.

[1] Melville Jacobs (personal communication) has suggested Coastal and Columbia
River Chinook as preferable to the familiar terms Lower and Upper Chinook.

The Wasco are little known to anthropologists; the Wishram are described in scattered papers, as well as in three more substantial publications by Sapir (1909), Curtis (1911), and Spier and Sapir (1930). Such sources, my own field data gathered with the help of co-workers during recent years, and an especially rich body of historical materials have provided the basis for the present analysis.

The selection and organization of materials for the study are based on the general framework provided by the culture change seminar. Consequently, data of potential comparative value for the study of change, including differential change, are emphasized. In the course of the analysis, special attention is paid to the question of the identity of the Chinookans and the role of outsiders in defining that identity. The changing nature of Chinookan identity is considered in the light of the relative lack of boundaries between sociocultural groupings. An adaptation of reference group theory is employed to discuss the puzzling fluctuation between Indian and White forms of behavior among recent Chinookans, as well as the persistence of Indian characteristics 150 years after White contact. Throughout the study, forms of behavior are related whenever possible to the situations in which they occurred. In analyzing the major changes in Chinookan life, it has been convenient to view the culture of any one period as if it were a system. By discussing the replacement of one system by another, it is thus possible to minimize the use of unique events as explanatory devices. These approaches and methodological concepts are discussed more fully and explicitly in relevant sections of the case study and are partially recapitulated in the conclusions.

To provide comparable treatment with the other chapters in this volume and as a convenience in analysis, four cultural periods have been delineated, as shown in Table 7. Although certain historical *events* are indicated in the table, the periods do not necessarily begin or end with such events (or points in calendar time). Rather, the periods indicate the predominance of differing sociocultural processes and were established in those terms.

Period I: Pre-Horse Culture

The "period" of Pre-Horse Culture may be regarded as beginning with the arrival of the ancestral Wasco-Wishram in the area; it ends with the appearance of the horse in the mid-eighteenth century (Haines 1938: 430, 436). This period is postulated largely as a device to provide perspective for the later periods—for example, to suggest that significant changes were occurring before the arrival of the Whites. *This involves the assumption that there were Upper Chinookans living along the Columbia River east of the Cascade Mountains prior to the arrival of the horse. *Considering the nature of the later culture, it is reasonable to make the further assumption that the primary economic adjustment was to the river rather than to the hinterland.

Since no Whites visited the area during this period, historical documents are naturally lacking. However, other kinds of evidence on the

TABLE 7

WASCO-WISHRAM CONTACT HISTORY

Period	Approximate Dates	Events
IV Part-Time Indian Culture	1920——	1955 The Dalles Dam under construction 1941–45 World War II 1938 Indian Reorganization Act accepted at Warm Springs 1930–39 Depression
III Modified Wasco-Wishram Culture	1858–1920	1917–18 World War I 1873 Warm Springs Scouts in Modoc War 1866–68 Paiute campaign 1865 Second Warm Springs treaty
II Augmented Wasco-Wishram Culture	1750–1858	1857–58 Warm Springs Reservation settled 1855 Yakima, Warm Springs treaties signed; Yakima War begins 1842 Major U.S. immigration begins 1838 Methodists at The Dalles 1811 Astoria founded 1805–6 Lewis and Clark 1792 Gray at mouth of Columbia
I Pre-Horse Culture	——1750	1730–50 Horses reached eastern Oregon and Washington

period may soon become available. In view of recent linguistic research by Hymes, Swadesh, and others, one can anticipate that glottochronological dates will be forthcoming. Preliminary archeological work was done some years ago by Strong, Schenck, and Steward

---

* Sentences (and parts of sentences) marked with asterisks contain statements based on data from later historical periods; such statements can only be established by inference for the period in question. (This corresponds to the practice whereby linguists use asterisks to mark forms that are reconstructed or unattested in actual speech.) The material selected to be added by this inferential method: (1) is intended to round out the picture of the culture in a particular way; and/or (2) is especially significant in terms of the cultural changes and continuities to be described later.

(1930). When results of recent archeological research by parties from the Universities of Oregon and Washington are published, the prehistoric picture will be further clarified.

The adoption of horses must have been a gradual process, and the precise date for the first use of a horse by an Upper Chinookan is not especially important in this context. Haines (1938: 430) suggests 1730 as a date for the arrival of horses in eastern Washington, and they would have reached the Wasco-Wishram subsequent to that time. The early effects were, presumably, a certain increase in the mobility of the Chinookans as well as an increase in the ease with which other horse-riding peoples could visit them (cf. Fuller 1941: 25). The extent of the changes in economy, religion, and social structure can only be a subject for speculation.

Period II: Augmented Wasco-Wishram Culture

The major type of change which occurred in this cultural period was the addition of new cultural materials. The period is defined as extending from the mid-eighteenth century to the late 1850's, when the Indians moved to reservations. The culture is described in some detail in order to provide a basis for discussions of change. The description does not refer to a single point in time, but rather to a span of years roughly in the middle of the period. Much of the information is drawn from the journals of the 1805–6 Lewis and Clark expedition, with supplementary material from fur traders' accounts, especially for the years 1811 to 1814. Sources referring to the 1830's and 1840's, such as Lee and Frost (1844), Brewer (1929), and Wilkes (1844), are used principally to amplify earlier indications of the existence of particular cultural elements, as well as to document their persistence. These sources are also used in discussions of change within the period.

Wascos and Wishrams are rarely differentiated in the sources, and, since the two were so similar, they are described as if they constituted a single group during this period. The description refers to the Wasco and Wishram proper (cf. Spier and Sapir 1930: 159–68), excluding the closely allied peoples to the west.

SETTLEMENT PATTERN AND POPULATION

The nature, size, and location of Wasco-Wishram communities varied appreciably from season to season and year to year. The first distinction to be made in understanding this variability is to contrast the camps that were established when the people were away from the river with the somewhat more stable communities on or near the banks of the Columbia. During the spring, when the women, as an alternative to fishing, dug edible roots in the uplands away from the river, temporary camps were established whenever it was difficult to return home at night (cf. Thwaites 1905: IV, 293, 294, 296; Brewer 1929: 61). In the fall, families or households camped in the mountains to enable the women to pick huckleberries and the men to hunt (Thwaites 1905: III, 158; Lee and Frost 1844: 158).

The communities located near the river were almost always described by travelers as "villages," though some might equally well be designated "camps." They were clusters of multifamily dwellings, scattered rather than conforming to a pattern (Thwaites 1905: III, 154; cf. Frémont 1845: 187). During the winter, when the fish were not running, the people occupied sheltered sites away from the river bank (Thwaites 1905: III, 154; cf. Cox 1957: 218; Lee and Frost 1844: 163). In the spring, house clusters were erected conveniently near important fishing sites (Thwaites 1905: IV, 289, 300; cf. Gass 1810: 199–200; cf. Brewer 1929: 53; cf. Lee and Frost 1844: 242). *As the river rose and fell, and as the species of fish ascending the river changed, certain of the households or families would shift again.

*Neither houses nor households were named. Numerous names of "villages" have been recorded by ethnographers (Curtis 1911: 180–81; Spier and Sapir 1930: 164–73)—many more, in fact, than are mentioned in any one of the historical accounts. It is clear that these were not names of villages that existed simultaneously. The lists of names include winter and summer variants and are essentially lists of village sites, occupied during certain years but not others (Thwaites 1905: III, 154). About thirty such names of Wasco and Wishram sites have been recorded by anthropologists; it is sufficient to identify two of them in this paper. The principal Wishram village site at the head of the Fivemile Rapids was called *Nixluidix* (later Spedis and Spearfish in English) (Thwaites 1905: III, 154; Wilkes 1844: 388). *The name Wasco was derived from *wasqu*, the name of the most important village site on the Oregon side (Curtis 1911: 181; Spier and Sapir 1930: 168).

Wascos and Wishrams crossed the river for fishing and for hunting (Thwaites 1905: III, 158; cf. IV, 289). It is not clear from the historical accounts whether or not winter villages were ever erected on the "wrong" side of the river; *it seems likely, however, that in the early nineteenth century Wascos often "became Wishrams" and lived on the Washington side when fishing was suspended so that they could protect themselves from attacks by the Northern Paiutes (cf. Thwaites 1905: III, 163, 169–70, 171).

Clark mentions twenty or twenty-one houses at Nixluidix; he estimated three families per house (Thwaites 1905: III, 151, 154, 155). Farther down the river Lewis and Clark note villages of eight, seven, and eleven houses. In one case there is an estimate of thirty inhabitants per house (*ibid.*: 166, 169, 170). Lee and Frost state that twenty or thirty people sometimes occupied a house (1844: 181), and Wilkes mentions forty or fifty in mat-covered summer dwellings (1844: 383).

Spier and Sapir, combining data from Lewis and Clark with their own, arrive at a rough estimate of a thousand to fifteen hundred for the total Wishram population at the beginning of the nineteenth century (1930: 169–70). Because of ecological variability and the problem of defining the boundaries of groups, it is impossible to achieve a more accurate estimate than this. However, Spier and Sapir's figures may well include some Wascos. The historical data suggest that the Wasco population was smaller than the Wishram but do not provide a basis for any estimate of its absolute size.

Toward the end of the period, disease and other factors modified the size and distribution of the population of the area appreciably. Curtis (1911: 172) states that the Wishrams had declined from 400 to 199 by 1854. Smallpox was blamed for the decline (Commissioner of Indian Affairs 1857: 351). An 1854 figure for the Wascos was 300, but a few years later figures as high as 475 were reported (Commissioner of Indian Affairs 1859: 435).

From the previous discussion it is clear that there would have been considerable variation in the population size at any one village site. Furthermore, a discussion of population would be misleading if no mention were made of visitors to Wasco-Wishram territory. Ross (1904: 129) estimated that the total population at a Fivemile Rapids village swelled to 3,000 during the summer fishing and trading season. Even if this figure is inflated, it is evident that visitors could outnumber the local inhabitants.

SIGNIFICANT OUTSIDERS

In this case study, as in others in the volume, relations with outside groups are emphasized in the analysis of change. Consequently, the Indians and non-Indians who were significant to the Wasco-Wishram will be discussed in advance of the rest of the culture. The network of relationships stretching hundreds of miles in every direction could be discussed as a single system; Anastasio (1955) has described traditional group interrelationships on the Columbia Plateau using this approach. The whole area is a *single* system only from the point of view of an outside observer. If one is concerned, as in this case study, with a particular group, then another approach—analysis of the societal interrelationships as defined (explicitly or implicitly) by *that group*—may prove more useful (cf. Pike 1954: 8–28). In making this choice, it will be necessary to pay passing attention to the interrelationship systems as defined by the *other groups*. Nevertheless, the principal concern here is with one aspect of Wasco-Wishram culture: regularities in behavior toward outsiders, including expectations regarding the behavior of those outsiders.

Before discussing interrelationships on a group by group basis, a few general points should be made. The Wasco-Wishram had many more contacts with outside groups than did most American Indians. The relations included trade, recreation, marriage, and war. In spite of the fact that the Wasco-Wishram had both canoes and horses and were potentially quite mobile, the historical records indicate that outsiders came to them much more than they went to outsiders (cf. Spier and Sapir 1930: 224).

Other Chinookans; Western Oregon.—The Wasco-Wishram were in continual communication with other Chinookan-speaking villagers down the Columbia. Mutually intelligible dialects extended for many miles (Thwaites 1905: III, 164, 185; IV, 280 *et passim*). Cultural similarities and a sense of identity were sufficiently strong to cause old people today to recollect having heard that there once were "Wascos" (or "Wishrams") all the way to the mouth of the river. This is an expression of the intergrading of essentially similar peoples, despite the pseudo-tribal names, such as Cascades and Clackamas, in the literature.

There was much travel along the river. Parties from upriver (e.g., Wasco-Wishram) could pass the Cascade rapids, about halfway to the Willamette, without portaging. They left their own canoes at a village above the rapids and borrowed other canoes below for use until they returned (Thwaites 1905: IV, 269–70). Sometimes the portage was made instead (Thwaites 1905: III, 180, 183–84). News and trade goods passed rapidly up and down the river

(Franchère 1904: 275, note 82; Lee and Frost 1844: 38; Brewer 1929: 61). A man in Wishram territory told Hunt, who had been traveling overland, about the destruction of the ship "Tonquin" at Vancouver Island not many months before (and about a visit to a fur post on the Okanagan River) (Hunt, in Stuart 1935: 305). Items such as wappato (*Sagittaria*) roots and trade beads were obtained from the west in exchange for Wasco-Wishram goods: root bread, pounded salmon and bear-grass (*Xerophyllum*) for basket-making (Thwaites 1905: III, 180; IV, 260).

Most of the relations with such western Oregon groups as the Kalapuya occurred through other Chinookans. In the latter part of the period, Indian relations to the west were of less importance, since in 1830 and the following years a malaria epidemic raged in western Oregon and along the Columbia. The great majority of the Indians west of The Dalles, Chinookans and others, were destroyed, and the Wasco and Wishram populations were also affected (Cook 1955: 303–16, 321–22).

Local Sahaptins.—Wasco-Wishram territory was the site of the greatest Indian market activity in the whole region (Thwaites 1905: IV, 289; cf. Hosmer 1902: II, 149–53; Spier and Sapir 1930: 224); this was a result of the fact that it produced the greatest exchangeable surplus of fish (cf. Hunt, in Stuart 1935: 305). Nearby Celilo Falls would have been the only rival in importance. The proximity of the two, as a matter of fact, was undoubtedly of mutual benefit in attracting greater numbers of visitors to the area as a whole (Thwaites 1905: IV, 307).

Most of those with whom the Wasco-Wishram traded spoke some dialect of Sahaptin. Sahaptins were scattered on all sides of them in. somewhat the way Navahos surround the Hopi villages, and a variety of kinds of contacts occurred. Perhaps interaction was most frequent with the Sahaptins at Celilo Falls. Smaller and more temporary settlements were found between Celilo Falls and the Wasco-Wishram villages (Thwaites 1905: III, 153–54). *Although little is said of it in the early historical literature, a Sahaptin village site named Tenino was at the head of the Fivemile Rapids on the Oregon side, thus immediately opposite Nixluidix and adjacent to Wasco settlements. To the south, in Tygh Valley and at Sherar's Bridge on the Deschutes, were the Tygh (*taix*), at least subsequent to the expulsion of the Molala (Murdock 1938: 397, 398). To the north of the Wishram

lived a number of groups who later became known collectively as
the Yakima. To the northwest and the west were the Klickitat; some
Klickitat villages were interspersed among Chinookan villages along
the Columbia, while other settlements were inland. To the east on
the north side of the river were people sometimes known as *sḱin* in
the literature (Thwaites 1905: IV, 305; Spier 1936: 16–17, 19, 25–26,
42–43).

These then are the Sahaptin "bands" and villages which had the
closest relations with the Wasco-Wishram in the early nineteenth
century. (It would be inappropriate to designate them as tribes, since,
like the Chinookans, they lacked the formal political unity often implied by that term.) The Sahaptins had a culture clearly of the
Plateau type (Ray 1939: 145 *et passim*). On a trait-by-trait basis it
did not differ greatly from the culture of the adjoining Upper
Chinookans. Emphases within the culture, however, were significantly different; for example, the Sahaptins spent much more time away
from rivers, relying more heavily on roots, berries, and game, as opposed to fish.

*Surpluses of meat, and perhaps also roots and berries, were traded
to the Wasco-Wishram in exchange for preserved fish. Except for
those who spent considerable time fishing at Celilo, and possibly for
a few of the Klickitats, the local Sahaptins could not obtain enough
fish through their own efforts to supply their needs (Thwaites 1905:
IV, 289, 305).

Other goods reached the Wasco-Wishram through local Sahaptins.
Some of the groups to the north obtained White goods directly or
indirectly from maritime fur traders at an early date and passed these
on to the Chinookans (Thwaites 1905: IV, 289); *slaves were
among the commodities given in exchange by the Chinookans. Trade
with Sahaptins at Celilo probably was not primarily in food items,
but rather in standard trade goods; the Wasco-Wishram supplied
European items, canoes, and the like, and the Sahaptins passed on
Indian trade items received from the east and slaves from the south
(cf. Ross 1904: 129).

While trade could occur at any time during the year, it was especially heavy from spring through fall. The Wasco-Wishram area
evidently resembled a continuous village market and celebration, with
many hundreds of outsiders coming and going. Local Sahaptins and
others traveled freely in and through the territory, except perhaps

those with whom there were specifically hostile relations (Thwaites 1905: III, 152, 162; IV, 284). Trade was important indeed *and was often carried out through a system of established trading partners. Ross (1904: 129) regarded gambling as even more important than trading; whether he was right or not, gambling opportunities certainly attracted outsiders to the area. Opportunities for singing, dancing, and meeting members of the opposite sex may also have drawn visitors to the Wasco-Wishram villages (Ross 1904: 127–130). *Intermarriage with outsiders, e.g., other Chinookans and local Sahaptins, was evidently frequent, especially in the upper classes (cf. Curtin, in Sapir 1909: 242–44).

The several kinds of interrelationships with local Sahaptins that have been sketched were of sufficient importance to the Wasco-Wishram that it is not surprising that they continued to pay a great deal of attention to these particular outsiders during later historical periods.

Distant Sahaptins.—Most of the other Indians with whom the Wasco-Wishram had significant contact also spoke Sahaptin languages and dialects; some of these were rather divergent from the speech of the nearby groups. Although documentation is not available in these cases, visitors probably came from the following eastern groups: *John Day, *Umatilla, *Wanapam, *Walula, and possibly *Palus (cf. Spier and Sapir 1930: 224–28; Murdock 1938: 397); visitors are known to have come from the Cayuse (Lee and Frost 1844: 176–77) and the Nez Percé (Brewer 1929: 114). In exchange for preserved fish and trade goods, such as beads, the Wasco-Wishram received skin clothing, buffalo robes, and horses from these more distant Sahaptins. Since some of them visited the Plains for buffalo hunting and trade, and others were in contact with those who made such visits, certain types of goods reaching the Wasco-Wishram had crossed the Rocky Mountains (Lee and Frost 1844: 163). During this period and thereafter Plains Indian cultural complexes were slowly disseminated to the Wasco-Wishram, especially by the Nez Percé (cf. Gunther 1950: especially pp. 177–78).

Relations with the Nez Percé and the Cayuse deserve special mention because of assertions by Whites that these two groups controlled the nature of the relationships (e.g., peace versus war) among all of the other Indians in the region (Ross 1956: 126). Groups of Nez Percé appeared in the capacity of traders (Hosmer 1902: II, 150), but in the early nineteenth-century records they also serve as guides, interpreters, and general protectors of the Whites who were traveling along the Columbia (Hosmer 1902: II, 493, 494, 495; Thwaites 1905: III, 152; IV, 297). Fighting of limited scope sometimes occurred between Nez Percé and Upper Chinookan groups; peace could be reestablished by negotiation (Thwaites 1905: III, 152, 156; Henry 1897: II, 853, 856, 879).

The Cayuse were also reported to have been opponents in battles (Henry 1897: II, 853, 856, 879, is probably referring also to them) and were said to use superior military strength to obtain special privileges from the Wasco-Wishram. Nevertheless, reports of tribute in salmon or forced sale at low prices because of fear of the Cayuse (Lee and Frost 1844: 176–77) are difficult to believe; they suggest European misunderstandings of the relations between the groups. David Douglas (1904: 328–29) told of being rescued by a Cayuse leader from some threatening Indians near Celilo Falls; Douglas said the Cayuse were the terror of all the other tribes in the area but staunch friends of the Whites. In any case, the relations between the Cayuse and the other groups in this area were completely disrupted following the Whitman massacre in 1847.

The Sahaptin-speaking Klamath and Modoc near the California border were also intermittently in contact with Upper Chinookans. There is a report of early fighting with the Klamath (Lee and Frost 1844: 177); such incidents were possible, but trade rather than war characterized most relations with the Klamath (cf. Spier 1930: 24). *From somewhat later evidence, it seems that slaves (Allen 1850: 259), water-lily seeds (a valued trade item), bows, and beads (Spier 1930: 27, 40, 41) were brought north; horses, salmon, blankets, and parfleches were given in exchange (Spier 1930: 27, 40, 41, 235, 236). *Relations with Modocs may have been more consistently hostile.

No evidence exists that the Wasco had any significant contacts with the Molala despite their relative accessibility (Murdock 1938: 397–98).

Paiutes and Others.—While the Wasco-Wishram were almost always at peace with each other and with some of their neighbors, for example, other Chinookans and the nearby Sahaptins, and only sporadically, or situationally, involved in raiding relations with certain of the more distant Sahaptins, there was traditional enmity with the Paiutes in southeastern and central Oregon. In spite of accounts from modern Paiutes that trade sometimes occurred with Sahaptins and Chinookans along the Columbia, there is abundant evidence that most relationships involved bloody fighting, without any expectation of negotiations (Thwaites 1905: 163, 169–70; cf. Stuart 1935: 53; Lee and Frost 1944: 177; Murdock 1938: 398–99). Wishram fights with the Paiutes were usually defensive, as were many of those of the Wasco, although individual Wishrams or small groups sometimes joined Wascos or their Sahaptin allies on offensive raids into central Oregon (Spier and Sapir 1930: 228–35; cf. White Salmon Indians, Thwaites 1905: IV, 280–81). Fighting also resulted at times from chance encounters during hunting and gathering trips (Thwaites 1905: III, 158).

While Interior Salish were known (cf. Hunt, in Stuart 1935: 305; Spier and Sapir 1930: 224–25), they were relatively unimportant to the Chinookans. *Plains tribes were evidently known in the same hazy way that the groups near the Oregon and Washington coasts were. *Modern informants believe that Plains Indians, called Sioux and Blackfoot, made the journey west in order to trade, and there are traditions of Wasco trips to the Plains. *Perhaps individuals did join, for example, Nez Percé buffalo-hunting expeditions on rare occasions (cf. Anastasio 1955). Such travels were scarcely possible until after the introduction of horses. The Shasta, Achomawi, and Atsugewi will be mentioned later in connection with raiding for slaves.

Relations with Whites.—The categories of Whites who were of greatest significance during this period arrived in the following order: (1) Lewis and Clark's party, 1805–6; (2) fur traders of the early nineteenth century; (3) missionaries of the 1830's and after; and (4) immigrants or settlers. From the point of view of the Indians, the distinction between explorers and fur traders was of little consequence. In contrast, the importance of the traders as a dynamic influence had waned by the time the missionaries arrived; the latter were a new kind of outsider. During the 1840's and 50's, many new categories of Whites, partially differentiated by the Indians, passed through the area or settled in it.

None of the early relations with the Whites were traumatic or even very dramatic from the point of view of the Indians in the area. The appearance and spread of horses could hardly have been associated with Whites. In the late eighteenth century, trade goods and information about the maritime fur traders seeped into the interior, preparing the Indians for the appearance of the White people themselves.

Modern Chinookans and Sahaptins insist that French traders or explorers were the first to appear in the area. It is remotely possible that they are right, but "history tells us" that Lewis and Clark were the first Whites to visit the section of the Columbia Valley with which we are concerned.

It would be an understatement to say that the appearance of Lewis and Clark caused no excitement, but their reception was a far cry from the literary stereotype of "white gods awing natives." Crowds of visitors frequently accumulated at their camps. Our only evidence comes from the members of the party itself, but one can infer that the goods they carried and the fiddling and dancing of the men were among the most intriguing characteristics of these travelers (Thwaites 1905: III, 156; IV, 289). In general, Lewis and Clark seem to have been treated much the same as members of any strange Indian group who had come to visit and trade: Chinookan chiefs met with them; they were offered food and lodging in a sporadic way; and hard bargaining was the response to their requests for horses and provisions (Thwaites 1905: III, 151–70; IV, 288–312). During the years that followed, other travelers received essentially the same treatment. It is significant that the Indians were not afraid of the Whites under normal circumstances and would consequently approach them unarmed (Cox 1957: 270). Probably, the Wasco-Wishram attitudes toward the early Whites were most like those toward certain "distant Sahaptins," in contrast to their attitudes toward local Indians, Paiute enemies, or supernatural beings.

In the thirty years following the Lewis and Clark visit, practically all of the contacts with Whites were with travelers connected in one way or another with the fur trade. The first permanent trading post in the region was Astoria, founded in 1811 at the mouth of the Columbia by Astor's Pacific Fur Company. It was soon sold to the Northwest Company, which also maintained a number of other posts far up the river (Johansen and Gates 1957: 122–41). Following the merger of the Northwest Company with the Hudson's Bay Company in 1821, headquarters for operations on the lower Columbia were shifted to Fort Vancouver, just north of the present city of Portland (*ibid.*: 143–54). This brought a major trading post within visiting distance for the Wasco-Wishram (Hines 1885: 150). A short-lived trading post was established by an American in the Dalles area in the late 1820's (Wyeth 1899: 175). In the early sources, "the Dalles" means the rapids above the modern city of The Dalles.

The personnel of the fur companies was most heterogeneous. The officers were overwhelmingly of Scotch ancestry, whether the United States, Canada, or the British Isles had been their previous homes. The largest group among the men was composed of French Canadians, but native Hawaiians and Iroquois (and other eastern Indians) were also employed in appreciable numbers (Ross 1956: 91).

The French, especially, had close relations with certain Northwest Indians. In contrast, none of the fur people spent much time with the Wascos and Wishrams, and intermarriage was not as frequent as it was near the coast or farther in the interior. Lewis and Clark's party, incidentally, saw one "half white" child at Nixluidix (Whitehouse, in Thwaites 1905: VII, 180); it was presumably conceived somewhere down the river. Only one reference to an Indian-White couple, during the late 1820's, was noted in the fur trade accounts of the Wasco-Wishram area (Wyeth 1899: 175). In general, early White relations were transient and limited.

Until the arrival of the missionaries, the Whites actually wanted relatively little from the Wasco-Wishram. Primarily, they were anxious that they be peaceful and predictable. Intermittently, they wanted to hire their services and to obtain food, canoes, and other articles from them. Sometimes they wanted horses to ride or to eat. They found it easy to buy dogs for food. Although they complained of the prices, they also bought salmon in various forms, root cakes, berries, and the like (Thwaites 1905: III, 166, 170; IV, 293 *et passim;* Hunt, in Stuart 1935: 306; Cox 1957: 218).

To establish and maintain the desired relations with the Indians the early Whites met and smoked with leaders, made friendly speeches, distributed gifts, and made restitution (although reluctantly) on the few occasions when Indians were killed in disputes. Gifts and payment consisted most frequently of tobacco, but other trade items of the usual sort also changed hands (Thwaites 1905: III, 156 ff.; IV, 288–90 *et passim;* Hunt, in Stuart 1935: 306; Stuart 1935: 58–59).

From the point of view of the Indians the passage of Whites through the territory had its unfortunate aspects. They received a few presents, as well as trifling payment for assistance in portaging and other services, but they did not receive goods in any quantity. These

Indians had few furs to trade to the Whites. At the same time, the Indians above and below them were receiving valued articles, including guns, through trade (cf. Seton 1935: 194). Cox (1957: 257) stated that, because of this situation, the Indians in the Dalles-Celilo area were generally the sufferers in attacks from the others. Whether the Wasco-Wishram were really at a relative disadvantage or not, they claimed that the treatment they were receiving from Whites was unjust (Seton 1935: 194).

From 1806 into the missionary period and beyond, the Wasco-Wishram (and the Sahaptins at Celilo) had a reputation as thieves, and as being otherwise untrustworthy. Lewis and Clark mention the loss of such things as a knife, trade tomahawks, and spoons (Thwaites 1905: IV, 304–5, 308). Lewis struck one thief several times and had him thrown out of camp. This was the first such act of violence in the several years of the expedition (Gass 1810: 201–2). In order to control thefts, Lewis and Clark appealed to chiefs, excluded Indians from camp, and threatened shooting and house-burning (Thwaites 1905: IV, 308–9 *et passim*).

In both the Cascade area, with which we are not concerned, and in Wasco-Wishram territory itself, numerous incidents involving property occurred later while fur traders were traveling along the river. Hunt's party lost an axe, two guns, and a horse. Moreover, the equivalent of a confidence game—a story of an impending attack by another group—was, evidently, attempted as a means of obtaining horses from them (in Stuart 1935: 306). Other "confidence games" were reported subsequently (for example, Hines 1885: 157–58). Information is not sufficient to establish whether or not such episodes represent ordinary Wasco-Wishram business practices employed with other Indians.

During the period 1811–14, there were numerous incidents at the Cascade and Wasco-Wishram portages of the Columbia, which were much more serious from the White point of view than the sporadic thefts. Armed Indians would appear, sometimes blocking the use of the portages. Full scale attacks seemed imminent (Ross 1904: 195–96). Whole bales of goods, rather than individual articles, were stolen. Canoes were damaged during portaging operations. During one of the most serious "attacks" of this nature, John Reed was seriously wounded and two Indians were killed in struggles over some goods (Stuart 1935: 55–59; Franchère 1904: 274–76; Ross 1904: 187–88).

A close look at the incidents reveals that the shooting was usually done by the Whites; harassment or defense, rather than lethal intentions, would explain the rare occasions when the Indians actually used their weapons. The throwing of stones was more characteristic (Ross 1956: 77–78).

There are suggestions in the fur travelers' accounts that the belligerency was based on a desire to establish an effective tribute system at the portages (Ross 1904: 187–88; 1956: 90). Envy and fear regarding the enrichment of other Indians are also mentioned. While such concrete gains would undoubtedly have pleased the Wasco-Wishram, a somewhat more general interpretation seems possible: they were attempting to cause the Whites to "pay attention to them." This could be phrased psychologically, but much the same thing is said by positing: the Wasco-Wishram had defined themselves as *the* important people. In a number of traditional ways visitors and travelers had paid attention to them. They could be generous or parsimonious, belligerent or gentle, as they saw fit. The Whites were ignoring them when they could, and, in general, acting without reference to them. The harassing behavior of the Indians can be interpreted, then, as attempts to maintain or re-establish their position of importance. Furthermore, as important people, they would in the course of things expect to receive more of the valuable trade goods. In general terms: as important people they could cause things to happen (cf. Adams 1958 for a comparable analysis of Cascade data).

This interpretation may help to explain the thefts as well as the more spectacular incidents. We can presume that a trading people would operate within a well-understood system of property, including rules of inviolability. That certain kinds of property could be left unguarded is clear from the fact that valuable dried fish was stacked in the open (Thwaites 1905: III, 155). The thefts from Whites would arise, then, not from a fundamental lawlessness (or from defining the Whites as enemies) but rather from a temporary dislocation of relations which might be remedied if pressure were applied, for example, through thefts or "incidents." These would serve to re-establish, not to break, relationships.

The indications are that the Upper Chinookans much preferred to negotiate over issues than to fight about them; this was true even when the Whites had engaged in killing (Stuart 1935: 58–59; Ross 1904: 187–88). Such negotiations, of course, represented clear examples of attention being paid to them. Furthermore, they served to maintain the initial understanding of the relationship: that of a bargaining structure in contrast to one of conflict (as with the Paiutes).

Especially after the Hudson's Bay Company began to operate in the area, relations with the Indians became regularized from the White point of view (Lamb in McLoughlin 1941: lvii; Minto 1889: 132). Thefts occurred during Hudson's Bay and missionary times (Douglas 1904: 368; Lee and Frost 1844: 165, 178), but it became increasingly possible to discover the particular offenders and to punish them. Travelers no longer faced a whole group of apparently greedy and hostile Indians at the portages. There is no evidence that the Indians had yet redefined their own position with reference to the Whites, nor were they being "held in check" by force. Instead, the Indians had learned how to take into account the peculiarities of this new "tribe"—the Whites, who were not just like the Nez Percé or any other strangers. The Whites had learned to act predictably, for example, to pay for goods and services in a way that was understood by the Indians (cf. Chittenden 1935: I, 18).

By 1838 when the Methodists arrived at The Dalles to found their mission, the Wascos and Wishrams were prepared to co-operate with them in a variety of ways. Unlike the fur traders, but like the Indian Service employees to come, the missionaries were concerned with civilizing the Indians, that is, changing their whole culture to make it identical with their own. Neither the first missionaries nor the later Presbyterians and Catholics at The Dalles had the resources or the influence to effect changes in more than selected aspects of the culture. A school was established, but was probably of little importance (Allen 1850: 124). Religion, technology, and perhaps language seem to be the areas in which their impact was the greatest; these are discussed in pages to follow. If the attitudes expressed in Lee and Frost's book (1844) are representative, the missionaries were covertly hostile to the Indians and overtly so to their culture. Data are lacking on Indian attitudes toward the missionaries, beyond the fact that in certain ways they found them impressive.

The Whites did not constitute a stable entity toward whom the Wasco-Wishram could make an easy adjustment; they continued to change in quantity and in qualitative characteristics. Missionary families and even retired fur traders began to turn into settlers in Oregon and Washington. Especially after 1842, successive years brought increasing numbers of emigrants from the East, whose intention was to settle in the Oregon country. There were over 1,000 in the spring emigration of 1843; in 1844 there were nearly 1,500 arrivals; and in 1847 over 4,000 arrived (Fuller 1941: 132, 133, 143, 145). The numbers are even higher in the 1850's, with an estimated 11,000 to 12,000 arriving in the single year 1852 (*Oregon Statesman* 1854: 2). Almost all of the immigrants passed through or near the growing community of The Dalles. Traders and others joined the missionaries there (Kerns 1917: 187); when a fort was erected about 1850 (Clark 1935: 59; cf. Fuller 1941: 158), soldiers were added to the types of Whites which the Indians needed to take into account.

With the arrival of these new Whites, many of the Wasco-Wishram cultural systems would no longer "work." Even though most of the immigrants traveled on to settle in western Oregon and Washington, the Indians had lost control. For example, they were at a loss to deal with squatters and with the increase in killings by Whites (Coan 1922: 3). The results of the Wasco-Wishram awareness of the new situation will be discussed in the introduction to the next cultural period.

The Importance of Outsiders.—Before concluding this discussion of the relations of Wasco-Wishram to outside groups, a few general points should be made. Outsiders were traditionally an extremely important aspect of Chinookan culture. Whether one considers the beginning or the middle of the nineteenth century, the people spent much of their time interacting with various categories of strangers and other outsiders. This characteristic is not unique with the Wasco-Wishram—for example, it would be shared with other trading peoples. Nevertheless, the Chinookan involvement with *meaningful outsiders* was important in the dynamics of the culture we are examining; this remained true in later historical periods.

THE REST OF THE CULTURE

Wasco-Wishram culture has been classified as an easterly extension of the Northwest Coast area (e.g. Kroeber 1939: 30, Map 6; Drucker 1955: 7). With greater ease it can be classified with the Plateau (Ray 1939: 145). There is no need, of course, to consider such taxonomic questions here; cultural elements were shared with both areas.

The economy, social organization (excluding external relations), and certain other aspects of the culture are now to be described, primarily as they existed during the early part of the nineteenth century.

Technology, Economy:—Edible roots were staples and were dug in considerable numbers by the women, mainly during the spring (Thwaites 1905: IV, 290; Brewer 1929: 59, 61; Lee and Frost 1844: 181). Food preparation from roots included boiling, baking, and sun-drying (Thwaites 1905: IV, 291). Roots were also formed into thin cakes, which when dried were easily preserved (Lee and Frost 1844: 181) and which served as trade items (Thwaites 1905: IV, 293; Ordway 1916: 303).

Huckleberries were picked in the late summer and fall (Brewer 1929: 57) and were eaten fresh or stored in dried form (cf. Thwaites 1905: III, 166; Lee and Frost 1844: 158, 181). Cranberries (Ordway 1916: 303) were less important. Acorns were pit-baked, then buried in mud for an extended period (Lee and Frost 1844: 181). A lichen resembling "Spanish moss" was used as a food, probably baked (Lee and Frost 1844: 156).

There was, of course, no cultivation of food crops, but tobacco was grown in this area; *later evidence attributes it specifically to the Wishram (Curtis 1911: VIII, 173). The tobacco seeds were planted among ashes provided by the burning of a dead tree, log, or stump (cf. Douglas 1904: 269–70).

Before the end of the period, certain Wascos, if not Wishrams, began to do some sporadic farming, or gardening (Lee and Frost 1844: 175–76; Meacham 1878*a*: 6). *Family traditions among modern Wascos indicate that corn and potatoes were the principal crops. After 1838, the missionaries at The Dalles were growing these foods, in addition to wheat, oats, peas, and other vegetables (Brewer 1929: 54–62, 111–19). The Indians were provided with an easy source of seeds and instruction in farming. For example, in 1839 some Indians shared several acres with the missionaries. The theft of potatoes from missionary gardens is another indication that Wascos appreciated garden produce (Lee and Frost 1844: 175–76).

The importance of salmon in trade has already been made clear; they also formed a staple in the local diet (Thwaites 1905: IV, 290). Fishing from scaffolds erected over the white water in the vicinity of falls and rapids was the principal technique for catching salmon; the nets used had handles from fifteen to twenty feet long. The salmon were killed by being clubbed on the head (Hunt, see below in Stuart, 1935: 305; Lee and Frost 1844: 196–97). Other fishing techniques, such as seining and spearing (Thompson 1916: 496, cf. 519; Wilkes 1844: 384), were also employed.

Much of the salmon was placed on racks and wind dried (Thwaites 1905: III, 155; Hunt, in Stuart 1935: 305). *Smoking, common near the sea, was not necessary for the preservation of the salmon and was employed only during damp weather late in the fall. A highly concentrated product, called "sugar salmon" today, was prepared by pounding specially dried fish in mortars and packing it tightly in bags lined with fish skin (Lee and Frost 1844: 181; Wilkes 1844: 384; cf. Thwaites 1905: IV, 289). Some indication of the amount of fish produced can be gained from the Lewis and Clark estimate of 10,000 pounds of fish stacked on the rocks at Nixluidix, in addition to the quantities stored in the houses (1905: III, 152, 155). At the beginning of the next fishing season, there were still many stacks, perhaps 100, remaining (1905: IV, 288, 289). Wyeth (1899; 175) estimated that one chief he visited had four tons of dried salmon. Other fish, such as sturgeon, were of most importance when salmon were not running (cf. Wilkes 1844: 383).

Hunting, a secondary activity with the Wasco-Wishram, provided food and skins in limited quantities. Among the animals eaten were deer (Ordway 1916: 304), elk (Lee and Frost 1844: 158), and bear (Whitehouse, in Thwaites 1905: VII, 180; Wyeth 1899: 175). *Meat was probably preserved by drying, but the quantities on hand were so limited as to escape mention in the early sources. In addition, animal fats, such as "bear oil," were preserved (Thwaites 1905: III, 162). Snares were among the hunting techniques and were used, for example, for wolves or coyotes (Thwaites 1905: III, 159).

Animal skins were used (*for bedding and) for clothing. Robes of deer, elk, and mountain-goat skin were commonly worn. Men often wore leggings, moccasins, and shirts. The shirts were already decorated with beads as well as quillwork by 1806. Loin cloths were of small skins, such as fox. A leader returning from a hunting and war expedition was dressed in a war jacket and cap, as well as leggings and moccasins. Most of the women wore a "truss," or breechcloth, though some wore "long shirts." Many items of clothing were like those of the Nez Percé and other Plains-influenced groups and were obtained in exchange for salmon and other goods, rather than made locally (Thwaites 1905: III, 158; IV, 284, 289). Often, little or no clothing was worn; it was regarded as decoration, like face paint, *and might well have been an indication of rank in the sociocultural system (Wilkes 1844: 383, 388). European clothing was highly valued (Lee and Frost 1844: 164–65).

The introduction of horses in the mid-eighteenth century by more easterly Indian groups was used, it will be remembered, to mark the opening of the cultural period being discussed. By the beginning of the nineteenth century the limit of horses was about twenty-five miles downstream from the Wasco-Wishram; heavy vegetation and a reliance on river transportation were deterrents to their further spread. Lewis and Clark found Chinookans, as well as Celilo Sahaptins, asking much more for horses than did most groups farther up the Columbia, suggesting that the animals were still regarded as scarce, despite the numbers to be seen (Thwaites 1905: IV, 280, 291, 295, 307). Early information on horse techniques and on accoutrements is limited: by 1805–6 more horses were still obtained through trade and through raiding the Paiutes than were raised locally; the technique of gelding was not in use in 1806; the Indians knew how to swim horses across the Columbia; they were used by war parties and to transport goods; by 1841, if not earlier, enthusiasm for horse racing was great enough to lead to fights (Thwaites 1905: III, 158; IV, 289–90, 301; cf. 281; Stuart 1935: 58; Wilkes 1844: 386). *Horses were symbols of wealth, as well as a means for the exploitation of wider areas away from the river; these opportunities were exploited more by Sahaptins than Chinookans. By the 1840's a few cattle were evidently being raised by the Wasco-Wishram (Allen 1850: 277).

The canoes were of several specialized types, and being trade articles, were not necessarily made by the Wasco-Wishram. A skifflike form was used to cross the Columbia (Ordway 1916: 304); there were also much larger ones with a raised bow and stern (Thwaites 1905: III, 166–67; Hunt, in Stuart 1935: 36).

Baskets were made in a variety of forms; they were used for storing berries and pounded fish, as water buckets, and for stone-boiling meat and fish. There were also containers made of bark (Thwaites 1905: III, 155, 165, 166; Wilkes 1844: 384). Mats were used in the construction of buildings, for example, in lining houses, and were put down for sleeping (Gass 1810: 155; Thwaites 1905: IV, 290).

The Wasco-Wishram made several types of buildings—for residence and/or for drying and storing fish. Clark and others describe large plank houses, which were obviously related historically to those of the Northwest Coast. Fireplaces were located under the ridgepole, smoke escaping through an opening left for that purpose in the bark roof (Thwaites 1905: III, 152, 154–55; Lee and Frost 1844: 180–81; Wilkes 1844: 382). The earlier historical accounts attribute mat-covered summer dwellings to Celilo Sahaptins; 1841 is the earliest mention of them for the Wasco-Wishram (Wilkes 1844: 383), suggesting that a change had occurred.

Many items of European manufacture had reached Wasco-Wishram territory even before Lewis and Clark made their visit. The majority of these had undoubtedly come from the maritime fur traders at the mouth of the Columbia, with Lower Chinookans, and such groups as the Cascade villagers, as intermediaries (Thwaites 1905: III, 166). Lewis and Clark mention seeing the following items in the Wasco-Wishram area: swords, guns, brass tea kettles, jackets, scarlet and blue cloth, brass thimbles, and beads (Thwaites 1905: III, 166, 169; IV, 296, 304). Interestingly enough, Lewis himself took advantage of the availability of such goods by giving elkskins, canoes, and some "old irons" to the Indians in exchange for a gun and some beads (Thwaites 1905: IV, 304). As the century progressed, the quantity and variety of European goods increased markedly.

The division of labor involved little formal specialization beyond shamanism and leadership. *Slaves were assigned jobs defined as disagreeable, for example, procuring wood and water. Women gathered plant food, and men fished and hunted (Lee and Frost 1844: 181). Women processed salmon (*and meat, after the initial butchering) (Wilkes 1844: 383). The activities of the sexes were to a degree complementary; Lee and Frost (1844: 158) mention elk hunting during the huckleberry season. Certain tasks, such as portaging (Thwaites 1905: IV, 269–70), were shared by men and women. Wilkes (1844: 388), writing about Nixluidix, says, "Their women seemed to be of more consequence than is usual among savages, and some of them even took command over the men." The men referred to may have been slaves, of course. *notice qualification - white, of course,*

During this period, the Whites offered the Indians a variety of kinds of wage work. It has already been made clear that the Wasco-Wishram were employed intermittently at the portages, carrying goods and canoes. In these and in other capacities in which they worked for the fur traders, they did not always function satisfactorily as employees (Work 1920: 111). In view of the kinds of economic arrangements to which they were accustomed—slavery, and kin group utilization of resources—it would be surprising if they had understood either the White role of employee or that of employer; furthermore, they had not been accustomed to extended contractual relationships.

Following the establishment of the mission and settlement at The Dalles, new kinds of work became available. Timbers for mission buildings were cut and transported by the Indians (Lee and Frost 1844: 152). Subsequently they sawed lumber (Lee and Frost 1844: 162) and aided in the mission farming enterprises (Brewer 1929: 60, 61, 112, 115).

In the Columbia River area the fur traders traveled almost entirely by water and provided their own transport. When missionaries and others arrived, the Indians began to perform a variety of services related to transportation. They rented horses (Lee and Frost 1844: 152) in addition to selling them. They also made canoes available. Increasingly, the Whites hired Indians to paddle for them (abundant references, for example, Frémont 1845: 188; Lenox 1902: 54). Wasco-Wishram also served as guides for trips overland (Lee and Frost 1844: 155–60; Frémont 1845: 197–98; Commissioner of Indian Affairs 1871: 127; Brewer 1929: 112). In some of the instances cited, they also functioned as porters, hunters, or in other capacities. Written messages were carried by Indians, usually by canoe (Brewer 1929: 114).

Initially, Whites gave the Indians such things as tobacco and clothing in payment for the goods and services they were receiving. By the 1840's the Indians were beginning to request "dollars" on occasion (Frémont 1845: 197). It is obvious that certain kinds of employment not only gave the Indians greater familiarity with the Whites and their culture, but also provided the means whereby the Indians could learn White techniques and roles. Only a limited number of roles could be learned, however, as long as the general framework of Wasco-Wishram culture remained unchanged.

Pieces of land in The Dalles area came to be regarded as the property of individual Wascos before the end of the period. This was a response to the beginnings they were making in gardening, as well as to the expectations of the Whites with regard to land. The nature of the rights to fishing sites is not clear in the early sources (cf. Curtis 1911: 90); ideas about these rights may have been transferred to tillable land. As the number of Whites increased, new problems and arrangements arose. Some Indians sold their claims, receiving goods in payment (Brewer 1929: 62). Other Indians found their claims being used by squatters without recompense (Chinook 1853; Commissioner of Indian Affairs 1854: 492). There were also cases in which payment was expected but had not been received even years after the Indians were sent to the Warm Springs Reservation (Meacham 1878a: 6).

Social Organization.—It should already be clear that the Upper Chinookans lacked maximal, formalized political structures which one could easily interpret as "tribal" organization. Moreover, there was no *tribal group* with sharp boundaries separating it from the adjacent groups. The difference between Sahaptins and Chinookans was clear to the Wasco-Wishram, though the distinction was often of little importance. Among the Upper Chinookan villagers themselves, distinctions between groups were made even less rigidly or consistently. In a somewhat different context, Curtis (1911: 85) says of the Wishram: "to a remarkable degree they lacked the tribal instinct."

A pertinent question at this juncture is: what functions would sharp boundaries and broad political integration have for the Wasco-Wishram? It was important for them to co-operate in defense, and for this a special form of leadership existed (see below). In contrast, for example, to peoples with major irrigation systems, or fish weirs which spanned large rivers, the Wasco-Wishram had no joint endeavors which required co-operation or obedience from a large group. Family groupings or small parties could undertake all of the fishing, hunting, and gathering activities. Nor were there functions outside the technological realm which required such co-operation.

Despite the lack of tribal organization, the Wasco-Wishram had a system of leadership (or behavioral regularities resembling leadership) that permitted the Europeans to perceive "chiefs" among them. The number of such chiefs, their functions, and the territorial scope of their influence are not easily determined. Lewis and Clark believed there were two "nations," each headed by chiefs, on the Washington side of the river. Both nations were viewed as having: (1) a principal, great, or first chief; (2) one or more second, or inferior, chiefs (Thwaites 1905: III, 156, 157, 158, 162; IV, 260, 288–89, 294). Later writers during the fur trade period sometimes speak of a single "chief" (Cox 1957: 80, 270), and at other times of "chiefs" (Hunt, in Stuart 1935: 306; Wyeth 1899: 183) with reference to a single village or limited area.

"Chiefs" met and smoked with important visitors (Thwaites 1905:

III, 156, 158; IV, 288–90; Cox 1957: 80), gave presents or exchanged them with visitors (Thwaites 1905: III, 158; Cox 1957: 80), provided food and lodging (Thwaites 1905: III, 169; IV, 289–90, 294; cf. Curtis 1911: 87), and made speeches addressed to their own people and to visitors (Thwaites 1905: IV, 304; Seton 1935: 194). Most of these functions were directed toward a specific type of transient outsider: those defined as "visitors." The European travelers (who were defined as visitors by the Wasco-Wishram) did not record other functions.

Since it is difficult to disentangle the qualities *projected* upon the native leaders or functionaries by the White writers from the patterns of leadership that the Wasco-Wishram themselves experienced, some reconstruction will be ventured: *Mature men became leaders, if they belonged to families of high prestige who had previously produced such leaders (cf. Minto 1900: 300; cf. Curtis 1911: 87). *The number of such "chiefs" at one time was related to the number of men in the appropriate families. *Leadership was not necessarily an active matter; the mere presence of a chief could identify a situation as one in which executive, judicial, and other "tribal" functions were taking place (cf. Curtis 1911: 87–88). *Even when the actual decision-making activity was assumed by others, the presence of "chiefs" apparently legitimized the decisions; the chiefs were then *responsible* for them. *The prestige and power of particular chiefs may have been a function of the extent to which they actually did make decisions or initiate action.

Some historical sources mention "principal men," with the implication that they were leaders of lesser rank (Thwaites 1905: IV, 290; Allen 1850: 277). There were also special functionaries who made announcements in the villages (Allen 1850: 278).

Political control of Indians by Whites did not become especially important or "effective" during this period. The Hudson's Bay Company, the missionaries, and subsequently a few governmental agents exercised influence (Lamb, in McLoughlin 1941: lvii; Allen 1850: 192–93, 216, 277–79; Commissioner of Indian Affairs 1850–58). The fact that the Indians placed their own interpretations on White political principles (Hines 1885: 156–57) made little difference to either group until after the 1840's. The introduction to the next period will sketch the events after Indians and Whites began to feel substantial conflicts in interests.

*War leadership was the responsibility of men with special supernatural power for invulnerability and bravery. This was demonstrated during spirit dances, for example, by slicing off folds of skin with a knife; survival of a self-inflicted wound established the possession of such a guardian spirit (cf. Lee and Frost 1844: 164). One man, who claimed invulnerability, became "chief" (probably a war leader) after covering the entire front of his body with such scars and after shooting himself through the chest (Townsend 1905: 359–60).

Offensive warfare was undertaken by task groups, who were not necessarily all Wasco or Wishram. Departure for war was preceded by singing, dancing (not Plains-type "war dancing"), and other ritual activities. Stuart (1935: 58) mentions the drinking of the blood of horses. While the task groups could be formed specifically for war, hunting parties became involved in fights—or war parties hunted (Thwaites 1905: III, 158; Ordway 1916: 304; see Anastasio 1955, on task groups in this area).

Weapons included knives, war clubs, spears, bows, arrows, and quivers (Thwaites 1905: III, 169; Hunt, in Stuart 1935: 306; Stuart 1935: 57; Ross 1956: 92; Franchère 1904: 275; Lee and Frost 1844: 177–78). As indicated above, guns had become available through trade by 1805–6. Protective jackets made of split wooden rods were worn (Whitehouse, in Thwaites 1905: VII, 180).

Fingers *and other body parts were taken from dead enemies as trophies (Thwaites 1905: III, 169–70). While these evidently enhanced the owner's prestige, they would not affect his class membership.

*Later data indicate that there were four quite distinct social classes: the chiefly families, rich people, poor people, and slaves. Chiefs might or might not be wealthy. In 1806 the "principal chief" at Nixluidix owned more horses than all the rest of his "nation"; the "second chief" was poor, if a lack of firewood and the limited repast offered Clark was an indication (Thwaites 1905: IV, 298, 294). Not surprisingly, other aspects of behavior varied with class affiliation: for example, a member of one of the two higher classes resisted conversion to Christianity on the grounds that most converts were lower-class people (Lee and Frost 1844: 185; cf. Allen 1850: 260).

Slaves were obtained from the south in raids or were traded to the Wasco-Wishram by the Klamath. Shastas, *and Achomawi-Atsugewi or Pit Rivers, were the typical groups from which slaves were taken

(Allen 1850: 259; cf. Spier 1930: 27, 40, 41, 236). Unless Lee and Frost (1844: 177) made a mistake in identification, the Klamath themselves sometimes became slaves. *Probably any war captives, for example Paiutes, were kept or sold as slaves on occasion. *The Wasco-Wishram were not only slaveholders but also slave dealers, trading them to the north and probably also down the Columbia.

Slaves were sometimes tied to dead bodies and left with them in the charnel houses (Minto 1900: 300). In general, however, their lives were not especially unpleasant (cf. Curtis 1911: 88–89). They became involved in many everyday activities; one slave boy was described as the regular companion of a chief's son (Allen 1850: 259–60). Townsend (1905: 360) tells of a slave who killed a leader "in a fit of jealousy," but it seems more likely that he was following the orders of his owner (cf. Curtis 1911: 88). *From later evidence, it seems that slaves were important not only in terms of the heavy work they did, but also for the prestige they brought their owners.

Family organization during this period can be described only by reconstruction from later data. *We can assume bilateral structuring and a Hawaiian kinship system. *There were no clans. *Predominantly patrilocal residence was modified by special circumstances (cf. Spier and Sapir 1930: 262–65, 221).

*Those living in the large Wasco-Wishram houses were usually related in some manner; there were also visitors—for example, Sahaptin traders—and slaves. Clark's statement (1905: III, 155) that each house appeared to be occupied by three families suggests that there were about three fireplaces to each house. *We can speculate that the relatives who cooked and ate together would sometimes function as a family unit, while at other times a larger group would be mobilized.

Life Cycle.—The life cycle of individuals is very poorly documented in the sources for this period. *Omens and restrictions on the behavior of parents were associated with birth. *Small children were kept fastened to cradleboards much of the time. The heads of children of both sexes were flattened by being pressed between boards lashed together (Thwaites 1905: III, 165; Gass 1910: 156; Wilkes 1844: 388).

*The piercing of a child's ears and naming were events marked by feasts and the distribution of presents to guests; the amount given may have been related to the class position of the family. *Comparable ritual activity accompanied the replacement of one name by another at any time later in life. *The lives of growing children were punctuated with similar ceremonies sponsored by their families. *These occurred whenever a child performed an important economic activity for the first time: catching a salmon, killing a deer, or gathering a specified quantity of a plant food. *Young children of both sexes were sent out on guardian spirit quests. *Puberty for girls was marked by dancing and gift distribution; there was no ceremony for boys.

In arranging marriages, parents sought a spouse who was of high prestige, *wealthy, or skilled in the important economic techniques, such as hunting (cf. Curtin, in Sapir 1909: 248). Property, such as slaves, was given to the bride's family to "buy" the girl; the amount given was related to the prestige and wealth of the families (cf. Curtin, in Sapir 1909: 249). *Since the bride's family gave property in return, the transaction was a ceremonial exchange, rather than a purchase (cf. Curtis 1911: 89–90); nevertheless, the exchange may not have been an equal one. Polygyny occurred, and the number of wives was roughly proportional to wealth; Townsend (1905: 359) mentions a leader with six wives (cf. Curtis 1911: 89).

*As Wasco-Wishram adults of both sexes (Hines 1885: 190) grew older, they might become more actively engaged in shamanism. Men often increased their leadership activities, *with the probable exception of war leadership. *The training and disciplining of children were recognized as especially appropriate tasks for older people.

Lamentation and other ritual activities were customary after a death (Lee and Frost 1844: 165; Allen 1850: 277). The hair of survivors was cut (cf. Curtin, in Sapir 1909: 255). Townsend (1905: 360) reported that a man gashed his leg following the death of a chief, but it is not clear how common this was. Burial with personal possessions was practiced, but frequently bodies were placed in wooden charnel houses on islands in the Columbia (Thompson 1916: 519; Wyeth 1899: 175; Lee and Frost 1844: 196; Allen 1850: 261–62). The corpses were wrapped in skin robes, somewhat in the manner of an infant on a cradleboard (Ordway 1916: 342, regarding an island a few miles down the river from the heart of Wasco-Wishram territory). *The bones, or the naturally formed mummy, were rewrapped after an interval.

Death necessitated a variety of social readjustments; *the levirate or sororate involved a series of interactions between families (cf. Allen 1950: 277–78). Property not destroyed or deposited with the dead was distributed (Thwaites 1905: 165), and arguments sometimes arose over the distribution (Lee and Frost 1844: 164–65). Payment was expected from the individual or group considered responsible for a death (Stuart 1935: 58–59; Ross 1904: 187–88; cf. Lee and Frost 1844: 242–44). Vengeance killings and feudlike successions of killings sometimes occurred (Townsend 1905: 360; Allen 1950: 277).

Archeological and other evidence indicates an extreme preoccupation with death in this area (Strong 1945), *which can be seen in the use of skeleton-like figures as design elements, the necessity for special supernatural powers for those who had dealings with dead bodies or ghosts, and the destruction of property following a death. A group ceremony, involving "a solemn dance" and lasting at least four or five days, was held "in remembrance of their departed dead" (Brewer 1929: 54–55).

Ceremonials, Supernaturalism, Curing.—It is not surprising that the arrival of the salmon in the spring was marked by ceremony. Lewis and Clark (Thwaites 1905: IV, 300, 302) describe it as a time of rejoicing; the first fish was cut into pieces and distributed to the children. This description could be suspected of being a Euro-American projection of the idea of a harvest festival, were it not for the fact that later data indicate that first products ceremonies were indeed times of celebration. Aside from Christian activities, the only other ceremonialism recorded for this period concerned guardian spirits, war, and death. *There may have been additional first products ceremonies; inadequacies in the documentation of life cycle rites have already been indicated.

*Among the supernatural beings of importance to the Wasco-Wishram, few if any were "deities" with broad powers and of concern to the whole group. There were anthropomorphic creatures, such as the blind "men" believed to inhabit Mount Hood (Lee and Frost 1844: 157–58). Water monsters lived in the Columbia; they, as well as supernatural forms of the more familiar animals, approached children who were on lonely vigils and became their guardian spirits (Curtin, in Sapir 1909: 248–63). *There was no difference between the guardian spirits of shamans and of others, though shamans could be expected to have more spirits and to have established their position not only through winter spirit ceremonials but also through preliminary curing activities. *Spirits could be called upon to protect individuals from danger. Townsend (1905: 286–89) mentions the singing of a "prayer" by an Indian who was terrified by a storm on the Columbia; this was presumably a power song, rather than an aspect of any of the other "revealed religions" to be described later.

Midwinter was the time for "spirit dancing" by shamans and others with supernatural power. Shamans were hosts (Lee and Frost 1844: 163), but potential shamans may also have filled this role. The dance sessions usually lasted five nights in each house. A long pole, suspended horizontally, was swung against a plank to provide a rhythmic beat. One by one, individuals with power songs would dance and invoke their guardian spirits. If a dancer fell unconscious, he was revived by a shaman. The spirit dances were accompanied by displays of shamanistic skill or power, such as the eating of fire and the drinking of blood from self-inflicted wounds (Lee and Frost 1844: 163–64; cf. Townsend 1905: 359–60).

Curing was the most important activity of shamans. *Illnesses could arise from "natural causes," but they were more commonly ascribed to other humans, living or ghostly (cf. Lee and Frost 1844: 179). *There were no witches in the sense of a distinct status. Killing through sorcery was within the power of shamans, but they might function the next day as conscientious curers. This appears to be an example of an intricate pattern of role differentiation congruent with those in other areas of activity, such as trading relations. Those who were believed to have killed someone through magic, however, could expect to be killed by a relative of the deceased (Brewer 1929: 54; Lee and Frost 1844: 179; Hines 1885: 190).

Shamans were paid in advance for their cures, but the fee was usually returned if the patient died. In a curing session the shaman led in the singing of one or more of his power songs; a group of helpers provided accompaniment by beating with sticks on long poles laid on the ground. In the most common type of cure, the shaman knelt by the patient and sucked out the intrusive object causing the illness. Helpers pulled the shaman away from the patient. After a period of unconsciousness the shaman mastered the disease object and ejected it from his own body (Lee and Frost 1844: 179–80).

The early historical documents do not provide data on non-shamanistic curing or on sweat bathing.

Shamanism was a specific form of a more general pattern that can best be labeled an "active supernatural world." Throughout the area, it was believed that one or another aspect of the supernatural world could intrude in human affairs and give individuals specific instructions of personal or group relevance. For example, a man "of Chenook [*sic*] descent" (Lower Chinook?, Wasco or Wishram?) living near the Dalles, became violently ill with an eye inflammation sometime prior to 1838. While apparently dead, he received a supernatural visitor who caused his recovery. He was regarded as having been returned to life miraculously and was given a new name (Lee and Frost 1844: 155). Whatever the man's ancestry, the reaction to his return was viewed in terms of the local culture and is relevant here. This was undoubtedly not a manifestation of the guardian spirit complex, but rather was an example of another kind of revealed religion similar to those—"Longhouse," Feather, and Shaker—which became important through the acceptance of prophets during the next period.

The Indians had already received some instruction in Christianity by 1836. The "first chief" of the Indians from "the La Dalles" told the Reverend Samuel Parker (1846: 259–60) that he had been praying but that his heart was worse rather than better. Furthermore, "He said, a white man gave them a flag, and told them to set it up on a pole, on Sundays, and meet and pray, sing their songs, and dance around the pole bearing the flag; and they had done so a long time. He wished to know if this was right."

It seems likely that the Indians at The Dalles had received such instruction from other Indians, rather than directly from Whites (cf. Spier 1935). Two interesting points are involved here: that this particular leader, at least, was aware of a problem or a difficulty of some sort; and that the Whites had at this stage become important and trustworthy enough to be sources of the kinds of religious information normally disseminated by native prophets.

Parker understood dancing in its function of making Christianity acceptable to the Indians. He told the chief, however, that dancing on the Sabbath was wrong and that he should disregard this part of the previous instruction. Soon thereafter a chief reported that the dancing had indeed been stopped; as a result, when they prayed for deer before hunting, God sent deer to satisfy their wants (Parker 1846: 261).

The same superficial success occurred when the Methodist mission was established in 1838, forming the nucleus for the city of The Dalles. Large numbers of the Indians in the area did attend the meetings called by the missionaries and many were "converted" to the new religion (Lee and Frost 1844: 182–87 *et passim;* Allen 1850: 260). Certain converts traveled with one of the missionaries to a Klickitat village and to western Oregon to aid in the Christianizing of other Indians (Lee and Frost 1844: 190, 195).

Conversion was viewed by the Wasco-Wishram as the acceptance of a new set of instructions and powers from the "active supernatural world," comparable to those which members of their own group had received. This is made explicit in the story of the conversion of John Mission, a Wasco, as he told it to Meacham (1878*a:* 6). The Indians became disillusioned when the new religion did not protect the converts from danger (Lee and Frost 1844: 241–42). The missionaries were discouraged by the fact that the Indians followed the ritual forms of Christianity more closely than its morality (Lee and Frost 1844: 241–42; Wilkes 1844: 382–83; Hines 1885: 159).

Art, Recreation.—Painting and carving of wooden objects were common (Thwaites 1905: III, 166, 169). Beads and quills were used in decoration. Singing was associated with shamanism and war, as well as being an accompaniment to certain gambling games and recreational dancing (Thwaites 1905: IV, 298; Ross 1904: 127–28). The only two forms of instrumental accompaniment which were reported both involved the beating of poles or sticks against wood (Thwaites 1905: IV, 298; Lee and Frost 1844: 163). *Dancing was a major ritual activity, undoubtedly accompanying most ceremonies. It was recorded in connection with shamanism, war, and recreation. Thompson (1916: 495) was greeted by dancers at the Fivemile Rapids, but their identity and intentions are not clear.

Gambling was an absorbing interest of the people; it was also one of the reasons that visitors assembled in the area. The only two games described in the early literature were gambling games. In April, 1806, the Wishram beat the Klickitats in a bone game, or stick game, much like that played today; the stakes were the kinds of articles which also figured in trading relations (Thwaites 1905: IV, 298–99). Horse racing, *with betting, has already been mentioned.

Although liquor was linked in the minds of the Whites with gambling as immoral, it came to be associated by the Indians with recreational activities. Whiskey became regularly available at The Dalles around 1852 (Commissioner of Indian Affairs 1854: 285–86; 492); its relation to cultural change is not clear, however, except as an example of an added cultural element.

Language.—Throughout this period most of the communication between Whites and Indians was in the trade language known as
Chinook Jargon (for example, Lee and Frost 1844: 153). Although
words from a number of Indian languages had gone into the formation of this jargon, the largest part of the vocabulary was drawn from
Lower Chinookan. *The number of French and English words in
the language increased during this period; in general, these named
such things as European plants, animals, and manufactured articles.
As befitted their position as traders, Wasco, Wishram, and Cascade
Indians often spoke more than one dialect of Chinookan and one or
more of Sahaptin (Stuart 1935: 37, 51, 53). By 1812, at least one
man at Nixluidix knew some English, and the number increased slowly during the period (Hunt, in Stuart 1935: 305; Frémont 1845: 197).

THE CULTURE AS A WHOLE

In terms of this study, the most significant aspects of Wasco-
Wishram culture during the period were: (1) the exploitation of a
strategic location; (2) the production and export of large surpluses
of salmon; (3) an appreciation for a diversity of imported articles;
(4) manifold and frequent relations with outsiders, so classified that
the Whites could be included within the system; (5) a lack of emphasis on political structuring; (6) a lack of concern with sociopolitical boundaries. Most of these general statements could also be
phrased in terms of Wasco-Wishram themes, values, or world view.
Such approaches would undoubtedly bring into sharper focus the
fact that a kind of cosmopolitanism was present.

If the Chinookans of the period had been asked to indicate which
were the most significant aspects of their own way of life, in contrast
to that of their Sahaptin neighbors, they might have stressed the importance of wealth and inherited rank. These preoccupations, however, do not appear to have been so crucial to cultural change as the
items listed above.

By the end of this period, there were already numerous differences
in the extent to which individuals were participating in White culture. The range of *information* about it may have been even greater
than the range of *participation*. One Wasco, for example, left The
Dalles with Frémont in 1843 and traveled east to Washington and
Philadelphia. When he returned home several years later, he was not
only literate, but had become a potential source of an array of new

cultural characteristics (Frémont 1845: 197, 290; Palmer 1857). As situations changed, certain items of information possessed by such individuals were accepted by others as relevant to themselves and thus became functional in new phases of participation in White culture.

Most of the changes during the period were *additions* to the culture, derived from the Whites; there were also a few elements diffused from Indians to the east. Even though there had been some losses, the essential structure of the traditional Wasco-Wishram culture had persisted and was still operative. Even the losses or replacements were not necessarily "permanent." They had occurred on the level of overt behavior; replaced Indian techniques and artifacts were latently present in that they were still regarded an alternatives and could be employed if the new ones were unavailable or ineffective. I suggest that significant permanent losses presupposed modifications elsewhere in the Wasco-Wishram cultural system (or in the Chinookans' evaluation of their own system) which were more fundamental than the changes that had yet occurred. These modifications were already under way in the closing years of the cultural period just described, but they are most conveniently discussed in introducing the next period.

Period III: Modified Wasco-Wishram Culture

The period now to be delineated, that of *modified* Wasco-Wishram culture, extended roughly from 1858 to 1920. It opened at a time when significant losses and replacements of elements of the earlier culture were becoming possible. At the close of Period III many of the Wascos and Wishrams had ceased to behave consistently as Indians, except in specific situations.

In the description of the previous period there were indications that from time to time Wasco-Wishram culture did not function as it traditionally had. The frequency of such instances increased as the numbers and characteristics of the Whites continued to change. Usually it was necessary for the purposes of the analysis to describe Period II "as if other things were equal," that is, as if all conditions were stable, even though this was less and less true with the passage of time. Crucial to the emergence of new Wasco-Wishram behavioral patterns, which were adapted to the changed circumstances, were changes in the Indians' definitions of their own cultural situation and that of the Whites. Certain events of the 1840's and 50's can be understood in terms of these ⌈redefinitions⌉ Indian groups throughout the Northwest were responding to the influx of the Whites in diverse ways. The Cayuse War has already been mentioned; there was later fighting in southwestern Oregon. While the Yakimas and Klickitats were becoming restive, the Chinookans and most north central Oregon Sahaptins were, in the main, reacting in another way: they were concluding that life as they had known it would no longer continue and could not be maintained by any efforts of their own.

It is suggested that many of the Indian groups in the Northwest were acting as if they were experiencing one or another variant of cultural crisis, which is the shared feeling that one's own culture is going to change; the feeling may or may not be accompanied by the idea that there are ways to affect the change—to facilitate it, hinder it, or to re-establish previous conditions. The existence of such a crisis does not imply the presence of "disorganization" on either a personal or a cultural level. The integrity of behavioral systems is not necessarily disturbed either by changes in interpretations of them or by the appearance of alternative systems.

When treaties proposing to move the Indians to reservations in Oregon and Washington were offered in 1855, they were signed by the Chinookans without great opposition. This can be seen as a type of reaction to the crisis. Various Sahaptin groups also signed the 1855 treaties. As part of a complex series of events (not to be detailed here), many Sahaptins, particularly the Yakimas, fought against the Whites in 1855 and for a period thereafter. This can best be understood as another of the several possible solutions to the cultural crisis as they were experiencing it. There is evidence that many of the Indians were aware of the options open to them. The Chinookans explicitly rejected the "Yakima solution": Wishrams in the berry patches near Mount Adams hurried to The Dalles to be near home and near the Whites; other Chinookans made comparable moves (cf. Commissioner of Indian Affairs 1857: 372). Having surrendered their arms, they "sat out" the Yakima War under close surveillance. They were safe enough so long as they stayed in camp at The Dalles; elsewhere they were in danger both from hostile Sahaptins and from irresponsible volunteer soldiers, who were inclined to shoot any Indians they encountered (Thompson 1855; Commissioner of Indian Affairs 1856: 756).

The interpretation of the data for these years has been based on the assumption that the signing of the treaties by the Wasco and Wishram was more than just a "political" act dictated by immediate circumstances. The treaty-signing, the neutrality during the war, and the move to the reservations indicated that the Whites were no longer viewed as a visiting Indian group. The Chinookans recognized that they must take the Whites into account even in regard to the most fundamental aspects of their own culture. The Wasco-Wishram may or may not have ceased to define themselves as *the* important people; however, the superiority of their culture as a moral order was no longer unquestioned—they saw it as no longer functioning as before and saw that there were possible alternatives to it. In differing ways, both the Whites and the local Sahaptins thus represented significant points of reference in the making of choices. As the discussion proceeds, the importance of these changes should become clear.

Oregon Sahaptins moved to the new Warm Springs Reservation in 1857, but many Wascos waited until 1858, when they were more certain that conditions there would be as they had been planned at the time the 1855 treaty was signed. The Wishram moved north to the area of the present Yakima Reservation at about the same time.

In the century following the establishment of the reservations, the spatial separation between the Wasco and Wishram was greater than in the past. The cultures were highly similar at the time of separation and remained so despite the fact that the two peoples had distinct, though similar, sets of experiences. In contrast to the previous period, the sources for the last two cultural periods usually distinguish between the Wasco and the Wishram.[2] Throughout the rest of this case study, the two groups are differentiated whenever relevant; the hyphenated form "Wasco-Wishram" is not used for the later periods. The terms Wasco and Wishram came to have an expanded meaning in certain situations during the third period: Upper Chinookans from

[2] Data in the ethnographic writings of Curtis (1911) and Spier and Sapir (1930) refer mainly to the early part of Period III. Other Wishram sources for this study were modern informants living at Spearfish and at Warm Springs. The documentary history of the Wishram was not examined in detail for the later two periods. For the Wasco, not only published sources such as the Reports of the Commissioner of Indian Affairs, but also national archival materials in Washington, D.C., and Seattle, were used extensively. The memories and family traditions of certain older Wasco informants went well back into the nineteenth century, and there were numerous informants at Warm Springs for the early part of the twentieth century. Data from informants will be presented without citation of the source.

down the Columbia, for example, from Hood River, were becoming assimilated to the Wasco group while they lived at Warm Springs; Indians from the Cascades and White Salmon were similarly assimilating to the category "Wishram" at Yakima and Spearfish. It should also be noted that the customary intermarriages between Chinookan and non-Chinookan Indians continued. In addition, an increasing number of individuals whose fathers or grandfathers were White (or Hawaiian, Negro, and the like) were maturing; if they were Indian culturally, they were regarded (in most situations) as members of the Wasco or Wishram group.

The description of the culture of this period will be referable, as before, to no single point in calendar time. In general, the statements pertain to the years around 1900; when statements refer to earlier or later times, this is indicated or is clear from the context.

SETTLEMENT PATTERN AND POPULATION

At Warm Springs the Wascos settled close to the agency, about two miles west of the Deschutes River on Shitike Creek. At first they occupied multiple-family dwellings (sometimes called "longhouses" in English) of types which had been customary along the Columbia. An old Wasco informant said, "The people wanted to live all together in a bunch, but they separated them and taught them . . . everything about farming."[3]

The system of settlement soon approximated quite closely the hopes of the agents and of "Washington" (cf. Secretary of the Interior 1859: 98–99). Wasco families moved on to small plots of land between the agency and the Deschutes and up Shitike Creek from the agency. The Sahaptin Teninos made a corresponding move up Tenino Creek, which joins Shitike Creek at the agency. From the White point of view, the rest of the Sahaptins did not "settle" anywhere in the first decades following the treaty; they had rather temporary camps here and there in the northern part of the reservation and in traditional locations off the reservation.

Subsequent to the 1880's, Wascos began to clear even more extensive farms or ranches north and west of the agency, on Miller Flat and then Sidwalter Flat. These localities were atop the lava plateau,

---

[3] The governmental policy here—dispersal—is the same as that later applied to the Mandan and many others. It contrasts with the policy toward the Navahos at Bosque Redondo.

in contrast to the semimoist creek bottom land they were farming at first. A few Wascos moved south of the agency—to Dry Hollow and to the Seekseequa Creek valley. The latter area, about fifteen miles from the agency, was assigned principally to the Paiutes, however, who settled on the reservation in the 1870's and 1880's.

When the Wishram moved to the Yakima Reservation in the 1850's, they found farming difficult and began to return regularly to the Columbia to fish. Subsequently, farming—raising grain, hay, stock —became a meaningful way of life to many of them. In addition to reservation land, which became increasingly valuable through irrigation, other government land in areas north of the Columbia became available.

Both root-digging and berry-picking were at least as easy on the reservations as they had been when the Chinookans were living along the Columbia. The Warm Springs Reservation was acceptable to the Indians in part because of the accessibility of such foods. Since roots could often be dug on one-day trips on horseback, or even on foot, there was no necessity of establishing camps. Wascos continued to travel to the Mount Hood area for berries and for hunting, but they now increasingly joined Sahaptins in exploiting mountainous country farther to the south. Mount Jefferson, with its berry patches, forms part of the western boundary of the reservation. Correspondingly, Wishrams were close to upland root areas, as well as to familiar berry patches in the Mount Adams area.

It was much more difficult, of course, for both Wascos and Wishrams to exploit Columbia River salmon if their winter housing was on the two reservations. At first, the agents accepted the Indians' plea that they needed to return to the river in order to survive. Friction with Whites along the Columbia, and the belief that Wasco farming operations would succeed if fishing were curtailed, led an Indian Agent, J. W. P. Huntington, to effect the signing of a second treaty with Warm Springs Indians in 1865. This treaty limited the freedom of movement of the Indians and included a provision in which fishing and other rights were relinquished. All the evidence suggests, however, that the treaty had not been properly interpreted to the signers and that there was probably deceit involved in the failure to make the document clear (Commissioner of Indian Affairs 1869: 161; Secretary of the Treasury 1888). Despite the treaty, the Warm Springs Sahaptins and Chinookans, like Yakima Reservation

Indians, continued to fish at the Columbia. The treaty was not important except as a basis for intermittent arguments between Indians and Whites even as late as the 1950's.

The fishing camps of the Chinookans during this period were temporary, for the most part. They could be in the traditional rocky places, right next to the river, since the growing White settlement in the area around The Dalles was concentrating in places more suitable for permanent building. When commercial fishing became more important, toward the end of the period, some Chinookans began to spend the entire year at the river. A few Wascos built permanent structures beside the river and on islands near the Oregon bank. An even higher percentage of the Wishrams built permanent structures in and near the old village of Nixluidix. This community was subsequently known in English as Spedis (from the name of a Wishram man) but has more recently been called Spearfish.

Aside from the two reservations, Spearfish came to be the most important Chinookan settlement. It was conveniently situated for fishing, but it also provided one of the better places for both Wascos and Wishrams to live if they wanted to be away from the reservations. It can be noted parenthetically that the several possibilities for residence—reservations, off-reservation farms, and fishing settlements—could serve as indicators of a person's definition of himself. For example, residence at Spearfish could indicate a lack of co-operation with the government's plan to make progressive farmers of the Indians.

There were no marked fluctuations in the total size of the Wasco or Wishram population during the period. In 1910, there were 274 Wishrams; of the 242 Wascos, 54 were in the state of Washington, mainly at Spearfish (Census 1915: 82).

SIGNIFICANT OUTSIDERS

Other Chinookans; Western Oregon.—Most of the remnants of Indian groups in western Oregon and Washington had been moved to reservations near the coast, making them relatively inaccessible to the Wasco and Wishram. Exceptions would have been individual families who returned to familiar areas near the Willamette or Columbia rivers. Wascos also encountered Chinookans and others while picking hops in the Willamette Valley (Smith 1878) and on occasional visits to the Grande Ronde and Siletz Reservations.

Local Sahaptins.—The Sahaptins with whom the Wasco and the

Wishram shared the Warm Springs and the Yakima Reservations were already well known to them, of course.

The numerous Sahaptin groups on the Yakima Reservation need not be differentiated here; among those who settled there were families that had spent at least a few seasons on the Oregon side of the Columbia. On the Warm Springs Reservation, the largest group had been associated with Tygh Valley. The Teninos were more numerous than the John Days; other Sahaptins came and went from the reservation, though they were never there in appreciable numbers. During trips to the Columbia River to fish or during quasi-permanent periods of residence at the river, Sahaptins were also encountered. They concentrated at Tenino and on both sides of the river at Celilo Falls. Klickitats retained an attachment to localities farther down the river.

There is no evidence that the establishment of the reservations led to any immediate change in the relations between the Upper Chinookans and the Sahaptins. When appropriate, trading in horses, food, and other commodities continued. Intermarriage became increasingly common; the earlier marriages at Warm Springs with non-Chinookans were generally with the Teninos, who were more available and who were undergoing processes of acculturation paralleling those of the Wasco. As the period advanced, joint political activities vis-à-vis the Whites increased in frequency. The Wascos and Wishrams also became involved in religious movements which had had their origin among the Sahaptins. On a more general level, the presence of the Sahaptins was increasingly important to the Chinookans in defining their own identity.

Distant Sahaptins.—While the same groups of Sahaptin-speaking Indians listed for the previous period were still known to the Wasco and the Wishram, there were shifts in the frequency and importance of the interactions. The Nez Percé, Umatilla, and Klamath were the most significant. The Wanapam, Walula, Paluse and Molala were known but were unimportant. The distinction between distant and local Sahaptins had changed somewhat since the previous period. Certain families or larger groupings who had lived some distance from The Dalles, such as some of the people in the John Day Valley and at Rock Creek, moved to one or another of the reservations; others from the same groups lived away from the reservations and were in contact with the Wasco or the Wishram only during visits.

Relations with the Sahaptins to the east, especially the Nez Percé, resembled those of the previous period: trade continued even though the items traded and the methods of transportation changed with time. For example, it became possible for the Indians to the east to travel by boat, wagon, and railroad in order to fish at Celilo Falls or to trade near The Dalles. To illustrate shifts in trade articles, one could cite the replacement of buffalo robes by Nez Percé cornhusk bags.

Because of military operations against them following the Whitman massacre and population loss through disease, the Cayuse lost their power and importance in the area (Commissioner of Indian Affairs 1860: 781–82). Increasingly they merged their identity with the Nez Percé and Umatilla and ceased to be a significant group so far as the Wasco and Wishram were concerned. The Umatilla proper, and other Sahaptins on the Umatilla Reservation, had more frequent relationships with the Wasco than with the Wishram (Spier and Sapir 1930: 227). This may have been true of the Umatilla during the previous period, but documentation is lacking.

In the earlier part of the period, relationships with the Klamath, for example the trade in slaves, continued on the traditional basis (Mitchell 1869). Subsequently, the visits of the Klamath to the Columbia River and to the Warm Springs Reservation became more and more sporadic. Following World War I, trading expeditions in the old sense no longer occurred, though other relationships, such as kinship ties, might lead to visits.

Relationships with the Modocs, which had never been as close as with the Klamath, were limited to the participation of the Wascos in the fighting against them in the Modoc War of the 1870's.

Paiutes.—Following the establishment of the Warm Springs Reservation, Paiute groups engaged in a series of raids which were demoralizing to the agency personnel and the Indians (Commissioner of Indian Affairs 1859: 757–58; 1866: 79). Neither retaliatory raids nor the stationing of soldiers on the reservation eliminated the danger. In 1866, Wascos and Sahaptins from the reservation were recruited into a group known as the Warm Springs Scouts. Under army command, the scouts inflicted decisive defeats on the Paiutes in central Oregon (Shane 1950: 297–98). As a consequence of the Bannock War in the late 1870's, the potential threat of the Paiutes, as well as certain more easterly Shoshoneans, was eliminated by capture, imprisonment, and resettlement. Subsequently, certain of the Paiutes (some of whom had never raided in the area) settled in the southern part of the reservation. It is questionable whether this would have been accepted by the Wascos and Sahaptins had their political attitudes been more "chauvinistic" and had they been more legalistic about their rights. During the remaining years of the period, the Paiutes were scarcely assimilated into any of the networks of relationships which existed among the other peoples on the reservation.

Other Indians.—Certain Wascos and Wishrams traveled extensively and from time to time encountered other Indians. For example, stories are told today of cattle drives through Plains country and elsewhere. Conversely, strange Indians visited the Columbia River area. Periods spent in boarding schools not only led to increased information about other Indians but sometimes also to persisting relationships: friendships and marriages. None of these distant peoples—Salish (Curtis 1911: 180), Plains Indians, or others—was of consequence to the whole Wasco or Wishram group.

Relations with Whites and Other Non-Indians.—Relationships with Euro-Americans of a variety of kinds had become much differentiated by this period. There were soldiers on the reservations in the early years, along with administrators, technicians, teachers, and missionaries. While towns of any consequence were slow to appear in eastern Oregon near Warm Springs, The Dalles continued to grow and was regularly visited by the Wascos (cf. Meacham 1875: 147). Yakima and Goldendale, as well as The Dalles, were increasingly important for the Wishrams. Portland, which was within traveling distance for the Chinookans, was becoming a major city.

In general, the Whites who were most significant were those on the reservations and those connected directly or indirectly with ranching. Even in the towns, the men in the livery stables, harness shops, and feed yards were of greater importance than, say, bankers. The most significant characteristic of the Whites on the reservations was their single-minded insistence on acculturation.[4]

Individual Indians met other kinds of Whites—at distant boarding schools, on visits to Portland, and on cattle drives. Certain Warm Springs Indians brought back descriptions of the eastern seaboard

[4] Acculturation is used in this case study to refer to the learning of cultural content, including evaluations, from an outside group. Assimilation involves participation in the social relations of the other group; with complete assimilation, the identity of the ego group (in this case, Indians) is lost.

and even of "the crowned heads of Europe," as a result of a tour with Buffalo Bill's Wild West Show.

Increasing numbers of Indians worked for wages off the reservation; for example, men did harvesting and women did domestic work. Most such employment, however, simply brought them into closer contact with the kinds of Whites they also encountered in other connections.

Such non-Indian minority groups as Negroes, Chinese, and Finns became known, or better known. They were often called by Chinook versions of the English names; special characteristics were attributed to each group, for example, that Finns (like Indians) appreciated salmon heads.

As Indian behavior came to approximate that of the Whites in increasing numbers of situations, the Indians could not help but experience the phenomena usually labeled "prejudice" and "discrimination." The Whites were in effect saying, "Become civilized"; however, barriers to participation in White civilization appeared whenever Indians began to assume certain White roles. The importance of these barriers is difficult to assess for the third cultural period; certainly they were significant during the fourth period.

The Concept of "The Indian."—The pattern of relationships with outside groups, then, shifted in a number of respects. New kinds of Indians and non-Indians became identifiable, but the most significant change lay in the outside reference points from which the Wascos and Wishrams could view themselves. The category "Indian" became meaningful to them, that is, they came to appreciate the ways in which the Whites grouped them with Sahaptins and others. In certain situations "we" now included not only one or another grouping of Upper Chinookans, but also Sahaptins and any other Indians who were around. The consequences of these changes will become clearer later in this study.

THE REST OF THE CULTURE

Technology, Economy.—It was suggested earlier that a difference between the Wasco-Wishram subsistence activities and those of the local Sahaptins lay in the higher percentage of the Chinookan diet derived from salmon, as opposed to plant food and game. Quantitative data are lacking, but it is plausible that the shift to the Yakima and Warm Springs areas, with their available supplies of land products, caused a shift toward a Sahaptin-like balance of production. Phrased differently, the Wasco and Wishram came to be more typical Plateau Indians, at the expense of certain characteristics they had shared with coastal peoples. This same point could be made for aspects of culture other than subsistence.

Ethnobotanical work (French n.d.) with both Chinookans and Sahaptins on the Warm Springs Reservation has led to the conclusion that the former did not learn to exploit as many kinds of plants in the area as did the latter. This holds whether one is considering food or other uses of plants, such as medicine. Nevertheless, the Wascos did learn to use, or to use more extensively, plants which had not been available near the Columbia. For example, a starchy root (*Lomatium canbyi* C. & R.) was common enough on the reservation to permit it to become a staple; it is rare or absent near the Columbia. Corresponding shifts in plant use occurred among the Wishram who moved to the Yakima Reservation.

Bitterroot was extensively dug; other important foods that required digging included members of the Lily family, such as onions and camas, and members of the genus *Lomatium*, such as "cous" and the species mentioned above. Both the roots and young shoots of sunflower-like plants were eaten; a few other species also provided greens.

The most significant fruits were members of the genus *Vaccinium*, which includes cranberries and various blueberries and huckleberries; gooseberries and currants; and members of the rose family, such as strawberries, service berries, and chokecherries. Other foods included a few kinds of nuts and seeds, mushrooms, and the black lichen already mentioned.

Toward the end of the period the use of certain of these plant foods decreased, and some of them came to be ignored by particular families. The gathering of the sunflower-like *Balsamorhiza* became infrequent, for example, but other wild foods were exploited as vigorously as ever. Purchased foods, government "rations," and garden produce were sporadically available as supplements and alternatives to the traditional diet.

It has already been indicated that Wasco farming, or gardening, had begun in the previous period at nearly the earliest possible moment considering the available knowledge about the techniques. This was in marked contrast with many Indians in the United States, though not with certain others on the Northwest Coast (Suttles 1951) and on the Columbia Plateau. Previous experience with plant control techniques, for example, growing tobacco, may have been important in this acceptance, but stress should also be laid on the fact that fishing had already encouraged relatively settled village life among these Indians. In The Dalles area it had been possible to fish and still pay attention to garden plots not far distant. On the reservations farming operations among both Wascos and Wishrams were strongly encouraged by the Whites, who considered the industrious use of land a highly moral activity. To the extent that the Indians desired to maintain and strengthen their relations with the Whites, they found farming a means of eliciting favorable and meaningful responses. Insofar as farming *activity* can be dissociated from cultural concepts regarding property, it is unlikely that Euro-American ideas of property were conveyed to the Wasco and Wishram.

Even in the absence of the Whites themselves, agriculture on a limited scale was undertaken at Spearfish; grain raised for hay was perhaps the most important type of crop. Gardening was also attempted but came to be regarded as too much trouble because of attacks by grasshoppers and rodents.

The disruption of the annual fishing cycle by the move to the reservation has already been noted. With a growing tendency to concentrate only on the big salmon runs in the spring and fall, the exploitation of fish species other than Chinook salmon decreased. The Indian fishing complex had been efficient and was simply modified or supplemented by items from White culture. For example, Indian hemp (*Apocynum cannabinum* L.) was only gradually supplanted by European twine and net. Scaffolds were of the familiar shape, but nails and lumber were becoming available to aid in building. The coming of the fish hatcheries provided the Indians with a new source of fish; they preserved the salmon that had been stripped of eggs and milt (Geer 1912: 451–52). Salting was added to the preservation techniques (Commissioner of Indian Affairs 1858: 615). At the time of the transition to the next period, when commercial fishing was beginning to be important, fish wheels mounted on scows and other purely European inventions began to be adopted.

Hunting was an activity shared by the Whites and the Indians. The Whites *expected* the Indians to hunt and would scarcely disapprove unless it interfered with farming or some other valued activity. Consequently, no marked decrease in hunting—already only a secondary activity for the Chinookans—would be expected. The data are insufficient to establish the point, but it may be that with improved weapons and easy access to hunting areas, the amount of game killed actually increased. Meat was customarily shared both with relatives and non-relatives; surpluses of venison, especially, were preserved by drying.

Decorated and undecorated items of hide and buckskin continued to be made in a variety of forms; others were received in trade. There was a gradual decrease in the manufacture of such articles, but even more significant were shifts in meaning. Clothing, like jewelry, had long served as decoration and to enhance the wearer's prestige. These functions continued, but the ownership and use of such items also came to signify the owner's orientation toward Indian culture. The Wasco and Wishram knew that those who wore buckskin, beads, and feathers were Indians. It will be remembered that European clothing was already becoming available before Lewis and Clark. First the missionaries, then the Indian Service, actively encouraged the wearing of "citizen's dress" (many sources, for example, Commissioner of Indian Affairs 1881: 153). The everyday clothing of the majority of the men and women came to resemble closely that of the ranchers in the area. (Incidentally, the conformity related to outer garments; the Indians did not necessarily wear White underclothing.) In hair styles and in details of clothing the members of certain families continued to be identified as Indians. During celebrations and on special occasions buckskin clothing and other items of Indian decoration were often worn by participants, especially those involved in Sahaptin-oriented religious movements.

Horse-breeding had grown in importance during the nineteenth century, and certain individuals on the reservations and at Spearfish became specialists in it. Horses were often sold to Whites; for example, they were driven across the mountains from the Warm Springs Reservation for sale in western Oregon (Nash 1881: 118–20).

Cattle-raising increased in importance during the course of the period. Only one man, part Sahaptin, raised sheep at Warm Springs; there were also a few hogs.

An assortment of new manufactured articles, too numerous to list, was accessible to the Wascos and the Wishrams, and there were traditional as well as newly-learned motives for availing themselves of innovations. The additions represented more than simply the acquisition of manufactured articles. For example, the management of a sawmill on the Warm Springs Reservation was in the hands of some Wascos; informants today indicate that these "old-timers" quickly became skilled in working with machinery. Through vocational training in schools and in an apprentice system, the number of skills proliferated. Correspondingly, there was a decline in the exercise of Indian technological activities no longer appropriate: canoes were no longer made and the manufacture of small articles either began to disappear or to become by default the specialty of a few individuals. Baskets and matting were made by fewer and fewer women. This did not mean that matting, for example, was to disappear during the period; it continued to be useful in building temporary structures along the Columbia. When the quantities of such items were insufficient for the needs of the Wascos or the Wishrams, it was possible to obtain them from Sahaptins.

Multiple- and individual-family houses of Indian types began to be replaced on the Warm Springs Reservation by wooden structures more or less approximating White standards (Commissioner of Indian Affairs 1869: 162). Toward the end of the century some quite "respectable" frame houses began to appear on the reservation and subsequently at Spearfish.

Those who were accumulating money began to hire others to work for them or to make things for them. They bought such items as moccasins, which once might have been received in trade or made by someone within the household—perhaps a slave.

Older and indigent people were cared for in a variety of ways. When fish were being caught in abundance, some would often be given away. Furthermore, an old man had the right to take the initiative and "bum" a fish; by tapping his hip, he indicated that the one just caught was to be his. Food other than fish, as well as such items as clothing, was provided for those who needed it. Commonly, older people were asked to live with a family to whom they might or might not be related. They performed light work, such as child care and instruction, and sometimes provided companionship for family members.

Kinship and other obligations were increasingly met by gifts or indefinite loans of money; those who were achieving some measure of financial success by White standards found it difficult to refuse pleas for assistance from other Indians. When such informal disbursement was coupled with the formal gift-giving on ceremonial occasions, it is not surprising that few Chinookans became outstandingly prosperous.

One might anticipate that people who had done as much trading as the Wasco-Wishram would go into business—become entrepreneurs, perhaps shopkeepers—in the new towns and on the reservations. Chinese emigrants established businesses all over the world, often with far fewer resources. The only real example that has been discovered of a comparable Chinookan businessman is that of a "highly-acculturated" Cascade Indian, Jake Andrews, who had a fish market in The Dalles early in the twentieth century. White prejudice against Indians is a possible explanation for the scarcity of Chinookan (and Sahaptin) businesses. Still, the reservations and the Spearfish area could have supported small stores, comparable to those in Pueblo villages. A more adequate explanation is possible if we analyze the activity of entrepreneurs: their basic motivation, that is, profit; their knowledge of the specific techniques involved; and their capacity for sustained responsibility and tolerance for routine at specified times and places. There is abundant evidence that the Wasco-Wishram had traditionally appreciated profit and actively sought it. Business techniques could have been learned, just as other White techniques were learned. Chinookan Indians impress Whites as quite "responsible," compared, for example, with Sahaptins, in such matters as keeping appointments. Nevertheless, the kind of abstract or impersonal "responsibility" involved in keeping a store open from day to day and season to season, whether there are many customers or not, was evidently not congenial; seasonal production techniques, such as fishing and farming, seemed more worthwhile.[5]

Social Organization.—It has already been made clear that the modern Wascos and Wishrams were of heterogeneous origin and that there had previously been no strong political organization on any level. On the reservations there were conditions which one might expect would build tribal organization and unity: (1) close physical proximity of Chinookans to each other; (2) the presence of culturally contrasting Sahaptins to serve as an "out-group;" and (3) activities on the part of the agents based on the assumption that they were dealing with "tribes." Despite these and lesser considerations operating in the

[5] Helen Codere has suggested that the problem of extending or refusing credit to other Indians might have become acute had such businesses been established.

direction of unity, "tribes" in any consistent sense did not develop. There was no substantial basis for tribal organization in the Indians' own activities. The behavior of the agents was not consistent: sometimes they felt that the whole reservation, rather than any one linguistic-cultural grouping, should constitute a tribe. Furthermore, they were pledged to de-tribalize the Indians as soon as possible.

"Chiefs" and chiefly families from various villages had moved to the reservations following the signing of the treaties. Even had the Whites not been involved, the problem of selection of leaders for the two heterogeneous collections of Chinookans would have been complex; the White agents added to this complexity by appointing men to positions of leadership without necessarily paying attention to traditional Indian criteria of selection. Commonly, there were a number of chiefs alive at any one time, and there were diverse and even contradictory reasons for attributing the office to them. To illustrate with Wasco data, men were called chiefs in certain situations, who: (1) were regarded as chiefs at the time the reservations were established; (2) signed the 1855 and/or 1865 treaty; (3) were descended from chiefs; (4) were selected by Indians as chiefs; or (5) were appointed chiefs by representatives of the Indian Service. To complicate matters further, the Indian agents usually appointed a Wasco as chief of the whole reservation with (nominal) authority over more than just the Chinookan-speaking group. During the middle part of the period, the office of chief of police, often held by Wascos, was an important one in terms of power, and this office became partially assimilated to the concept of chief in the minds of the Indians.

The coexistence of such a variety of political principles and functionaries, coupled with the cultural variability within and between the tribal groupings on the reservation, might seem to provide an excellent basis for factionalism. While there were occasional differences on issues, for example religion, the evidence indicates that there was no factionalism in any of the usual meanings of that term. Perhaps a crucial missing element for the appearance of factionalism was an assumption (and correlated overt behavior) that there *ought* to be unity (cf. French 1948).

A cultural loss that deserves mention is that of the somewhat nebulous political independence the Indians had had before the treaties. During Period III the Whites made many important decisions relating to the affairs of the Indians; such decisions, however, were often of types the Indians themselves had never made. When it *was* appropriate for the Wascos and Wishrams to consider a question, the decisions were usually reached in meetings, rather than by an individual leader. Such meetings were attended by the several kinds of chiefs and other leaders; ordinary men and women often participated, depending on the subject at issue. The Indians were periodically opposed to specific acts of the federal government, for example, certain projected solutions to a dispute about the north boundary of the reservation. However, the activities of the Indians occurred within limits acceptable to the Whites, if not established by them.

Among the kinds of political functions exercised by the Indians were certain judicial ones, especially in areas of interpersonal relations. At Warm Springs, Wascos sometimes served as Indian Judges. Crimes of violence and adultery had traditional Chinookan definitions (Spier and Sapir 1930: 213–16), however, and were handled by the Indians themselves even during those periods in which there was no Indian Service sanction for judicial activity. To illustrate: the ethnographic sources and modern informants agree that during the nineteenth century adultery was considered a matter of great seriousness (Curtis 1911: 89; Spier and Sapir 1930: 213–14, 216–17). In the traditional system, payments, beatings, and even sanctioned killings were inflicted upon parties guilty of adultery. In the settlement of these cases, chiefs, in conjunction with other leaders, exercised real authority and dispatched men who had supernatural power for war (or violence) to carry out decisions. It is not possible now to determine exactly how much of the punishment system was operative on the reservations, but there is no doubt that severe punishments were still inflicted (Commissioner of Indian Affairs 1872: 366). It appears that the waning powers of native leadership were maintained or even strengthened in such domestic matters, in contrast to external relations, because of support from Christian ideology.

After the establishment of the reservations, Chinookans were not involved in warfare or raiding along the Columbia or to the north in Washington. Reference has already been made to Paiute raids on the Warm Springs Reservation and to participation of the Warm Springs Scouts in U.S. military campaigns against the Paiutes and the Modocs. There was no further fighting until a few individuals were recruited during World War I.

During the campaigns against other Indians, certain Wasco cultural patterns relating to warfare were maintained (Sapir 1909: 205–27). For example, the Modoc fighting was preceded by dancing of the traditional type. In addition, some of the men who fought and who were leaders had the special supernatural powers for invulnerability. When no fighting was under way, these men were feared by other Indians in their own community because they were aggressive, self-confident, and perhaps irresponsible. Presumably due to White influence, the practice of establishing one's own invulnerability through self-inflicted wounds was not maintained. Also abandoned were bows and arrows and other weapons less efficient than guns.

Data from this cultural period make it possible to amplify the previous brief reference to class structure. The four classes were defined on the basis of differing criteria; perhaps the easiest way to under-

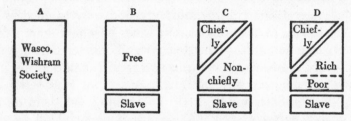

Fig. 1.–Wasco-Wishram class structure

stand the structure is to focus on the system of distinctions involved in it. In Figure 1, the whole society (A) can be seen as having consisted of two groups: the free people and the slaves (B). This was the most fundamental distinction in the system. Next in importance was the distinction between the chiefs and their families on the one hand and the rest of the free people on the other (C). The final distinction was between the poor and rich non-chiefly families (D), with some of the latter not only being wealthier than certain chiefly families (Spier and Sapir 1930: 211–12), but having high prestige of a somewhat different sort. To illustrate, one role available to members of the rich families was that of "statesman," to use an informant's term, indicating forms of leadership that emphasized performance rather than hereditary position. Movement from one class to another occurred, but the data suggest that, during the nineteenth century, such movement was largely confined to the two middle groups. The chiefly and the slave groups were separated from the others by caste-like distinctions.

In the search for a spouse within one's class it was common to select from outside groups, such as Sahaptin families.

Political and economic conditions following the establishment of the reservations led to a growing discrepancy between the native conception of the class system and the network of relationships between the actual Wasco-Wishram families. Enough marriages crossed class and ethnic lines that it became difficult to rank the descendants. New bases for prestige existed along with the old ones.

Slavery persisted until well into the reservation period. For example, the Warm Springs agent reported in 1869 that the Wascos were holding eighteen Pit River slaves sold to them by the Klamath several years earlier. At that time, two other Pit Rivers had already left the reservation and were working in The Dalles (Mitchell 1869). Under federal law, slavery was illegal in these years following the Civil War, and this in part effected the freeing of the Indian slaves. In addition to those who moved to off-reservation localities such as The Dalles, there were others who returned to their original tribes. The remainder stayed on the reservations as legal residents with low prestige.

The bilateral kinship structuring imputed to the Wasco and Wishram during Period II is adequately documented for the present period (Spier and Sapir 1930: 262–66). It is doubtful on theoretical grounds whether any important changes took place between Periods II and III; certainly there were no such changes within the later years of the third cultural period. Both the Whites and the Sahaptins, who were the outside groups of greatest importance to the Chinookans, had kinship systems which were roughly similar. Contacts with Whites were not of such a nature that the differences in details of kinship terminology were brought into sharp focus; the terms were not particularly vulnerable to processes of change. One of the four Chinookan grandparent-grandchild reciprocal terms was sometimes replaced by a Sahaptin term (Spier and Sapir 1930: 262, 263). Sahaptin-Chinookan bilingualism was sufficiently common that such Sahaptin alternatives also existed in other aspects of the terminology for social relationships, for example, in regard to ceremonialism.

The move to the reservation, intermarriage, illegitimacy, and the imposition of White legal principles could all be "handled" by the Chinookan bilateral system. The fact that the kinship terminology could be extended indefinitely provided "emergency" arrangements for the mobilization of relatives.

Both inheritance and residence were flexible enough in the traditional culture to present no difficulties in the face of White-derived changes. Sometimes the traditional patrilocal residence pattern could be preserved on the reservations. White pressures toward individual parcels of land and small households functioned to encourage neolocal residence; comparable deviations from the patrilocal pattern had evidently occurred for some time among the Chinookans. The increase in neolocal residence was not accompanied by a disappearance of extended family relationships.

To sum up, within the third period ("modified Wasco-Wishram culture") family structures and functions changed less than many other aspects of the culture; by inference, they represented persistences of even older sociocultural regularities.

Life Cycle.—The Whites lacked the resources or the motivation to modify Wasco and Wishram birth practices appreciably during this period. Expectant fathers and mothers continued to avoid certain activities and engage in others in order to protect and influence the destiny of the child. Omens were still associated with childbirth (Spier and Sapir 1930: 255). Head-flattening became less and less frequent and was abandoned during the period; cradleboards continued to be used. The use of wooden masks to frighten disobedient children (Spier and Sapir 1930: 257) was discontinued.

Certain life cycle ceremonies persisted unchanged throughout the period, others were sponsored by fewer and fewer families, and still others were abandoned. A typical pattern for a life cycle ceremony involved a dinner by the host family for any visitors, including non-Chinookans, who chose to attend (cf. Spier and Sapir 1930: 258–62). Gifts were distributed to the guests. Sometimes the latter responded by dancing in honor of the one whose status was changing; speeches were also made by guests. On certain occasions gift exchanges rather than gift distributions occurred.

The life cycle ceremony marking the acquisition or change of a name was one of those which was mentioned for the previous cultural period, but which could not be documented at that time level. Evidently there was little change in naming practices during this third period. However, the ceremonial piercing of children's ears for the insertion of ornaments became less frequent during the latter part of the period (cf. Spier and Sapir 1930: 261). This meant the abandonment of the ceremony for infants; the ears of the girls, at least, were still pierced, but often not until adolescence.

Ceremonies marking a child's first performance of an important economic task, for example, catching a salmon, may have been somewhat less frequent as the period progressed. The girl's puberty ceremony was abandoned by all or almost all families; this loss may be related to the fact that the Sahaptins had previously paid little formal attention to puberty. Sahaptins performed ritual activities corresponding to all the other ceremonies mentioned for the Wascos and Wishrams; participation as guests in the Sahaptin activities may have facilitated the continuation of ceremonial performances by the Chinookans themselves.

The tasks set for children began to change as the period progressed; for example, fewer parents hired old men to instruct their children, discipline them, and send them on power quests.

In contrast to the Sahaptins, whose children attended school only sporadically during the period, Wasco families were quite conscientious about sending their children to school. The fact that many of them lived near the agency may have facilitated this at first, but education came to be appreciated as providing means for dealing with Whites in general while satisfying the expectations of the agency personnel. Day schools and a boarding school were built at Warm Springs. Children from the reservation were also sent to a western Oregon boarding school located first near Forest Grove and then at Chemawa, near Salem.

The Indian agents perceived a system of bride purchase in Chinookan wedding practices and worked to institute changes. The native system of gift exchange persisted throughout the period but was evidently modified in particular instances (Commissioner of Indian Affairs 1872: 366). The expectations regarding the activities of potential spouses undoubtedly changed with other changes in the economy, for example, a successful young farmer was seen as a desirable son-in-law. Polygyny persisted in wealthy and chiefly families until late in the nineteenth century. Its abandonment was regarded as a victory by Whites on the reservations; it had been viewed by them as one of the most conspicuous examples of barbarous practices among the Indians (Meacham 1875: 165, 174–77; Commissioner of Indian Affairs 1872: 366).

Although the activities of mature and elderly people may not have changed greatly, respect for them as exemplars of ideal behavior and as sources of valued knowledge undoubtedly declined.

Religious changes influenced some of the practices associated with death. For example, the Longhouse Religion (discussed below) included new mourning practices, such as songs to be sung before the burial. The depositing of bodies on islands in the Columbia persisted well into the period among those living along the river. On the reservations, burial in cemeteries, and other White-derived practices, became the norm.

Ceremonials, Supernaturalism, Curing.—In the later years of this period much of Chinookan ceremonial activity was carried out jointly with Sahaptins; the latter were usually the hosts. For example, those living at Spearfish ceased to hold First Salmon Ceremonies but continued to participate in the ones held by Sahaptins at Celilo Falls.

As in the previous period, guardian spirits were of greater significance to the Wascos and Wishrams than any other form of supernatural being. Among anthropomorphic spirits were water monsters and cannibal women (Spier and Sapir 1930: 236–38); nothing was recorded from the period regarding the blind humanoids of Mount Hood. Evidently, supernatural figures associated with Christianity either assumed no great reality for the Wasco and Wishram or else were assimilated to guardian spirit ideas; clearly formulated theistic concepts were not characteristic of the other religions in which the Wasco and Wishram participated (cf. Jacobs 1955: 289).

The details of the shamanism–guardian spirit complex did not change greatly during the course of the period; the changes were principally on other levels: the nature and extent of participation in the complex. Not only were the missionaries and Indian agents vigorously opposed, but shamanistic curing was even declared illegal, and arrests were made. More significant was the fact that shamanism was usually defined by the Indians as inconsistent with the new cultural systems in which they were participating. Many Indian converts to Christianity ceased to participate in the complex; certain converts to the Shaker Church and to the Feather Religion evidently behaved similarly. (The latter two religions, having curing aspects, were alternatives to shamanistic medicine.) While older Wascos and Wishrams continued to sing power songs and to become shamans, fewer children had guardian spirit experiences in the latter part of the period.

Sweat bathing was employed for purification as well as for curing. In addition to the cures by use of plant materials, which are to be expected in any American Indian group, cures and other concrete ends were sought by means of secret verbal formulas. No data are available on changes in these non-shamanistic practices, but it is to be presumed that they decreased somewhat in frequency. White medicine began to be important to the Indians as the period progressed (Commissioner of Indian Affairs 1875: 355).

A complex of religious practices, involving singing, dancing, and prophecy, was widespread in the area during the nineteenth century. Spier (1935) decided that this complex showed Christian influence but had an aboriginal base, which he named the Prophet Dance. Evidently, the Sahaptins who moved to the Warm Springs Reservation, as well as the Yakimas, were already followers of forms of this complex (for example, see Wyeth 1899: 247–48). About 1870 some of the Sahaptins at Warm Springs became influenced by the teachings of Smohalla, a prophet of the central Washington area who had "returned to life" with vigorous new teachings (Meacham 1875: 155, 156; 1878*b:* 82; Commissioner of Indian Affairs 1872: 362, 365). The Smohalla form of the religious complex was nativistic and anti-White (Meacham 1878*b:* 82; Mooney 1896: 716–31). In time, the Smohalla movement began to decrease in militancy and to merge again with other Prophet Dance-type religious activities. It is convenient to refer to all of the later nineteenth century forms as the "Longhouse Religion," on the basis of the more or less aboriginal structures in which meetings were held.

It is not clear whether forms of the Prophet Dance or Longhouse Religion existed among the Wasco or Wishram at any time prior to the last quarter of the nineteenth century. If not, however, it is easy to identify a basis in the religion of the previous period for the adoption of the Longhouse Religion (cf. Spier and Sapir 1930: 251–54). For example, reference was made to the "active supernatural world," to the First Salmon Ceremony, and to a preoccupation with death, all of which were prominent in the Longhouse Religion.

The second half of this period was a time of religious conversions among Wascos and Wishrams. Modern informants believe that the latter part of the nineteenth century, rather than earlier, was the time of the establishment of the Longhouse Religion among the Chinookans. The Wishrams were more affected than were the Wascos; with

Sahaptin instruction, according to informants, they began to hold "worship dance" ceremonies in longhouses of their own. Sahaptins often joined them in the services. During the first part of this century there were three longhouses in use at Spearfish, and they also existed on the Oregon side of the Columbia, for example, at Hood River. There is no evidence that Wascos erected longhouses of their own at Warm Springs, but they participated with Sahaptins.

A Klickitat named Jake Hunt began to preach a new version of the Longhouse Religion following a supernatural experience about 1904 (DuBois 1938: 21–22). Since he had been a member of the Shaker religion, it is not surprising that curing was part of his new Feather Religion ceremonialism. Traveling from reservation to reservation, he made a number of converts, including Wascos at Warm Springs. Wishrams were also converted, perhaps especially during the final years of Jake Hunt's life when he was living at Spearfish. The Feather Religion, except for the curing, was essentially a variant of the Longhouse Religion; Chinookan participation in it can be interpreted as a clear case of Sahaptin influence on them.

Modern informants indicate that the Chinookans who were participating in Feather-Longhouse activities were overtly nativistic. They were emphasizing their Indian ancestry, but were doing so in conjunction with a group they recognized to be more Indian than they were. The Sahaptins were sometimes called the "chosen people" or "first people" by the Wishrams, since they were recipients of special instructions from the supernatural world. Chinookan participation was unstable in that it required nativistic motivation and an identification with Sahaptins, both of which were intermittent. It is not surprising then that late in the period other religions and secular activities began to supplant Longhouse-Feather activities for most of the Wascos and Wishrams.

The Shaker religion was older than the Feather Religion, having been founded by a Puget Sound Salish Indian on the basis of a supernatural experience in the early 1880's (Gunther 1949; Barnett 1957: 3–44 ff.). This religion spread slowly and began to be important to Wascos and Wishrams in the early part of the twentieth century. Once conversions began at Yakima, along the Columbia, and at Warm Springs, the other revealed religions began to lose members to the Shakers. For example, regular Sunday services in one of the Longhouses at Spearfish ceased about 1915 because so many participants had become Shakers.

One focus of activity in the Shaker religion is curing. While this is analogous to shamanistic curing, in that supernatural power is involved, group rather than individual activity is the basis for the therapy. Both in paraphernalia—such as candles—and in morality—for example, rules against smoking and drinking—the Shaker religion reveals strong Christian influence. In some of its manifestations Shakerism could even be called a form of Christianity, but the Indians viewed it as a separate revelation. There is an ambiguity here which may have been functional for the Wasco and Wishram: on the one hand, they could perceive their religious activity as Christian and White-oriented; on the other hand, the Indian origin of the religion supported the separate identity of Indians (cf. Pope 1953). Which aspect was dominant varied in accordance with situational demands.

All of the Wascos and Wishrams participated in one or another of the revealed religions (cf. Smith 1878). After the middle of the period, Christianity had become the residual category; those who were not active converts to Shakerism or a Longhouse group were Christians. As a matter of fact, many regarded themselves as affiliated with more than one of the revealed religions. Christianity itself became stabilized by the end of the period; while it was no longer increasing in importance, neither was it disappearing.

Art, Recreation.—A few art forms disappeared during this period. More commonly the knowledge of the activity persisted, but the frequency of its occurrence decreased with the passage of time. The number of new art forms was small, considering the rapidity of change in the culture.

With the disappearance of the earlier woodworking technology—associated with housing, canoes, household utensils, shamanism, and death—was a disappearance of the carving and painting which had embellished the articles. The use of quills in decoration also disappeared.

Although fewer baskets were made in the later years of the period, traditional decoration persisted. The same point can be made regarding the songs and instrumental music accompanying shamanism and other ritual activity: the forms persisted but occurred less frequently.

The singing and dancing connected with Shakerism and the other religions were, of course, new to Chinookan culture. Recreational and quasi-recreational songs and dances continued to be diffused to Yakima, Spearfish, and Warm Springs as part of a westward spread of Plains traits. Items of costume and other decorations in Plains style also increased (cf. Gunther 1950). A related process was an increase in the amount of beadwork, resembling that of the Plains in general.

Oral literature was not mentioned for the previous period because documentation was lacking. During the third period both Wasco and Wishram myths and tales were recorded by Curtin and by Sapir (1907; 1909). A conspicuous feature was a recounting of the travels of Coyote up the Columbia River; he tricked as well as helped the myth-age people and announced certain characteristics of the world of humans that was to follow. In general, Wasco and Wishram myths have few features not widely distributed in the region (Sapir 1907). There are no data on changes in oral literature during the period.[6]

The number of types of native games, including gambling games, decreased with the passage of time. Horse racing and the bone (or stick) game continued to prove fascinating and to serve as important ways for members of different groups to interact. Certain individuals refrained completely from gambling, as well as drinking, in the name of religious regulations; it would be difficult to assess the over-all frequency of these activities.

Language.—The multilingualism previously mentioned continued during this period. Many adult Wascos and Wishrams knew English and the local type of Sahaptin in addition to their native speech and Chinook Jargon. (Sahaptins and Whites rarely, if ever, learned Chinookan, incidentally.) A few Wascos and Wishrams learned even more distant languages, such as Nez Percé, which were useful for visiting and trading. There was prestige attached to knowing languages and perhaps aesthetic satisfaction; while serving as an army scout, one Wasco learned a certain amount of Delaware from a fellow scout. While this was not a "practical" accomplishment, it provided a basis for pride and prestige.

Linguistic materials gathered during the period (Sapir 1909; Curtis 1911) reveal that a number of vocabulary items had been added. No single process dominated Chinookan linguistic acculturation. There

---

[6] Jacobs (personal communication) has commented: "I believe strongly that in your third period myths were retained while tales tended to be forgotten. Myths were Indianist, ego-enhancing, still possessed of glamor and truth. Tales were not ego-enhancing by comparison."

were new coinages using native morphemes, borrowings from English and Sahaptin, and the addition of new meanings to old forms.

THE CULTURE AS A WHOLE

At the conclusion of the last period a series of points about the economy and the sociopolitical structure was made. The changes which occurred during the third period were of such a nature that these generalizations were still more or less "true" but had become less significant. To illustrate: the Wascos and Wishrams were still fishermen who engaged in trade and who did not emphasize the boundaries between themselves and others. However, the culture had been modified by losses in content and by the addition of a series of new complexes derived from Euro-American culture. These related to farming, to domestic life, and to ideological activities.

In contrast to the end of the previous period, losses had occurred in the content of Wasco and Wishram culture which were "permanent." Many earlier Indian techniques were no longer understood by the average adult.

The variant of European culture to which the Wascos and Wishrams were most thoroughly exposed had agriculture (principally stock and grain ranching, rather than farming) as its focal activity. Many of the Indians learned to act in a way that approximated this cultural pattern quite closely. Other, more "urban," variants of European culture were becoming important to the Whites and these in turn were to influence the Indians during the years that followed.

The learning of White culture was accompanied by changes in self-conceptions. The outward form of these changes could be quite dramatic, consisting as they did of public "conversions" to the White way of life. The instances cited in the literature are of individuals who became Christians, but the conversions included more than Christianity. The converts said, "From this point on I will be a White man" (Meacham 1875: 172–79; cf. Meacham 1878a: 6). In certain situations indeed they were "White" in culture.

The Chinookans who had been "educated" in a White sense were among those who were admired and respected by the Wascos and the Wishrams. Ironically, perhaps, one reason for admiring them was that they were able to use their White-derived education in defense of Indians against White encroachments. It should be noted, however, that the admiration was new only in relation to the kinds of information possessed by the educated person. The Chinookans had long admired those who possessed knowledge, for instance, of other languages and customs, even when the knowledge was not immediately useful.

To an increasing extent, the activities defined as Indian in which the Wascos and Wishrams engaged were limited to those which were shared with the Sahaptins. Indian culture in general was giving way to that of the Whites, but the presence of the Sahaptins, who remained a significant group to the Chinookans, contributed to the maintenance of certain of the Indian cultural systems.

Period IV: Part-Time Indian Culture

Three characteristics mark the Chinookan culture during this final period, 1920[7] to the present: (1) the Indians were enmeshed in the money-oriented economy of the Northwest; (2) the Chinookan "communities" on the reservations had so dwindled in importance that the Wascos and Wishrams were about as likely to interact with Sahaptins or Whites in any given situation as they were with Chinookans; and (3) in many situations, the Chinookans did not behave like Indians at all.

No cultural crisis comparable to the one in the mid-nineteenth century accompanied the opening of the period. The transition was gradual, with certain individuals and families beginning to display the above characteristics even before World War I, and with others continuing to exemplify the modified Indian culture of Period III well past 1920. Heterogeneity characterized Chinookan culture during both the nineteenth and twentieth centuries; except sporadically in such areas as religion, a person could act in a thoroughly Indian or a thoroughly White manner without eliciting serious negative sanctions from others. As a consequence, it is impossible to sketch *the* culture of the period. The name for the period, "Part-Time Indian Culture," refers to the fact that all of the Chinookans act on occasion as Whites act, and yet all act as Indians in other contexts.

SETTLEMENT PATTERN, MOBILITY

The beginning of this period was not marked by radical changes in patterns of settlement. During the period, no new types of localities

---

[7] The year 1920 has been chosen as an arbitrary date for the beginning of the fourth cultural period. This period is presumably still continuing, since there are no obvious criteria for marking its close. Statements in the present tense refer to 1955, the year preceding the seminar which stimulated this volume; they hold equally well for the time of writing, two years later.

became important as places of residence for Indians. However, families and individuals shifted rather frequently from one to another of the possibilities: Spearfish, Celilo, the reservations, off-reservation farms, and such urban centers as Portland. This mobility might begin at an early age; children who were sent away to schools (for example, Chemawa in western Oregon) were then often employed by a series of White families as domestics and laborers.

On the reservations, White-introduced systems for ownership and use of land had yielded a moderate degree of stability in family residence. However, families or family members frequently came to have rights to more than one piece of land and more than one house; alternation between them became common. As a result of intermarriage, complexities of inheritance, and the like, the neat geographic segregation of the "tribes" on the Warm Springs Reservation became blurred. For example, the area near the Warm Springs Agency was no longer occupied primarily by Wascos. After 1930 the population in this area increased markedly, partly in response to new opportunities for wage work. A typical Euro-American town did not develop, however. Houses were built in clusters, sometimes called "villages" by the Indians. The location of the clusters has often been determined by the location of public utilities: water and power lines. The composition of the clusters has been determined by no single factor. Relatives sometimes live side by side, but neighbors may have nothing more in common than the fact that they both needed an agency area house at a time when a new plot of land became available for building. No single section of the area has been utilized for White-owned stores, service stations, and restaurants, with the result that these are scattered from the agency across the eastern reservation boundary.

In 1949, a major highway linking Portland with eastern Oregon was completed through the reservation. Few of the through travelers stop, except to patronize the White restaurants and service stations; in general, the highway has made little difference to the Indians, except to facilitate automobile travel for them. Even with less adequate roads, the Indians have long been going by automobile to and from their farms and places of employment. A typical Wasco family today may live near the agency and have one or more members working for wages for a lumber company or the government. Farming operations can still be carried on even by the wage workers after a short drive to a piece of land owned by a family member.

Modified forms of the traditional annual cycle for fishing, hunting, and gathering are still followed by some families. These activities, along with agricultural wage work in western Oregon, can now take place easily and with little or no advance planning. For example, after finishing her housework, a woman can decide to load the children in the car and go out for an afternoon of root-digging. Families "run down to The Dalles" to get some fish.

THE WASCO AND WISHRAM GROUPS

In 1950 census records,[8] 485 persons (244 men and 241 women) are listed as at least partly Wasco in ancestry; this is just over 47 per cent of the total reservation enrolment. Of these 485, however, only 64 have no other Indian "mixture," though some are partly White in ancestry. There are 335 persons designated Wasco and Sahaptin in varying degrees. The remaining 86 are descendants of marriages with Paiutes, non-local Indians, and other non-Whites. From the point of view of this study it is important to note that these census figures are a more or less accurate reflection of a person's ancestry but give no reliable indication about his present cultural identity or affiliation.

SIGNIFICANT OUTSIDERS

It would be impractical as well as unnecessary to discuss, or even list, all of the kinds of outsiders known to the present-day Chinook-ans. They have learned many of the ways in which Whites categorize non-Indians, and their attitudes toward the categories are similar to those held by Whites in Oregon and Washington. All of the Indian groups in the Northwest region discussed in previous sections are still familiar to most adults; of these only Plateau Sahaptins and Paiutes are of any great significance, however. Paiutes from Burns and Sahap-tins from reservations to the east continue to visit Warm Springs and Yakima during celebrations. The Paiute group at Warm Springs has dwindled in size but occupies a stable position in the social system of the reservation.

The mass media of communication, as well as other mechanisms dis-cussed previously, have brought other Indians in the United States to the attention of the Chinookans. Pan-Indian attitudes are transitory, however, among Chinookans—in part because of the isolation of the

---

[8] These figures were compiled by Kathrine French from original records at the Warm Springs Agency. Comparable figures for Wishrams were not obtained at Yak-ima, and published U.S. Decennial figures no longer indicate "tribal" affiliation.

Northwest from major centers of modern Indian activity and in part because political consciousness is not highly developed in any modality of Chinookan life.

The frequency of intermarriage has increased to such an extent that at Warm Springs in recent years a majority of Wascos are married to non-Wascos. In a great many of these cases the marriages are to other Indians, such as Sahaptins and Paiutes, and these marriages are the occasion for no special comment. The relations between the families of the bride and the groom are approximately the same as they would be within, say, the Sahaptin or Chinookan populations. This is an illustration of the fact that the reservation, rather than the linguistic grouping, has become the effective subsociety. Wascos and Wishrams living away from the reservations and away from Spearfish have often married non-Indians. Such spouses tend to be members of other minority groups, for example, Oriental- and Mexican-Americans. At least two Wasco men have married middle-class White women. These families are living on the Warm Springs Reservation, as are those of several of the other mixed marriages.

One result of past marriages with Sahaptins, for example with the Tenino group near the Warm Springs agency, has often been the loss of Chinookan culture, including language. Particularly when the woman of an intermarrying pair has been Sahaptin, the children have been raised to speak her language, as well as English, but they have learned only a smattering of Chinookan. In another generation, Wasco culture, if not identity, is gone.

The Chinookans have now become familiar with a much larger number of cultural types among Whites than earlier. These include not only the rural people of eastern Oregon who were significant during Period III, but also business and professional people, laborers, and technicians. White prejudice and discrimination have continued to provide barriers to participation in certain Euro-American activities, though these barriers are not especially strong near the reservations or elsewhere in the Northwest. A marked change in relations with Whites is the near disappearance of the zeal for the rapid acculturation of the Indians on the part of the Whites on the reservations.

With about 150 years of contact with the Whites, and with Chinookans now displaying so many cultural characteristics which are similar to those of the Whites, it would evoke little surprise in an anthropological context if the Chinookans as a group were to be labeled "quite acculturated." An attempt might be made, furthermore, to classify individuals into groups ranging from the most acculturated to the least acculturated, indicating the defining characteristics of each class. Such an approach has sufficient utility and familiarity that it was found convenient to employ it in minor ways in this case study. An analogous kind of thinking would be involved if notice were to be taken of the frequency with which Chinookans not only interacted with Sahaptins but also displayed cultural regularities similar to those of the Sahaptins; a strong case could be made for the proposition that the "more Indian" of the Chinookans had become "assimilated into" the Sahaptin group. There is no doubt that a degree of identification with Sahaptins is present, for example, in many ceremonial contexts. Furthermore, self-conceptions in a broader sense appear to be involved: Wishrams, for example, will often label themselves as "Yakima" on first acquaintance. On the other hand, in contexts in which comparisons are being made, Chinookans may still proudly identify themselves as Wascos or Wishrams—this behavior occurs even with those whose knowledge of Chinookan culture and speech is scanty. On the question of establishing classes based on "degree of acculturation," there would be great difficulty in dealing adequately with the fact that the behavior of a given individual varies from that which is "very Indian" to that which is "hardly Indian at all." Even establishing subclasses within the acculturation classes would not permit a satisfactory interpretation of the types of variability displayed today among the Chinookans.

Throughout this case study, variability in the behavior of individuals and variability between individuals has often been handled by relating the differing kinds of behavior to differing kinds of situations, as defined by participants. Such attention to the situational contexts for behavior, taken alone, is inadequate. Further theoretical constructs are necessary to understand why the Chinookans appear to be inconsistent in their definitions of situations. For example, it is not clear why the apparently most acculturated of the Chinookans do not always define situations as White persons would; similarly, those whose behavior is often quite Indian will inexplicably act like Whites in a situation which, "objectively" defined, appears to call for Indian behavior.

At various times in the preceding pages, it has been suggested that the local Sahaptins, and subsequently also the Whites, were of special significance to the Chinookans. It has been implied that the Wasco and Wishram often act with reference to these Sahaptins and the Whites. It is now time to discuss a conceptual framework or approach —that of reference groups—which has been used as a general orientation.

Reference group theory was initiated by Hyman (1942) and has been elaborated by other social psychologists and sociologists.[9] This approach is concerned with the sociocultural determinants of behavior, but it is not limited to analyzing relationships between the actor and groups of which he is a member. On the basis of both empirical research and theoretical considerations, it has become clear that actors frequently make comparative judgments with regard to their own situation by using others who are unlike themselves as reference points. This does not necessarily mean that they imitate, take the roles of, or model themselves after members of the other group. They may, in fact, make unfavorable comparative judgments regarding the other group, which then provides examples of behavior to be avoided. Groups to which the actor belongs can also serve as reference groups.

Apparent inconsistencies in Chinookan behavior may be made comprehensible by assuming that every Chinookan, from the "least acculturated" to the "most acculturated," commonly uses three points of reference: Chinookan, Sahaptin, and White. Depending upon how he categorizes a situation, a Chinookan will employ one or more of these in making evaluations, for example, regarding appropriate behavior at an Indian celebration. It is with decreasing frequency that the Chinookans consider only the behavior of other Chinookans in relation to their own; the employment of Sahaptin and White reference groups has increased in importance with the passage of time.

In order to indicate the kind of reference group the Sahaptins provide, it would be useful to list some of the characteristics attributed

---

[9] The writer is indebted to John Pock for suggesting the use of this approach. An excellent introduction to the literature on reference groups is provided by Merton (1957: 225–386). An article by Turner (1956) is also of special significance. Beginnings have been made in utilizing the concept in the study of non-American cultures (Eisenstadt 1954); papers employing the reference group approach have been read at scholarly meetings (e.g., Basehart 1956; Hughes 1957), but the adaptation of the approach to anthropology has scarcely begun.

"Reference point" seems preferable to "reference group" as a general term, since the objects of reference for behavior can be symbols, institutions, persons, and other cultural structures not subsumed under the term group (cf. Merton 1957: 302 *et passim*). In these pages, however, "reference group" is practically always quite appropriate.

to Sahaptins by Wascos and Wishrams in the course of field research: they are viewed as physically large and strong, untidy, gregarious, clannish, irresponsible, "nomadic," slow to learn, conservative, uncivilized, and above all "Indian." The statements on which this list was based were almost all made in a comparative context, with explicit comparisons with Chinookans being frequent.

The Chinookan definitions of White characteristics were less often made explicit, possibly because of the group membership of the field workers. Whites are "set in their ways." They work hard but are faced with responsibilities, such as heavy taxes, which Indians may avoid. They possess power and knowledge. They are trustworthy in business dealings; on the other hand, they frequently break promises, as exemplified by treaties with Indians.

The Chinookan picture of their own group changes with changing contexts. In general, they regard themselves as less "Indian" than the Sahaptins and less "civilized" than the Whites.

The utility of reference group concepts in reconciling apparent inconsistencies in Chinookan behavior may be suggested by an example. Suppose that shamanism is mentioned in the course of a conversation between a Wasco and a White agency employee. If, as is likely, the Chinookan employs the Whites as a reference standpoint, he may say something like, "Some of them [certain Indians] are still pretty superstitious. They still follow the old ways." This would be an honest reflection of his attitudes in that context. Now suppose this same Wasco were to be invited by a friend to attend a winter power ceremony. On arriving, he finds that participation is general; Indian norms, best exemplified by Sahaptins, are operating. With Sahaptins as a reference group, and defining himself as a member of the reservation community, he may participate in the singing and dancing. He would not exclude the possibility that he might have a supernatural experience while a shaman is singing.

The anthropologists of fifty years ago frequently predicted that in a relatively few years the cultural identity of groups like the Wascos and Wishrams would be gone. Perhaps at this point some light can be thrown on why it has persisted to the extent that it has. In contrast to some of the Indian groups considered in this volume, Chinookan identity is not being sustained to any appreciable extent by allusion to a heroic past; nor is it any longer being sustained by frequent, meaningful interactions between Chinookans. It seems relevant, however, that the Chinookans quite frequently refer to the Sahaptins as being like the Chinookans of some distant time in the past. The Sahaptins are serving in comparative situations to define that which is Indian. The Whites provide a contrasting reference point. The existence of a distinct Chinookan identity today is being interpreted here as being to a large extent a function of the existence (from the point of view of the Chinookans) of *more than one* contrasting outside point of reference. The integrity and maintenance of the Chinookan identity have been contingent upon the routinization of these outside anchorage points.

Both Sahaptin and White cultures have been changing, yet changes in Chinookan behavior do not consistently follow one pattern or the other. Neither is the emerging Chinookan behavior to be considered some kind of compromise between the two. It can be suggested that the analysis of Chinookan cultural change, as well as the synchronic analysis of a particular time level, is enhanced by the reference group concept. The use of reference group theory appears to be compatible with the "levels of integration" approach (Steward 1955), which has often been implicit in this case study. Such a combination has implications for what is meant by "cultural change." Activities that are viewed as "change" may amount to "shifts" from one sphere (level) of activity to another with appropriate shifts in reference points. Diachronically considered, when these "shifts" are more readily and more frequently made, or when they have become differentiated, "cultural change" has occurred.[10] The relevance of reference group theory to cultural integration and dynamics is further explored in the concluding sections of this study.

THE REST OF THE CULTURE

Technology, Economy.—The pattern of utilization of wild plants has changed markedly; younger people, especially, may not take the trouble to gather wild foods at all. For most others, gathering has become a spare-time activity of no real consequence. A few older women, however, still dig as many roots and pick as many berries as possible during the season.

The number of species gathered has been sharply reduced. The

[10] In effect, this means that a "new" cultural item has been "created" because it calls for subsequent rearrangement, which a synchronic analysis would reveal (cf. Steward 1955). (This suggestion and others regarding the paragraph above were made by John Pock.)

only roots still dug by Wascos with any regularity are bitterroot, *Lomatium canbyi*, *Lomatium cous*, and *Perideridia gairdneri*. Of the fruits, only one type of huckleberry (*Vaccinium membranaceum*) and chokecherries are still picked with any frequency at all.

Farming changed little until after World War II, when it became almost completely mechanized. Farmers not only own trucks and tractors nowadays, but many of them also own combines for threshing grain. With changes in transportation, marketing, and food preservation, few if any Chinookans plant gardens any longer.

Despite decreasing utility, horses in appreciable numbers are still raised. Cattle are of far greater monetary importance; with government assistance, the quality of the herds has improved steadily during recent years.

The percentage of Wascos and Wishrams engaged in farming or ranching has decreased since the previous cultural period. Cash, rather than subsistence, has increasingly been the motive for this activity, as is also the case with other economic endeavors. Canneries along the Columbia River began to buy fish from Indians even before the beginning of the final period. Following World War I, an increasing number of Chinookans abandoned farming and other activities in order to specialize in one form or another of commercial fishing.

Indian fishing by traditional methods has been protected by the treaties. Even with scaffolds and nets, which are slight modifications of the aboriginal types, it has been possible for a fisherman to earn, say, one hundred dollars a day during the height of the season. It is also possible for a man to catch enough fish during a week end to provide for the needs of his family throughout the winter. It is not surprising that Wascos and Wishrams still know an amazing amount about the various kinds of salmon and the appropriate uses for each part of each type. The building of a major dam at The Dalles during the 1950's will, however, almost erase the importance of fishing.

An old Wasco man who died in 1951 had supplemented his diet to quite an extent by hunting, mainly deer, even in his later years. For most other Wascos and Wishrams, however, hunting has become an occasional activity involving only a few of the animals and birds once hunted. It is probable that the remaining ones include no types of game that Whites do not also hunt.

A few women still make buckskin from deer hides by traditional methods that include the use of animal brains, and even tools with chipped stone heads, in the softening process. Buckskin is made into moccasins, gloves, and other articles, often with beadwork decoration. Some women obtain their hides and buckskin from other Indians; leather tanned by Whites is also purchased sometimes for use in making Indian-style articles. The making of buckskin items is a specialty on the Warm Springs Reservation and has persisted long after the abandonment of basket-making and most other native techniques of manufacture. Many families, however, cherish Indian artifacts they have inherited or received through trading.

Although the overwhelming majority of Wascos or Wishrams dress like the White residents of the area, some variability is still present. Very old people still wear moccasins regularly. A special jumper, known as a wing dress and worn over an inner dress, identifies a few older women as followers of the Longhouse-Feather Religions. Middle-aged and older women do not cut their hair; they commonly cover it with a bright kerchief. While there are no longer men with braids, some of the oldest wear their hair longer in back than do Whites. Especially at times of celebration, many women wear expensive "Indian-style" shawls and beads; some of their jewelry originates in the Southwest. When participating in dances, young people as well as older men and women often wear Plains-derived costumes. Many more Sahaptins than Chinookans have long hair and customarily wear moccasins, wing dresses, and other articles of clothing that mark them as Indian.

As might be expected, vocational specialization among Chinookans increased during this period, and many now work in semiskilled positions, such as driving trucks for the two commercial lumber companies that are permitted to cut timber on the Warm Springs Reservation. Occasionally they go into business for a brief period, for example, service station management; one man attempted to operate independently as a barber. Such business and service activities, however, do not last long because of problems of credit and motivation discussed previously.

Once the Chinookans became involved in commercial fishing and farming, they were affected by national and regional economic fluctuations. For example, the depression of the 1930's was a difficult time for many families, but the employment opportunities provided by the Indian Civilian Conservation Corps and a return to traditional subsistence activities alleviated distress. The Indians shared in the generally prosperous conditions during and following World War II. Salmon brought good prices from the canneries. Those on the reservations benefited directly or indirectly from high or relatively high prices paid for lumber, cattle, and grain. Per capita payments and increases in tribal treasuries from timber sales provided benefits supplementary to the direct gains from individual sales. A few Wascos and Wishrams are now well off, though not really wealthy. Welfare arrangements provided by the tribes, the federal government, and the states and counties have kept families at the lower end of the scale from suffering. There has been a decrease in traditional Indian "welfare" arrangements; old people, for example, are sometimes sent to nursing homes rather than being cared for by relatives.

As family income rose in recent years, so too did spending. A few Sahaptins and Chinookans in the area have bought powerful cars and other high-prestige consumers' goods. This kind of spending, however, is uncommon. Most automobiles are of the lower-priced makes, and many are secondhand. A new truck, or farm machinery, has taken the money that might have gone into a more expensive car. Gradually, families have been acquiring electric refrigerators and washing machines, in line with changing standards of household needs. Generally speaking, choices have been made in the direction of capital goods rather than prestige symbols.

In contrast to the Sahaptins, Wascos take pride in their houses when they conform to White standards. Consequently, there are houses that are not recognizably Indian, either from the outside or in regard to furnishings. Older farmhouses, shacks, and tents continue to be used, especially for supplementary housing.

Before closing this discussion of economic activity, it might be noted that Sahaptins periodically remind the Chinookans of the Indian way to accomplish a task—or define it for them—by using such things as wooden net hoops, lashed pole fishing scaffolds, or older types of horse equipment. Many Chinookans who work for wages and who have little to do with Indian material culture and subsistence activities could still employ many of these were appropriate occasions to arise.

Social Organization.—It should be clear that only in a restricted sense can the term "tribe" be applied to any Chinookan grouping or structure. As a matter of fact, behavior is about as likely to occur in terms of newer geographic groupings as in terms of the entities Wasco and Wishram. For example, Wascos, Paiutes, and Sahaptins living in the Warm Springs agency area sometimes form a co-operative group, in opposition to the Sahaptins living in the northern part of the reservation. Issues concerning the dates and the arrangements for the annual Root Feast and Berry Feast (first products ceremonies, plus rodeos, and other innovations) are debated between groupings having such a territorial base.

The ambiguities regarding the forms and principles of Chinookan leadership did not disappear during the fourth period. For example, it was not always clear whether or not there was a Wasco or a Wishram chief. Since such chiefs would have little power under any circumstance, the question was not really one of great importance and has been discussed by the Indians only sporadically. The political history of the Yakima Reservation as such was not examined in connection with this project, and the few points now to be made about Warm Springs may or may not apply to the Wishrams and to the Yakima Reservation. Wascos have continued to hold positions of leadership in regard to the reservation as a whole, not simply their own linguistic group. Following the acceptance of the Indian Reorganization Act by the Warm Springs residents in 1938, the Wasco membership on the elected Tribal Council has been out of proportion to their total numbers. Furthermore, most, if not all, the elected chairmen of the council have been Wascos. They are believed by everyone on the reservation to be better educated and to be more skilful in dealing with outsiders than Sahaptins or Paiutes.

Following an election, a man was formally installed in 1953 as Wasco chief, which gave him a lifetime position on the Tribal Council. His prestige and abilities were such that he was regarded as a suitable choice, even though many of the Wascos who voted for him were not certain of the nature of his claim to chiefly ancestry.

Although Whites have provided the context for warfare in the twentieth century, the traditional supernatural powers for danger are still attributed at times to veterans of World Wars I and II. The safe return of at least one Wasco veteran from World War II, with an enemy weapon as a trophy, was celebrated by his family with a ceremonial dinner and a distribution of gifts.

The traditional principles of class stratification continue to be one of the means whereby the Chinookans classify themselves and others. However, there have been enough generations in which marriages have crossed class and ethnic lines that practically every Chinookan has ancestors of high prestige as well as others without it. Consequently, there is the possibility for almost everyone to define his own position advantageously and that of anyone else disadvantageously. Principles of stratification are almost more important on a verbal level than they are in terms of the choice of one's associates and differential access to power, prestige, and possessions. Wascos or Wishrams today quite often call attention to their own "royal ancestry," that is, their descent from chiefs. Wealth in the family during past or present times is also a basis for pride. In speaking of the past, a Wishram said, "Rich people had the power. I like it that way." In other contexts, Chinookans make democratic statements comparable to those of most Americans in the region.

In a conceptual sense, slavery has not disappeared completely: to have had a slave ancestor is equivalent to having had a known Negro ancestor among White Americans in the North. The fact is "remembered" in certain critical situations and ignored in others.

It has already been suggested that there were never great differences between the Chinookan bilateral kinship system and that of the Sahaptins or the Euro-Americans. The similarity limits the kinds of changes to be expected. Now that English has become the customary language for the majority of those with Chinookan ancestry, English kin terms, both vocative and referential, are used. Moreover, this is not a literal rendering of the Chinookan terms into English; the Anglo-American system of distinctions is understood and used. By contrast, in speaking English a few older people may refer to a cousin as "brother" or "sister" following the Hawaiian-type Chinookan system. Chinookan speakers, especially men, now sometimes become confused about details of the original system. An increasing number of Sahaptin terms are used as alternatives for Chinookan ones. In general, when speaking Chinookan the kinship terminology of the nineteenth century is employed.

Residence continues to be determined by a variety of factors not contained within the kinship system. Households have grown smaller during the twentieth century, but family and other kinship obligations have not decreased correspondingly. Unattached people continue to live with their relatives, though not with the same frequency as formerly. Kin relationships that are still understood form the basis for a complex pattern of innovative and traditional behavior. For example, certain obligations to one's affinal kin are periodically observed. On the other hand, a man will sometimes use a Chinookan kin term to another man as if he were invoking a traditional relationship but with aggressive banter as his motive.

Life Cycle.—Birth and childhood are now dominated by Euro-American medical, nutritional, and educational practices. Omens and restrictions connected with birth are still remembered, but they are not taken seriously by younger people. Older relatives and the Indian midwives who are still employed on occasion are likely to perpetuate traditional customs; for example, part of an infant's umbilical cord may be preserved in a buckskin bag. Even some of the "most acculturated" families still use cradleboards.

Children are rarely named in the traditional ritual manner. Informally, they still receive Indian names inherited from ancestors; parents simply begin to call their children by such names without "paying the public" to sanction the act. Children are no longer disciplined and instructed by hired functionaries, told myths in a formal manner, or sent on power quests. Although Wascos and Wishrams rarely sponsor life-cycle ceremonies for their own children, the potentiality for them is maintained by Chinookan participation in Sahaptin ceremonies. If a Chinookan ceremony is desired at some future time even those familiar only with Sahaptin ceremonies can always "translate" them to Chinookan culture.

Throughout the period, the Indian expectation was that every child would attend school. Following World War II, arrangements were made so that Warm Springs students were enrolled in the public high school at Madras. A few individuals had attended college previously, but a system has now been established whereby students are supported by the tribe; those who do not graduate must repay the advances as if they had been loans, while the graduates repay nothing.

Most marriages today occur at the initiative of the couples themselves, ideally but not invariably with the consent and support of their relatives. At least one marriage in recent years, however, was arranged by an older woman in the traditional manner. Especially when Sahaptins are related to either the bride or the groom, the customary ceremonial exchange of gifts takes place; nowadays the exchange is expected to be an equal one.

One feature of the life of young people today which is somewhat difficult to assess is "the problem of deciding between Indian and

White ways." While they are still in school, they rarely define this as a serious problem. Subsequently, the feeling that there is a problem or conflict in this area sometimes waxes strong. Moves to Portland and other off-reservation areas may be interpreted by the young people themselves as mechanisms toward removing the stigma of being reservation Indians. That this is *defined* as a conflict situation, rather than *being* one in some objective or absolute sense, is demonstrated by the fact that no resolution to the conflict is ever achieved. Yet, as they pass through their twenties, Wascos and Wishrams cease to have an acute concern with the question. Their lives become more and more stable, but continue to exemplify both White and Indian behavior, depending upon the situation.

Sometimes older people feel self-conscious in the homes of their "highly acculturated" grandchildren. Despite their fears, however, the younger people do not reject them. For middle-aged and elderly persons, there are new variants of the traditional functions: the care and informal education of children, political leadership, religious activity, and the exemplification of the cultural heritage. It is not uncommon for an older woman to be given the custody of one or more of her grandchildren temporarily or permanently. Such an arrangement provides her with companionship, while at the same time reducing the responsibilities of an active young mother who may be attempting to work for wages during her child bearing years. The importance of grandparents in child care is traditional in Chinookan culture and may contribute both to cultural stability and to tolerance of cultural heterogeneity.

The preoccupation with death has persisted even in the Wasco and Wishram families whose behavior most frequently follows White norms. Both White and Indian style funerals are elaborate. Commonly, at least perfunctory attention is paid to the levirate or sororate and to restrictions on the behavior of the surviving spouse. Many families also distribute gifts at a ceremony signifying the end of mourning; evidently this practice was recently adopted from Sahaptins.

Ceremonials, Supernaturalism, Curing.—As can be expected, little ceremonial activity, including religious activity, occurs with Chinookan sponsorship alone. Chinookans are, however, intermittent participants in the whole range of activities on the reservations, from shamanism to all-reservation "celebrations." Sometimes they are mere spectators; sometimes they participate as vigorously as the Sahaptins; sometimes at Warm Springs a Chinookan leader has planned some special reservation event, then failed to appear to take part in it.

Many traditional conceptions of the supernatural world are still known to the Chinookans, yet it is often difficult to decide what the beliefs of a given individual actually are. Actions, including verbalizations, based on such conceptions, vary with situations. For example, the drowning of four men in the Columbia in 1952 was tentatively attributed to a water monster by certain people; they themselves might not know whether or not they "believed in" water monsters under less dramatic circumstances. The same point can be made for omens and the individual supernatural experiences which still occur.

During the course of this last period, shamans were dying or ceasing their practice faster than they were being replaced. Many adults had no power songs at all. Soon after World War II, one might have predicted that only Sahaptin shamans, and not many of them, would be available in a few years. However, the situation on the Warm Springs Reservation would now suggest that Wasco shamanism will continue to persist for some time. Certain Wascos were participating regularly in winter spirit dances sponsored by Sahaptins. At least one Wasco has been serving as host himself. A World War II veteran, of predominantly Wasco ancestry, has not only been singing but has actually begun shamanistic practice. There are at least two Wishram shamans—older people—still alive.

The number of uses for supernatural power and the number of people involved in its use decreased markedly during this period, as might be expected. Shamanism functions as a specialized supplement to other kinds of curing. Guilt and anxiety, chronic illness, and certain conditions not helped by Euro-American medicine are sometimes treated by shamans. Those who would not ask a man with power to deal with any other kind of situation might hire one to cope with the danger surrounding a death in the family. Shamans are still feared, and deaths and other events are still explained by reference to their supernatural powers. Even those who are skeptical about modern claimants to power may assert that in former times "when they were more Indian inside" they were really able to perform cures and cause deaths. In other words, the reality of power is not questioned by them.

Sweat bathing, native drugs, and verbal formulas are still employed, but numerous alternatives have been available. They have included Euro-American doctors, hospitals, and clinics; these surely had been patronized by all Wascos and Wishrams who were living at the end of the period. In addition, Shakers, Feather Religion followers, and fundamentalist Christians have engaged in curing. A few Wascos have patronized a Chinese herbalist. It has been a common practice to move from one to another of these alternatives, depending upon the patient's or the family's diagnosis of the illness and evaluation of the efficacy of types of cures.

Only a few Chinookans are active participants in Longhouse Religion activities, which, as a matter of fact, have also declined among Sahaptins. Earlier, Jake Hunt's personal misfortunes (DuBois 1938: 20–21, 27–28) and other factors led to a decline in the importance of the Feather Religion. Sahaptin and Chinookan believers ceased to carry on regular "worship services" but sometimes joined Longhouse Religion people when they were singing and dancing. A few individual Feather men would also periodically gather others together for curing sessions, thus functioning somewhat in the manner of shamans. One Wasco at Warm Springs did this occasionally until near the time of his death in 1951. A Klickitat at Yakima is still holding comparable services in which Chinookans participate.

In the early part of the period, individual Wascos and Wishrams were being converted from Presbyterianism or from the Longhouse-Feather Religions to Shakerism. There were Shaker churches and home services wherever there was an appreciable Chinookan population. At Warm Springs it was understood that Shakerism was predominantly a Wasco religion. Following World War II, some Wascos became dissatisfied with the Shaker Church and ceased to participate actively. One reason for dissatisfaction was that large numbers of Sahaptins were being converted and were inadvertently effecting changes.

While conventional Christian churches (Presbyterian at Warm Springs) have retained certain of their Chinookan members, other people have joined fundamentalist congregations for a while in somewhat the same spirit that they have joined religions labeled as Indian.

Members of certain families now participate in no religion and have little interest in the supernatural; these are essentially the same people who fail to appear at non-religious public ceremonies. One such Wasco, for example, now labels people of his type as being "not very religious."

Art, Recreation.—The decoration of manufactured articles is now limited to beadwork on cloth and buckskin. Traditional designs are employed, but commonly the designs are inventions within a traditional framework. Perhaps Chinookan women are among those of the area who also employ commercially designed needlework patterns in making beaded bags. As has already been indicated, other decorated articles made in the past or made by other Indians continue to be preserved and valued. These include, for example, silverwork and basketry from British Columbia and articles of clothing from the Plains. Both Chinookan and Sahaptin women regularly buy any pleasing articles of Indian manufacture they encounter in curio and secondhand stores. Like other Americans, Indians are now more likely to be collectors and passive consumers of the arts than to be creators.

Although songs and dances of many types have persisted, Chinookan participation usually is limited to joining the audience. Nevertheless, there are individual Wascos and Wishrams who participate in all the forms of religious and recreational dancing practiced by the Sahaptins. Periodically, a group of Wascos will perform the complex Wasco Dance, which is regarded as a specialty of the group. Euro-American dancing by young people sometimes precedes Indian-style dance festivities, but naturally the former more commonly occurs in such separate contexts as school activities.

Television is available at Warm Springs, and movies are regularly attended by Indians throughout the area. Comic books and similar mass literature are read by young people.

Few, if any, Chinookans know more than fragments of the traditional body of oral literature. Most adults have heard many more stories than they now remember. While full evenings of storytelling no longer occur, story episodes are still discussed and narrated informally on occasion.

Horse racing has declined in importance for both Sahaptins and Wascos, but rodeos of the familiar Western type regularly constitute part of the program during first fruits celebrations and on national holidays. The only aboriginal game that has survived in the area is the bone game or stick game, largely limited to these times of celebration. Chinookans may bet on the outcome of these games, but their active participation in gambling is usually limited to the card games which occur at the same time.

Many of the Indian-oriented activities not obviously classed as recreational or aesthetic do fulfil these functions today. For example, if Chinookans decide to watch the ceremonial exchange associated with a marriage or a Longhouse religious ceremony, pleasure can be derived from the evocation of memories and pseudo-memories of past times. Such ceremonies not only fulfil manifest functions but also serve, for Chinookans and Sahaptins alike, to symbolize Indian identity.

Language.—As the period progressed, there was a growing number of individuals who did not have adequate control of the Wasco-Wishram language. The effects of intermarriage with Sahaptins and the increasing importance of English have already been made clear. Chinookan parents feel no effective responsibility to teach their children Wasco-Wishram or even to use it in their presence so that they can learn it. Those younger people who have learned Chinookan are those who have been raised in a family that includes one or more elderly persons who prefer to speak it rather than English or Sahaptin.

Sometime during the middle of the period it was no longer regarded as necessary to translate the speeches at reservation meetings into Chinookan; English or Sahaptin would suffice for the remaining older Chinookans, as well as for the younger ones. Probably all living Chinookans now speak English. Chinookan has not dropped out of use entirely, however. A few individuals know it better than they know English, and certain older women prefer it in speaking to each other.

The several processes of change within the language already mentioned have continued to operate. For example, many English words with Chinookan affixes are now used in speech.

THE CULTURE OF THE LATEST PERIOD

As in the third cultural period, Chinookan behavior during the latest or fourth period was in some respects Indian and in other respects White. There are significant differences between the two periods, however. During the third period, many Chinookans were strongly motivated toward learning White culture. They, as well as those who were less strongly motivated, had only a partial understanding of one rural variant of that culture and were exemplifying

White behavior largely within a Wasco-Wishram cultural context. During the fourth period, many more of the significant kinds of interaction were taking place with Whites and Sahaptins. White contexts for Euro-American cultural behavior were much more thoroughly understood, despite the fact that the spread of urbanization and commercial activity meant that the available White culture was much more complex and difficult to understand.

Much of the Indian behavior during the fourth period has occurred in conjunction with Sahaptins and tends to consist only of those activities which the Sahaptins are perpetuating. The Chinookans have the Sahaptins as an important reference group, along with the Whites and the Chinookans themselves. To an appreciable extent the Sahaptins are serving to define and preserve Indian culture for the Chinookans. The "part-time Indian culture" of the fourth period is thus in some senses a Sahaptin-Chinookan culture, with the Chinookans exemplifying a variant of it. Indian behavior in a limited sense is being perpetuated in such areas as technology, class attitudes, family responsibilities, religious and secular ceremonialism, supernaturalism, music, and recreation. Many of these activities are likely to continue among Chinookans as long as they also persist among Sahaptins and as long as the Chinookans are interacting with such Sahaptins.

Conclusions

Changes in the culture of the Chinookan-speaking Wasco and Wishram have been analyzed in terms of four periods, the first of which was entirely prehistoric and was not assigned a beginning date, and the last of which was regarded as still continuing. The interpretation employed historical reconstruction, traditional anthropological concepts, and certain constructs adapted from sociology. In order to try to eliminate the use of unique historical events to "explain" cultural changes, the culture of each period was viewed as a system. This approach to culture made it possible to regard the emergence of a new period as predicated in the elements of the earlier period. In other words, the new system characterizing the next period was seen as coming into existence while the previous system was still functioning. Thus, the new system could not have taken the form it did had its previous organizational principles been different, had the previous system encompassed all of the behavior that was occurring, had the Chinookan perception of the intrusive and dynamic influences (for example, the Whites) been different, and had the non-Chinookan cultural systems remained the same. It will be noted that the second and third points can be more or less subsumed under the other two.[11]

Before turning to some of the special problems of interpretation, it is appropriate to summarize the analysis of cultural change as it was presented for each period.

Compared with most American Indians, the Chinookans were relatively wealthy and relatively sedentary. Their villages were located near fishing sites; these they utilized so as to yield large surpluses of salmon, defined as a commodity for trade. They were visited annually by outsiders whom they categorized, on one level of abstraction, into named groups, for example, Nez Percé. The evidence indicates that on another level—in a trading context—these same visitors were reclassified in terms of whether or not they were potential "customers" or trading partners. These "levels," or complexes of activities, permitted a given Chinookan to perceive an identical situation or person, such as a White explorer, in terms of alternative modes of orientation.

Even in the eighteenth century, horses and White-manufactured goods were beginning to circulate through the network of trading relationships. When the Lewis and Clark party appeared in 1805, followed soon by fur traders and then missionaries, the Wasco-Wishram dealt with these newcomers in terms of their existing definitions of appropriate behavior toward outsiders. The Whites were treated as if they were a new group of Indians, who might or might not be customers, and who had no more right than any (other) Indian group to ignore the strategic importance of the Chinookans. Such minor instances of violence as occurred can be understood as representing Indian attempts to effect White recognition of this importance. The Whites frequently threatened violence but never initiated it in an organized fashion at any time during Wasco-Wishram history.

During the course of the cultural period which ended about 1858, the principal process of change was the addition of White-derived behavioral forms to Chinookan culture; these included overt forms of religious behavior and the use of White trade goods. The cultural

---

[11] The question has been raised whether the systematic nature (or the integration) of the culture of each period should not have been empirically demonstrated. Such demonstration was not necessary to the analysis, since the concept of system was a methodological device employed to delineate each period effectively. This simplified the subsequent task of considering the dynamics of interperiod relationships.

regularities which had been "lost" were still remembered and still existed as potential alternatives at the close of the period.

The Wasco-Wishram were beginning to realize even before the 1850's that their culture was not functioning in its traditional manner. Their response to this cultural crisis was to redefine their relationship with the Whites. By signing treaties in 1855 and moving to reservations, the Wasco and the Wishram signified, in effect, their acceptance of White cultural hegemony. Both on the reservations and in Chinookan communities elsewhere, significant aspects of Indian behavior were replaced by corresponding behavioral forms of White origin. Incomplete information about White culture and discrimination on the part of the Whites served as checks on acculturation. Furthermore, the behavior of Whites toward "Indians" produced a situation in which the Chinookans saw themselves as similar to the Sahaptins and to other Indians. Many Chinookans symbolized their identity as "Indians" by joining Sahaptins in new religious movements that were appearing.

A new period, labeled as that of "part-time Indian culture" can be defined as beginning about 1920. During this most recent period, the Chinookans have alternated between activities which are identifiably Indian and other behavior shared with Whites; this is in spite of the fact that Chinookan society—in the sense of frequent and meaningful interactions among Chinookans to the exclusion of others—has largely ceased to exist.

No single interpretation will suffice in explaining the aspects of culture which have persisted among the Chinookans. In understanding the persistence of religious forms, including shamanism, it seems best to focus on the relationship these forms bear to the identity of the Chinookans. This is no simple matter, since a single religious complex, such as Shaker activities, can function to express both the Indian and the White-oriented aspects of Chinookan identity. Identifiably Indian items of material culture have persisted for several reasons. Some of these items are religious equipment, for instance, the sticks used to accompany shamanistic singing; others are ornamentation, such as dance costumes, suitable for an Indian role in public celebrations as well as in religious contexts. The Chinookans today, however, are much more frequently owners and observers of the products and manifestations of Indian culture than they are creators.

White expectations regarding Indians are useful in explaining the existence or persistence of some other aspects of Chinookan culture. For example, the Whites expect Indians to have chiefs, and in a sense the Wascos and Wishrams do have chiefs. The provisions of the 1855 treaty permitted the Indians to fish in their traditional manner. Since legal and economic considerations exclude other techniques (fish wheels and various kinds of traps are now illegal), a modified form of the aboriginal scaffold and net fishing complex has persisted.

Other interpretations for the persistence of traditional culture are not inconsistent with that discussed by Bruner (1956), namely: those patterns of behavior learned early in the course of enculturation are the most resistant to change. The continuation of traditional foods, Chinookan speech, and certain regularities in family life could all be interpreted as symbols of Indian identity, but the fact that these are learned early in life may help to explain why they are suitable as symbols.

No ultimate "explanation" is provided by the hypothesis that any aspect of culture which has persisted among the Sahaptin neighbors of the Chinookans has a high probability of occurring as a counterpart in Chinookan behavior. It does, however, provide an immediate explanation for certain aspects of Chinookan cultural stability. At least, in employing the other interpretations suggested above, it is necessary to take the significance of Sahaptin culture to the Chinookans into account.

Throughout the case study, the importance of outsiders to the Chinookans was emphasized; in all but the earliest years the Whites as well as the local Sahaptins were of special consequence. In explaining the significance of groups who were neither enemies, like the Paiutes, nor fellow Chinookans, it was convenient to employ a version of reference group theory. It was suggested that the existence of the Whites and the Sahaptins permitted the Chinookans to establish two distinct outside "anchorage points" which operated to stabilize Chinookan identity. They have neither consistently emulated either group, nor have they consistently avoided White or Sahaptin behavioral forms. A common characteristic of many choice-making situations has been the use of either or both of the reference points in making comparisons with their own position. Obviously, the Chinookans would not share so many traits and patterns with Euro-American culture had the Whites not been such a significant part of their environment. At the same time, it was suggested that the

Sahaptin anchorage point has been of critical importance in the persistence of the Indian aspects of Chinookan life.

It is now appropriate to raise certain comparative questions. Some Indian groups, for instance, Eastern Cherokees of North Carolina (Gilbert 1955), have preserved their identities and other aspects of their culture in isolation from other Indians. They have not had groups comparable to the Yakima and Warm Springs Sahaptins who could be utilized as anchorage points. Other relatively isolated groups, such as the Klamath of southern Oregon, have changed more rapidly and thoroughly in the direction of White culture than have either the Eastern Cherokees or the Chinookans. Additional theoretical considerations are necessary to understand such differences.

It has been pointed out that the Wasco and Wishram lacked any high degree of political integration. At no time did there exist a group or a series of groups which had well-defined "boundaries." Following the treaties in 1855, the Upper Chinookans from below The Dalles—the Cascade, Hood River, and other groups—merged smoothly with the Wasco and Wishram populations. This easy assimilation supports the interpretation that the previous distinctions among the various upriver and downriver peoples had never been especially significant. Even the distinctions between Chinookans and Sahaptins, in spite of the language difference and the differences in cultural emphases, had never reached the level of importance exemplified, say, by the differences between most Plains tribes. Only the distinction between Paiutes on the one hand and Sahaptins and Chinookans on the other was of great consequence. This distinction involved a traditionally hostile relationship but did not presuppose political unity and loyalty among any of the groups.

The lack of boundaries between groups was paralleled by a lack of boundaries within the groups of the area. Except for class lines, there was no significant segmentation in Chinookan social organization. Clans, societies, and other structures which could have served as native models for the structuring of tribal grouping, were absent. The class structuring probably served to de-emphasize linguistic and other cultural boundaries, since a common and desirable marriage was between a young Sahaptin and a young Chinookan of comparable class position.

The lack of political integration was discussed in relation to the lack of significant functions for larger groupings: the economy required no broad integration, and the predominantly defensive patterns of warfare did not depend upon forms and organizations which were Chinookan to the exclusion of the Sahaptins.

The existence of political boundaries appears to bear a relationship to the kinds of changes which occurred among the Indians treated in this volume. During the course of the 1956 seminar, it became apparent that the Navaho, Kwakiutl, and Chinookan populations were similar in failing to emphasize political boundaries and also in displaying comparable types of cultural change. All three groups had added, replaced, and lost cultural materials; fusional or isolating (compartmentalizing) utilization of European materials has been absent or unimportant. The other three peoples studied—Yaqui, Pueblo, and Mandan—emphasized the boundaries between themselves and others and also displayed fusional and isolating processes of change during certain periods.[12] In the diverse treatments of the cases in the present volume, the contrast between the (relatively) "unbounded" and "bounded" groups, and the similarities among the three examples of each, may have been somewhat obscured. Nevertheless, the contrast between the two types is noteworthy.

In the case of a bounded group, such as the Yaqui or a Rio Grande pueblo, "boundary maintaining mechanisms" (Social Science Research Council Seminar 1954: 975–76) preserve the integrity of the whole group. Even at a time when there is no political unity, attitudes appropriate to such unity still exist. For example, if a New Mexico pueblo is split into factions, there is a high probability of political structuring within each faction, as well as of claims by each faction that it *ought* to represent the whole people (French 1948). It is not appropriate here to discuss the bounded type at length; the crucial point is that the boundary around the entire group, or the identity

[12] These cultural processes are elucidated in the concluding chapter of this volume, as well as in several of the case studies.

Spicer has called attention to the fact that fusional processes like those of Yaqui culture appear to have been involved in the formation of the Shaker religion and other movements in which the Chinookans participated. To the extent that fusion is important, the correlation sketched above is weakened. Perhaps these considerations are relevant: the fusing or amalgamation of Indian and White elements in these religions occurred elsewhere, among (unbounded) Salish and Sahaptin groups. The religions were defined as *new* revelations from the supernatural world. The fact that certain content is shared with Whites, for example, bells and candles, is recognized by participants; they do not claim that the religions are aboriginal, only that the revelations were made to Indians. The differences between the Yaqui and the Northwestern processes are sufficiently great that further detailed study would be required to decide whether fusion (in Spicer's sense) can be a significant process among "unbounded" groups.

of the group, is a significant point of reference for its members. Not surprisingly, the ancestors, or a past identity of the group, such as the Eight Towns of the Yaquis, may also be a significant anchorage point.

For the unbounded groups, neither past nor present identities are of great significance as points of reference. Parents do not insist that their children learn Wasco (or Kwakiutl or Navaho) in order to preserve the distinction between their group and all others. Persons are rarely excluded from participation in some activity solely on the basis of a lack of membership in a maximal grouping such as a tribe. Participation in a particular activity may be inappropriate—but for other reasons, such as sex or age.

The Eastern Cherokee, who were mentioned earlier, appear to be a bounded group like the Yaquis, Pueblos, and Mandans; they were able to preserve their culture even in a situation of marked isolation from other Indians because the boundaries or political integration functioned to permit the integrity of the group itself to serve as an anchorage point. Even were the Mandans not in contact with the Hidatsa and the Arikara, they might well have been able to survive as Mandans; comparable points could be made for the Pueblos and Yaquis. In contrast, the relatively unbounded Klamath culture is approaching extinction after a comparatively short period of White contact. The small local Modoc and Paiute communities have not been defined as anchorage points by the Klamaths.

In the nineteenth century the Kwakiutl were exposed to fewer intensive White pressures than were the Wasco and Wishram. The "collapse" of Kwakiutl culture in the twentieth century, or, rephrased, the relatively low probability of the appearance of overtly Indian behavior among Kwakiutls today, is not surprising in view of the fact that they are an unbounded group without an outside Indian anchorage point.

The unbounded culture of the Navahos represents a somewhat special case, since, for reasons of isolation and population size, the overwhelming majority of social relationships for the average Navaho have been with other Navahos. Were political consciousness to continue to grow, they might become a bounded group like the Pueblos. Or, some other anchorage point for them may appear; otherwise, their future cultural history may resemble that of the Klamath and the Kwakiutl in many respects.

It would be legitimate to ask: if the Wascos and Wishrams use the

Sahaptins as an Indian anchorage point, what serves the corresponding function among the Sahaptins themselves? The Chinookans are
not suitable for this, because they have been consistently "less Indian" than the Sahaptins. In the first place, like the Navahos, many
Sahaptins have lived in relative isolation from the Whites. Furthermore, it is not circular reasoning to suggest that the Yakimas, Warm
Springs Sahaptins, and more easterly groups such as the Umatilla and
Nez Percé serve as Indian reference points for each other. With automobiles to facilitate travel, frequent comparative judgments on norms
of behavior are possible. If the Sahaptins were to be investigated in
terms of problems of persistence and change, attention could be paid
to the possibility that the area-wide religious movements of the Longhouse type might have been serving some of the identity-preserving
functions that sociopolitical integration has served among groups
east of the Rockies and in the Southwest. Nevertheless, Sahaptin
culture is now changing rapidly, and with these changes there is a
waning of the usefulness of the Sahaptins as an Indian reference group
for the Chinookans.

No other Indian group studied in the seminar has exemplified exactly the same relationship with the Whites and with another Indian
group as held for the Chinookans. Furthermore, the extraordinary
importance of outsiders to the trading Chinookans may have facilitated their later use of more than one group of non-Chinookans in
defining their identity. Consequently, comparative research beyond
the scope of the tribes represented in this volume will be necessary
to test the usefulness of the interpretive framework employed in this
study.

REFERENCES CITED

ADAMS, BARBARA
  1958 "The Cascade Indians: Ethnographic Notes and an Analysis of Early
        Relations with Whites." B.A. thesis, Reed College.
ALLEN, A. J. (compiler)
  1850 *Ten Years in Oregon. Travels and Adventures of Doctor E. White
        and Lady, West of the Rocky Mountains.* . . . (2d ed.) Ithaca.
ANASTASIO, ANGELO
  1955 "Intergroup Relations in the Southern Plateau." Ph.D. dissertation,
        University of Chicago.
BARNETT, H. G.
  1957 *Indian Shakers: A Messianic Cult of the Pacific Northwest.* Carbon-
        dale, Ill.

BASEHART, HARRY W.
1956 "Reference Group Theory and the Analysis of Segmentary Systems." Fifty-fifth Annual Meeting of the American Anthropological Association, Santa Monica, Calif.
BREWER, HENRY BRIDGMAN
1929 "Log of the Lausanne–IV, V." JOHN M. CANSE (ed.). *Oregon Historical Quarterly*, XXX, 53–62, 111–19.
BRUNER, EDWARD M.
1956 "Cultural Transmission and Cultural Change," *Southwestern Journal of Anthropology*, XII, 191–99.
CENSUS, BUREAU OF THE
1915 *Indian Population in the United States and Alaska, 1910*. Washington.
CHINOOK, WILLIAM
1853 [Copy of] Letter from an Indian of the Waskopan Tribe–named William Chincuch. Waco [*sic*] Dalles of Columbia, November 30, 1853. Washington, National Archives, File Oregon, 1853, P179.
CHITTENDEN, HIRAM MARTIN
1935 *The American Fur Trade of the Far West.* 2 vols. New York.
CLARK, ROBERT CARLTON
1935 "Military History of Oregon, 1849–59," *Oregon Historical Quarterly*, XXXVI, 14–59.
COAN, C. F.
1922 "The Adoption of the Reservation Policy in Pacific Northwest, 1853–1855," *Quarterly of the Oregon Historical Society*, XXIII, 1–38.
COMMISSIONER OF INDIAN AFFAIRS
1850–1900 *Annual Reports of the Commissioner to the Secretary of the Interior*. Washington (various editions).
COOK, S. F.
1955 "The Epidemic of 1830–1833 in California and Oregon," University of California *Publications in American Archaeology and Ethnology*, XLIII, 303–25.
COX, ROSS
1957 *The Columbia River*. EDGAR I. STEWART and JANE R. STEWART (eds.). Norman, Okla.
CURTIN, JEREMIAH. (See Sapir 1909.)
CURTIS, EDWARD S.
1911 *The North American Indian*. FREDERICK WEBB HODGE (ed.). Vol. VIII. Norwood, Mass.
DOUGLAS, DAVID
1904–5 "Sketch of a Journey to the Northwestern Parts of the Continent of North America during the Years 1824–25–26–27," *Quarterly of the Oregon Historical Society*, V, 230–71, 325–69; VI, 76–97, 206–27.
DRUCKER, PHILIP
1955 *Indians of the Northwest Coast*. American Museum of Natural History, *Anthropological Handbook No. 10*, New York.
DUBOIS, CORA
1938 *The Feather Cult of the Middle Columbia*. "General Series in Anthropology," No. 7. Menasha.

EISENSTADT, S. M.
1954 "Reference Group Behavior and Social Integration: An Explorative Study," *American Sociological Review*, XIX, 175–85.

FRANCHÈRE, GABRIEL
1904 *Narrative of a Voyage to the Northwest Coast of America in the Years 1811, 1812, 1813, and 1814.* REUBEN GOLD THWAITES (ed.). *Early Western Travels, 1748–1846*, VI, 167–410. Cleveland.

FRÉMONT, J. C.
1845 *Report of the Exploring Expedition to the Rocky Mountains in the Year 1842, and to Oregon and North California in the Years 1843–44.* Printed by order of the House of Representatives. Washington.

FRENCH, DAVID
1948 *Factionalism in Isleta Pueblo.* American Ethnological Society, *Monograph No. 14.* New York.
n.d. Wasco-Wishram ethnobotany. MS.

FRENCH, KATHRINE and DAVID
1955 "The Warm Springs Community," *American Indian*, VII, 3–17.

FULLER, GEORGE W.
1941 *A History of the Pacific Northwest.* (2d ed. rev.) New York.

GASS, PATRICK
1810 *A Journal of the Voyages and Travels of a Corps of Discovery, under the Command of Capt. Lewis and Capt. Clarke . . . during the Years 1804, 1805 & 1806.* Philadelphia.

GEER, T. T.
1912 *Fifty Years in Oregon.* New York.

GILBERT, WILLIAM H., JR.
1955 "Eastern Cherokee Social Organization," in *Social Anthropology of North American Tribes.* (Enl. ed.) FRED EGGAN (ed.). Chicago.

GUNTHER, ERNA
1949 "The Shaker Religion of the Northwest," in *Indians of the Urban Northwest.* MARIAN W. SMITH (ed.). New York.
1950 "The Westward Movement of Some Plains Traits," *American Anthropologist*, LII, 174–80.

HAINES, FRANCIS
1938 "The Northward Spread of Horses among the Plains Indians," *American Anthropologist*, XL, 429–37.

HENRY, ALEXANDER
1897 *New Light on the Early History of the Greater Northwest: The Manuscript Journals of Alexander Henry . . . and of David Thompson . . . 1799–1814.* ELLIOTT COUES (ed.). 3 vols. New York.

HINES, GUSTAVUS
1885 *Wild Life in Oregon.* New York.

HOSMER, J. K. (See LEWIS and CLARK 1902.)

HUGHES, CHARLES
1957 "Reference Group Concepts in the Study of a Changing Eskimo Culture," in *Cultural Stability and Cultural Change*, Proceedings of the 1957 Annual Spring Meeting of the American Ethnological Society.

HUNT, WILSON PRICE. (See STUART 1935.)

HYMAN, HERBERT H.
1942   *The Psychology of Status.* "Archives of Psychology," No. 269.
INTERIOR, SECRETARY OF THE
1860   *Report of the Secretary of the Interior, December 1, 1859,* in *Senate Exec. Doc.,* 36 Cong., 1 sess., 1859–60, pp. 91–113. Washington.
JACOBS, MELVILLE
1955   "A Few Observations on the World View of the Clackamas Chinook Indians," *Journal of American Folklore,* LXVIII, 283–89.
JOHANSEN, DOROTHY O., and CHARLES M. GATES
1957   *Empire of the Columbia: A History of the Pacific Northwest.* New York.
KELLY, GAIL MARGARET
1955   "Themes in Wasco Culture." B.A. thesis, Reed College.
KERNS, JOHN T.
1917   "Journal of Crossing the Plains to Oregon in 1852," *Transactions of the Forty-second Annual Reunion of the Oregon Pioneer Association,* pp. 148–93. Portland.
KROEBER, A. L.
1939   *Cultural and Natural Areas of Native North America.* Berkeley.
LEE, DANIEL, and J. H. FROST
1844   *Ten Years in Oregon.* New York.
LENOX, EDWARD HENRY
1902   *Overland to Oregon in the Tracks of Lewis and Clarke.* ROBERT WHITAKER (ed.). Oakland.
LEWIS, MERIWETHER, and WILLIAM CLARK
1902   *History of the Expedition of Captains Lewis and Clark.* JAMES K. HOSMER (ed.). Vol. II. Chicago.
1905   *Original Journals of the Lewis and Clark Expedition 1804–1806.* REUBEN GOLD THWAITES (ed.). Vols. III, IV, VII. New York.
McLOUGHLIN, JOHN
1941   *The Letters of John McLoughlin from Fort Vancouver to the Governor and Committee. First Series, 1825–38.* E. E. RICH (ed.). London.
MEACHAM, A. B.
1875   *Wigwam and War-Path.* (2d ed. rev.) Boston.
1878*a*   "John Mission (Indian)," *Council Fire,* I, 6.
1878*b*   "Another Cloud," *Council Fire,* I, 82.
MERTON, ROBERT K.
1957   *Social Theory and Social Structure.* (Rev. enl. ed.) Glencoe, Ill.
MINTO, JOHN
1889   "The 'Good Old Doctor,' Doctor John McLoughlin," *Transactions of the Sixteenth Annual Reunion of the Oregon Pioneer Association for 1888,* pp. 123–36. Portland.
1900   "The Number and Condition of the Native Race in Oregon When First Seen by White Men," *Quarterly of the Oregon Historical Society,* I, 296–315.
MITCHELL, W. W.
1869   Letter to A. B. Meacham, Superintendent, Indian Affairs, Salem, Oregon, from W. W. Mitchell, Bvt. Capt. U.S.A., Indian Agent, Warm Springs Agency, October 12, 1869. Seattle, Federal Records Center, File #11076, Agent's letter-book 1869–74, pp. 9–10.

428 *Perspectives in American Indian Culture Change*

MOONEY, JAMES
  1896 "The Ghost-Dance Religion and the Sioux Outbreak of 1890," *Fourteenth Annual Report*, Bureau of American Ethnology, 1892–1893, Part 2, pp. 641–1136. Washington.

MURDOCK, GEORGE PETER
  1938 "Notes on the Tenino, Molala, and Paiute of Oregon," *American Anthropologist*, XL, 395–402.

NASH, WALLIS
  1882 *Two Years in Oregon*. (2d ed.) New York.

ORDWAY, JOHN
  1916 *The Journals of Captain Meriwether Lewis and Sergeant John Ordway Kept on the Expedition of Western Exploration, 1803–1806*. MILO M. QUAIFE (ed.). "Publications of the State Historical Society of Wisconsin," *Collections*, Vol. XXII. Madison.

Oregon Statesman
  1854 April 25, p. 2, col. 7. Salem, Oregon.

PALMER, JOEL
  1857 Letter, May 19, 1857. Washington, National Archives, File Oregon and Washington, 1857, p. 496.

PARKER, SAMUEL
  1846 *Journal of an Exploring Tour beyond the Rocky Mountains*. (5th ed.) Auburn.

PIKE, KENNETH L.
  1954 *Language in Relation to a Unified Theory of the Structure of Human Behavior*. Part I. Preliminary edition. Summer Institute of Linguistics, Glendale.

POPE, RICHARD K.
  1953 "The Indian Shaker Church and Acculturation at Warm Springs Reservation." B.A. thesis, Reed College.

RAY, VERNE F.
  1939 *Cultural Relations in the Plateau of Northwestern America*. "Publications of the Frederick Webb Hodge Anniversary Publication Fund," Vol. III. Los Angeles.
  1942 "Culture Element Distributions: XXII Plateau," University of California *Anthropological Records*, VIII, 99–258.

ROSS, ALEXANDER
  1904 *Adventures of the First Settlers on the Oregon or Columbia River, 1810–1813*. REUBEN GOLD THWAITES (ed.). Cleveland.
  1956 *The Fur Hunters of the Far West*. KENNETH A. SPAULDING (ed.). Norman, Okla.

SAPIR, EDWARD
  1907 "Preliminary Report of the Language and Mythology of the Upper Chinook," *American Anthropologist*, IX, 533–41.
  1909 *Wishram Texts, Together with Wasco Tales and Myths*. Collected by JEREMIAH CURTIN and edited by EDWARD SAPIR. "Publications of the American Ethnological Society," Vol. II. Leyden.

SETON, ALFRED
  1935 "Life on the Oregon," *Oregon Historical Quarterly*, XXXVI, 187–204.

SHANE, RALPH M.
1950 "Early Explorations through Warm Springs Reservation Area," *Oregon Historical Quarterly*, LI, 273–309.
SMITH, JOHN
1878 "Letter to A. B. Meacham, January 24th, 1878," *Council Fire*, I, 42–43.
SOCIAL SCIENCE RESEARCH COUNCIL (Summer Seminar on Acculturation)
1954 "Acculturation: An Exploratory Formulation," *American Anthropologist*, LVI, 973–1002.
SPIER, LESLIE
1930 "Klamath Ethnography," University of California *Publications in American Archaeology and Ethnology*, XXX, 1–338.
1935 *The Prophet Dance of the Northwest and Its Derivatives: The Source of the Ghost Dance.* "General Series in Anthropology," No. 1. Menasha.
1936 *Tribal Distribution in Washington.* "General Series in Anthropology," No. 3. Menasha.
SPIER, LESLIE, and EDWARD SAPIR
1930 "Wishram Ethnography," University of Washington *Publications in Anthropology*, III, 151–300.
STEWARD, JULIAN H.
1955 *Theory of Culture Change: The Methodology of Multilinear Evolution.* Urbana.
STRONG, WILLIAM DUNCAN
1945 "The Occurrence and Wider Implications of a 'Ghost Cult' on the Columbia River," *American Anthropologist*, XLVII, 244–61.
STRONG, WILLIAM DUNCAN, W. EGBERT SCHENCK, and JULIAN H. STEWARD
1930 "Archaeology of the Dalles-Deschutes Region," University of California *Publications in American Archaeology and Ethnology*, XXIX, 1–154.
STUART, ROBERT
1935 *The Discovery of the Oregon Trail; Robert Stuart's Narratives of His Overland Trip Eastward from Astoria in 1812–13 to Which Is Added: . . . Wilson Price Hunt's Diary of His Overland Trip Westward to Astoria in 1811–12.* PHILIP ASHTON ROLLINS (ed.). New York.
SUTTLES, WAYNE
1951 "The Early Diffusion of the Potato among the Coast Salish," *Southwestern Journal of Anthropology*, VII, 272–88.
THOMPSON, DAVID
1916 *David Thompson's Narrative of His Exploration in Western America, 1784–1812.* J. B. TYRRELL (ed.). The Champlain Society. Toronto.
THOMPSON, R. R.
1855 Letter to Joel Palmer, Superintendent of Indian Affairs, Dayton, Oregon. Agency Office, Dalles, Dec. 19th, 1855. Washington, National Archives, File Oregon, 1856, p. 61.
THWAITES, REUBEN GOLD (editor)
1905 *Original Journals of the Lewis and Clark Expedition, 1804–1806.* Vols. III, IV, VII. New York.

TOWNSEND, JOHN K.
  1905   *Townsend's Narrative of a Journey across the Rocky Mountains, 1834.*
         REUBEN GOLD THWAITES (ed.). *Early Western Travels,* Vol. XXI.
         Cleveland.
TREASURY, SECRETARY OF
  1888   Indian Fishing Privileges. Letter from the Secretary of the Treasury.
         . . . House of Representatives, 50 Cong., 1 sess., v. 26, *Ex. Doc. No. 183.*
TURNER, RALPH H.
  1956   "Role-taking, Role Standpoint, and Reference-Group Behavior,"
         American Journal of Sociology, LXI, 316–28.
WHITEHOUSE, JOSEPH. (See Lewis and Clark 1905, VII.)
WILKES, CHARLES
  1844   *Narrative of the United States Exploring Expedition during the Years
         1838, 1839, 1840, 1841, 1842.* Vol. IV. Philadelphia.
WILKES, GEORGE
  1845   *The History of Oregon, Geographical and Political.* New York.
WORK, JOHN
  1920   "John Work's Journal of a Trip from Fort Colville to Fort Vancouver
         and Return in 1828." WILLIAM S. LEWIS and JACOB A. MEYERS (eds.).
         Washington Historical Quarterly, XI, 104–14.
WYETH, NATHANIEL J.
  1899   *The Correspondence and Journals of Captain Nathaniel J. Wyeth,
         1831–60.* F. G. YOUNG (ed.). *Sources of the History of Oregon,* Vol. I.
         Eugene.

CHAPTER 7

Kwakiutl

By Helen Codere

The Southern Kwakiutl are the famous "Kwakiutl" of the North Pacific Coast of North America. They are known to social science through field work and publication of Franz Boas extending over some fifty years. Since Boas termed them the "Kwakiutl," after placing them in relation to other groups, the same usage will be followed in this account.

The Southern Kwakiutl lived on the shores of the waterways between northern Vancouver Island and the mainland from Cape Mudge in the south to Rivers Inlet in the north. They spoke a language of the Wakashan stock as did their neighbors the Northern Kwakiutl (the Bella Bella and Rivers Inlet groups spoke Hē'iLtsuq and groups farther to the north spoke Xa•isla') and the Nootka on the Pacific Ocean side of Vancouver Island. According to Swadesh (1948: 106), the linguistic differentiation for Southern and Northern Kwakiutl is as great as that between English and Dutch, and Nootka and Southern Kwakiutl are as far apart as English and a Scandinavian tongue. The Southern Kwakiutl are in the Northwest Coast culture area, and many basic features of their culture are ones they hold in common with the other cultures of the area from Puget Sound to Alaska. Kroeber (1917, 1923) has pointed out that the Northwest Coast lacks certain generic North American culture traits, most notably the entire agricultural complex, and that it possesses certain distinctive specializations in the institutionalization of property and social ranking and in woodworking and plastic art. He considers that Asiatic influences were perhaps "more potent than Nuclear (Middle) American ones in the specific shaping of Northwest Coast culture" (1947). What Kroeber (1923) calls the deeply different outlook and direction of development of the Northwest Coast is a fact important to this comparative study of culture change, since such similarities of cultural process as may be seen between the Kwakiutl case and any of the other five North American Indian cases may be due that much less to continuous historical interrelationships and intercultural influences in precontact North America than to the fundamental nature of culture and of cultural change.

While the Southern Kwakiutl were allied with all the other cultures of the area and especially closely with the cultures of their neighbors, they had their own characteristic version of everything in the cultural inventory from technology to social institutions and the world of art and ideas. To specify at this point, however, would be inconsistent with the plan and meaning of the joint inquiry in which a "culture" is not to be considered apart from its history. A full cultural historical exposition makes up the main body of this chapter. Here it is sufficient to note that the Southern Kwakiutl were a culturally distinct and relatively homogeneous group who, however, did not, and do not think of themselves as a unified people or "nation" but as divided into village groups. Since the local group designation is of primary importance, a map giving village locations is included.

In the Kwakiutl homeland partially submerged rugged mountains rise steeply from the sea, and it is only along the shoreline that some level land is likely to be found. The mountains rise over 4,000 feet on Vancouver Island and over three times that height on the mainland opposite. High and strong tides run in the many channels, fjords, and inlets of the tortuous coastline. The climate is mild for the 50° north latitude, for it is ameliorated by the Japanese current flowing just off the continental shelf. It is also wet with an average annual rainfall of about 100 inches. If, however, any lengthy period of bright sunny days is rare even in the summer months, any winter temperature below freezing is of even briefer duration.

Marine life of all kinds is abundant. On the shores and beaches there are edible seaweeds, clams, mussels, crabs, sea-eggs, abalone and barnacles; in the sea there are herring, halibut, cod, and salmon, and seals and sea lions attracted to these waters by the abundance of the

MAP 12

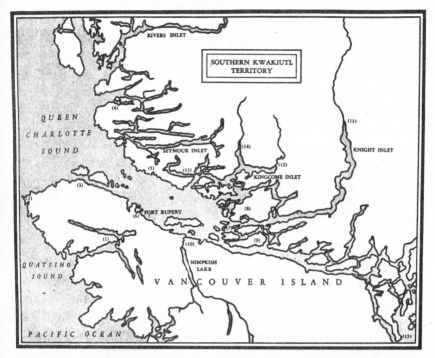

SUBDIVISIONS OF THE SOUTHERN KWAKIUTL*

Name	Official Spelling	Geographical Location (See map numbers)†
Koskimo Subdialect		
Lā'ṣq'ēnôx	Klaskino	Klaskino Inlet (1)
Gua'ts'ēnôx	Quatsino	Quatsino Sound (1)
Qo'sqēmôx	Koskimo	
Gō·p'ēnôx		
Newettee Subdialect		
Naô'mg·ilisala		Cape Scott (2)
La'Lasiqoala	Nuwitti	Newettee (3)
Kwakiutl Subdialect		
Goasi'la	Quawshelah	Smith Inlet (4)
Nā'q'oaqtôq	Nakwakto	Seymour Inlet
		Blunden Harbour (5)
Kwa g·uł	Kwakiutl, Kwawkewlth	Fort Rupert (6)
Ma'malēleqala	Mamalillikulla	Village Island (7)
Qoē'xsôt'ēnôx	Kwilkwisotenok	Gilford Island (8)
Lau'itsîs	Tlawitsis	Cracroft Island (9)
NE'mqic	Nimpkish	Nimpkish River,
		Alert Bay (10)
T'Ena'xtax	Tanakteuk	Knight Inlet (11)
A'wa iLala		Knight Inlet
Ts'āwatEēnôx	Tsawataineuk	Kingcome Inlet (12)
Guau'aēnôx	Kwawwawainuk	Drury Inlet (13)
Haxuā'mis		Wakeman Sound (14)
Lē'kwîltôq	Lekwiltok	Cape Mudge (15)

* The Kwakiutl names are taken from Boas (1897:329–31).

† The numbers following the general geographical location designate the site of the chief village on the map.

fish. Great runs of oulachen and salmon take place seasonally up many of the fresh-water streams. The salmon runs of the different species (*Oncorhynchus keta, O. kisutch, O. tschawytscha, O. nerka*) occur from early spring to early winter.

The land is as rich in its resources as the sea. It is densely forested, and high trees, mostly conifers, rise from a heavy, tangled undergrowth and a ground cover of dank, thick moss. The most important species of tree are red cedar, yellow cedar, hemlock, Douglas fir, and yew. Many types of berries and other plants, such as nettles, grow in clearings or on the edges of the forest. The land animals include bear, mountain goat, deer, wapiti, and the smaller North American forest animals.

Introduction to Kwakiutl Culture History

The century and a half of Kwakiutl culture history shows a single outstanding development, the rise and fall of the potlatch. The earliest period of Kwakiutl history is one in which the potlatch is present as an institution but in competition with other institutions on a fairly equal basis. The middle period is the one in which the potlatch came to be the central and all-encompassing institution. This is also the period for which we have rich ethnographic materials and which we are tempted to think of as "classical" and most characteristic of Kwakiutl culture. In the final period the potlatch as an institution died, a fate that has been met by many other highly specialized and elaborated institutions.

Kwakiutl cultural development was continuous, so that the divisions between the successive periods are not sharp, although they are marked by some significant event that is at least the beginning of new altered conditions in the world surrounding the Kwakiutl, what we in the seminar have called the contact community. The types of changes that occurred in Kwakiutl culture, changes that were, of course, not limited to those directly connected with the potlatch but that extended throughout the whole culture, were the results of both changes in the contact community and of every preceding change in the culture.

The period names and dates are: the Pre-Potlatch Period from about 1792, when Vancouver recorded the first known European contact with the Kwakiutl, until 1849, when the Hudson's Bay Company established a post in Kwakiutl territory at Fort Rupert; the

Potlatch Period from about 1849 to the mid-1920's and the onset of most unfavorable economic conditions; and the Post Potlatch Period which began in the mid-twenties and continues to the present. A synoptic table (Table 8) of the periods, datable historical events, types of contact community, and types of change summarizes Kwakiutl culture history for the convenience of the reader.

TABLE 8

KWAKIUTL CONTACT HISTORY, 1770–1955

Periods	Events	Contact Communities	Types of Change
III Post-Potlatch (1921–1955)	1951 Revised Indian Act (not specifically forbidding potlatching or winter dancing) 1942 Pacific Northwest Coast Fishermen's Association joins Native Brotherhood 1936 Pacific Coast Native Fishermen's Association 1921 Low point in Kwakiutl population; economic depression	British Columbia Canadian-American Contact Community (degree of impact): Local version of British Columbia cities Mass media of national culture	Assimilation to Canadian-American culture: Acceptance of White models Specialization in White economy No institutional retentions (Part-time use of old language) Non-institutional persistences of old culture, e.g., social status–property relationship
II Potlatch (1849–1921)	1921 Great Village Island potlatch 1911 First gas (power) boats 1895 Japanese in fishing and canning 1880 Canneries in area 1881 Kwawkewlth Agency set up	II*b*. Alert Bay Center of Contacts: Agency, mission, fishing industry; Areal Contacts: Seasonal occupational mobility World Contacts: Occasional travel	Kwakiutl Cultural Specialization–Full Cultural Specialization in the Potlatch: Exploitation of non-Kwakiutl economy Secularization Numerous additions of European goods to material culture
	1880 Reserves allotted 1876 Indian Act forbidding potlatching and winter dancing 1867 Indian Liquor Ordinance 1858 British Columbia Gold Rush 1849 Fort Rupert established	II*a*. Fort Rupert Center of Contacts: Fort Rupert trading post Visits to Victoria Increased Indian movement in area with increase in peaceful and non-peaceful contacts	Increasing Cultural Specialization of Focus: Increase and elaboration of the potlatch Increase in secularization End of Kwakiutl localism and beginning of over-all system of social ranking End of warfare as an institution.
I Pre-Potlatch (1770–1849)	1835 Coal discovered in Kwakiutl territory 1811 "Tonquin" massacre 1792 Vancouver 1778 Cook 1770 Maritime traders	Contacts with Visiting Traders: Hudson's Bay Company, 1830 Maritime traders, 1770	Addition of European goods to material culture
		Indian Contacts: Trade, fighting, intermarriage	Addition of an idea (the idea of crests) which was causing changes in cultural interests, emphases, and organization

The Pre-Potlatch Period: 1792–1849

From 1792, when Vancouver, Menzies, and an unknown journalist all recorded descriptions of the Nimpkish village of the Kwakiutl on the first known contact of Kwakiutl and Europeans, there is cultural information on these people. It was not until the last quarter of the nineteenth century that there was thorough and competent ethnography; at that time Jacobsen, Dawson, and Boas all did professional work with the result that for Kwakiutl there is cultural documentation of high quality as well as much cultural information in such various historical sources as travelers', traders', and missionaries' accounts, and in official reports. There is no question that if Boas, for example, had mature adult informants or access to them through a younger interpreter in the 1880's and 1890's, these adults would have seen, lived in, and been socialized in Kwakiutl culture before 1849, when the establishment of Fort Rupert by the Hudson's Bay Company created the first conditions of steady contact with White settlers. Boas says, "My accounts of personal reminiscences of the Kwakiutl go back to approximately 1850, and a number of earlier dates are well authenticated, so that many details of their history can be traced back to the beginning of the nineteenth century" (1940: 448). Therefore, meticulous handling of the available cultural data makes it possible to re-create Kwakiutl culture before 1849. The picture that follows is imperfect in its failure to cover all aspects of the culture, but it is for the most part a re-creation and not a reconstruction, since it has been based primarily on dated materials or on data that can be connected with them. The account of Kwakiutl culture begins in every possible instance with some part of the description of the Nimpkish village given by Vancouver, Menzies, and the unknown journalist in 1792 and then expands the description with materials either of known date or of an approximate date that surely places them in this period.

COMMUNITY ORGANIZATION

Vancouver (1798: 346) counted thirty-four houses in the Nimpkish village, and both he and Menzies estimated a population of five hundred (Vancouver: 348; Newcombe: 88). The houses were arranged in street-like rows on the steep bank of the shore of the river near its mouth. The typical Kwakiutl village plan was that of a single row of houses along a strip of seashore. The Nimpkish village was, however, typical in its general settlement pattern—a sizable population closely concentrated and distributed among a relatively few great houses of a substantial and permanent sort. Vancouver (1798: 345) arrived at the Nimpkish village on the twentieth of July, and it is probably this summer date that accounts for the large population of that village then, the number of canoe groups he saw on the move just before, and the "depopulation of the North side of the straits" that he noticed (1798: 348). The large villages such as that of the Nimpkish were virtually abandoned more often than not at various times in the summer, unless, as in the case of the Nimpkish who were in possession of an excellent salmon stream, there was some abundant local resource in season. No village had the entire inventory of resources that the people felt necessary to their level of living: it might have a stream in which salmon but not oulachen ran; it might be near a herring pond but have very poor berry patches. The summer months in which there was great variety in such abundant seasonal resources were ones in which the "winter" villages were periodically deserted for camp sites near some valued resource and in which the people were busily on the move.

EXTERNAL RELATIONS

Both Vancouver and Menzies were interested in the European trade goods they saw and in the behavior of the people as evidence of possible previous contact with Europeans. They establish with certainty that the Nimpkish had an overland trade route to Nootka territory, but the question of direct contact is not settled. The manner of the Kwakiutl was very relaxed, even "jocular," and matter of fact with the visitors. This might suggest previous experience with Europeans, but only if we are inclined to share the characteristic view of European voyagers that the outlander should be awed and thrown into confusion on a first meeting. There was a great variety of trade goods, including many muskets, in the possession of the people. Most, if not all, of these goods had come from Nootka. The trade with the men of the "Discovery" was conducted by the Kwakiutl in orderly and sophisticated fashion. The way in which the women dunned the visitors for buttons and other trinkets and the fact that a chief, like Maquinna of Nootka, supervised the trading of his people's furs suggested to the visitors that a pattern had been set for dealing with their kind. The business sophistication shown by the Nimpkish could be evidence either of earlier European contact or of the important trade experience of the Nimpkish among all the other Kwakiutl by virtue of their monopoly of the route to Nootka. This overland route was the old "grease" (oulachen oil) trail. Oulachen do not run up the streams of the West Coast of Vancouver Island and their oil was a valuable commodity. The Nimpkish were in command of this trail;

not even the Nootka seem to have used it. The Nimpkish could, therefore, have developed much trade experience before the coming of Europeans to the Coast and could have been receiving European goods from Nootka in trade for oil and furs almost fifteen years before Vancouver's visit. They might have learned much about Europeans indirectly in the process. In any case the Nimpkish struck a hard bargain with Vancouver's men. Newcombe (88) claimed that sea-otter skins were procured from the Nimpkish at "more than double the value [he] ever saw given for them on any other part of the Coast" and Vancouver (1798: 348) noted that the people "were well versed in the principles of trade." In the later years of the pre-1849 period business ability and successful trade relations with Europeans seem to characterize all the Southern Kwakiutl. This has been described fully (Codere 1950: 21–23), but one extraordinary fact should be repeated here: the Hudson's Bay Company had occasion to regard the Kwakiutl as real competitors. Not only were they canny buyers and sellers, but they were also middlemen who did such things as peddle Hudson's Bay guns from Fort Langley in the south to the Indians of the northern area in which the company had been able to maintain a dearer price for them.

Before 1849 Europeans in this area were visiting traders with whom the Kwakiutl dealt briefly and a few at a time. Before 1825 (Wike 1952: 1) there were the ill-famed maritime fur traders and after that the predominant group was Hudson's Bay Company men of honorable reputation. There is certain evidence, throughout this period and even before 1825, of peaceful trade relations.

Such data set a puzzle, however, for the maritime fur trade on these coasts was in general full of violent incidents in which the Indians retaliated for the predatory acts of the traders who were so avaricious about sea-otter skins that they forced the trade at gun point or captured and ransomed Indians for furs. It seems likely that such incidents happened in Kwakiutl territory. It is possible that the Kwakiutl of the village of Newettee were involved in the most famous of all of these incidents, the destruction of the "Tonquin" in 1811 (Dawson 1887: 8).

It seems that Southern Kwakiutl and European relations were predominantly peaceful and businesslike with only occasional violent incidents. This also seems to be the general character of Kwakiutl relations with other Indian peoples, although the situation is quite different in the relative sizes of the groups concerned. The Southern Kwakiutl were a sizable population in an area of exceptional population density (Kroeber 1947: 143). According to Wilson Duff (1957: personal communication) who has recently made a detailed study of the Indian populations of British Columbia, estimated populations for 1835 are:

Southern Kwakiutl	
Lekwiltok (1700)	7,500–8,000
Northern Kwakiutl	2,700
Nootka	7,500
Coast Salish	12,000
Bella Coola	2,000
Haida	6,000
Tsimshian	8,500

The Lekwiltok, the southernmost of the Southern Kwakiutl, seem to have been the only warlike Kwakiutl group and the only one to have engaged in territorial conquest. They pushed southward into Coast Salish territory to their present villages at Cape Mudge and Campbell River in post-contact times. There is a strong possibility that they may have been able to do this because they obtained guns through the Nimpkish before they were available to the Salish of the Gulf of Georgia (Taylor and Duff 1956: 63–65). Once settled in their new villages, they were in command of a natural maritime bottleneck comparable to a narrow mountain pass. They not only continued their depredations on the Coast Salish to the south, but they also preyed upon all maritime traffic, an activity that was to increase with the growth of Victoria as a trading center and a center of attraction to visiting Indians from the North. The Lekwiltok were, however, an exceptional Southern Kwakiutl group in many ways. The more usual pattern of Southern Kwakiutl relations with other Indian peoples was one of peace, broken occasionally by unplanned acts of violence against some party of canoe travelers or head-hunting raids in which a Southern Kwakiutl group from another area than that of the raiders might be in almost as much danger as a group having a different language and culture. Retaliatory expeditions were planned against Tsimshian, Haida, Bella Coola, and Bella Bella for violent acts they had committed in either organized raids or in chance meetings of travelers.

The peculiarly Kwakiutl and unwarlike nature of these expeditions is well illustrated by one that was made about 1835 (Boas 1897: 426–29, 664). The Bella Coola had attacked a Kwakiutl village which was at the time host to important visitors from other villages. Many people had been killed. A very large "war" party of thirty-two canoes was made up of men from all the Kwakiutl groups involved and their stated purpose was revenge: "Now Kwakiutl we will soar up and catch in our talons the Bi'luxla. We will be the great thunderbird" (Boas 1897: 427). They had not been out more than two days, however, when one of the war leaders suggested that instead of the Bella Coola they attack the Awikeno, a Northern Kwakiutl group of Rivers Inlet and a group closely allied to them. The war leader who wanted "to play with the Awikeno" was overruled. Almost immediately the lead canoes met with a party of six Bella Bella canoes. They learned through friendly conversation that there were great chiefs with important ceremonial equipment in the party, and they assured the Bella Bella that they would not harm them but would only compete with them ceremonially. When the impetuous and undiscriminating war leader arrived in his canoe, he almost immediately started the killing of the Bella Bella; all of the other Kwakiutl joined in and all agreed that they "had done a great thing." After that the Kwakiutl had the names of the Bella Bella chiefs and the hamatsa or Cannibal Dance, which was to become one of their most important ceremonies.

Kwakiutl "warfare" consisted of incidents of this sort, although in many cases the retaliation was even more indiscriminate and generalized, for instance, when a raid was planned to wipe away sorrow over the death of a relative from natural causes. Such a raid was made by a Nimpkish chief on the Nootka about 1850 (Curtis 1915: 120–21); his daughter had died and a rival chief, whose mother was Nootkan, seemed to him to rejoice rather than sorrow over the death. These cases describe Kwakiutl relations with other Indian peoples. There was peace (intermarriage, trade, the ability to communicate across language boundaries, the possibility of cultural interchange), but the peace was broken by sporadic acts of violence and destructiveness. In this period before 1849, there seem to have been two functions of such unwarlike raiding: to maintain the status quo by upholding the reputation of a group to be reckoned with and to augment the importation of valued cultural items, principally of a supernatural and ceremonial sort.

ECONOMIC AND SOCIAL ORGANIZATION

The Kwakiutl exploited their rich environment with great industriousness and technological skill. Not only were their methods of production adequate to maintain one of the highest levels of living in pre-Columbian America, but also their methods of distribution guaranteed that all were well fed, well housed, and well equipped with everything needed in daily living from canoes to wooden household dishes of all sorts, from fishing gear for each kind of fish to specialized tools like a woman's spade for digging lily bulbs. The development and use of storage techniques and containers for perishables and the manufacture of standardized and pluralized, or many times duplicated, durables show lavishness and an absence of any ceiling for production. (See the detailed descriptions in Boas 1897, 1906, and 1921 and the discussion of these in Codere 1950.) All Kwakiutl were producers—even children contributed in such simple things as berry-picking—and specialists, mountain-goat hunters, canoe-makers, carvers, seem to have carried on their specialty in addition to a generalized round of subsistence and everyday production. A fundamental division of labor in manufacturing was that men worked with rigid materials and women with fibers, but this division meant that many final products, such as a fishing line and hook were a combination of the skills and efforts of both. In food production the women seem to have collected the immobile plant crops and relatively immobile seafoods such as clams, and men fished and hunted. The distribution system for everyday goods and produce gave an abundance to everyone and involved no invidious distinctions in consumption, but full exposition of the social system is required for understanding the handling of prestige goods and particularly surpluses.

Boas (1940: 356–69) has given a detailed description of Kwakiutl social organization. The following is an attempt to use his description historically with the help of other historical data in order to see the pre-1849 situation.

Kwakiutl social organization, somewhat paradoxically on first glance, was both lineage-based and bilateral. The paradox disappears on close examination of the organization. Two things were of paramount importance to the people, and it can be seen that bilaterality would double the possibilities in both cases. A lineage claim was necessary, first, for any position of social rank with its accompanying crests and privileges and, second, for the use of lineage properties such as hunting and gathering grounds, fishing stations, and house sites. Thus, rights to the use of both important intangible and real property derived from lineage inheritance. Children seem to have been assigned to either the mother's or the father's lineage, and the parents' decision was based upon the central principle of placing each successive child in the position of highest rank available in either lineage. Secondary principles influencing the decision were that the male line was favored, if the parents were of equal rank; that certain crests and privileges, such as the "house name," could never pass out of the lineage by marriage; and that certain other privileges had that express plan of inheritance, always passing from a man to his daughter's son, and actually exercised by the man's son-in-law. Lineages were connected with particular villages and, for the most part, there were both lineage and village exogamy. It can be seen that these bilateral kin ties would have the effect of expanding both economic and social opportunities for the individual as well as of allying the different villages.

The units of Kwakiutl society were in order of their increasing size and inclusiveness:

1. The man and wife, who usually belonged to different lineages and different villages and who lived together with their unmarried children in a great house in which they had their own quarters and fireplace.

2. The household, which consisted of couples and their children. The household was headed by a senior male member of the lineage to which the house belonged and for the most part consisted of male members of the lineage with their wives and children. Often some of its male members were living for a period in the house of the wife's lineage and similarly the household contained some of the women of its lineage with their husbands of another lineage.

3. The lineage, or *numaym*, as Boas decided to call it (1940: 359–60) because of its peculiar character. Boas anglicized the Kwakiutl (>nE>mē'm) "of one kind." The numaym was usually identified with just one village and in possession of at least one great house.

4. The village, which consisted of at least one but more often several affiliated numayms.

5. The confederacy, which was the uniting of two or more villages to form a new village. Drucker introduced this useful term (1955: 117–18). We know that confederacies were established in historical times after

1849. They are included here for completeness, but the question of whether they existed before 1849 must be discussed.

The numaym is the fundamental unit of the system. It is character-ized by having a particular mythic geographical point of origin, an identification with a particular village often coinciding with its mythic location, and by the social differentiation of its membership according to rank and authority, if authority is understood to be qualified at all points by the necessity for co-operation of all its mem-bers in their relations within the numaym and with other numayms.

The description given would seem to fit the Kwakiutl for the en-tire historical period up to recent years. Certain difficulties arise, however, out of the dearth of the pre-1849 record and the fact that not long after that date there was such a drastic reduction in their number that it may have caused some change in social organization. These difficulties must be discussed and the historical data considered in order to clarify the picture of pre-1849 Kwakiutl social organ-ization.

Boas thought that the intermediate position of the Kwakiutl be-tween the matrilineal tribes of the north and the patrilineal Coast Salish to the south accounted for such mixed features of the Kwaki-utl system as the transfer of some hereditary privileges from a man to his daughter's son (1924: 329–30). He also thought that the Kwa-kiutl had obtained the concept of crest privileges from the north and that the first crests had probably been obtained in marriages of Kwa-kiutl men with northern women, presumably before the historical period. In an earlier publication (1920: 367) he considers, perhaps incorrectly, that the whole artistic development of the crest was probably not older than the middle of the last century, or about 1850.

The reports of Vancouver and Menzies are consistent with many of the important features of Kwakiutl social organization that have been mentioned and therefore give a dating of 1792 for them. Van-couver and Menzies witnessed protocol and behaviors that indicated at least three levels in a hierarchy of respect and authority. There were "Cheslakees" (Vancouver 1798: 347) the undoubted chief, the villagers whose trade with the visitors was supervised by Cheslakees (Newcombe 1923: 86–87), several near relations of Cheslakees who greeted the landing party ceremonially and took them through the village, and, last, "an elderly chief, to whom Cheslakees and every other person paid much respect" (Vancouver 1798: 347) and in whose house the official reception with its speeches, singing, and ceremony took place. The elderly chief also made the presentation of a strip of sea-otter skin to each member of the visiting company. Both journalists noted that the great houses were inhabited by several families, each one of which had a separate private compartment. These details are, however, only consistent with what we know Kwakiutl social organization to have been at a later date; they are not full or definite substantiation. For this it is fortunately possible to turn to the texts of family histories in which the founding of Fort Rupert by the Hudson's Bay Company is mentioned. By following the generations back, it is even possible to make fair estimates of dates, although it is only necessary here to see whether pre-1849 Kwakiutl social organization shows special characteristics. Based on two such lengthy and detailed accounts (Boas 1921: 836–85; 951–1002), the general features of Kwakiutl social organization that have been given are confirmed, and there are also certain important additions to the pre-1849 description that can be made.

In the family histories not only is the lineage of central importance, but it is emphasized again and again that a man of high rank in one lineage sought out high-ranking princesses of other lineages to marry. The account is largely taken up with these matters and with the reciprocal gift relations of the man and his father-in-law and the assignment of the children to positions in his own and his wife's or wives' numayms. There is elaborate specification and enumeration of the names, crests, and privileges transferred and of the tangible property distributed at the time. It seems, therefore, that crests must have been of importance before 1849; and there is some reason for thinking that they may have also been important in 1792, because the generations mentioned in the family histories would project back further than that and because Vancouver mentioned (1798: 346) painted house fronts and Cheslakees' house "distinguished by three rafters of stout timber raised above the roof, according to the architecture of Nootka."

One difference between the pre-1849 picture and that of the next period is that the various concerns of the people before 1849 seem to be of roughly equal importance. The family histories seem to treat in equal detail and as matters of equal interest: supernatural experiences and treasures, names, crests such as the right to use a certain type of house dish, privileges (really crests also) such as the right to put on the performance of a certain dance or ceremony, and distributions of property. It is only after "the white men came to Fort Rupert" that accounts of potlatches take up most of the contents of the family history.

A second point of contrast between the pre-1849 social organization and that of the next period can be detected in the family histories. This contrast is in the character of intervillage relations. There is detail in the family histories indicating that the numayms of the various villages were ranked. This detail includes such information as that about "good marriages" with princesses of another village where it is clear that the princess was in a high-ranking numaym in the village. "Bad" marriages to slaves are also mentioned in the histories in order to account for the worthless position of a numaym or branch of a numaym. The histories, however, contain nothing that suggests that the particular numayms or villages fall into any over-all scheme of social ranking. The villages seem in general to have been of equal rank, and it was as desirable to marry into one village as another. The greatest men in the numaym seem to be those who made such alliances by marrying princesses "all over the world." There is no rank order of villages for these sequences of marriages.

THE POTLATCH

In this pre-1849 period the Kwakiutl "potlatch" does not seem to be so developed or striking an institution that there is need for a distinctive term for it. There is nothing remarkable about the giving of gifts or even of ceremonialized giving in human society; and marriages, comings-of-age, and meetings with other villagers or outsiders are so frequently the occasion for gifts that Kwakiutl practices before 1849 seem less particularly Kwakiutl than human. The peculiarly Kwakiutl element, well established before 1849, was that all transfers of the intangible property, the names and crests they considered so important, were accompanied by distributions of real property. These transfers were made within the parental numayms or on marriages, so it might be expected that the numaym and all its household or households would be involved in both the distributions made and the gifts received by one of its members. The property distributed was surplus property or a copper shield that had a value in surplus property. Food surpluses were used in the feast-giving that invariably accompanied the potlatch, and the goods distributed were surpluses of blankets of fur, mountain goat hair, and cedar bark, mats, canoes, and slaves. Blankets were the most common and important potlatch item and the occasional slave who could be regarded as of little economic value was the least important.

Vancouver and Menzies give us the earliest description of a Kwakiutl potlatch. Vancouver records that when he gave presents to Cheslakees and some of his near relations they seemed greatly pleased. Later Vancouver and his party were entertained in one of the great houses and, as part of the ceremonies, all of them were "presented with a strip of sea-otter skin; the distribution of which occupied some time" (1798: 347). Neither Vancouver nor Menzies was impressed by the size of the distribution and neither considered it a mark of any special courtesy or consideration that they were given the very sea-otter skins that the Nimpkish knew they valued above anything else they had to trade and that were at that very time being traded at high prices. There seems, however, to have been a roughly equal exchange in which neither group lost or gained. If Vancouver's gifts were desirable items but not of great value, so were the potlatch strips, or in Menzies' account "slips," of otter skin.

The family histories are a source of information of the pre-1849 Kwakiutl potlatch. The potlatches in one of them (Boas 1921: 836–85) have been inventoried (Codere 1950: 92–93), and their common features are seen. It is notable that the many European trade goods in Kwakiutl hands before 1849 do not appear as potlatch items in this period. Vancouver gives a list of trade goods he saw among the Nimpkish: beads, hawk's bells, trinkets, buttons, muskets. He also lists goods the men of the "Discovery" gave in trade: sheet copper, blue cloth, and woolen jackets and trousers. Other outstanding features of the pre-1849 potlatches are the relatively small distributions and the fact that they remain about the same size from generation to generation. During the six generations before 1849, each of about twenty years (there is no record of the potlatches many years before this or until the fabulous first three generations of the account), five of the ten potlatches mentioned are 170–220 blankets in size, in a size range of 75–287 blankets, and there is no trend toward increasing the size; the two relatively small potlatches of the account were given in the later years.

CEREMONIALISM AND SUPERNATURALISM

As a basis for any sound statements about Kwakiutl supernatural-ism and ceremonialism before 1849, it is necessary to review the de-velopmental sequence worked out by Boas.

At first, according to Boas, or as far back as the reconstruction can be pushed, the Kwakiutl lived in patrilineal descent groups (1897: 336; 1924: 329–30), shared the widespread North American Indian guardian spirit concept and type of supernatural belief (1897: 336–37; 662), and shared also general North American and Northwest Coast literary materials and motifs (1897: 662–63). Boas's statements also imply that they were probably much concerned with warfare (1897: 664) and in all likelihood possessed some religious ceremonial-ism in connection with war. This interpretation corresponds with the situation Wike (1952) considers must have at one time character-ized the Northwest Coast and the Kwakiutl. Wike's interest is in the significance of the dead in Northwest Coast culture, although an im-portant part of her work is concerned with warfare, head-hunting, and cannibalism. However, it was probably at this time that the Kwa-kiutl originated elaborate ceremonials that were intimately connected with the methods, spirits, and symbols of war. Boas states that the Kwakiutl originated the ceremonials that were later to spread over the whole area (1897: 660–61) and that the rituals and the secret so-cieties that performed them "had their origin in methods of warfare" (664).

The Kwakiutl then got the idea of hereditary crests from the matrilineal people of the North (Boas 1897: 336–37, 662; 1924: 329–30; 1920: 367–68), and a series of complexly interconnected devel-opments was set in motion. Guardian spirits became crests inherited through the female line by the device of a man's passing on the right to use a ceremony to his son-in-law, who would have one of his rela-tives re-enact it and who would finally transmit it to his daughter's husband. The person who re-enacted the guardian spirit incident had to be initiated into the appropriate secret society for that type of ceremonial, and the initiation involved the seclusion of the initiate while presumably under the influence of the spirit and his being "tamed" or freed from the spirit's hold by the ceremony. The reli-gious significance of the ceremony seems to have been attenuated and no longer resembled the individual and often intense nature of guardian spirit relationships so common in the rest of North America. Family histories and guardian spirit legends, in so far as they were separate from family histories, were reworked to give historic validity to a supernatural ancestor and his crests for each numaym and to record the transmission of the now altered guardian spirit ceremonials from a man to his son-in-law as crests (Boas 1897: 337, 662–63). It was still possible, however, to obtain a man's family names and rank or such ceremonial crests as he had by killing him in warfare. In the latter case it is not clear on the face of it how a man would know the details of the ceremonial he had obtained. Usually the father-in-law had the dance ceremony put on for the son-in-law's benefit. Since, however, a man did put on the ceremonies he obtained in warfare, it seems justifiable to conclude that their connection with warfare was still very intimate. Perhaps obtaining ceremonials in war involved a re-creation of their original spiritual significance which could therefore sanction any innovation or use of known ceremonial detail.

The cannibal ceremony and warfare were closely connected, and it is clear that one form of the ceremony was taken over by the Kwakiutl from the Hē'iLtsuq (Bella Bella) about 1835 (Boas 1897: 664). It seems probable that there was some kind of ceremonial cannibalism long before that date. In one of the family histories (Boas 1921: 951–1002) the exact nature of the cannibal ceremony is not clear, but in another (836–85) there is no doubt. The cannibal ate a slave and this particular cannibal was in the fifth ascending generation starting with a man who was old enough to marry around the time of the founding of Fort Rupert. This would date the ceremony about 1769. Also, the nature of many of the supernatural beings who were thought to preside over the winter ceremonials, for instance, BaxbakuālanuXsī'wae (the first one to eat man at the mouth of the river, that is, in the north) is cannibalistic and does more than suggest that the Kwakiutl had the idea of cannibalism from early times. When, therefore, the Kwakiutl received certain Cannibal Dance ceremonials from the Bella Bella about 1835, they were a revival of something they had had earlier—a form of the ceremony that was somehow more impressively organized or equipped—or they were simply a sufficiently recent acquisition of a crest, which like most crests was distinctive from others only in details and not in fundamental type, so that it was particularly memorable to informants in 1894 and 1895.

The latter alternative seems more consistent with the whole picture of development.

One further point deserves notice. If Boas' ideas about the influence of northern cultures on the Kwakiutl are correct, and there seems no reason to doubt them, it is possible to look at the reconstruction from the point of view of the relations of all the groups, including the perhaps fairly isolated Coast-Salish-like village groups of the early Kwakiutl. Once the idea of hereditary crests as desirable social distinctions came in, acquiring the ones that other lineage groups in the same locality possessed became important, as did having rarer crest distinctions. The family histories contain many instances of the desire of one numaym to have some crest they saw in possession of another and of cases of marriages "far outside" (Boas 1940: 368), for example, to Bella Bella, Bella Coola, or Tsimshian to obtain crests. There are also cases in which a lineage did not want some crest to go out of the lineage by marriage, other cases in which it was opposed to having the crest go to some particular lineage. In spite of the fact that the desire for crests was the motive for some acts of violence both between Kwakiutl groups and between the Kwakiutl and those of other cultures, it must be also considered as a powerful force for making and maintaining peaceful relations in the area.

In other words, it seems possible to look at the reconstruction from another point of view. In the early days the Kwakiutl may have consisted of relatively small and isolated groups for which success in warfare was important to assure survival. Such prestige as any group might have perhaps consisted of having to be reckoned with offensively and defensively in war. It would then be small wonder that warlike or cannibalistic supernatural beings played an important part as guardian spirits or that ceremonialism would develop about them. The idea of hereditary crests from the north might have taken on importance because it involved both prestige and a method of peaceful affiliation of groups through intermarriage. This is not to say that there were no intergroup marriages before; it is rather a question of reinforcing the reasons for making them, consequently increasing their number and finally enlarging the entire area over which relations of peace and prestige could exist. As we shall see, the Kwakiutl never reached anything like political unity, but in later years it seems that they were very different from the Coast Salish, who had no structural unification of any kind.

Before 1849, for at least a half century, Kwakiutl religious beliefs and practices revolved around violent and warlike supernaturals—at a rather remote and safe distance. Neither these supernaturals nor the supernatural ancestors of the various numayms were close to the people or were thought to help or hinder them in their daily living; the only time the relationship was close was when one man killed another and then became ceremonially possessed. Other beliefs are indicated by the fact that they prayed to the sun as individuals for general blessings and success, to the weather for help in what they were doing, to the animals they killed for some desirable trait, such as industriousness, that was characteristic of the animal, to plants they gathered for good success in using them medicinally to help a sick relative. Their prayers seem to be more the assertion of human hopes than supplications, expression of rapport, or acknowledgment of supernatural powers (Boas 1930: 182–210). As Boas says, the Kwakiutl were aggressive in their relations with the supernatural (1935: 183). They believed in the power of evil people to work successful sorcery with such things as the hair combings of the living and a corpse, usually stolen from its burial place. They also had shamans and believed to a degree in their power to cure.

Their beliefs were not unified into any system or any philosophical whole. This is equally true of the legends about supernatural beings. Boas states (1897: 395–96) that even for the most important spirits of the winter ceremonial it is not clear "in what the gift of the spirit consists" (396); that "fundamental mythological concepts are very self-contradictory" (1935: 177); and that the mythology has elements "that have never been worked into a system" (1940: 447–48). No religious unification could thrive when the people were primarily interested in putting supernaturals in a human context that would give historical validity to the assumption and display of crests. A group discussion of the question "who is the great creator of man, of our ancestors, of all our tribes" is completely confused and inconclusive when each of the members of the various numayms recounts the historical supernatural origin of his numaym but is unable to relate it to the other origin stories to anybody's satisfaction (Boas 1935: 177–78). The ceremonies relating to their beliefs were the most organized part of their religious life, yet as a reading of *The Social Organization and the Secret Societies of the Kwakiutl Indians* will demonstrate and as Boas stated, these ceremonies are in a state of "enormous complexity and confusion" (1924: 331).

The concept of secularization has been rarely applied to any so-called primitive people and must be used with care. If it is taken to mean the assignment of the supernatural to a relatively unimportant role in the culture, while interest and value become centered in the non-religious area or in some non-religious aspect of the culture, the concept of secularization can apply to the Kwakiutl even before 1849. The interest in crests was certainly an overwhelming one by that date. If the Cannibal Dance ceremony that came from the Bella Bella as a hereditary crest about 1835 was the source of interest and excitement to the people that it seems to have been, then they were less secularized than they were to become in later years. It must be remembered, however, that the interest and excitement were aroused by its being a new, or revived or impressively elaborated crest, as well as its being a ceremonial or horrifying drama. The growth of potlatching in connection with Kwakiutl ceremonial life was to take secularization much further in the years after 1849, so in this period it should be considered a process that has been definitely set in motion but that was to continue.

CURING AND NON-SUPERNATURAL KNOWLEDGE

The Kwakiutl had a vast body of secular or non-supernatural knowledge. Their ethnobotany and ethnozoology have not received systematic study, so there are no measures of their knowledge in these areas as there are for other groups, such as the Navahos, but their operations in their environment show control based upon an intimate acquaintance with the land and sea and all their products. If they had some curious notions, for example, that they lived on the shores of a great river, we should not be surprised: this notion had some basis because tidal currents in their area have a northward set and because the navigational problems are river-like, with strong currents, eddies, and tidal overfalls.

Their pharmacopoeia was extensive and furnished them with specifics for most of the familiar bodily complaints. The various preparations, usually from plants, were made by a close relative and the only supernatural element involved was the familiar matter-of-fact type of prayer, in this case, to the effect that it was hoped that the medicine would work. Medical technology went so far as to include treating the burns of children with some blood from one of the parents and treating extensive and severe burns by encasing the patient in the blubbery skin of a seal (Boas 1930: 209–45).

Their close watch on nature was, after all, the enabling condition of their complex and productive type of economic life. They knew when fish ran or spawned and the stage of growth when kelp could best be used as oulachen oil storage bottles. They knew the seasonal rhythms and so wasted little or no productive time through miscalculation of harvest times for plant or animal crops.

Boas's *Geographical Names of the Kwakiutl Indians* (1934) is documentation of the extent to which they knew the physical features of their country, and many of the place names indicate the availability of some local resource. During a tour of the entire Kwakiutl region in 1955 the book still had value as a natural resources Baedecker; the place called "Having Porpoises" lived up to its name and, had the tour been at an earlier date, so would have "Tswade" or "Having Oulachen."

Kwakiutl month names were predominantly names of some gathering season, for instance, "Near-to-Oulachen-Fishing-Season" (Boas 1905–9: 413). From four different Kwakiutl groups Boas received twelve month names which indicated that the name of one moon really covered two, and he thought that some kind of readjustment was made in mid-winter.

All their technology was impressive and indicated knowledge of the material dealt with, whether it was spreading a dugout canoe with steam and uric acid, making the four sides of a wooden box out of one board, or raising and setting house posts weighing tons. Their understanding of storage problems was particularly important and remarkable. They stored quantities of fish, fish spawn, oil, meat, tallow, berries, and seaweeds. There were usually at least several ways of storing just one species of fish, depending on the amount of fat in it when taken and the cuts that could be handled in different ways for different results in taste, type of cooking required, and length of time it could be kept (Boas 1921: 223–41, 305–77).

THE ARTS

Kwakiutl art before 1849 exhibited the features that were so exuberantly developed after that date. Again, northern influences in the crest idea and in animal symbolism and design are to be credited as the stimulus to Kwakiutl cultural change. As Boas pointed out (1927: 280–81), it would be impossible to decide whether the idea of social standing or the use of animal designs to symbolize it gave the prime impetus, for the two seem to have reinforced one another at every possible point. Except for many common and everyday objects which were decorated with the earlier geometric type of Kwakiutl design, their art was a crest art. Boas claims that there was no painting of crests on house fronts until about 1860 (1927: 289), but Vancouver's report makes this doubtful. On the point of whether their designs were geometric or representational, he is either misleading or recording a not too uncommon type of European rejection of Northwest Coast art:

... The houses ... were arranged in regular streets; the larger ones were the habitations of the principal people who had them decorated with paintings and other ornaments, forming various figures, apparently the rude designs of fancy; tho it is by no means improbable, they might annex some meaning to the figures they describe, too remote or hieroglyphical for our comprehensions. (1798: 346.)

I would conclude that the graphic and plastic art of the Kwakiutl was probably a full crest art in the years from 1792–1849, and, if one type of crest, the painted house front, did not exist in 1792, Vancouver at least saw smaller carvings and paintings of a crest nature on Kwakiutl house fronts.

There is no description of the nature of the musical art of the people before 1849, but there is ample evidence that the literary arts had also been brought under the crest idea. The results seem to have been not to stimulate but to inhibit and depress literary developments. Boas documents very fully in *Kwakiutl Culture as Reflected in Mythology* (1935: 171–90) how all the Kwakiutl stories having to do with people and human society suffer from having motivations restricted to the desire to obtain crests, from plots of little variety and a coherence based only on stringing together as "history" the incidents upon which crest privileges could be based. It might have been that, as the crest idea became increasingly important and as the chief occasion for telling myths and legends became the public one of transferring the privilege or displaying it, legends were gradually stripped of anything but the crest details they regarded as appropriate for the occasion. Something of this sort is necessary to explain the relentless and unvarying purpose of their main literary art. In only their animal stories are there human interest, variety, and imagination.

SUMMARY

In sum, Kwakiutl culture between 1792 and 1849 was a culture in flux. It is not possible in many instances to determine whether important changes occurred before or after 1792, but it is clear that they were in progress after that date. It is also clear that the changes had their original impetus in the idea of crests imported from the northern people. A concept of social distinctiveness and differentiation of an individual and his kin, and this distinctiveness symbolized through artistic, literary, ceremonial, architectural, and rhetorical devices, was changing the structure and the functional interrelationships of the culture. Exuberant developments in some areas, such as ceremonialism and the graphic arts, can be traced to the crest idea, as can changes in the character of associated areas, such as religion.

Also before 1849, it was characteristic of the Kwakiutl that crests were transferred on public occasions made memorable not only by the feasting and ceremony that accompanied them but also by the distribution of some notable amount of real property. These pre-1849 potlatches seem, however, to have been relatively modest and similar in size, limited to a few types of goods conveniently appropriate for distribution. There seems to have been no idea that the size of the potlatch had any relation to the prestige of the donor and his crests or to any system of social ranking or public notoriety throughout the culture.

The Potlatch Period: 1849–1921

The years from 1849 to about 1921 in Kwakiutl culture history seem best characterized as the Potlatch Period. During these years the Kwakiutl potlatch not only came to have unique features and extraordinary size, but it also came to be the central and predominating institution in the culture. Closely connected with the potlatch were other major tendencies at work during these years: a continual and sharp decline of Kwakiutl population; a similarly sharp increase in the numbers of white Europeans in the area and in the frequency and intensity of contacts with Whites; and, last, a marked increase in the material wealth of the Kwakiutl as a result of their ability to take advantage of the expanding economy of their area.

Although these developments, with all the cultural changes they will be seen to involve, run through the entire period, it is useful to subdivide it according to the villages that were the centers of both the White and the Kwakiutl influences that were to bring about changes in Kwakiutl culture. From the date of its establishment by the Hudson's Bay Company in 1849 until about 1880, Fort Rupert was the important Kwakiutl village. In 1881 the Kwakiutl Agency and mission were set up at Alert Bay.

The founding of Fort Rupert was followed immediately by changes in Kwakiutl culture, particularly by changes in the social rank organization of the people and changes in potlatching. Unusual opportunities were available to the people of the various numayms and villages that moved to Fort Rupert while it was being set up. They benefited from the presence of the fort by being near at hand, and, probably, by mediating trade between the company and visiting Kwakiutl and other Indians. The result was the exaggeration of the wealth and social importance of the "Fort Ruperts" and a great increase in potlatching generally. This Fort Rupert subperiod was peaceful and business-oriented. Warfare and raiding ended about 1865. Among the new opportunities open to the Kwakiutl were those connected with the boom city of Victoria in the south. Mission, agency, and other governmental influences were not directly present in the Kwakiutl area, although from 1867 on legislation and plans were being set up on general policy toward Indians, liquor, and Indian lands. With the establishment of the agency and mission in Alert Bay, what the Kwakiutl had seen casually as visitors to Victoria suddenly became a permanent part of the local scene along with a school, sawmill, canneries, and the Royal Canadian Mounted Police. During this Alert Bay subperiod potlatching increased in frequency, in the numbers of people present, and in the size of the distributions made. Winter dancing also continued, although, as in the case of potlatching, successful evasion of the law prohibiting it depended upon holding it away from Alert Bay. The period ended with a great potlatch, one of the largest ever given and one of the first to be followed by measures enforcing the Indian Act or the law against potlatching and winter dancing. This dramatic series of events involved the Royal Canadian Mounted Police, native informers jealous of the potlatch-giver, and pressures brought to bear on the agency by a highly missionized half-Kwakiutl. The great 1921 potlatch and the events connected with it coincided with the end of the period of expanding economy. The Great Depression started a decade early for the Kwakiutl, who were caught in an economic squeeze caused by the technological change-over to gas boats, and it was to continue through the thirties and long enough to bring the Kwakiutl potlatch, one of the world's unique institutions, to an end.

COMMUNITY ORGANIZATION AND EXTERNAL RELATIONS

Immediately after 1849 the settlement pattern and community organization of the Kwakiutl underwent a significant change. For the first time there was a center in the Kwakiutl area, one village that was of outstanding size, influence, and importance. Before that date there is nothing to suggest that any Kwakiutl village had more than local prominence. When Fort Rupert was being built by the Hudson's Bay men, groups from four different Kwakiutl villages moved there. Thus was formed the Kwakiutl Confederacy, as Drucker has called it, and, although it is clear that earlier in the history of the people there must have been both amalgamations of numayms and even villages, as well as the splitting of these groups, this amalgamation was at least one of the largest in numbers of groups involved, if not the greatest, that had ever been made. It is not clear in every detail, but it seems the case that the members of the Fort Rupert Confederacy had particularly easy access to the economic advantages offered by the trading post and the visiting Indians attracted to it. There were employment and trade opportunities at the post, and it does not seem unlikely that the "Fort Ruperts" were able to profit as interpreters, middlemen, and entrepreneurs in relations with other Kwakiutl and northern Indian visitors, so that they were for a time not only the largest Kwakiutl group but also the most wealthy.

The Southern Kwakiutl numbered an estimated 7,500–8,000 in 1835 (Duff 1957); in 1882 the first agency census gives their number as 2,264. This startling decline was due primarily to disease. There was smallpox in 1837, 1862, and 1876; and measles, influenza, venereal disease, and tuberculosis continued the diminution. Medical measures and the gradual acquisition of immunities did not bring about an upward trend until about 1924, when the population numbered only a little over a thousand.

While similar steep declines were taking place among the other Indian populations of the Coast, the population of Whites was increasing at an overwhelming rate in the Kwakiutl area itself and particularly in the area to the south which the Kwakiutl began to visit with increasing frequency and which became a part of their social and economic world. When Mayne visited Fort Rupert in the 1850's, he saw only the officer and eight other Hudson's Bay men at Fort Rupert. Even in the early days of the Alert Bay Agency the White group living among the Kwakiutl was small. In contrast the city of Victoria on the southern tip of Vancouver Island became a metropolis almost overnight, and it attracted the Kwakiutl and all the Indians of the area as visitors. It increased from 500 in 1856 to over 25,000 when the Fraser River gold rush came in 1858. Although some of the

TABLE 9

KWAKIUTL AND BRITISH COLUMBIA POPULATION, 1881–1921

Year	Southern Kwakiutl	Chinese	Japanese	Total British Columbia
1881.........	2,264 (1882)	4,383	....	49,459
1911.........	1,208	27,774	4,738	392,480
1921.........	1,039 (1924)	39,587	9,021	524,582

population of the gold rush was a temporary gain and many of the American miners were to return to the States, other immigrants—White, Chinese, and Japanese—swelled the total southern British Columbia population, as Table 9 shows.

Kwakiutl contacts with the Hudson's Bay traders at Fort Rupert seem to have been harmonious and profitable for all concerned. It is difficult to assess the effect that the small settlement of Hudson's Bay men had upon the culture. Company policy had long been to conduct business with Indians as they were, not to revolutionize their way of life, and this seems to have held at Fort Rupert. In the 1850's, Mayne visited the post and estimated that its business must have been very profitable with costs of about £600 and an income from the fur trade of almost ten times that amount (1862: 184–85). The activity of the village must also have been very great, for Mayne says that there were generally from two to three thousand Indians there, and many of these would have been visitors (1862: 243). Certainly the Hudson's Bay garden that was fertilized with some 3,000 salmon purchased from the Indians with an equal number of leaves of tobacco was never to have any cultural impact on the completely non-agricultural Kwakiutl (Mayne 1862: 183). The tale Mayne tells of some of the company men's joining in the drinking party that took place when some Indians had brought back a quantity of liquor from Victoria (1862: 208) also suggests that the men of the company were the friends and not the mentors of the Kwakiutl. This is borne out by an incident in 1851. The company was accused of insufficient co-operation with the governmental authorities in the south in not helping bring to swift punishment the Indians who murdered three White sailors who had deserted ship near Fort Rupert. The best interpretation of the complex reports of this incident seems to be that the Hudson's Bay men on the spot knew the people, Indian and White, involved and knew the circumstances and would have found little sense in going by even a well-tried book to say nothing of the brand new book of British governmental authority in the region.

About fifteen years after the establishment of Fort Rupert, John Lord described its layout and equipment as deserving of the name of fort in everything but the use to which it had ever been put. He records that the only time the cannon was fired was in a comic opera attempt to impress the Indians, who promptly brought the cannon ball back from the woods to trade for something nearer to their fancy. (Lord 1886: 164). The chief direct cultural influence of the men of the fort on the Kwakiutl seems to have come about because one of them had married a Tsimshian woman, and their children were to become the famous Hunt family of Fort Rupert, a family that was thoroughly Kwakiutl and which had crests from the Tsimshian that were valuable in Kwakiutl eyes.

Relations with other Indians also took place at Fort Rupert, but the most important contacts seem to have taken place in the course of visits to Victoria, which attracted Indians from the entire Northwest Coast and which caused an unprecedented amount of Indian traffic in the area.

From 1858 on, Victoria offered opportunities of which the Kwakiutl, like all the Indian people of the Coast, seem to have been quick to take advantage. It seems likely that the city, with its large and cosmopolitan population, was itself a source of interest and excitement. Indian men held temporary jobs as laborers, and Indian women earned wealth as laundresses and prostitutes. Around 1864 and 1865 a Tlawitsis Kwakiutl was reported to be sending his wife down to Victoria as a prostitute two times a year. On each of these visits she was said to have earned at least one bale of blankets. A bale contained fifty blankets and was worth about $125 at the time (George Hunt n.d.).

Boas described the miserable conditions under which the Indians lived during their stays in Victoria (1891: 76); but apparently they were able to put up with squalor and filth in order to return home with wealth and liquor.

Trouble with other Indians in Victoria or on traveling to and from Victoria often occurred. A typical incident took place around 1860. A Kwakiutl chief was murdered by a Songhie in Victoria. On the trip home the Kwakiutls captured and carried off a Nanaimo woman (Mayne 1862: 208). Back at Fort Rupert the Kwakiutls held a drinking bout with the liquor they had bought in Victoria and decided to make war on the Songhies to avenge the death of their chief, but when the government gunboat anchored offshore and the officials waited for sobriety to prevail, they turned the Nanaimo woman over to the authorities and forgot about their war plans (Mayne 1862: 208–9). For every incident of this sort, and there were none after 1865, there must have been many peaceful contacts with other Indian peoples. While in Victoria the Kwakiutl bought coppers from northern Indians. At Fort Rupert also there seems to have been an increase in the peaceful relations they had as buyers and sellers and as hosts and guests. Although government gunboats figured in the incident mentioned above and in a punitive expedition to the Nawitti Kwakiutl in 1852, these shows of force seem not to have been necessary to keep the peace among people for whom, as Hawthorn says, war was "more a horrifying concept than a practice" (Hawthorn, Belshaw, Jamieson 1958: 37).

Kwakiutl contacts with Whites during the years between 1849 and 1881 seem to have been relatively infrequent except at Fort Rupert, where there was a small group of Whites permanently in residence. The Kwakiutl also had the initiative in most interactions with the exception of the very infrequent visits made to their territory by government gunboats. The interactions themselves seem to have been

mostly secular, commercial, and profitable to both sides. The interactions with other Indians were largely of this same sort, but there
is evidence of an increase also in unanticipated scrapes and brawls.

The establishment of the Kwawkewlth Agency in Alert Bay in
1881 marks the beginning of important changes in the type of contact
community confronting the Kwakiutl in their homeland. It was not
the end of a laissez faire era in Kwakiutl-White relations for the very
good reason that many factors apart from the nature of Kwakiutl
culture stood in the way of law enforcement and Westernization,
but from the beginning it was a well-planned and expansive extension
of Canadian culture and Canadian government into this area. Re-
serves had been set up on the sound and equitable principle that the
Indians should retain title to any lands they had used. The Indian
Liquor Ordinance had been made law in 1867. The Indian Act of
1876 contained provisions that prohibited both potlatching and winter
dancing, provisions that were specifically directed against the Kwakiutl and other groups of the Northwest Coast. The first missionary,
A. J. Hall, spent two years at Fort Rupert learning Kwakiutl in preparation for the founding of the mission in Alert Bay. The technology of
salmon canning, developed from the 1860's on, had been the fishing
industry's preparation for the establishment of canneries at Alert Bay
and other places in Kwakiutl territory, Rivers Inlet, Smith Inlet,
Bones Bay, and Knight Inlet.

While Alert Bay grew very quickly into a town with western
Canadian industries, schools, police, and government representatives
which also established themselves or exerted some influence elsewhere
in the Kwakiutl area, the Kwakiutl remained the greater part of the
local population throughout this period. Mission, agency, and cannery personnel were few in number. To the south, however, the
non-Indian population growth was prodigious. The construction of
the transcontinental railway began in 1880 and thousands of immigrants were attracted to the province. The tremendous economic expansion begun then continues to this day. The Kwakiutl continued
their visits to the cities—Vancouver became the large and magnetic
place—and frequently included the hop fields and the salmon fisheries
of the Fraser in their round of seasonal occupations.

In Boas's report on his visit to Victoria published in 1891 there is
the only record known to me of how the Indians, including the
Kwakiutl, felt about the Chinese, who formed the chief part of the

non-Western immigration in the early years of this period. Boas said that the Indians had a deadly hatred for the Chinese, despised them, and considered themselves to be infinitely above them. It is an interesting question whether the Indians were mirroring local White attitudes toward the Chinese, since there seem to have been no Chinese at all or at most a few cannery workers in Kwakiutl territory and the Chinese were never to compete with the Kwakiutl to the extent that the Japanese did in the fishing industry. In the 1890's the Japanese came to British Columbia. By 1896 some 6,000 Japanese fishermen made up a quarter of the labor force in the industry and by 1901 Japanese women were employed in many canneries (Gladstone 1953: 29). Salmon fishing for canneries was a particularly attractive and profitable type of employment for the Kwakiutl. Kwakiutl fishermen knew the local waters; the women packed the fish in the cans; many of the children did light work; and all lived in the barracks provided by the canneries. The employment was on their own initiative, and there were alternatives to manipulate according to the place they liked to go, the cannery they liked best or thought most profitable to work for, and the pattern they wanted to follow including other seasonal activities such as those connected with fishing and gathering for their own subsistence. In this pre-1921 period there is every reason to think that the Japanese did not compete with the Kwakiutl to any serious extent; a look at Kwakiutl income figures over these years would seem to prove this (Codere 1950: 45), but there were occasions for friction and in some cases diminished profits. There were violent Fraser River strikes in 1900 and 1901 involving Kwakiutl and Japanese as well as other Indians and White fishermen. However, in 1907 Indian women working in the canneries demanded and received higher wages, and, in 1912, Indian drag seiners at the Nimpkish Kwakiutl village demanded and received a higher price for their sockeye salmon. These successes indicate that Japanese competition was not severe for the Kwakiutl until after the First World War (Gladstone 1953: 29–30).

The general description of the attitudes of Indians and Whites toward one another given in *The Indians of British Columbia* (Hawthorn, Belshaw and Jamieson 1958: 58–60) cannot be improved on for the Kwakiutl. The Whites saw the Indian as a "person to be Westernized by a policy determined and administered by the Whites, as the proper charge of the churches for schooling, as a desired . . .

worker or as a soul to be saved, as a nuisance because of contrasting morals and institutions," and "as the Vanishing Red Man." Kwakiutl concepts of Whites seem to be those that in general are ascribed to the Indians before 1850: the Whites were "desirable for trade supplies," were "granted superiority only in a limited number of technical fields," and "not granted any superiority in social fields." Before 1921, however, the groundwork was certainly being laid for "widespread and general distrust" of Whites and for the attitude that keynotes many of their relations today, "The Whites claim their superiority gracelessly; the Indians grant it in a like manner." As the same report points out, the Indians saw not only White group characteristics but individual differences, and it is best at this point to summarize the main types of Kwakiutl-White interrelations with this in mind.

The job of agent during this entire period must have been one of maximum frustration, since apart from the task of collecting and keeping up to date a large statistical record, one of the agent's main duties was to try to prevent potlatching under well-nigh impossible circumstances. Only the people at or near Alert Bay were under anything like close supervision by the agent, whose budget frequently prevented him from making more than a yearly round of all the Kwakiutl villages in any case. If he got any hint of a potlatch gathering, and he seldom did in a population solidly behind keeping such news from him, he found the geography of the land on the side of the lawbreakers. Potlatching throughout the period has been fully documented (Codere 1950: 81–86), and winter dancing was to continue just as active as potlatching until after 1895. All the agents became more or less resigned to it, some, as my informants have made clear to me, with better grace and humor than others. All the agents from 1881 on are remembered as individuals by Kwakiutl living today, and I have heard many anecdotes about them. One actually helped once to tow some Kwakiutl canoes that he knew perfectly well contained a group on its way to potlatch. Another named his gas boat "Chief," to the people's scorn. Another, Halliday, wrote a book (1935) which offended their sensibilities by claiming that Indian women were bought and sold "like cows." The critical wrath expressed seems justified because the very woman named as having the kind of plural marriage career that proved the "like cows" charge was in fact a noteworthy monogamist. The agents mostly kept statistics and exhorted the people to send their children to school, not to potlatch, not to live in great houses, and not to go to Victoria. There was little else they could do for or against the interests of the people. They could only get along with them or fail to do so, as the case might be, so that the relationship seems to have been more or less reduced to an interpersonal one.

The relationship between the people and their missionaries was again largely a personal one that brought about no changes in the institutions of their culture during this period. The missionaries, nevertheless, did leave an inheritance that seems to have compounded interest for later years. The first missionary knew both Chinook Jargon and Kwakiutl after a fashion and translated evangelical hymns and even a song or two like "Frère Jacques" into Kwak^ʔwala. As late as 1913, and there would probably have been a similar report in later years were it not for the curtailment of all agency reporting during and after the war, the results of missionary labors are flatly labeled "negative" (Canada, *Annual Report on Indian Affairs* 1913: 229).

A school was started in 1881 in a room at the mission. Ten years later a school was built, and soon afterward an industrial school and a girls' home were completed. School attendance was frequently very brief and interrupted, and a glance at the biography of Smoke from Their Fires (Ford 1941) reveals this and some of the reasons behind it. Through the years, however, the attendance figures were fairly large, especially as a proportion of the total Kwakiutl population which was declining to a figure not much over a thousand by 1921. In 1896 an average daily attendance of 42 is claimed for all schools, in 1905 an attendance of 43, and in 1916 it is claimed that of the 183 Kwakiutl children of school age 130 attended school (Canada, *Annual Report on Indian Affairs* 1881–1921). If by 1914 there were some 241 Kwakiutl who spoke English and 96 who could write it, this is impressive. There is no question that literacy was valued and had utility. Indians who were educated during this period are proud of their literacy. They kept potlatch records and accounts and could conduct their business operations that much more cannily. The attitude was that school was for intellectual labors over the three R's, and trouble came up again and again, as it did in the school career of Smoke from Their Fires, over the assignment of time to housekeeping or industrial tasks calculated to teach moral or vocational lessons. The result seems to have been literacy and that alone for this period.

ECONOMIC ORGANIZATION

In the Potlatch Period, and as the condition for there being a Potlatch Period, Kwakiutl wealth was increasing progressively. Partly because of Kwakiutl habits of industriousness and partly because the Kwakiutl yearly round of migratory and seasonal occupations fit the new contact conditions to the point of exploiting them, material wealth poured into the hands of the people.

In the Fort Rupert subperiod from 1849 to 1881 the chief sources of income were the sale of furs to the Hudson's Bay Company, employment by the company, and temporary jobs, including prostitution, in the city of Victoria. A flood of new goods was added to their material culture, and of these the most remarkable were the cheap gray-white woolen blankets acquired in quantities far beyond any need. They were used instead as a medium of exchange and as the main property distributed in potlatches. The people also date the end of their nakedness from 1849. Although Vancouver saw some European clothing among them and traded clothing to them earlier, general replacement of their old minimal and optional attire does not seem to have taken place until after 1849 and, if we are to believe a visitor in the 1860's, was still optional for some at that time (Lord 1866: 170). Tea, coffee, and liquor were added to make a list of beverages whereas before they had only used water. Biscuits and molasses were added to their diet. From 1881 to the end of the period the increase in incomes and the constant additions of material goods continued. A potlatch account book of the 1920's gives a full list of Canadian-American consumer goods of the time:

pails	clocks	gas boats
teapots	watches	shawls
basins	bedsteads	silks (?)
cups	trunks	sweaters
washing tubs	hand sewing machines	coats
looking glasses	treadle sewing machines	jackets
glassware	canvas boxes	hats
bowls	camphor boxes	underskirts
hardware	dressers	stockings
cake plates	gramophones	towels
lamps	pool tables	dresses
guitars	gas boat engines	buttons
violins		

In addition to these goods, masks, headdresses, blankets, button blankets, silver bracelets and many other more "Indian" goods were listed, almost all of which would, however, have taken cash to buy.

Throughout the period the old economic organization persisted. The people continued to get not only their own subsistence but also their accustomed surpluses of fish, oil, and other foods. The old custom of moving according to a pattern of seasonal occupations from spring to winter continued, although many of these jobs were now paid for in cash or blankets and some went farther afield, even as far as the hop yards of the Fraser River Valley. In this there were, of course, changes in the selections made from larger numbers of alternative temporary occupations. It seems to have been the handicrafts that suffered in the consequent redistributions of production time. Agency reports show that the number of Indian-made canoes decreased from the turn of the century, being replaced first by European rowboats and then, after about 1912, by gas boats. The acquisition of European household goods and tools is frequently noted in the agency reports and, although no figures are given, much replacement must have occurred during this period. Nothing else, considering the life span of material objects, would account for their paucity at the present time.

The Kwakiutl economic year of about nine months of industrious production followed by three months of winter vacation from most production continued throughout this period. The vacation months became so filled with travel, potlatches, and ceremonial that this again may have contributed to the neglect of the handicraft production that had been carried on previously in the longer periods of time spent in the "winter" villages. Kwakiutl business and enterprise filled the greater part of the year. The people seem to have been capable of turning any economic opportunity to their advantage, whether it was a bounty on hair seals that could be collected by turning in the noses of a species of seal rather easier to hunt, filling a temporary and lucrative demand for rat-fish oil to grease logging skids, or going to fish salmon in some locality that promised an exceptional yield and profits for a particular year.

Industriousness and entrepreneurial flexibility were habits they carried over from the past into the new expanding economic opportunities, and the result was wealth of the kind they wanted for clear purposes of their own. To understand these purposes or how their new and increasing wealth could serve them, it is necessary to know the nature and changes in Kwakiutl social organization from 1849 on.

SOCIAL ORGANIZATION

Changes in social organization began with the founding of Fort Rupert when most of the population from four Kwakiutl villages migrated there to be near the post and formed a confederacy. The groups making up the confederacy were ranked one to four in social greatness and the "Fort Ruperts" as a group were ranked first of all. Before this time there is nothing in the family histories to indicate that there was a Kwakiutl-wide system of socially ranking the various villages, the numayms that made them up, or the individual standing places in the numayms. Even when the history is told at a later date by some one who wishes to claim its great social importance, braggadocio about ancestors is confined to general claims of their greatness and of their achievement of "firsts," such as being the first man to give a potlatch in connection with a seal feast. Only the facts that this over-all ranking process was taking place shortly after the founding of Fort Rupert and that all the villages and numayms were busy getting and justifying a place in the system can explain the resulting organization recorded by Boas in the 1890's and which he regarded as "of recent growth" (1897: 333).

Many of the difficulties of the system can be blamed upon the later upsets in the rank order of positions that may have occurred. The record shows unsuccessful attempts, for example, to advance the rank of a position by giving an enormous potlatch with the proceeds of prostitution, but some may have been successful. However, only the emergence of an over-all system from a number of local ones among a people greatly interested in social rank could explain both its general features and its discrepancies. The Kwakiutl villages became ranked from one to thirteen, or nineteen if the Lekwiltok are included. The Lekwiltok were clearly drawn in late according to Chief William Assu, and their extreme southerly position might be the reason.

Kwakiutl numayms according to Boas (1897: 333) were substituting honorific names like "the rich ones," "the great ones," "those who receive first" for their old names as late as about 1865. The instability in the rank order of about 658 positions among the people and the tendency to match certain villages and numayms in potlatching (Boas 1897: 342) out of the over-all order can be explained if that order is seen as emergent. The clearest case, however, is that there was nothing to suggest that the four village "tribes" who settled together at Fort Rupert were the first ranking and the greatest among all the people before that time. What seems to have happened is that the wealth they were first to get among the people because of their new location at the fort established the claim that they were the greatest of all. The other local groups had similar ambitions for the wide recognition of their own social worth. The system grew with such complications that the people themselves recognized that only a few talented individuals could keep all its details straight.

The severe population decrease beginning well before the establishment of Fort Rupert may have played its part in these developments. A greater and greater proportion of the population could hold one of the limited number of positions of social rank throughout this period. This may have been a stimulus to interest in social rank with the participation in all the ceremonial, social, and potlatching activities that such a position made possible.

THE POTLATCH

What seems to have happened immediately after 1849 is that crests became less important than the property distributions that validated them, while the interest in social status and worth not only continued but may even have become of greater importance, since it could be asserted and recognized over the whole Kwakiutl area by an increasing proportion of the population. Immediately after the founding of Fort Rupert, potlatches increased in size and included European goods, at first mainly woolen blankets. Increase in the size of inventory, including more and more European goods, in the numbers of people to whom property was given, and in the frequency with which they were given was to continue up to 1921. The greatest potlatch known before 1849 was a distribution of 320 blankets. By 1869 there is one of 9,000 blankets, in 1895 one of over 13,000 blankets (Codere 1950: 89–97), and the one ending the period in which the value of the goods distributed was over 30,000 blankets.

The various financial devices that helped to sustain and maximize the potlatch system must have been developed after 1849, for in the family history accounts there is no hint of them before that time. Before 1849 the people did have "coppers," or copper shields, whose worth was in terms of the amount of property that had been distributed when they last changed hands, but it is only after that date that there is evidence that a copper could only be obtained for double the amount distributed at its preceding sale. George Hunt's history of twenty-one coppers (n.d.) shows this to be the case for the ten coppers which have a history sufficiently detailed to include the amounts paid in the sequence of transactions. The twenty-one coppers would be a good sample of all Kwakiutl coppers at the time, for they were the ones that happened to be in Alert Bay when the Royal Canadian Mounted Police confiscated them along with other potlatch and winter dance paraphernalia on the occasion of the first all-out and moderately successful enforcement of the Indian Act in 1921. Boas suggested that this geometric progression of potlatch receipts that had to be returned to the giver at double their value held for all of Kwakiutl potlatching (1897: 343). However, informants have denied this geometric progression. When a man gave a potlatch, he had only to return the amount he had received from another in a potlatch with something over and above what he had received, and this increment did not have to be double in amount. There was, however, an increment in all potlatches and a 100 per cent increment in those at which coppers changed hands. People were able to raise the always increasing amounts necessary both by earning more wealth and by lending what they had to one another at high rates of interest. The development of the concept of interest and interest rates and of a credit potlatch economy ensued.

A description of some of the preparations for the 1921 potlatch of Daniel Cranmer will illustrate what was involved. First, Daniel Cranmer had very good earnings for the several years he was planning for his great potlatch. In one of the years alone he recalls that he earned over $6,000, mostly from commercial fishing. In the careful record book he kept there are three types of account: his loans of property to individuals who probably had to get property together for a potlatch they were giving, with a record of their repayment with interest, loans made to him, and the amounts of property he had received from various people when they had given potlatches. The latter part of the book is devoted to the complex matter of deciding who of the some 300 recipients at his potlatch was to get what property in what amounts. Daniel Cranmer's preparations ran from 1913 to his potlatch in 1921, and he was involved in many other potlatch matters along with long-range planning for his great potlatch. He advanced money to people planning to buy a copper, an advance that was lucrative for him because it would be well repaid. He also accepted part payments, really options, on coppers that he owned. Others, as well as he, used their literacy to keep written accounts of all their financial debits, credits, and involvements. The wonder is that any potlatcher could keep track of the inevitable complexities and detail without such written records, although many did.

It is necessary to picture a Kwakiutl potlatch world of finance developing during this period with increasing size and complexity. Its connection with a "real" Kwakiutl economy was tenuous. Subsistence activities, subsistence surpluses, and the absence of invidious distinctions in levels of everyday living continued as in pre-White days. It was the expanding European economy of the area that was "real" for sustaining the potlatch. Throughout these years the Kwaw-kewlth agents had a sorry time, noting with approval, and sometimes even with envy, how much European property the people were acquiring but how all or most of it was being circulated (their word was "squandered") in the vast potlatch system (Codere 1950: 81–86). In fact, to answer the Lynds' question for Middletown, "Why do they work so hard?" with regard to the Kwakiutl of the 1920's and before seems easy. Their earnings from European sources and their potlatch were mutually reinforcing.

Their development of such financial devices as credit and interest in connection with potlatching must have come from the general business skill which they seem to have had even in the time of Vancouver. Some of this, as is probably the usual case, verged on sharp practice. What, for example, could be an easier way to wealth than to fake a copper by getting a $4.50 copper sheet from the White men in Victoria, making one, and passing it off as bought from a northern Indian? As the people point out, coppers are just like checks, worth nothing as paper and ink, worth often very much as a claim on credits. To forge one would be just like forging a check today, and in the history of the twenty-one coppers mentioned there were two forgeries made about 1864 and 1869 which were successful in becoming worth very much on successive transactions and seven which brought the original forger from 50 to 100 blankets and continued to circulate thereafter as known forgeries for that fixed amount.

Kwakiutl ethnography contains many accounts of actual potlatches. The procedures used and the nature of the potlatch as a great social occasion are fully revealed (Boas 1897). Because Daniel Cranmer's 1921 potlatch at Village Island shows the same general features that are shown in these earlier accounts, but also the greater size, scope, and complexity of potlatching characteristic of the later years of the Potlatch Period, some details are in order. The following is his summary of the main events of this potlatch:

The potlatch was at Village Island, because that was away from the agent and that is where my wife's relatives were. People came from all over, from Lekwiltok to Smith's Inlet. The invitation was given to all the chiefs of all the tribes. Only a few Nimpkish went, however, because they were afraid of the agent there. Three to four hundred men, women and children turned up.

The first thing that was done, was that all the things I gave were transferred over to me from my wife's side. The chiefs of her tribe made speeches. Those who made the speeches, my wife and her relatives and I were in button blankets.

That night a dance was given. Hamats!a and others. H. M. was my hamats!a.

The second day a xwéxwe dance with the shells was given to me by the chief of Cape Mudge. I gave him a gas boat and $50. cash. Altogether that was worth $500. I paid him back double. He also gave some names. The same day I gave Hudson's Bay blankets. I started giving out the property. First the canoes. Two pool tables were given to two chiefs. It hurt them. They said it was the same as breaking a copper. The pool tables were worth $350 apiece. Then bracelets, gas lights, violins, guitars were given to the more important people. Then 24 canoes, some of them big ones, and four gas boats.

I gave a whole pile to my own people. Return for favors. Dresses to the women, bracelets and shawls. Sweaters and shirts to the young people. To all those who had helped. Boats brought the stuff over from Alert Bay to Village Island by night (This was to evade the Agent). This included 300 oak trunks, the pool tables and the sewing machines.

Then I gave button blankets, shawls and common blankets. There were 400 of the real old Hudson's Bay blankets. I gave these away with the xwéxwe dances. I also gave lots of small change with the Hudson's Bay blankets. I threw it away for the kids to get. There were also basins, maybe a thousand of them, glasses, washtubs, teapots and cups given to the women in the order of their positions.

The third day I don't remember what happened.

The fourth day I gave furniture: boxes, trunks, sewing machines, gramophones, bedsteads and bureaus.

The fifth day I gave away cash.

The sixth day I gave away about 1000 sacks of flour worth $3 a sack. I also gave sugar.

Everyone admits that that was the biggest yet. I am proud to say our people (Nimpkish) are ahead, although we are the third, Kwag·uł, Mamaleleqala, Nəmgəs. So I am a big man in those days. Nothing now. In the old days this was my weapon and I could call down anyone. All the chiefs say now in a gathering, "You cannot expect that we can ever get up to you. You are a great mountain" [Field notes 1951].

Because potlatching was for the purpose of establishing and aggrandizing social worth, there is a tendency to depreciate statements made about a potlatch by the potlatch-giver himself. In this case, however, other informants who were not related to the potlatch-giver confirm the report as does the potlatch account book.

Since a constant expansion in potlatching could not take place without a concurrent expansion in the amount of wealth, the system was in delicate balance. It was to end as a system when Kwakiutl earnings from European sources dried up. This began in the 1920's and continued unremittingly through the Great Depression of the 30's. Even before the 20's there were some signs of strain, signs that the expansion in earnings was not quite keeping up with the constant increases demanded by the potlatch, especially the potlatch connected with the purchase of a copper. In the Hunt history of twenty-one coppers there are several coppers which were getting so expensive by 1900 that they could be sold and purchased only with difficulty. One, for example, was bought originally from a Tsimshian in 1864. It changed hands about every seven years and went from 100 to 250 to 500 blankets and approximately doubled thereafter on every exchange. By the time its price was about 4,000 blankets several men held it temporarily with an option in hopes of raising the rest of the property needed for title. The man who finally bought it faced the same difficulty in getting buyers. By the time the price was about 8,000 blankets the device of an immediate sale at the same price was used (a type of sale that did not bring much credit to the short-time owner of the copper). By the time the history ends the proper price of the copper was 16,000 blankets, and there had been no clear prospect of sale for some time.

The development of the potlatch system must be viewed as the substitution of the wealth rivalry—a sort of metaphorical warfare—of the potlatch for the physical violence that had frequently occurred earlier in the relations of the various Kwakiutl groups with one another and with other Indians. The Kwakiutl themselves saw this development, and their phrases describe it better than any others could: "When I was a young man I have seen streams of blood shed in war. But since that time the white man came and stopped up that stream of blood with wealth. Now we are fighting with our wealth" (Boas 1897: 571). The thesis has been presented at length in *Fighting with Property* (Codere 1950: 118–29).

Kwakiutl wars, internecine or otherwise, since 1792 seem never to have been more than scrapes and brawls in which a few men were lost or taken captive or a few heads or captives brought back in triumph. This was the case for either an organized war party of several hundred men or the chance meetings of a couple of hunters with a canoe group of strangers or a few defenseless berry-pickers. That for the most part only small-scale destructions occurred would not mean, however, that the people lived in any security. Elaborate defensive measures, such as sleeping on the roofs of the great houses, were sometimes taken by villagers fearful of a surprise attack. As Boas said, Kwakiutl groups both sought a reputation for atrociousness for themselves and feared it in others (1939: 684–88). The impression is that the people lived uneasy; that even if there was little to fear from neighboring villages or more distant villages containing relatives by marriage, there were not only travelers and war parties from the northern people to fear, there were also intervillage enmities, rivalries between numaym chiefs even in the same village, and the ever-present possibility that a bereavement would be the occasion for an expedition to get someone "to die with those who are dead" and "to let someone else wail." Such expeditions were indiscriminately murderous: ". . . even if they should be relatives they do not take mercy on them in war. They would kill whomever they might see paddling by in a canoe. Therefore no member of the tribe goes out paddling when they know that warriors are traveling about" (Boas 1921: 1375).

The Kwakiutl seem to have stopped their internecine wars first. Then all warfare ceased by about 1865. The effect of European gunboats and policing measures in helping to bring this about is uncertain, but what is certain is that it was of small account compared with the effect of European wealth and that the result was a great new day for the Kwakiutl: "In olden times we fought so that the blood ran over the ground. Now we fight with button blankets and other kinds of property and we smile at each other! Oh, how good is the new time!" (Boas n.d.; see also 1897: 580–81). Therefore, in spite of all the rivalry in potlatching, the rivalry described so well by Ruth Benedict in *Patterns of Culture* (1934: 173–222), it must be seen as a great social change that occurred in Kwakiutl culture during the Potlatch Period and to a large extent as the exuberant development of a larger social world in which there were peace, security from physical violence, and an opportunity to establish social worth among all the people rather than among only those of close kinship or the immediate locality.

CEREMONIALISM AND SUPERNATURALISM

Changes in Kwakiutl religion and ceremonialism during the Potlatch Period are consistent with the developments that have been described. They, too, are involved in "fighting with property instead of with weapons," and they perhaps display the shift from any actual physical violence to symbolic representations of violence even more clearly than does potlatching. The most remarkable development was that Kwakiutl culture became secularized, a development, granting the difficulties in the concept of secularization, that had begun before 1849 but that was to approach completion well before 1921.

Boas' eyewitness account of almost three weeks of winter dance ceremonial at Fort Rupert in 1895 shows the nature of the ceremonies and the non-religious context in which they were held (1897: 544–606). The point of the entire proceedings seems to have been the rivalry through potlatching of the Kwakiutl of Fort Rupert and those of Koskimo. These and other potlatch activities seem to overwhelm all else. Not only was each dance presentation accompanied by a potlatch, but also the meetings were continually interspersed with speeches referring to past potlatches and promising future potlatches and with announcements of a dunning nature, calling in loans publicly and often naming the debtor. When past ceremonials are referred to, it is in connection with the history that justifies the hereditary crest right or in speeches about the amount of property given when the ceremony was last put on by its owner. It was the potlatching crest owners who were completely in charge of the dance ceremonies. "Their" Hamatsas (Cannibal Dancers) or other dancers (usually younger relatives) not only became "inspired" at their decision to put on the ceremony, but they were also carefully instructed in the dramatic details of their performances; they were expected, for example, to go into their ecstasy at certain cues and to be strictly controllable, becoming duly tamed in the ceremonial order of events. These and other theatrical aspects of the performance were elaborated. Songs were rehearsed before they were publicly presented. Theatrical gimmicks were used, for example, two ends of a blade fixed to a hoop that closely fit over a woman's shoulder so that she appeared to be cleaved by the monstrous weapon. There is much evidence of theatrical spectacle in these descriptions but almost none of religious feeling. One of my informants who danced as a Cannibal at about this time confirmed their unreligious nature. It could be that for the actual dancers, who were supposedly kidnapped by the spirit of the ceremony, possessed by the spirit and "tamed" or brought back to normal after their ecstasy at the end of the ceremony, there might at least be some religious involvement. However, one informant, a great potlatcher, told a story of a contrived kidnapping by an uncle, a boring stay in seclusion in the woods, and a matter-of-fact following-out of ceremonial directions. Other informants' comments suggest that the theatrical impact of some of these ceremonies was considerable, but the best that can be made of it is that some performances were so successful as to produce a "suspension of disbelief," and the presumption is that there must have been disbelief in the first place.

Joyce Wike shares the view that Kwakiutl ceremonies of this period were theatrical and non-religious (1952: 97). She was the first to my knowledge to point out that all Northwest Coast cultures, presumably excepting the Coast Salish, might be best understood as having been secularized in the mid-nineteenth century through the potlatch. The process seems to me to have begun before then, with the acquisition and transmission of ceremonials as crests, and to involve another shift from that of horror and fear of actual physical violence to the evocation of horror by theatrical presentations which simulated and symbolized physical violence. Ford considers the bloodthirsty ceremonials of the Kwakiutl a needed outlet for aggression among a people who were "never even remotely bloodthirsty in their day to day relationships" (1941: 26), but, since potlatching so obviously did provide an outlet as well as a channel for aggression, the historical shift away from physical violence provides a better explanation of late nineteenth century Kwakiutl culture.

In the early days of Fort Rupert there was a killing of a Nanaimo slave by Cannibal Dancers, Fool Dancers, and Bear Dancers. All the people who participated in this murder are alleged to have died within five years as a result of the curse placed upon them by the wife of the murdered man (Boas 1897: 439). In the memory of Boas' 1895 informants other incidents of this violent character had occurred. By the time of Jacobsen's visit in 1881, he is assured that killings in connection with the Cannibal ceremony had been replaced by eating bits of the flesh of a corpse (Jacobsen 1895: 47). In later ceremonial procedures the Cannibal also bit the arm of one of the witnesses or, perhaps a better phrase would be, one of the members of the audience. The injury was slight, but there was careful prearrangement about whom he would bite and the indemnity that would be paid. In other words actual violence was being eliminated from the ceremonials long before 1895 and what was being substituted for it was its theatrical representation. The story of the effectiveness of the curse might reveal the truth of how the people felt about physical violence, and this in turn would seem partly to explain its virtual elimination from Kwakiutl life during this period.

The final transformation seems to have been the translation of all the ceremonial from the language of warfare to that of potlatching. This happened between 1849 and 1895. Ceremonial procedures and symbols connected with war and physical violence are assigned a metaphorical equivalent in potlatching and "fighting with property." An illustration from the description of the 1895 winter dances follows:

The Koskimo are the first to enter. Each man carries as many hemlock wreaths as he has killed enemies during war expeditions. They also carry bows and arrows. Then they step up into the middle of the house and throw one wreath after another into the fire, calling the name of the enemy whom it represents. As soon as a wreath is thrown into the fire they call "yē," and all repeat this cry. At the same time they shoot arrows into the fire. This ceremony is called yi'lxoa, which means placing the head of an enemy on a pole. The fire is called XusE'la which means fighting place. The whole ceremony is called al Xts aliL wā'lastEm (carrying blood into the house and giving away much property) or k• āg• euLaxsta'la (sharp edge of a knife). *At present the wreaths represent the number of coppers which a man has given away. They have taken the place of heads, because according to the usages of the Kwakiutl, a man who has given away a copper by doing so becomes a victor over his rival. They also throw paddles into the fire, the meaning of which is that they send a canoe to call their rivals to a festival, in which they are going to show their greatness.* (Boas 1897: 522; italics mine.)

As was the case in potlatching, the Kwakiutl seem to have been well aware of the changes in their culture and to have expressed them in a way that cannot be improved upon. At the Winter Ceremonials of 1895 Boas saw the performance of a new Fool Dancer and learned that the man who was his predecessor in the last performance of the same crest dance had killed a chief of the Nanaimo and many other men. Boas says the speaker referred to this when he told the audience: "The time of fighting has passed. The fool dancer represents the warriors, but we do not fight now with weapons; we fight with property" (Boas 1897: 601).

It is a puzzle to determine the degree and extent of belief or disbelief in supernatural power controlled by shamans and sorcerers during this period. The most detailed reports are George Hunt's (Boas 1930: 1–56), and he seems to have been extraordinary in both seeking out knowledge of these matters and receiving it with a thoroughgoing skepticism: "I desired to learn about the shaman, whether it is true or whether it is made up and . . . they pretend to be shamans" (Boas 1930: 1). As he learned the ways of the shaman and became one himself, he gathered only evidence that it was all lies and tricks and pretense. Whether most Kwakiutl were as hardheaded as he is a question, but there must have been widespread skepticism. I have heard informants scoff at the alleged powers of the sucking shaman, and there was a fearless contempt of their supposed powers in such accounts as that of Hā'daho (Boas 1930: 277–78) whose pretense was exposed, who was ridiculed mercilessly, and who died of shame without even the comfort and support of his near relatives. In Hā'daho's case it was his use of a theatrical trick that led to his downfall, and this suggests that the changes that had occurred in ceremonial life had led to the suspicion that all ceremonies were of a theatrical nature and relatively empty of any supernatural meaning.

The performances witnessed by Jacobsen and Boas were demonstrations of sleight-of-hand or contrived dramas in which a "thrower of sickness" caused and cured illness in a member of the audience with whom arrangements had been made in advance. Furthermore, these performances were in a potlatching context. George Hunt's dealings with other shamans and with non-shamans show that the former feared exposure and lacked faith in themselves to a far greater extent than the latter feared or respected them.

Again it is necessary to take George Hunt's personality into account. He was either a man of extraordinary courage, or he was sustained by something outside Kwakiutl culture, such as Boas' stimulus to his intellectual curiosity, or Kwakiutl culture itself must have developed his secure skepticism. It seems to me that Kwakiutl culture must have played some part in supporting him when he confronted sorcerers in the woods and when he sought them out to make inquiries about their methods (Boas 1930: 278–83). All Kwakiutl myths and stories which must in any case be fairly ancient contain the remarkable lesson that human beings can always confront the supernatural fearlessly, aggressively, and successfully; but this is the equivalent of saying that strictly human powers have precedence and control over all others.

George Hunt not only acted in ways that were consistent with this attitude, but evidence from other sources indicates that such an attitude was quite generally held. In the period from 1849 to 1921 there are several recorded attempts to cast a spell on rivals in rank and potlatching. In the usual case the sorcery was discovered and canceled by the simple means of destroying the machinery of sorcery, which consisted of some association of the bait, the Kwakiutl called it "game," from the victim and a graveyard corpse. Kwakiutl society was set against sorcery, and social controls operated to eliminate it. There is a remarkable incident reported in the biography of Smoke from Their Fires. The head chiefs at Fort Rupert held a secret meeting at which they declared that a sorcerer in the village was "not fit to be alive." Among them they raised the sorcerer's fee in blankets, arranged for some of the young men to get some of the sorcerer's excreta for bait, and then told him that one of them wished the death of another chief in the village because of potlatch rivalry. The sorcerer then killed himself by sorcery, because he used his own bait (Ford 1941: 99). While the incident on the face of it shows that the idea of bewitching a rival was plausible enough to trap a sorcerer, it also shows the extent to which sorcery was under control. It seems to me also to show that the Kwakiutl could be said to be aware that human hate and ill-will, and not the supernatural, was the power of sorcery.

In conclusion, skepticism about the beneficent supernatural powers controlled by shamans seemed widespread and, while there was less disbelief in the malevolent powers of sorcerers, this is not the same as saying that there was widespread or intense belief in supernatural power.

CURING AND KNOWLEDGE

When the shocking population decrease was occurring during this period and when especially the young along with the elderly were being carried off by infectious diseases, an increase in supernatural curing or some revolution in medical techniques would seem likely and understandable. However, neither of these things happened. Various European medicines were distributed by first the Hudson's Bay Company and later the agency. None of them seems to have had any fad or gained any importance and in view of their dubious efficacy there seems to be no good reason why they should. The people did co-operate in having themselves vaccinated against smallpox, but apart from that and the addition of a few Western medicines, including patent medicines, to their old list of specifics there were no changes. Their old cures and their old pragmatism persisted.

There were undoubtedly extensive additions to knowledge during this period, but their nature and their effect on the culture is difficult to assess. Some of them do not seem to have become important until recent years. The knowledge the women gained of salmon canning would be an example of the latter. Literacy, mentioned earlier, seems to have brought no change during this period except in what it contributed to potlatch accounting. Knowledge of home brewing made a dubious cultural contribution.

Knowledge of the world was certainly brought back by the Kwakiutl who attended the Chicago Exposition in 1893 and those who sailed on sealers that called into ports as distant as Japan. I recall my eager anticipation when I had an opportunity to hear what an elderly Kwakiutl had thought of Japan. The answer was unenlightening as far as his reactions to Japanese culture were concerned, but typically Kwakiutl: "Very good, very nice, everything cheap."

There may have been one increase in knowledge during this period that would afford, if it occurred, a classic case of the ability of the people of any culture to expand their own concepts when they have a reason for doing so. This was the Kwakiutl number system which by the time it was recorded had the means of expressing large numbers (Boas 1947: 276–80). The question demands careful study, but there is at least the possibility that the system expanded with the increase in the enumerations necessary for the potlatch after 1849. There is no use of numbers in the thousands or ten thousands in the myths or family histories which deal with an earlier time.

ART

In the Potlatch Period, Kwakiutl art was exuberant and was almost entirely devoted to crest representations. In the Pre-Potlatch Period art in ceremonial and myth seems to have been of the crest variety, but there is some question about the graphic and plastic arts. The decision was that they, too, were a crest art at the time, but in spite of Vancouver's report of the painted house fronts at the Nimpkish Village, the evidence for this was not conclusive. Boas may very well have been correct in thinking that the whole, graphic and plastic, artistic development of the crest was not very old and probably not older than the middle of the past century (Boas 1920: 327). In any case there was abundant artistic activity after 1850 in the painting of house fronts, in the carving of the so-called totem poles, and in the production of head masks, rattles, speakers' staves, and other paraphernalia for the winter dances and potlatches.

After about 1860 the people began acquiring sawn lumber in quantity. This they soon put to use for house fronts whose large, smooth areas were painted with complex crest designs. There are excellent illustrations of these house fronts in Boas (1905: Plate XXX, p. 44; XXXVII, p. 517). The people also used sawn lumber to make wings, fins, beaks, and other protuberances on the house posts and crest poles, so that this sculpture broke away from the form limitations of the cylindrical tree trunk.

Kwakiutl masks of this period were often gadgety; not only were the beaks of the various bird masks made so that they could be opened and shut and vibrated by the dancer's manipulation of the proper strings, but some masks were almost unbelievably mechanized with fins that could be made to flop, little fish or other figures that could be made to revolve, and faces within faces that could be exposed, again by pulling the proper strings, so that an animal head could be opened to reveal a bird, a fabulous being, or a man.

Probably judgments of the art of any culture, even when made by specialists or students of the culture, should never be articulated, since they must be subjective. Boas in *Primitive Art* permitted himself no statement that did not have a demonstrable basis. Therefore to relate some over-all reactions to Kwakiutl art of this period may be gratuitously irrelevant and wrong. Philip Drucker (1955: 161–85) has, however, published enthusiastically commendatory judgments of Wakashan (Nootka and Kwakiutl) art and has made invidious comparisons between Wakashan art and the art of other Northwest Coast cultures from Puget Sound to Alaska. Under these circumstances and because other and contradictory judgments might contribute to understanding the Kwakiutl of this period, there may be some point in recording the other view. What Drucker commends in Wakashan art as vigorous, imaginative, and freed from certain formal limitations can also be regarded as undisciplined to the point of lacking a necessary restraint. Paul Wingert seems to express such ideas in the comparisons he makes of Coast Salish and Kwakiutl art (Wingert 1949: 119–23). Audrey Hawthorn and I share the view that much Kwakiutl art of this period is, compared to earlier Kwakiutl art, of a rococo, unrestrained, artistically less effective type. A stimulus such as the crest idea in Kwakiutl culture can both inspire and smother an art. By the twentieth century its stultifying effect seems apparent; the quality of artistic production seems to bear a predictable correlation with the importance of quantity production of crest designs or forms as well as with the requirements of distinctive gadgets and embellishments on crests. Much further thought and study is necessary to make any firm statements, but meanwhile there is a possibility that Kwakiutl art in the Potlatch Period was developing characteristics that seem consistent with other aspects of the culture; if, for example, religious life became secularized, why should art not lose some of its aesthetic purpose?

SUMMARY

The Potlatch Period from 1849 to 1921 takes its name from the predominant institution of Kwakiutl culture during that time. Interest in potlatching was the major preoccupation of Kwakiutl life and all other interests were relegated to a secondary and subservient position. Even the interest in social rank and the idea of crests which symbolized it, an idea which came from the northern people at an earlier time and which stimulated important changes in the culture, were given a secondary and derivative cultural position. Distributions of real property in potlatches became necessary not only to validate and uphold the use of any social position and its crests but also to meet a new requirement. Each distribution had to be greater than the last; each potlatch receipt had to be returned with an increment when the recipient took the role of donor and distributor, which he was obliged to take at cost of diminishing the worth of the ranked position he held and customarily transferred to an heir during his lifetime. The activities of the people were enthusiastically directed toward earning the wealth from European sources that was required to sustain the potlatch and to manipulating this wealth among themselves in ways that could bring about the concentration of impressive amounts in the hands of each man long enough for him to give potlatches in his turn.

Potlatches gave the people ever greater occasions for sociability and social drama. Relations between Kwakiutl individuals of various groups and villages which either just did not exist in the past or existed on a tenuous or even precarious basis became firm and filled with possibility. Although these relations were frequently rivalrous, the rivalry seems to have gone to destructive lengths only in a few flagrant cases. For the most part, individuals had the opportunity of achieving a position of social rank that would be recognized "all over the world" and of playing a role in a system of positive interrelationships that included the entire Kwakiutl population perhaps for the first time in history. The potlatch was social excitement and potentiality that replaced the relative isolation, hostility, and anxiety of an earlier day. No wonder, then, that the Kwakiutl could say of the change from fighting with weapons to fighting with property, "Oh, how good is the new time!"

Post-Potlatch Period: 1930–55[1]

Kwakiutl prosperity ended in the 1920's with a series of economic difficulties many of which were to continue and be intensified throughout the long years of the depression. The potlatch depended upon the relation of the Kwakiutl to an expanding European economy. When first the relation was disturbed and then the economy depressed for a decade, the potlatch as an institution and as a system requiring constantly increasing amounts of wealth was to end.

In 1921 there was a sharp, though brief, economic recession and Kwakiutl incomes suffered. Early in the 1920's there was a change-over to gas boats in fishing; the Kwakiutl not only bore the cost of this change, they were also unable to get credit to help finance it. There was a change in the earlier system of cannery-rented boats and equipment; such equipment as the canneries still had for rent was so obsolete that those who used it could not expect to compete successfully against better-equipped fishermen. Japanese competition in the

---

[1] The section on the Post-Potlatch Period or the recent period in Kwakiutl life draws again and again on the work of the Indian Research Project directed by Dr. Harry B. Hawthorn, Professor of Anthropology at the University of British Columbia. The results of the research appear in H. B. Hawthorn, C. S. Belshaw, S. M. Jamieson, *et al., The Indians of British Columbia, a Study of Contemporary Social Adjustment* (Berkeley: University of California Press; Vancouver: University of British Columbia, 1958). The great value of this work is in its comprehensive survey of the entire area. The research included a series of studies of Indian communities and a number of studies by specialists of demography, resources, occupations, industries, housing, family, education, crime, law enforcement, social welfare, politics, administration, and other topics. The Kwakiutl were included in all phases of the research, and Alert Bay was one of the communities studied. In my field work among the Kwakiutl in 1951 and 1955 I made every effort to acquire some fair sample of the vast materials, especially the statistical materials, that are needed for understanding any community today. I also had the fullest co-operation from the hospital, the agency, cannery officials, and others in this endeavor. In spite of this, my record could be no more than a small sample and that for the Kwakiutl alone. The work of the Indian Research Project has included the collection and collation of all the available statistical materials, so it is not only possible to get from it more material that is specifically Kwakiutl than any one individual could obtain under most conditions, but it is also possible to compare the Kwakiutl with other Indian groups, and this process invariably raises fruitful questions and leads to discoveries that might not otherwise have been made. The specialist studies of the Indian Reearch Project were also of immense value, particularly in the many historical summaries, for example, the Indians and the fishing industry. Anyone working in this area now has the great good fortune to be able to use the specific kind of background history that is needed for an understanding of culture or of culture change. References to *The Indians of British Columbia* are numerous in this section but are still all too few. I should not have drawn many of the conclusions I did without the stimulus of this report. The report illumined so much in my own field notes and gave such a helpful context to my data that I have drawn relatively firm conclusions where I should otherwise have drawn tentative ones.

fishing industry became severe. The number of canneries in the Kwakiutl area was reduced, decreasing the employment opportunities for Indian fishermen and women cannery workers alike. All these difficulties were but a prologue to the Great Depression.

In the long period of diminished incomes and wealth that the Kwakiutl experienced along with most of the people of the world, they were perhaps fortunate that they did not also experience destitution and grinding economic want; but the inability to obtain wealth made it pointless or impossible to potlatch. Even when sufficient wealth was accumulated for a potlatch distribution, and a few large potlatches were given as late as the thirties, recipients were unable to raise the funds for a potlatch with the necessary increase in return gifts. Those few who stubbornly potlatched became self-righteously embittered at the failure of their debtors to repay them and refused to continue to "just give away property for nothing." Those who were unable to potlatch rankled at reminders of their debts and felt the bitterness of their dilemma. The younger people who had not yet taken a place in the potlatch saw the system as the source of all the troubles and unhappiness around them. By the time prosperity returned in the forties, the potlatch as a system was broken.

Economically the Kwakiutl were the beneficiaries of World War II; the war shortage of labor, the removal of the Japanese from the fishing industry from 1941 to 1948, and very high prices for salmon all contributed to their welfare. But the new prosperity did not bring back the potlatch. In the period of hard times and on into the postwar period there were thoroughgoing cultural changes directed toward assimilation into Canadian-American culture. In recent years assimilation has been rapid and brought the Kwakiutl very close to the condition of being another local version of Western culture distinguished, as every other version is, by its special historical past and the qualities of its particular region.

The main problems faced by the Kwakiutl today are no different from those faced by any individual or group in Western culture; they are the ones connected with industrialization, with urbanization, with the impact of mass media on the local life, with finding status and status criteria. The remainder of this study will be largely concerned with the Kwakiutl of the 1950's and will show the extent and nature of the changes that have taken place in the culture and good hopes for the future—along with the anthropological regret that so much that was dramatically different and facilely stimulating to thought has perished.

COMMUNITY ORGANIZATION AND EXTERNAL RELATIONS

At the present time Alert Bay is the major Southern Kwakiutl village and contains a third of the population. There are nine other villages, none of which can compete with Alert Bay in size or in facilities and several of which are remnant populations rather than fully functioning communities. The latter includes famed Fort Rupert, the only village aside from Alert Bay that neighbors a White settlement. All look to Alert Bay for necessary services and in many cases for all social excitement. The two Lekwiltok villages are omitted here because their extreme southerly location and ties with middle and southern Vancouver Island continue as in the past to give them a special and separate position among the Southern Kwakiutl.

Today one village, Kingcome, outstrips Alert Bay in vigor and pride in itself as a community, but this does not alter the over-all development which was that of the increasing dominance of Alert Bay over the life of the people at the expense of the community life of the other once independent and fully functioning villages. This development began with the founding of the agency at Alert Bay, progressed with the growing White settlement there, and was probably nearly completed by the thirties, when commercial fishing in the area took on its present organized character, with Alert Bay as its local center. During the fishing season, which lasts the greater part of the year from spring to late fall, only women, children, and the aged are in the villages. The fishing week lasts from Sunday evening through Thursday, but only the fishermen living in Alert Bay are sure to spend the weekends fairly regularly with their families and to make frequent calls into the port for boat servicing or for moorage during the important part of the season when the fish are running in Johnstone Strait.

The contact community in which the Kwakiutl now live is the total White Canadian-American cultural world. The Kwakiutl live with that part and version of the White world that is represented locally, and with the extended experience of it that is offered by the mass media, visits to Vancouver and other cities to the south, and an ever increasing number of years spent in school.

The Southern Kwakiutl, again omitting the Lekwiltok, numbered

1,482 in a 1954 census. Their number, together with that of all the other Indian people of British Columbia, makes up only slightly over 2 per cent of the total population of the province. In the northern Vancouver Island census district, the Kwakiutl and other Indians of the area form only 13 per cent of the population. The population of Alert Bay is about 1000; half the total is Kwakiutl and half White. The Kwakiutl stopped "vanishing" about 1921 and the increase in their numbers that began then has continued steadily. At present they are a growing and very young population; over 60 per cent of the people are under twenty-one. The part of the White population with which the Kwakiutl have most contact has characteristics peculiar to a frontier. There is a large group of loggers and fishermen temporarily in the area each season and a large group made up of cannery, agency, church, police, medical, school, and other personnel who may stay for lengthy periods but who have no intention of staying permanently.

Alert Bay on Cormorant Island is on the main channel of Johnstone Strait, provides much good harborage, has a long gravel beach, and, for this area, considerable level land. Having few natural advantages besides those listed, which were then irrelevant, it is easy to understand why it was not a village site of the Kwakiutl in pre-White days. The long, curving beach is divided sharply into a White and an Indian half. In the Indian half there are Indian residences, the agency, the Anglican church, several stores, one of the two fish company wharves, and schools, including the Indian residential school. In the White half are almost all the White residences and all the main community services: wharves, the high school, stores, the bank, the post office, two hotels with their two beer parlors, the hospital, the light plant, the community hall, two movie houses, restaurants, the fire house, and the police station. Alert Bay is a steamship stop and a seaplane base, and, though it has few tourists, it is a point of call for travelers of every description from social workers and visiting public health nurses to salesmen of *The Book of Knowledge*, ready-made eyeglasses, or Wearever pots and pans.

White and Indian general concepts of one another are listed in the recent *Indians of British Columbia*, which included the Kwakiutl. The list forms an excellent summary of Kwakiutl-White attitudes. White concepts of the Indian are the following:

—the Indian is seen as not vanishing at all
—as a person with an increasing say in his own future
—as headed for assimilation
—as having outgrown some of the forms of guardianship by Government and Churches
—as an economic factor of varied desirability
—as a neighbor of varied desirability and acceptance.

(Hawthorn, Belshaw, Jamieson, *et al.* 1958: 60.)

A point is made in this source about the general "graceless" claim to superiority made by the Whites and the equally graceless acceptance of the claim on the part of the Indians (59). This applies with few exceptions in White-Kwakiutl relations today. The more specific Indian concepts of the Whites selected and quoted from the same source are:

—increasing acceptance of the fact of White power
—increasing acceptance of White technical superiority . . . which became a fact as communities became more and more directed towards White goals
—a feeling that the contest for dominance had not been a fair one
—a questioning of the probity of the Whites, especially by those Indians who realized that Indian culture had possessed general technical and social superiority under the earlier set of conditions
—a belief, which more sophisticated Indians still attempt to hold, in the Utopian quality of pre-White existence
—the enjoyment of Indian superiority when it exists. This now occurs where the traditional techniques continue to work, as in some aspects of hunting and fishing, and where new Indian communities possess better facilities or better organization than adjoining White ones. Again the possession of an additional language is a point of superiority, which can often be employed, as can more occasionally, knowledge of the traditional culture
—Indians have generally a more realistic concept, related to sharper observations and analysis of White society and its divisions than Whites hold of Indians
—Whites are seen as differing both as groups and individuals, with differing actions and attitudes
—this is countered by widespread and general distrust, wait-and-see attitude and dislike
—Whites are regarded as failing to extend courtesy, justice, fair dealing and friendliness to Indians

—the advantages of identification with White society are often rejected by a person but sought for his children

—there is a somewhat similar ambivalence toward intermarriage, assimilation and even the less far-reaching processes of acculturation.

(Hawthorn, Belshaw, Jamieson, *et al.* 1958: 60.)

On the basis of these general Kwakiutl-White attitudes, which have so much in common with any majority-minority group attitudes, it should not, perhaps, be surprising that the Kwakiutl in their turn look down upon whomever they can. There is widespread anti-Asiatic prejudice which was bolstered by the long-standing competition of the Japanese in the fishing industry and the events of World War II. This goes to the lengths of violently repudiating the ancient pre-historical connection of the Indians with Asia, though this is in part a response to the allegations of prejudiced Whites that Indian loyalty was suspect because of this ancient "blood tie." What is truly to be marveled at from a scientific viewpoint is that today anti-Semitic statements are not uncommon. That few Kwakiutl have ever seen a Jew is beside the point. They borrow the idiocy from the dominant White group and, like the Whites, derive from it what status comfort they can.

To describe interrelations in detail, it will be necessary to show the specific reciprocal White-Indian roles in their context of economic, political, religious or social organization, because in the recent Post-Potlatch Period these major aspects of living no longer have separate and functioning Kwakiutl and White parts as they did in earlier periods. In all their specific role interrelations with Whites the Kwakiutl show ambivalence, sensitivity about social status, and, more than occasionally, self-hate. The hospital doctor's office, which maintains a weekly schedule of service to logging companies and a nearby island community has received more than one telephone inquiry, "What day do we native folk come to the office?" Mussy little children are called "Dirty Indians" by their Indian mothers or sisters. Clothes, houses, house furnishings, kitchens, and kitchen equipment are praised as being "just like White's." "Dumb Indian" jokes about ridiculous failures in using equipment or in behaving knowingly are told. To run the gamut of reaction, two Kwakiutl college students can make sophisticated fun with the idea of the Whites holding a fertility dance at the community hall on a national holiday.

Kwakiutl relations with other Indian peoples have not been extended, as has been the case with many New World Indian groups, into any pan-Indianism. Kwakiutl interest in Indian people living elsewhere has been recent and has been pretty much limited to such White-Indian questions as kinds of Indian liquor laws. The Kwakiutl have wanted such information to bolster their own arguments and own local interests. I got the impression in 1951 and 1955 that many of the adults were learning for the first time and without much enthusiasm that their level of living and their school and other facilities were way above those of many Indians and particularly the Indians of interior British Columbia.

The Kwakiutl have, however, made common cause with the other coastal Indian people who, like them, are dependent on the commercial fishing industry. In 1936 the Kwakiutl from Alert Bay to Cape Mudge organized the Pacific Coast Native Fishermen's Association "to protect the interests of all the Indians engaged in the fishing industry" (Hawthorn, Belshaw, Jamieson, *et al.* 1958: 111–12). This can be regarded, I think, as the first united political action of the Kwakiutl. This organization, which had been established because of the economic troubles of the period and because of the Kwakiutl feeling that they had been disadvantaged by White leadership in a strike, soon joined with the Native Brotherhood of British Columbia. For many years the president of the organization was a Kwakiutl. Its chief function has been to negotiate collective bargaining agreements for the Indians in the fishing industry. The brotherhood brings the Kwakiutl into closest contact with the Bella Bella and other northern neighbors.

Over the years the Kwakiutl have had occasion to meet many Indian and "Native" people; they prefer the word "Native" for themselves indicating proprietary rights stemming from original settlement of the country. World's fairs, coronations, visiting royalty, special government conferences have all broadened their contacts. It is my impression that the knowledge gained in this way had not had much impact until recent years, that it has not been effectively transmitted to others by those who had the opportunity to do so. It might be, however, that, like so much of the learning of White ways that was going on but not much put into practice during the Potlatch Period, it has been latent and will show results in time. It will have to be proved out by future events but it seems likely that, for instance, some of the recent meetings of councilors from the different Kwa-kiutl bands with councilors from all the Indian groups of the province will result in important cross-cultural education as well as in clari-fications in "Indian"-White relations and in "Indian" policies and attitudes.

ECONOMIC ORGANIZATION

No one of the major aspects of living and of culture is at present separate and functioning as Kwakiutl rather than White. Of these major aspects the economy shows so few Kwakiutl characteristics that it is necessary to describe the local version of the White econ-omy. For some time the Kwakiutl have been completely dependent upon the commercial fishing industry for their living. In the larger sense this also means that their economic welfare is a derivative of the general condition of Canadian economy and that the Kwakiutl have no determination of the financial and technological developments that affect their income or that affect the price of the processed goods they must acquire as consumers. Kwakiutl specialization in commer-cial fishing has been a continuous process from the 1920's on. The changes in the industry that have since occurred have called the turn at every point in producing both the specific character of Kwakiutl economic circumstances at any one time and the general specializa-tion and almost complete dependence that has come about.

Since the 1920's the fishing industry has eliminated the casual fish-erman, become decentralized, and undergone technological changes requiring larger and larger amounts of capital investment. The first mechanization occurred in the twenties with the changeover to gas boats and has continued to the present with power-driven drums and winches for manipulating the net. Radio-telephones, echo sounders, and radar are also now necessary for succcessful competition in the industry. Canneries no longer operate in the Kwakiutl area but have been consolidated. Large refrigerated packers collect the fish and take it to the processing plants in the southern cities. The employ-ment that the Kwakiutl once found so congenial because of its ac-cessibility, its family opportunities, and its independence has lost many of these characteristics. The captain and crew of a purse seiner are often kin and are subject to no direct supervision while they are working, but there is publicity about the size of catches and acci-dents to boats or their expensive equipment that is disciplinary in effect. Today the Kwakiutl fish in local and familiar waters only part of the season. In 1955 there were about 150 Kwakiutl owners of fishing boats (Hawthorn, Belshaw, Jamieson *et al.* 1958: 114), but, even in the few cases where this meant clear ownership rather than an equity in a perhaps very heavily mortgaged boat, an accident to a $2,000 nylon net or a bad season could quickly end independence. In 1955 over 200 Kwakiutl were employed in the fishing industry and received wages, a share of the profits of the catch, or some combination of the two. Aside from some work in the logging industry, which in most cases was done in addition to fishing, there were only a few other cases of non-fishing employment for Kwakiutl in 1955: one man operated a truck (Hawthorn, Belshaw, Jamieson, *et al.* 1958: 78–81) and three men were employed by the Provincial Museum as carvers. There are a few conspicuously successful Kwakiutl fishermen, one of whom was estimated to have interests in fishing and other enterprises with a capital value of roughly $95,000 (Hawthorn, Belshaw, Jamieson, *et al.* 1958: 171). Whether even he can keep ahead of the game and avoid the small-business squeeze is a question, for the fishing industry is one of corporate and consolidated economic power. While such cases as his excite the envy and the admiration of the local Whites, most Kwakiutl earn relatively modest incomes and are dependent upon fish company credit for needed equipment and supplies during the season and for groceries during some part of the non-fishing season. They have no more control over their fortunes than is suggested by the fact that the Indians in the British Columbia fishing industry have been a minority since 1913 (Gladstone 1953: 30).

The Kwakiutl have also lost control in that relatively small area left to the individual in the management of financial and business affairs within the over-all system. Up to this period they were characterized by business skill and enterprise; now they are characterized by dependence and passivity in business matters. In recent years the agency has been paternalistic and managerial in regard to the business and financial enterprises of the people. The agency not only intervened but took over business operations like accounting, obtaining credit, seeing that legal questions were settled or clarified. Such help was available to those who asked for it, and, though they benefited economically, they did not benefit by learning to operate by themselves, for the help was not given in any educational form. Without agency recommendation it was nearly impossible to obtain credit or to operate successfully. This situation seems to have come about in part as a legal administrative matter and in part because of the role played by all government services since the depression. The managerial activities of the agency may be curtailed in the future. If they are, it should have two important beneficial effects on the Kwakiutl: it should enable them to make use of such business skills as they still have, and it should smooth relations in a community riddled with resentments about paternalistically conferred favors (Hawthorn, Belshaw, Jamieson, *et al.* 1958: 487–88).

Today the economic position of women is anomalous. A younger woman is occasionally cook on a family seine boat, a few keep store, one teaches school. A few elderly women help their husbands in very small-scale fishing operations or in old-time pursuits such as catching oulachen and rendering their oil. Most women are unemployed except as homemakers and, although the youth of the population and the size of many families mean that there is much homemaking to be done, their definition of the job is a relatively limited one.

Up to the 1920's and probably much later in the depression years, there was much domestic production of food in which women played a vital part. Today the amount of domestic production in Alert Bay is unimpressive, and although there is more of it in other villages with better resources near at hand, self-sufficiency in food supplies is a thing of the past. Figures on domestic production of food in Alert Bay and in Kingcome Inlet show the range of Kwakiutl practices in 1954–55. In a sample of sixteen Alert Bay households, about a quarter of the Alert Bay population, two households had no domestic production. About 3,500 pounds of canned salmon had been produced along with 250 pounds of canned deer, about 100 pounds of frozen fish, and some canned berries. Only three households obtained fresh berries, clams, and abalone (Hawthorn, Belshaw, Jamieson, *et al.* 1955: 432). In Kingcome Inlet in a sample of eleven households forming half the population of the village, domestic production was both more various and greater in amount. Only in one household was it limited to the canning of salmon. The list is extensive:

Canned salmon	
Potatoes	for all households
Vegetables	
(mostly peas and carrots)	
Smoked salmon	for 7 households

Deer
Dried seaweed   } for 5 households
Canned or dried berries

Dried salmon   for 3 households

Bear
Canned clams   } for 2 households
Oulachen oil

Cranberries
Wild crabapples
Canned oulachen   } for 1 household
Smoked oulachen

(Hawthorn, Belshaw, Jamieson, *et al.* 1955: 436.)

There are marked differences between Alert Bay and Kingcome and the other more remote villages in the amount of collecting and gathering activity. A few salal berries were picked by the women in Alert Bay, but apart from that there were no additions of wild foods to the diet except for the occasional seal or sack of clams the men brought back to the village at the end of the fishing week. In Kingcome the villagers were busy with fishing and berrying. The children were healthier in Kingcome according to public health officials; a better diet seems part of the explanation.

The presence of certain foods like oulachen oil and the large amounts of salmon used both show that something of the diet of the people is not entirely White; yet today, for the most part, they could not and would not live without many Canadian staples, all of which have to be bought at high prices in this area. The planting of vegetables at Kingcome is an extraordinary and recent development.

Craft production of all tools, utensils, house furnishings, and clothing has ceased and the people have to go into the market for practically everything they wear and use. One or at most two dugout canoes for river work may be made a year; a few men have made halibut hooks of steel on the old Kwakiutl pattern; but the craft production of women is confined to some sewing, the crocheting of antimacassars, table covers, and small door curtains with "Eagle" and "Thunderbird" designs and the knitting of the heavy sweaters sought by Whites but little used by the people themselves. Unlike many New World Indian peoples the Kwakiutl have not selected a costume for themselves from the White possibilities. The men wear "suit clothes" for any formal appearance; and for their work they wear the high rubber boots, heavy woolen pants and shirts, and rubber coats and hats that make up the standard Northern European fisherman's costume. Elderly women occasionally wear bright shawls and pendant golden "Eagle" earrings, but the dress of women in general is not different from that of Canadian women. Teen-agers and young people keep in step with the latest styles. The use of special White children's dress seems relatively recent, for instance, garments like snow suits and dresses for little girls. Girls from five to ten still occasionally wear the low-waisted and long garments they got as hand-me-downs, but some feeling attaches to this as a sign of poverty or being old-fashioned.

House interiors in this area, Indian and White alike, have far to go before they attain the genteel perfection and the mechanized heights of convenience of the women's magazines, but they are on their way. No great house of the few that are still standing is at present being lived in. Almost all houses are of light frame construction, built by the owners themselves and intended for single family occupancy. Those built recently, even two in the most remote and inaccessible village of all, Kingcome, are one-story suburban in design and are equipped with running water, radios, washing machines, irons, hot water heaters, oil stoves, and lights, even though there is no electric power in the village. In Alert Bay electric equipment replaces the Coleman irons, kerosene-powered washing machines, and battery radios of a place like Kingcome; and home freezers, phonographs, and at least as long ago as 1955 two tape recorders add to the list. Much of the housing and equipment is substandard from the point of view the Kwakiutl share with the Whites. A complex background of migration from outlying villages to Alert Bay for the fishing season, or permanently, and agency arrangements for financing new housing accounts for much of this. The important point is that no Kwakiutl is living in Kwakiutl housing; it is either standard or substandard White housing for the area and occasionally excels the White standard. The Kwakiutl features, if any, are mere touches: a crocheted "Eagle" over the glass door panel, a school painting of a crest design on the wall, a copper or a painted box, though usually such things are kept in a closet or attic with what few masks, button blankets, and dance paraphernalia the people still possess.

SOCIAL ORGANIZATION

The nuclear family of parents and their children was always of importance in Kwakiutl social organization, but formerly it had dependable formal extensions into the numayms of both the husband and the wife. These extended kin associations have been peeled away along with coresidence. The nuclear family is now the important unit for economic welfare and social status. Relatives still help one another and exchange gifts and hospitality, but the pattern of these reciprocities is that of modern industrial society which makes a limited place for close kinship ties whether Kwakiutl, nineteenth-century European, or whatever. There is in part institutional substitution for kinship services in such things as family allowances granted all Canadians, and the welfare, health, and other services especially available to Indians. In many cases the people feel that the collection of every possible governmental benefit is both necessary as good business practice and as a prideful claim on White indebtedness to the Indian for lands and resources. In part their specialized, even over-specialized, cash economy has resulted in attaching an exaggerated price to kin disbursements. A home-produced two-pound can of salmon is, for instance, thought of as having a grocery store value whether it is opened for the family table or given as a gift. This magnifies the generosity that is still highly valued by the people but that is practiced mostly within the nuclear family or between parents and the families of their married children. Older women can large quantities of salmon for their married daughters, and married and unmarried working sons give expensive presents to their parents and brothers and sisters at the end of the fishing season.

Social differentiation among the Kwakiutl has taken new forms and the complex but orderly ranking system lives on only in the memories of a few older people. It is difficult to make an estimate, but, considering the sample of the young people I have known, I should say that fewer than half have proper Indian names and that none of them have the most important type of name, that representing the ranked standing place and used when giving a potlatch, and that none knows securely what their rank would be. The anthropologist today has to be wary of "Indian names" for something that sounds all right, "bi′nətsə," will turn out to be "Peanuts." The old style names, those that are given to young people of different age grades, pertained to a particular standing place and were validated by a potlatch of an older relative, are still being conferred, though very infrequently. Younger people are in general ignorant of the system and the meaning of their names and so ambivalent about them that those who have them keep them secret even from one another. The younger people who are aware that they could hold great names face the dilemma of wanting social status but being psychologically and culturally unable to pot-latch, the one means of using these names for social status. The best proof of this is the standard pattern of the young men's fighting to-day, in which two young fishermen who have been drinking quarrel about whose father had the biggest name in the old days. The quarrel ends in a fist fight in which usually at least one of them falls off the dock into the cold water. They are not able to claim social rank in their own name, or to sustain the claim by fighting with property in the potlatch, or, it appears, even to introduce sufficient content into their arguments about their fathers' rank to reach a verbal conclusion.

The feeling for social rank and its connection with wealth exists today, but it is an extremely complex question to decide what is a carry-over from earlier Kwakiutl culture and what is essentially European. It is useful to review the character of potlatching in Kwakiutl history and to consider some present-day aspects of the culture that may be modern forms of potlatching and the establishment of social status rather than what they most seem to be, simply a somewhat Kwakiutl version of contemporary Western society in which the most important basis of differentiation is probably wealth, with its use almost as important as its amount. The point was made earlier that sizable property distributions, often made with considerable ceremony, were world-wide in occurrence. Their history is also ancient and their continuity into modern industrial society unmistakable. During one period in Kwakiutl history they were developed into a central institution subserved by the rest of the culture and elaborated by further special developments, for instance, finance and a system of social ranking. This period has ended with the end of the potlatch as a system. The great day of the potlatch is over, but how are we to interpret certain features of contemporary Kwakiutl society: as specific cultural inheritances from the Potlatch Period, or as instances of assimilation to the way of Western society, or both?

There is no difficulty in assigning the potlatch activity of a few elderly people today. It is the continuation of the Kwakiutl past, for those few who are living in the past. It is a difficult thing for these elderly people to accumulate the property necessary to potlatch and only the special luck of a longer earning career in fishing than might have been expected or special opportunities in working for anthropological institutions has made it economically possible. The gatherings and the distributions are very small compared to earlier days; few younger people attend and none give potlatches themselves. Cash is frequently all that is given away and this use of the conveniences of Canadian paper money is also an indication of the perfunctory quality, the constricted size of the potlatching group, and the inability to make impressive displays of goods anyway. Several hundred dollars worth of clothing and housewares might make a fairly impressive display, but there is no longer the same easy potlatch solution to what to do with the potlatch gift of a dozen sugar bowls, ten sweaters, and so on. Even these few magnificently stubborn oldsters bow to the new conditions when they prefer to give cash rather than decide what each recipient might like or need in the way of goods, a decision that would have been unnecessary in the old days.

As far as younger people are concerned there is no doubt that they are no longer interested in the potlatch as a way to social status. In a great potlatching family, one in which the younger people have more knowledge of the old days and more reminders of them than in most families, there is both ignorance of the potlatch and revulsion about potlatch distributions of property. In this family a teen-age son asked his mother why a friend of his had no Indian name. His mother showed reluctance about telling him and he finally hit on the answer himself, "It's because his father never gave a bazaar." The most frequently used Kwakiutl word for potlatch is "p!esa." A young woman of this same family was described by her parents as not being able to stand the idea that the property she saw piled about the house about fifteen years ago was going to be given away in a potlatch, yet this young woman has profound loyalties to her family and pride in the great social positions once held by her parents in the old system.

Social use of wealth seems apparent in some present-day patterns of consumption. When a great chief of the old days plays a more important part in the financing of the Native Brotherhood banquet than his own resources and comparative wealth seem to justify, it seems to be straight out of the Kwakiutl past.

The case of the Wearever dinners is difficult to assign to anything

Kwakiutl, since it was so complicated by the social novelty of having two young White salesmen prepare the meal in Indian homes. However, in Alert Bay the Wearever sales in about two weeks in 1951 were in the thousands of dollars. At the Wearever dinner observed in the field, the women seemed obliged to buy the $250 sets of pots and pans to uphold their social status. The same kind of pressure would probably be present at an all-White Wearever dinner, but it is doubtful whether it would be so great that almost every woman present would give in to it. The old potlatch, like the Wearever dinner, was visible evidence of the buying of goods far beyond consumption needs. There is further evidence that contributes to the probability that White social status was bought along with the pots and pans, and this would be in the old pattern as well as in the new.

Modern Kwakiutl patterns of consumption show other mixed Kwakiutl and White features. Lemert has set out the thesis that the use of alcohol by Kwakiutl and other Northwest Coast people is of a type that can be seen to have potlatch connections. He considers drinking to fill the social vacuum left by the dying-out of the potlatch and particularly the once full opportunities for spending in the potlatch (Lemert 1954: 323). There are serious doubts about Lemert's interpretation as far as the Kwakiutl are concerned. There are many complicating factors (Codere 1957: 1304) in the nature of the liquor laws, the White contact community, and contemporary Kwakiutl culture. There is, however, no question that Kwakiutl today do drink to assert their social equality with Whites, as well as for other reasons, and that any kind of spending behavior connected with social status has a general connection with the earlier potlatch days. But the Kwakiutl also drink to express aggression against Whites by flaunting their scoff-law drunkenness, so that their drinking cannot be seen as any simple matter of spending to achieve social status.

Much present-day acquisition of goods and handling of consumer durables seems again to be a complex synthesis of old and new elements. There is extravagance in buying and carelessness in use that might be connected with potlatching days when spending was grandiose and when the goods bought circulated from hand to hand like money and did not have to be used with great care in order to retain their potlatch value. Expensive presents given within the family are one form of excessive liberality. This usually occurs, as do sprees of all sorts, at the end of the fishing season and is encouraged by the fish-company practice of paying off in a lump sum after deducting company store charges. The consumption life of clothing, houses, expensive home equipment, and personal possessions like watches seems often to be unduly short. Maximizing the level of living by careful buying and use of consumer goods, particularly consumer durables, is not widespread among the people today, although there are a few families whose consumption practices would make those of the average American family seem stupidly wasteful. The important thing in potlatch days was what the object had cost on purchase, and this may be the background of some Kwakiutl consumption habits today. The reason might also be in part that local White practices do not offer much of a model. Frontier carelessness is common in the area: stoves are overloaded and equipment knocked around; and the Kwakiutl who gets salt water in his $100 wrist watch or whose failure to strain outboard-motor fuel results in early and irreparable damage has plenty of White precedent for his negligence.

It is too early to tell with certainty, but there is evidence of Kwakiutl assimilation to a contemporary White pattern of consumption in acquiring goods symbolic of social status in the White community. Houses and home equipment "just like White" are admired. Lack of indoor plumbing, electricity, and a battery of appliances signifies low social status, while such equipment and all the home furnishings that go with it is the ideal. Achievement of the ideal can be valued above comfort. In one case a family acquired a white enamel stove of the heavily insulated sort that is used in Vancouver homes for burning trash. The stove was wanted and needed for heat but was kept even when it did that job unsatisfactorily because it went with the other white enamel kitchen equipment: stove, refrigerator, hot-water heater and washing machine. Freezers have been acquired in some Kwakiutl homes even though the people uniformly dislike frozen fish and fish is mostly what there is to freeze. The conflicting views of Kingcome and Alert Bay are interesting in this context. Kingcome had a low rank in the old potlatch heirarchy and in Nimpkish eyes continues to be socially low because of its lack of modern facilities, for until recently there was no water supply except the glacial river and there is still no village electric plant. Some Kingcome villagers accept Alert Bay's evaluation of them. The ones who do not and who are leaders in the community are precisely the ones who have the most "modern" homes and who had the greatest enthusiasm and did the most work on the symbolic new water system.

Social status in any case does not carry over from the old system. There is an interesting recent study of whether the Nimpkish of Alert Bay admitted band transfers according to the old potlatch rank of the villages of the migrants (Pineo 1955). What this study shows is that Nimpkish women who married men of outlying villages wished to remain in Alert Bay or return to live there because of its conveniences, facilities, social activities, and prestige. Marriage preferences and admitted band transfers coincide as much with village size, geographical nearness to Alert Bay, and relative wealth of villages as with the old rank order of villages; and the high place of Kingcome and Quatsino among the preferences violates the old order.

Kwakiutl intermarriage with Whites has recently been taking place with increased frequency. About 1950 a White woman married into the Kwakiutl community; however, the marriage of White men by Kwakiutl women is more usual. In 1954 there were fourteen marriages recorded; seven of these were within the Kwakiutl population and seven of Kwakiutl women with White men. Parents seem to desire these marriages for their daughters and to take pride in them. In some cases they seem to have the glamour and social status meaning of the old crest marriages "far outside." They seem to form proof for the people of social status equivalent to that of Whites and such proof is valued.

In the old days social and political leadership were integrated in what was also a fairly well-integrated community. Nowadays there are only remnants of the earlier situation. There seems today to be only one village in which community life and pride is strong and which seems to have real social and political leadership. The force at work, however, is a kind of nineteenth-century progressivism and neither this community's enthusiasm nor the effectiveness of its leadership derives from the old culture, especially from the old system of social rank.

Perhaps the most important figure among the Kwakiutl in recent years was the President of the Native Brotherhood. He was a man who could have had a chief's name, but he never potlatched. The older men scorned him for this, perhaps regarding him with more contempt than they would have if he had come from less high-ranking origins and had no chiefly pretensions. The younger men neither held his failure to potlatch against him nor, as far as I could see, thought of his assumed chiefly status as depending on his father's great name rather than his own success as a politician. He was one of the two customary chiefs representing bands; the remaining ten Kwakiutl bands were represented by elected councilors. The only other band with a customary chief was a remnant band, and in 1951 and 1955 there was grumbling about the chief's lack of literacy, his failure to operate in the contemporary situation, and the irrelevance and meaninglessness of his old-time chiefly status under the new conditions. If the brotherhood president had not been a man who could dispense important favors and get things done because of his office, his sizable band would probably have had council leadership long ago.

Qualifications for election to council membership seem today to be solid citizenship, competence in dealing with Whites, and interest in the job. The system does not yet function successfully in the various band communities, most of which are somewhere in between Alert Bay with its many unsolved or half-solved community problems and Kingcome with its spirit of progressivism and its effective community co-operation. Alert Bay had more problems to solve than any other Kwakiutl village in recent times, and too much was somehow left to the agency located there. The result in the largest and most important Kwakiutl village is lack of community planning, cohesiveness, leadership, and achievement.

Social leadership seems even more dispersed and unorganized than political leadership. Such as it is, it seems to be in the hands of the more assimilated and the more prosperous. The one case of real social domination in recent years was that of an elderly and extremely churchly woman who had a very great effect on the women of Alert Bay. She was only part Kwakiutl in origins and had from her youth been completely set against the old life, particularly the potlatch. Her knowledge of the language, said by some to be very imperfect, nevertheless gained her status as a lay preacher and interpreter of the Bible. Her influence was pretty much confined to her own very large family until the end of her days in 1951. The long extended drama of her preparations to meet her Maker produced a religious revival and, since her own religion was full of behavioral precepts of the old-time missionary sort, there was indeed less drinking and smoking, or at least more guilt in such behavior, for a time, along with greatly increased hymn-singing about the house and participation in church affairs.

Social leadership today seems to be consumption leadership, though it is dangerous to risk assessing the nature of developments that are at present in progress and cannot be seen in full perspective. At least the force people seem to follow is the desire for modern consumption goods, and the people they want to emulate are those who have them. It is too risky to say categorically that these goods symbolize social status for the people today or that such symbols would also indicate the desire to be fully participant in the modern world, but other evidence strongly supports these possibilities.

CEREMONIALISM AND SUPERNATURALISM

There are still some ceremonial performances, but they take place in new contexts and have new and different meanings in Kwakiutl society. They also perpetuate, however, knowledge of the use of masks and of old ways of handling the body in dance, for younger people take part in them.

Several years before 1951, dances were held again after a long interruption. The context was novel; it was the putting on of a benefit dance for the hospital in Alert Bay. The first one was initiated by a woman who ranked high in the old system. The greatest difficulty that she said she had to overcome was that at first the old chiefs were confused and thought that putting on the dance would have to involve potlatching as it did in earlier days. The only potlatch was in the turning over of the proceeds of the show to the hospital. A master of ceremonies announced the dances and explained them to the audience and according to tape recordings ended each with a proper "emcee" flourish, "Come on folks, let's give the Raven a hand." It was not apparently because of lack of enthusiasm for the hospital but probably lack of community feeling and leadership that after 1951 the benefit ceremonial was discontinued. In 1954 an old-style ceremonial complete with potlatch was sponsored by the Provincial Museum in Victoria. The occasion was the completion of a Kwakiutl great house for the museum. In 1955 the Kwakiutl who had directed the building and the carving in Victoria decided to put on a winter ceremonial as a business venture. The summer tourist season was chosen as the time and a baseball park was rented. The venture was not financially rewarding, although it may have an honorable place in Kwakiutl history in preserving some aspects of the old traditions. The most remarkable feature of these recent ceremonials seems to be the fact that younger people can both be persuaded to dance in them and can do so successfully. Several of the young dancers in the ball park ceremonial were typical present-day teen-agers who were thoroughly ignorant about the old days. The rehearsals they were put through were strenuous. Older men demonstrated the proper motions and use of masks and after a time their performance was fairly duplicated. Although some younger people have said they could not imagine taking part in an Indian dance unless they were drunk, some can and do. There may be vital cultural latency here, sufficient continuity of an old tradition to use it and maintain it and even to build upon it in the future.

In general it can be said that the Kwakiutl have made an easy transition into today's secular society, although there are both individuals and groups for whom Protestant religious beliefs and observances are neither nominal nor perfunctory. The Kwakiutl were missionized by the Anglican Church from about 1880, but missionaries and agents alike were deeply disappointed in the results as recently as World War I. At present almost all Kwakiutl are Anglican in religious affiliation. A few might be described as doubters and a small minority group recently became devoted followers of the Pentecostals, although the intensity of their interest was diminishing in 1955.

Kwakiutl official and public Protestantism has gone so far as to interfere, apparently unwittingly, with economic interest. Some Indian people both to the north and the south of the Kwakiutl on the coast were missionized by the Roman Catholic Church. The Native Brotherhood with its ideal of including all the Indians of the province and forming an effective political group, but with its more limited functions as an Indian fishermen's union, is disadvantaged by its strongly Protestant cast. Possible non-Protestant membership is turned away apparently unintentionally by the Brotherhood use of "Onward Christian Soldiers" as an official hymn and other such unnecessarily denominational or, for that matter, religious usages (Hawthorn, Belshaw, Jamieson, *et al.* 1958: 475–76).

The Kwakiutl have, however, made a firm connection between Anglican religious observances and public life. The church seems now to give public validations, such as those once conferred by potlatches, before witnesses. Christening, confirmation, marriage, and burial are church affairs of importance for most of the people, although not all the villages have churches and instead depend upon the visits of the mission steamer. In the five villages which have churches, and this includes the four largest Kwakiutl villages, the church is part of community life. Church organizations like the choir for the younger people and the Woman's Auxiliary, or "W.A.," as it is always called, are particularly important. Even in a small village without a church there will be a happy buzz of activity one afternoon as the "W.A. Ladies" bake things and sell them to one another. In Kingcome, where the church has almost no recreational or social competition, it is of outstanding community importance. There in 1955 the W.A. Ladies even gathered informally with all their children to discuss the general problems of living in the village and the need for special precautions because the men were away fishing. Children were warned not to go to the end of the village where the river was deep and not to fool around the canoes that were needed to get supplies or, perhaps, help. The pockets of small boys were turned out and emptied of matches or any other dangerous item. These warnings were afterwards observed by the children. Kingcome is extraordinary in the extent to which it uses church organizations and connections in community matters, but Alert Bay still finds the "W.A." important. There its activities seem to be focused on the yearly bazaar, and on this occasion the efforts of Kwakiutl women to compete successfully with the White churchwomen is dramatically apparent. Even if it were not made obvious by the division of the tables at the bazaar into a White and an Indian half, comparisons of the quality and amount of handiwork, other contributions, and money brought in would explain the excitement of the Kwakiutl women and the effort and often the money they had spent.

CURING AND KNOWLEDGE

Kwakiutl pragmatism about curing techniques has carried over into the modern period. There is little to indicate that the Kwakiutl were much impressed with Western medicine until after antibiotics came into general use, but that factor plus the expansion of hospital facilities in Alert Bay after World War II has produced real enthusiasm among the people. The whole medical area is of exceptional interest in showing the "Kwakiutl" and the "White" in contemporary Kwakiutl life.

The Kwakiutl have some special health problems. Dentition is very poor. Low blood counts are common. There are a number of cases, among them some individuals who are extremely obese, that are characterized by the local doctor as "qualitative malnutrition." The frequency of respiratory ailments, especially among young children, is very high. The Kwakiutl come to the hospital whatever the difficulty and bring and leave their children there with confidence. Many of them regard the hospital as the only suitable place for childbirth. They are altogether docile and co-operative patients except when it comes to following home nursing and dieting directions and ill such less dramatically and specifically medical procedures that form the daily living complement of modern medical technology. It is when a cure is stubborn and requires co-operation away from the hospital that the people may revert to their old-time specifics. Ratfish oil for an ulcerated leg is an example.

The Kwakiutl are acquiring an increasing amount of education. The youth of today's population and the present high attendance record indicates a strong and continuous trend in this direction. Eight of the ten Kwakiutl villages have grade schools. In one of these, nearby White schools are used; in three there are only one-room grade schools. Kwakiutl children who do not have access to school facilities in their own villages, and this number would include many of high-school age, attend the new high school in Alert Bay and, while they do so, live with relatives or at the Anglican church residency. Until the Alert Bay High School was built, young people had to leave home and board out, often with strangers, while attending school in Victoria or Vancouver. Few did so, but there are at the present time two young people who not only gained high-school diplomas under these difficult conditions but also attended the university. Some of these developments are too new to assess in any way. A few parents have seen education for their children as a way for them to escape dependence upon the uncertain fishing industry and as a way to better and more varied living opportunities. The amount of education coincides precisely with the degree to which White living habits and standards have been accepted. This cannot be an occasion for any surprise when the goal of the White-managed Indian grade schools is assimilation for the Indian and when further schooling is schooling in Western culture.

The old art of the people is not conserved and little new is being produced except under White patronage. There is only one carver living in the Kwakiutl area and spending most of his time at his art; he was an elderly man of failing eyesight in 1955. The greatest artistic activity of recent years has been taking place in the south where first the Museum of the University of British Columbia and then the Provincial Museum employed a Kwakiutl carver. Lately two younger men have been working under his direction. This enterprise has been connected with the activities of the Committee for the Preservation of Totem Poles; rotted poles collected from often uninhabited village sites have been duplicated and sounder poles repaired. Other accomplishments have been the repairing of masks and carvings and the building of the Kwakiutl great house in Victoria.

Recent Kwakiutl carving has made use of shiny modern enamels of all colors applied over a white base. These bright colors have had an adverse effect on the definition of the carvings over which they were applied. In the south the anthropologists in time convinced the Kwakiutl artisans of the superiority of the old subdued reds, blacks, and blues, but in the Kwakiutl area itself what little is being done has a new garishness even when the underlying workmanship is fine. Younger men can still carve clean-cut toy boats for their children, and they usually know how to reproduce an old crest design with pen and ink. Women's crafts seem to have almost completely disappeared and given way to crocheting, embroidering, and knitting. A crocheted "Thunderbird" with its zigzag squares bears only a courtesy resemblance to the old design.

Some of the people keep some masks and other objects like button blankets in dead storage in their homes. Many have nothing from the old days among their possessions, and there is no attempt to conserve the monumental carvings that still stand in some villages or to protect them from the weather or from children with knives and hatchets. The task of conservation of both objects and techniques has been accepted by anthropology. From one point of view this is a highly artificial situation; from another it might very well prove to be merely a temporary trusteeship. Since two younger Kwakiutl men have submitted to training by an elder carver and since some value is still attached to old objects, there is reason to think that latent skills and interests still exist.

LANGUAGE

With almost no exceptions Kwakiutl today know and use their own language as well as English. The older people can charge the younger with speaking an indifferent and simplified Kwak'wala, but even those who say they want their children to speak good English, and therefore speak English at home, can also add with assurance that the children will learn Kwak'wala quickly enough when they play in the village.

The linguistic changes that have occurred require much further study and cannot be detailed here. It is important, however, to consider that no matter how drastic these changes may prove to have been, the language itself is viable still, though there seems to have been much contraction in the number and types of situations in which its use is still comfortable and appropriate.

CONCLUSIONS

Kwakiutl culture has not been described generally. What has been set out is Kwakiutl culture of the Pre-Potlatch, the Potlatch, and the Post-Potlatch periods. The divisions are rough, in the sense that it would be possible to introduce further subdivisions; but they are operational in that there is no doubt that the Kwakiutl cultures of the three periods are different and that the periods order the changes that have taken place in the lives of the continuous and overlapping generations of the people called the Kwakiutl. There can be no sense in regarding the Kwakiutl culture of any one period or date as "Kwakiutl culture," although there certainly might be a powerful temptation to do so and to select the period during which the people evidenced the most dramatic differences in their way of life from all other ways of life and, therefore, seemed most to deserve a special and distinguishing label. If this were done, it would be simple to choose the Potlatch Period as "Kwakiutl culture," interpret the Pre-Potlatch Period as becoming the Potlatch Period and the Post-Potlatch Period as one of loss, disintegration and degeneration of the "classical culture." Such an interpretative model would have many precedents in the historiography of peoples, polities, empires, cultures, and arts, not the least of which are those based upon an organic or anthropomorphic version of the general model. The problem with such an interpretation as applied to the Kwakiutl case seems to be that of making a meaningless and confused distinction between culture and change. The moment the dynamism that is now generally recognized as being a feature of culture and the continuity that is generally recognized as a part of change are admitted, Kwakiutl culture as a whole can be seen. It has lost its distinctiveness in recent years only because of the historical fact that many of its basic features and persistences happen to be very much like certain fundamental features of contemporary Canadian-American life. The genuine-enough differences in the local, special-interest, special-background, or other groups that exist in modern society are difficult to analyze or even see. There is the danger of being misled by appearances. In the early days of contact with the people of other cultures Europeans could not see even the humanity of the non-European because of the differences in costuming, stage-setting, and other superficials. Today the problem is one of exaggerating the cultural homogeneity of the Western industrial world and considering the absence of superficial distinctions the evidence of sameness.

Some general matters of definition are in order here to clarify the concepts that will be used in the analytic discussion of Kwakiutl culture change. All cultures are open systems and all are dynamic. No culture is known to have a unique content, and the assumption that content must have been admitted into a particular culture from another culture in order to produce at least some of the shared content that exists is borne out in every instance by history or prehistory when investigation has been possible. A cultural system is dynamic to the point that the distinction between the structure of the system and its functioning is neither necessary nor valid, since no cultural structure exists without functioning and no cultural function takes place randomly without any structural form. Cultural systems vary in their degrees of integration according to whether it takes relatively large or relatively small changes to disrupt, dissociate, or disintegrate the system; the more integrated, the greater the changes that can be met without disorganization.[2] Throughout the presentation of the

[2] I am indebted to Walter Buckley for many of these ideas and for some of the phrasing of them. The definition of cultural integration is borrowed directly from him, although put in somewhat more compressed form. Walter Buckley's unpublished manuscript is entitled "Social System Models and General Systems Theory."

Kwakiutl case the concepts of culture and change have been used crudely and categorically because the emphasis was on the setting out of data. Discussion of either the theoretical implications of the case or of its over-all meaning, an answer to the question of what in general happened, requires a general view with a statement of its terms and assumptions.

The question of what has been persistent and what non-persistent in Kwakiutl culture since 1792 is fundamental, and it is equally important to determine the relationship of persistent and non-persistent elements to changes in the conditions or nature of the contact world of the Kwakiutl at various points in time. Table 10 has been prepared to summarize Kwakiutl cultural persistences in three rough cultural categories: material culture, institutions, and interests. The facts are clear; the only full persistences are in the category of interests: social status and its maximization; the social status–property relation; profitable economic ventures; abhorrence of physical violence; pragmatism in curing, religion, human relations, and technology. These interests seem to hold as much for the Kwakiutl of 1955 as for those of the early days of the historical record, and they seem never to have diminished. It might be possible to take this group of interests and work out in terms of their meanings and interrelationships some one or several Kwakiutl "values," but it does not seem clear how to reach this level of philosophic generalization or how useful it would be to do so. What is startling is that Kwakiutl interests differ very little from those that are thought to comprise the Protestant ethic. The chief contrast is that the Kwakiutl interest in non-violence in physical relations and the Kwakiutl interest in results seem to have higher positions by far in the respective hierarchies of interests of the two groups. Both war, or any other kind of physical violence, and mysticism seem more alien to the Kwakiutl. From such a general overview Kwakiutl culture could be seen to have sustained one great change beginning with the importation of the idea of crests from the northern people probably before the coming of the European into the area. Around this idea the culture became reorganized, highly specialized, and developed a sharp focus. The general part played by the conditions of contact was to maximize the cultural specialization in the potlatch at one period and to destroy the potlatch at a later time, but to continue to sustain the people's central interest in social status and its tangible and visible material proofs and validations. In such a picture the non-persistence of any Kwakiutl institution or any item of material culture, except in the form of remnants, latencies, behaviors sustained by outside patronage, and occasional transmissions from the memories of the elderly, is altogether unimportant. The only thing that is important is that Kwakiutl culture has remained integrated around central interests for the past century and a half. The

TABLE 10

KWAKIUTL CULTURE: PERSISTENCES AND NON-PERSISTENCES

KWAKIUTL CULTURE	PRE-POTLATCH 1792–1849	POTLATCH 1881 1921	POST-POTLATCH 1921–1955	KWAKIUTL-CANADIAN CULTURE, 1955
Material Culture:				
Great Houses				Single Family House
Canoes				Power Boats
Mats and Fur Robes				Blankets, European Clothing
Minimal Clothing				European Clothing
Containers of Wood, etc.				Metal, Glass, etc.
Tools of Stone, Wood, Beaver Teeth				Iron and Steel
Native Foods				Limited Canadian Menu
Institutions:				
Potlatch				?Church Bazaar, Wearever Dinner, etc.?
Winter Ceremonial				New Context, Infrequent
Lineage Groups				Nuclear Family
Crest Art				Under Anthropological Patronage
Religious Beliefs				Christianity-Nominal Non-Mystical Protestant
Migratory Diversified Economy				Commercial Salmon Fishing. Settled, Specialized within Canadian Economy
Village Social Life				Commercial Entertainment. Limited Hospitality
Warfare				Limited Interest and Participation in Modern National Wars
Slavery, War Captives				Nothing. No substitute
Kwakiutl Monolingualism				Bilingualism. Kwakiutl-English
Interests:				
Social Status and Its Maximization				
Social Status-Property Relation				Persistent. Fully Present Today
Profitable Economic Ventures				
Abhorrence of Physical Violence				
Pragmatism in Curing, Religion, Human Relations, Technology				

non-persistences in institutions and material culture cannot be stated in such an exaggerated form in any case, since the language is still spoken and there are so many things that still can be and occasionally are re-created. Anachronisms like a winter ceremonial held in a ball park in the summer as a commercial venture in the Canadian entertainment field or a house woodpile with the puncheons sawed by a modern chain saw and split with a set of yew wedges show persistences even if full vigor, maximum intensity or frequency, or dependability of association and context are absent.

This very broad interpretation of Kwakiutl cultural change and cultural persistence goes too far. At least it extends to a point that puts verification beyond the scope of the data covered. For example, the scholarship and analysis of Western civilization that supports the idea of a characterizing "Protestant ethic" seem both solid and brilliant. There is also no question about the character of those agents and missionaries who recorded their own point of view along with their judgments of the Kwakiutl. But while they may seem imbued with Tawney's Protestant ethic, there seems to be no way of establishing whether it was predominant in the contact world of the Kwakiutl from about 1850 on. Is a Kwakiutl prostitute in Victoria of the 1860's a good example of Kwakiutl pragmatism in human relations and of Kwakiutl enterprise for economic profit being furthered by a White world with a Protestant ethic? After all, the White world set up the business opportunity, built and rented the shacks, and ran the quarter of town that was the business location of prostitution; both groups made use of the income and property gained to further group cultural interests chiefly of a social sort. Because this and other questions are open to some argument, it seems better to return to a level of generalization and interpretation that is more secure.

A detailed summary of persistences and changes in relation to contact conditions is in order. In the Pre-Potlatch Period, probably before the first direct European contact in 1792, Kwakiutl culture was in a period of lively reorganization and change. The idea of crests or symbols of distinctive social status in art, mythic literature, rhetoric, and ceremonial and the peaceful method of obtaining crests by intermarriage were being enthusiastically and thoroughly integrated into the culture. Whether some increase in the possibility of peaceful, rather than uneasy, relations with outsiders sparked this change cannot be known. European contact seems to have amounted to little beyond the addition of European goods to the material culture inventory. It may also, however, have added to economic opportunities and thereby furthered peaceful relations among both local Kwakiutl groups and Kwakiutl and outsiders.

In the next period, the Potlatch Period, complex and manifold changes occurred; they seem to have been the further development of processes already set in motion as affected by new contact conditions. They involved integrative cultural reorganization, cultural specialization, and cultural loss, the last only in the sense that once important phases of culture were set aside in ways that were consistent with the integrative reorganization. Warfare and everything directly connected with warfare ceased almost immediately with the beginning of the period. Part of this development seems the outcome of processes begun earlier; part, an unimportant part, the result of some European action to suppress hostilities in the region; part, the most important part of all, the interplay between the constantly increasing economic opportunities of European contact conditions and the increased specialization in the potlatch. By 1880 Kwakiutl culture was already transformed. The over-all system of social ranking that developed with potlatching had brought all the Kwakiutl local groups into closer and probably more exciting social relations, and the potlatch secularization of religious and ceremonial life seems to have begun. Ceremonial life seemed to be in a transitional state. It took over or retained the idea of warfare and violence that remained after their practice had ceased and made theatrical play with their themes. Potlatching in connection with putting these on as crest ceremonials did not yet overwhelm them or in its turn take over their war symbolism. The first replacement rather than mere addition to material culture comes at this time, when woolen blankets replaced those of fur and cedar bark. Woolen blankets began to be acquired in such numbers that they soon became a symbolic good and a currency.

In the second part of the Potlatch Period, from 1880 on, all these developments intensified and the chief effect of the contact world on them was the continuously expanding economy of the area. The Kwakiutl became a highly specialized culture in which every institution and preoccupation subserved the potlatch. Religion and ceremonialism became further secularized. Crests which had been of primary importance earlier gradually seem to have become less so. Without the property validations of potlatching they were nothing, and their worth was measured by the size of potlatch distributions. Drucker claims that the "Eagles" were the fabricated crests of the *nouveaux riches* (1955: 128–29) and, although the nature of the "Eagles" is not certain, there were some attempts to fabricate a position of rank complete with its crests. Kwakiutl culture seems to have been such that, if a great potlatch validated a claim, it became real. Through their successful exploitation of the expanding European economy, the Kwakiutl obtained quantities of many kinds of European consumer goods; many of these became a kind of money circulating rapidly in the potlatch donations and in the preparatory loans for potlatches. Subsistence activities were relatively unaffected, but craft production was. New tools, utensils and other goods were not merely adding to inventory but were replacing their craft-made counterparts. From 1880 on, non-economic aspects of Western culture were much more important features of the contact world than they had been before. Representatives of Western culture knew what changes they wanted in Kwakiutl culture. The chief one was the abandonment of potlatching; then came paganism, such savage ways as marrying without religious sanction, and such prematurely civilized ways as earning money sinfully in the flesh pots of the south. About the only method they had to effect cultural change was exhortation, a notably frail device, especially when coupled with cheers and encouragement for the industrious pursuit of economic gain that was having the unplanned and unwitting, but really pervasive effect of strengthening the potlatch at every point. Nevertheless, knowledge of the Western world and its ways was being acquired, and the effects show in later years, although not within this period. If one of the missionaries of the time were able to return for a look at the people today, he could be permitted at least a moment of satisfaction about the Kwakiutl use of "Onward Christian Soldiers" interfering with the strength of the Indian fishermen's union and, therefore, with their best economic interests.

In the Post-Potlatch Period from 1921 to the present, the most drastic changes occurred, or give the appearance of having occurred, and the conditions of contact seemingly account for them all. Difficulties with their relation to the Western economy, followed by the European and world depression, ended the potlatch as an institution. With it all other Kwakiutl institutions ceased functioning as such. It might be possible to claim that this was the end of Kwakiutl culture and that the remainder of their history is simply that of rapid assimilation to White Canadian culture. This is oversimplified, since the facts are remarkable and complex, and appearances can be deceptive. Were the Kwakiutl such an extraordinary people that when all the institutions of their culture collapsed they turned away from it almost immediately and joined White Canadian culture? The years between about 1930, or even 1921, and today are amazingly few for changing from one culture to another. The importance of the potlatch until 1921 is too undeniably great to make it seem credible that there were dozens, even hundreds, of individuals secretly against it, hoping to leave it, and just as secretly deeply affected by the exhortations of agents and missionaries and preparing themselves in every way to take over the new culture when the opportunity came. Yet, if the potlatch were as important as all the evidence shows, why would there not have been more trouble, disruption, and confusion at its ending? Fifteen years, from about 1925 through the thirties, seems the maximum time allowance for breaking away from the old culture. A few potlatches including one or two large ones were given as late as the thirties. What marvels of perspicacity would have been involved, if the majority saw their cultural situation factually without the distortions of regrets or hopes and took rationally appropriate action. "That's finished. Now we shall become Canadians." And so they did within the next fifteen years.

To interpret the picture with the maximum caution, such a quick and relatively painless loss of an old culture followed by an equally painless and quick and seemingly competent taking on of a new one— all this within thirty years—seems almost impossible. There is then only one adequate explanation of what did happen and that is that Kwakiutl and European culture were profoundly alike, and alike in such fundamental ways that reports of the death of Kwakiutl culture are greatly exaggerated, change to a new culture was not anywhere nearly so drastic as appearances indicate, and the new culture had more the appearance than the reality of newness and difference. The conclusion that Kwakiutl culture and Western European culture must be profoundly alike seems to be required by the facts. Once accepted, it resolves major difficulties of interpretation about what has happened.

It does, however, set a problem of terrifying difficulty. How can such similarities, assuming they exist, be seen, measured, demonstrated? Particularly, how are they to be perceived and described by any participant in the two cultures concerned? An earlier statement about the similarity of interests in the two cultures was tentatively withdrawn because it immediately generated such questions as whether the Kwakiutl were really confronted with a Protestant ethic in their contact world, assuming a Protestant ethic to describe certain realities of Western culture conveniently. The difficulty of this question is now an insignificant part of the total problem. Yet this account must end with the promise to work at this total problem and the hope that some other student of the case, too, will do so. It should not be an occasion for surprise that a study of culture history must stop at the point where a deeper and more comprehensive analysis of a culture than any yet made becomes necessary. It is particularly to be expected that it is the analysis of so-called Western culture that is required, when the history of a non-Western culture is traced to the present with its inevitable relation to a Western contact world.

REFERENCES CITED

BENEDICT, RUTH
  1934 *Patterns of Culture.* Boston.
BOAS, FRANZ
  1891 "Ein Besuch in Victoria auf Vancouver," *Globus*, LIX, 75–77.
  1897 "The Social Organization and Secret Societies of the Kwakiutl Indians," *Report of the U.S. National Museum for 1895*, pp. 311–738. Washington.
  1909 "The Kwakiutl of Vancouver Island," *Memoir of the American Museum of Natural History*, VIII, 307–515 (The Jesup North Pacific Expedition). New York.
  1920 "The Social Organization of the Kwakiutl," *American Anthropologist*, XXII, 111–26. Reprinted in *Race, Language and Culture*, 1940.
  1921 *Ethnology of the Kwakiutl. Thirty-fifth Annual Report*, Bureau of American Ethnology. Washington.
  1924 "The Social Organization of the Tribes of the North Pacific Coast," *American Anthropologist*, XXVI, 323–32. Reprinted in *Race, Language and Culture*, 1940.
  1927 *Primitive Art.* Oslo.
  1930 *The Religion of the Kwakiutl Indians.* Columbia University "Contributions to Anthropology," Vol. X, Part 2. New York.
  1933 "Review of G. W. Locher: The Serpent in Kwakiutl Religion: A Study of Primitive Culture." Reprinted in *Race, Language and Culture*, 1940.

1934 *Geographical Names of the Kwakiutl Indians.* Columbia University "Contributions to Anthropology," Vol. XX. New York.

1935 "Kwakiutl Culture as Reflected in Mythology," *Memoirs of the American Folklore Society*, Vol. XXVIII. New York.

1938 "Methods of Research," in *General Anthropology*, edited by FRANZ BOAS. Boston.

1940 *Race, Language and Culture.* New York.

1947 *Kwakiutl Grammar with a Glossary of the Suffixes.* Edited by HELENE BOAS YAMPOLSKY, with the collaboration of ZELLIG S. HARRIS. *Transactions of the American Philosophical Society*, XXXVII, Part 3, 203–377. Philadelphia.

n.d. "Kwakiutl Ethnology," manuscript.

BOAS, FRANZ (ed.)

1938 *General Anthropology.* Boston.

CANADIAN GOVERNMENT PUBLICATIONS

1872–1955 *Annual Report on Indian Affairs.* Ottawa.

1950 "An Act respecting Indians." Department of Mines and Resources Indian Affairs Branch. Ottawa.

CODERE, HELEN

1950 *Fighting with Property: A Study of Kwakiutl Potlatching and Warfare 1792–1930.* American Ethnological Society, *Monograph 18.* New York.

1951 "Field Notes," September to December, Alert Bay and Fort Rupert.

1955 "Field Notes," May to August, all Kwakiutl villages and village sites.

1955 "Review of Edwin M. Lemert: Alcohol and the Northwest Coast Indians," *American Anthropologist*, LVII, 1303–5.

1957 "Kwakiutl Society: Rank without Class," *American Anthropologist*, LIX, 473–86.

CRANMER, DANIEL E.

n.d. "Potlatch Account Book 1913–1921," manuscript.

CURTIS, EDWARD S.

1915 *The North American Indian.* Vol. X. Norwood.

DRUCKER, PHILIP

1939 "Rank, Wealth, and Kinship in Northwest Coast Society," *American Anthropologist*, XLI, 55–65.

1955 *Indians of the Northwest Coast.* American Museum of Natural History, *Anthropological Handbook*, No. 10. New York.

DUFF, WILSON

1957 Personal communication.

FORD, CLELLAN S.

1941 *Smoke from Their Fires: The Life of a Kwakiutl Chief.* New Haven.

GLADSTONE, PERCY

1953 "Native Indians and the Fishing Industry of British Columbia," *Canadian Journal of Economics and Political Science*, XIX, 20–34.

HALLIDAY, WILLIAM

1935 *Potlatch and Totem.* Toronto.

HAWTHORN, HARRY B., CYRIL S. BELSHAW, S. M. JAMIESON, *et al.*

1958 *The Indians of British Columbia: A Study of Contemporary Social Adjustment.* Berkeley and Vancouver.

HOWAY, F. W. (ed.)
1914   "A New Vancouver Journal," *Washington Historical Quarterly*, Vol. V, No. 3.
1915   "A New Vancouver Journal," *Washington Historical Quarterly*, Vol. VI, No. 1.
HUNT, GEORGE
n.d.   "History of Twenty-one Coppers from Alert Bay," manuscript.
JACOBSEN, ADRIEN
1884   *Reise an der Nordwestküste Amerikas 1881–1883*. Leipzig.
KROEBER, ALFRED L.
1917   "The Tribes of the Pacific Coast of North America," *Proceedings of the Nineteenth International Congress of Americanists*. Washington.
1923   "American Culture and the Northwest Coast," *American Anthropologist*, XXV, 1–20.
1947   *Cultural and Natural Areas of Native North America*. Berkeley.
LEMERT, EDWIN M.
1954   *Alcohol and the Northwest Coast Indians*. University of California "Publications in Culture and Society," Vol. II, No. 6. Berkeley.
LORD, JOHN K.
1886   *The Naturalist in Vancouver Island*. London.
MAYNE, RICHARD C.
1862   *Four Years in British Columbia and Vancouver Island*. London.
NEWCOMBE, C. F. (ed.)
1923   "Menzies' Journal of Vancouver's Voyage April to October 1792," *Memoir Number 5. Archives of British Columbia*. Victoria.
PINEO, PETER
1955   *Village Migrations of the Modern Kwakiutl*. Honours Essay. University of British Columbia.
RICH, E. E. (ed.)
1941   *Letters of John McLoughlin from Fort Vancouver to the Governer and Committee. First Series, 1825–1838*. Toronto.
SAGE, WALTER N.
1930   *Sir James Douglas and British Columbia*. Toronto.
SWADESH, MORRIS
1948   "A Structural Trend in Nootka," *Word*, IV, 106–19.
TAYLOR, HERBERT C., and DUFF, WILSON
1956   "A Post-Contact Southward Movement of the Kwakiutl," *Research Studies*, State College of Washington, XXIV, 56–66.
VANCOUVER, GEORGE
1798   *Voyage of Discovery to the North Pacific Ocean and Round the World*. London.
WIKE, JOYCE
1947   "The Effect of the Maritime Fur Trade on Northwest Coast Society." Unpublished Ph.D. thesis. Columbia University.
1952   "The Role of the Dead in Northwest Coast Culture," in SOL TAX (ed.), *Selected Papers of the Twenty-ninth International Congress of Americanists*. Pp. 97–103.
WINGERT, PAUL
1949   *American Indian Sculpture: A Study of the Northwest Coast*. New York.

CHAPTER 8

Types of Contact
and Processes of Change

By Edward H. Spicer

The growth of a general understanding of cultural change among anthropologists has seemed slow and unsatisfactory. There is a widespread feeling that we have no really useful concepts, that there is no theory worthy of the name, for comparing and understanding the many instances of change with which we are acquainted. It is true, nevertheless, that there has been a discernible advance, ever since Tylor, toward something like a systematic approach. A decisive step beyond the insights of Tylor and the uncertain gropings of Boas came in 1936 in a brief memorandum instigated by the Social Science Research Council. Put together by Robert Redfield, M. J. Herskovits, and Ralph Linton, it purported to be no more than a sort of check list for students interested in the study of acculturation (Redfield *et al.* 1936). Its publication in the *American Anthropologist* immediately stimulated discussion and set two of its authors to critical reappraisal of its implications.

The impetus which the memorandum gave to studies of acculturation has been great, although its influence has not often been explicitly stated. Aside from the many descriptive studies which followed its suggestions, the most important formulations deriving in some way from it have been Linton's sketch of acculturative types and processes (Linton 1940: 463–520), Malinowski's conception of contact institutions (Malinowski 1945), Herskovits' theory of cultural focus (Herskovits 1948: 542–60), the Wilsons' development of Redfield's theory of cultural change (Wilson 1945), Keesing's bibliographic summary (Keesing 1953), the 1954 report of the SSRC Seminar on Acculturation (Broom *et al.* 1954), and Carnegie Institution's 1955 Seminars in Archaeology (Wauchope 1956). To say that all these contributions derive directly from the 1936 memorandum and from it only would be to ignore a large amount of significant work and thought, most important among which has been the program for the study of culture contact instituted in 1931 by the International Institute of African Languages and Cultures (Malinowski *et al.* 1938). The memorandum did nevertheless focus studies in a fruitful new way, because its authors faced the problem, if they did not solve it, of differentiating the significant factors in situations of cultural contact. The inadequacies and undeveloped implications of the memorandum constituted a point of departure for the needed comparative work on which theoretical growth has depended.

The subsequent proliferation of acculturation studies has at times seemed, as Kroeber has intimated, little more than a fad (Kroeber 1948: 426). It has been difficult to see any consistent growth of understanding; yet the fact is that important general ideas have taken form. Credit for cutting through the tangle of descriptive data and specific formulations accrues heavily to Ralph Linton. It was Linton who, attempting to follow out suggestions for comparative studies in the 1936 memorandum, began to see the fundamental distinctions between types of contact situations (Linton 1940). His awareness of the important differences between directed and non-directed contacts, inadequate though his formulation was, laid a foundation for understanding the apparent overwhelming variety in the results of contact. It was also Linton's pioneer effort to sketch a model of what he called the process of "culture transfer" in terms of acceptance, diffusion, and modification which gave further systematic basis for the analysis of acculturation phenomena. His description of the process tended to ignore the distinction he had made with reference to contact type and hence remained too general for greatest utility, but it outlined the necessary concepts. It is indeed from these early broad formulations that the current understanding of acculturation phenomena has steadily proceeded. It is not too much to say that the very large amount of descriptive and analytical work in the light of Linton's and related ideas has already led to a vantage ground from which the study of contact change assumes a systematic character. The six instances of change reported here will be presented with reference to the framework of general ideas which has developed over the past twenty-five years.

The Analysis of Contact

When members of societies with different cultures come into contact, an adaptation immediately begins which may be looked at as the operation of two interrelated processes. On the one hand, the members of the societies interact with one another, and, to the extent that they develop working relations and a sense of common identity, a single society develops out of the contact situation; the process of the growth of a common social system may be regarded as a form of social integration. On the other hand, the beliefs and customs of the members of the differing societies must, as a result of contacts of individuals who hold them, be adjusted to one another or, that is to say, made compatible to an extent that enables the members of the societies to get along; this process of adjustment of beliefs and customs from differing traditions may be regarded as a kind of cultural integration. Essentially, from this standpoint, what we are concerned with in the study of "culture contact" are processes of social and cultural integration which the coming-together of members of different societies sets in motion.

It is clear from the many instances of contact which have been studied that not every situation leads to the production of a single society out of those juxtaposed nor to the growth of a common culture. On the contrary, what has been most interesting about contact situations has been the wide variety in the results of contact. Every contact involves some degree of social and cultural integration, but there is a wide range in what become more or less stabilized situations with varying degrees of integration.

The distinction which Linton saw between directed and non-directed situations (Linton 1940: 501) in culture contact remains basic in any attempt to develop generalizations in the field of acculturation. The reason why it is fundamental is that, fully understood, it makes clear the two most general classes of contact situation. What takes

place in one class of situation involves quite different cultural processes from those which operate in the other. In recognizing the distinction, therefore, a clear basis for comparison is provided.

In both directed and non-directed situations members of one society interact in some manner with members of another society; the situations differ in the character of this interaction. In directed contact
the societies are interlocked in such a way that the participants in one
social system are subject not only to sanctions in their own but also
to those operative in the other system. In other words, directed contact involves interaction in specific roles between members of two
different societies and effective control of some type and degree by
members of one society over the members of the other. Further, if the
situation is one of directed contact, members of the superordinate society have an interest in changing the behavior of members of the
subordinate society in particular ways. The interest may be limited to
a single feature, or it may be ramified to the whole range of cultural
behavior. Whatever the extent or intensity of interest of the superordinate society, the members of the subordinate society are in some
degree subject to influence not only from their own culture but also
from another. It is highly misleading to think of what happens in
terms of the metaphor "borrowing," unless we remind ourselves that
true borrowing requires the borrower to act in terms of another's interests and values. Understood in this way, a situation of directed
contact is one in which the change which takes place has determinants from two distinct cultural systems.

Contacts between members of societies with different cultures may,
of course, occur without the establishment of one society in a superordinate position over the other. All such contacts may be considered
as falling into the other general category of contact situations, namely, non-directed. There is interaction between members of the different societies, as in directed situations, but there is no control of one
society's members by the other. Hence the effective influence of the
interests, sanctions, and values of each culture is confined to a single
society.

It may be objected that if a single trait or pattern from one society
is transferred to another this constitutes "effective influence" from
that society on the other. It is true, to be sure, that every instance of
diffusion or transfer is an instance of a kind of influence of one cul-

ture on another. The whole field of study of contact phenomena is, in fact, delimited on this general basis: What happens to innovations in a given culture when they derive from alien cultures or from situations created by the contact of societies? The point that we are making here is that within this broad field we may distinguish two fundamentally different kinds of contact conditions. In one, the nondirected type, although the innovations may derive directly from one culture, they are accepted and integrated into another culture in accordance with the cultural interests and principles of integration which obtain in the latter. In the other, or directed, type the two systems of interests and integration are linked through the kind of social relations established; accordingly any transfer of culture elements originates and proceeds under conditions which are not set *exclusively* by either one of the cultural systems involved. We believe that this distinction is of fundamental importance and will aid considerably in the discovery of general propositions.

To summarize, the decisive criteria for distinguishing the two major classes of contact situations may be indicated. (1) If definite sanctions, whether political, economic, supernatural, or even moral, are regularly brought to bear by members of one society on members of another, one condition for directed contact is met. (2) If, in addition, members of the society applying the sanctions are interested in bringing about changes in the cultural behavior of members of the other society, then both necessary conditions for directed contact exist. To illustrate, if one society wants to change another, but has not the power, the situation may be treated as non-directed contact. Further, if a society is in a superordinate position and has no interest in changing certain features of the subordinate society's culture, what takes place in those areas of culture may closely resemble what happens in non-directed situations. However, whenever the superordinate society is interested in changing some features of culture, the total situation is best treated as one of directed contact, for it may be assumed that there will be some relation between what happens in the areas not under attack and what happens in those that are.

We may illustrate from the six cases presented in this volume more precisely what we mean by directed and non-directed contact and, in doing so, perhaps lay a basis for showing how the distinction is significant. To hold that the trapper and trader contacts of the Kwakiutls, the Mandans, or the Wascos and Wishrams were basically like the missionary contacts of the Pueblos or Yaquis would be to misunderstand our viewpoint. Although they appear similar, in that a few individuals isolated from their societies established contacts and maintained them in isolation, the nature of the roles assumed was quite different. This was true not only in respect to such matters as marriage but also in the fundamentally important matter of authority. We may in fact describe the early Mandan period of fur-trading as non-directed contact, whereas the Jesuit period among the Yaquis, for example, was definitely directed. The contrast is apparent in that the missionaries assumed and were accorded high authority in the Yaqui communities, had a program for change, and established organization and sanctions for carrying it out. The missionaries were, moreover, replaced from time to time by other missionaries, so that there were always individuals who had been socialized in a different culture enmeshed in the affairs of Yaqui communities; trappers' sons, on the other hand, had often been socialized either in Indian-oriented families or the mixed institutions of the trading posts. The contrast in the situations lay not only in the different cultural interests of trappers and missionaries but also in the structure of the contacts in which they were involved with the Indians. French trappers and Jesuit missionaries in northern New Spain were by no means equivalent agents of change.

To illustrate further, it may be said that Navahos did not experience any directed program of change until the time of incarceration at Fort Sumner. From that time on there was directed contact, but this has varied extremely in regard to intensity and to extent of the contacts for Navahos. In these terms, the Yaquis experienced an alternation—from directed contact in the Jesuit missions to non-directed during the Autonomous Period and back again to directed during the Relocation Period. The question may be raised whether the Mexican efforts to change the Yaqui town system during the 1800's did not constitute directed contact. Undoubtedly the known Mexican hostility to the colonial town system was an important influence for re-orientation of Yaqui culture; however, the re-orientation took place in communities in which there was no effective linkage of Yaqui and Mexican social systems. Yaqui culture developed under conditions of growing isolation through the nineteenth century as the linkages which had existed during the Jesuit period broke down. The Yaqui folk culture came into existence under conditions in which a single cultural system increasingly governed the processes of change. In the case of the Kwakiutl we should perhaps draw the line between the Fort Rupert and Alert Bay phases of the Potlatch Period. Until the establishment of the Alert Bay settlement, there was no effective directed contact; from that time on there was directed contact, although of relatively low intensity for the latter phase of the Potlatch Period. Like the Kwakiutls, the Wascos and the Mandans experienced relatively short periods of directed contact: in the case of the Wascos only after the establishment of the reservations following 1855, and in the case of the Mandans only after the permanent establishment of the agency in 1868. In contrast, the Rio Grande Pueblos have been continuously since 1598 in a situation of directed contact, with the exception of the few years following the Pueblo Revolt and another short period preceding 1848. Looked at in this way, it becomes apparent that our data are not all readily comparable. There are two general types of contact which should be distinguished from each other. As instances of directed and non-directed contact, we may classify them as follows:

Non-directed	Directed
Pueblo I	Pueblo II, III, IV, V
Yaqui I and III	Yaqui II and IV
Mandan I, II, III	Mandan IV and V
Navaho I, II, III	Navaho IV
Wasco-Wishram I and II	Wasco-Wishram III and IV
Kwakiutl I and Phase A of II	Kwakiutl Phase B of II and III

One useful way of looking at this distinction is in terms of "interference" in the action of cultural systems. From the point of view of members of a superordinate society, it often appears that something interferes with the changes they wish to bring about; members of the subordinate society appear stubborn, or stupid, or just barbarian; they will not accept obviously better ways of doing things. Also, from the point of view of members of the subordinate society it often appears that the moral order is being interfered with; new ways are presented, or forced, which, because they have not been selected by the subordinate society, have no meaning or have negative value; they interfere with established ways and yet they must be lived with and an adjustment made to them. There are degrees and kinds of interference. There may be a degree of compatibility and similarity between cultures in contact, as in the case of the Kwakiutl, such that the directed change does not appear to be interference.

It is the specific nature of the interference in the subordinate society's cultural system which can be related to the various results of contact. On the one hand, in non-directed contact there is no interference; on the other hand, under conditions of directed contact a number of different kinds of interference may develop. An understanding of the relationship between the form of linkage of the social systems and the effects of contact depends on the development of some sort of classification of directed contact situations. It is in such situations that the greatest variety of change appears. While the seminar reported here did not attempt a universal classification of directed contact situations, it frequently came up against the problem of comparing one directed contact with another and under that impetus considered, if it did not codify, some of the factors which appeared important in our cases.

We considered, for example, the apparently similar situations of the Yaquis in the 1600's and the Navahos in the early 1900's. There were about the same number of Indian Bureau subagents among the Navahos as there were Jesuit missionaries among the Yaquis; moreover, there was close agreement in the ratio of agents of change to Indian population, for the Navaho population was not much smaller prior to 1910 than the Yaqui in 1690. The very great differences in influence of the members of the dominant society must be related to other differing factors, such as settlement pattern, cultural interests of the dominant Anglo-Americans, communication, and effective sanctions. Again, if we compare the two instances of most intensive missionary contact, namely, the Rio Grande Pueblos and the Yaquis, it is apparent that important differences existed in only three of the above factors, namely, settlement pattern, communication, and sanctions, for cultural interests and population ratios were similar. It was variation in these which would appear to account for the strikingly different results. As comparisons along these lines developed in the seminar, we did not find it easy to agree on a terminology which called attention to what we began to see as significant combinations of factors.

The seminar often discussed these variables in terms of what was called the "contact community." What we meant by "contact community" was the social relations (considered in the widest sense) obtaining among members of the societies in contact at any given time. The concept led to analysis of contacts along the following lines: In what social structures did the participants in the different social systems interact? In what social structures did they not jointly participate? What was "the strategy," or, that is to say, what were dominant society members interested in changing and how? And what was the response of the subordinate group in relation to such programs? In attempting to answer such questions, the seminar began to distinguish among contact communities as they succeeded one another in each tribe's contacts.

There were often profound changes in the nature of the successive contact communities. Thus, for Yaquis the contact community in Jesuit times was uniform and relatively stable, once the "concentration" had taken place, and the contact interaction was intensive, consistent, and strongly structured; during dispersal, on the other hand, the contact community for the Yaquis was immensely varied and contact roles were often inconsistent. In the attempted delineation of "periods," or phases, the seminar found itself aiming at division of the sequence of contacts into segments within each of which the character of the contact conformed to a pattern distinguishable from that in preceding or following segments.

As the seminar went about the business of defining periods in this sense, we began to see more clearly some similarities and differences which appeared to be significantly related to differing results of contact. Attention focused repeatedly on variation in the following factors: (1) the nature of the structural linkage with the dominant society, whether ecclesiastical, political, economic, or other, and the nature of the combination of these different institutional linkages (cf. Loomis n.d.: 38–40); (2) the kinds of roles, with their accompanying sanctions, assumed by members of the superordinate society in the contact communities; and (3) the nature of the subordinate society's social structure in terms of stability, whether new types of communities were in process of formation or not. There were obviously other factors not taken into account in a consideration of only such criteria, but these seemed often of primary importance in our data.

affect women

By using them it became possible to speak, for example, of "structurally stable communities under coercive control of closely linked political and ecclesiastical agents." This would obviously apply to the Rio Grande Pueblos during Period II and not to the Yaquis during Period II. The differences to which such labeling called attention seemed significantly related to the results of contact.

However, terminology of this sort, while giving some degree of precision, was cumbersome. Since we did not arrive at simple labels for types of contact community, we contented ourselves with the more conventional period names as given in the descriptions above, for example, Mandan Reservation Period, Kwakiutl Post-Potlatch Period, Pueblo Spanish Exploratory Period. These terms have the virtue of being more concrete but in that very quality failing to call attention to the significant similarities in the various contact communities. It will be our purpose in what follows to point out some of these similarities.

At what might be regarded as the generic level we could distinguish some five types of contact community, as follows: (1) Spanish mission, (2) fur trade, (3) United States reservation, (4) Canadian reservation, and (5) urban segment. The labels employed, besides giving rather concrete images of community forms, also may be interpreted as taking into account in some degree the three important factors mentioned above, namely, linkage, role pattern and sanctions, and structural stability.

The Spanish mission contact community, for example, could be defined as a type involving linkage through ecclesiastical and political interests, intimate face-to-face roles with strong coercive sanctions, and structural stability. In contrast, the fur trade contact community involved a purely market linkage, non-coercive roles, and structural stability. The United States reservation was a contact community built on political and economic linkage, coercive roles, and structural reorganization. The Canadian reservation was similar but with more structural stability. The urban segment was characterized by linkage in economic and a variety of other areas without administrative centralization, highly variable role networks, and urban structural instability.

Once characterization of such generic types was made, we were struck forcibly by the differences in contact results in our examples of both mission and reservation communities. The effects of contact were notably different on Pueblos and Yaquis, and yet these different effects came about in Spanish mission contact communities. These facts led to distinction between Jesuit and Franciscan mission communities. It was apparent that the general characterization above fits the missions in New Mexico but not the Jesuit missions among the Yaquis. In the latter political linkage was weak and coercive sanctions relatively mild. The Franciscan mission communities were structurally stable, but the Jesuit communities shifted from scattered rancherias to compact towns. Obviously, here were two subtypes of the mission communities, and the differences appeared to be of great importance in influencing cultural change. The generic type of "mission community" could be useful only in contrasting at a very general level what happened in the Spanish mission communities with what happened in, for example, fur trade or reservation communities.

To illustrate, the Spanish mission community differed from the other types mentioned in the following ways. It differed from the fur trade community fundamentally in that it was a community in which directed contact prevailed. It was to be distinguished from the reservation community chiefly on the basis of the different kinds of linkage with the superordinate societies. While both involved a range of linking roles with much in common as regards authority and sanctions, the areas of culture on which interest in change was focused differed considerably. Fraught with conflict though it was, in the mission community the integration of ecclesiastical and political roles was close and systematic. In the U.S. reservations, while there was some attempt to relate these at first, after 1896 there was increasing separation. The reservation emphasis on secular education for Indians resulted in very different influences from those emanating from religiously focused schools, often for a selected few. The U.S. focus on economic resource development differed markedly from the simple improvement of techniques brought about by the missionaries. The point is that the differences in dominant society interests were highly important in the contact results.

This was true despite the fact that in both reservation and mission communities there were systematic efforts to remake the Indian social structure. In the mission communities, the program was one of "reduction," that is to say, reorganization of the local group at a wider level, as the basis for integration into the national state. On the reservation there was the same general concern to reorganize the local group, but here it took the form of conformity to north European settlement pattern, namely, the isolated farm homestead; thus the Indians were reduced to a narrower level of integration of the local group as the basis for national incorporation. Where the Spanish mission carried through a reduction program, it resulted generally in extensive change; where this was not done because of pre-existing settlement pattern, as in the case of the Rio Grande Pueblos, change took a very different and more limited course. Wherever the reservation system was carried through to produce the homestead type community, there were generally great cultural losses and strong trends toward assimilation.

Thus, there would seem to be some value in recognizing and defining these broad types of contact communities. Moreover, it would appear that they may be differentiated with respect to the three criteria listed above, namely, systemic linkage, role and sanction patterns, and structural stability. While the seminar did not arrive at a universal classification of types and subtypes of contact communities, it is suggested that such a classification, employing at least these three features, is wholly feasible and that its definition would be an important foundation for further advance in acculturation theory. The manner in which results of contact may be related to such factors as stability of the subordinate society's structure, the nature of sanctions employed, and the areas of cultural interest of the dominant society will become clear as we proceed to a consideration of the examples of cultural integration from our data.

Processes of Contact Change

The sequence of events which takes place in a contact situation may be looked at from any of several different points of view. What the sequence leads to, or produces, is not a particular and unitary result, but rather a new or persisting state of the cultures in contact. Since any given state of a cultural system has many features and aspects, the sequence of changes may be looked at from many standpoints. It may be viewed in terms of a process of social integration, or the development of a common social system; of cultural integration, or the development of common culture; of, more narrowly, cultural reorientation; or as any of numerous other processes discernible in cultural systems. Because a considerable amount of discussion in the seminar was devoted to the subject, we shall here pay special attention to a certain kind of cultural integration, viewed both as process and as result.

What we mean by cultural integration in this analysis is only one aspect of the general process. We are limiting our attention to one characteristic phenomenon of contact situations, namely, the combination of traditional elements from different cultures. The elements of a given cultural system, under conditions of contact, may be augmented, replaced, or combined in a variety of ways with elements of another system. Students of acculturation, particularly in the United States, have paid a great deal of attention to the forms of tradition combination and have frequently attempted to classify the results of contact in such terms.

It appeared to the members of the seminar that we could distinguish fairly easily in our materials four kinds of tradition combinations. Our cases included several very clear and interesting examples of the various types. In some instances, for one of the defined periods or phases one kind of combination was dominant; sometimes the same process was important through several phases of contact. Yet wherever data were adequate, it was clear, even though one process might be operative in most areas of culture, other processes were also in operation.

One type conformed to what Vogt has called "the incorporative model." Here was a process which strongly characterized Navaho response in several phases of contact, in fact, Vogt was inclined to believe, throughout Navaho contacts up to the present. It was a type of tradition combination which flourished under conditions of nondirected contact, such as those characterizing Navaho contacts until the Fort Sumner subphase. Prior to that time Navahos had incorporated sheepherding, weaving, clothing styles, and numerous other selected elements from neighboring groups into what remained a distinctive and simple cultural system. The incorporative form of tradition combination, or what we shall here call incorporative integration, has been characteristic of Navahos through many different circumstances of contact. There is a strong suggestion that the process continues even under conditions which appear unfavorable to it. However, closer study of the most recent phase of Navaho culture history, as Vogt suggests, may require modification of this view. At any rate, in his data the Navahos generally constitute one of the clearest and most spectacular instances of incorporative integration.

What is meant specifically by "incorporative" in this sense? Vogt's description seems adequate, but let us recapitulate briefly. By incorporation is meant the transfer of elements from one culture system and their integration into another system in such a way that they conform to the meaningful and functional relations within the latter. It is implied that the borrowing system is not disrupted or changed in fundamental type. It remains, as Vogt has pointed out for the Navahos, with social system fundamentally unchanged and with essentially the same values, despite the enrichment of content. In the incorporative process nothing important to the pre-Spanish Navaho cultural system was replaced by the innovations from the Pueblos or the Spaniards. What superficially appeared to be extreme change, such as the adoption of a new subsistence pattern in sheepherding, turned out rather to be a reinforcement of the interest in hunting and the tendency for moving about which had been important elements in Navaho culture for a long time. In other words, incorporative integration is a type of tradition combination which results in totally new forms being accepted into a culture in such a way that they enhance the existing organization of that culture.

This process is not one which operates ordinarily under conditions of directed contact. It is a process limited to situations in which one cultural system comprises the cultural determinants. Once directed contact is established, incorporative integration is supplanted by some other process, at least in those areas of the culture where directed influences are strong and important. It may be pointed out that there are instances of incorporative integration in other cases besides the Navaho. One of the more notable is that of the Yaquis in their third phase of contact, during the Autonomous Period. Specifically we may point to the adoption of Mexican techniques of warfare and adaptation of these to the folk culture of the river towns. Similarly the Mandan purchase and performance of Arikara ceremony during Period III is an example of incorporative integration. Incorporation also appears to be the dominant process among the Kwakiutl during the Pre-Potlatch and early Potlatch Periods. Incorporation here had to do chiefly with items of material culture and cash payments from the fur traders and others which in their new abundance served to enhance the gift exchange customs. This resulted in the proliferation of the potlatch into a unique and complex institution, but entirely within the compass of the pre-existing Kwakiutl values and social system. The pre-Spanish contacts of Rio Grande Pueblos were characterized by incorporation. The "incorporative model" thus helps in the description of several of the contact changes and points to conditions of contact which were decisive in its development.

In direct contrast to incorporative we might speak of assimilative, or replacive, integration, a familiar-enough form of response under certain conditions of directed contact. What is actually meant by "replacement" has not usually been made clear. In the 1936 Social Science Research Council memorandum the phenomena were subsumed under the label "acceptance." It is clear from our data that "acceptance" is insufficient as a characterization of process in such cases. Acceptance is involved in incorporative integration also. What is important is that there be acceptance of meanings as well as forms by the subordinate society. But even this is hardly sufficient to indicate the nature of the process of assimilative integration. Both acceptance and replacement are involved in the process; however, the distinctive feature consists in the acceptance and replacement of cultural behaviors in terms of the dominant society's cultural system. This means an absence of modification which harmonizes what is accepted with a divergent system. Individuals select among alternatives in the contact situation as if they were participants in the dominant culture.

One of the most striking examples comes from the Kwakiutl in their final phase. Here, as Codere indicates, the process was facilitated by the similarity in the cultural interests and orientations of Kwakiutl and Canadians. The new forms of fishing and of acquiring goods, as well as the specific goods themselves, could be easily included in Kwakiutl behavior in terms of the native system of meanings and functions. Choice among alternatives could be made with reference to ends already well-established in Kwakiutl culture, as one might choose among alternatives in a non-contact situation.

It appears also that the Wascos have undergone a process of assimilation since the foundation of the reservation. French says that all

Wascos are able to behave like White men in some situations. The fact that the replacement is not complete, that Wascos are also still to be observed behaving like "Indians," will be considered below. Yaquis in the relocation phase in Arizona have certainly been undergoing assimilation. The assimilation has in fact proceeded so far that Yaquis tend increasingly to adjust the core of the old folk culture—the religious observances and beliefs—to the dominant culture, rather than the reverse. It appears even that persistence of the distinctive ceremonialism depends heavily on the interest in it in the dominant society. In Period V of Mandan contact history it is apparent that the process of assimilation assumes importance. By this time Mandan and Hidatsa society and culture had merged, and under conditions of altering settlement pattern and an Anglo-directed program focused on economic change, various elements of the merged Indian culture were replaced at an increasing rate.

Assimilation and incorporation might be regarded as the poles of process in contact change; in the former the determinants of the change insofar as they are cultural come to be the nature of the superordinate society's culture, in the latter the determinants are also from a single culture, but since there is no superordination of societies, there is no replacement of cultural system determinants. One may imagine North American Indian societies generally going through a series of stages in cultural adjustment beginning with incorporation and ending with assimilation. It is true that a number of groups have progressed in such stages, but the great majority of Indians in the area of what is now the United States have not, and in fact exhibit at present clearly neither dominantly incorporative or assimilative tendencies. In the seminar we noted two other types of cultural integration besides the two mentioned.

These other two processes come into operation and either may become a dominant process under conditions of directed change. They are a result of different kinds of directed contact conditions. One that has been discussed in some detail is that of fusional integration. The essentials of fusion are that elements of two or more distinct cultural traditions be involved, that they be combined into a single system, and that the principles in terms of which they combine not be the same as those governing the cultural systems from which they come. The process may result in a variety of combinations of form and meaning, a common one, as illustrated in the Yaqui case, being the combination of forms from the dominant society with meanings from the subordinate. The essential is simply that whatever the specific form of combination the principles which guide it are neither wholly from one or the other of the two systems in contact.

The Yaqui example of fusion has already been sufficiently elaborated above. It may be seen as having taken place under circumstances characterized by the continued selection of innovations from Spanish culture by Spanish-socialized missionaries and the continued acceptance of these in some form by communities in which Yaqui local group structure was altering in type. The relationship of conditions to results seems clear enough in the Yaqui instance. There are numerous other examples of fusion in the data. An interesting one consists of the complex fusion of religious beliefs and rituals in the Shaker and other cults among the Wasco-Wishram (see Barnett 1957). In every case there are examples of fusion, for fusion may take place with reference to a subsystem within a cultural whole or with reference to even smaller segments. Thus, we have some instances of fusion in the Rio Grande Pueblo culture, despite the general importance of another process.

It is an interesting fact that one of the sharpest contrasts in process and result is to be found in connection with Yaquis and Pueblos, both of whom underwent contact in mission communities. Nevertheless we should not lose sight of the fact that there were also many similarities in the results of Spanish contacts in the two groups. We might mention the similar wide range in the aspects of culture affected and the consistent strong influence in the area of religion for all the Pueblo villages as well as for each of the Yaqui towns. It is nevertheless in the area of religion that the great contrast between Yaqui and Pueblo response to similar strong influences appears most clearly.

Dozier has discussed the concept of compartmentalization, which we shall here for purposes of uniformity in terminology refer to as isolative integration. What is meant is a keeping-separate within a realm of meaning of elements and patterns taken over from the dominant culture. This took place in the way described by Dozier for the Pueblos, but it was also characteristic of limited areas in the other instances. In isolative integration the accepted elements lack linkage with other complexes, despite serving very similar or identical functions. The lack of linkage leads to their being isolated within the culture in a distinct subsystem of meanings, hence the term "isolative integration." Obviously the process is quite different from fusion, despite the fact that both cultural systems in contact continuously influence the developments.

The four processes discussed have to do with the alteration of a culture under conditions of contact. We may describe the results of the operation of these processes respectively as incorporation, replacement, fusion, and compartmentalization. The processes and results take place with respect to any of the cultures in a contact situation. The processes are cultural and the discussion of them given here must be regarded as being carried on at the level of analysis of cultural systems. The data may be considered also with reference to processes of social integration, by which is meant the participation of individuals from different societies in a common social system. Many of the phenomena involving such processes have to do with maintenance or loss of identity by members of the societies concerned, aspects of which have been treated in Broom *et al.* (1954).

The Mandan case illustrates a process of social integration under conditions of non-directed contact. At no time in Mandan history were the Hidatsas dominant over the Mandans or vice versa. As Bruner points out, members of the two societies had by 1950 merged into a single society on the reservation. Some Mandans, it is true, preserved some degree of distinctive identity, but it was clear that the dominant process was resulting in the creation of a new common sense of identity as Indian for descendants of both Mandans and Hidatsas. The members of what had been two different societies were participating in common social structures without distinction. Intermarriage, the restructuring of local groups, and the formation of common church congregations had contributed to the emergence of a single reservation society with progressive loss of distinction between tribal groups. Bruner has spoken of this development as a merging of societies.

The Mandan instance raises the question whether the merging involved was not the same phenomenon as what has been called fusion in the case of the Yaquis. The answer appears to be that the phenomena were quite distinct. Superficially the cultural effects of Spanish-Yaqui contact might appear to be closely similar to, or identical with, those of Mandan-Hidatsa contact. However, the Mandan and Hidatsa cultural systems, in contrast with those of the Spanish and Yaqui, were very nearly, if not wholly, identical. The combination of elements from the two Indian cultures involved no growth of a new integrative system; it seems doubtful, in fact, that under conditions of non-directed contact the two Indian cultures could have emerged in the way that they did if they had contrasted in type. Moreover, it must be pointed out that the fusional integration of culture which took place among Yaquis during the Jesuit period depended on the continued sharp separation of Spanish and Yaqui societies. The Yaqui sense of distinct identity increased, rather than diminished, during the period of Jesuit contact, despite the fusion of so many Spanish innovations into their culture. It is in this fact that we see a basic difference from the Mandan-Hidatsa situation. The processes of social integration were not at all alike, even though the cultural processes bore some superficial resemblance.

Another type of social integration received some attention in the analysis of the Wasco-Wishram case. In the final period of contact took place what French describes as the growth of a Part-Time Indian Culture. We take this to mean that what might be called bicultural behavior appeared among the Wascos and Wishrams (cf. Polgar 1960). That is, in somewhat the same manner that an individual may learn a language in addition to his mother tongue, so a Wasco learns the system of behavior of Whites. For example, in a situation in which most actors are non-Wasco, he may behave in accordance with their ways; in another he may behave Indian-wise under the influence of an Indian-dominated situation. In complex situations of other types, Wasco behavior may contrast with that of others who are present. Shifts in language use, according to the communication requirements of a given situation, are of course familiar in the behavior of persons who are bilingual. The Wasco case calls attention to the existence of similar employment of elements of culture other than language.

The contact response involved here is of a different order from that in fusion and isolation. There we were talking about cultural processes operating to alter cultural systems. Here we are talking about more purely social processes operating to encourage and permit dual participation in cultural systems. In contrast with the others so far discussed, this process does not directly involve any development or change of cultural systems. We are, therefore, here considering a type of social, rather than cultural, integration.

The condition fundamental for the development of biculturalism is one which permits or encourages enculturation of individuals in the subordinate society in the patterns of the superordinate. There must further be opportunities for exercising those behaviors so learned in continuing situations in such a way as to insure continued practice in them. The Wasco-Wishram illustrate this type of situation. Several generations of schooling in White schools and working on White jobs preceded the Part-Time Indian Culture Period. Moreover, there was great mobility for those who wished it after residence was taken up on the reservation, especially in connection with fishing and off-reservation wage work. It was necessary also that there be some rewards in connection with behaving like an Indian, and this was true on the Warm Springs Reservation. Of course, once biculturalism was established, Indian parents participated in the teaching of both cultures to their children.

Bicultural adjustment took place in a number of other instances. It was characteristic of the Yaquis during both the Autonomous and the Relocation Periods. Yaquis steadily gained broad experience of Mexican culture during the nineteenth century as they were forced to work outside Yaqui country to keep alive; the conditions of mobility were there, albeit without an organized school system involved, as in the case of the Wascos. In terms of numbers who elected to exercise their Yaqui behaviors and defend the homeland as against those who behaved like Mexicans during the crisis we know little, but many did not choose to fight. Yaqui biculturalism continued down to the 1950's, as individual assimilation proceeded to step up in tempo; we have noted the phenomenon of constant return to participation in the fully revived Yaqui culture of Sonora and also the partially revived Yaqui culture of the Arizona urban segments. In situations permitting even more mobility perhaps than those of the Wasco-Wishram, the Yaquis, or at least a large number of them, were bicultural in a similar way. Biculturalism was also operative in the last periods of contact for the Mandan; however, there was a lesser degree of mobility than in the other two cases, particularly with respect to off-reservation employment.

It is not presumed that these five types of acculturative processes exhaust the possibilities. These are well illustrated in the present material. The seminar in the course of its work did not clearly see other types. We have applied such terms as incorporative, assimilative, fusional, isolative, and bicultural quite consciously as similar to concepts now current in linguistic science. They imply the conception of cultural systems, as well as social systems, in the same sense that linguists think of languages as systems.

It may be that this goes too far. Certainly it has hardly been demonstrated that the whole round of cultural behavior of any community or group of communities constitutes a coherent system. This has been a common anthropological assumption for some years, but recently there have been growing uncertainties in this regard and a tendency to assume less comprehensive systems within the whole of a people's cultural behavior (Keesing 1958: 410–12). It does not seem to us that if investigation moves more in this direction it would require abandonment of either our terminology or our concepts. They would apply in, for example, subsistence systems or security systems, as well as in whole cultural systems; they might in fact be more usable in that way than in connection with "cultures as wholes."

Sequences of Type in Contact Change

In an effort to attain clarity, we have spoken as if it were possible to characterize any given contact situation as exhibiting a dominant process of cultural or social integration. While it did turn out in the material examined that this was sometimes the case, it was also obvious that in other instances it was not. Even in situations where there was what could be designated as a dominant process, as in the Jesuit period of Yaqui contact and in the post-revolt phase of Rio Grande Pueblo contact, there were clearly other processes. This was a result of the differential influence of the dominant cultural system in the subordinate system. The varying cultural interests of the dominant society and the different character of relations in the parts of the social system resulted in the simultaneous operation of differing processes. What we have called a dominant process existed only in the sense that the same process appeared to affect elements of culture in several different areas of cultural interest.

The seminar group tended at times to fall into the easy error of labeling the whole sequence of change for a given Indian tribe in terms of the results of a single dominant process. Thus there was a tendency to think of the Yaquis throughout their contact history as exemplifying a fusional adjustment, the Rio Grande Pueblos as isolating, and so on. It was true in these cases that in successive contact situations there was continuing evidence of the effects of what had been a long-existing dominant process. This led us to overlook the inauguration or intensification of other processes. Certainly in the case of the Yaquis, those elements of the nineteenth-century culture which persisted in the urban segments in Arizona still obviously exemplified the results of fusion of Spanish and aboriginal elements. Nevertheless the process of assimilation had begun to dominate by the 1950's, and fusion was no longer important. In the case of the Rio Grande Pueblos the shift in contact situation during the later Anglo-American Period was a less marked change from previous situations than in the case of the Yaquis, but even so it was clear that isolative integration was no longer taking place in respect to Pueblo-Anglo contacts. The illusion of continuity in process was a result of failure to analyze thoroughly the whole set of new conditions and changes.

The fact remained that there was some continuity. The Navahos appeared in spite of the inauguration of directed change during the late phase of the Anglo-American Period to be characterized still by an incorporative adjustment. The Yaquis even in the Relocation Period tended to accept and fuse cultural elements in language and minor features of religion. A pattern of response once worked out seemed to persist under conditions not obviously favorable. This suggested the importance of a given cultural response as a determinant of change on into situations which had altered from those under which the type of response had developed. The important consideration is to determine the limits in terms of contact conditions within which the given type of integration process can continue to operate.

For example, it would seem that the fusional type of integration is inhibited to the extent that strong coercive means are employed by the dominant society and to the extent that the social system of the subordinate society is disrupted. While the process of fusion in Yaqui culture set in motion during the Jesuit period continued to operate in the Autonomous Period with respect to elements which Yaquis had learned from the Jesuits, it did not operate with respect to the cultural elements which Mexicans were offering. Elements presented by Mexicans were rejected wholesale, not fused, and those elements of Mexican culture selected by Yaquis were incorporated. Further, the fusional process was greatly inhibited in the Yaqui Relocation Period as the social unit of the town and its complex of organizations were disrupted. There was, in other words, a set of conditions in which fusion could no longer operate as a dominant process. This would seem to be the case also in respect to the later phases of Navaho contact. Among those Navahos whose participation in contact social structures such as Tribal Council and Mormon church was direct and intensive, the incorporative process was no longer dominant. Conditions had changed beyond the limits where it could operate, despite the fact that those Navahos whose contacts were different and less intensive were able to some extent to continue incorporating English words and some patterns of behavior into their cultural system.

Change in process dominance, or shifts in the balance of processes, was a marked feature of the data. Thus in all cases of Indian contact with Europeans—Spanish or Anglo-American—an initial period was characterized by extensive taking-over of material items and formal elements of cultural behavior offered by the European group. In all six cases this was evident. French speaks of this initial contact period as giving rise to an "Augmented Wasco-Wishram" culture. There was a phase of "Spanish innovation" early in Yaqui contacts. The Pueblos impressed the Spaniards in the 1630's as docile and rapidly assimilating people. The Mandans were receptive at first. The Kwakiutl enthusiastically incorporated blankets and other goods into their potlatching.

Members of the seminar were struck with this similarity in initial phases regardless of the specific forms of contact. There was the dominance of what might be called, in fact, a process of additive integration; nothing important was replaced in these initial phases. This took place under conditions of both directed and non-directed contact. However, it was apparent that such general acceptance of novelties (mostly material culture) gave way to responses describable in terms of the processes outlined. An initial honeymoon of contact shifted to a situation in which one or another of the processes described came into operation. If it remained a situation of non-directed contact, then incorporative integration became clearly established. If directed contact crystallized with permissive programs of change in incompletely dominated social systems, then fusion became important. The "additive" process, never of course very fully described in the documents because of the imperfect acquaintance of the contacting groups, seems important to note as an unstable condition characteristic of initial contacts between Indians and Europeans before the crystallization of clearly structured contact relations.

There appear also to be certain easy transitions from dominance of one process to dominance of another. A notable such transition consists of that from fusion to assimilation, exemplified in the case of the Yaquis in their fourth phase of contact. The fused form of Yaqui culture at the end of the nineteenth century constituted a steppingstone, as it were, to the assimilative acceptance of religious and other forms of cultural behavior as the conditions of contact changed resulting in more complete dominance by the non-Indian society. The process of reinterpretation of Yaqui fusions in accordance with the meaning system of Catholicism was strongly operative in Arizona. In Sonora this was even true, though in a different way, in the relations between church and town. Unquestionably the written tradition of Spanish, more fully developed than the Yaqui, played an important part. One suspects that something like this was involved in connection with Mandan political organization in the transition to the reservation phase. In contrast with isolative integration, fusion seems to lend itself to such transition. It is apparent however that the nature of the dominant culture in comparison with the subordinated one is of great importance.

This does not mean that fusional integration results in a necessarily unstable condition. It grows out of situations in which for one reason or another political and other controls have not been established commensurate with the dominant society's interest in bringing about certain changes. Only in that sense is it an unstable condition. It need not necessarily give way either to incorporative integration, as it did in the case of the Yaquis in Period III, or to assimilation, as it did in Yaqui Period IV. Whether it is replaced by another dominant process depends entirely on whether there is a sufficient shift in the contact conditions, but it is certainly true that fusion must be regarded as an unsatisfactory condition by proponents of programs of directed change who have assimilative objectives.

Several times we have alluded to the importance of "culture types" in encouraging or limiting the operation of a given cultural process. The seminar did not get much involved in the important problem of typing cultures with respect to significance for the processes of tradition combination. Suffice it to say that the "primitive fusion" of Yaqui culture in the nineteenth century was a specially tight organization of cultural elements; yet it turned out to be readily dissolvable under new conditions. The intensity of its prescriptions remained for Arizona Yaquis, but limited to a single set of complexes of the cultural whole of the river towns. In other words, the definition of a cultural whole as rigid or loose seems to depend on the functioning of that culture in a given set of contact circumstances. Rigidity in the sense of a coherent organization does not seem necessarily to be a persistent quality regardless of contact conditions, nor does looseness of organization. French indicates a conception of Wasco-Wishram culture as loosely structured and suggests that this condition persisted throughout the phases of contact. It appears also, however, that conditions favorable to looseness of structure have persisted throughout. In reverse this has been the situation for the Rio Grande Pueblos. It appears then that the integrative type is more likely to be a product of given contact conditions than it is a determinant of the kind of change which takes place.

It remains to consider whether there are, as Elkin has suggested, any recurrent sequences of change in contacts between non-literates and Europeans. Our data suggest that it is meaningless to posit such invariant sequences without explicit statement of the conditions of contact as well as of the nature of the cultures in contact. The Australian sequence is well described by Elkin (1951) and many of the phenomena are obviously present in American Indian contact situations, including our cases. However, one can see that the sequence of changes for the Australians could have been altered at many points. The described sequence seems to rest heavily on such special and overarching conditions as population decline for Australians, disruption of local group structure, economic and religious interests of the dominant group, and the kind of integration in the national culture. In a general way many of these conditions are repeated in certain phases for our six groups, but nowhere is there evidence that Elkin's sequence is inherent in the contact of European and native cultures and must develop regardless of conditions once contact has been established.

Differential Change

Considerable effort was expended by the seminar in making lists of most and least persistent traits and in comparing these from case to case. As this was done it became clear that the same group sometimes changed rapidly its ceremonial interests and practices and under other conditions clung desperately to them; under some circumstances material culture items were replaced or changed rapidly while little else changed, but in other situations social structure and religion changed rapidly while material culture underwent small change. In some circumstances there was rapid change in all aspects of culture at the same time; under other circumstances there were marked differentials. The conclusion seemed inescapable that the seminar would have to content itself with something less than generalizations applying to all kinds of culture elements under any kinds of contact conditions. In short, the comparative analysis carried out by the seminar led to an abandonment of a search for generalizations framed in terms of a universal differential susceptibility to change of aspects of culture.

It was true that when lists were made of persistences for each group over the whole span of their contacts there appeared to be a general conclusion. Technological changes had taken place extensively in all the Indian cultures, to the point in fact that none could be said to have preserved much of their technology beyond some items connected with ritual interests. Linguistic structure, on the other hand, was notably persistent. Nevertheless there were exceptions: the Mandans lost their language without losing a sense of distinctive identity or features of their social organization; the Yaqui language showed not only lexical but also structural changes. One of the weaknesses of the approach in terms of aspects of culture over the whole span of contacts was that it obscured the differences from phase to phase. Most notably for those groups which had contacts with both Spaniards and Anglo-Americans it seemed to obscure the differences in material culture and ceremonial change under Spanish as compared with Anglo-American directed change.

The view of differential change developed in the seminar has been set forth in this chapter. It is a view which recognizes as an important problem the discovery of regularities in the sequences of change which take place in cultures in contact. Comparison of the data in the six cases led to treating the material not as six, but as some twenty-two, instances. It was not found that the regularities could be stated in terms of aspects of culture, but it was apparent that when stated in terms of cultural or social processes some cross-cultural generalizations emerged. These generalizations had to do with types of contact conditions favorable for the operation of the various processes identified. The analysis of the case materials has been presented with the aim of pointing out recurrent regularities in the association of process with type of contact. The seminar is well aware that its analytical work and its efforts toward generalization have far from exhausted the possibilities in the data with which it worked. It is hoped that the detailed presentation of materials in accordance with a common plan will result in other students' seeing significant relations which the seminar missed and that what the seminar did see can be built on for the better understanding of cultural change.

REFERENCES CITED

BARNETT, H. G.
1957 *Indian Shakers: A Messianic Cult of the Pacific Northwest.* Carbondale, Ill.

BROOM, LEONARD, BERNARD J. SIEGEL, EVON Z. VOGT, and JAMES B. WATSON
1954 "Acculturation: An Exploratory Formulation," *American Anthropologist,* LVI, 973–1000.

BRUNER, EDWARD M.
1957 "Differential Culture Change: Report on the Interuniversity Summer Research Seminar, 1956," *Items, Social Science Research Council,* Vol. II, No. 1.

COLSON, ELIZABETH
1953 *The Makah Indians.* Minneapolis.

ELKIN, A. P.
1951 "Reaction and Interaction: A Food Gathering People and European Settlement," *American Anthropologist,* LIII, 164–86.

HANKS, LUCIEN M. and JANE
1950 *Tribe under Trust: A Study of the Blackfoot Reserve of Alberta.* Toronto.

HERSKOVITS, M. J.
1948 *Man and His Works: The Science of Cultural Anthropology.* New York.

KEESING, FELIX M.
1953 "Culture Change," *Stanford Anthropological Series, No. 1.* Stanford, Calif.
1938 *Cultural Anthropology: The Science of Custom.* New York.

KROEBER, A. L.
1948 *Anthropology: Race, Language, Culture, Psychology, Prehistory.* New York.

LINTON, RALPH (ed.)
1940   *Acculturation in Seven American Indian Tribes.* New York.
LOOMIS, CHARLES P.
n.d.   "Social Systems, Their Activities, Elements and Processes," manuscript.
MALINOWSKI, BRONISLAW
1945   *The Dynamics of Culture Change.* New Haven.
MALINOWSKI, BRONISLAW, *et al.*
1938   "Methods of Study of Culture Contact in Africa," *International Institute of African Languages and Cultures Memorandum,* Vol. XV. London.
NEWCOMB, WILLIAM W., JR.
1956   "The Culture and Acculturation of the Delaware Indians," *Anthropological Papers No. 10,* Museum of Anthropology, University of Michigan, Ann Arbor.
POLGAR, STEVEN
1960   "Biculturation of Mesquakie Teenage Boys," *American Anthropologist,* LXII, 217–35.
REDFIELD, R., R. LINTON, and M. J. HERSKOVITS
1936   "A Memorandum on the Study of Acculturation," *American Anthropologist,* XXXVIII, 149–52.
STERN, THEODORE
1952   "Chickahominy: The Changing Culture of a Virginia Indian Community," *Proceedings of the American Philosophical Society,* Vol. XCVI, No. 2. Philadelphia.
WAUCHOPE, ROBERT
1956   "Seminars in Archaeology 1955," *Memoir of the Society for American Archaeology,* No. 11.
WILSON, G. and MONICA
1945   *The Analysis of Social Change Based on Observations in Central Africa.* Cambridge, England.

Index

Acceptance of innovation, 8, 31

Acculturation: definition of, 379; degree of, 402; situations, 94, 197; studies of, 2, 518

Acoma, 121, 124, 287, 299

Addition of culture elements, 35, 141, 149, 229, 341, 371, 397, 417, 418, 422, 435, 511, 539

Age-grade system (Mandan), 204, 225

Agents, Indian, 218, 233–34, 239, 240, 254, 256, 309, 385, 391, 462

Alternatives, cultural, 29, 33, 86, 229, 268, 327, 371, 372, 414

Anglo-Americans, 75–91, 95, 151–84, 280, 307–24, 349, 373

Annuities, 209, 234, 239, 240, 245, 247, 250

Apaches, 42, 72, 81, 95, 100, 132, 135, 136, 137, 142, 144, 154, 161, 279, 280, 286, 287, 289, 291 ff., 302, 304–5, 307, 308, 312, 314

Arikara, 187, 189, 190, 201, 203, 207, 208, 209, 213, 214, 218, 230, 234, 235, 238, 248, 253, 258, 259, 423

Art: Kwakiutl, 452–54, 479–81, 505–6; Wasco-Wishram, 369, 395, 415; Yaqui, 16, 18, 25, 63

Assimilation, cultural, 7, 8, 74, 254, 269, 317, 379, 421, 435, 498, 504, 531

Assiniboin, 197 ff., 208, 209, 213, 217–18

Associations; see Sodalities

Athabascan languages, 282, 284

Athabascan tribes, Southern, 278, 283, 287, 288, 304

Attitudes, interethnic, 42, 74–75, 142, 145, 237–38, 256, 300, 302, 404, 461, 485–87

Banderas, Juan, 8, 40–43, 46, 56, 57, 64

Bella Bella, 440, 448, 449

Bella Coola, 439–40, 449

Biculturalism, 536

Blackfoot, 2

Boas, Franz, 431, 436, 441, 443, 447, 449, 453, 459, 460, 473, 476, 480, 517

Boundary-maintaining mechanisms, 147, 422–23

Buffalo, 190, 191, 215, 219, 220, 223, 233, 246, 285, 287, 303, 347

Bureau of Indian Affairs, 168, 169, 233, 238, 245, 250, 251, 252, 255, 307, 315, 316, 386

Cacique, 112, 122, 170

Cahita language, 10, 20, 22

Cajeme, 8, 41, 45–46, 56, 64, 65, 67, 69, 77

Cannibal Dance, 440, 448, 451, 474, 475

Carson, Kit, 312 ff.

Catholic Church, 42, 58, 76, 252

Cebolleta, 298, 299

Ceremony; see Religion

Change, differential, 3, 542; mechanisms of, 188; types of, 3, 5, 6, 528

Change, economic, 24, 30, 35, 37, 45, 50, 65, 82, 86, 98, 165, 174, 177, 215, 228, 242

Cherokees, 421, 423

Cheyenne, 205, 209, 218